On

aroυ

Pacific

Northwest

THOMAS COOK

On 5 July 1841 Thomas Cook, a 32-year-old printer from Market Harborough, in Leicestershire, England, led a party of some 500 temperance enthusiasts on a railway outing from Leicester to Loughborough which he had arranged down to the last detail. This proved to be the birth of the modern tourist industry. In the course of expanding his business, Thomas Cook and his son, John, invented many of the features of organised travel which we now take for granted. Over the next 150 years the name Thomas Cook became synonymous with world travel.

Today the Thomas Cook Group employs over 14,000 people across the globe and its Worldwide Network provides services to customers at more than 3000 locations in over 100 countries. Its activities include travel retailing, tour operating and financial services – Thomas Cook is a world leader in traveller's cheques and foreign money services.

Thomas Cook believed in the value of the printed word as an accompaniment to travel. His publication *The Excursionist* was the equivalent of both a holiday brochure and a travel magazine. Today Thomas Cook Publishing continues to issue one of the world's oldest travel books, the *Thomas Cook European Timetable,* which has been in existence since 1873. Updated every month, it remains the only definitive compendium of European railway schedules.

The *Thomas Cook Touring Handbook* series, to which this volume belongs, is a range of comprehensive guides for travellers touring regions of the world by train, car and ship. Other titles include:
Touring by train
On the Rails around France (Published 1995)
On the Rails around Britain and Ireland (Published 1995)
On the Rails around Europe (Second Edition Published 1995)
On the Rails around the Alps (Published 1996)
On the Rails around Eastern Europe (Published 1996)
Touring by car
On the Road around California (Second Edition Published 1996)
On the Road around Florida (Second Edition Publication 1997)
On the Road around Normandy, Brittany and the Loire Valley (Published 1996)
On the Road around the Capital Region (Published 1997)
On the Road around the South of France (Published 1997)
Touring by ship
Greek Island Hopping (Published annually in February)
Cruising around Alaska (Published 1995)
Cruising around the Caribbean (Published 1996)

For more details of these and other Thomas Cook publications, write to Thomas Cook Publishing, at the address on the back of the title page.

ON THE ROAD AROUND THE

Pacific
Northwest

The fly-drive guide to
Oregon, Washington
and British Columbia

Fred Gebhart
and Maxine Cass

A THOMAS COOK TOURING HANDBOOK

Published by Thomas Cook Publishing
The Thomas Cook Group Ltd
PO Box 227
Thorpe Wood
Peterborough PE3 6PU
United Kingdom

Text:
© 1997 The Thomas Cook Group Ltd
Maps and diagrams:
© 1997 The Thomas Cook Group Ltd

ISBN 0 906273 95 1

Managing Editor: Stephen York
Project Editor: Deborah Parker
Editorial Assistant: Leyla Davies
Copy Editor: Wendy Wood
Map Editor: Bernard Horton
Maps drawn by Caroline Horton
Colour maps drawn by RJS Associates

Cover illustration by Adam Green
Text design by Darwell Holland
Text typeset in Bembo and Gill Sans using
    QuarkXPress for Windows
Maps and diagrams created using Macromedia
    Freehand and GSP Designworks
Printed in Great Britain by Fisherprint Ltd,
    Peterborough

ABOUT THE AUTHORS

Fred Gebhart has lived in the West for more than 40 years, interrupted by extended sojourns in Europe and West Africa. He has logged thousands of miles in the Pacific Northwest as a child as well as an adult, travelling by foot, horseback, bicycle, sailboat, RV and car. A freelance photojournalist for 16 years, Fred covers the Western United States for publications in Asia and Europe while focussing on Australasia for US readers between collaborations in *On the Road Around..* series titles with his wife, Maxine Cass. He has also contributed to other books and written computer software manuals. Fred's passion is scuba diving, a love more happily consummated in tropical climes than in the chilly waters of the Pacific Northwest.

Maxine Cass, born in California, has studied Medieval History at the University of California, lived in Greece and Senegal, and become a widely-published photojournalist and author in the forty-some years she has lived in the West. Maxine contributes to travel and business publications in Asia, Canada, Europe and the US between book collaborations with her husband, Fred Gebhart. *On the Road Around the Pacific Northwest* is their third *Thomas Cook Touring Handbook*. Others include *On the Road Around California* and *On the Road Around Florida* (with Eric and Ruth Bailey), as well as *A AAA Photo Journey to San Francisco* on her own. Between research trips around the world, Maxine gardens and shares the indulgences of a cat with her husband and series co-author at their home in San Francisco, California.

PHOTOGRAPHS

All photographs for this book have been taken by Maxine Cass, with the exception of the following, which were taken by Fred Gebhart: colour section opposite p. 224: page (iv); colour section p. 288: page (i), (iii) Aquabus, and (iv); back cover.

ACKNOWLEDGEMENTS

The authors and publishers would like to thank the following people and organisations for their assistance during the preparation of this book:

Toni Anderson, Cedarbrook Herb Farm; Brenda Baceda, Tourism Asociation of Vancouver Island; John Bateman, Tourism British Columbia; David Blanchard, Seattle Kings County News Bureau; Camden Brewster, Crater Lake National Park; Deidre Campbell, The Empress Hotel; Heather Chapman, Tourism Vancouver; Sharon Clarno, Gold Beach CC; Chris Christensen, Eagle Point Inn; The Claremont Hotel; Robin Cogdill, Everett Area CVB; John Cooper, Bellingham-Whatcom Co CVB; Maureen Cumming, BC Ferries; Heather Day, Tourism Victoria; Sherie Dennis & Shireesh Sharma, Cowlitz County Dept of Tourism; Tricia Dice, Coulee Dam CC; Leigh Dienert, Florence CC; Diane Duca, Edmonds VB; Timothy Egan; Kim Fisher-Cowan, The Dalles Area CC; Julie Gangler, Tacoma-Pierce County VVB; Lloyd & Lou Gebhart; Barbra Glover, Yakima CVB; Kris Gonzalez, Thomas Cook Financial Services N. America; Governor Hotel; Barb Gower, Lake County CC; Maria Greene, Tourism British Columbia; Spencer Grigg, City of Moses Lake; Leah Hammer, Ravenscroft Inn ; Rickie Hart, The Marquee House; Rick Hert, North Olympic Peninsula VCB; Irene Hoadley, Salem CVA; Natalie Inouye, CVA Lane County; Linda Johnson, Burns CC; Kim Kaminski, Newport CC; Andrea Klaas, Hood River CC; Gene Kurtz, Rosebury VCB; Lesley Lacey, Thomas Cook Financial Services N. America; Sara Ledoux, Kimpton Hotel & Restaurant Group, Inc; Georgia Marshall, Sage County Inn; Charleen Maxwell; Paul & Virginia McCarthy; Marion McLean, Vancouver (WA) CC; Pat McMillan, Klamath County Dept of Tourism; Bruce Miller; Linda Miller, Kitsap Peninsula VCB; Charlie & Julie Mitchell, Grants Pass; Heidi Niblack, Bay Area CC; Glenna & Jack O'Neil; Julie Petretto, Medford/Jackson County VCB; Beth Pine, Klickitat County Tourism; Poi; Christine Potter; Connie Pound, Baker City VCB; Mary Ellen Quesada; Buddy & Stephanie Mays; Louis Richmond, Richmond Public Relations; Ruth Roberts, Tourism British Columbia, London; Roger Rocka, Astoria/Warrenton CC; Sally Sederstrom and Karen Runkel, Oregon Tourism Commission; Eve Sheehy, Wallowa CC; Charlotte Skinner, 2310 Lombard Bed & Breakfast; Rich Skinner, Kathleen Dunlap, Ann Stevens, SDS International; Mary Ann Stark, Tillamook CC; Jerry Stevens; Dennis Strayer, Oregon Caves National Monument; Linda Swearinger, Redmond CC; Sweetbrier Inn; Maureen Thomas, Ontario CC; Barb Thompson, Toppenish CC; Dawn Tryon, Washington County CC; Monte Turner, Oregon Parks & Recreation Dept; Esther Veltkamp, Sequim-Dungeness Valley CC; Deborah Wakefield, Portland Oregon Visitors Association; Westin Hotels & Resorts; Martha Lou Wheatly, Spokane Regional DVB; Carrie Wilkinson-Tuma, Washington State Division of Tourism; Tara Woolley, Whistler Resort Association.

5

CONTENTS

ROUTES AND CITIES

In alphabetical order. For indexing purposes, routes are listed in both directions – the reverse direction to which it appears in the book is shown in italics.
See also the Route Map, p. 8, for a diagrammatic presentation of all the routes in the book.
To look up towns and other places not listed here, see the Index, p. 348.

REFERENCE SECTION

7

8

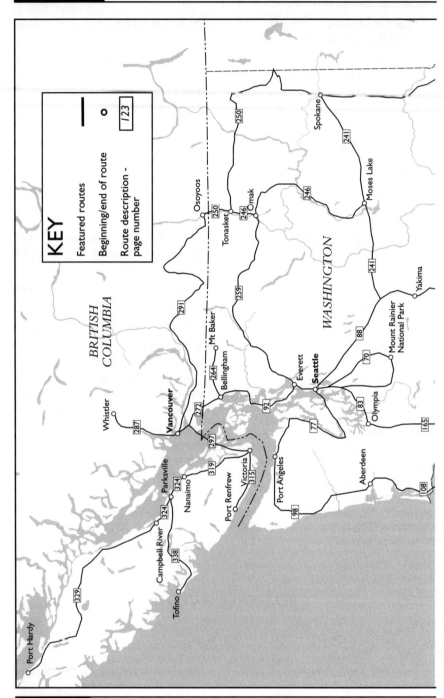

KEY

Featured routes

Beginning/end of route

Route description -
page number

123

BRITISH
COLUMBIA

WASHINGTON

Port Hardy
Tofino
Campbell River
Nanaimo
Parksville
Whistler
Vancouver
Port Renfrew
Victoria
Port Angeles
Aberdeen
Olympia
Seattle
Everett
Bellingham
Mt Baker
Tonasket
Osoyoos
Omak
Spokane
Moses Lake
Yakima
Mount Rainier
National Park

329
338
324
324
319
287
291
297
272
264
315
98
92
77
83
165
108
70
88
259
250
246
246
250
241
241

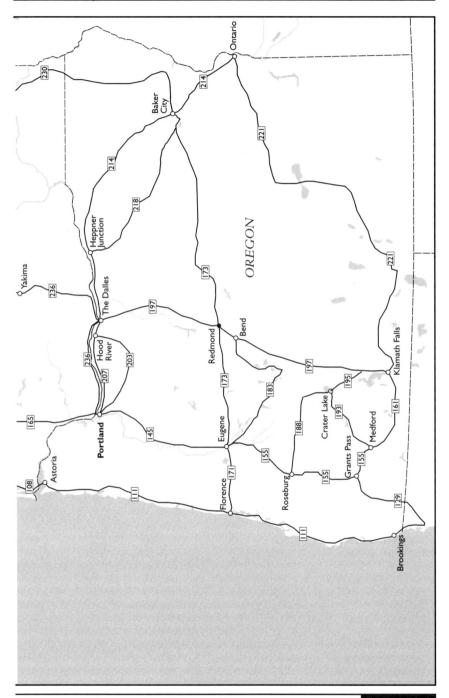

INTRODUCTION

Greys and greens predominate along the narrow strip of land from the Cascade Range west to the Pacific Ocean. The rain forests of the western sides of the Olympic Peninsula and Vancouver Island are among the wettest places in North America. Jibes about the residents of Portland, Seattle and Vancouver rusting as quickly as their bicycles ring true during the seemingly endless days of winter drizzle broken by rain and occasional snow.

The land east of the Cascades is another world – sunny plains and rich valleys that give way to deserts as dry and as harsh as any on the continent. Wheat fields wave unbroken from horizon to horizon beneath snow-capped peaks. Water is a precious resource, a giver of life, crops and hydroelectric power.

Seattle and Vancouver are gateways to the world, but nature remains an overriding presence. Piles of volcanic ash are a reminder of the thunderous eruptions of Mount St Helens nearly two decades ago; the ethereal images of Mts Adams, Baker, Hood, Rainier and a dozen other white-capped Cascade peaks floating on the horizon, are a daily reminder that nature may yet exact another volcanic toll.

There's a tension in the Pacific Northwest, an uncertain balance between old and new, a struggle for dominance between nature and humanity. Settled by religious fanatics and intolerant nationalists, it has become one of the most socially progressive corners of the continent. Native Americans, deliberately and systematically deprived of land, liberty and life by government policy, have re-emerged as a potent political, economic and cultural force.

This birthplace of Greenpeace and the original vision of ecotopia remains heavily dependent upon the exploitation of rapidly disappearing natural resources. Dense rain forests that once stretched unbroken from Pacific Ocean to Cascade crest are being reduced to scattered patches inside protected parklands. The Columbia River dam system is paradoxically one of the most stunning civil engineering projects ever conceived and one of the most environmentally devastating ever built. The endless runs of salmon that once ascended every river and stream have dwindled to yearly trickles in the wake of overfishing and overzealous timber cutting.

The more successful sections of the Pacific Northwest have already cut themselves loose from the old cycle of resource exploitation in favour of computers, wine, medical products and other new industries. The recreational lure of forests, mountains and fish attracts the engineers, technicians, venture capitalists and dreamers of this cutting edge world.

It's not the first time that a new wave of immigrants has changed life in the Pacific Northwest. Change overtook Native Americans in the form of traders and fur trappers in the 18th century, themselves displaced by farmers and lumbermen in the 19th. Nature plays her own role in the perpetual tug-of-war, sometimes defeated, in taming the Columbia River with a spate of dams, sometimes victorious, as when Mount St Helens resculpted the face of south-western Washington in 1980.

The paradox, the tension between using resources now or conserving them for the future, will bring change and the passing of a way of life that many hold dear. If the Pacific Northwest breaks with tradition and favours conservation, it will preserve the awesome natural scenery that has been the stuff of legend since humans first saw it more than 10,000 years ago.

Fred Gebhart and Maxine Cass

HOW TO USE THIS BOOK

ROUTES AND CITIES

On the Road around the Pacific Northwest provides you with an expert selection of over 40 recommended routes between key cities and attractions of Oregon, Washington and the neighbouring area of British Columbia, each in its own chapter. Smaller cities, towns, attractions and points of interest along each route are described in the order in which you will encounter them. Additional chapters are devoted to the major places of interest which begin and end these routes, and some circular routes explore regions of particular interest. These route and city chapters form the core of the book, from page 58 to page 342.

Where applicable, an alternative route which is more direct is also provided at the beginning of each route chapter. This will enable you to drive more quickly between the cities at the beginning and end of the route, if you do not intend to stop at any of the intermediate places. To save space, each route is described in only one direction, but you can follow it in the reverse direction, too.

The arrangement of the text consists of a chapter describing a large city or region of interest first, followed by chapters devoted to routes leading from that place to other major destinations. The first city to be covered is Seattle (pp.58–66), followed by Seattle Circuit circular drive (pp.67–69) and then routes from Seattle: Seattle to Mount Rainier (pp.70–76), Seattle to Port Angeles (pp.77–82), Seattle to Port Angeles (pp.77–82), Seattle to Olympia (pp.83–87), Seattle to Yakima (pp.88–91) and Seattle to Bellingham. Olympia Peninsula is described in the next chapter, as the routes head south along the Pacific Coast to cross Oregon, then Washington and finally British Columbia.

The order of chapters thus follows the pattern of your journey, beginning in the region's major gateway of Seattle, covering Oregon and heading north to Washington, before crossing the Canadian border to Vancouver and southern British Columbia. However, you can just as easily work backwards going south. To find the page number of any route or city chapter quickly, use either the alphabetical list on the **Contents** pages, pp. 6–7, or the master **Route Map** on pp. 8–9.

The routes are designed to be used as a kind of menu from which you can plan an itinerary, combining a number of routes which take you to the places you most want to visit.

11

WITHIN EACH ROUTE

Each route chapter begins with a short introduction to the route, followed by driving directions from the beginning of the route to the end, and a sketch map of the route and all the places along it which are described in the chapter. This map, intended to be used in conjunction with the driving directions, summarises the route and shows the main intermediate distances and road numbers; for a key to the symbols used, see p.13.

DIRECT ROUTE

This will be the fastest, most direct, and sometimes, predictably, least interesting drive between the beginning and end of the route, usually along major highways.

SCENIC ROUTE

This is the itinerary which takes in the most places of interest, usually using ordinary highways and minor roads. Road directions are specific; always be prepared for detours due to road construction, adverse weather conditions, etc. The driving directions are followed by sub-sections describing the main attractions and places of interest along the way. You can stop at them all or miss out the ones which do not appeal to you. Always ask at the local tourist information centre (usually the Convention & Visitors Bureau or Chamber of Commerce) for more information on sights, lodgings and places at which to eat.

 SIDE TRACK

This heading is occasionally used to indicate departures from the main route, or out-of-town trips from a city, which detour to worthwhile sights, described in full or highlighted in a paragraph or two.

CITY DESCRIPTIONS

Whether a place is given a half-page description within a route chapter or merits an entire chapter to itself, we have concentrated on practical details: local sources of tourist information; getting around in city centres (by car, by public transport or on foot as appropriate); accommodation and dining; post and phone communications; entertainment and shopping opportunities; and sightseeing, history and background interest. The largest cities have all this detail; in smaller places some categories of information are less relevant and have been omitted or summarised. Where there is a story to tell which would interrupt the flow of the main description, we have placed **feature boxes** on subjects as diverse as 'The Oregon Trail' and 'The Pig War'.

Although we mention good independently owned lodgings in many places, we always also list the hotel chains which have a property in the area, by means of code letters to save space. Many travellers prefer to stick to one or two chains with which they are familiar and which give a consistent standard of accommodation. The codes are explained on p. 344, and central booking numbers for the chains are also given there.

MAPS

In addition to the sketch map which accompanies each route, we provide maps of major cities (usually the downtown area), smaller towns, regions, scenic trails, national parks, and so on. At the end of the book is a section of **colour road maps** covering the Pacific Northwest, which is detailed enough to be used for trip planning and on the road. The **key to symbols** used on all the types of map in this book is shown on p. 13.

THE REST OF THE BOOK

At the front of the book, **Driving Distances** is a tabulation of distances between main places, to help in trip planning. The use of the **Contents** and **Route Map** pages has already been mentioned above. **Travel Essentials** is an alphabetically arranged chapter of general advice for the tourist new to the Pacific Northwest, covering a wide range subjects such as accommodation and safety or how much to tip. **Driving in the Pacific Northwest** concentrates on advice for drivers on the law, rules of the road, and so on. **Background Pacific Northwest** gives a concise briefing on the history and geography of this fascinating region. **Touring Itineraries** provides ideas and suggestions for putting together an itinerary of your own using the selection of routes in this book. At the end of the book, the **Conversion Tables** decode US sizes and measures for non-US citizens. Finally the **Index** is the quick way to look up any place or general subject. And please help us by completing and returning the **Reader Survey** at the very end of the text; we are grateful for both your views on the book and new information from your travels in the Pacific Northwest.

12

KEY TO MAP SYMBOLS

Route diagrams

City maps

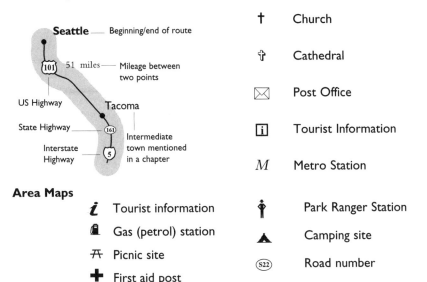

Seattle — Beginning/end of route

51 miles — Mileage between two points

US Highway — Tacoma

State Highway

Interstate Highway

Intermediate town mentioned in a chapter

†   Church

⑂   Cathedral

⊠   Post Office

⑂   Tourist Information

M Metro Station

Area Maps

i   Tourist information

🛢   Gas (petrol) station

🌂   Picnic site

➕   First aid post

☏   Public Telephone

🏛   Park Ranger Station

▲   Camping site

(S22)   Road number

------   Hiking trail

13

KEY TO PRICE DESCRIPTIONS

It is impossible to keep up to date with specific tariffs for lodging and accommodation or restaurants, although we have given some general advice under 'Cost of Living' in the Travel Essentials chapter p. 22). Instead, we have rated establishments in broad price categories throughout the book, as follows:

Accommodation (per room per night)
Budget   Under $35
Moderate   Under $90
Expensive   Under $150
Pricey $150 and higher

Meal (for one person, excluding drinks, tip or tax)
Cheap   Under $5
Budget   Under $10
Moderate   Under $20
Pricey   Over $20

ABBREVIATIONS USED IN THE BOOK
(For hotel chains, see p. 344)

Bldg	Building (in addresses)	Jan, Feb	January, February, etc.
Blvd	Boulevard	min(s)	minute(s)
Dr.	Drive (in addresses)	Mon, Tues	Monday, Tuesday, etc.
Fwy	Freeway	Rd	Road (in addresses)
hr(s)	hour(s)	Rte	Route, e.g. Rte 450
Hwy	US or State Highway, e.g. Hwy 1	St	Street (in addresses)
I-	Interstate Highway, e.g. I-95	SR	State Road, e.g. SR 197

THOMAS COOK TOURING HANDBOOKS
The perfect companions for your holiday

These route-based guides are crammed with practical information and maps. From advice on road laws to ideas for accommodation and sightseeing, they contain all the information you need to explore the USA by car.

On the Road around New England   Price: £10.95

40 routes with side-trips and scenic drives throughout this varied region. The area covered stretches from New York up to northern Maine, with side trips into Canada to visit Montreal and Quebec.

On the Road around Florida   Price: £10.95

With clear city and regional maps and honest sightseeing advice, this book will help you to get the most out of your visit to Florida. Over 30 routes combine famous and more unusual sights.

On the Road around the Capital Region USA
Price: £12.95

The historic heartland of the USA boasts dramatic scenery and major cultural sites. Washington, DC as well as Virginia, Maryland and parts of Pennsylvania and Delaware are covered. Includes 16 pages of colour photography.

On the Road around the California, 2nd edition £12.95

Thirty-five driving routes have been thoroughly re-researched for this second edition. The Grand Canyon, Bryce Canyon, Tijuana and Las Vegas have all been covered, as well as the whole of California. Includes 16 pages of colour photographs.

These publications are available from bookshops and Thomas Cook UK retail shops, or direct by post from Thomas Cook Publishing, Dept (OWN/PNW), PO Box 227, Thorpe Wood, Peterborough, PE3 6PU, UK. (Extra for postage and packing.)
Tel: 01733 503571/2.
Published by Passport Books in the USA.

TRAVEL ESSENTIALS

The following is an alphabetical listing of helpful tips and advice for those planning a Pacific Northwest holiday.

ACCOMMODATION

The Pacific Northwest offers accommodation of every price level imaginable, from five-star hotels and posh resorts to youth hostels and campsites. *Where to Stay in Oregon, Oregon Lodging Association, 12724 S.E. Stark St, Portland, OR 97233; tel: (503) 255-5136*, lists several hundred possibilities. *Oregon Bed & Breakfast Directory, Box 1283, Grants Pass, OR 97526; tel: (800) 841-5448 or (541) 479-5879*, is the largest Bed and Breakfast guide for the state. *Oregon Bed & Breakfast Guild, Box 3187, Ashland, OR 97520; tel: (800) 944-6169*, lists members state-wide who meet strict criteria. *Oregon Guest House Guide, 955 16th St N.E., Salem, OR 97301; tel: (800) 636-7455 or (503) 581-1057*, lists rental houses, cabins and condominiums around the state.

Washington State Lodging & Travel Guide, Washington State Division of Tourism, Box 42500, Olympia, WA 98504; tel: (360) 753-7180, lists accommodation for the entire state. *Washington State Bed & Breakfast Directory, 2442 N.W. Market St, #355, Seattle, WA 98107; tel: (800) 647-2918*, lists Bed and Breakfasts around Washington.

British Columbia Accommodations, Tourism British Columbia, 1117 Wharf St, Victoria, BC V8W 2Z2; tel: (800) 663-6000 or (604) 663-6000, makes free bookings for lodging across the province; have a credit card ready to confirm advance bookings by telephone. *B&B Inns of BC, Western Canada Bed & Breakfast Inns Association, Box 74534, Vancouver, BC V6K 4P4; tel: (604) 255-9199*, lists WCBBIA-approved members in BC. *Best Canadian Bed & Breakfast Network, 1090 W. King Edward Ave, Vancouver, BC V6H 1Z4; tel: (604) 738-7207*, lists Bed and Breakfasts across Western Canada.

Local tourist offices also provide lodging lists and telephone numbers, but generally cannot make bookings. Where available, local lodging services are noted in the text.

Accommodation can be extremely hard to find in major tourist destinations during high season, which is usually late May (Memorial Day weekend in the US) to early September (Labor Day weekend in the US and Canada), plus weekends and major public holidays. Exceptions are Vancouver and Victoria, where high season runs from early May–Sept to match the Alaska cruise ship season; and ski resorts, where high season prices arrive with the first good snowfall.

Expect to pay as much as 60% over low season rates during the high season. It is sometimes possible to avoid the higher tariffs by travelling during the shoulder season, one or two weeks before or after high season, when crowds are smaller and rates lower. It is also possible to travel out of season, but many attractions, especially in smaller towns, close when high season ends.

Thomas Cook or any other good travel agent can handle room bookings when purchasing air tickets and car or other local transportation. All-inclusive fly-drive arrangements, and 'do-it-yourself packages' such as Thomas Cook's *America for the Independent Traveller* programme, can provide hotel coupons, exchangeable at a range of hotel chains, which guarantee a pre-paid rate at participating chains, although they do not guarantee rooms – it's up to you to phone ahead as you go, or take a chance on availability. It is particularly important to pre-book the first and last nights' stay to avoid problems when connecting with international air flights.

It is also important to confirm pre-booked rooms by telephone if you will arrive after 1800. Many hotels and motels automatically cancel bookings at 1800, especially during high season, even if rooms have been guaranteed with a credit card. The best time to make the

15

reconfirmation is 1600–1800 the day of the late arrival.

Throughout the book, we have indicated prices of accommodation in a comparative way by using terms such as 'moderate' and 'pricey'; see 'How to Use This Book', p.11, for an explanation of what these descriptions mean. British Columbia prices are quoted in Canadian dollars; Oregon and Washington prices are quoted in US dollars.

Hotels and Motels

Hotel rates are quoted for single or double occupancy; children usually stay cheaply or for free with parents.

Once in North America, you will find that most chain hotels and motels have toll-free reservation telephone numbers. The list on p. 344 gives a selection of these, along with the abbreviations used in the text of this book to indicate which chains are present in the town or city being described.

Advance bookings generally require a voucher or credit card number to guarantee the booking. Ask for discounts if you're disabled, a senior, a motoring club member, or travelling off season. When checking in, always ask if there's a cheaper room rate than the one you pre-booked. It's often cost-effective to find lodging day by day, especially in off-peak seasons.

Motels are often the best bet. Literally, 'motor hotels', motels are one- to three-storey buildings with a modest version of a hotel's accommodation and facilities. Most belong to nation-wide chains which enforce service and safety standards.

Independent motels may not be quite as fancy, but offer even lower prices. Motels fill up fast during high season, but last-minute rooms are usually available in the off season, especially during the week. The *AAA TourBook* volumes for Oregon/Washington and Western Canada/Alaska list thousands of motels and hotels; thousands more are just as comfortable and affordable. Check the motels that line major highways entering most cities and towns. Special prices are often noted on roadside signs.

Budget hotels in Canada are often acceptable, but those in US cities tend to be dim, dirty and dangerous. Look for a motel or youth hostel instead.

Bed and Breakfast

In the Pacific Northwest, Bed and Breakfast can be a homey alternative to institutional seeming hotels and motels, but they are seldom the bargain lodgings of their English cousins, especially in major cities. They *may* be appropriate for budget travellers in more rural areas. The accent is more often on luxury than on value, particularly in Portland, Seattle, Vancouver and Victoria. The typical urban Bed and Breakfast is a refurbished room in a Victorian mansion, complete with chintz curtains, down comforter, fireplace, bric-a-brac atop antique furniture, and private facilities. If 'Victorians' are in short supply, any ordinary mansion will do, even a converted garage or barn, so long as it's suitably luxurious. Bed and Breakfast accommodation in smaller towns and rural areas is much closer to the original concept. In some remote areas, it may be the only choice other than camping.

Breakfasts vary, but the standard includes fruit juice, coffee or tea, an egg dish, homemade bread and a sweet.

Camping

Camping means a tent or a recreational vehicle (RV) in a rural campsite. KOA, Kampgrounds of America, is a private chain of RV parks that also accept tents. Many other campsites are public, most operated by federal, state or provincial authorities. Overnight fees range from $7 to more than $20, depending on location and season. Standard facilities include a fireplace for barbecues, food storage locker, tent site, nearby showers/toilets, and, during high season, daytime guided hikes and evening educational programmes around a large campfire.

The latest wrinkles in camping: the **yurt**, a permanent, round tent modelled on traditional Mongolian nomad tents; **tepees** and **covered wagons**. All three are available at selected parks in Oregon through **Reservations Northwest**; *tel: (800) 452-5684* or *(503) 731-3411.* Cost is $25 per yurt per night for up to five people, including beds, mattresses, table and lights.

Many state and provincial park campsites

can be reserved in advance. In popular parks, they must be. For Oregon parks, **State Park Campsite Reservations and Information**; *tel: (800) 452-5684 or (800) 551-6949*. For Washington parks, **Washington State Parks & Recreation Commission**; *tel: (800) 452-5687 or (800) 233-0321*. For BC parks, **Discover Camping**; *tel: (800) 689-9025 or (604) 689-9025*.

Youth Hostels

Hostelling International *(HI)* was created for tight budgets. Most Pacific Northwest hostels provide a dormitory-style room and shared bath for $8–$16 per night. Some have family rooms, all offer discounts to local attractions. The downside: there are an extremely limited number of hostels in the region. And when two or more people are travelling together and can share a room, cheap motels may be even cheaper than hostels.

Airports

Travelers Aid desks provide tourist information; **airport information** booths and touch-screen information kiosks cover airport facilities, airport-to-city transport and local accommodation. For flight information and bookings, contact individual airlines, not the airport.

All major airports have foreign exchange and banking services as well as car hire facilities. Secondary airports have cash machines (ATMs) and car hire desks, but seldom currency exchange facilities. Public transportation to the nearest city is usually available, but seldom practical in terms of routes or time. Luggage trolleys are generally free for international arrivals; elsewhere, there is a $1–1.50 charge. Be prepared for long walks through terminals on arrival – moving walkways are few and far between, even at the largest airports.

Specific airport arrival information is given in the chapters dealing with the major airport cities.

BICYCLES

Cycling is popular for countryside day touring – less so for overnight trips, due to geography. Bikes can be hired by the hour or the day in most wine country and urban areas as well as in major parks.

For serious bikers (as cyclists are called in the Pacific Northwest), biking tours are available at all levels, from easy day trips to arduous pulls over the Cascades or up to Whistler Resort. On-your-own bike tours are also possible, but beware of unexpected distances and mountains between towns.

Many highways also have narrow or non-existent verges, which can make a cycling nerve-wracking experience as well as dangerous in heavy traffic. Local law generally requires cyclists to wear protective helmets while riding.

BORDERS

Customs and Immigration officials are paid to take their jobs very seriously. Both Canada and the United States have had problems with illegal immigration, most often visitors who overstay tourist and student visas. US and Canadian citizens need only proof of identity and residence to cross the border, but nationals of other countries generally need a valid passport and visa to enter either country.

US Customs and Immigration has a reputation as one of the most unpleasant travel experiences the world has to offer. It can be for citizens returning home as well as for first-time holidaymakers. Canadian as well as US C & I officials have *carte blanche* to ask any question, search anyone or anything, and do it in any manner they see fit, however unpleasant. In reality, most inspectors are polite to a fault, but the only defence against an inspector who got up on the wrong side of the bed is to have passport, visa, proof of support, and return ticket in order.

A car or RV can be a liability when crossing the border: the diligent search can extend to your vehicle. Canadian officials are especially diligent checking US-registered vehicles for firearms which are legal in the US but banned in Canada. They also show a keen interest in Canadian-registered vehicles which may have ventured south on a shopping spree and could well owe customs duties.

There are generally no restrictions on taking rental cars across the border in either direction, but check when making your initial car rental booking and again when picking up the vehicle. It is also wise to ensure that vehicle insurance purchased in one country is valid in the other.

Both the US and Canada prohibit the importation of weapons, narcotics, or certain non-approved pharmaceutical products. Carry doctors' prescriptions with documentation (such as a doctor's letter) to prove that medications are legitimate.

BUSES

Greyhound Bus Lines, *Customer Service, 901 Main St, Dallas, TX 75202; tel: (800) 231-2222*, provides information on long-distance bus services between major cities. There are discounts for seniors (over 55), disabled travellers, helpers and children (under 12) riding with a full-fare adult. The **International Ameripass** offers special discounts for adult travellers not resident in North America. Greyhound passes are obtainable through Thomas Cook travel shops in the UK.

If you're buying tickets locally ask for the **Domestic Ameripass**, which, depending on distance travelled, may be more economical. Local transportation companies listed in the telephone directory under individual cities and towns provide local service. Thomas Cook publishes bi-monthly timetables of North American buses in the *Thomas Cook Overseas Timetable* (full details on p. 38).

CAMPERS AND RVS

It's the freedom of the open road, housekeeping on wheels, a tinkerer's delight, a large machine hurtling down slopes and ploughing up grades. An RV, caravan, or motorhome provides a kitchen, sleeping and bathroom facilities, all integrated atop a lorry chassis.

Fly-drive holiday packages usually offer the option of hiring an RV. The additional cost of hiring an RV can be offset by the economics of assured lodging for several people, space for meal preparation and eating, plus the convenience of comfort items and souvenirs stored nearby. RVs are cramped, designed to stuff you and your belongings into limited space. The economics work only if advance planning assures that the pricey spur-of-the-moment

allure of a hotel shower or unplanned restaurant meal doesn't overcome RV campers! Factor in the cost of petrol – an RV guzzles 3–4 times more than a medium-sized car.

Always get operating manuals for the vehicle and all appliances before leaving the RV hire lot, and have someone demonstrate how *everything* works. Systems may be interdependent, or more complex than anticipated. Be prepared to pre-plan menus and allow additional time each morning and afternoon/evening to level the RV (perfect levelling is essential for correct operation of refrigerators), hook up or disconnect electricity, water and sewer hoses and cable television plugs. As at home, some basic housecleaning must be done; also allow time for laundry at RV parks.

Buy a pair of sturdy rubber washing gloves to handle daily sewer chores. Pack old clothes to wear while crawling under the vehicle to hook up and disconnect at each stop – many RVers carry a pair of overalls. Without hook-ups, water and electricity are limited to what you carry with you from the last fill-up or battery charge. If you camp in a park without hook-ups, locate the nearest restrooms before dark. Using showers and toilets in RV parks or public campsites will save time cleaning up the RV shower space and emptying the toilet holding tank. Have a strong torch (flashlight) handy.

When you move out on the road, expect anything that's not secured to go flying, or to shake, rattle, and roll. Quickly get into a routine of allotted tasks and assign a handy spot for maps, snacks, cameras and valuables.

RV travel information: **Recreation Vehicle Industry Association (RVIA)**, *Dept. RK, PO Box 2999, Reston VA 22090-0999; tel: (703) 620-6003*. To plan RV camping, request *Go Camping America* from **Camping Vacation Planner**, *PO Box 2669, Reston VA 22090; tel: (800) 477-8669*, covering the US and Canada.

Camping clubs offer RV information for members; some, including the **Good Sam Club**, *PO Box 6060, Camarillo CA 93011; tel: (805) 389-0300*, offer roadside assistance for breakdowns and tyre changing. Many camping clubs publish magazines or newsletters with tips on operating and driving an RV. For a hilarious insight into RV travel, find a copy of *Out West, 9792 Edmonds Way, Suite 265, Edmonds WA 98020; tel: (206) 776-1228; fax: (206) 776-3398; email: outwestcw@aol.com*, a periodic tabloid with bizarre pictures of signs and stories about Western characters. The publisher packs his family and computer into an RV for several weeks at a time, and they deliver a flavourful picture of the best and the worst of home-on-wheels travel.

Campsite directories and state/provincial tourist office guides list private RV park locations, directions, size, number of pitches, hook-ups, laundry, on-premises convenience stores and showers. Directories cover parks in the US and Canada. Popular directories include: *Trailer Life Campground & RV Services Directory*, TL Enterprises, *2575 Vista del Mar Dr, Ventura, CA 93001; tel: (805) 667-4100*, ($19.95); *Woodall's Campground Directory (Western Edition), 13975 W. Polo Trail Dr, Lake Forest IL 60045; tel: (800) 823-9076*, ($13.70); *Wheelers RV Resort & Campground Guide, 1310 Jarvis Ave, Elk Grove Village, IL 60007; tel: (708) 981-0100*, ($15.50); *Kampgrounds of America (KOA) Directory, PO Box 30558, Billings MT 59114-0558; tel: (406) 248-7444* ($3 or free at KOA campsites).

The **AAA** and **CAA** have directories and maps for Pacific Northwest campsites. See 'Parks Information' in this chapter for campsites on state, provincial or federal land.

CANADA

A valid passport is required for entry into Canada, but no visa is required for citizens of Australia, New Zealand, Republic of Ireland, South Africa, the UK or the US. US and Canadian citizens need only proof of identity and citizenship to cross the border in either direction, but a passport remains the easiest documentation. Citizens of countries other than Canada and the US who plan to return to the US after visiting Canada should check with US immigration officials that their visa, if one is required, permits a return.

Canada imposes a 7% **Goods & Services Tax**, or **GST**, on nearly all purchases, including accommodation and meals. In addition, provinces impose sales taxes of 4%–12% on

selected goods, meals and accommodation. Visitors may apply for a **refund** of GST paid on most products taken out of Canada and on accommodation of less than 30 days. To qualify for a refund, your total purchases must be for a minimum of $200 ($14 in tax), you must have original receipts and each individual receipt must show a minimum of $3.50 in tax.

The refund application may be obtained from Canadian Customs and tourism offices, department stores, hotels, and tourist infocentres. Refunds can be given at certain duty-free shops, at some foreign exchange bureaux, or by post: **Visitor Rebate Program**, *Revenue Canada, Summerside Tax Centre, Summerside, PE C1N 6C6; tel: (800) 668-4748 or (902) 432-5608*. Duty-free shops and Revenue Canada return the entire rebate, but only after you've already left the country. Currency exchange bureaux pay cash on the spot, but charge a commission, usually $5 or 15%, whichever is more. Unless you're planning a quick return to Canada, it's usually simpler to pay the commission and get the cash to spend before you leave.

National holidays include New Year's Day (Jan 1); Good Friday (Apr); Easter Monday (Apr); Victoria Day (late May); Canada Day (Jul 1); Labour Day (early Sept); Thanksgiving (mid Oct); Remembrance Day (Nov 11); Christmas Day (Dec 25) and Boxing Day (Dec 26).

CHILDREN

The Pacific Northwest, with its many natural attractions, is both ideal for travelling with children and welcoming. From museums to transport, check for children's rates, often segmented by age, e.g. under 3 yrs free, 6–12 yrs $3.00, 12–18 yrs $4.00. A student card must be shown to use student rates.

Travelling with children is never easy, but preparation helps. *Travel with Children*, by Maureen Wheeler (Lonely Planet) is filled with useful tips. Kids get bored and cranky on long drives. Pack favourite games and books, and pick up a book of travel games. A traditional favourite is to count foreign, i.e. non-local, licence plates. The winner – always a child – gets a special treat later in the day. If the children are old enough, suggest that they keep a detailed travel diary. It will help them focus on the Pacific Northwest instead of what they might be missing back home. A diary also helps them remember details later to impress friends and teachers. Collecting anything, from postcards to admission tickets, adds a new dimension to travel.

Any driving destination in the region is equipped for children of all ages, from nappies to video games. Most hotels and motels can arrange for baby-sitters, though the price may be steep. Many motel chains allow children under 12, 14, and sometimes up to 18, to stay free in their parents' room. A rollaway child's bed, usually called a cot, usually comes at no or low cost.

Meals can be difficult, but picnic lunches offer flexibility. It's also a good idea to carry a small cooler filled with ice, cold drinks and snacks, especially in hot weather. Most towns have coffee shops with long hours, children's menus and familiar fast-food names. If the children like McDonalds at home, they'll like Big Macs in the Pacific Northwest – and vice versa.

CLIMATE

Climate is what you expect, weather is what you get. Expect grey skies west of the Cascade Range and blue skies to the east, but weather can change abruptly on either side of the mountains. Rain and snow are more likely October to April, but don't be surprised at a downpour in August. Fog is common along the coast all year. Portland, Seattle and Vancouver are known for cloudy skies and rain all year round, but the sun shows itself for at least a few minutes most days May–Sept. Sunshine is a treasured experience on the western side of the Olympic Peninsula and the west coast of Vancouver Island, where tall mountains wring rain from prevailing winds off the Pacific Ocean. The San Juan Islands, the Gulf Islands and Victoria, sheltered by those same mountains, are much drier and sunnier.

The Pacific Ocean moderates temperatures west of the Cascades. Expect greater extremes east of the range, colder in winter and hotter in summer. Summer is also fire season. Forest fires may be allowed to burn unchecked unless human lives or major property damage are threatened. Regular burning is a natural renewal mechanism and necessary for the regeneration of many forest species. If a patch of forest has not burned in several years, deliberate fires, called controlled burns, are set during wet weather to burn out accumulated dead growth and prevent later conflagrations. Smoke-

Average Temperatures					
	Portland	Seattle	Spokane	Vancouver	Victoria
JANUARY					
Highest	44°F/7°C	46°F/8°C	31°F/-1°C	43°F/6°C	43°F/6°C
Lowest	33°F/1°C	37°F/3°C	19°F/-7°C	34°F/1°C	36°F/2°C
APRIL					
Highest	62°F/18°C	59°F/15°C	59°F/15°C	59°F/15°C	55°F/13°C
Lowest	42°F/6°C	44°F/7°C	36°F/2°C	43°F/6°C	43°F/6°C
JULY					
Highest	72°F/22°C	75°F/24°C	84°F/29°C	75°F/24°C	68°F/20°C
Lowest	52°F/11°C	56°F/13°C	55°F/13°C	55°F/13°C	52°F/11°C
OCTOBER					
Highest	63°F/17°C	60°F/16°C	59°F/15°C	59°F/15°C	57°F/14°C
Lowest	45°F/7°C	48°F/9°C	38°F/3°C	44°F/7°C	46°F/8°C

jumpers, airborne fire-fighters who parachute into remote areas to fight fires, and water bombers are at their busiest in late summer.

CLOTHING

Summers can be blisteringly hot in the interior and shivery in coastal fog. Winters are cool to freezing throughout the Pacific Northwest. In any season, take plenty of layers, from shorts for the beach and interior valleys to jumpers and jackets for the mountains. Cotton and wool, worn in layers, are the region's favourite fibres. One layer is cool, several layers are warm. Adding and removing layers makes it easier to stay comfortable no matter how many times the weather changes in a single day. Umbrellas and lightweight rain gear are indispensable along the coast.

What to pack is a constant question. Informality is the norm throughout the Pacific Northwest, with the exception of a handful of elegant city restaurants which require jackets and ties for men. Sneakers (trainers), sandals and hiking boots are far more common than wingtips and high heels, even in fancy hotels. When in doubt, leave it at home. Pacific Northwest clothing prices are cheaper than almost anywhere outside the Third World, especially in Oregon, which does not have a sales tax. But do take good, broken-in walking shoes.

COFFEE

Coffee has become something closer to a religious experience than a hot drink in the Pacific Northwest. Espresso carts are a way of breakfast, lunch and tea time on city pavements from Medford to Tofino. Motorists stuck in traffic jams jump out for a quick shot of espresso to speed the drive home while petrol stations sell cappuccino and latte along side the motor oil and tyre chains. Drive-through espresso stands have become common in most urban areas. Even McDonalds restaurants have installed espresso machines.

The caffeine craze began when three University friends in Seattle named a 1971 coffee shop for the steadfast first mate of the *Pequod* in Herman Melville's *Moby Dick*. Starbucks introduced espresso to the masses and mush-roomed to become the largest coffee roastery in North America.

Urban residents are fiercely loyal to their chosen brand. Expect descriptions such as 'strong', 'nutty', 'smooth', ' delicate' etc. **Espresso** is the basic brew, black and thick. **Cappuccino** is espresso mixed with hot milk, topped with milk foam and a dusting of chocolate or cinnamon. **Latte** is similar to cappuccino, without the foam or the spice dusting. And if coffee is too strong for your taste buds, most coffee bars offer more than a dozen flavours, from vanilla and hazelnut to banana and coconut. The latest wrinkle is iced coffee drinks, often whipped.

CONSULATES

Australia: *602-999 Canada Place, Vancouver, BC V6C 3E1; (604) 684-1177 and 1 Bush St, 7th Floor, San Francisco, CA 94104; tel: (415) 362-6160.*

Canada: *Plaza 600, Suite 412, Seattle, WA 98101; tel: (206) 443-1372.*

New Zealand: *Box 51059, Seattle, WA 98115; tel: (206) 525-0271, and 1200-888 Dunsmuir, Vancouver, BC V6C 3K4; tel: (604) 684-2177.*

Republic of Ireland: *655 Montgomery St, San Francisco, CA 94104; tel: (415) 392-4214.*

South Africa: *50 N. La Cienega Blvd, Suite 300, Beverly Hills, CA 90211; tel: (310) 657-9200, and Suite 3023, 3 Bentall Center, 595 Burrard St, Box 49096, Vancouver, BC V7X 1G4; tel: (604) 688-1301.*

UK: *First Interstate Center, Seattle, WA 98101; tel: (206) 622-9255, and 800-1111 Melville, Vancouver, BC V6E 3V6 ; tel: (604) 683-4421.*

US: *1075 W. Pender St, Vancouver, BC V6E 2M6; tel: (604) 685-4311.*

COST OF LIVING

Oregon does not have a local sales tax, although Washington and British Columbia do (GST in BC); all three have hotel/lodging taxes. The combined levy, however, is less than the VAT charged in most of Europe. Prices are always marked or quoted *without tax*, which is added at time of purchase (see 'Sales Taxes', p. 33).

Petrol prices are a special bargain, about $1.25 per US gallon (4 litres), or about $0.30

21

per litre in Oregon and Washington, about $0.60 per litre in BC. Lodging and food prices are similar in either US or Canadian dollars: Motel rooms cost $30–$70 per night; hotels from $50 up. Restaurant meals, including soup or salad, main course, dessert, beverage, and tax are about $10–$20 per person for lunch; $20–$25 for dinner. National, state and provincial parks charge $4–$20 per vehicle entrance; most museums charge $2–$5 per person.

CURRENCY

US dollars are the only currency accepted in Oregon and Washington; Canadian dollars the only currency accepted in British Columbia. *Some* shops and restaurants near the US-Canada border accept currency from the other country, but only at a substantial discount.

US banknote denominations are $1, $2 (very rare), $5, $10, $20, $50 and $100. All bills are the same colour, green and white, and the same size. Take great care not to mix them up. The only differences, apart from the denominations marked on them, are the US president pictured on the front and the designs on the back. There are 100 cents to the dollar: coins include the copper 1-cent piece, 5-cent nickel, 10-cent dime, 25-cent quarter, 50-cent half-dollar (rare), and a seldom-seen Susan B. Anthony dollar which is almost identical to the quarter.

Canadian banknotes come in $1, $2, $5, $10, $20 and $100 denominations, all the same size but each a different colour. $1 and $2 bills are being replaced by coins. $1 coins are popularly called 'loonies' for the image of a loon, a type of duck, on the original issue. $2 coins, a small silvery disk surrounded by a golden disk, have not been named. There are 100 cents to the dollar: coins include the copper 1-cent piece, 5-cent nickel, 10-cent dime and 25-cent quarter. Size and weight of US and Canadian coins are slightly different and seldom work in vending machines or coin-operated telephones in the other country.

Banks can exchange foreign currency or travellers' cheques, but expect delays in small town branches as they telephone the main office in search of exchange rates and procedures. Don't even both trying to exchange

coins: it costs banks on both sides of the border more to collect and process them than they're worth. Better to seek out one of the Thomas Cook locations (or Marlin Travel in Canada) noted in this book; to contact Thomas Cook offices in the US, *tel: 1-800-CURRENCY* (toll-free). A number of Thomas Cook locations offer MoneyGram, a quick international money transfer service. Traveller's cheques from well-known issuers such as Thomas Cook are acceptable everywhere and can be used like cash or changed easily. To report Thomas Cook travellers cheque losses and thefts; *tel: (800) 223-7373*, (toll-free, 24-hr service).

For security reasons, avoid carrying large amounts of cash. The safest forms of money are travellers cheques and credit or debit cards. Both can be used almost everywhere. If possible, bring at least one, preferably two, major credit cards such as **Access (MasterCard)**, **American Express**, or **Visa**. (Thomas Cook locations offer replacement and other emergency services if you lose a MasterCard.) Nearly all US shops accept both MasterCard and Visa, but smaller shops in BC may accept only one of the two.

Plastic is the only acceptable proof of fiscal responsibility. Car hire companies require either a credit card imprint or a substantial cash deposit before releasing a vehicle, even if the hire has been fully prepaid. Hotels and motels also require either a credit card imprint or a cash deposit, even if the bill is to be settled in cash.

Some shops, cheaper motels, small local restaurants, and low-cost petrol stations require cash. Automated teller machines, or **ATMs**, are a ubiquitous source of cash through withdrawals or cash advances authorised by debit or credit card. **Star** and **CIRRUS** are the most common international systems used in the region, but check terms, availability, and PIN (personal identification number) with the card issuer before leaving home. Expect to pay transaction fees to both the bank which owns the ATM and your own bank for each transaction.

CUSTOMS ALLOWANCES

Personal duty-free allowances which can be taken into the USA by visitors are 1 litre of spirits or wine, 120 cigarettes and 100 (non-

Cuban) cigars and up to $100 worth of gifts.
Personal duty-free allowances which can be
taken into Canada by visitors are 1.14 litres (40
ounces) of spirits or wine or 8.5 litres (300
ounces, 24 bottles/cans) of beer or ale, 50 cigars, 200 cigarettes and 400 grams (14 ounces) of
loose tobacco. On your return home you will
be allowed to take in the following:
Australia: goods to the value of A$400 (half for
those under 18) plus 250 cigarettes or 250 g
tobacco and 1 litre alcohol.
Canada: goods to the value of C$300, pro-
vided you have been away for over a week and
have not already used up part of your allowance
that year. You are also allowed 50 cigars plus
200 cigarettes and 1 kg tobacco (if over 16) and
40 oz/1.14 litres alcohol.
New Zealand: goods to the value of NZ$700.
Anyone over 17 may also take 200 cigarettes or
250 g tobacco or 50 cigars or a combination of
tobacco products not exceeding 250 g in all
plus 4.5 litres of beer or wine and 1.125 litres
spirits.
South Africa: Goods to the value of 500
Rand. Anyone over 18 may also take 400 cigarettes and 50 cigars and 250 grams tobacco plus
2 litres wine and 1 litre spirts, plus 50 ml perfume and 250 ml toilet water.
UK: The allowances for goods bought outside
the EU and/or in EU duty-free shops are: 200
cigarettes or 50 cigars or 100 cigarillos or 250 g
tobacco + 2 litres still table wine + 1 litre spirits or 2 litres sparkling wine + 50 g/60 ml perfume + 0.5 litre/250 ml toilet water.
US: The allowances for goods bought outside
the US are: US$400 worth of goods, including
1 litre of spirits or wine and 200 cigarettes or
100 (non-Cuban) cigars.

Street prices for alcohol, tobacco, perfume
and other typical duty-free items beat most
duty-free shops in Oregon, Washington or
BC. Follow the locals into chain supermarkets
and drug stores (Safeway, Fred Meyer and others) and discount stores (Target, K-mart, and
Wal-Mart are the most common). Prices are
generally lower in Oregon and Washington
than in BC.

DISABLED TRAVELLERS

Access is the key word. Physically challenged is

synonymous with disabled. Physical disabilities
should present less of a barrier in the Pacific
Northwest than in much of the world. Federal,
state and provincial laws generally require that
all businesses, buildings and services used by the
public be accessible by handicapped persons,
including those using wheelchairs. Every hotel,
restaurant, office, shop, cinema, museum, post
office and other public building must have
access ramps and toilets designed for wheelchairs. Most cities and towns have ramps built
into street crossings and most city buses have
some provision for wheelchair passengers. Even
many parks have installed paved pathways so
disabled visitors can get a sense of the natural
world.

The bad news is that disabled facilities aren't
always what they're meant to be. Museums,
public buildings, restaurants and accommodation facilities are usually accessible, but special
automobile controls for disabled drivers are seldom an option on hired vehicles.

Airlines are particularly hard on disabled
passengers. Carriers can prevent anyone who is
not strong enough to open an emergency exit
(which weighs about 45 lb, 20.5 kg) or has
vision/hearing problems from sitting in that
row of seats – even if it means bumping them
from the flight. Commuter airlines sometimes
deny boarding to passengers with mobility
problems on the grounds that they may block
the narrow aisle during an emergency.

Some public telephones have special access
services for the deaf and disabled. Broadcast
television may be closed-captioned for the
hearing impaired, indicated by a rectangle
around a double cc in a corner of the screen.

North American Information: SATH
(Society for the Advancement of Travel for the
Handicapped), *347 5th Ave, Suite 610, New
York NY 10016; tel: (212) 447-7284.*

UK Information: RADAR, *12 City
Forum, 250 City Rd, London EC1V 8AF; tel:
(0171) 250 3222* publish a useful annual guide
called *Holidays and Travel Abroad* which gives
details of facilities for the disabled in different
countries.

DISCOUNTS

Reductions and concessions on entrance fees

and public transport for senior citizens, children, students, and military personnel are common. Some proof of eligibility is usually required. For age, a passport or driving licence is sufficient. Military personnel should carry an official identification card. Students will have better luck with an International Student Identity Card (ISIC) from their local student union, than with a college ID.

The most common discount is for automobile club members. Touring guides from AAA (Automobile Association of America) and CAA (Canadian Automobile Association) affiliates list hundreds of member discounts throughout the Pacific Northwest. Always ask about 'Triple A discounts' and 'CAA discounts' at attractions, hotels, motels and car hire counters. Most recognise reciprocal membership benefits. Some cities will send high-season discount booklets on request, good for shops, restaurants or lodging.

DRINKING

Hollywood movies to the contrary, you must be 21 yrs old to purchase or to drink any kind of alcoholic beverage in Oregon and Washington and 19 in BC. Beer, wine and spirits are sold in supermarkets in Oregon and Washington, in government-run **Liquor Stores** in BC. Beer is also sold at breweries and wine at wineries throughout the region.

Opening hr for licensed establishments, usually called bars, lounges, pubs, saloons or taverns, vary by locale, but it is seldom difficult to find a drink between 0800 and 0200 any day of the year.

Convenience stores in Oregon and Washington sell beer, wine and sometimes spirits, but prices are higher than in supermarkets.

Laws against drinking and driving are very strict, and very strictly enforced with fines and imprisonment. If stopped under suspicion of Driving Under the Influence (DUI), the police officer will ask you to choose between one of three tests: breath, blood, or urine. Refusing to submit to a sobriety test is tantamount to admitting that you are drunk. Any liquor, wine or beer container in a vehicle (RVs excepted) must be full, sealed, and unopened – or in the boot.

EARTHQUAKES

Earthquakes are less frequent in the Pacific Northwest than in neighbouring California and Alaska, but not unknown. Archaeological evidence, Native American accounts, and Settler diaries all record major quakes in Oregon, Washington and BC, although not in recent years.

If you feel a mild earthquake, treat it like an amusement park ride. If items start falling from shelves, lamps sway or it becomes difficult to walk because of a quake, take cover. Crawl under the nearest solid table for protection against falling objects. If there's no table handy, brace arms and legs in an interior doorway. Stay away from windows, bookcases, stairs or anything else that could fall or break. *Don't* run outside. Glass, masonry and live power lines could be falling.

If driving, pull off the road and stop – it's almost impossible to control a vehicle when the road won't hold still.

Once the quake is over, treat it like any other civil emergency. Make sure everyone is safe and provide all help possible to the wounded. And get ready for the next shake. *There are always aftershocks.*

ELECTRICITY

The Pacific Northwest uses 110 volt 60 hertz current. Two- or three-pin electrical plugs are standard. Electrical gadgets from outside North America require plug and power converters. Both are difficult to obtain in the US and Canada because local travellers don't need them, although BC hotels often have a supply of converters for their UK clientele.

Beware of buying electrical appliances for the same reason. Few gadgets on the North American market can run on 220 V 50 Hz power. Exceptions are battery-operated equipment such as radios, cameras, and portable computers. Tape cassettes, CDs, computer programmes, and CD-ROMs sold in the Northwest can be used anywhere in the world.

North American video equipment, which uses the NTSC format, is *not* compatible with the PAL and SECAM equipment used in most of the rest of the world. *Pre-recorded* video tapes sold in the US and Canada will not work with other equipment unless specifically marked as compatible with PAL or SECAM. *Blank* video tapes purchased in North America, however, *can* be used with video recorders elsewhere in the world.

Discount store prices on blank video cassettes are very reasonable, especially in Oregon, which has no sales tax.

EMERGENCIES

In case of emergency, ring 911, free from any telephone. Ambulance, paramedics, police, fire brigades, or other public safety personnel will be dispatched immediately. See also under 'Health' on the next page.

If you lose your Thomas Cook travellers' cheques; *tel: (800) 223-7373*, (toll-free, 24-hr service). In the event of loss or theft of a MasterCard card, or for assistance with other card–related emergencies, call MasterCard Global Service at *1-800-307-7309* (toll-free 24-hr service).

FOOD

Eating in the Pacific Northwest has revolved around salmon and berries for centuries. To a large degree, it still does. It's hard to find a restaurant in the region that doesn't have salmon on the menu. Chum, Coho, Chinook, dog, silver, king and other types of salmon are seen more as a birthright than just another fish.

Local and menu reference to seafood is often by place name, e.g. 'Willapas' or 'Elliot Bays' for Washington oysters from those two areas. 'Dungeness' is Dungeness crab, 'rainbows' are rainbow trout, and so on.

Increasing overfishing, combined with rampant habitat destruction from logging, land reclamation and housing construction, has decimated natural stocks. There's a growing likelihood that the fillet on your plate came from a fish farm and not from a wild fish fighting its way upstream to spawn. The same is true of oysters, clams, mussels, trout and many other types of seafood.

Berries have fared better in the modern world. More raspberries, blackberries and blueberries are grown and consumed in the Pacific Northwest than almost anywhere else in the

world. Oregon agronomists have developed the marionberry, a sweet, magenta-coloured blackberry variant that is widely used for pies and jams. But the top of the berry heap belongs to the huckleberry, a kind of tart wild blueberry that has so far resisted every attempt at domestication. Add apples, peaches, pears, cherries, hazelnuts, wine grapes, hops, and dozens of other introduced crops, and Northwestern cooks are faced with a bounty that much of the world can only dream about.

North American pioneer traditions demand huge portions, beginning with breakfast and coffee cups that are never allowed to go empty. Thinly-sliced bacon and eggs cooked to order (fried, boiled, poached) come with hash browns (shredded fried potatoes) or chips. Toast, a flat 'English' muffin with butter and jam, or a bagel with cream (farmer's) cheese and lox (smoked salmon slices) may be served alongside. Variations or additions include pancakes, French toast (bread dipped in egg batter and lightly fried), and waffles. Fresh fruit, yoghurt, cereal, and porridge are other possibilities. A 'continental breakfast' is juice, coffee or tea, and some sort of bread or pastry.

Hotels and some restaurants offer Sunday brunch, usually 1100–1400, with all-you-can-eat self-service buffets heaped with hot and cold dishes. The economical Sunday brunch also includes coffee, tea, orange juice and cheap 'champagne' (sparkling wine).

Menus offer similar choices for lunch and dinner, the evening meal. Dinner portions are larger and more costly. Most menus offer appetisers (starters), salads, soups, pastas, entrées (main courses), and desserts. Northwesterners expect salads to be fresh and crisp and sauces light and tasty. Cooking oils are not light on the palate, so avoid fried fish and ask instead for grilled seafood. Ice cream or sherbet is a lighter dessert choice.

For hearty eating, try a steak house where salad, baked potato, and beans accompany a thick steak, be it beef or salmon. Italian restaurants serve pizza, pasta, seafood and steaks, with heavy doses of tomato and garlic. Mexican cooks use thin wheat or corn tortillas as the base for beans, rice, cheese, tomatoes, spicy sauce, and other ingredients. The Chinese cuisine

25

offered in Chinatowns is Cantonese with bean sprout chow mein and fried rice. More authentic Chinese dishes can be found with regional variations, from spicy Hunan to rich, meaty Mandarin. Bite-size dim sum (filled dumplings) or any variety of won ton soup make a filling lunch. Japanese, Vietnamese and Thai food are other easy-to-find Asian cuisines.

The melting pot of cuisines in major cities includes Basque, French, German, Spanish, Cuban, Ethiopian, Salvadoran, Indian and a hundred others.

Perhaps *beignets* or Chinese finger food came first, but America made fast food an international dining experience. Fast food is quick and economical. Food is ordered, paid for, and picked up from a service counter, all within a few minutes. Some fast-food outlets have drive-through service, where the driver pulls up to a window, orders from a posted menu, pays, and gets the meal, all without leaving the vehicle. Hamburgers, hot dogs, tacos, fried chicken, and barbecue beef are common offerings. McDonalds' golden arches and KFC's grinning chubby colonel are easy to spot. Other fast food chains include A & W, Arby's Roast Beef, Burger King, Carl's Jr, Del Taco, Domino's Pizza, Jack-in-the-Box, Little Caesars Pizza, Pizza Hut, Subway and Taco Bell. All are cheap.

The budget rung of the price ladder includes chain restaurants such as Chevy's (Mexican), Denny's (common along freeways and usually open 24 hrs), Olive Garden (Italian), Red Lobster (seafood), Sizzler and White Spot (in BC). Denny's and White Spot are open for breakfast, lunch and dinner, the others for lunch and dinner only.

A new movement throughout the region is certification of organically grown (without pesticides) produce. Be prepared to pay a premium for these fruits and vegetables.

GAMBLING

Gambling is illegal in the Pacific Northwest, but only under the wrong circumstances. Oregon, Washington and BC have highly advertised lotteries, casinos on and off Indian Reservations, legal card rooms in some areas and bingo in church halls everywhere.

HEALTH

Hospital emergency rooms are the place to go in the event of life-threatening medical problems. If a life is truly at risk, treatment will be swift and top notch, with payment problems sorted out later. For more mundane problems, 24-hr walk-in health clinics are available in urban areas and many rural communities.

In BC, government-run programmes provide health care for all, including visitors. Non-Canadians must pay for treatment, but prices are a bargain compared to most other industrialised countries. Not so in the US.

Some form of **health insurance** coverage is almost mandatory in order to ensure provision of health services in Oregon and Washington. Coverage provided by non-US national health plans is *not* accepted by US medical providers. The only way to ensure provision of health services is to carry some proof of valid insurance cover. Most travel agents who deal with international travel will offer travel insurance policies that cover medical costs in the USA – at least $1 million of cover is essential.

Bring enough prescription medication to last the entire trip, plus a few extra days. It's also a good idea to carry a copy of the prescription in case of emergency. Because trade names of drugs vary from country to country, be sure the prescription shows the generic (chemical) name and formulation of the drug, not just a brand name.

The Pacific Northwest is basically a healthy place to visit. No inoculations are required and common sense is enough to avoid most health problems. Eat and drink normally (or at least sensibly) and avoid drinking water that didn't come from the tap or a bottle. Most ground water, even in the high mountains, is contaminated with *giardia* and other intestinal parasites.

Sunglasses, broad brimmed sun hats, and sunscreen help prevent sunburn, sun stroke, and heat prostration. Be sure to drink plenty of non-alcoholic liquids, especially in hot weather. Too little water is a particular problem when travelling from the coast to the dry interior.

AIDS (Acquired Immune Deficiency Syndrome) and other sexually transmitted diseases are endemic in the Pacific Northwest as they are in the rest of the world. The best way to avoid sexually transmitted diseases (or STDs, as they're usually called) is to avoid promiscuous sex.

In anything other than long-term, strictly monogamous relationships, the key phrase is 'safe sex'. Use condoms in any kind of sexual intercourse – they're *very* strongly encouraged by prostitutes plying the sex trade throughout the region. Condoms can be bought in drug stores, pharmacies and supermarkets, and from vending machines in some public toilets.

Rabies is another endemic disease. It's most likely to afflict those who try to hand feed the squirrels and chipmunks that haunt many parks, but end up being bitten instead. If bitten by an animal, try to capture it for observation of possible rabies, then go to the nearest emergency medical centre. You must seek *immediate* treatment – if left too late the disease is untreatable and fatal. Squirrels and chipmunks also carry fleas that transmit bubonic plague.

Don't wear shorts for hikes through the inviting grasslands, forests and mountains. Instead, cover up with long trousers, long-sleeved shirts, and insect repellent. The risk of contracting **Lyme Disease** from ticks which thrive in moist climates is rising by the year.

Lyme Disease is frequently misdiagnosed and usually mistaken for rheumatoid arthritis. Typical symptoms include temporary paralysis, arthritic pains in the hand, arm, or leg joints, swollen hands, fever, fatigue, headaches, swollen glands, heart palpitations and a circular red rash around the bite up to 30 days later. Early treatment with tetracycline and other drugs is nearly 100% effective; late treatment often fails. Symptoms may not appear for three months or longer after the first infected tick bite, but the disease can be detected by a simple blood test.

Pacific Northwest ticks also carry Rocky Mountain spotted fever, Colorado tick fever and tularemia. All are treatable, but it's easier to avoid the diseases in the first place. Cover up while hiking and check skin for ticks at midday and again in the evening. Look for tiny dark dots, 2–5.5 mm (0.08–0.2 in) long. Ticks especially like to hide in hair on the head and at the back of the neck.

HIKING

Walking is a favourite outdoor activity, especially in park areas. The same cautions that apply anywhere else are good in the Pacific Northwest: know the route; carry a map, compass and basic safety gear; carry food and water. It's also wise to stay on marked trails. Wandering off the trail, easy to do in the forest, adds to erosion damage.

Lyme Disease (see above) can be avoided by wearing long trousers and sleeves. The most common hiking problem is **Poison Oak**, found primarily in southern Oregon and north along the coast into Washington. This oak-like plant is usually a shrub, sometimes a vine and always a trailside hazard. Variable leaf shapes make the plant difficult to identify, although the leaves always occur in clusters of three and usually look like rounded oak leaves. Leaves are bright, glossy green in spring and summer, bright red in fall, and dead in winter – but not forgotten.

All parts of the plant, leaves, stems, and flowers, exude a sticky sap that causes an intense allergic reaction in most people. The most common symptoms are red rash, itching, burning, and weeping sores. The best way to avoid the problem is to avoid the plant. Second best is to wash skin or clothing that has come into contact with the plant immediately in hot, soapy water. If you are afflicted, drying lotions such as calamine or products containing cortisone provide temporary relief, but time is the only cure.

Wildlife can also be a problem. **Cougars** (also called bobcats, mountain lions and pumas) would rather run than fight, but can be vicious if defending a den or accidentally cornered. Avoid hiking alone and never let small children run ahead or fall far behind. If you meet a cougar, *never* try to run or hide – you won't escape and either behaviour signals that you're prey. Instead, be aggressive. Stand your ground. Try to appear larger by raising your arms or opening up a jacket. Should the lion approach, shout and throw sticks or stones. Show that you're ready to fight. And if attacked, fight with all you've got. Pummel, kick, hit with anything hard, and try to scratch the lion's eyes. Prove

27

that you're not an easy target, and the lion will probably look for something easier – like a hare.

Bears are a more serious threat. They're large, strong, fast-moving, always hungry, and smart enough to connect humans with the food they carry. Parks and campsites have detailed warnings on how to safely store food to avoid attack. When possible, hang anything edible (including toothpaste) in bags well above the ground or store in metal lockers. *Never* feed bears as they won't know when the meal is over. Shouting, banging pots, and throwing stones usually persuades curious bears to look somewhere else for a meal.

Coyotes are common, if somewhat shy, inhabitants throughout the region. About the size of a small German shepherd dog, coyotes prey on mice and small rodents. You're most likely to see them hunting in open fields or meadows early and late in the day, or near cleared roads in winter.

Few people in the Pacific Northwest ever see **snakes** outside a zoo. The only poisonous snake native to the region is the **rattlesnake**, found only in drier areas east of the Cascades. Only a handful of people each year across North America die from rattlesnake bites, usually while trying to catch them. 'Rattlers' are harmless if left alone (as all snakes should be). The markings vary with the species, but all have diamond-shaped heads and rattles in their tails. Most, but not all, rattle a warning. In the wild, look where you're walking; don't put hands or feet on ledges which you can't see; and before sitting down, make sure a rattler hasn't already claimed the spot.

HITCH-HIKING

In an earlier, more trustful era, hitch-hiking was the preferred mode of transportation for budget travellers. Today, hitch-hiking or picking up hitch-hikers is asking for violent trouble, from theft to physical assault and murder. *Don't do it.*

INSURANCE

Experienced travellers carry insurance that cov-

ers their belongings and holiday investment as well as their bodies. Travel insurance should include provision for cancelled or delayed flights and weather problems, as well as immediate evacuation home in the case of medical emergency. Thomas Cook and other travel agencies offer comprehensive policies. Medical cover should be high – at least $1 million. Insurance for drivers is covered in more detail in 'Driving in the Pacific Northwest', p. 37.

LANGUAGE

English is the official language in Oregon and Washington, English and French in BC, but recently arrived immigrants speak dozens of languages. Spanish, Chinese (both Cantonese and Mandarin), Tagalog, Vietnamese and Korean are spoken widely in urban areas and are often used on neighbourhood billboards and in other advertising. Some hotels have bilingual signs in English/Spanish or English/Japanese.

English can create its own difficulties. Canadian English is a hybrid of British spelling and grammar with American vocabulary and usage. The Queen's English is universally understood and occasionally spoken, but Canadians read, hear and use more Americanisms than Britishisms, e.g. 'taking a vacation' rather than 'taking a holiday'. A selection of commonly encountered terms which may be unfamiliar or have a different meaning in the Pacific Northwest are set out in the box on p.30. The next chapter, 'Driving in the Pacific Northwest', also provides a glossary of motoring terms.

LUGGAGE

Less is more where luggage is concerned. Porters don't exist outside the most expensive hotels and luggage trolleys (baggage carts) are rare outside airports. Trolleys are free for international arrivals in Portland, Seattle, Vancouver and Victoria, but must be hired almost everywhere else. Luggage has to be light enough to carry. The normal luggage allowance is 2 pieces, each of 70 lb (32 kg) maximum, per person.

Luggage must also fit in the car or other form of transport around the Pacific Northwest. North Americans buy the same cars as Europeans, Australians and the rest of the world, not the enormous 'boats' of the 1960s. If it won't fit in the boot at home, don't count on cramming it into a Northwest rental car.

MAPS

The best all-round maps are produced by the **American Automobile Association** (AAA) and **Canadian Automobile Association** (CAA) distributed through their local affiliates. State, regional, county, and city maps are available free at all association offices, but only to members. Fortunately, most motoring clubs around the world have reciprocal agreements with AAA and CAA to provide maps and other member services. Be prepared to show a membership card to obtain service.

Rand McNally road maps and atlases are probably the best known of the ranges available outside the USA, in the travel section of bookshops and more specialist outlets. Once in North America, the **Gazetter®** series from **DeLorme Map Co.**, *Rte 1, Freeport, ME; tel: (207) 865-4171,* provide excellent upcountry maps.

US Geological Survey quadrangle (topographic) maps show terrain reliably. In BC, logging companies often provide the most accurate and up-to-date off-road maps through travel info centres and timber industry information centres, but getting lost in the wilderness is a genuine possibility even with the best of maps in hand. If you are thinking of driving off the beaten track, always carry a topographic map and compass in addition to any other maps and guides. **Sierra Club** and **Wilderness Press** publish the most up-to-date and reliable backcountry maps and guides. Outdoor supply shops and good booksellers carry maps.

Before leaving civilisation behind, compare every available map for discrepancies, then check with forest or park personnel. Most are experienced backcountry enthusiasts themselves, and since they're responsible for rescuing lost hikers, they have a vested interest in dispensing the best possible information and advice.

MEETING PEOPLE

North Americans are friendly, at least on the

How to talk Northwest

Alternate means 'alternative', not 'every other', sometimes a source of confusion when reading timetables.

Americano 'American' coffee, usually weak and served in a mug or large cup.

Barrista The person, not always female, who works behind an espresso bar. 'Barrister' still refers to a lawyer admitted to the bar.

Bed & Breakfast (or 'B&B') Overnight lodging in a private home, usually with private facilities and often more expensive than nearby hotels and motels.

Cappuccino Espresso mixed with steamed milk, topped with foam and sprinkled with ground cinnamon or chocolate.

Caulk boots Pronounced 'cork boots', heavy boots worn by lumbermen with sharp spikes in the soles to provide traction in the forest.

Chips Crisps, usually made from potatoes, but also from corn, taro, cassava, rice or other starches.

Cream soda A sweet, lightly-flavoured carbonated drink.

Downtown City or town centre.

Espresso Dark, strong coffee served in a tiny cup, also called a 'shot' of espresso.

Fries Chips, usually, but not always, made of potatoes.

Goeduck Pronounced 'gooey duck', a large clam with a long, thick neck, usually used for soup.

Grange A rural self-help organisation of local farmers.

HBC Hudson's Bay Company.

Holiday A public holiday, such as Christmas or Boxing Day, not a private holiday, which is a vacation.

Jo-jo potatoes Chips cut large, often with the skins left on, also called 'cottage fries'.

Latte Espresso mixed with steamed milk.

Lodging The usual term for accommodation.

Micro-brewery (also called brewpubs) small, artisanal breweries which sell their beer on the premises, usually with food.

Mocha Espresso mixed with steamed milk and chocolate.

Natural ingredients Food that has been grown, processed and prepared without pesticides or other chemical additives.

Nordic skiing Cross-country skiing.

Northwest Cuisine Anything the chef wants it to be, as long as it's expensive, but usually based on locally-grown foods, especially fish, vegetables and fruits.

Organic Foods and other products grown and processed without artificial fertilisers, pesticides or other synthetic chemical products.

Outlet shopping Shopping at large stores specialising in factory overruns at reduced prices. In many cases, factory outlets are simply low-priced retail stores selling direct from the factory.

Parkade A parking garage.

Parking lot A car park or parking garage.

Prairie schooner The type of covered farm wagon used by settlers travelling across North America in the 19th century.

Resort A fancy hotel which specialises in leisure activities such as golf, tennis and swimming.

Road Kill Literally, animals killed by passing cars, but usually used to describe bad restaurant food.

Shooter A raw oyster, usually swallowed whole. Originally a small glass, or 'shot' of whiskey or tequila drunk in one swallow.

Smokejumpers fire-fighters who are parachuted in to remote areas .

Tailgate party A picnic, usually at a football game, held in the stadium car park.

Telemark skiing downhill skiing.

Thunder egg Hollow balls of solidified lava filled with agates, formed 60 million years ago; usually cut in half for sale to display the sparkling agates inside.

Vamping Van camping.

Victorian A term used to describe buildings built between the middle of the 19th century and 1915.

Water bombers Planes used to drop water on forest fires.

Wrinkle trend.

surface. As in much of the world, asking for directions, map in hand, is a useful 'icebreaker'. Friendliness does not extend to inviting new acquaintances to their homes, however. A bed and breakfast is an excellent place to meet 'locals' on holiday. Sports events, casual restaurants and bars can be meeting places, but most local people are wary of approaches by strangers. Professional associations, sports or interest clubs welcome visitors from abroad; contact well in advance for meeting times and venues. Check Fri or Sun newspapers for listings of events and attractions. Street fairs and farmers markets, increasingly popular in the Northwest, bring out crowds with a variety of interests.

OPENING HOURS

Office hours are generally 0900–1700, Mon–Fri, although some tourist offices also keep Saturday hours. Most banks and other financial institutions are open 1000–1600 Mon–Thur, 1000–1800 on Fri, and 0900–1300 Sat. ATMs (cashpoints) are open 24 hr.

Small shops keep standard business hours. Large shops and shopping centres open at 0900 or 1000 Mon–Sat and close at 2000 or 2100. Opening hours are slightly shorter on Sunday.

Many restaurants, museums, and legitimate theatres close on Monday, but most tourist attractions are open seven days a week in summer. Many tourist attractions are closed Sept–May.

PARKS INFORMATION

Much of the Pacific Northwest is publicly owned. The degree of protection and the type of uses varies, but camping is generally permitted only in marked campgrounds. For specific national and state/provincial parks, monuments, and seashores, see the appropriate description among the recommended routes throughout this book. For general information on national parks, monuments and seashores in Oregon and Washington, contact the **National Park Service Regional Headquarters Office, Pacific Northwest Regional Office**, *83 S. King St, Seattle, WA 98104; tel: (206) 442-4830.*For US Forest Service lands, contact **US Forest Service Pacific**

Northwest Region, *Box 3623, Portland, OR 97208; tel: (503) 326-2877.* For Bureau of Land Management facilities, contact **Bureau of Land Management OR/WA State Office**, *1300 NE. 44th Ave, Box 2965, Portland, OR 97208; tel: (503) 280-7001.* For information on National Wildlife Refuges and other Fish and Wildlife areas throughout the Western US, contact the **Fish and Wildlife Service Pacific Region**, *911 NE. 11th Ave, Portland, OR 97232; tel: (503) 872-5270.* For state parks information and advance bookings, contact **Reservations Northwest**; *tel: (800) 452-5687* or *(503) 731-3411.*

There is a charge for entry to National Parks as well as many state and regional parks. Campsite fees are almost always additional. In winter, some state parks may not require fees. Senior and disabled persons should ask if discounts apply. If visiting more than four or five US National Parks, monuments, or historical sites for which entrance fees are charged, purchase a **Golden Eagle Passport** for $50, which covers the holder and one other person. Blind and disabled travellers can request a free-of-charge Golden Access Passport upon arrival.

Canada has a similar scheme for its National Parks, **Canada's Great Western Annual Pass**, $35 per person or $70 per family from individual parks or **Parks Canada Service Centre**, *Rm 220 Canada Place, 9700 Jasper Ave, Edmonton, Alberta T5J 4C3; tel: (800) 748-7275.*

PASSPORTS AND VISAS

All non-US citizens must have a valid full passport (not a British Visitor's Passport) and, except for Canadians, a visa, in order to enter the United States. Citizens of most countries must obtain from a visa from the US Embassy in their country of residence in advance of arrival. In the UK, your local Thomas Cook branch can advise on and obtain US visas (which last the life of your passport).

Citizens of Britain, New Zealand and Ireland may complete a visa waiver form, which they generally receive with their air tickets if the airline is a 'participating carrier'. Provided nothing untoward is declared, such as a previous entry refusal or a criminal

31

conviction, which would make application for a full visa mandatory, the waiver exempts visitors from the need for a visa for stays of up to 90 days. It also allows a side-trip overland into Mexico or Canada and return

Note: Documentation regulations change frequently and are complex for some nationalities; confirm your requirements with the nearest US Embassy or consulate at least 90 days before you plan to depart for the USA.

POLICE

To telephone police in an emergency, ring 911. There are many different police jurisdictions within the Pacific Northwest, each with its own force. See also under 'Security' on the next page and 'Police' in the next chapter. In BC, nearly all public safety and crime issues are handled by local police.

The Royal Canadian Mounted Police, the RCMP or 'Mounties' of cinema and television fame, are a national force which seldom deal with local problems. Mounties only wear their famous red dress uniform for formal functions and occasional public appearances. Yes, you *may* ask a Mountie for help.

POSTAL SERVICES

Every town has a least one post office. Hours vary, although all are open Mon–Fri, morning and afternoon. Postal Service branches may be open Saturday or even Sunday. Some hotels sell stamps through the concierge; large department stores may have a post office; and supermarkets like Safeway sell stamps at the checkout counter. Stamp machines are installed in some stores, but a surcharge may be included in the cost. For philatelic sales, check major city telephone directories under US Postal Service and Canada Post. Postal rates are lower in the US than in Canada.

Mail everything going overseas as Air Mail (surface mail takes weeks or even months). If posting letters near an urban area, mail should take about one week. Add a day or two if mailing from remote areas.

Poste Restante is available at any post office, without charge. Mail should be addressed in block lettering to your name, Poste Restante/General Delivery, city, state, postal code, and United States of America or Canada (do not abbreviate). Mail is held for 30 days at the post office branch that handles General Delivery for each town or city, usually the main office. Identification is required for mail pickup.

PUBLIC HOLIDAYS

North America's love affair with the road extends to jumping in the automobile for holiday weekends. Local celebrations, festivals, parades, or neighbourhood parties can disrupt some or all activities in town.

See the CANADA section for Canadian public holidays. The following public holidays are celebrated in the US: New Year's Day (1 Jan); Martin Luther King Jr Day (third Monday in Jan); Lincoln's Birthday (12 Feb); Presidents' Day (third Monday in Feb); Easter (Sunday in Mar/Apr); Memorial Day (last Monday in May); Independence Day (4 July); Labor Day (first Monday in Sept); Columbus Day or Indigenous Peoples Day (second Monday in Oct); Veterans Day (11 Nov); Thanksgiving Day (last Thursday in Nov); and Christmas (25 Dec).

Post offices and government offices close on public holidays. Some businesses take the day off, though department and discount stores use the opportunity to hold huge sales, well advertised in local newspapers. Petrol stations remain open. Small shops and some grocery stores close or curtail hours.

Call in advance before visiting an attraction on a public holiday as frequently there are special hours. National and state/provincial park campsites and lodging must be reserved in advance for all holidays. Easter, Thanksgiving, and Christmas are family holidays, where accommodation is available and may even be

---

Colour section (i): On the Road around the Pacific Northwest, pioneer style.
(ii): Seattle (see pp.58–69); Seattle at night; dining on the waterfront. (iii): The Hammering Man and Seattle Art Museum; inset, a Pike Place Market fishmonger.
(iv): Crystal River at Mount Rainier National Park (p.75); inset, a totem pole in front of the Seven Cedars Casino at Sequim (p.80).

WE PACK
FISH & CRABS
FOR AIR
TRAVEL
FOR UP TO
48 HRS.

discounted (to fill hotels and motels). Other holidays are 'mobile', so book early.

SALES TAXES

There is no sales tax in Oregon. Washington has a sales tax, currently 8%, added to most purchases and itemised separately on the bill. BC levies GST (Goods & Services Tax), currently 7%, on almost every purchase. All three jurisdictions add local taxes on accommodation. There may also be special taxes or fees on rental cars.

SECURITY

Throwing caution to the winds is foolhardy anytime, and even more so on holiday. BC prides itself on a law-abiding tradition which began with no-nonsense judges sent from England to bring law and order to brawling gold mining towns in the last century. The US, by contrast, has a far more violent traditional culture that prizes easy access to firearms. Dial 911 on any telephone on either side of the border for free emergency assistance from police, fire and medical authorities.

Millions of people travel in perfect safety each year in the Pacific Northwest. So can you if you take the following common-sense precautions.

Travelling Safely

Never publicly discuss travel plans or money or valuables you are carrying. Use caution in large cities, towns, and rural areas. Drive, park, and walk only in well-lit areas. If unsure of roads or weather ahead, stop for the evening and find secure lodging. Sightsee with a known companion, or in a group. Solo travel, in urban areas or in the countryside, is not recommended.

The best way to avoid becoming a victim of theft or bodily injury is to walk with assurance and try to give the impression that you are not worth robbing (e.g. do not wear or carry expensive jewellery or flash rolls of banknotes). Use a hidden money-belt for your valuables, travel documents and spare cash. Carrying a wallet in a back pocket or leaving a handbag open is an invitation to every pickpocket in the vicinity. In all public places, take precautions

with anything that is obviously worth stealing – use a handbag with a crossed shoulder strap and a zip, wind the strap of your camera case around your chair or place your handbag firmly between your feet under the table while you eat.

Never leave luggage unattended. At airports, security officials may confiscate unattended luggage as a possible bomb. In public toilets, handbags and small luggage have been snatched from hooks, or from under stalls. Airports and bus and train stations usually have lockers. Most work with keys; take care to guard the key and memorise the locker number. Hotel bell staff may keep luggage for one or more days on request, sometimes for a fee – be sure and get receipts for left luggage before surrendering it.

Concealing a weapon is against the law. Some defensive products resembling tear gas are legal only for persons certified in their proper use. Mugging, by individuals or gangs, is more of a problem in the US than in Canada. If you are attacked, it is safer to let go of your bag or hand over the small amount of obvious money – as you are more likely to be attacked physically if the thief meets with resistance. *Never resist.* Report incidents immediately to local police, even if it is only to get a copy of their report for your insurance company.

Driving Safely

Have car hire counter personnel recommend a safe, direct route on a clear map before you leave with the vehicle. Lock all valuables and luggage in the boot or glove box so that nothing is visible to passers-by or other drivers. Don't leave maps, brochures, or guidebooks in evidence – why advertise that you're a stranger in town?

Always keep car doors and windows locked. Do not venture into unlit areas, neighbourhoods that look seedy, or off paved roads. *Do not stop* if told by a passing motorist or pedestrian that something is wrong with your car, or if someone signals for help with a broken-down car. If you need to stop, do so only in well-lit or populated areas, even if your car is bumped from behind by another vehicle. If your car breaks down, turn on the flashing emergency lights, and if it is safe to get out, raise the bonnet and return to the vehicle. Do not split passengers up. Lights on emergency vehicles are red or red and blue, so do not stop for flashing white lights or flashing headlights. Ask directions only from police, at a well-lit business area, or at a service station.

At night, have keys ready to unlock car doors before entering a parking lot. Check the surrounding area and inside the vehicle before entering. Never pick up hitch-hikers, and never leave the car with the engine running. Take all valuables with you.

Sleeping Safely

When sleeping rough, in any sort of dormitory, train, or open campsite, the safest place for your small valuables is at the bottom of your sleeping-bag. In train sleeping carriages, padlock your luggage to the seat, and ask the attendant to show you how to lock a compartment door at night. If in doubt, it's best to take luggage with you.

In hotels, motels, and all other lodging, lock all door locks from the inside. Check that all windows are locked, including sliding glass doors. Ground-floor rooms, while convenient, mean easier access by molesters intent on breaking in. Never leave the room at night without leaving a light on. Lights deter prowlers, and when you return, any disturbance to room contents will be visible.

Use a door viewer to check before admitting anyone to your room. If someone claims to be on the hotel staff or a repair person, do not let the person in before phoning the office or front desk to verify to person's name and job. Money, cheques, credit cards, passports and keys should be with you, or secured in your hotel's safe deposit box. When checking in, find the most direct route from your room to fire escapes, elevators, stairwells, and the nearest telephone.

Documents

Take a few passport photos with you and photocopy the important pages and any visa stamps in your passport. Store these safely, together with a note of the numbers of your travellers cheques, credit cards, and insurance documents

(keep them separate from the documents themselves). If you are unfortunate enough to be robbed, you will at least have some identification, and replacing the documents will be much easier. Apply to your nearest consulate (see 'Consulates' in this chapter for addresses and phone numbers).

SHOPPING

Pacific Northwest souvenirs include wines; dried, tinned or smoked salmon; apples, cherries and other dried fruits; honey; berry jams and syrups; Oregon filberts; prepared mustards, oils, and condiments and the ubiquitous T-shirts. Clothing can be a bargain, particularly at discount or factory outlet stores. Pottery work is particularly fine; dishes and other small items made of local myrtlewood are ubiquitous in coastal Oregon. Cameras and other photo equipment can be a fraction of UK prices, but do your homework on prices before you go, and shop around when you arrive. Native American souvenirs include wood and stone carvings, rugs, masks, baskets and jewellery incorporating silver and gold.

Tape cassettes, blank video tapes, CDs, computer programs, and CD-ROMs sold in the Pacific Northwest can be used anywhere in the world. For more information on electrical goods, see 'Electricity' in this chapter.

SMOKING

Lighting up is out in public buildings and public transportation. All plane flights in North America are non-smoking, and some hire cars are designated as non-smoking. Most hotels/motels set aside non-smoking rooms or floors; bed and breakfast establishments are almost all non-smoking. Restaurant dining regulations vary by locality; some forbid all smoking; others permit it in the bar or lounge only; some have a percentage of the eatery devoted to smokers. Smoking is prohibited in most stores and shops. Always ask before lighting a cigarette, cigar, or pipe. When in doubt, go outside to smoke. Smoking is more common in rural areas than in larger cities.

TELEPHONES

The North American telephone system is

divided into local and long-distance carriers. Depending on the time of day and day of the week, it may be cheaper to call New York than to call 30 miles (48 km) away. After 1700, Mon–Fri, and all weekend, rates are lower. Useful phone numbers are provided throughout this book.

Public telephones are everywhere, indicated by a sign with a white telephone receiver depicted on a blue field. Enclosed booths, wall-mounted, or free-standing machines are all used. If possible, use public phones in well-lit, busy public areas.

Dialling instructions are in the front of the local white pages telephone directory. For all long-distance calls, precede the area code with a *1*. In emergencies, call *911* for police, medical, or fire brigade response. *0* reaches an operator. For local number information, dial *411*. For long-distance phone information, dial *1*, the area code, then *555-1212*. There will be a charge for information calls.

Pay phones take coins; local calls cost $0.20–$0.25. An operator or computer voice will come on-line to ask for additional coins if needed. Most hotels and motels add a stiff surcharge to the basic cost of a call, so find a public telephone in the lobby.

Prepaid phone cards are now widely available at grocery and convenience stores. Before you travel, ask your local phone company if your phone card will work in North America. Most do, and come with a list of contact numbers. However, remember that the USA has the cheapest overseas phone rates in the world, which makes it cheaper to fill pay phones with quarters than to reverse charges. A credit card may be convenient, but only economical if you pay the bill immediately.

For comparison, local call rates:
coin $0.20–0.25
direct dial, calling card $0.35
operator–assisted, calling card $0.95

800 and *888* numbers are toll-free. Like all long-distance numbers, the 800/888 area code must be preceded by a *1*, e.g. *1-888-123-4567*. Some telephone numbers are given in letters, i.e. *1-800-VAN-RIDE*. Telephone keys have both numbers and letters, so find the corresponding letter and depress that key. A few numbers have more than seven letters to finish a business name. Not to worry, US or Canadian phone numbers never require more than seven numerals, plus three for the area code.

Dial an international operator on 00 for enquiries or assistance.

For international dialling, dial 011-country code-city code (omitting the first 0 if there is one)-local number; e.g., to call Great Britain, Inner London, from the USA or Canada, dial: 011-44-171-local number. Some country codes:

Australia 61
New Zealand 64
Republic of Ireland 353
South Africa 27
United Kingdom 44

TIME

Oregon, Washington and British Columbia share a time zone, GMT -8 hrs, called Pacific Standard Time (PST). From the first Sunday in April until the last Sunday in October, clocks are advanced one hour to Pacific Daylight Time (PDT), GMT -7 hrs. Ontario, Oregon is one time zone east in Mountain Standard Time, GMT -7 and Mountain Daylight Time, GMT -6, depending on the season.

35

Time in the Pacific Northwest (PST)	8 a.m.	12 p.m.	5 p.m.	12 a.m.
Time in				
Auckland	4 a.m.	8 a.m.	1 p.m.	8 p.m.
Cape Town	6 p.m.	10 p.m.	3 a.m.	10 a.m.
Dublin	4 p.m.	8 p.m.	1 a.m.	8 a.m.
London	4 p.m.	8 p.m.	1 a.m.	8 a.m.
Perth	Midnt	4 a.m.	9 a.m.	4 p.m.
Sydney	2 a.m.	6 a.m.	11 a.m.	6 p.m.
Toronto	11 a.m.	3 p.m.	8 p.m.	3 a.m.

Thomas Cook and AAA

The Thomas Cook Group has formed an alliance with AAA which, from 1 January 1997, gives visitors to the United States who have purchased their travel arrangements with Thomas Cook access to the benefits of the Thomas Cook Worldwide Customer Promise at AAA travel agency locations.

The courtesy services available under this arrangement include changes to airline reservations and ticket revalidation, hotel and car rental reservations, travel planning and emergency local phone assistance, all free of agency service charges.

The American Automobile Association (commonly referrred to as AAA, pronounced 'Triple A') is one of the largest leisure travel businesses in the United States. Made up of nearly 1000 travel agency locations across the country, AAA is operated by local Automobile Clubs which in turn are affiliated with the AAA. With branch office locations numbering from one to over 70, the AAA travel agency offices are ready to serve the Thomas Cook customer.

To find the nearest AAA travel agency location, check the local phone directory or Yellow Pages when travelling in the United States. Washington and Oregon are covered by three AAA affiliates: AAA Oregon/Idaho, AAA Washington and the Inland Automobile Association.

To make use of these courtesy services in Canada, travellers should visit the nearest Thomas Cook location or office of Marlin Travel. Travel agency offices of the CAA (Canadian Automobile Association) also provide these benefits.

TIPPING

Acknowledgement for good service should not be extorted. That said, tipping is a fact of life, to get, to repeat, or to thank someone for service.

Service charges are not customarily added to restaurant bills. Waiters and waitresses expect a tip of 15% of the bill before taxes are added on. In luxury restaurants, also be prepared to tip the maitre d' and sommelier a few dollars, up to 10% of the bill. Bartenders expect the change from a drink, up to several dollars.

Hotel porters generally receive $1 per bag; a bellperson who shows you to the room expects several dollars; in luxury properties, tip more. Room service delivery staff should be tipped 10–15% of the tariff before taxes, unless there's a service charge indicated on the bill. Expect to hand out dollars for most services that involve room delivery.

Some hotels have a chambermaid name card placed in the room: it's a hint for a tip of a few dollars upon your departure, but never required.

Ushers in legitimate theatres, arenas, and stadiums are not tipped; cinemas seldom have ushers, nor are tips expected. Do not tip Oregon petrol station attendants who are required by law to pump petrol for customers as a safety measure.

TOILETS

There is nothing worse than not being able to find one! *Restroom* or *bathroom* are the common terms in the US and *washroom* in Canada; *toilet* is acceptable in both. Canadians usually recognise *WC*, Americans usually do not. Whatever the term, most are marked with a figure for a male or a female; *Men* and *women* are the most common terms. Occasionally, a restroom may be used by both sexes.

Facilities may be clean and well-equipped or filthy. Most businesses, including bars and restaurants, reserve restrooms for clients. Petrol stations provide keys for customers to access restrooms. Public toilets are sporadically placed, but well-marked. Parks and roadside rest stops have toilet facilities.

TOURIST INFORMATION

Each state and province is responsible for its own tourism promotion. Request information well in advance. **Oregon Tourism Commission**, *775 Summer St NE., Salem, OR 97310; tel: (800) 547-7842 or (503) 986-0000;*

fax: (503) 986-0001. **Washington State Division of Tourism,** *Box 42500, Olympia, WA 98504; tel: 800-544-1800 or (360) 753-5630.* **Tourism British Columbia,** *802-865 Hornby St, Vancouver, BC V6Z 2G3; tel: (800) 663-6000 or (604) 663-6000; fax: (604) 660-3383.*

Canada also has an active federal tourism promotion office, usually located in Canadian Consulates around the world. In the UK, **Tourism British Columbia** is located at *British Columbia House, 3rd Floor, 1 Regent St, London, SW1Y 4NS; tel: (0171) 930-6857.* The United States currently lacks a tourism promotion office.

Oregon has official State Welcome Centers in **Astoria, Brookings, Klamath, Lakeview, Ontario, Portland/Jantzen Beach, Seaside, Siskiyou** and **Umatilla.** This book also gives addresses and telephone numbers of tourism offices in regions, cities and towns along specific routes.

TRAINS

AMTRAK is the official passenger train transportation company in the United States; *tel: (800) 872-7245.* Main routes along the coast run from California to Portland, Seattle and Vancouver as well as from the east into Portland and Seattle. **VIA Rail** handles passenger traffic in Canada; *tel: (888) 842-7245.* Primary routes run north to Whistler or east to Kamloops and onward across the Rockies. Trains do not stop at each town en route, so check if there is a stop at your destination.

Train times for many AMTRAK, VIA Rail and local services are published in the *Thomas Cook Overseas Timetable* (see under 'Useful Reading' in this chapter).

AMTRAK sell a Far West Rail Pass, which gives 15 or 30 days of unlimited train travel on their system in the West at prices in the range of $170–250. This is available from Thomas Cook in the UK through **Leisurail,** *tel: (01733) 335599.*

TRAVEL ARRANGEMENTS

Given the fact that most of the world's international airlines fly into Portland, Seattle or Vancouver, and the ease of hiring cars at air-

ports, the Pacific Northwest is an ideal destination for independently-minded travellers. However, the many types of air ticket and the range of temporary deals available on busy routes make it advisable to talk to your travel agent before booking to get the best bargain.

In fact, taking a fly-drive package such as one of Thomas Cook's own, or one of the many others offered by airlines and tour operators, is usually more economical than making all your own arrangements. All include the air ticket and car hire element; some also follow set itineraries which enables them to offer guaranteed and pre-paid en route accommodation at selected hotels. Programmes such as Thomas Cook's *America for the Indepenent Traveller* allow the flexibility of booking the airline ticket at an advantageous rate and then choosing from a 'menu' of other items, often at a discounted price, such as car hire, hotel coupons (which pre-pay accommodation but do not guarantee availability of rooms) and other extras such as excursions.

USEFUL READING

Most British and international colour-illustrated guidebook series feature one or more volumes on the Pacific Northwest. If you are considering using trains, buses or ferries for any part of your trip, the *Thomas Cook Overseas Timetable* (published every 2 months, £8.40 per issue) is indispensable. For more details of this and other Thomas Cook publications see p.14 and p.245

If you are arranging your own accommodation as you travel, a comprehensive guide such as the *AAA/CAA TourBook for Oregon and Washington* and *Western Canada and Alaska* or one of the *Mobil Regional Guides* can often be obtained through specialist travel bookshops outside North America. The *AAA CampBook Northwestern* covers RV and tent camping areas in Oregon and Washington.

Books you can buy in the Pacific Northwest include:

Atomic Marbles & Branding Irons: A Guide to Museums, Collections, And Roadside Curiosities in Washington and Oregon, by Harriet Baskas and Adam Woog, 1993, Sasquatch Books, Seattle.

Backroading Vancouver Island, by Rosemary Neering, 1996, Whitecap Books, Vancouver.

Exploring Washington's Past: A Road Guide to History, by Ruth Kirk and Carmela Alexander, Revised Edition, 1995, University of Washington Press, Seattle.

The Good Rain, by Timothy Egan, 1991, Vintage Books, New York.

A Traveler's Guide to The Historic Columbia River Highway, edited by Ken Manske, 1994, Manske & Associates, Gresham, Oregon.

Just East of Sundown: The Queen Charlotte Islands, by Charles Lillard, 1995, Horsdal & Schubart, Victoria.

The Living, by Annie Dillard, 1992, HarperCollins, New York.

Looking at Indian Art of the Northwest Coast, by Hilary Stewart, 1979, Douglas & McIntyre, Vancouver/Toronto.

Middle Puget Sound & Hood Canal and *South Puget Sound*, by Marge & Ted Mueller, 1990 and 1996, The Mountaineers, Seattle.

More English than the English: A Social History of Victoria, by Terry Reksten, 1986, Orca Book Publishers, Victoria.

Native Peoples of the Northwest: A Traveler's Guide to Land, Art, and Culture, by Jan Halliday & Gail Chehak, 1996, Sasquatch Books, Seattle.

Northwest Indian Travel Guide and Map, Affiliated Tribes of Northwest Indians, 825 NE. 20th Ave, Suite 310, Portland, OR 97232; tel: (503) 230-0293; fax: (503) 230-0580.

Northwest Trees: Identifying & Understanding the Region's Native Trees, by Stephen F Arno, 1977, The Mountaineers, Seattle.

Official Guide to Pacific Rim National Park Reserve, by JM MacFarlane et. al., 1996, Blackbird Naturgraphics, Inc., Calgary, Alberta.

Oregon Atlas & Gazetteer® and *Washington Atlas & Gazetteer®*, 1991 and 1995, DeLorme, Freeport, Maine.

Oregon Discovery Guide and *Washington Discovery Guide*, by Don & Betty Martin, 1995, Pine Cone Press, Columbia, California.

Oregon Scenic Drives, by Tom Barr, 1995, Falcon Press, Helena, Montana.

Sexless Oysters and Self-Tipping Hats: 100 years of Invention in the Pacific Northwest, by Adam Woog, 1991, Sasquatch Books, Seattle.

Totem Poles, by Pat Kramer, 1995, Altitude Publishing Canada Ltd, Canmore, Alberta.

Washington for the Curious: A By-the-Highway Guide, by Rob McDonald et. al., 1996, The Curious Corporation, Hailey, Idaho.

Washington State Parks: A Complete Recreation Guide, by Marge & Ted Mueller, 1993, The Mountaineers, Seattle.

The West Beyond the West: A History of British Columbia, by Jean Barman, Revised Edition 1996, University of Toronto Press, Toronto.

WEIGHTS AND MEASURES

Officially, the USA is converting to the metric system. In truth, few people have changed. (A few road signs show both miles and km.) The non-metric US measures are the same as Imperial measures except for fluids, where US gallons and quarts are five-sixths of their Imperial equivalents. Canada has long since joined the metric majority of the world.

WHAT TO TAKE

Absolutely everything you could ever need is available, so don't worry if you've left anything behind. In fact, most North American prices will seem low: competition and oversupply keeps them that way. Pharmacies (chemists), also called drug stores, carry a range of products, from medicine to cosmetics to beach balls. Prepare a small first aid kit before you leave home with tried and tested insect repellent, sun-screen cream, and soothing, moisturising lotion. Carry all medicines, glasses, and contraceptives with you, and keep duplicate prescriptions or a letter from your doctor to verify your need for a particular medication.

Other useful items to bring or buy immediately upon arrival are a water-bottle, sunglasses, a hat or visor with a rim, an umbrella and light rain gear, a Swiss Army pocket knife, a torch (flashlight), a padlock for anchoring luggage, a money belt, a travel adapter, string for a washing line, an alarm clock and a camera. Those planning to rough it should take a sleeping bag, a sheet liner, and an inflatable pillow. Allow a little extra space in your luggage for souvenirs.

DRIVING IN THE PACIFIC NORTHWEST

This chapter provides hints and practical advice for those taking to the road in the Pacific Northwest whether in a hire car or RV, or in their own vehicle.

ACCIDENTS AND BREAKDOWNS

Holidays should be trouble-free, yet **breakdowns** can occur. Pull off to the side of the road where visibility is good and you are out of the way of traffic. Turn on hazard flashers or indicators, and, if it is safe, get out and raise the bonnet. Change a tyre only when safely out of the traffic flow.

For emergencies; *tel: 911* (free) from any telephone to reach the appropriate highway patrol, police, fire or medical services. Emergency call boxes are placed about every half a mile on some highways and can be used to report breakdowns or a need for petrol. Give your phone number, location, problem and need for assistance.

Earthquakes are a rare but potentially devastating driving hazard – see p.24 for specific advice.

If involved in a **collision** or an **accident**, stop immediately. Telephone the nearest police agency without delay if there are injuries, deaths or physical damage to vehicles or other property. Oregon, Washington and BC require drivers to provide their own drivers licence number, vehicle licecse number, vehicle registration number, insurance carrier and policy number, and contact information to the other driver(s) involved in the accident. It's also wise to obtain contact information for any passengers in the other vehicle. You will also have to provide full information to the police if an official investigation is required.

Accidents must also be reported to your car hire company and your own insurance carrier.

Accidents involving vehicles registered in British Columbia must be reported to the provincial-owned **Insurance Corporation of British Columbia (ICBC)**; *tel: (800) 661-6844* or *(604) 661-6844*, which insures all BC vehicles.

Fly-drive travellers should bear in mind the effects of **jet lag** on driver safety. This can be a very real problem. The best way to minimise it is to spend the first night after arrival in a hotel near the airport or in the nearest city and pick up your hire vehicle the next day, rather than picking up the car and setting out on a long drive within hours of walking off the plane.

CAR HIRE

Hiring a car or RV (camper – see 'Travel Essentials', p.18 for more information) gives you the freedom of the road with a vehicle you can leave behind after a few weeks. Whether booking a fly-drive package with an agency or making independent arrangements, plan well in advance to ensure that you get the type and size of vehicle your heart desires. Free, unlimited mileage or kilometrage is common with cars, less so with RVs.

Sheer volume in airport rental car turnover means that it is almost always cheaper to pick up the vehicle from an airport than from a downtown site, and to return it to the airport. A surcharge, called a *drop fee*, may be levied if you drop the vehicle off in a different location from the place of hire. When considering an RV, ask about one-way and off-season rates.

You will need a valid credit card as security for the vehicle, even if the rental is pre-paid or is being paid for in cash. Before you leave the hire agency, ensure that you have all documentation for the hire, that the vehicle registration is in the glove box and that you understand how to operate the vehicle and all of its accessories.

39

For RVs, also get instruction books and a complete demonstration of all systems and appliance and how they affect each other. Using a microwave oven, for example, can interfere with other electrical appliances in some RVs. On other RVs, it is possible to exhaust the engine battery by running the refrigerator or other appliances unless you first trip a special safety switch.

Avoid hiring a car that exhibits the hire company name on a window sticker, on the fender (bumper) or license plate frames. It's advertising for criminal attention.

Car size terminology varies, but general categories range from small and basic to all-frills posh: sub-compact, compact, economy, mid-size or intermediate, full-size or standard and luxury. Sub-compacts are often over-subscribed. Expect to choose between two- and four-door models. The larger the car, the faster it accelerates and the faster it consumes petrol. Some vehicles are equipped with four-wheel drive (4WD or 4X4), unnecessary except for off-road driving, which is not covered in this book.

Standard features on North American hire cars usually include automatic transmission, air conditioning (a necessity for summer and desert driving) and cruise control, which sets speeds for long distance highway cruising, allowing the driver to take his or her foot off the accelerator. However, even with cruise control engaged, it is necessary to pay constant attention to steering.

DIFFICULT DRIVING

Deserts

Tackling a desert is like approaching a snowy mountain: preparation is essential. Insist that your car has air conditioning and a good heater. Winter in the Pacific Northwest desert is cold. High deserts can get significant rain and even snow in mid-summer. By March, daytime temperatures are high; occasional thunderstorms unleash torrents of summer rain. Most of the time, deserts sizzle in the daylight. Plan to arrive at desert lodging or campsite well before dark. Temperatures plummet once the sun sets.

Basic safety precautions include making sure that the vehicle's engine and cooling system are in good working order, tyres are properly inflated and the petrol tank filled. All travellers should carry extra water, snacks, a torch and warm clothing in case of trouble.

If the car breaks down on a freeway or major highway, pull off the roadway and raise the bonnet. One person should walk to the nearest yellow emergency telephone, no more than a mile away in many cases, call for help, and return to the car to wait. All other passengers should stay with the car until help arrives. Not only is the car likely to be the only shade within sight, but breakdown lorries will be looking for a stranded vehicle, not for a person walking along the highway.

Carry at least 2–4 litres of bottled drinking water for each person in the vehicle. If you're stranded or need to replenish a hiking water bottle, the extra will seem like liquid gold. A warm sleeping-bag may come in handy should you need to camp out unexpectedly. If stranded in the desert (or the mountains), *stay with your vehicle* – airborne searchers can spot a car or RV far more easily than a person.

Sandstorms can reduce visibility to nil. Pull over and park until the storm has passed, preferably in a spot slightly above the surrounding terrain. RV drivers are sometimes tempted to park along the sides of the roads or in dry river beds called washes. This is not safe. One of the worst desert and mountain hazards is a flash flood, or gulleywasher, caused by sudden rainstorms, sometimes miles upstream and unseen, that create raging floods that wash down dry riverbeds carrying away anything not cemented in place. In park areas, always check with a ranger or warden for safe camping areas.

If venturing into the desert, have sunscreen cream, sunscreen lip protection, lotion for dry skin, sunglasses, a hat and clothing that can be worn in layers. Also take a backpack to carry documents, water, snacks and extra clothes. Long underwear will be welcome in winter.

Skin can burn even in the desert winter; wear long trousers for comfort. Wearing sandals, you risk sunburned feet and are vulnerable to rattlesnakes. When hiking, wear comfortable boots with good traction.

Fog

Fog is frequent along the Pacific coast, the Columbia Gorge and most interior valleys all year. It can be treacherous to drive in, resulting in several chain-reaction mass collisions each year. Never use bright headlamps in fog, the high beams blind oncoming drivers, the driver ahead of you and reflect back in your own eyes like a mirror. Use low beam headlamps instead. Driving with only parking lights illuminated is generally illegal.

Winter

The Cascade Range is a formidable barrier, and never more so than during winter snow storms. Visibility can be nil due to high winds and blowing snow. Some mountain passes simply close for the season, e.g. McKenzie Pass near Sisters and Chinook Pass, SR 410 to Mt Rainier. To check road conditions; *tel: (541) 889-3999* (Oregon); *(900) 407-7277* (Washington, 1 Oct–15 Apr, $0.35 per min); or *(800) 663-4997* (British Columbia). The **Northwest Avalanche Center** compiles snow avalanche conditions and issues warnings as necessary; *tel: (503) 326-2400* (Oregon) or *(206) 526-6677* (Washington).

The speed limit when using chains or other traction devices such as snow tyres or studded tyres is generally 25–30 mph. Even if chains are not required, snow and adverse conditions often require caution and slower than normal driving speeds. Allow extra time to get to and through mountain areas. Local radio stations broadcast weather information. Lorry drivers and truck stops are also excellent sources of information for conditions ahead. *Never* drive where snow has fallen or is anticipated without carrying chains or other traction devices and knowing how to install them.

Accelerating or braking sharply when roads are wet, snowy or icy is almost certain to throw your vehicle into a skid. When meeting oncoming traffic on narrow roads, the driver going uphill always has the right of way – if one vehicle has to back up to a wider spot in the road, it is safer to back uphill than downhill. If you get stuck in snow or mud, don't spin the wheels, but rock the car gently backward and

forward by changing from forward to reverse gears until you begin to move. Accelerate and brake gently.

When hiring a vehicle for winter mountain driving, be sure that chains or other traction devices are included. Rental cars generally are not equipped with snow tyres or studded tyres. After a snowfall, authorities post signs at checkpoints indicating that chains are required. Failure to install chains can result in a fine – or in getting stranded. In mountain areas, petrol station attendants and independent entrepreneurs will install chains for a fee, but only if you already have a set. Pull over for installation and get a receipt for the service as well as the installer's badge or identification number. The speed limit when chains are required is 25–30 mph.

Useful items for winter driving are an ice scraper, a small shovel for digging out, warm sleeping bags and extra clothing in case of long delays. Keep the petrol tank at least half-full so you'll be able to go back should a road close unexpectedly. Keep warm and conserve fuel if stalled, but keep the car ventilated inside.

SnoParks are officially designed public parking and recreation areas during the snowy season, usually 15 Nov–April, for Oregon, Washington, Idaho and California, but not British Columbia. If SnoPark signs are posted, parking requires a daily or seasonal permit, sold at sporting goods stores, gas stations, outdoor recreation stores, ski resorts and other outlets; *tel: (503) 945-5281* (Oregon) or *(206) 586-0185* (Washington). Permits are valid for all four participating states.

DISTANCES

Point-to-point distances can be vast in the Pacific Northwest. To estimate driving time, plan on an average speed of 50 mph, without stops, slower in cities and mountains. AAA maps include charts with approximate driving times between major points. Use the sample driving distances and times of p. 343 as guidelines, but allow for delays and stops. In Oregon and Washington, highway mile markers show distances border to border, which make it easy to keep track of progress.

DOCUMENTATION

Your home country driving licence is valid in Oregon, Washington and British Columbia, but most car rental companies require that drivers be at least 25 years of age. Some companies accept younger drivers, but only upon payment of an additional fee. All three jurisdictions require that drivers carry their driving licenses with them at all times while operating a vehicle. An **International Driving Permit** is helpful if your own driving licence is not in English, but is not required. If using your own automobile insurance, be sure to carry proof of cover.

INFORMATION

Automobile or motoring club membership in your home country can be invaluable. AAA and CAA clubs provide members of corresponding foreign clubs travelling to North America the reciprocal services that AAA/CAA members are eligible to receive abroad. Auto club services include emergency road service and towing; maps, tour guide books and specialist publications; touring services; road and camping information; and discounts to attractions and accommodations. In general, if it is free to you at your home club, it should be free to you at AAA/CAA offices.

Thomas Cook has formed and alliance with the AAA to provide services for its customers travelling in the US – see p.36.

The AAA/CAA may charge for some services, such as maps and tour books. Emergency breakdown road service may not be available to some non-North American club members. For information on reciprocal clubs and services, contact your own club or request *Offices to Serve You Abroad, American Automobile Association, 1000 AAA Dr., Heathrow, FL 32746; tel: (407) 444-7000.* Carry your own club membership card with you at all times.

MOTORCYCLES

If *Easy Rider* is still your idea of North America, so be it. Motorcycles provide great mobility and a sense of freedom. Luggage space is limited, however; vast distances can make for long days in the saddle; and potholes, gravel, poor roads, dust, smog and sun are constant touring companions.

Hire motorcycles locally by finding a telephone directory listing. Helmets are required by law for both driver and passenger. By custom, most motor-cyclists turn on their headlamps even in the daytime to increase their visibility.

PARKING

Public parking garages, parking lots and parkades (car parks) are indicated by a blue sign showing a 'P' with a directional arrow. Prices are posted at the entrance. Some city centre lots charge per 20 mins to disguise exorbitant rates. Many car parks in BC accept credit cards as well as cash. Oregon and Washington car parks generally require payment in cash.

In civic centres, shopping and downtown areas, coin operated parking meters govern kerbside parking. The charge and time limit varies with the location. Compare parking garages against meter charges for the more economical choice.

Kerbs are colour-coded throughout the Pacific Northwest: *Red* means no stopping or parking for any reason at any time; *Blue* is for disabled parking, permitted only with a special permit; *White* is for passenger pick-up and drop-off only, no parking; *Green* is for limited-time parking as indicated on the kerb (usually 10 mins); *Yellow* is a commercial zone for lorries and delivery vehicles with commercial number plates. White, green and yellow zones may be enforced only during specific hours such as Mon–Fri 0800–1800, check the kerb or nearby signs.

No parking is allowed within 15 ft/5 m of a fire hydrant, within 3 ft/1 m of a disabled person pavement ramp, in bus stop areas, in an intersection or zebra crossing (crosswalk), on the pavement, blocking a driveway or on a freeway except in emergencies.

If you park in violation of times and areas posted on kerb signs or on signposts nearby, expect to be issued with a citation – a ticket that states the violation, amount of the fine and how to pay it. If you do not pay, the car hire company will charge the ticket amount, plus any penalties for late payment, against your credit card. Fines range from a few dollars to several hundred dollars, depending on the violation and the locality.

Valet parking at garages, hotels, restaurants and events may be pricey. The parking attendant will expect an additional tip of $1–$5 when returning the car. Leave the car keys with the valet attendant, who will return them with the car.

PETROL

Petrol (gas) is sold in US gallons (roughly four litres per gallon) in Oregon and Washington and in litres in BC. Posted prices include tax. Prices can vary by 100% depending on location. In areas with many stations, there can be strong price competition. Prices tend to be lower in and near urban areas and on the US side of the US-Canada border. In mountain or desert areas, prices can be astronomical.

Some stations offer full service, filling the petrol tank, washing the windscreen and checking motor oil, usually for about $0.40 more per gallon. Most motorists use the more economical self-service.

Two exceptions: in Oregon, state law requires that attendants, not customers, dispense petrol, but attendants may or may not check oil or wash the windscreen. Attendants are not tipped. In BC, where self-service is the norm and all petrol stations in the same area post uniform prices, some stations offer full service to try to lure customers away from their competitors. Full service attendants do not expect a tip, but a few may suggest 'topping off', or filling, the motor oil unnecessarily. Non-brand name petrol stations in BC sometimes offer discounted prices at the pump even though prices posted on advertising signs match the prevailing rate in town.

Nearly all North American cars and RVs require unleaded petrol. Leaded petrol is generally unavailable due to environmental controls. The three fuel grades are regular, super and premium. Use regular unless the car hire company recommends otherwise. A few vehicles use diesel fuel.

When petrol stations are more than a few miles apart, road signs usually indicate the distance to the next services. Open petrol stations are very well-lit at night; many chain stations are open 24 hr.

Most stations accept cash, credit cards and travellers cheques in local currency. Some stations accept only cash and may require payment before filling the tank. Many stations, especially in urban areas, do not accept $50 or $100 bank notes because of counterfeiting and security concerns.

POLICE

Police cars signal drivers with flashing red or red and blue lights, and sometimes a siren. Respond quickly, but safely, by moving to the right side of the road. Roll the driver's side window down but stay in the vehicle unless asked to get out. You have the right to ask an officer – politely – for identification, though it should be shown immediately. Have your driver's license and car registration papers ready for inspection when requested.

Officers normally check computer records for vehicle registration irregularities and the driver for theft, criminal records, or other driving violations. If cited for a violation, arguing with the officer will only make a bad situation much worse.

ROAD SIGNS

International symbols are used for directional and warning signs, but many are different from European versions; all language signs are in English; in British Columbia, official signs are English/French bilingual. Signs may be white, yellow, green, brown or blue.

Stop, give way, do not enter, and wrong way signs are *red* and *white*. *Yellow* is for warning or direction indicators. *Orange* is for roadworks or detours (temporary diversions). *Green* indicates freeway directions. *Brown* is an alert for parks, campsites, hiking, etc. *Blue* gives non-driving information, such as radio station frequency for traffic or park information, or services in a nearby town.

Speed limits and distance are primarily shown in miles in the US, kilometres in Canada. Dual-system signage is occasionally posted in US National Parks and Washington/British Columbia border areas. Speed limit signs are *white* with black letters.

43

Traffic lights are red, yellow and green. Yellow indicates that the light will shortly turn red; stop, if possible, before entering the intersection.

A favourite (and highly illegal) trick is to *jump* the red light, that is, enter the intersection when the signal is yellow and about to turn red. Major cities have installed cameras which photograph the licence plate of any car running a red light. Police can cite you if you enter an intersection and you will not be clear of the intersection before the light turns red.

It is permitted to turn right at a red traffic light if there is no traffic coming from the left, i.e. as if it were a 'give way' sign, unless there is a sign specifically forbidding it ('No Turn on Red'). A flashing yellow light, or hazard warning, requires drivers to slow down; flashing red means stop, then proceed when safe.

ROAD SYSTEM

The US Interstate Highway System was built in the 1950s to streamline cargo transportation across the USA. Federal funds maintain the interstates, which are usually the smoothest roads available. **Interstate** highways, designated I-(number) in the text, are the straightest and usually the least scenic route from point to point.

Freeways, often called expressways elsewhere in the USA, are motorways with controlled access. **Highways** have cross traffic interrupting the flow. East–west roads have even numbers, e.g., I-82, I-84, I-90; North-south roads are odd, e.g. I-5, Hwy 97, Hwy 101.

Rest areas, commonly along highways, have restrooms with toilets and public telephones and are usually landscaped. Picnic tables are provided in scenic areas and rest stops of historic or geographical interest have explanatory signs or maps. Use caution when leaving your vehicle at night and carry a torch (flashlight).

Local roads can range from satin-smooth to pitted, depending on local spending. Unpaved roads indicated on maps or described in this text may be treacherous. Ask at a petrol station or a truck (lorry) stop about local conditions before venturing on them. Car hire companies may prohibit driving on unpaved roads.

RULES OF THE ROAD

Lanes and Overtaking

Drive on the right. Vehicles are left-hand drive. The lane on the left, the *Number 1 Lane*, is fast; the right is slowest, and cars enter or leave traffic from the right (unless otherwise indicated by signs). Overtake other vehicles on the left side. A solid white line at least 4 ft from the kerb marks a special lane for bicycles, usually labelled 'Bike Lane'.

Cars may and will pass you on both sides in a multi-lane road. For many drivers from the UK, this is the most unexpected and most confusing feature of North American roads. Use direction indicators when changing lanes, but don't be surprised if other drivers don't bother. Never turn against a red arrow traffic signal.

Make right turns from the right-hand lane after stopping at stop signs or traffic lights. Turn left from the most left-hand lane of lanes going in your direction, unless the turn is prohibited by a no-turn sign. Do not drive in areas marked for public transportation, such as bus lanes or trolley tracks, or in pedestrian walkways.

If the centre line down the middle of a two-way road is a double solid line, overtaking is not allowed. Overtaking is permitted if the centre line is broken. Always overtake on the left. Highways in mountainous areas or along long narrow stretches, have occasional overtaking lanes. Driving or parking on pavements is illegal.

Main road drivers have the right of way over cars on lesser roads, but at the junction of two minor roads, cars to your right have the right of way when arriving at the same time you do.

Freeway Driving

Lanes are numbered from left to right: number one is the extreme left-hand lane closest to the centre, number two is the next lane to the right, and so on. An 'exit' or 'off ramp' is the slip road leading off the freeway; an 'entrance' or 'on ramp' leads onto the freeway. 'Metering lights' are traffic signals controlling ramp access, found only in congested urban areas.

When freeway traffic does flow, it flows

smoothly and quickly. The posted speed limit is generally 65 mph in the US and 100 kph in BC; 5–10 mph or kph faster is common in the fast (furthest left) lane. The safest speed is that which matches the general traffic flow in your lane, regardless of the posted speed limit. If you are exceeding the posted speed limit, however, you may be ticketed even if other traffic is keeping to the same speed.

When entering a freeway, *don't stop* on the ramp unless access is controlled by a traffic signal. Accelerate on the ramp and merge into the freeway flow. Cars that stop on the ramp are likely to be hit from the rear.

Freeways may have **car-pool** or **HOV** (high occupancy vehicle) lanes for vehicles carrying several passengers. Road signs will specify the number of passengers required to use those speedier lanes. Car-pool lanes are normally marked with a white diamond symbol painted on the roadbed. Special bus lanes are also marked.

Horns
Horns should be sounded only as a safety warning, and never near a hospital.

Pedestrians
Pedestrians have the right of way at all zebra crossings and at all intersections, whether or not a pedestrian crossing is marked. In other places, vehicles have the right of way. Visitors from California, where pedestrians have the right of way at all times, are a special hazard in the Pacific Northwest; they tend to step blithely off the kerb in mid-block expecting traffic to halt. Some towns and cities cite pedestrians for jay-walking, crossing in the wrong spot. If a vehicle is involved in an accident with pedestrian in a zebra crossing, the presumption of error usually lies with the driver.

Speed Limits
The standard speed limit on major highways and freeways is 65 mph in Oregon and Washington and 100 kph in BC. Faster or slower speed limits may be posted on some sections. Traffic generally flows faster than the speed limits, but police may ticket any driver exceeding the speed limit irregardless of traffic

conditions. You may not see the patrols. Many jurisdictions patrol open country by aeroplane and nearly all use radar or laser devices on the highway and in towns.

Regardless of posted speed limits, police can invoke basic speed laws which hold that no one may drive faster than is safe for local conditions. To exceed posted speeds for mountain driving and around bends is to court disaster.

In towns, the speed limit near schools is generally 25 mph for Oregon and Washington, 30 kph in BC. Slow for railway crossings when you cannot see at least 400 ft in both directions.

Seat Belts
Seat belts must be worn in Oregon, Washington and BC by the driver and all passengers. In addition, children under four years or 40 pounds (Oregon), 3 years (Washington) or 18 kg (BC) must ride in approved child safety seats. RV passengers outside the driving area are not required to wear seat belts, but should be safely seated while the vehicle is in motion.

Vehicle Insurance
Oregon, Washington and BC require that all vehicles on the road be insured. Minimum required cover in Oregon is $25,000 per person bodily injury and property damage liability, $10,000 personal injury protection and $25,000 uninsured motorist protection; in Washington, $25,000 bodily injury and $10,000 property damage and liability; and in BC, $200,000 third party liability protection. Vehicles found to be without proper insurance cover may be (and are) impounded until insurance is obtained and penalties paid.

In practice, considerably more cover is desirable. Overseas visitors hiring a car are strongly advised to take out top-up liability cover such as the Topguard Insurance sold by Thomas Cook in the UK, which covers liability up to US$1 million. (This is not to be confused with travel insurance, which provides cover for your own medical expenses – see p. 28.)

Car rental agencies try to sell their own insurance to renters, called collision damage waiver, or CDW, and loss damage waiver,

45

Some Pacific Northwest Driving Terms

Big rig A large lorry, usually a tractor pulling one or more trailers.

Boulevard stop Slowing at a stop sign, but not coming to a complete halt.

Crosswalk A marked pedestrian crossing or zebra crossing.

Connector A minor road connecting two freeways.

Curve Bend.

Divided highway Dual carriageway.

Diversion A detour or temporary alternate route, usually to avoid construction.

DUI Driving Under the Influence, usually of alcohol.

Exit Slip road leading off a freeway, also called an *off ramp*.

Fender Bumper.

Freeway Motorway.

Garage or *parking garage* car park.

Gas(oline) Petrol.

Grade Gradient, hill.

Highway Trunk road.

Hood Bonnet.

Metering lights Traffic signals controlling access to freeways, bridges, etc.

Motor Home Motor caravan or camper.

Off ramp Slip road leading off a freeway, also called an *exit*.

On ramp Slip road leading onto a freeway, also called an *entrance*.

Pavement The road surface. A UK 'pavement' is a *sidewalk*.

Pull out Lay-by.

Ramp Slip road.

Rent Hire.

Rubberneck(er) One who impedes traffic by slowing down to peer while driving past the scene of an accident or some other unusual event.

RV (recreational vehicle) Motor caravan.

Shoulder Verge.

Sidewalk Pavement.

Sig-alert An official warning of unusually heavy traffic, usually broadcast over local radio stations.

Shift(stick) Gear lever.

Switchback Serpentine road.

Tailgate Driving too closely to the vehicle immediately in front.

Tow truck Breakdown lorry.

Traffic cop Traffic warden.

Trailer Caravan.

Truck Lorry.

Trunk Boot.

Unpaved road Rough gravel or dirt road – check car hire restrictions on driving unpaved roads.

Windshield Windscreen.

Yield Give way.

LDW. Refusing CDW makes the renter personally liable for any damage to the vehicle. US and Canadian drivers using their own or hired vehicles should ask their insurance company if their coverage extends to Oregon, Washington and BC and meets the required minimum insurance cover. If not, arrange for insurance before departing. In addition, some credit cards provide insurance cover for car rentals; check with your credit card issuer for details.

CDW is strongly recommended for drivers from outside North America, and often required as part of a fly-drive package. Sometimes it is paid for when booking the hire abroad, sometimes it is payable locally on picking up or returning the car. Special hire rates occasionally include CDW.

Vehicle Security

Lock it when you leave, lock it when you're inside and don't forget the windows. Never leave keys, documents, maps, guidebooks and other tourist paraphernalia in sight. Be mindful of anyone lurking in the back seat or in the house part of an RV, especially at night. Watch other drivers for strange behaviour, especially if you're consistently being followed. Never leave the engine running when you're not in the vehicle. Keep car keys with you at all times and always park in well-lit areas.

BACKGROUND
PACIFIC NORTHWEST

Ignore the 49th parallel. Geography, history and outlook link the two US states and one Canadian province of the Pacific Northwest to each other more strongly than to the rest of their respective countries. Nature, not politics, defines the north-west, a region bound by the interlocking influences of Pacific Ocean, Cascade mountains and salmon.

GEOGRAPHY

Nature's Bounty

It's no accident that modern utopian writers have cast the Pacific Northwest as an *Ecotopia* that blends nature and economics. Europeans who arrived in the 18th-century found a land so bountiful that even hunters and gatherers had the leisure and the wealth to create one of the richest and most artistic cultures on the continent.

Lumbermen revelled in endless forests, a bottomless treasure trove waiting to be tapped. Farmers found some of the most fertile farmland in North America in the shadow of the soaring, glacier-capped peaks of the Cascade Range. Merchants grew wealthy from commerce across the Pacific Ocean. Nature, it seemed, had conspired to create a land that was as rich as it was beautiful and as hard to reach as it was rewarding.

When the tide is out, the table is set, said early settlers of the immense shoals of oysters, clams, mussels and other shellfish that lined every beach, bay and shoreline. Great runs of salmon choked every river and stream from spring to autumn. To Native Americans, the silvery fish was as much god as food, revered even as they

were eaten fresh, roasted, smoked, dried and rendered. Two centuries of overfishing and forest destruction have reduced the mighty runs to an annual trickle, but salmon, or least the ideal of salmon, unify an otherwise divided region.

The Land

The volcanic Cascades split the Pacific Northwest. To the west lie the lush forests and mighty rivers of popular imagination, a land where steady rain reduces the rainbow to shades of grey and green. To the east, the sun blisters increasingly arid forests, grasslands and deserts laced with rivers that once brought salmon nearly 1000 miles inland to spawn.

The first humans who migrated into the region 10,000–20,000 years ago prospered. Coastal rain forests supported a diversity of life seldom seen outside the tropics. From ten-inch banana slugs to 10-ft grizzly bears and 300-ft trees, nearly everything that lived was useful. The red cedar tree alone provided the raw material for baskets, clothing, tools, canoes, houses, roof shingles, religious objects and works of art. Drier valleys supported immense fields of camas lilies – rich, starchy bulbs that grew with little tending. Desert rivers teemed with salmon and trout, the plains with game. Nature's larder seldom ran empty.

Trade

What couldn't be obtained locally was readily available via trade routes that stretched eastward across flinty deserts to the Rocky Mountains and beyond. Early White explorers who expected to traverse a forbidding, empty land found networks of trails criss-crossing every mountain range. When **Simon Fraser** journeyed down the river which bears his name in 1808, tribes far inland knew the annual trading schedules of ships visiting Vancouver Island.

47

Nature's bounty gave Pacific Northwest tribes the leisure to develop immensely complex societies. Ritual and art became highly varied and valued. Among the Haida, Chinook, Coast Salish, Kwakiutil, Nootka and other groups, power and respect were measured by the wealth given away in great **potlatch** ceremonies (See Seattle–Port Angeles, p.82). White traders complained that Native Americans were the sharpest bargainers they had ever encountered.

HISTORY

Early Explorers

When the outside world first learned of the Pacific Northwest isn't clear. A Chinese manuscript from 217 BC tells of an accidental voyage west to a land of towering trees and red-faced men. Chinese and Japanese shipwrecks along both the Oregon and Washington coasts have been dated to the 5th century AD, matching ceramics excavated up the Columbia River.

Sir Francis Drake may have sailed as far north as Vancouver Island on his round-the-world voyage to plunder Spanish possessions in 1577, but **Juan de Fuca**, a Greek sailing for Spain in 1592, gets credit as the first European to visit the Pacific Northwest. In the early 1700s, Danish captain **Vitus Bering** sailed east from Russia to Alaska for the Tsar and turned the world's attention to the Pacific Northwest.

China prized the thick, silky fur of the sea otter. When Bering discovered huge sea otter populations in Alaska, Russian merchants rushed to trade with Native Americans for pelts. By the 1770s, Spain was laying its own claims. A 1774 voyage north from Mexico got as far as the Queen Charlotte Islands and Nootka Sound, on the west coast of Vancouver Island. The next year, **Bruno de Heceta** and **Juan Francisco de la Bodega y Quadra** returned. Heceta noted, but didn't explore, 'the mouth of some great river', the Columbia.

The English had their own commercial interests. For more than two centuries, Britain had searched for a northern sea route to Asia. Parliament had a standing reward of £20,000, a considerable fortune, for discovery of a route from Hudson's Bay west to the Pacific Ocean.

James Cook, the first European to visit Australia, New Zealand and Hawaii, went looking for the fabled Northwest Passage.

While anchored in Nootka Sound in 1778, Cook bought sea otter pelts for warm clothing and bedding. He was killed the next year in Hawaii without finding the Northwest Passage. Neither did his second-in-command, **Charles Clark**, who stopped at Macau on the way back to England. The well-worn otter skins fetched such high prices that the crew nearly mutinied to return to Nootka, but the expedition sailed home.

The Nootka Convention

Accounts of Cook's voyage set off a rush by traders despite the strong territorial claims of both Spain and Russia. Merchants from the newly-independent United States of America sailed for the Pacific Northwest almost as soon as the war with England ended in 1783. British traders made the trip as well.

The fur rush nearly brought war between England and Spain, but diplomacy prevailed. The Nootka Convention of 1790 granted joint trading rights. In preparation for final settlement of land claims, both countries mounted expeditions to explore and map the coast.

Spain sent Bodega y Quadra. Britain sent **George Vancouver**, who had visited Nootka as a midshipman under Cook. Vancouver missed the region's biggest feature, the Columbia River, first charted by American trader **Robert Gray** in 1792, establishing US claims. England and Spain lost interest in the area as war consumed Europe and overhunting killed the otter trade. In 1819, Spain ceded its Pacific Northwest interests to the United States in return for American recognition of Spanish title to California and the Southwest.

The Columbia River

The inland fur trade was more successful. European demand for beaver pelts to make hats spurred the **Hudson's Bay Company** (HBC), run from London, and its Montreal-based competitor, the **North West Company**. NWC partners Alexander Mackenzie, Simon Fraser and David Thompson pioneered northern routes to the Pacific Coast from the

1790s–1810s; Americans **Meriwether Lewis** and **William Clark** explored west from American territory 1804–1806. All were searching for the Columbia.

Mackenzie reached the mouth of the Bella Coola River in 1793, the first non-Native to cross the continent north of Mexico. Fraser fought through treacherous rapids to the sea in 1808, only to realise that he, too, was too far north. The Fraser River was too perilous to become a major trade route. In 1811, Thompson finally made his way to the mouth of the Columbia, only to discover American traders building Fort Astoria.

The NWC took over Astoria during the War of 1812, then built Fort Vancouver 100 miles upriver at the confluence of the Columbia and Willamette Rivers. At war's end, the 49th parallel divided the US and British America east of the Rockies; the two powers jointly occupied the Pacific Northwest. When the HBC absorbed the NWC in 1821, England had an economic monopoly spanning North America, but neither country exercised political control west of the Rocky Mountains.

Manifest Destiny and the Oregon Trail

Four years later, Britain and America agreed to recognise Russian authority south to 54°40′. The HBC established and expanded posts at Spokane, Okanogan, Nisqually, Langley, and elsewhere to block American movement west. **Manifest Destiny**, the idea that God had ordained America to occupy the continent, was gaining strength in the US. American missionaries began filtering into the Pacific Northwest to 'civilise the savages'. Their reports of rich farmland began to attract attention.

The HBC was also expanding. The company established farms along the Columbia River and Puget Sound to supply inland forts and for export to Alaska, Hawaii and Asia. Dr John McLoughlin, chief factor at Fort Vancouver, directed American settlers south into the Willamette Valley, hoping to maintain British control north of the Columbia River. HBC wanted the Columbia itself, the major route to its most profitable fur territories in present-day British Columbia.

But just in case, HBC governor George

Simpson moved HBC headquarters to Fort Victoria, on the southern tip of Vancouver Island, in 1841.

It was a prescient move. The US Navy visited the Pacific Northwest in 1841, ostensibly on a goodwill mission. US Army surveyors laid out a wagon route across the Rockies. In 1843, the US Senate declared Oregon Territory, the vast expanse west of the Rockies between California and Alaska, to be American and the first official **Oregon Trail** settlers headed west. The lure was free land, 640 acres for every white male US citizen plus 320 acres for his wife. The Organic Act and the later Land Donation Act effectively blocked land ownership by Native Americans, Blacks, Asians and non-citizens, but boosted land settlement by families. Today Oregon and Washington remain overwhelmingly White, a sharp contrast to California and British Columbia.

The Gold Rush

Tensions escalated when James Polk swept America's 1844 presidential election on the slogan of '54°40′ or fight!'. Britain, which had reaped few profits from the Pacific Northwest, agreed to extend the US boundary along the 49th parallel to the coast, then through the Strait of Juan de Fuca to the Pacific. The 1846 Treaty of Washington swelled the tide of Americans flooding west. California's 1848 gold rush sparked demand for grain and timber, demand which continued to grow when gold was discovered in Oregon, Washington and BC after 1850. In 1852, settlers north of the Columbia won their own government as the Territory of Washington. Oregon, more heavily populated, became a state in 1859, Washington in 1889.

BC was a late starter. The HBC were more interested in commerce than community. In 1849, Britain leased Vancouver Island to the company to establish a viable colony. The California gold rush fostered lumber mills. Commercial shipping and Royal Navy ships at Esquimalt, next to Victoria, supported coal mining at Nanaimo. World-wide demand kept salmon canneries busy. But the HBC was singularly unsuccessful at attracting permanent settlers.

49

The only practical access was a brutal, five-month voyage from England around the tip of South America. Oregon and Washington, where acreage was far cheaper, were accessible overland. Even Victoria, HBC's capital on Vancouver Island, remained a small, if prosperous, town in a vast forest.

Gold made the difference. The HBC had suppressed news of gold discoveries since at least 1850 in order to maximise profits and discourage American migration north. When word of gold finds on the Fraser River got out in 1858, hordes of American miners flooded north, raising fears that America would annex territory that was British on paper but outside all control in practice. The fears were warranted. The largely-American mining population began circulating petitions calling for changes to mining regulations and government. The US sent a special commissioner to the gold fields to protect American interests. The commissioner reported that it was only a matter of time until Vancouver Island and the mainland became American by force of population, unless Washington wanted to act sooner.

Territorial Claims

London moved first. In June, 1858, the House of Commons created the mainland colony of New Caledonia. Queen Victoria changed the name to British Columbia. On November 19, a provisional government, headed by **James Douglas**, was installed at Fort Langley. Key officials were dispatched from England. Royal Engineers promptly moved the capital to New Westminster, now part of Greater Vancouver, a site more defensible against American invasion. Gold Commissioners maintained strict order in the gold fields, a sharp contrast to pervasive lawlessness in US gold camps.

Miners needed food. In 1860, the colony offered prospective settlers 160 acres at bargain prices. The entire Fraser Valley was under cultivation within nine years. Cattle ranches sprang up even as drovers brought thousands of head north from Washington. Merchants prospered, but every economic downturn brought renewed calls to join the United States, the nearest economic power.

BC and Vancouver Island colonies were combined in 1866, but talk of the State of British Columbia increased when the US purchased Alaska from Russia in 1867. The US tried to claim BC as compensation for British support of the Confederacy during the US Civil War. Britain declined, citing the need for a Royal Navy base in the region. BCers equivocated.

Douglas and other leaders were firmly British in outlook, but BC depended on business decisions made in San Francisco, not London. The working population were either American immigrants or Canadian-born with little love for Britain or rule from afar. It wasn't until Britain pushed BC to join the new Dominion of **Canada** in 1870 that pro-American feelings subsided, assuaged by promises of a transCanada railway and economic links to the east. When the railway finally arrived in 1885, an obscure lumber town called Vancouver blossomed into the region's most successful and cosmopolitan city.

Railways also recast Oregon and Washington. Seattle and Portland became major junctions between rail and sea transport. The US government awarded huge swaths of land to railway builders, who sold forested tracts to timber companies such as Weyerhaeuser, which agreed to build mills near the railway lines. Other lands were sold to immigrant farmers, especially in sparsely-settled Washington. Railway owners made fortunes from construction, further fortunes selling land and still more hauling farm and timber products.

Native Americans were the biggest losers. Otter traders imported smallpox, measles and other diseases which decimated tribes throughout the region. Government saw only an empty land waiting to be settled. The HBC generally purchased tribal lands, but purchase terms were routinely violated. Colonial and Dominion officials treated First Nations bands as children, appropriating lands and resources 'for their own good'. The US government forced tribes to abandon their lands and relocate by treaty, then broke treaty terms and called in Army troops when the tribes objected. Courts in both countries are still dealing with tribal claims to land, fishing rights, timber and other property taken under questionable circumstances.

Panic and Recovery

The boom times ended with the **Panic of 1893**. The stock market crash reverberated in bank and railway failures, which brought down businesses dependent on capital and transportation, but the Yukon gold rush of 1898 boosted a recovery that was already under way. The economy boomed again after World War I as irrigation systems spread into the Okanagan, Yakima and other valleys, once thought too dry for successful farming. The rise of hydroelectric power spurred the spread of manufacturing. The good life in the Pacific Northwest looked to get even better.

Even the US stock market crash of 1929 and the ensuing world-wide depression hit the Pacific Northwest with less force than many other regions. Manufacturing suffered, but many residents were able to turn to farming, fishing and other subsistence pursuits. The Government helped too, with civil engineering projects and grand irrigation schemes for the Columbia and other rivers. Bonneville Dam, completed in 1938, rescued Portland's shipyards, aluminium smelters and other industries. Grand Coulee Dam, completed in 1941, did the same for Seattle.

World War II brought prosperity to most, and persecution to some. Hysterical American and Canadian officials shipped ethnic Japanese populations to bleak inland prison camps.

The perfection of the chainsaw during the 1940s helped the timber industry leap into the post-war housing boom. Irrigation schemes delayed by the war came on line in the 1950s, turning vast patches of eastern desert green with mint, maize, wheat and a dozen other crops.

The Environmental Struggle

Population growth also brought questions. Natural resources, furs, fish, timber and minerals, developed the Pacific Northwest, but the resources were visibly disappearing. So was the natural beauty that had lured so many westward.

Sea otters, beaver, and most other fur animals had already been driven to the brink of extinction. Dams, bad forestry practices and overfishing destroyed salmon runs. Timber companies cut far more trees than they planted. Mines, metal refineries and paper mills dumped toxic wastes in the nearest waterway and vented poisonous fumes into the air.

The last patch of virgin forest near Victoria was reduced to splintered stumps. Mt Rainier began to fade behind layers of brown smog. Residents revolted.

Oregon, Washington and BC tightened environmental and land use controls while pushing their national governments to do likewise. A new economic model began to emerge, however tentatively, that forests, rivers, ocean and mountains are resources to be renewed, not treasure troves to be looted and discarded. It's a model often clothed in references to mother earth and Native American struggles, but it's based on the same harsh economics that killed the sea otter trade, the beaver trade, most of the fishing business and nearly all of the timber companies: When the resource is used up, the industry dies.

The environmental struggle to preserve natural resources for long-term use has produced groups such as BC's Greenpeace and landmark laws like Oregon's Bottle Bill, America's first mandatory deposit on containers to reduce waste and pollution.

Outdoor recreation is replacing lumbering in many locales. Sport fishing is more lucrative than commercial fishing. Aircraft, computer software and recreation companies such as Boeing, Microsoft, Intel and Nike, bring in more money than ship building. And the Pacific Northwest remains more closely linked to itself and to the Pacific Rim than to the rest of North America.

TOURING ITINERARIES

Much of the pleasure of a driving holiday lies in tailoring your itinerary to match your tastes and interests. By dividing the Pacific Northwest into recommended routes, this book is intended to make it easy and pleasurable to plan your ideal tour. By linking several of our routes, you can create a trip to suit your tastes and be confident of following a tried and tested path which introduces you to the best the route has to offer.

This chapter begins with some practical advice on tour planning, followed by two ready-made itineraries designed to show you as much as possible of the Pacific Northwest's tremendous variety in a two- or a three-week trip. Feel free to vary our suggestions, using the full range of information contained in the route descriptions. The remaining pages suggest features you can use to create a variety of self-planned theme tours.

PRACTICAL HINTS

Here are a few tips to make routes easier to plan and more fun to follow:

1. Use the most detailed maps possible. The colour map section at the end of this book is useful for planning and following the basic routes, but a more detailed road map is indispensable, especially if you intend to wander from the outlined routes, a practice we highly encourage. If you don't already have a good set of road maps, stop at the nearest AAA/CAA office as soon as possible after arriving in the Pacific

Northwest and pick up maps for the areas you will be touring. For still more detail, buy a copy of *DeLorme Mapping's Atlas & Gazetteer* for the area you will be touring from any major bookseller.

2. Don't schedule too much driving each day. Allow a conservative 50 miles per hour of freeway driving and 35 miles each hour on secondary roads to allow for the inevitable unplanned stops. It's better to have more time to explore along the way than to be pressed to arrive each evening. Route descriptions in this book give information about driving times as well as distances–driving on secondary roads in deserts and mountains can be surprisingly slow.

3. Check weather and road reports. Most paved roads in the Pacific Northwest are open all year, but some major mountain passes across the Cascade Range are closed from Oct/Nov until May/June, depending on the weather. Other passes, including such crucial routes as I-90 between Seattle and Yakima, may be closed for several days following major winter storms. Fire, flood and mudslides also close roads without warning.

4. Unless accommodation is pre-booked, plan to arrive each night with plenty of time to find a place to sleep. Advance bookings are essential for Ashland, the Columbia River Gorge, Crater Lake, the Oregon Coast, Portland, Vancouver (BC), Victoria, Whistler and the entire region in summer and at holiday weekends.

5. Allow time at the end of the trip to get back to the departure city (most likely Portland, Seattle or Vancouver) the day before a scheduled flight home. Airlines

don't hold planes for a single carload of late arrivals. Passengers travelling on cheap fares who miss a flight will likely be faced with buying a new ticket home–at full price.

6. Give serendipity a chance by not planning in too much detail. Allow time to spend a few extra hours–or an extra day–in some unexpected gem of a town or to turn down an interesting side road. If you want your days pre-planned in 15-min increments, you'll be happier on a fully escorted coach tour than on a self-drive holiday.

THE BEST OF THE PACIFIC NORTHWEST

The following circular tours start and end in Seattle, but can be reversed or picked up in Portland, Vancouver or any other convenient spot. Routes in Southern Oregon can easily be combined with California routes outlined in the second edition of Thomas Cook's *On The Road Around California*.

These tours combine several recommended routes, with a few digressions and short-cuts added. Suggested overnight stops are in bold type. Adapt the tours freely or use the same cut-and-paste method to personalise your own tours.

14 Days

For those who want (or need) to 'do' the Pacific Northwest in one whirlwind bout of driving, it can be done. Just be sure to allow a few days at home to recover!

Day 1: **Seattle** (pp. 58–66)
Day 2: Seattle to Port Townsend and ferry to **Victoria** (Seattle–Port Angeles, pp.77–82, Victoria, pp. 301–310)
Day 3: **Victoria**
Day 4: Victoria to **Nanaimo** (Victoria–Nanaimo, pp. 319–323)
Day 5: Nanaimo to **Vancouver** by ferry (Vancouver, pp. 274–282)
Day 6: **Vancouver**
Day 7: Vancouver to Bellingham, Seattle, Snoqualmie, Cle Elum, Ellensburg and

Yakima (Bellingham–Vancouver, pp. 272–272, Seattle–Bellingham, pp. 92–97, Seattle–Yakima, pp. 88–91)
Day 8: Yakima to Toppenish and **Goldendale** (Portland–Yakima, pp. 236–240)
Day 9: Goldendale to Maryhill, the Columbia Gorge, Bingen/White Salmon, Stevenson, Vancouver and **Portland** (Portland–Yakima, pp. 236–240, Portland, pp. 134–141)
Day 10: **Portland**
Day 11: Portland to Salem and **Eugene** (Portland–Eugene, pp. 145–154)
Day 12: Eugene to Florence and **Newport** (Eugene–Florence, pp. 171–172, Astoria–Brookings, pp. 111–128)
Day 13: Newport to Astoria, Longview/Kelso and **Castle Rock** (Astoria–Brookings, pp. 111–128, Olympia–Portland, pp. 165–170)
Day 14: Castle Rock to Mt St Helens, Centralia, Tacoma and **Seattle** (Olympia–Portland, pp. 165–170, Seattle–Olympia, pp. 83–87)

21 Days

Three weeks is a more realistic, though still rushed, time to see much of the Pacific Northwest. If possible, add another one to two weeks to see the more remote and less travelled eastern reaches of the region.

Day 1: **Seattle** (Seattle, pp. 58–66)
Day 2: Seattle to Port Townsend and ferry to **Victoria** (Seattle–Port Angeles, pp. 77–82, Victoria, pp. 301–310)
Day 3: **Victoria**
Day 4: Victoria to **Nanaimo** (Victoria–Nanaimo, pp. 319–323)
Day 5: Nanaimo to **Vancouver** by ferry (Vancouver, pp. 274–282)
Day 6: **Vancouver**
Day 7: Vancouver to Hope and **Osoyoos** (Vancouver–Osoyoos, pp. 291–296)
Day 8: Osoyoos to Tonasket, Omak and **Coulee Dam** (Spokane–Osoyoos, pp. 250–258, Moses Lake–Tonasket, pp. 246–249)
Day 9: Coulee Dam to Dry Falls, Soap Lake, Ephrata and **Moses Lake** (Moses Lake–Tonasket, pp. 246–249)
Day 10: Moses Lake to Ritzville and **Spokane** (Yakima–Spokane, pp. 241–245)

53

Day 11: Spokane to **Colfax** (Spokane–Baker City, pp. 230–235)

Day 12: Colfax to Clarkston, Enterprise, Joseph, Hells Canyon, Halfway, Richland and **Baker City** (Spokane–Baker City, pp. 230–235)

Day 13: Baker City to Sumpter, Unity and **John Day** (Eugene–Baker City, pp. 173–182)

Day 14: John Day to Prineville, Redmond and **Bend** (Eugene–Baker City, pp. 173–182, Klamath Falls–The Dalles, pp. 197–202)

Day 15: Bend to Crescent, Chemult, Beaver Marsh and **Crater Lake** (Klamath Falls–The Dalles, pp. 197–202)

Day 16: Crater Lake to Steamboat, Roseburg, Cottage Grove and **Eugene** (Roseburg–Crater Lake, pp. 188–189, Eugene–Medford, pp. 155–160)

Day 17: Eugene to Florence and **Newport** (Eugene–Florence, pp. 171–172, Astoria–Brookings, pp. 111–128)

Day 18: Newport to Astoria (Astoria–Brookings, pp. 111–128)

Day 19: Astoria to Westport, Rainier, St. Helens and **Portland** (Portland, pp. 134–141)

Day 20: Portland to Longview, Mt St Helens and **Castle Rock** (Portland–Olympia, pp. 165–170)

Day 21: Castle Rock to Olympia, Tacoma and **Seattle** (Portland–Olympia, pp. 165–170, Seattle–Olympia, pp. 83–87)

THE MAJOR CITIES

Cities the world over have more in common than not. Even in the relatively unpopulated Pacific Northwest they're big, noisy, crowded and busy, which can be alluring beacons or flashing warnings.

The cities are listed in order on a circular tour, including the recommended connecting routes.

Seattle

Often called the Emerald City for the frequent rain that keeps trees, parks and lawns green all year, Seattle is equally the caffeine capital of America and the home of grunge music, all beneath a growing pall of pollution that veils the soaring majesty of Cascade peaks and Puget Sound. (Seattle, pp. 58–66, Seattle–Port Angeles, pp. 77–82).

Victoria

A reputation as being more English than the English still draws tourists hoping for a taste of Imperial glory, but Victoria has long since outgrown its colonial trappings. Isolated by a scenic ferry journey for which cruise ship passengers pay handsomely, the city sets its own leisurely pace amidst imposing architecture, a busy arts scene, baskets of cheerful flowers and the best urban weather in the region. (Victoria, pp. 301–310, Vancouver–Victoria, pp. 297–300).

Vancouver

Invigorated by a steady stream of immigrants from around the world, Vancouver thrives on the commercial bustle that Vancouver disdains. Created in part to stem America's northward expansionism in the 19th century, Vancouver has matured into the region's most diverse, most international and most vibrant city. (Vancouver, pp. 274–282, Bellingham–Vancouver, pp. 272–273, Seattle–Bellingham, pp. 92–97 and Seattle–Yakima, pp. 88–91).

Yakima

Yakima is a rarity in rural America, a farming community that has continued to prosper even as farming has become more mechanised. Traditional farm country conservatism is alive and well, tempered by a more recent wave of urbanites fleeing the impersonality of major cities for the more friendly rural atmosphere. (Yakima, p. 90, Yakima–Spokane, pp. 241–245).

Spokane

The largest city in the eastern part of the Pacific Northwest, Spokane is often cited as one of the most liveable cities in America. It was the first non-Native American settlement in the Pacific Northwest, which lends a sense of permanence, independence and enduring optimism. (Spokane, pp. 226–229, Spokane–Baker City, pp. 230–235).

Baker City

Oregon Trail immigrants rushed past what

would become Baker City on the way to the Willamette Valley. The discovery of gold brought them back, ranching and farming convinced them to stay. Baker City today has the rugged, windblown look of the last city on the edge of the desert, which is precisely what it is. (Eugene–Baker City, pp. 173–182).

Pendleton
Pendleton was a boisterous boomtown built on cattle, sheep and railroads that has survived long enough to boast about its youthful indiscretions. A quiet farming community today, it is luring back many of the best and brightest who fled to the big city and discovered that small cities are more comfortable places to raise their own families. (The Dalles–Ontario, pp. 214– 217, Klamath Falls–The Dalles, pp. 197–202).

Bend
Bend has become Eastern Oregon's recreation centre. Its small town atmosphere, skiing, hiking and fishing lured a generation of entrepreneurs from Portland, Seattle, San Francisco and Los Angeles who have turned Bend into one of the liveliest – and most expensive – cities east of the Cascades. (Eugene–Bend, pp. 183–187).

Eugene
Surrounded by farmlands, forests and mountains, Eugene is famous for its fine parks, miles of cycling trails and South Willamette Valley wineries. The University of Oregon gives the city a vibrant tenor and liberal outlook that sets it apart from cities of similar size in the region. (Portland–Eugene, pp. 145–154).

Salem
Salem is Oregon's gracious capital, thanks more to its many historic buildings and spreading trees than to its founding fathers, missionaries who turned to real estate development when they failed to win Native American converts. Wineries and covered bridges dot the surrounding Willamette Valley countryside. (Portland–Eugene, pp. 145–154).

Portland
Sitting astride the confluence of the Columbia and Willamette Rivers, Portland prefers to concentrate more on the beauties of nature than on the mundane reality of being the third largest port on the western coast of North America. The city prides itself on its parks, its recreational facilities and its roses, all fuelled by explosive growth in computers, running shoes, manufacturing and shipping in the metropolitan area. (Portland, pp. 134–141).

THE TOP TEN SIGHTS
Here are the top ten attractions people visit in the Pacific Northwest according to tourism offices in the region. They're less crowded during the winter months, but anyone looking for a crowd won't go wrong by sticking to these attractions.

1. **Victoria Inner Harbour** Most visitors come for the day from Vancouver, Seattle or a cruise ship. (Victoria, pp. 301–310).

2. **North Cascades Highway** One of the most spectacular drives in the region. (Everett–Omak, pp. 259–263).

3. **Oregon Coast** RV heaven in summer and nearly deserted in winter. (Astoria– Brookings, pp. 111–128).

4. **The Palouse** The most scenic farmland in North America. (Spokane–Baker City, pp. 230–235).

5. **The Columbia Gorge** The most scenic section of America's most scenic river. (Portland–Yakima, pp. 236–240 and Portland–The Dalles, pp. 207–213).

6. **John Day Fossil Beds National Monument** The earth stripped to its bare essentials. (Eugene–Baker City, pp. 173–182).

7. **Crater Lake National Park** The most perfect lake in the Pacific Northwest. (Crater Lake National Park, pp. 190–192).

8. **Mt Rainier** The mountain that dominates Seattle. (Seattle–Mt Rainier Loop, pg. 70–76).

9. **Mount St Helens** America's most famous modern volcano. (Portland– Olympia, pp. 165–170).

10. **Mt Hood** The symetrical peak dominates Portland and North-west Oregon, with rich farmland to the snow line and superb

skiing to the summit. (Portland–Hood River, pp. 203–206).

TOP PARKS AND MONUMENTS

Pacific Rim National Park, *west coast of Vancouver Island; tel: (250) 726-7721,* protects some of the most unspoiled scenery on Vancouver island. The Long Beach area, the most accessible of three units, stretches between Ucluelet and Tofino. The Broken Island Group protects a largely uninhabited cluster of islands in Barkley Sound, accessible only by boat. The West Coast Trail stretches 77 km between Port Renfrew and Bamfield, accessible only on foot and by permit.

Olympic National Park, *off US 101 on the Olympic Peninsula, Washington; tel: (360) 452-0330,* covers 900,000 acres of wilderness rain forest stretching from glaciers and snow–capped mountain peaks to the Pacific Ocean. More than 600 miles of trails run through forests teeming with wildlife. The Hoh Rainforest and Hurricane Ridge are accessible by car.

North Cascades National Park, *surrounding SR 20 45 miles east of I-5 from Burlington, WA; tel: (360) 856-5700,* is open all year, but SR 20, Washington's northern–most highway across the Cascade Range, is closed in winter. The highway is one of the most dramatic drives in the region, climbing from the coastal plain through rainforest to the high mountains and down to the near desert on the eastern slope of the Cascades.

Grand Coulee Dam, *on SR 155 at Coulee Dam, WA; tel: (509) 633-9265,* is claimed to be the most massive concrete structure in the world, 550 ft high, 500 ft wide at the base and 5223 ft long. The dam and powerhouses are open daily for self-guided tours. A free laser light show is shown on the face of the dam each night during summer.

Dry Falls State Park, *4 miles SW. of Coulee City on SR 17; tel: (509) 632-5583,* was once the largest waterfall in North America. During the last Ice Age, glaciers blocked the Columbia River, forcing it into a new channel, today's Grand Coulee. Until the glaciers retreated and the Columbia returned to its nor-mal channel, Dry Falls was a 3.5-mile wide

cataract plunging 400 ft to the riverbed below. The park is open daily, the interpretive centre is open May–Sept.

Mt Rainier National Park, *entrances off SR 706 and SR 410 east of Seattle; tel: (360) 569-2275,* protects Mt Rainier, a towering, glacier-clad volcano rising just east of Seattle. Forests cover the lower slopes, alpine meadows carpeting the upper reaches become a sea of wildflowers in spring and early summer, May–Aug depending on elevation. The Nisqually (south-west) entrance and the Nisqually-Paradise road are open all year. Other roads are closed in winter.

Columbia National Wildlife Refuge, *off SR 17 south of Moses Lake, WA; tel: (509) 488-2668,* is a 23,100-acre refuge for waterfowl. Wildlife viewing is best in spring and summer, but the eerie basalt formations and heavily eroded landscape is open all year.

Hells Canyon National Recreation Area, *north-eastern corner of Oregon off SR 86 and SR 350; tel: (541) 426-4978,* covers 653,000 acres along the Snake River in Oregon and Idaho, including Hells Canyon, the deepest gorge in North America. White water rapids alternate with deep, swift pools through most of the recreation area. The best way to view the canyon is by boat or along the *Hells Canyon Scenic Byway,* a loop from Baker City to Halfway and *Forest Service Road 39* to SR 82 near Joseph.

Columbia River Gorge National Scenic Area, *both sides of the Columbia River east of Washougal, WA and Troutdale, OR, to just west of the Maryhill Museum of Fine Arts, WA, and Biggs, OR; tel: (541) 386-2333,* covers the most scenic portion of the Columbia River. The Historic Columbia River Highway, Hwy 30, on the Oregon Side, passes 620-ft Multnomah Falls, but views are splendid from both sides of the river.

National Historic Oregon Trail Interpretive Center, *Flagstaff Hill, off SR 86 just east of Baker City, OR; tel: (541) 523-1843,* is the premier interpretive centre for the Oregon Trail, the overland route that took tens of thousands of settlers from the United States to the Oregon frontier in the mid 19th century. Displays, dioramas, costumed volunteers, live presentations and walking trails paint a vivid picture of immigrant life that is far different from the more familiar Hollywood version.

John Day Fossil Beds National Monument, *off Hwy 26 between John Day and Prineville, OR; tel: (541) 575-0721*, protects a variety of plant and animal fossils as well as stunning landforms in three separate units. Each of the three areas has unique and vibrantly coloured rock formations.

Newberry National Volcanic Monument, *south of Bend, OR; tel: (541) 593-2421*, is an enormous caldera containing two lakes, Palulina and East, separated by cinder cones and an obsidian flow.

Crater Lake National Park, *72 miles east of Medford off SR 62; tel: (541) 594-2211*, surrounds Crater Lake, a brilliant blue lake filling the bottom 1932 ft of an ancient volcanic crater. Rim Drive, which traces the crater rim, is a stunning loop drive. The south entrance and a single road to the rim are open all year; the north entrance and Rim Drive are closed beneath an average of 525 in of snow each winter. However, check with rangers in advance, as the road from the Visitor Center to the Rim may be open in winter.

Upper Klamath National Wildlife Refuges, *20 miles north of Klamath Falls, OR off Hwy 97; tel: (916) 667-2231*, is one of North America's oldest waterfowl refuges, established in 1908. Up to 500 bald eagles spend Nov–Apr hunting birds on the refuge.

Oregon Dunes National Recreation Area, *off Hwy 101, Florence–North Bend, OR; tel: (541) 271-3611*, covers 40 miles of sand dunes up to 25 miles wide. The dunes average 250 ft high. Off-highway vehicles churn much of the area; the best place to avoid them is near the Eel Creek Campground.

Mount St Helens National Volcanic Monument, *30 miles east of Castle Rock, WA on SR 504; tel: (360) 750-3900*, protects the volcano and the surrounding area devastated by the 1980 eruption that blew the top 1313 ft off Mount St Helens.

Fort Rodd Hill/Fisgard Lighthouse National Historic Site, *14.5 km west of Victoria, BC off Hwy 1A; tel: (250) 363-5933*, was a coastal artillery fortress until 1956. The 1860 Fisgard Lighthouse has become an automated beacon, but the old keeper's house is a museum.

San Juan Islands National Historic Park, *east of Friday Harbor on San Juan Island, WA; tel: (360) 378-2240*, preserves English and American military camps from the Pig War of 1859. The sole casualty during the 13-year stand-off over possession of the San Juan Islands was the stray pig which provoked the hostilities.

Porteau Cove Provincial Park, *30 km north of Vancouver on Hwy 99*, offers picnicking, fishing and scuba diving on scenic Howe Sound.

Manning Provincial Park, *between Hope and Penticton, BC on Hwy 3*, protects 67,000 hectares of mountains, forest and alpine meadows for hiking, fishing, horse riding, mountain biking, camping and Nordic skiing.

Lake Roosevelt National Recreation Area, *upstream from Grand Coulee Dam (along what used to be the Columbia River); tel: (509) 633-9441*. Thirty-four developed recreation areas offer swimming, boating, fishing and water skiing on this 130-mile long reservoir that stretches nearly to the Canadian border. The lake flooded Kettle Falls, once one of the most important Native American fishing spots on the Columbia River, and the remains of Fort Colvile, the last Hudson's Bay Company trading post in the United States.

Stanley Park, *downtown peninsula, Vancouver, BC*, is one of the world's finest urban parks with 80 km of roads and trails, gardens, an aquarium, restaurants, and splendid views of Vancouver from all sides.

Samuel H. Boardman State Park, *6 miles north of Brookings on Hwy 101*, possibly the most scenic section of the Oregon coast. The park protects coves, towering rocks battered by crashing surf and swirling fog mixed with stunning sunsets.

57

SEATTLE

Rainfall and mist-grown trees make Seattle the Emerald City, green dappled with the deep blue waters of Puget Sound and Lakes Union and Washington and rain-laden grey skies.

A society built on commerce, timber and fishing at Puget Sound's natural harbour on Elliott Bay is being transformed by Microsoft-fostered computer software industry and the aerospace giant Boeing Aircraft Corporation. Starbucks Coffee and its cohorts stoke the locals on caffeine. The result is a youthful population of forward-looking independent thinkers, rooted in pragmatic capitalism, living the good life at the north-western edge of the US.

58

TOURIST INFORMATION

Seattle-King County Convention & Visitors Bureau, *520 Pike St, Suite 1300, Seattle, WA 98101; tel: (206) 461-5800; fax: (206) 461-5855.* **Downtown Seattle Visitor Information Center,** *Washington State Convention & Trade Center, 800 Convention Place, Galleria Level; tel: (206) 461-5840,* open Mon–Fri 0830–1700 Sat–Sun 1000–1600 (Memorial Day–Labor Day), Mon–Fri 0830–1700 (Labor Day–Memorial Day). **Thomas Cook** location at *Westlake Centre, Level One, 400 Pine St,* open daily, offers sightseeing and transport information, dinner reservations and ticket sales.

WEATHER

The Emerald City moniker pays homage to misty green forests seen through legendary rain and occasional winter snow. Residents dress for, and expect, rain from Oct–Apr, though it may rain in summer too. Temperatures range from a low 37°F in Jan to nearly 80°F in July. Grey skies are credited for winter melancholy leading to play-in-the-sun behaviour when the sun does shine. Seattle sparkles in sunshine as shorts and T-shirts appear and sun-worshipping begins. For weather conditions; *tel: (800) 544-1965* or *(206) 464-2000, ext. 9902.*

ARRIVING AND DEPARTING

Airport
Seattle-Tacoma International Airport (Sea-Tac), *17800 Pacific Hwy S., Seattle, WA 98158, via I-5, Exit 154B; tel: (800) 544-1965* or *(206) 431-4444,* is about 10 miles from downtown. There are four **Thomas Cook Foreign Exchange** locations at the airport. A **Traveler's Aid** kiosk; *tel: (206) 433-5288,* is in the main terminal. Luggage carts cost $1.

Most major car hire companies operate from Sea-Tac. **Gray Line Airport Express**; *tel: (206) 626-6088,* operates 0540–2335 every 20 mins between two Sea-Tac terminal stops and eight downtown Seattle hotels, adults $7.50, $13 return, children 2–12 $5.50, $9.50 return. **Metro Transit**; *tel: (206) 553-3000,* bus nos 174/194 run every 30 mins from the lower level baggage claim, for $1.10–$1.60, depending on time of day. Taxis, shuttles and limos are available.

By Train
AMTRAK, *303 S. Jackson St; tel: (800) 872-7245,* connects to Seattle's **King Street Station** from Chicago, Los Angeles–San Francisco/Emeryville and Vancouver, BC.

By Bus
Greyhound Lines, Inc., *8th Ave and Stewart St; tel: (800) 231-2222* or *(206) 628-5526,* has bus connections. **Quick Coach Lines Ltd,** *tel: (800) 665-2122* or *(604) 244-3744,* offer 4-hour bus services from Vancouver to Seattle ($28) and Sea-Tac ($34).

By Boat
Victoria Clipper/Clipper Navigation;

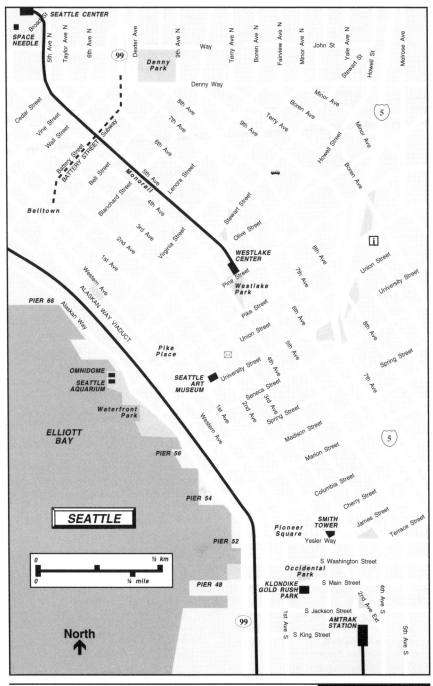

59

60

2701 Alaskan Way, Pier 69; tel: (800) 888-2535 or (206) 448-5000, passenger ferries connect Victoria, BC and Seattle. **Victoria Line**; *tel: (800) 683-7977* (US), *(800) 668-1167* (CAN), or *(206) 625-1881,* operate a car and passenger ferry mid May–Sept from Ogden Point, Victoria to Seattle Pier 48. **Washington State Ferries**: *tel: (800) 843-3779* or *(206) 464-6400,* connect to Puget Sound communities and the San Juan Islands.

GETTING AROUND

West of Lake Washington, Seattle is divided into 10 street name designation areas. Seattle has six *1st Aves,* but don't worry. Avenues run north–south, except in downtown, with directional indicators after the avenue name, e.g., *44th Ave S.W.* Streets run east–west, with the direction given before the street name, e.g. *S.W. Alaska St.* In the heart of downtown between *Denny Way* and *Yesler Way* (both east–west), no direction is given for avenues west of *Melrose Ave.* South-west and south sections are south of *Yesler Way*; north of *Denny Way* are west, north-west, north-east and east areas.

I-5 is east of downtown. It is paralleled to the west by SR 99, which bypasses the waterfront via overhead *Alaskan Way Viaduct* and continues south towards Sea-Tac. The West Seattle Freeway provides bridge access to **Alki Point**. Rush hour, 0700–0900 and 1530–1800, is horrific in every direction on all freeways.

Lake Union is north-east of downtown, connected to Puget Sound by the **Hiram M Chittenden 'Ballard' Locks**.

Once in Seattle, consider easy, cheap public transport. **Metro Transit**; *tel: (800) 542-7876* or *(206) 553-3000,* buses cover the city. Outside Seattle city limits is a second fare zone. Mon–Fri 0600–0900 and 1500–1800, adults pay $1.10 (1 zone), $1.60 (2 zones). Outside peak times, fares are $0.85 and $1.10. Children 5–17 pay $0.75 anytime. A weekend and holiday **All-Day Pass** is $1.70. Travelling toward downtown, pay the driver as you enter; from downtown, pay as you exit; bicycles ride free.

The 1.3 mile **Metro Tunnel** speeds passage of electric buses through downtown under *3rd Ave,* with artistically decorated station entrances near the Convention Center, Westlake Center,

Pioneer Square and International District. Buses are free 0600–1900 within the **Downtown Seattle Ride Free Area,** between *6th Ave, S. Jackson St, Alaskan Way* and *Battery St.*

The **Waterfront Street Car,** Metro route 99, runs every 20 mins daily from Pier 70 *(Broad St)* on *Alaskan Way* to *Pioneer Sq.* and the International District. Seattle imported five of Melbourne, Australia's green-and-cream trolleys to travel along the waterfront into the city's historic heart. Tickets are valid for 90 mins.

Parking can be dear downtown. **Downtown Seattle Association,** *500 Union St, Seattle, WA 98101; tel: (206) 623-0340,* has a free map of 58,000 parking spaces. **Shopper's Quick Park,** *Republic Parking, Rainier Square, 2nd Ave and Union St,* offer 1 hour parking for $2, 2 hours for $3, and 3 hours for $4. **Easy Streets,** $1 off tokens, available from merchants, give some car park discounts and some free Metro transport. Ask downtown merchants for a free token with each $20 purchase.

A legacy of the 1962 Seattle World's Fair, the **Monorail** is a fast way to travel from Westlake Center to **Seattle Center** 0900–midnight Memorial Day–Labor Day; off-season hours are 0900–midnight Fri–Sat 0900–2100 Sun–Thur, adults $1, children 5–12 $0.70.

Ferries

Though used by tourists, **Washington State Ferries,** *Colman Dock, Pier 52, 801 Alaskan Way; tel: (800) 843-3779* or *(206) 464-6400,* are for commuters and day trippers travelling from outlying areas and islands to downtown Seattle. WSF ferries ply Puget Sound to Vashon Island, Bainbridge Island and Bremerton. Call ahead for driving directions to the pier. Prices increase in summer. See p.58 'By Boat' for travel to Victoria, BC.

STAYING IN SEATTLE

Seattle, like any large city, requires caution as you move about. Avoid the Rainier Valley, south-east and east of downtown.

Accommodation

Seattle-King County CVB has an extensive *Lodging Guide,* and **Seattle Hotel Hotline**; *tel: (800) 535-7071* or *(206) 461-5882,* Mon–Fri

0830–1700 Apr–Oct, book lodging in down-town Seattle, University District, Bellevue and at Sea-Tac free of charge. Summer prices are high, but Nov–Mar, the CVB organises **Seattle Super Saver Package**, *same phone numbers*, with discounts of up to 50%. Most chains are represented amongst Seattle's 7000 rooms. The Greater Seattle area has another 14,000 rooms. A slightly cheaper alternative is to stay south of Seattle in Tukwila, Renton or near Sea-Tac on Pacific Hwy S. Book well in advance any time of year.

Seattle Bed & Breakfast Association, *PO Box 31772, Seattle, WA 98103-1772; tel: (206) 547-1020*, has information on a dozen historic inns. At the south end of Lake Union is moderate–pricey **Tugboat** *Challenger* **Bunk & Breakfast**, *1001 Fairview Ave N.; tel: (206) 340-1201*. The **Seattle International AYH Hostel**, *85 Union St; tel: (206) 622-5443; fax: (206) 682-2179*, is within easy reach of the waterfront and Pike Place Market.

Downtown, the **Claremont Hotel**, *2000 4th Ave at Virginia; tel: (800) 448-8601 or (206) 448-8600; fax: (206) 443-1420*, is expensive–pricey, with cosy, comfortable rooms near shopping and Pike Place Market. The pricey **Westin Hotel Seattle**, *1900 5th Ave; tel: (800) 228-3000 or (206) 728-1000*, has posh rooms in landmark round towers. **Inn at the Market**; *86 Pine St; tel: (800) 446-4484 or (206) 443-3600*, expensive–pricey, has wonderful views at Pike Place Market. **The Inn at Harbor Steps**, *1221 1st Ave; tel: (800) 234-1425*, expensive–pricey, is across from the Seattle Art Museum. Expensive and luxurious, the **Hotel Vintage Park**, *1100 5th Ave; tel: (206) 624-8000*, is a well-refurbished boutique hotel. **Best Western Pioneer Square Hotel**, *77 Yesler Way; tel: (206) 340-1234*, is an expensive, but excellent location in this historic district.

Eating and Drinking

Dining can be a sublime art in a city where local seafood, produce and beverages combine in a Northwest blend of Pacific Rim cuisine.

Hundreds of restaurants offer a choice of any cuisine. Follow your nose and budget; Seattle chefs invite adventurous dining.

There is no better introduction to Seattle's bounty than **Pike Place Market**, *85 Pike St; tel: (206) 682-7453*, 7 acres of food stalls, restaurants, crafts, produce and flower sellers, gift shops and fishmongers. Open year-round, the market draws hundreds of residents on weekends; arrive early on Sat morning to see the finest produce and fish. It's easy to enter anywhere and wander, but a stroll on *Pike St* towards the water reaches the famous yell-and-fish-throw performed by fishmongers at **Pike Place Fish** when a customer places an order. On the pavement nearby is the life-size bronze statue of **Rachel the Market Pig**.

The North Arcade, to the right, shelters food, produce, product, flower, herb and craft sellers. Huge bouquets of flowers may be purchased for a few dollars. Many sellers provide samples to passers-by. Don't miss **Le Panier Very French Bakery**, *1902 Pike Pl.; tel: (206) 441-3669*, for the best baguettes outside Paris, and no-nonsense **Starbucks**, *1912 Pike Pl.; tel: (206) 448-8762*.

Fullers Restaurant, (Sheraton Seattle) *1400 Sixth Ave; tel: (206) 621-9000*, is pricey, elegant, a spot for small portions, delicate sauces and exquisite service. **Painted Table**, (Alexis Hotel) *92 Madison St; tel: (206) 624-3646*, is named after its décor which resembles a bright, high-ceiling art galley with unique plates and pricey, fine food. Moderate–pricey **Wild Ginger Asian Restaurant & Satay Bar**, *1400 Western Ave; tel: (206) 623-4450*, may be the tastiest marriage of fresh ingredients in Pacific Rim recipes.

Alaskan Way has many choices. **Ivar's Acres of Clams**; *Pier 54; tel: (206) 624-6852*, is a traditional budget–moderate clam-house, bustling and basic. **Elliott's Oyster House & Seafood Restaurant**; *Pier 56; tel: (206) 623-4340*, is fine for moderate shellfish and fine-day outdoor relaxing on the pier. **Anthony's Pier 66**, *2201 Alaskan Way; tel: (206) 448-6688*, one of a chain, has three budget–pricey venues at the Bell Street Pier. Try salmon pot pie and cobbler at **Bell St Diner**.

Space Needle, *Seattle Center, 219 4th Ave N.; tel: (206) 443-2100*, has two revolving dining rooms 500 ft above ground level: the casual moderate **Space Needle Restaurant** and the formal moderate–pricey **Emerald Suite**.

61

Dahlia Lounge Restaurant, *1904 4th Ave; tel: (206) 682-4142,* has a dark *film noir* atmosphere. **Sit & Spin**; *2219 4th Ave; tel: (206) 441-9484,* is an urban launderette. Excellent budget vegetarian food meets counter-culture furniture and patrons. **Beth's Café**, *7311 Aurora Ave N.; tel: (206) 782-5588,* is a smoky, noisy 24-hour cheap–budget place with 12-egg omelettes and endless hash browns. **Chinatown**, in the International District has many good, budget Chinese restaurants.

Tillicum Village on Blake Island (State Park), *from Pier 55-56; tel: (206) 443-1244,* daily May–mid Oct, weekends mid Oct–Apr, includes a narrated harbour cruise, Native American cultural show and alder-smoked salmon dinner during a 4-hr tour. Pricey. **Redhook Ale Fremont Brewery** and **Trolleyman Pub**, *3400 Phinney Ave N.; tel: (206) 548-8000,* has good budget food, brews and $1 microbrewery tours in the 'Center of the Universe' Fremont District. **Hart Brewery & Pub**, *1201 1st Ave; tel: (206) 682-3377,* has tours with Thomas Kemper Lager and Pyramid Ales on draught. **Rainier Brewing Co**, *3100 Airport Way S.; tel: (206) 622-2600,* Mon–Sat 1300–1800, offers free tours of this major regional brewery.

Communications
Hotels and motels accept mail. **Sea-Tac Airmail Center,** *16601 Air Cargo Rd; tel: (206) 248-3176,* has all postal services. Parking is costly and scarce at the **Main Station**, *301 Union St; tel: (206) 442-6340;* walk, don't drive, to this post office.

Money
Thomas Cook Foreign Exchange; *tel: (800) 287-7362,* have Greater Seattle locations at: Westlake Center, see p.58; Sea-Tac Airport, see also p.58; and **Airline Ticket Center**, *10630 N.E. 8th St, Bellevue,* open Mon–Fri 0900–1730 Sat 1000–1400; and *906 3rd Ave.*

Dress
Wool, raincoats and umbrellas are winter wear. Jumpers and light jackets are useful for layering. Shorts, T-shirts, sandals and trainers appear for warm weather. Footwear is prized, perhaps due to Nordstrom department store's excellent shoe departments!

ENTERTAINMENT
Several local free papers – *Seattle Weekly* Wed 'Going On', *Eastside week* and bi-weekly *The Rocket; tel: (206) 728-7625* – list cultural and nightlife events. The *Seattle Times* Thur *'Tempo'* section has traditional area coverage. **Seattle Arts Hotline**; *tel: (206) 447-2787,* has recorded information on cultural events.

The Seattle-Tacoma music scene started in the 1950s, but it took local son Jimi Hendrix' 1960s success in Britain to make more than a few local fans notice. Punk was popular in the 70s, but it took 1990s grunge bands Nirvana, Pearl Jam, Alice in Chains, Soundgarden and Candlebox to put 'Seattle Sound' on the map.

In 1999, **Experience Music Project** interactive computers and instruments will let Seattle Center museum visitors make music while viewing Microsoft founder Paul Allen's 20,000-artefact collection of guitars, posters and albums. Make the current scene at **MOE's Mo'Roc'N Café**, *325 E. Pike; tel: (206) 324-2406* or *(206) 323-2373.*

SHOPPING
Made in Washington, *2221 2nd Ave; tel: (206) 728-0838,* stock a wide selection of local products and crafts. **Ralph's Grocery Deli**, *2035 4th Ave; tel: (206) 441-0700,* has a range of Northwest wines and beers. **Uwajimaya Market**, *519 6th Ave S.; tel: (206) 624-6248,* is crammed with Asian food and International district shoppers.

Westlake Center, *400 Pine St; tel: (206) 467-1600,* is the heart of the downtown shopping area, which includes **The Bon Marché** and **Nordstrom** department stores plus speciality stores like the original 1930 **Eddie Bauer** store and **Banana Republic**. **Stonington Gallery**, *2030 1st Ave; tel: (206) 443-1108,* has outstanding Northwest Native carving and artwork.

The **REI store**, *222 Yale Ave N.; tel: (206) 223-1944,* which sells outdoor clothing and equipment, also has a 65-ft indoor climbing tower with shifting light to imitate sun patterns, clothing tests under a simulated rain shower, a

580-ft mountain bike test track, a nature trail and a waterfall that increases with rain.

SIGHTSEEING

Imagine more hills, trees and a lumber mill rolling logs down a 'skid road' to take advantage of a protected harbour. From the original 1851 landing at Alki Bay, settlers moved to Elliott Bay and named their town Seattle after a friendly Duwamish Native chief, Sealth. Brides were brought and timbermen started families. Their fine wooden homes burned in the Great Fire of 1889.

Sturdy building materials were used in rebuilding the town, but it took the steamer *Portland's* July, 1897 offload of more than two tons of gold from the Yukon's Klondike to turn Seattle into a boom town. A steady stream of publicity touted Seattle as the only place to properly provision for and book a passage to Skagway, Alaska to begin the scramble over treacherous Chilkoot Pass to the Klondike Gold Rush. **Klondike Gold Rush National Historic Park**, *117 S. Main St; tel: (206) 553-7220*, open 0900–1700, is partnered with interpretative centres in Skagway and Dawson, and Whitehorse in Yukon Territory, Canada.

The historic park is an integral part of **Pioneer Square Historic District**, where gold prospectors were outfitted for the journey north. Ask rangers at the historic park information desk for the *Klondike Gold Rush* brochure, which includes a prospector's year's supplies list and an excellent map of graceful red brick and stone gold rush-era buildings around *Pioneer Sq.* In summer on Sun, join rangers for tours of the district. **Bill Speidel's Underground Tour**; *601 1st Ave, Pioneer Square; tel: (206) 682-4646*, is a comprehensive 1-hr tour of Pioneer Square history, squalor and colour.

A 1909 pergola and a bust of Chief Sealth stand in **Pioneer Square**. Peek in the door of **Merchants Café**, *109 Yesler Way; tel: (206) 624-1515*, across from *Pioneer Sq.*, to see the long bar, tile floors and embossed iron ceiling of Seattle's oldest eatery. **Grand Central Baking Company**, *214 1st Ave S.; tel: (206) 622-3644*, offer delicious roast vegetable sandwiches to be eaten by a fireplace in the red brick lined alley or outdoors overlooking totem poles in

Occidental Park. Or take a picnic lunch to **Waterfall Garden**, almost hidden one block east on *S. Main St.*

Metsker Maps of Seattle, *702 1st Ave; tel: (206) 623-8747*, has a huge selection of maps, globes and Northwest travel guides. **Elliott Bay Book Company**, *101 S. Main St; tel: (206) 624-6600*, is Seattle's rainy day magnet, famed for author readings. **Pioneer Square Mall**, *602 1st Ave; tel: (206) 624-1164*, has antiques.

In the years that followed the Gold Rush, the prospering commercial centre levelled 16 million cubic yards of dirt from hills in the Denny Regrade, now trendy **Belltown**, and constructed a new waterfront along *Alaskan Way*. In 1916, the **Hiram M Chittenden (Ballard) Locks–Lake Washington Ship Canal**; *tel: (206) 783-7059*, open 0700–2100, was constructed to connect Lakes Washington and Union with Puget Sound. Migrating salmon and steelhead navigate the **Fish Ladder** at various times from Apr–Dec. Walk across the locks to **Carl S English Jr Botanical Garden**, *3015 N.W. 54th St; tel: (206) 783-7059*, on the Ballard side.

The 42-storey **Smith Tower**; *Yesler Way and 2nd Ave; tel: (206) 443-2001*, was built near *Pioneer Sq.* in 1914, the tallest building outside New York City for decades, now offering an observation deck from 1000–1900. In 1916, The Boeing Company started in the Red Barn®, now part of the **Museum of Flight**; *9404 E. Marginal Way S.; tel: (206) 764-5720*, open 1000–1700 (Thur 1000–2100), adults $8 children 6–15 yrs $4, a showcase of 50 aircraft suspended under glass from metal rafters and the Boeing 707 Airforce One used by US presidents Eisenhower and Johnson.

Timber, aircraft production and exports to Asia kept the local economy moving and Seattle's downtown activity moved north from *Pioneer Sq.* The **1962 Seattle World's Fair** forced the little-known city to polish its attractions and added the **Space Needle** as its icon. **Seattle Center**, *305 Harrison St; tel: (206) 674-7200 or (206) 684-8582*, the old World's Fair site, includes the **Space Needle**, **Pacific Science Center**, **Children's Museum**, **Fun Forest Amusement Park**, and **Monorail**, and is a venue for opera, concerts and sports.

Salmon Country

To the early inhabitants of the Pacific Northwest, the annual salmon migration was more than a mystery of life, it *was* life. From the Chinook on the coast to the Nez Perce and other tribes living far inland, salmon were the staff of life. The rich, meaty fish were so important that a delay in the annual migration could mean mass starvation on land.

Five species of salmon live in the rivers and streams of the Pacific Northwest, plus two species of migratory trout. All are *anadromous*, spawning (laying eggs) in fresh water but spending at least part of their lives in the ocean, and all are distinct from Atlantic salmon. Homing instincts draw adult fish back from the Pacific Ocean. Fat from 2–5 years of gorging at sea, the fish fight their way upstream through hordes of fishermen, rapids, waterfalls and dams, to spawn in the same stream where they were born. By the time they arrive, the fish look ghastly, tattered, thin, often missing fins or eyes, but determined to reproduce.

The fish pair off, the female digging a shallow nest, or *redd*, in the gravel and laying 3000–5000 eggs. The male fertilises the gelatinous mass of eggs with *milt*, and the female covers the mass with gravel to protect the eggs from predators and from washing downstream. Salmon spawn once and die, their bodies an important food source for bald eagles, bears and other animals. Seagoing trout, **steelhead** and **cutthroat**, spawn and return to the sea.

Chinook (*Onchorhynchus tshawytscha*) or **king** salmon are the largest and most highly valued. Adults average 20–25 lbs, but 40–50 pounders are common. Larger rivers have separate runs in spring, summer and autumn. Fish are silver until close to spawning, when males turn a dark maroon or red; females become dark silver to black.

Coho (*O. kisutch*) or **silver** salmon average 6–12 lbs but grow to 25 lbs. Males turn brick red and females become a dull bronze during autumn migration.

Chum (*O. keta*) or **dog** salmon were named by early settlers who fed these fish to their dogs and saved the richer Chinook and sockeye for their own tables. Autumn migration.

Pink (*O. gorbuscha*) or **humpback** salmon usually spawn north of Puget Sound. Fish average 6–12 lbs; the males develop a pronounced humped back during the autumn migration.

The **Space Needle**; *tel: (800) 937-9582, (206) 443-2111 or (206) 443-2100,* has a 360° view from the 520-ft high **Observation Deck**, open 0800–midnight, adults $8.50, children $4, with dining and a gift shop.

Pacific Science Center; *tel: (206) 443-2001,* open 1000–1800 mid June–Labor Day; Mon–Fri 1000–1700 Sat–Sun 1000–1800 Labor Day–mid June, adults $7.50, children 6–13 $5.50, 2–5 $3.50, involves children in science exhibits. IMAX® and laser shows cost extra. The **Children's Museum**, *Center House; tel: (206) 441-1768,* $4.50, adds art and music to the interactive mix. Rides operate from mid Mar–Labor Day at **Fun Forest Amusement Park**, *tel: (206) 441-1768.*

Downtown

Highrises, offices, expresso bars, statues, sculpture, boutiques and department stores – public transport makes it easy for commuters and tourists to get to the clean inner city. While 76-storey **Columbia Tower** dominates the skyline, **Westlake Center Plaza** is the heart of downtown, an open space where office workers picnic and children play under a fountain.

A huge black Hammering Man sculpture marks the **Seattle Art Museum (SAM)** *100 University St; tel: (206) 654-3100,* open Tues–Sun 1000–1700, Thur 1000–2100, adults $6, with an outstanding collection of Northwest Coast Native American art. **Benaroya Hall** will open next door in late 1998 for **Seattle Symphony** performances. The **Frye Museum**, *704 Terry Ave; tel: (206) 622-9250,* open Tues–Wed Fri–Sat 1000–1700, Thur 1000–2100, Sun 1200–1700, free, has a large collection of 19th-century German art and American masters.

The renowned **Pilchuck Glass School**

Sockeye (*O. nerka*) or **red** salmon average 3–7 lbs, but can reach 15 lbs. Normally a metallic blue-black, maturing fish turn bright red with green head and tails as they move upriver mid summer–autumn.

No one knows how many salmon once moved up Northwestern waterways. Early explorers and settlers wrote of walking across rivers atop shoals of migrating fish. Just 150 years later, newspapers proclaim 10,000 Chinook returning to the entire state of Washington, a major victory in the fight to save salmon. The Hudson's Bay Company began exporting salmon from Fort Langley in 1835 and built its' first Fraser River salmon cannery in 1876. By 1900, Canadian canneries were beginning to close for lack of fish. The story was similar in Washington and Oregon, where a fish and game magazine warned in 1894 that 'It is only a matter of a few years when the chinook of the Columbia will be as scarce as the beaver that once was so plentiful in our streams'.

Overfishing was compounded by dam building. Fifty-five major dams block salmon migrations on the Columbia River alone. Fish ladders allow some fish to make their way over smaller dams, but other dams are impassable. Immature fish migrating downstream are sucked into powerplant turbines and turned to fish paste. Immense screens divert fish into traps to be captured and barged downstream. Reservoirs flood the shallow, fast-moving water salmon need for spawning. Logging adds to the destruction. Clear-cutting contributes to erosion, clogging gravel spawning beds with silt and smothering both eggs and young fish. Agricultural runoff, industrial waste and toxic drainage from roads and cities pollute streams and rivers.

Fish hatcheries release millions of fish each year to help replace the wild salmon and trout that have disappeared. But hatchery fish are less resistant to disease and less likely to escape predators than wild fish. Salmon are mired in controversy. In the end, the only way to restore salmon runs is to restore the habitat salmon need to reproduce and to limit the number of fish caught each year. The argument, and the mythical romance that still attaches to salmon, are graphically illustrated in *Ray Troll's Shocking Fish Tales: Fish, Romance, and Death in Pictures*, by Bradford Matsen and Ray Troll, 1993, Ten Speed Press, Berkeley, CA.

65

was founded near Seattle by Tacoma native Dale Chihuly, and the **Prescott Collection of Pilchuck Glass** is displayed at *1420 5th Ave.* **Emerald City Gallery**, (Westin Hotel), *1900 5th Ave, N. Lobby; tel: (206) 448-6336,* and **Seattle Glassblowing Studio & Fifth Avenue Glass Gallery**, *2227 5th Ave; tel: (206) 448-2181,* also have exquisite examples of this local craft.

Waterfront

Stroll *Alaskan Way* from **Pier 50–Pier 70** along Elliott Bay. There is metered parking beneath the Alaskan Way Viaduct across from the piers, full on weekends and holidays. The **Waterfront Street Car** is an easy driving alternative. **Washington State Ferries Colman Dock** occupies **Pier 52**. **Ivar's Acres of Clams** restaurant, the totem poles at **Ye Olde Curiosity Shop**; *tel: (206) 682-5844,* local

goods at **Exclusively Washington**; *tel: (206) 624-2600,* and kayakers fill **Pier 54**.

Piers 55–56 have jewellery and nautical gifts, **Elliott's Oyster House & Seafood Restaurant**, and is the dock for **Tillicum Village** tours. **Harbor Steps Park**, 104 wide steps with eight fountains descend from *1st Ave* across from the **Seattle Art Museum** down to *Western Ave* and *Alaskan Way*. There's more dining, parasailing and a carousel on **Pier 57**.

Stop at the **Seattle Aquarium**, *Pier 59, 1483 Alaskan Way; tel: (206) 386-4300,* open 1000–1900 Memorial Day–Labor Day, 1000–1700 Labor Day–Memorial Day, adults $7.15, children 6–18 $4.70, 3–5 $2.45, for large window views of Puget Sound fish. **Omnidrome**; *tel: (206) 622-1868,* shows OMNIMAX® films nearby; combined admission is discounted. **Waterfront Park** has fine areas for picnicking and summer concerts. Across from

Pier 59, **Pike Place Hill Climb** stairs ascend to **Pike Place Market**.

The **Bell Street Pier**, *Pier 66*, has dining, a rooftop observation deck, chandler and fresh seafood. **Pier 67** houses Seattle's only harbourfront hotel, **The Edgewater**, *2411 Alaskan Way; tel: (800) 624-0670 or (206) 728-7000*. Expensive–pricey, with dining. Catch the **Victoria Clipper** from **Pier 69** and *Spirit of Puget Sound; tel: (888) 774-7485 or (206) 443-1442*, bay cruises from **Pier 70**.

Belltown, or Denny Regrade
A skid row for decades between the waterfront, Seattle Center and downtown, Belltown is now filled with small restaurants, clubs, galleries and consignment clothing shops patronised by the grunge set and techno-heads.

Capitol Hill
Further east, elegant **Capitol Hill** is the center of gay life, with good restaurants, coffeehouses and shops. **Volunteer Park** is surrounded by lovely Capitol Hill mansions. The **Seattle Asian Art Museum**, *1400 E. Prospect St (Volunteer Park); tel: (206) 654-3100 or (206) 654-3255*, open Tues–Sun 1000–1700 Thur 1000–2100, adults $6, has excellent Pacific Rim collections. **Kado TeaGarden** within the museum is open weekends for teas and pastries. A conservatory and 75-ft moss-covered water tower complete the park. Just north of Volunteer Park are the **graves** of martial arts film stars **Bruce and Brandon Lee**, buried in **Lake View Cemetery**.

West of Lake Union are the posh homes of **Queen Anne**. **Kerry Park**, *W. Highland Dr.*, overlooks the Space Needle and downtown.

Fremont
Across the **Fremont Bridge**, Fremont is a self-described Seattle Left Bank, where a salvaged 53-ft rocket steams up at the Center of the Universe. 'Republic of Fremont' mottos like *delibertas quirkas* and 'Freedom to be Peculiar' flaunt the humour of this ultra-trendy district. The **Annual Solstice Parade** and the 31 Oct **Luminary Procession at Trolloween** let wacky locals act out in fun.

Lenin's statue watches over the **Fremont**

Sunday Flea Market; *tel: (206) 282-5706*, and the **Fremont Troll** munches a Volkswagen bug under the Aurora Bridge. **Redhook Ale Brewery** is an institution over 'a huge natural reservoir holding the largest proven beer reserve in the world'. Each month's **First Saturday Art Walk**; *tel: (206) 547-6551*, is a popular event 1600–1900, then costumed gallery shoppers retire to watch classic 'B' films at **Fremont's Almost Free Outdoor Cinema**, *607 N. 35th St; tel: (206) 634-2150*. **Fremont Business Association Chamber of Commerce**, *PO Box 31139, Seattle, WA 98103; tel: (206) 632-1500*, has an excellent free *Walking Guide to Fremont*.

Outdoors
Green Seattle is dotted with parks. **Discovery Park**, *3801 W. Government Way; tel: (206) 386-4236*, a former military base, encompasses Native American exhibits at **Daybreak Star Arts & Cultural Center**; *tel: (206) 285-4425*, 7 miles of hiking trails and scenic **West Point Lighthouse**. **Woodland Park Zoo**, *5500 Phinney Ave N.; tel: (206) 684-4800*, is open 0930–dusk. Wander through collections of oaks, hollies, rhododendrons, camellias and cherries at the free **Washington Park Arboretum**, *2300 Arboretum Dr. E.; tel: (206) 543-8800*, and the nearby **Japanese Gardens**. Native American artefacts draw visitors to the **Burke Museum**, *17th Ave N.E. and N.E. 45th St; tel: (206) 543-5590*, on the University of Washington campus. Walk through marshlands on the **Arboretum Waterfront Self-Guided Nature Trail**, near the University, and the **Museum of History and Industry (MOHAI)**, *2700 24th Ave E.; tel: (206) 324-1126*, open 1000–1700, adults $5.50, children 6–12 $3, 2–5 $1.

Gasworks Park graffiti-laced rusting pipes at the north end of **Lake Union** is popular with kayakers, sailors, kite-fliers and cyclists enjoying several bike trails on the **Seattle Bicycling Guide Map**; *tel: (206) 684-7583*. At the south end of Lake Union, the **Center for Wooden Boats**, *1010 Valley St S.; tel: (206) 382-2628*, open 1100–1800, is a mecca for sailors yearning to remember the days before technology gripped the Northwest.

SEATTLE CIRCUIT

Seattle is an isthmus bisected by water, dissected by green and punctuated by lakes. Geography mandates one-way streets, unexpected dead ends and streets which *should* connect. Residents take pride in navigating while cheerfully getting lost, crossing the wrong bridge or 'having an adventure'. Allow at least two days to complete this 53-mile circuit avoiding freeways and interstates, three–four days to museum-hop, hike or go on the water.

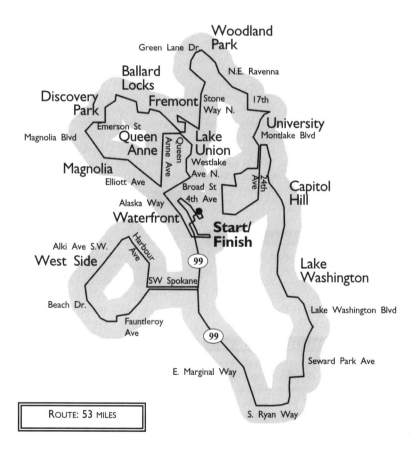

67

DOWNTOWN

Drive south on **Westlake Center's** *5th Ave* side past the Warner Brothers Studio Store, Banana Republic in the Coliseum Building and Eddie Bauer. On the right, Rainier Tower's base tapers inward. Turn right on *Seneca St*, then right again to go north on *4th Ave* for 0.9 miles past Westlake Center Plaza fountain to *Bell St*.

Turn left onto *Bell* for three blocks to **Belltown**, Seattle's alternative music club scene. Go left onto *1st Ave* heading south 1.4 miles to *S. Main St*. From *1st Ave*, divert right on *Pine* or *Pike Sts* to **Pike Place Market**, or continue to *S. Main St*, past 'Hammering Man' in front of the **Seattle Art Museum**, the **Harbor Steps** and **Pioneer Square**. *First Ave* narrows to two lanes at *Cherry St*.

Go left on *S. Main St* past Seattle's **Klondike Gold Rush National Historic Park**, **Occidental Park** and **Waterfall Garden** into **Chinatown/International District**. Seven blocks along *S. Main St*, turn right on *Maynard Ave S.* for one block, then right again onto *S. Jackson St*, past the Chinese gate at **Hing Hay Park**, **Uwajimaya Store** and the **King St Station**, heading towards the waterfront. The white **Kingdome** is on the left.

WATERFRONT

Turn right and drive one block north through the parking area under the Alaskan Way Viaduct to veer left onto *S. Main St*, then a quick right turn onto *Alaskan Way*. Follow *Alaskan Way* along Elliott Bay past the waterfront piers 1½ mile to *Broad St*.

LAKE UNION/QUEEN ANNE

Take *Broad St* right for 1.1 mile past the **Seattle Center** and **Space Needle**. Cross under the SR 99 overpass. Continue on *Valley St* for half a block to **Chandler's Cove** dining and the **Center for Wooden Boats** at **Lake Union**'s south end. Return on *Valley St*, veering right onto *Westlake Ave N.*, skirting the south side of the **Lake Washington Ship Canal** wharf buildings. Cross under the **Aurora Bridge**, where *Westlake Ave N.* becomes *Nickerson St.*

Turn left at *Florentia St* 0.3 miles beyond the bridge, then left up *Queen Anne Ave N.* Continue 2 miles south through the fashionable **Queen Anne** residential district, filled with posh cottages, barn-style mansions, cafés and restaurants. **Kerry Park** downtown overlook is 3 blocks right on *W. Highland Dr.* as *Queen Anne Ave N.* descends towards the **Seattle Center**. Turn right half a block on *Denny Way* to *Western*, which becomes *Elliott Ave W.* three blocks north. Continue straight on *Elliott Ave W./15th Ave W.* past the fine waterfront **Myrtle Edwards Park** jogging area.

MAGNOLIA/DISCOVERY PARK

Move to the right lane to cross Magnolia Bridge. For a fine view of **Mt Rainier** and the Seattle waterfront from Elliott Bay Marina near **Smith Cove Park**, follow signs 'Terminals 86–91 Magnolia' under the bridge. Otherwise, continue across Magnolia Bridge up *W. Galer*, veer right onto *Magnolia Blvd W.*, and follow *Magnolia Blvd* past **Magnolia Park**, magnificent views of downtown Seattle on the left and huge mansions. Turn right onto *W. Emerson* for 0.4 mile, left for 0.3 mile on *36th Ave W.* to *W. Government Way*. **Discovery Park** is left.

BALLARD LOCKS

From Discovery Park, follow *W. Government Way* 0.7 miles to *32nd Ave W.* Turn right onto *W. Fort St* for one block and left on *31st Ave W.* to *W. Commodore Way*. Walk through Commodore Park to reach the **Hiram M Chittenden (Ballard) Locks**.

Leaving the *Locks*, follow *W. Commodore Way* east, which veers south onto *21st Ave W.* Stop at **Caffè Appassionato**, *4001 21st Ave W.; tel; (206) 281-8040*, for an expresso, to see and smell coffee roasting and to enjoy an amusing history of coffee hung around the walls. Turn left onto *W. Emerson Place* and left again to **Fisherman's Terminal** for dining, fish and chips and a look at the commercial fishing fleet. Thirty-two species of fish taken from Puget Sound are depicted around the base of the **Fisherman's Memorial** for those lost at sea.

FREMONT/WOODLAND PARK

Stay in the right lane over the Emerson Viaduct

to *W. Nickerson St.* Go 1½ mile and turn left onto *4th Ave N.*, crossing the old-fashioned blue and pink metal **Fremont Bridge**, signed 'Welcome to Fremont, Center of the Universe. Set your watch back 5 minutes'.

On the Fremont side of the Lake Washington Ship Canal, look right to see the 'Waiting for the Interurban' statue of people waiting for public transportation. To find the **Fremont Troll,** turn left on *N. 35th St*, right on *Phinney Ave N.* for one block, right on *N. 36th St* two blocks, turn left back onto *N. 35th St*, go four blocks east under the Aurora Bridge and look left one block. Continue east on *N. 35th St*, then turn left on *Stone Way N.* for 1 mile.

Follow signs to the left to **Woodland Park Zoo**, or turn left onto *W. Green Lake Way N.* to wind through **Woodland Park**. Green Lake is a favourite North Seattle area for jogging, rollerblading, sailing and dog walking.

UNIVERSITY

Leaving Green Lake, jog left, east, onto *N.E. Ravenna Blvd* for 1 mile. Turn right on *17th Ave N.E.* going south ½ mile on tree-lined streets along Fraternity Row to the University of Washington Main Gate. **Burke Museum** is to the right of the entrance.

Go left on *45th St N.E.* for 0.7 miles, then right onto *Montlake Blvd N.E.* (SR 513) south through the UW campus. **Husky Stadium** is on the left. Take Montlake Bridge over the Lake Washington Ship Canal.

MONTLAKE/CAPITOL HILL

Take *24th Ave E.* south for 0.7 miles, turn right (west) on *E. Crescent Dr.*, then right on *E. Galer St* to *15th Ave E.* and the entrance to **Volunteer Park**. Take the park roundabout past the **Conservatory** and **Seattle Asian Art Museum**. Exit on *14th Ave E.*, go right on *E. Aloha St*, then left on *10th Ave E./E. Broadway* and **Capitol Hill**.

Continue south on *E. Broadway* 0.8 miles, then turn left on *E. Pike St.* Drive 0.3 miles east on *E. Pine St*, then veer left onto *E. Madison St.* Turn left (north) onto *23rd Ave E.*, which becomes *24th Ave E.* Keep to the right and turn

right onto *Lake Washington Blvd E.* for one block. Turn left onto *24th Ave E.* to the **Museum of Science and Industry (MOHAI)** and the **Arboretum Waterfront Trail**.

LAKE WASHINGTON

Continue south on *Lake Washington Blvd E.* through **Washington Park** with the **Arboretum** and **Japanese Gardens**. *Lake Washington Blvd* meets **Lake Washington** at **Denny Blaine Park**, one of several lakeside parks used by picnickers, sailors, rowers and joggers along the 6 miles south to **Seward Park Municipal Bathing Beach**. Take *Seward Park Ave S.* south for 2 miles, turn right on *S. Henderson St*, left onto *Rainier Ave S./51st Ave S.*, then turn right onto *S. Ryan Way* to cross west over I-5.

WEST SIDE

Following signs for 'Airport Way, Boeing Field,' turn right onto *E. Marginal Way S.*, going north 0.7 miles to the **Museum of Flight**. Continue north-west as *E. Marginal Way S.* becomes SR 99 going north. Stay in the right-hand lane to take a poorly marked exit 4.3 miles after the Museum of Flight. Follow 'West Seattle/Harbor Island' signs, turning left onto *S.W. Spokane St* under the West Seattle Freeway bridge. Turn right on *Harbor Ave S.W.* 2 miles to **Duwamish Head**, the best spot to photograph the Seattle skyline.

Follow *Alki Ave S.W.* past the **Birthplace of Seattle Monument** obelisk and seafood restaurants to **Alki Point** and **Alki Lighthouse**; *tel: (206) 217-6123,* open weekends and holidays May–Sept. Continue southeast along *Beach Dr. S.W.* 1½ miles, then make a series of left turns onto *S.W. Jacobson, S.W. Hudson St, Erskine St S.W.* and *California Ave S.W.* through West Seattle's business district. Turn right on *S.W. Alaska St*, then left onto *Fauntleroy Ave S.W.*, which gives onto the West Seattle Freeway Bridge towards downtown.

Follow signs to Hwy (SR) 99 and go 3 miles north. Take the *Seneca St* exit, go left on *1st Ave*, right on *Pike St* and left on *4th Ave* to return to **Westlake Center**.

SEATTLE–
MOUNT RAINIER LOOP

Mount Rainier National Park is the shining jewel of north-west Washington, a 14,411-ft snow-capped peak dominating the landscape for 100 miles in every direction. The high peak creates its own rain, fog and snow – it's a rare day when the peak is 'out'. The surprise is that the weather around the summit changes constantly, so it's possible to have stunning clarity on a drive along Mt Rainier National Park's main road.

This 160-mile loop from Seattle (which could start from Tacoma) can be driven in one gruelling day, but is best with one to two overnights in or close to the park. The east side, including Sunrise and Paradise, is closed in winter, but Crystal Mountain skiing, and the mountain in the distance make a Rainier excursion an adventure in any season.

ROUTE: 160 MILES

Seattle 5 miles
5 405 Renton
169 20 miles
25 miles Enumclaw
410
Puyallup 20 miles
161 20 miles
Eatonville 7
10 miles
Elbe 706
10 miles
Ashford
20 miles
Greenwater
410
Seattle–Yakima p. 88
30 miles
123
Mount Rainier National Park

ROUTE

Drive south from Seattle on I-5 to Federal way and take Exit 142B. Drive one block south on *348th St*, turn left onto SR 161, Enchanted Parkway. Cross over I-5 one mile south and continue on Enchanted Parkway S. to

Puyallup. Continue south on SR 161 to the SR 7 junction. Follow SR 7 along Alder Lake to **Elbe**, then continue straight on SR 706 around the south side of **Mt Rainier National Park**. Take SR 123 north, then continue north on SR 410 to **Enumclaw**. Go north on SR

169 to **Renton**, then go west on I-405 to I-5 at Tukwila, and return north on I-5 to Seattle.

GETTING THERE

For convenience, and to relieve traffic congestion in Mt Rainier National Park, 2 companies offer summer shuttle service from Sea-Tac Airport via the south side of the park: **Rainier Shuttle**; *tel: (360) 569-2331*, and **Rainier Overland, Inc.**; *tel: (360) 569-0851*.

Interstate-5 from Seattle to Federal Way is a corridor through hotels, dining and shopping malls. (See Seattle–Olympia, p. 83). **Federal Way** attractions include **Pacific Rim Bonsai Garden**, **Rhododendron Species Botanical Garden** and summer-only **Enchanted Village** and **Wild Waves Water Park**.

PUYALLUP

Tourist Information: Puyallup Area Chamber of Commerce, *322 2nd St S.W., PO Box 1298, Puyallup, WA 98371; tel: (800) 634-2334* or *(206) 845-6755*, covers lodging, dining and sightseeing.

Puyallup (pron: pew-al-up) – 'generous people', named after the local Native American tribe – was settled by Oregon Trail pioneer Ezra Meeker in 1862. Meeker made a fortune growing hops in the rich Puyallup Valley, then crop pests and the Panic of 1893 (see p.51) ruined him. Meeker retraced the complete Oregon Trail by wagon in 1906, at the age of 76, then flew the route by aeroplane in 1924. Restored **Meeker Mansion**, *312 Spring St; tel: (253) 848-1770*, open 1300–1600 Wed–Sun Apr–mid Dec, adults $2, children $1–$1.50, is 17 rooms of Victorian opulence with elegant fireplaces, stained glass, newell posts and trees, most shipped around Cape Horn.

A few old buildings remain; the Chamber of Commerce has a *Puyallup Walking Tour* brochure. Don't miss the wonderful sculpture of a grasshopper wearing tennis shoes on the police/fire department building, *W. Pioneer Ave and 3rd St S.W.* Saturday morning **Farmer's Market**, *Pioneer Park; tel: (253) 845-6755*, offers fresh flowers and produce May–early Sept. Raspberries and boysenberries boosted the economy after lice destroyed the hops. In 1923, the US Government declared Puyallup

ideal for flower bulb cultivation. Started during the Depression by a fourth generation Dutch bulb grower who was paid in bulbs, **Van Lierop Bulb Farm**, *13407 80th St E.; tel: (253) 848-7272*, open Feb–Oct, has daffodil and tulip fields blooming Feb–May. If in town Fri or Sat night in July–Aug, take in the open-air passion play *Jesus of Nazareth; tel: (206) 848-3577*, with 200 cast members assisted by legions of animals.

A long stretch of SR 161 has strip malls before the highway rises into forest. Follow signs east to outstanding **Northwest Trek**, *11610 Trek Dr. E., Eatonville, WA 98328; tel: (800) 433-8735* or *(360) 832-6117*, open daily 0930 and variable closing Fri–Sun Mar–Oct, and holidays Nov–Feb, adults $7.85, children 5–17 $5.50, 3–4 $3.50. The park, set in 600 acres of forest, is home to Pacific Northwest animals and birds. The denizens are cleverly divided between predator species and prey. A 50-min tram tour through the forest usually encounters free-roaming bison, bighorn sheep, Roosevelt elk, caribou, blacktail deer, moose, mountain goats, sandhill cranes and waterfowl. Predator species like grizzly and black bears, gray wolves, cougars, bobcats, eagles and owls are confined in large habitats elsewhere. The animals look real and wild; the forest, even in snowy winter, is thick and lush.

EATONVILLE

Tourist Information: Eatonville Visitor Information Center, *220 Center St, Eatonville, WA 98328; tel: (206) 832-4000*, has local and national park information.

Descend into a pretty valley. **Pioneer Farm Museum** and **Ohop Indian Village**, *7716 Ohop Valley Rd, Eatonville, WA 98328; tel: (360) 832-6300*, open from March–Thanksgiving, offers tours. Living history guides lead 1½ hour tours of the 1880s **Pioneer Farm**, adults $5.50, children 3–18 $4.50. Two afternoon tours of **Ohop Indian Village**, Sat–Sun in summer, adults $5, children 3–18 $4, or $9.50 and $8.50 for both, cover woodlands hunting and fishing, food preparation and wintertime crafts. The **Ohop Trading Post** (store) is an 1887 cabin.

Just after turning right onto SR 7, turn left

71

into the **Charles L Pack Experimental Forest**, *University of Washington, 9010 453rd St E., Eatonville, WA 98328-9407; tel: (360) 832-6531, drive through winter–summer, Mon–Fri 0800–1600.* UW's College of Forest Resources provides hands-on training for future resource managers, botanists and foresters. Unlike corporate-owned demonstration forests, Pack Forest has no agenda, no axe to grind and works to harvest timber, primarily Douglas-fir, while preserving habitat and recycling municipal sewage. Walking, hiking, and cycling are encouraged except during autumn hunting season.

Pass the small **La Grande Store** as SR 7 ascends to a viewpoint opposite a graffiti-filled rockface to overlook barely-visible **La Grande Dam,** part of the Nisqually River Project, one of the first hydroelectric dams in the west when it was built in 1912. Rebuilt in 1945, it supplies Tacoma with power.

Alder Dam, built in 1945, 1½ miles above La Grande Dam, has created a 3065-acre lake for **Alder Lake Park**, *50324 School Rd, Eatonville; tel: (360) 569-2778,* open Jan 4–Dec 19, $3. Camp pitches may be booked by post for Memorial Day–Labor Day weekends. **Stacel Point** picnic area is favoured by families for swimming, windsurfing, water-skiing, jet skiing, canoeing, kayaking and biking. Drive to the lookout at the end of the entrance road to see the dam and hydroelectric plant.

Sunny Beach Point, ½ mile beyond on SR 7 on the right, has another swimming beach; ancient stumps in the water look eerily like *tufa* (limestone columns). Picnic or pitch tents at **Rocky Point Recreation Area**, 3 miles east.

ELBE

In 1906, a German Lutheran congregation built a tiny white clapboard church, with a tall steeple surmounted by a four-ft iron cross made of railway nails. The local bishop still rides a bicycle to conduct summer services at the **Elbe Evangelische Lutherische Kirche**.

There's little pretension, some services and much railway preoccupation in Elbe, where SR 706 turns east toward the national park. The place to stay is **Hobo Inn**; *tel: (360) 569-2500,*

eight moderate variably-configured railway carriages. Look for an ostrich marquee over the entrance to **Mt Rainier Railroad Dining Co**, in railway carriages, with budget breakfast and lunch and moderate dinners, including Railroad Belt Buster Burgers. For imbibers, the Lounge Car's passionate pink leatherette booths evokes a 1950s diner.

Mt Rainier Scenic Railroad, *PO Box 921, Elbe, WA 98330; tel: (360) 569-2588; fax: (360) 569-2438,* daily June 15–Labor Day and weekends from Memorial Day, adults $8.50, children 12–17 $6.50, under 12 $5.50, runs 1½-hr excursions south to Mineral Lake, pulled by a steam locomotive engine.

Fern Hollow Gifts, in a railway carriage; *tel: (360) 569-2149 or (360) 569-2038,* sells tie-dyed clothing and unique earrings. Look for local residents selling huckleberry and fireweed honey sealed in straws and hand-made beeswax candles.

Continue east on SR 706 from Elbe. A sign posts open or closed conditions on SR 123 ahead; a sno-park is just beyond.

ASHFORD

Tourist Information: Six miles from **Nisqually Entrance**, Ashford has lodging, food, petrol and national park information. **Rainier/St Helens Tourism**, *PO Box 286, Ashford, WA 98304; tel: (360) 569-2628.* Fill up with petrol before entering the national park, as there is none inside.

ACCOMMODATION

Ashford's lodging includes **Mountain Meadows Inn Bed and Breakfast**, *28912 Hwy 706 E.; tel: (360) 569-2788,* in an old mill superintendent's home; eleven rooms at **Alexander's Country Inn**, *37515 Hwy 706 E.; tel: (360) 569-2300,* both moderate-expensive. **Gateway Inn**, *38820 SR 706 E.; tel: (360) 569-2506,* has moderate rooms.

EATING AND DRINKING

Alexander's, in **Alexander's Country Inn**, *37515 SR 706 E.; tel: (360) 569-2300,* has fine quality seafood at moderate prices. Try blackberry pie and 'healthy' fare at budget **Wild Berry**, *37720 SR 706 E.; tel: (360) 569-2628.*

72

State Route 706 briefly enters **Gifford Pinchot National Forest** before entering **Mt Rainier National Park** at the **Nisqually Entrance**.

MT RAINIER NATIONAL PARK

TOURIST INFORMATION

Mt Rainier National Park, *Park Headquarters, Tahoma Woods, Star Rte, Ashford, WA 98304; tel: (360) 569-2211,* 9 miles west of the Nisqually Entrance, has park, camping, wilderness, road and weather information and the free *Mount Rainier & Olympic National Parks Magazine* and *Official Map and Guide*. The park's *Tahoma* and *Snowdrift* (winter) newspapers cover park activities and programmes. *A Traveler's Companion to Mt. Rainier National Park,* by Robert Steelquist and Pat O'Hara, Pacific Northwest National Parks and Forests Association, Longmire, WA, 1987 and *Road Guide to Mount Rainier National Park,* by Barbara and Robert Decker, Double Decker Press, Mariposa, CA, 1996, are excellent driving guides.

There are several visitor centres in the park. **Henry M Jackson Memorial Visitor Center**, *Paradise; tel: (360) 569-2211, ext 2328,* is open year-round, daily 0900–1900 Sat–Sun May–mid Oct, holidays mid Oct–Apr, housed in a spaceship-shaped building with interpretative exhibits and magnificent views of Rainier and nearby escarpments. **Longmire**, open 0900–1700 in summer, has a museum, hiking information and backcountry permits. **Sunrise Visitor Center**; *tel: (360) 663-2425,* is open 0900–1800 Sun–Fri July–mid Sept, Sat 0900–1900. **Ohanapecosh Visitor Center**; *tel: (360) 494-2229,* open in summer, is on SR 123, south-east of this route.

Capt George Vancouver named the peak which dominated the sound his officers were charting after Admiral Peter Rainier. Puyallup and Nisqually tribespeople call it *Tahoma* and *Tacobet*, great volcano, a tribute to their reverence and fear of the fiery lake said to be at the top.

Think of Mount Rainier, and think of 100 inches of snow, frequent rain, fog, mist, and even occasional brilliant sunshine or starshine glinting from the summit. Alternating lava flows and pyroclastic ash and rock flows over the last million years have created a mixed surface stratovolcano. An eruption 5800 years ago, pushed a 100-ft high wall of mud to Puget Sound; another – 2500 years ago – created a second volcanic cone at the summit.

ACCOMMODATION

Mt Rainier Guest Services, *55106 Kernahan Rd E., PO Box 108, Ashford, WA 98304-0108; tel: (360) 569-2275; fax: (360) 569-2770,* books year-round stays at 25-room **National Park Inn at Longmire**, and mid May–early Sept at **Paradise Inn**, both moderate–expensive. Book early to stay in the park.

Five campsites, 564 pitches, are first-come first served; all accommodate RVs. Three, **Sunshine Point**, open year-round, **Cougar Rock**, summer–mid Oct, and **White River**, summer only, are along this route.

EATING AND DRINKING

National Park Inn at Longmire, *tel: (360) 569-2411,* has the only year-round restaurant in the park, open daily 0700–2000. From late May–early Oct, eat three meals or renowned Sunday Brunch in **Paradise Inn**; *tel: (360) 569-2413,* rustic log cabin decor dining room around a stone fireplace. Both are moderate, serve approximately the same meat, salmon, salads, and desserts, and accept no bookings. The **Glacier Lounge**, at **Paradise Inn**, is open 1200–2300 in summer.

Find fast food at **Sunrise Lodge**, late June–early Sept and at **Henry M Jackson Memorial Visitor Center**, May–Sept and Sat–Sun, holidays from Oct–Apr. May–Sept, **National Park Inn at Longmire** has takeout drinks and ice-cream. A good strategy for day trippers is to pack several meals in a cooler, or buy provisions at Ashford or the **Longmire General Store**.

SIGHTSEEING

Of two million annual visitors, 10,000 hikers attempt the snowy 14,411-ft summit of the dormant volcano. Half succeed. It's not a hike, but world-class mountain-climbing, requiring

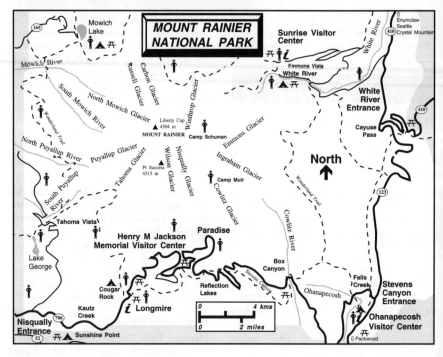

MOUNT RAINIER NATIONAL PARK

Mowich Lake

Sunrise Visitor Center

Mowich River

Emmons Vista
White River

White River Entrance

North Mowich Glacier
Russell Glacier
Carbon Glacier
Winthrop Glacier

South Mowich River

Liberty Cap
4304 m
MOUNT RAINIER
Camp Schuman

Emmons Glacier

Cayuse Pass

North Puyallup River
Puyallup Glacier

Tahoma Glacier

Wilson Glacier

Nisqually Glacier

Pt Success
4315 m

Ingraham Glacier

Camp Muir

Cowlitz Glacier

Wonderland Trail

North

South Puyallup River

Tahoma Vista

Henry M Jackson Memorial Visitor Center

Paradise

Cowlitz River

Box Canyon

Lake George

Cougar Rock

Reflection Lakes

Stevens Canyon

Ohanapecosh

Falls Creek

Stevens Canyon Entrance

Kautz Creek

i Longmire

0   4 kms
0   2 miles

Ohanapecosh Visitor Center

Nisqually Entrance

Sunshine Point

Packwood

Enumclaw
Seattle
Crystal Mountain
White River

skill and several days to cross some of the 26–75 (counts vary) glaciers spreading down Mt Rainier's flanks. It's recommended that climbers use a guide; check at **The Guide House at Paradise**; *tel: (360) 569-2227.*

Rangers lead Sat walks from the **White River Campground** to **Emmons Glacier**. For the less vertically inclined, sub-alpine wildflowers are in profusion around the **Jackson Visitor Center**, **Paradise** and **Sunrise** through summer.

The roads are deliberately narrow, slowing traffic and preserving scenic vistas in a timeless setting, albeit with summer congestion. Five miles from Nisqually Entrance is **Kautz Creek Trail Overlook**, a short walk to a stunning view of the mountain above water flowing through an area covered by a huge lahar mudflow in 1947. Vegetation and low elevation Douglas-fir, western hemlock and Western red cedar forest has returned, though an eerie hush remains despite the rushing waters.

Longmire, now a summer visitor centre, museum, with a general store, was discovered in 1883 by pioneer and mountain climbing guide James Longmire. In 1884, he built a medical spring resort and spa. The waters no longer flow, but huge boulders seem thrown about the wild-looking landscape. Across from the National Park Inn, walk the 0.7-mile **Trail of the Shadows** past Longmire-era ruins. Hire Nordic skis or snowshoes from the **Ski Touring Center**; *tel: (360) 569-2411,* to explored Longmire's ungroomed winter trails.

Take the lay-by to the right of **Cougar Rock Campground** and walk across the rustic bridge to the opposite bank of the Paradise River. White water hurtles over white boulders with craggy, forest-covered mountains behind. Stop at **Christine Falls Viewpoint** for a short walk to view 40-ft falls. One mile beyond, park on either side of the **Nisqually River Bridge** to see the silty white glacial river etching helix-shaped patterns in the grey rock below. In another mile, a sheer drop presents a green alpine meadow below a glacier, near a short, one-way loop road.

Narada Falls on the Paradise River is a

sheer 168-ft drop of clear water into a pool below. Two miles beyond, on the left side is **Glacier View**, part of the winding **Nisqually Glacier**, which can move 3-ft per day.

Jackson Visitor Center rangers, exhibits, snack bar and alpine paths beckon on the Paradise loop road. Rangers guide snowshoe walks late Dec–early Apr weekends.

Paradise was named in 1885 when James Longmire's wife, Martha, exclaimed at the carpet of wildflowers, 'It looks just like Paradise'! **Paradise Inn** lodge, restaurant, lounge and climbing guide facilities provide support for hikers and climbers striking out from the 5400-ft base. Paradise is the park's winter centre for snowshoeing, snowboarding and Nordic skiing. The roads east of Paradise close in winter.

Continue east on SR 706 3½ miles to aptly-named **Reflection Lakes**. Look for falls on the right at **Sunbeam Creek**. Louise Lake is left. Pass through a tunnel to **Stevens Canyon**. A tree-covered spine of rock along the ridge-top parallels the road. Another tunnel through the **Box Canyon Bridge** gives onto spectacular views of the grey-brown water rushing down the narrow, moss and fern-choked **Box Canyon of the Cowlitz**; a bridge overlook is left, a wayside exhibit in the direction of Mt Adams, right.

Falls Creek's beautiful Ohanapecosh River cascade is on the left near parking for the **Grove of the Patriarchs** trailhead. Turn left onto SR 123 at the **Stevens Canyon Entrance**. Drive north through towering, tree-lined canyon walls 11 miles to **Cayuse Pass**, at the SR 410 junction. State Route 410 goes east to Yakima (See Seattle to Yakima, p. 88) and continues north on this route.

Five miles north of the junction, turn left to the **White River Entrance**, and continue west to the **White River Campground**, staging area for 1½-mile hikes to **Emmons Glacier**. Return east 1 mile and drive 11 miles and 3000 ft up the narrow, switchback highway to 6100-ft **Sunrise**. A visitor centre, snack bar and paved meadow paths await, with Mt. Rainier's broad face as backdrop to sparse clumps of fir, whitebark pine and mountain hemlock.

Five miles north, turn right and drive 6 miles east to **Crystal Mountain Resort**, *One Crystal Mountain Blvd, Crystal Mountain, WA 98022; tel: (360) 663-2265.* A ski and snowboard resort with a marked number of difficult runs, the road remains open in winter. Local residents marvel over the **Silver Queen** and **Summit House** vistas when Mt Rainier is clear. On summer weekends, chairs lift hikers and mountain bikers part way up the mountain.

ACCOMMODATION

Year-round accommodation includes moderate **Alpine Inn**; *tel: (360) 663-2558; fax: (360) 663-0259;* **Crystal Chalet Condominiums**, **Silver Skis Chalet Condominiums**, **Quicksilver Lodge** and **Village Inn Hotel**, moderate–expensive; *tel: (360) 663-2558; fax: (360) 663-0145,* and summer RV camping; *tel: (360) 663-2300.*

EATING AND DRINKING

One chairlift runs to the 6872-ft **Summit House Restaurant**; *tel: (360) 663-2300,* for dining with views, popular at sunset in summer. In winter, have breakfast and dinner at **Rafters** or **Alpine Inn Restaurant**, cafeteria style lunch at **The Lodge**, **Summit House** or **Snorting Elk Deli**, snacks from **Rendezvous Snack Shop** and aprés-ski at **Snorting Elk Cellar**.

Back on SR 410, **Silver Creek Information Station** has Mt Rainier brochures. **Silver Springs Campground** is nearby. **Alta Crystal Resort**, *68317 SR 410 E., Greenwater, WA 98022; tel: (800) 277-6475* or *(360) 663-2500,* has all-year moderate–expensive chalets and log cabins within reach of **Crystal Mountain. The Dalles** campsite has 44 pitches.

GREENWATER

Traditionally a quick stop on the way to Mt Rainier, Greenwater's half dozen businesses and petrol station nestle at the confluence of the Greenwater and White Rivers, where 19th century pioneers struggling over the Cascade Mountains reached the end of the **Naches Trail**.

Purchase summertime Crystal Mountain lift tickets more cheaply than at the resort from

Wapiti Woolies, *Greenwater, WA; tel: (800) 766-5617* or *(360) 663-2268*, with high quality, but not inexpensive, hats and woollens. Simple French toast is served with local honey at budget **Buzzy's Greenwater Café**; *tel: (360) 663-2421*. Smoky **Naches Tavern**; *tel: (360) 663-2267*, has large milkshakes, burgers and a serious drinking bar.

Catherine Montgomery Interpretative Center, part of **Federation Forest State Park**, *49201 Enumclaw Chinook Pass Rd, Enumclaw, WA 98022; tel: (360) 663-2207*, has trails, picnicking and botanical gardens of Washington's coast, mountain, sub-alpine, alpine, yellow pine, bunchgrass and sagebrush forest zones. The interpretative centre with forest exhibits is open Apr 16–Oct, Wed–Sun 1000–1700. The trails are enjoyed by Nordic skiers.

The **White River** is on the left, restrained from flooding Puyallup farms by **Mud Mountain Dam**; *tel: (360) 825-3211*, open mid Mar–mid Sept, 2½ miles left. A large children's play area draws families for summer picnics. The dam is not full most of the year, so there's little engineering to marvel at. **Mt Baker-Snoqualmie National Forest, White River Ranger District Visitor Center**; *857 Roosevelt Ave E., SR 410; tel: (360) 825-6585*, open Mon–Fri 0800–1630, is on the right approaching **Enumclaw**. Turn right on *Griffin Ave*, SR 164, into downtown.

ENUMCLAW

Tourist Information: Enumclaw Area Chamber of Commerce & Visitor Information Center, *1421 Cole St, Enumclaw, WA 98022; tel: (360) 825-7666; fax: (360) 825-8369*, has information on lodging, including *BW* and area dining.

Enumclaw, (pron: E-numb-claw) settled by Norwegians and Danes, is set in an agricultural valley where dairy cows, deer and ostrich are farmed and thoroughbred horses are bred. Muckleshoot Native Americans camping nearby in ancient times were frightened by mountain noise, perhaps thunderstorms from visually dominant Mt Rainier, and afterward avoided the Enumclaw area, the 'home of evil spirits'.

Take *284th Ave S.E.* 6 miles north from Enumclaw to **Nolte State Park**, *36921 Veazie-Cumberland Rd; tel: (360) 825-4646*, open mid Apr–Sept for picnicking, forest hikes, swimming and fishing from Deep Lake's shore.

To continue the route, turn right (north) on *Porter St*, to *264th Ave S.E.*, State Route 169. The highway crosses 12-mile long **Green River Gorge Conservation Area**; *tel: (206) 931-3930*, which includes several state parks near SR 169. Find exciting Class III whitewater rafting and kayaking with camping at **Kanasket-Palmer State Park**, *32101 Kanaskat-Cumberland Rd, Palmer, WA 98051; tel: (360) 886-0148*. **Flaming Geyser State Park**, *23700 S.E. Flaming Geyser Rd, Auburn, WA 98002; tel: (253) 931-3930*, has but a six-inch flame, remnant of coal mine tests, but the park is known for hiking and picnic spots.

Black Diamond is an old coal mining town off SR 169. Wood-fired ovens at **Black Diamond Bakery**, *32805 Railroad Ave; tel: (360) 886-2741*, make it a mecca for bread fans. **Black Diamond Historical Society Museum**, *Railroad Ave at Baker St; tel: (360) 886-1168*, covers local mining in the former railway depot.

RENTON

Tourist Information: Renton Chamber of Commerce, *300 Rainier Ave N., Renton, WA 98055; tel: (253) 226-4560*. Renton has some lodging, including *Hd*; there's a larger selection of accommodation and dining in Seattle, Sea-Tac (see Seattle p.60), or Tacoma-Fife (see Seattle–Olympia p.83).

Boeing Corporation dominates Renton with 737 and 757 aircraft manufacturing and test field facilities, captured in exhibits at the **Renton Historical Museum**, *235 Mill Ave S.; tel: (425) 255-2330*. The *Spirit of Washington* Dinner Train, *625 S. 4th St; tel: (800) 876-7245* or *(425) 227-7245*, serves a delicious gourmet meal (lunch, brunch or dinner) during a relaxing 3½-hr return trip north past Seattle's Lake Washington to Woodinville, with a **Columbia Winery** or **Red Hook Brewery** stop.

Go west on SR 405 to **Tukwila**; take I-5 north to Seattle.

SEATTLE–PORT ANGELES

Begin with a ferry ride from Seattle to the grey naval ships filling Bremerton harbour. The direct 75-mile route to Port Angeles can take another three hours through heavy traffic up the Kitsap Peninsula to Dungeness Spit and Port Angeles, gateway to Olympic National Park. Shimmering Hood Canal and splendid rain forests west of Bremerton offer a longer, 115-mile scenic alternative. Both routes can include a 13-mile scenic side track to Port Townsend's magnificent Victorian homes.

DIRECT ROUTE

Take the ferry from Colman Dock, Pier 52, in Seattle, to **Bremerton**. Follow *Burwell St* (SR 304) west, then go right on SR 3. Turn left at Salisbury Point County Park, crossing the Hood Canal Floating Bridge. Continue west on SR 104 to Hwy 101; go north and west to Port Angeles.

SCENIC ROUTE

The scenic Hood Canal route also begins with a ferry from Seattle to Bremerton. From **Bremerton**, follow *Burwell St* (SR 304) west, then go left on SR 3 to the east end of the Canal. Follow SR 106 along the south side of the canal to Hwy 101, along the west arm of the canal, then west along the Strait of Juan de Fuca to Port Angeles.

BREMERTON

Tourist Information: Bremerton/Kitsap Visitor & Convention Bureau, *120 Washington Ave, # 101, Bremerton, WA 98310; tel: (360) 479-3588*, has area information.

Washington State Ferries, *Colman Dock, 801 Alaskan Way, Seattle, WA 98104-1487; tel: (800) 843-3779 or (206) 464-6400,* has 60-min auto and 50 min passenger-only ferries to Bremerton.

ACCOMMODATION

Bremerton is well-equipped with moderate lodging, including *BW, QI, S8.* Moderate **Highland Cottage**, *622 Highland Ave; tel: (360) 373-2235,* and expensive **Willcox House Country Inn**, *2390 Tekiu Rd; tel: (800) 725-9477 or (360) 830-4492,* are elegant bed and breakfasts.

SIGHTSEEING

Bremerton is a navy town, filled with Puget Sound Naval Shipyard workers, ships and submarines. **Bremerton Naval Museum**, *130 Washington Ave; tel: (360) 479-7447,* closed Mon except in summer, open 1000–1700 Mon–Sat Memorial Day–Labor Day, 1300–1700 Sun, is a good introduction to Puget Sound's first permanent US Naval base.

Naval Shipyard/Mothball Fleet Harbor Tours, *Kitsap Harbor Tours; tel: (360) 377-8924,* open 1100–1600 May 15–Sept and weekends, adults $8.50 children 5–12 $5.50, provide a narrated 45-min, close-up view of the grey giants from Sinclair Inlet. For a few dollars more, tour the **USS Turner Joy**, *Bremerton Boardwalk; tel: (360) 792-2457,* open daily May 15–Sept and Thur–Mon Oct–May 14. The destroyer saw Vietnam-era service in the Gulf of Tonkin. The self-guided tour includes a POW Memorial replica of a **Hoa Lo Prison** ('Hanoi Hilton') cell.

POULSBO

Tourist Information: Greater Poulsbo Chamber of Commerce, *19131 8th Ave N.E., PO Box 1063, Poulsbo, WA 98370; tel: (800) 416-5615 or (360) 779-4848; fax: (360) 779-3115.*

A century ago, Scandinavian immigrants prospered as farmers, loggers and fishermen. Poulsbo, now devoted to tourism, is visually and historically the closest thing to Norway outside Norway, with shops, galleries, cafés and tea-rooms along *Front St.* **Sluys Poulsbo Bakery**, *Front St; tel: (360) 779-2798,* has a devoted following for Poulsbo Bread, a whole-meal loaf based on the Biblical prophet Ezekiel's description.

Choose unglazed pottery and paint it, freeform or stencilled, then have it glazed and shipped home at **Dancing Brush**, *Front St; tel: (360) 598-3800.* **Bad Blanche**, *18890 Front St; tel: (360) 779-7788,* is an artistic furniture and antique emporium.

Liberty Bay is a popular venue for biking, canoeing and kayaking, **Olympic Outdoor Center**, *18971 Front St; tel: (360) 697-6095.* The **Marine Science Center**, *18743 Front St N.E.; tel: (360) 779-5549,* open Tues–Sat 1000–1600 Sun 1200–1600 June–Aug, Tues–Sat 1000–1600 Sept–May, has children's exhibits.

Thomas Kemper Brewery Tap Room & Grill, *22381 Foss Rd N.E; tel: (360) 697-1446,* serves a wide selection of beers and budget fare in a relaxed outdoor *biergarten* with summer concerts. Call ahead for tour schedules.

Kitsap Memorial State Park, *202 N.E. Park St, Poulsbo; tel: (360) 779-3205,* has camping and tidepooling on the Hood Canal, north of Poulsbo on SR 3. **Port Gamble** is east of the Hood Canal Floating Bridge via SR 104.

PORT GAMBLE

Tourist Information: Kitsap Peninsula Visitor and Convention Bureau, *2 Rainier Ave, Port Gamble, WA 98364; tel: (360) 297-8200.*

Port Gamble, an Historic District, is one of the few surviving company-owned towns, though its mainstay, the oldest operating sawmill in the USA, closed in 1995.

Port Gamble's Victorian homes, church, Masonic Temple and Country Store are perfectly preserved examples of what timber prosperity brought to the Northwest from the 1850s. There is no lodging; the Country Store sells drinks and snacks.

The **Port Gamble Historic Museum**, *Country Store lower level; tel: (360) 297-8074,* open daily 1030–1700 Memorial Day–Labor Day, Thur–Sun Labor Day–Memorial Day, adults $2, has rooms furnished as mill owners used them, from a ships cabin and office to a hotel lobby and bedroom. Evocative historic photographs and sound effects bring the exhibits to life. **Of Sea and Shore Museum**, *Country Store top level; tel: (360) 297-2426,* open Tues–Sun 1100–1600 May 15–Sept 15, Sat–Sun 1100–1600 Sept 16–May 14, has a fine shell collection.

Take SR 104 west across the **Hood Canal Floating Bridge** and a pleasant forest drive. Turn right on Hwy 101 and continue north to Fairmount.

SIDE TRACK TO PORT TOWNSEND

Drive north from Fairmount on SR 20 the 13 miles to Port Townsend.

PORT TOWNSEND

Tourist Information: Port Townsend Visitors Center, *2437 E. Sims Way, Port Townsend, WA 98368; tel: (800) 499-0047* or *(360) 385-2722,* has a wealth of information on this attractive Victorian-era seaport's lodging, dining, historic districts, museums and events; *tel: (360) 379-4636.* Request the free brochure, *Port Townsend, Washington's Victorian Seaport.*

ACCOMMODATION AND FOOD

Port Townsend has as many bed and breakfast inns as hotels and motels. Book in advance during summer and holiday weekends. Moderate–expensive **Ravenscroft Inn**, *533 Quincy St; tel: (800) 782-2691* or *(360) 385-2784,* is a replica 'old-style' bed and breakfast amongst historic originals, but the warm welcome, luxurious rooms and breakfasts are outstanding. The gables and turret of **Ann Starrett Mansion**, *744 Clay St; tel: (800) 321-0644* or *(360) 385-3205,* are quintessential Victoriana. Expensive.

Downtown, the **Palace Hotel**, *1004 Water St; tel: (800) 962-0741* or *(360) 385-0773,* offers moderate–expensive antique-

furnished rooms in an 1889 building that has been a tavern, railway office and brothel. Across the street on the waterfront is **The Belmont**, *925 Water St; tel: (360) 385-3007,* with moderate Victorian-style rooms above an 1880s saloon and restaurant. At the foot of *Water St* is moderate **Point Hudson Resort & Marina**, *Point Hudson Harbor, Port Townsend, WA 98368; tel: (800) 826-3854* or *(360) 385-2828.* **HI Olympic Hostel**, *Fort Worden State Park; tel: (360) 385-0655,* is open year-round, or camp at **Old Fort Townsend State Park**, *1370 Old Fort Townsend Rd; tel: (360) 385-3595.*

Fine dining establishments cluster on *Water St* downtown and along *Lawrence St* Uptown. Outstanding **Lonny's Restaurant**, *2330 Washington St; tel: (360) 385-0700,* specialises in moderate–pricey seafood. For Northwest cuisine, especially Sunday brunch, try moderate **Blackberries Restaurant**, *Fort Worden State Park; tel: (360) 385-9950.*

SIGHTSEEING

Named in 1792 by Capt George Vancouver for the Marquis of Townshend, Port Townsend's large, calm harbour rests in the rainshadow of the Olympic Peninsula. Farmers and timbermen took up residence, but the 1854 creation of the Puget Sound Customs District in Port Townsend brought rough bars, brothels and gambling. Seafaring men seeking respectability moved families from the nefarious waterfront to fancy houses in **Uptown**, a bluff with magnificent vistas of harbour traffic.

The boom crashed in the Depression of 1893. Several forts, including Worden, were built to protect Puget Sound. Port Townsend Paper Corporation began producing pulp and paper in the 1920s.

The Port Townsend Visitor Center has a self-guiding *Port Townsend Seagull Tour* covering the Downtown *Water St/Washington St* and Uptown Historic Districts. Commerce and entertainment clustered downtown, dignified and decorative red brick buildings now restored as hotels, restaurants, pubs, bookstores and up-market boutiques.

The 1891 **City Hall and Jefferson County Historical Museum**, *Madison and Water Sts; tel: (360) 385-1003*, displays historic photographs. **Ancestral Spirits Gallery**, *921 Washington St; tel: (360) 385-0078*, has superb Native American art. **Point Hudson**, a marina at the foot of *Water St*, is home to the **Wooden Boat Foundation**; *tel: (360) 385-3628*, a centre for ship building and repair. Steps by 1906 bronze **Haller Fountain** go to Uptown.

Uptown catered to the carriage trade. For tours of 1868 **Rothschild House** and gardens, *Jefferson and Taylor Sts; tel: (360) 379-8076*, Apr–Nov, and **Starrett House,** *744 Clay St; tel: (360) 385-3205*, daily 1200–1500. Walk or drive by the many lovely mansions, the imposing brick **Jefferson County Courthouse** 100-ft tall clocktower and a white lighthouse.

Fort Worden State Park, *200 Battery Way; tel: (360) 385-4730*, is the town's third historic district. Self-tour 12 perfectly restored rooms of the 1904 **Commanding Officer's House**, *end of Officer's Row*, Apr–Oct 15, $1. **Puget Sound Coast Artillery Museum**, *across the parade ground*, is open Feb–Nov. The **Marine Science Center**, *532 Battery Way; tel: (360) 385-5582*, has an aquarium and beach walks. Also in the park are rhododendron gardens, **Blackberries Restaurant**, a snack bar and Centrum's **McCurdy Pavilion** performing arts theatre; *tel: (360) 385-3102*.

Washington State Ferries, *tel: (800) 843-3779* or *(206) 464-6400*, runs 30-min ferries to Keystone on Whidby Island. **Port Townsend–San Juan Island** *P.S. Express, 431 Water St; tel: (360) 385-5288* offer day trips Apr–Oct to Friday Harbor, San Juan Island.

Circle Discovery Bay on Hwy 101. The Jamestown S'Klallam Tribe, named after a chief who guided an 1874 purchase of Dungeness area land, is based at **Blyn**, at the end of crab-rich Sequim Bay. **Seven Cedars Casino**, *270756 Hwy 101; Sequim, WA 98382; tel: (360) 683-7777* or *(800) 458-2597*, occupies a Northwest Coastal Native clan-house building; the seven cedars are totem poles in front. The **Salish Room** has budget–moderate specials, including all-you-can-eat Dungeness crab feasts. **Northwest Native Expressions**; *tel: (360) 681-6757*, gallery in the casino, has outstanding Native art, also at *1033 Old Blyn Hwy; tel: (360) 681-4640*.

SEQUIM

Tourist Information: Sequim-Dungeness Valley Chamber of Commerce, *1192 E. Washington, Hwy 101, PO Box 907, Sequim, WA 98382; tel: (360) 683-6197*.

ACCOMMODATION

Sequim is a less noisome alternative to Port Angeles. The Chamber of Commerce has a Lodging Association list; *tel: (800) 737-8462*. Chains include *BW, EL* and *Hd*. **Glenna's Guthrie Cottage Bed & Breakfast**, *10083 Old Olympic Hwy; tel: (800) 930-4349* or *(360) 681-4349*, has cosy, expensive rooms in an old farmhouse. **Sequim Bay State Park**, *1872 Hwy 101 E., Sequim, WA 98392; tel: (360) 683-4235*, has camping; *tel: (800) 452-5687*.

EATING AND DRINKING

Seven Cedars Casino **Salish Room** has excellent quality, variety and price. The usual assortment of fast food clutters Hwy 101. Dungeness Crab, famed on the Pacific Coast, is a sweet, succulent 6–7 inch crab named after Sequim's coastal area. **The Three Crabs**, *11 Three Crabs Rd; tel: (360) 683-4264*, has moderate seafood. **Alder Springs Smoked Salmon,** *61 River Road; tel: (360) 683-2829*, offers samples of its smoked salmon, oysters, turkey and chicken.

SIGHTSEEING

Sequim (pron: sqwim), Clallam for 'quiet water', has turned from commercial fishing and agriculture to tourism with a bow toward water activities and lavender farming. Olympic Peninsula rainshadow, less than 15 ins of rain annually, is a strong draw for retirees and crafts-oriented entrepreneurs. Downtown murals portray local life a century ago.

Dungeness Recreation Area/Clallam County Park; *3 miles north on Kitchen Dick Rd; tel: (360) 683-5847*, individual or family $2, has camping and hiking along 5½-mile **Dunge-ness Spit**, the world's longest natural sand hook. The views of the Strait of Juan de Fuca, and, in clear weather, the Olympic Range, are superb. Birders have 200 species to identify. **Sequim Bay Tours & Charters**, *2577 W. Sequim Bay Rd, John Wayne Marina; tel: (360) 681-7408*, run past the lighthouse on the end of the spit to circle **Protection Island**, favoured by gulls, May–June.

Bell Hill, a posh housing estate, offers panoramic views of the spit, strait and moun-tains. **Cedarbrook Herb Farm**, *1345 Sequim Ave S.; tel: (360) 683-7733*, open Mon–Sat 0900–1700 Sun 1000–1600 Mar–Dec 23, Squim's pioneer lavender producer, offers a huge variety of beautiful herb wreaths, dried flowers and hand-crafted gifts. **Lost Mountain Winery**, *3174 Lost Mountain Rd; tel: (360) 683-5229*, produces sulfite-free red wines.

Museum & Arts Center, *175 W. Cedar; tel: (360) 683-8110*, open 0900–1600, displays mastodon bones from local cliffs. Retired ani-mal kingdom actors wander the drive-through **Olympic Game Farm**, *1423 Ward Rd; tel: (800) 778-4295 or (360) 683-4295*.

PORT ANGELES

Tourist Information: Port Angeles Chamber of Commerce Visitor Center, *121 E. Railroad, Port Angeles, WA 98362; tel: (360) 452-2363*, has town information.

Ferry: The *M.V. Coho* runs a 95-min, year-round passenger and vehicle ferry to Victoria, BC. **Black Ball Transport, Inc.**, *101 E. Railroad Ave, Port Angeles, WA 98362; tel: (360) 457-4491; 430 Belleville St, Victoria, BC V8V-1W9; tel: (604) 386-2202; or 10777 Main St, Suite 106, Bellevue, WA 98004; tel: (206) 622-2222*. **Victoria Express**; *tel: (800) 633-1589 or (360) 452-8088*, mid May–mid Oct, takes 55 mins.

ACCOMMODATION AND FOOD

The Visitor Center has lodging information for this gateway to Olympic National Park. Mill effluent often blights the air, an invitation to overnight elsewhere. Chains include *BW, RL* and *S8*. Moderate motels line *1st St* and *E. Front St*, Hwy 101. A dozen bed and breakfasts,

a **KOA Kampground** and camping at **Salt Creek County Park**, *Clallam County Parks Dept, 223 E. 4th St, Port Angeles, WA 98362; tel: (360) 417-2291*, round out the offerings.

The Visitor Center has a list of restaurants. The yellow steeple of a former church marks **Bonny's Bakery**, *502 E. First St; tel: (360) 457-3585*, serving budget baked goods.

SIGHTSEEING

Port Angeles is a paper and plywood mill and harbour town where logs await shipment to Asia. Clallam and Makah artefacts and local his-tory are displayed at **The Museum of the Clallam County Historical Society**, *223 E. 4th St; tel: (360) 417-2364*, open Mon–Fri 1000–1600. The Chamber of Commerce has a *Downtown Port Angeles Walking Tour* brochure. **Port Angeles Trolley**, *Railroad Ave, west of the Visitor Center; tel: (800) 858-3747 or (360) 452-4511*, has narrated tours of town, including 3-mile-long Ediz Hook. A viewing tower and **Arthur D Feiro Marine Laboratory**; *tel: (360) 452-3940*, open 1000–2000 mid June–Labor Day, Sat–Sun 1200–1600 Oct–June, adults $2, children 6–12 $1, displays tidal crea-tures in tanks, near the ferry landing and Visitor Center. A **Waterfront Trail** traces Ediz Hook, with views of ships, kayakers and windsurfers.

BELFAIR

Tourist Information: North Mason County Visitor Information Center, *E. 22871 SR 3, Belfair, WA 98528; tel: (360) 275-5548*, has information on accommodation, recreation and fishing on the east end of the Hood Canal. Behind the adjacent **Mary E Theler Community Center**; *tel: (360) 275-4898*, is a 3.8-mile trail through pristine **Theler Wetlands**, freshwater estuaries, salt marshes and forest at the junction of the Hood Canal and the Union River.

Camp, via a 3-mile detour on SR 300, at **Belfair State Park**, *N.E. 410 Beck Rd, Belfair, WA 98528; tel: (360) 275-0668*; camping; *tel: (800) 452-5687*. Turn onto SR 106, following the south side of the east arm of Hood Canal.

In summer, stop where the sign says 'one stop hopping for night crawlers' at **Sunset Beach Grocery & Deli**, *17151 Hwy 106,*

81

Belfair (Sunset Beach); tel: (360) 275-2500, to buy a dozen fresh Hood Canal oysters, cheap. Fall–winter visitors to **Twanoh State Park**, *E. 12190 Hwy 106, Union, WA 98592; tel: (360) 275-2222,* can dip (net) smelt, pick oysters and dig for clams. Camping Apr 15–Sept.

Alderbrook Inn, *E. 7101 Hwy 106, Union, WA 98592; tel: (800) 622-9370* or *(360) 898-2200,* is a posh, expensive resort with golf, watersports, and moderate–pricey dining. Wooden **Dalby Waterwheel**, covered with moss, is a **Union** landmark. **Union Country Store** has provisions near **Hood Canal Marina**, or stop in summer at **Hunter Farm Produce Stand**, marked by flower greenhouses. Union is at the east end of the canal's **Great Bend**, or curve north. Cross the Skokomish River to Hwy 101.

OLYMPIC NATIONAL FOREST

Tourist Information: The Olympic National Forest, *1835 Black Lake Blvd S.W., Olympia, WA 98502-5623; tel: (360) 956-2300,* skirts much of the Hood Canal's west arm. **ONF** work closely with **Olympic National Park** (see Olympic Peninsula p.101) to co-ordinate camping, hiking and recreation, shellfish regulation and information on flora, fauna and waterfalls, and has prepared a *Points of Interest Along Hood Canal* flyer. **Hoodsport** and **Quilcene** have ONF district offices.

Turn right on Hwy 101 to **Skokomish Indian Reservation**, marked by fireworks booths. Like many Washington Native Americans, the Skokomish sell fireworks for Independence Day celebrations, although non-tribal jurisdictions forbid the practice. Stylised Northwest animals decorate the Indian Arts Shop and totem poles stand in front of **Twin Totems General Store** in **Potlatch**. Alder-smoked salmon is for sale.

Potlatch State Park, *N. 21010 Hwy 101, Shelton, WA 98584; tel: (360) 877-5361,* was once a tribal meeting place for **potlatch**, celebrations of life events, reparations, or apologies marked with an exchange of clothing, shells and food. Camp, picnic, walk along the shore, kayak, canoe, scuba dive or gather shellfish.

One mile north, the monolithic building below silver pipes is Tacoma City Light

Hydroelectric Plant. **Tacoma Public Utilities Salt Water Park** has picnic tables on the canal side. **Hoodsport Winery**, *N. 23501 Hwy 101, Hoodsport, WA 98548; tel: (360) 877-9891,* open 1000–1800, serves Washington State wines.

Shelton–Mason County Chamber of Commerce, *230 W. Railroad, Box 666, Shelton, WA 98584; tel: (800) 576-2021,* provides lodging and recreation information for the south-west Hood Canal, including **Hoodsport** and **Lilliwaup**. **Hood Canal Ranger District**, *150 N. Lake Cushman Rd, PO Box 68, Hoodsport, WA 98548; tel: (360) 877-5254,* has recreation information and hires budget cabins in **Olympic National Forest**. **Sunrise Motel & Resort**, *N. 24520 Hwy 101; tel: (360) 877-5301,* and **Glen-Ayr Motel**; *Hwy 101; tel: (360) 877-9522,* both moderate, are built over the water.

Hama Hama Oyster Farm & Seafood Store, *Lilliwaup,* open 0900–1730, sells a wide variety of Hood Canal seafood. Hama Hama River bridge crosses a beautiful estuary. **Eldon** and **Duckabush** have services. **Triton Cove** and **Dosewallips State Parks**; *tel: (360) 796-4415,* have camp pitches.

Greater Quilcene/Brinnon Chamber of Commerce, *PO Box 774, Quilcene, WA 98376; tel: (360) 765-4999,* covers recreation along this 20-mile north-western canal area. **Brinnon** services include moderate **Bayshore Motel**, *306142 Hwy 101, Brinnon 98320; tel: (800) 488-4230* or *(360) 796-4220,* and cheap delicious home-made clam chowder at **Geoduck Restaurant & Lounge**, *307103 Hwy 101; tel: (360) 796-4430.*

Hwy 101 briefly moves west of the canal. Autos, but not RVs, can turn right onto FR 2730 to drive to viewpoints and trailheads at the summit of 2804-ft **Mt Walker**, with fair weather views to Seattle, Mt Baker and Olympic Range peaks.

Stop at **ONF Quilcene Ranger District**, *295142 Hwy 101 S, PO Box 280, Quilcene, WA 98376; tel: (360) 765-3368,* open 0800–1630, for detailed hiking and camping information and two free audio cassette driving tours of Olympic National Forest. Continue north on Hwy 101 to rejoin the direct route.

SEATTLE–OLYMPIA

Most I-5 travellers drive 60 miles from Seattle, Washington's economic and cultural centre, to its capitol city, Olympia, in one hour. Despite the urban sprawl along this heavily-used interstate corridor, Tacoma, the city in-between, is undergoing a renaissance of old districts with a young, flourishing arts community.

ROUTE: 60 MILES

ROUTE

Take I-5, Exit 164, from downtown Seattle south to Exit 105, Olympia. I-5, Exit 164, is a convenient starting point from downtown Seattle, but join I-5 at any Seattle slip road and go south. Hwy 99 parallels I-5, ¾ mile west.

From Exits 161–158, **Boeing Field/King County International Airport** is on the right. Take Exit 158 west, then turn right (north) onto *East Marginal Way S.* to the **Museum of Flight** (see Seattle, p.63). **Southcenter** is the huge shopping area on the left at Exit 154. Exit 154B goes to **Seattle-Tacoma International Airport (Sea-Tac)**.

Federal Way, Exits 143 and 142, is crammed with services and shopping malls. **Greater Federal Way Chamber of Commerce**, *344004 16th Ave S., Suite 105, Federal Way, WA 98063; tel: (253) 838-2605*, provides local information. This area is also a convenient provisioning stop for visitors to Mt Rainier National Park (See Seattle to Mt Rainier Loop, p.73).

Rides and water slides are the lures to **Enchanted Parks**, *36201 Enchanted Pkwy S.;* *tel: (253) 661-8001* or *(253) 925-8001*, open mid May–Labor Day, a complex with side-by-side **Enchanted Village** and **Wild Waves Water Park**. The **Pacific Rim Bonsai Collection**, *Exit 142A E., 33663 Weyerhauser Way S.; tel: (253) 924-3153,* open Fri–Wed 1000–1600 Mar–May, Sat–Wed 1100–1600 June–Feb, is a free glimpse of over 60 lovely bonsai trees from North America and North Asia. The nearby **Rhododendron Species Botanical Garden**, *2525 S. 336th St; tel: (253) 927-6960,* open same hrs, adults $3.50, spreads 2000 varieties over 24 acres, with vibrant spring colours. I-5 turns west near Fife.

TACOMA

Tourist Information: Tacoma-Pierce County Visitor & Convention Bureau, *906 Broadway, Tacoma, WA 98402; PO Box 1754, Tacoma, WA 98401; tel: (800) 272-2662* or *(253) 627-2836; fax: (253) 627-8783,* has a useful *Visitors Guide* to area lodging, dining and attractions, including Mt Rainier National Park. The **Tacoma Visitor Information Center**, *Freighthouse Square Public Market, 440 E. 25th St, Phase #4B, Tacoma; tel: (253) 272-*

83

7801, is open daily. Two widely available free newspapers cover the Tacoma nightlife and arts scene: *Tacoma Weekly*, published Thur, and *Tacoma Voice*, every other Thur.

GETTING AROUND

Pierce Transit; *tel: (800) 562-8109 or (253) 581-8100*, provides bus service for the area, including express (direct) service to Seattle and Olympia.

ACCOMMODATION

Tacoma's proximity to Sea-Tac insures plenty of chain lodging in Fife, Tacoma and South Tacoma, though rooms should be booked in advance during summer and at holiday weekends. Find *BW, CI, DI, EL, Hd, M6* in Fife. **Royal Coachman Inn**, *5805 Pacific Hwy E., Tacoma/Fife, WA 98484; tel: (800) 422-3051 or (253) 922-2500*, has moderate rooms conveniently at I-5, Exit 137. *RM* and *Sh* are in downtown Tacoma; South Tacoma has *BW, DI, HJ*, and *TL*. A **Greater Tacoma Bed & Breakfast Reservation Service**, *3312 N. Union Ave, Tacoma, WA 98407; tel: (800) 406-4088 or (253) 759-4088*, books local inns.

EATING AND DRINKING

American-to-ethnic fare is widely available in the Tacoma metropolitan area. Several restaurants are outstanding. The **Boathouse Grill**, *5910 N. Waterfront Dr., Port Defiance Park; tel: (253) 756-7336*, has moderate fare with great views. **The Swiss**, *1904 S. Jefferson Ave; tel: (253) 572-2821*, is a 1913 multiple-room corner restaurant, brewpub, nightly music club and gathering place for students and businesspeople with Chihuly glass displayed in back. Hearty, tasty budget fare is hand-prepared, and bartenders suggest brews to 'marry' with the food. **Mitzel's American Kitchen**, *5402 Pacific Hwy E., Fife; tel: (253) 926-3144*, has excellent budget–moderate traditional American fare like stews, pot pies, roast beef and pasta. In Steilacoom, the **Bair Drug & Hardware Company Restaurant**, *1617 Lafayette St; tel: (253) 588-9668*, a 1906 soda fountain, open 0900–1600, serves old-fashioned ice-cream concoctions. **E.R. Rogers Restaurant**, *1702 Commercial St, Steilacoom; tel: (253) 582-0280*,

has pricey Northwest seafood in an 1891 Victorian Mansion with views of Puget Sound.

SHOPPING

The Pacific Northwest Shop, *2702 N. Proctor, Tacoma, WA 98407; tel: (253) 752-2242*, has a fine selection of Washington and Oregon products and handicrafts, including preserves, wines and pottery. **Freighthouse Square**, *25th and E. D St; tel: (253) 272-2011*, has shops, a food court, railway maps and memorabilia in the historic Milwaukee, St Paul and Pacific Railroad freighthouse. The **Museum Store**, *Washington State History Museum, 1911 Pacific Ave; tel: (253) 798-5880*, has a wide selection of *objets d'art*, souvenirs and books.

SIGHTSEEING

Tacoma spans the south end of Puget Sound. Point Defiance juts north into the sound, with Commencement Bay to the south-east, Dalco Passage eastward, and The Narrows on the west. The **Tacoma Dome**, a sports and concert venue, is clearly visible from I-5.

In 1792, George Vancouver's men explored the sound. Lt Peter Puget was charged 'to chart the sea in the forest' to its southern limits; Vancouver named Puget's maze of waterways Puget Sound. In 1833, the British returned with a HBC fur trading post, Fort Nisqually. Native Americans, Puyallup and Nisqually, called the area 'Mother of Waters', *Tacobet*, later changed by White settlers to Tacoma.

Lumbering in the 1850s brought sawmills to the sound, and a desire for railways to link Washington timber and wheat to Eastern US markets. The Northern Pacific Railroad designated Tacoma as its western terminus, and the city boomed with timber, coal and wheat 'exports' for a quarter century until the Panic of 1893 (see p.51) depressed business nation-wide.

The demand for lumber didn't flag for long. Weyerhauser Timber Company set up headquarters in Tacoma. Architecturally classic Union Station was built in 1911 by Northern Pacific Railroad, and the opening of the Panama Canal in 1914 increased business in Commencement Bay. Modern Tacoma is one of the world's larger container ports.

Tacoma Walking Tours, *Tacoma*

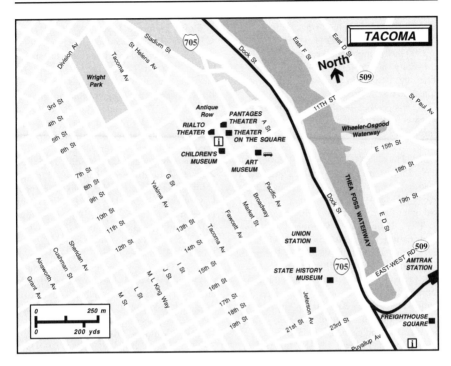

Architectural Foundation; tel: (253) 594-7839, conducts 1- to 1½-hour tours of historic downtown sights in summer. If in the area the third week of the month from 1700–2000, take a self-guided tour of downtown art galleries and venues, **Tacoma 3rd Thursday Artwalk**, *904 Broadway Plaza; tel: (253) 591-5191.*

Tacoma's sights can be explored via a partial circuit. Take I-5, Exit 133, going north. The multi-shaded blue and white diamond pattern wooden roof of the **Tacoma Dome** is on the right, giving its name to the **Dome District**, characterised by old red brick warehouses.

The **Washington State History Museum**, *1911 Pacific Ave; tel: (888) 238-4373 or (253) 272-3500*, open Mon–Wed, Fri–Sat 0900–1700, Thur 0900–2000, Sun 1100–1700, Memorial Day–Labor Day, Tues–Wed Fri–Sat 1000–1700, Thur 1000–2000, Sun 1100–1700, Sept–Memorial Day, adults $7, Children 13–17 $5, 6–12 $4, 3–5 $3, is an excellent introduction to state and Northwestern development, Native Americans' fate, industry and agriculture. The exterior resembles the adjacent arches

of Union Station; inside, several floors have stage-set dioramas, with mannequins narrating experiences on subjects such as the Oregon Trail, railway construction, visiting a general store, immigrant farmworkers, shipbuilding, Grand Coulee Dam construction and Japanese internment, among many others. A South Coast Salish (Native) Plank House, made with traditional materials and tools by a Native American craftsman, shows the life of Puyallup and Nisqually peoples, with hand-carved benches, woven cattail mats, baskets with nuts and fruits, narrated stories by tribal elders. Listen to Chief Joseph speaking in 1897, recorded on an Edison wax cylinder.

Union Station, *1717 Pacific Ave; tel; (253) 572-9310*, built in 1911 by New York's Grand Central Station architects, is now the Federal Courthouse. The rotunda, open Mon–Fri 1000–1600, summer Sun 1300–1600, with tours Thur at 1300, forms a perfect dome. Dale Chihuly, the glass artist who founded the **Pilchuck Glass School**, was born in Tacoma. The 164 panes of glass under the north arch have 27 Chihuly bursting orange butterfly-like 'Monarch' forms. A cobalt blue glass chandelier of 2500 shells hangs from the dome's peak. The University of Washington Tacoma Campus is discreetly housed in renovated brick warehouses across the street.

A few blocks north in the **Broadway Theater District**, the **Tacoma Art Museum**, *12th Ave at Pacific Ave; tel: (253) 272-4258,* open Tues–Wed Fri–Sat 1000–1700, Thurs 1000–1900, Sun 1200–1700, adults $5, students $3, has a stunning permanent collection of Dale Chihuly's glass, which he selected. Exhibits change, covering rock & roll and other forms of 19th and 20th century art.

The **Broadway Center for the Performing Arts**, *901 Broadway; tel: (253) 591-5890,* includes three stages. The **Pantages Theatre**; *tel: (253) 591-5894,* began as an elegant vaudeville house and now hosts legitimate theatre, dance, ballet, opera, symphonies and comedy. The Beaux Arts **Rialto Theater**; *tel: (253) 591-5890,* has a youth symphony, chamber orchestra and cinema. The Tacoma Actors Guild plays at **Theatre on the Square**; *tel: (253) 272-2145.* **Antique Row** stores are next door on *Broadway.* Youths explore the human body at **Children's Museum of Tacoma**, *925 Court C; tel: (253) 627-2436.*

Stadium Historic District, just north, is named after **Stadium High School**. The French-style château with turrets was built as a hotel. This is an area of posh homes and great views. In **Wright Park**, the free 1908 **W W Seymour Botanical Conservatory**, *316 S. G St; tel: (253) 591-5330,* open 0800–1620, is a Victorian-style glass building sheltering hundreds of exotic and tropical plants.

Original Tacoma was further north, in the **Old Town Historic District**. Follow *Ruston Way* north-west along Commencement Bay, past several parks forming a popular walking greenbelt. West is the **Proctor District**; *tel: (253) 752-2242* or *(253) 759-5773,* North Tacoma's trendy shopping area centred around several blocks of *Proctor St,* kept youthful by University of Puget Sound students. Take in a film at the 1923 **Blue Mouse Theatre**; *tel: (253) 752-9500,* browse for antiques or shop at the **Pacific Northwest Shop**.

Point Defiance Park, *5400 Pearl St; tel: (253) 305-1000,* 5-mile loop drive, much of it through 400-yr-old forest, is closed to cars Sat until 1300 to encourage joggers, walkers and bicyclists. Spectacular viewpoints of Vashon Island, Dalco Passage, Gig Harbor, the Narrows and Narrows Bridge are at every turn around the peninsula. Along with ancient trees are seven gardens: Japanese, rose, iris, herb, rhododendron, dahlia and Northwest native.

The most popular draw is **Point Defiance Zoo & Aquarium**; *tel: (253) 591-5337* or *(253) 591-5335,* open 1000–1900 Memorial Day weekend–Labor Day, 1000–1600 Labor Day–before Memorial Day, 1000–1700 Apr, May, Sept weekends, adults $6.75, children 5–17 $5, 3–4 $2.50. The zoo specialises in Pacific Rim country animals. Afternoon shark feeding offers floor-to-ceiling views through tank windows. Spot beluga whales through an underwater passage. Green and blue poison dart frogs and golden lion tamarins are amongst endangered species on display.

Fort Nisqually Historic Site; *tel: (253) 591-5339,* open daily June–Aug, Wed–Sun Sept–May, adults $1.25, children $0.75, is an historic reconstruction of the HBC trading fort established a few miles south in the 1830s. Costumed living history interpreters take the parts of French-Canadian trappers, clerks and officers in the trading room where beaver skins and pelts were exchanged for goods and furnishings, and spin belt cloth, string beads, fire black powder weapons and answer questions. The 1851 granary building is an original, with hand-hewn logs. The Factor/Officer Dwelling House, the other original building, contains a small museum.

Also in Point Defiance Park, **Camp 6 Logging Exhibit**; *tel: (253) 752-0047,* has steam logging equipment and offers occasional train rides. **Never Never Land**; *tel: (253) 591-5845,* is 32 fairytale character sculptures nestled in the woods.

Drive south on *Narrows Dr.,* then turn right onto SR 16 and continue across the 1950 **Tacoma Narrows Bridge** for a pleasant drive to see Mt Rainier rising above the posh sailboat marinas, kayaking and dining at **Gig Harbor**. **Gig Harbor/(Key) Peninsula Area**

Chamber of Commerce, *3125 Judson St, Gig Harbor, WA 98335; tel: (253) 851-6858.*

The original bridge over The Narrows, 'Galloping Gertie', proudly erected in 1940, collapsed spectacularly four months later in a windstorm that Washingtonians remember as a nauseating series of roadbed lurches.

Just south of the bridge on the Tacoma side is **Titlow Beach**, a favourite scuba diving site for spotting 100-lb giant Pacific octopus. Walking paths through wetlands and forest offer red fox, wood ducks and Canada geese at the **Nature Center at Snake Lake**, *1919 S. Tyler St; tel: (253) 591-6439.*

Steilacoom, (pron: Still-a-come) at the south end of Puget Sound, is Washington's first incorporated town. Amongst the 32 historic buildings are **Bair Drug and Hardware Store**, (see Eating and Drinking, p.84); **Nathaniel Orr Home & Pioneer Orchard**, *1811 Rainier St; tel: (253) 584-4133*, $1; **Steilacoom Historical Museum** in the **Town Hall**, *Main and Lafayette Sts; tel: (253) 584-4133*, covering pioneer history; and **Steilacoom Tribal Cultural Center and Museum**, *1515 Lafayette St; tel: (253) 584-6308*, open Tues–Sun 1000–1600, adults $2, a restored 1903 church, has a reconstructed archaeological dig, and a family account of how it maintained tribal identity for generations.

McChord Air Force Base Museum, *I-5, Exit 125, Bldg 192, McChord Air Force Base, Tacoma, WA; tel: (253) 984-2485 or (253) 984-2419*, open Tues–Sun 1200–1600, has aircraft on display outside with uniforms and fighter interceptor squadron memorabilia inside.

Fort Lewis Military Museum, *I-5, Exit 120, Bldg 4320, Main Gate, Fort Lewis, WA; tel: (253) 967-7206*, open Wed–Sun 1200–1600, displays US Army I Corps uniforms and equipment in the former Fort Lewis Inn.

Nisqually National Wildlife Refuge, *100 Brown Farm Rd, via I-5 Exit 114, Olympia, WA 98516; tel: (360) 753-9467*, $2 per car, with 5½ miles of trails, is bird heaven for bald eagles, red-tail hawks, great blue herons and migrating ducks and geese. **Tolmie State Park**, *6227 Johnson Point Rd N.E. via I-5, Exit 111, Olympia, WA 98506; tel: (360) 753-1519*, has a 2½-mile boardwalk loop trail through saltwater marsh; an offshore artificial reef lures scuba divers and fish.

OLYMPIA

Tourist Information: State Capitol Visitor Information Center, *PO Box 1967-SG, Olympia WA 98507; tel: (800) 753-8474* or **Greater Olympia Visitors and Convention Bureau**, *316 Schmidt Pl., Tumwater, WA 98501; tel: (360) 357-3370.*

ACCOMMODATION AND FOOD

The state capitol caters to bureaucrats and business visitors. Lodging includes *BW, Hd, RM, S8*, four bed and breakfasts, and RV parks. Try local moderate seafood or fresh pizza while watching an aquarium and Fish Tale Ales brewing at the **Fishbowl Pub**, *515 Jefferson S.E.; tel: (360) 943-3560*, or snack on fresh produce at the **Farmer's Market**, *401 N. Capitol Way; tel: (360) 352-9096*, Thur–Sun 1000–1500 Apr–Oct. Moderate **Olympia Oyster House**, *320 W. 4th Ave; tel: (360) 943-8020*, specialises in the rare local Olympia oyster.

SIGHTSEEING

87

Begun as an Oregon land claim, Olympia became the Washington Territorial capitol in 1853 and defended that honour against other cities in the state until 1890. The **Washington State Capitol Campus**, *Capitol Way between 11th and 14th Aves*, is the prime visitor attraction, for **tours**; *tel: (360) 586-8687*. The 1928 **Legislative Building**, which has the House and Senate Chambers, resembles the US Capitol Building. The rotunda's bronze Tiffany chandelier weighs 5 tons; a small car could fit inside. The **State Reception Room** would not be out of place in a French *palais*. Outside, the **Capitol Conservatory**, open Mon–Fri 0800–1500, has flower displays. Book in advance for Wed tours of the Governor's home, the **Executive Mansion**. **Washington State Capitol Museum**, *211 W. 21st Ave; tel: (360) 753-2580*, covers Olympia's development as the state capitol. **Percival Landing**, *Water Street, between Thurston and 4th Ave; tel: (360) 753-8380*, is a riverfront park along Budd Inlet, a boardwalk with interpretative signs and a few waterfront dining spots.

SEATTLE–YAKIMA

The 135 miles between Seattle and Yakima are among the most heavily-travelled holiday routes in Washington. Seattlites drive east to escape grey skies for desert sunshine and the many wineries of the Yakima Valley. Yakimites drive westward for ocean sports and the urban amenities of Seattle. In winter, avid skiers from both sides of the Cascade Range make for Snoqualmie Pass and one of the busiest skiing resorts in the state. Allow 3 hours for the journey in good weather, a full day in heavy snow.

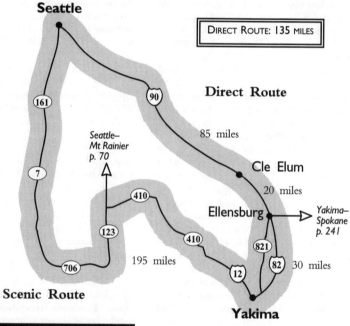

Seattle

DIRECT ROUTE: 135 MILES

Direct Route

85 miles

Cle Elum

20 miles

Seattle–
Mt Rainier
p. 70

Ellensburg → Yakima–Spokane p. 241

195 miles   30 miles

Scenic Route

Yakima

ROUTE

DIRECT ROUTE

From Seattle, take I-5, Exit 164A, to I-90 eastbound and **Ellensburg**. Drivers in a rush can take I-82/Hwy 97 south from Ellensburg to Yakima; those with more time can take the more scenic Rte 821 instead. Either way, leave Seattle with a full tank of petrol. Prices escalate sharply between Seattle and Ellensburg.

SCENIC ROUTE

Follow the Mt Rainier circuit (see p. 70) from Seattle to the junction of Hwys 410 and 123, on the east side of **Mt Rainier**. Take Hwy 410 over **Chinook Pass** and south to Yakima. The pass and portions of Hwy 410 are closed in winter.

SEATTLE TO CLE ELUM

Go east from I-5 at Exit 164A, following signs to I-90 E. Take *Lake Way Tunnel* onto the floating **Mercer Island Bridge** and cross Mercer Island through another curving tunnel. Cross the East Channel Bridge to Bellevue, a dormitory community. On the left is the greensward of **Mercer Slough Nature Park**.

Continue east on I-90, the Sunset Highway. Take Exit 15 north to **Lake Sammamish State Park**, *20606 S.E. 56th St, Issaquah, WA 98027; tel: (425) 455-7010,* a popular wind-surfing, water-skiing, jogging and fishing area. An 1880s railway connection to **Issaquah**, **Greater Issaquah Chamber of Commerce**, *155 N.W. Gilman Blvd, Issaquah, WA 98027; tel: (425) 392-7024,* south-east of the lake, made mining local coal periodically productive, along with hops and dairy farming. Salmon run Sept–Oct at **Issaquah State Salmon Hatchery**, *125 W. Sunset Way; tel; (425) 392-3180.* **Washington Zoological Park**, *Exit 15 to 19525 S.E. 54th St,* *tel: (425) 391-5508,* tends endangered and threatened animal species. A Boehm's Candies sign on an alpine chalet building marks the ascent towards the Cascade Range.

Exit 22, left (north) through Preston to Fall City is a scenic drive leading to **The Herbfarm**, *32804 Issaquah-Fall City Rd, Fall City, WA 98204; tel: (206) 784-2222,* a moderate–pricey Northwest cuisine restaurant amidst 17 display gardens. Follow signs to **The Salish Lodge at Snoqualmie Falls**, *SR 202, PO Box 1109, Snoqualmie, WA 98065-1109; tel: (800) 826-6124* or *(425) 888-2556,* pricey accommodation and restaurant near the 268-ft falls. The falls overlook is free, a stunning vista of water rushing seemingly from below the lodge. **Puget Sound and Snoqualmie Valley Railroad**, *SR 202 via Exit 27; tel: (425) 746-4025,* based at the **Snoqualmie Depot**, runs seven-mile return tours Apr–Oct, Sat–Sun. The **Snoqualmie Winery**, *1000 Winery Rd via Exit 27, Snoqualmie, WA 98065; tel: (425) 888-4000,* open 1000–1630, has stunning views from the tasting room.

North Bend Visitor Information Center, *Exit 31; tel: (206) 461-5840,* has information on Washington's most popular scenic hiking trail and hang gliding launch area part way up 4167-ft Mt Si (pron: sigh), a local winter ski area. Though the area shows effects of past timber clear-cutting, North Bend-Snoqualmie was the location for the TV series *Twin Peaks*. Stop a few miles east of North Bend at **Twin Falls Natural Area** on the Snoqualmie River South Fork to hike 1½ miles down to an overlook.

Forested mountains loom ahead; the massif to the left is craggy and regal. There are exits to many recreational areas and campsites in **Mt Baker-Snoqualmie National Forest**, *21905 64th Ave W., Mountlake Terrace, WA 98043; tel: (425) 775-9702.* **Snoqualmie Pass**, 3022 ft, gets heavy snow despite its low elevation as precipitation backs up against the west face of the Cascade Range.

Take Exit 54 to the **Snoqualmie Pass Ski Area**; *tel: (206) 236-1600,* a spectacular 65-run, four area locale on the west slopes. The season begins Oct–Dec with first snowfall. Check the **Snoqualmie/North Bend Avalanche Report**; *tel; (206) 442-7669,* before venturing to this ski area favoured by Seattle residents. Alpine skiing facilities are at **Alpental/Ski Acres/Snoqualmie/Hyak**; *tel: (206) 232-8182.* **Ski Acres/Hyak Cross-Country Center**; *tel: (206) 434-6646,* has Nordic skiing information, with trails from Hyak/Gold Creek Sno-Park. **Best Western Summit Inn**, *SR 906, Snoqualmie Pass, WA 98068; tel: (800) 557-7829* or *(206) 434-6300,* has lodging. **Wardholm West Bed and Breakfast**, *861 Yellowstone Rd; tel: (206) 434-6540,* is a moderate alternative .

Pull over on the lay-by 3 miles east for an expansive view from the north end of **Keechelus Lake**. Mining and logging left stumps poking eerily from glassy waters surrounded by mountains and wildflowers. Steep, glacier-formed **Mountain Valley** is north.

Cross **Kachess Lake Dam. Lake Easton State Park**, *Box 26, Easton, WA 98925; tel: (509) 656-2330,* is right (south) from Exit 70. Most facilities and camp pitches are on the north side. Fish for trout and swim in summer; snowmobile or Nordic ski in winter.

Cross the Yakima River to **Iron Horse**

89

State Park, a 102-mile long, 100-ft-wide former railway right-of-way which begins near Easton and roughly parallels Hwy 90 east to **Wanapum Dam** (See Yakima–Spokane, p. 241). The highway descends through foothills to cattlelands beneath the clear skies of Eastern Washington.

Take SR 903 left at the outskirts of Cle Elum to **Roslyn**, the best-known town in Alaska – that isn't there. Roslyn, a very Western-looking town with brick and wooden storefronts, was the stand-in for Cicely in the TV series *Northern Exposure*. Before TV crews inspired tourism, Roslyn had been a major coal-producer and the site of a major industrial action broken by imported Black labourers.

The Brick, a corner tavern, is a lively place to have a beer, hear live music and be seen. Several real buildings were used in *Northern Exposure*, including **The Old Company Store**, *101 E. Penn Ave; tel: (509) 649-2557*, which sell over-priced T-shirts and souvenirs based on the series. Stroll around the small downtown to soak up the atmosphere and find several wall murals including a huge, but lifelike, James Dean and motorbike.

CLE ELUM

Tourist Information: Cle Elum Chamber of Commerce, *Box 43, Cle Elum, WA 98922; tel: (509) 674-5958*.

The town name means 'swift water' in the language of the local Native American group, the Kittitas, from the Yakima River that tumbles through town. A favourite summer activity is the 4-hr raft trip downstream to the town of Thorp. Rubber rafts, canoes and return transportation can be hired in Cle Elum.

Once a busy mining and mill town, the modern world passed Cle Elum by. Much of the brick town centre remains almost untouched. The **Cle Elum Historical Telephone Museum**, *221 E. First St; tel: (509) 674-5702*, displays working telephone equipment dating back to 1901. **New Carpenter Museum**, *302 W. Third St; tel: (509) 674-5702*, is a fully furnished 1914 home. Both are open Memorial Day–Labor Day. Continue south on I-90 to **Ellensburg** (see p. 242) and take I-82 south to Yakima.

Scenic alternative: From Ellensburg, take Hwy 821 south to I-90 and Yakima. See Yakima–Spokane, p. 241.

YAKIMA

Tourist Information: Yakima Valley Visitors & Convention Bureau, *10 N. 8th St, Yakima, WA 98901; tel: (800) 221-0751 or (509) 575-1300; fax: (509) 575-6252*, open daily, has complete area information.

ACCOMMODATION AND FOOD

The busiest city in Central Washington, Yakima has *BW, DI, M6, QI, RL, S8, TL* and *VI*. The budget–moderate **Rio Mirada Best Western**, *1603 Terrace Heights Drive; tel: (800) 521-3050 or (509) 457-4444*, has a prime location near I-82, the city centre and the Yakima Greenway. Less expensive motels are clustered off I-82 Exit 31 along *N. 1st St*.

Britain's Real Ale movement first took root in America in Yakima in 1982. **Grant's Brewery Pub**, *32 N. Front St; tel: (509) 575-2922*, in the old train station, budget–moderate, remains one of the most popular drinking and eating spots in the region. Look for 6–8 beers, all brewed on premises, bangers, Scotch eggs and sandwiches, accompanied by live blues and jazz at weekends.

Other local favourites include **Bésame Mucho**, *104 E. Chestnut Ave; tel: (509) 454-4522*, for budget Mexican, **Santiago's Gourmet Restaurant**, *111 E. Yakima Ave; tel: (509) 453-1644*, for moderate–pricey Mexican, **Deli de Pasta**, *7 N. Front St; tel: (509) 453-0571*, for budget–moderate Italian and **Gasperetti's Restaurant**, *1013 N. 1st St; tel: (509) 248-0628*, for moderate Italian.

SIGHTSEEING

Missionaries came to the Yakima area in the 1840s, but the Yakima and other Native American bands in the region fiercely resisted White settlers who coveted their lands. Once US Army troops had solved the 'Indian Problem' with the Yakima Indian War of 1855–7, ranchers drove cattle into the desert valley. Farmers soon followed, lured by 300 days of sunshine each year and the promise of easy irrigation turning sagebrush into verdant fields. Streams and rivers flow through the low-lands in most valleys, but the Yakima River flows along the higher, western side of the valley. Gravity, not mechanical pumps, fed water into early irrigation channels. By the 1870s, orchards and fields had displaced cattle. A century later, Yakima County ranked first in North America in the number of fruit trees, first in the production of apples, mint, winter pears and hops and very near the top in the production of wine grapes.

A century of agricultural success has left Yakima with a rich architectural heritage. The former **train depot**, *32 N. Front St*, has become a brewpub and retail shops. Across the street, the **Opera House** has been refurbished into restaurants and more shops. The **Yakima Electric Railway Museum**, *306 W. Pine St; tel: (509) 575-1700*, offers public rides May–Oct on one of America's earliest regional trolley systems, the Yakima Valley Transportation Company (YVT). The YVT uses original equipment and facilities dating back to 1909; the 1910 maintenance building and museum is open during operating hours.

The **Yakima Valley Museum**, *2105 Tieton Dr.; tel: (509) 248-0747*, open daily, houses one of America's largest collections of carriages, coaches, wagons and early motorised vehicles as well as Native American artefacts and reconstructions of early farms, homes and shops. The museum has also recreated the Washington, DC office of Yakima-born US Supreme Court Justice William O Douglas, who died in 1980. Hometown conservatives twice tried to impeach Douglas for his articulate and persuasive advocacy for personal freedom, social justice and environmental causes. The museum also maintains the **HM Gilbert Homeplace**, *2109 W. Yakima Ave*, a fully-furnished 1890s farmhouse, open Apr–Dec.

Washington's Fruit Place, *105 S. 18th St, Suite 103 in Sarg Hubbard Park; tel: (509) 576-3090*, open Mon–Fri 0800–1700, Sat 0900–1700 May-Dec, sponsored by the apple industry, offers free samples of apples and apple juice with large servings of apple propaganda. Just outside the centre is the **Yakima Greenway**; *tel: (509) 453-8280*, a 10-mile park along the Yakima River. Heart of the park is a

Wineries

The Yakima Valley has one of the largest concentrations of vineyards and wineries in the Pacific Northwest. The **Yakima Valley Wine Growers Association**, *Box 39, Grandview, WA 98930*, publishes a free brochure of the two dozen wineries dotting the hills along I-82 south-east of Yakima. Hot summers generally produce better red wines than whites, but don't ignore Yakima whites. Area Chardonnay, Chenin Blanc, Gewürztraminer, Muscat, Riesling, Sauvignon Blanc and Semillon win nearly as many awards as Cabernet Sauvignon, Lemberger, Merlot, Pinot Noir, Sirah and Zinfandel.

Portteus Vineyards, *5201 Highland Dr., Zillah, WA 98953; tel: (509) 829-6870*, specialises in reds but also produces a rich chardonnay. **Hyatt Vineyards**, *2020 Gilbert Rd, Zillah, WA 98953; tel: (509) 829-6333*, produces some of the most powerful reds in the valley with one of finest views from its outdoor picnic area. **Covey Run Vintners**, *1500 Vintage Rd, Zillah, WA 98953; tel: (509) 829-6235*, one of the largest producers in the valley, has reliable wine and stunning vistas across rolling vineyards from an outdoor deck. **Bonair Winery**, *500 S. Bonair Rd, Zillah, WA 98953; tel: (509) 829-6027*, produces a unique mead from peppermint honey as well as the more familiar range of *vinifera* wines. Bonair's shady picnic ground surrounding a small pond is particularly restful in summer.

7-mile walking and cycling path from Harlan Landing, near Selah, through Yakima to *Valley Mall Blvd*, near the town of Union Gap.

The **Central Washington Agricultural Museum**, *4508 Main St, Union Gap, WA 98903; tel: (509) 457-8735*, open daily 0900–1700, is an astounding hodge-podge of ancient agricultural equipment, from horse-drawn cultivators to early tractors, and thousands of hand tools.

SEATTLE–BELLINGHAM

The 90 miles from Seattle to Bellingham take just 90 min on I-5. Even the 130-mile scenic route by way of Whidbey and Fidalgo Islands takes under half a day if you turn a blind eye to the alluringly scenic stops around nearly every corner. Two days would be better, with overnights in Coupeville, Oak Harbor or Anacortes, but try to avoid the weekend exodus from Seattle.

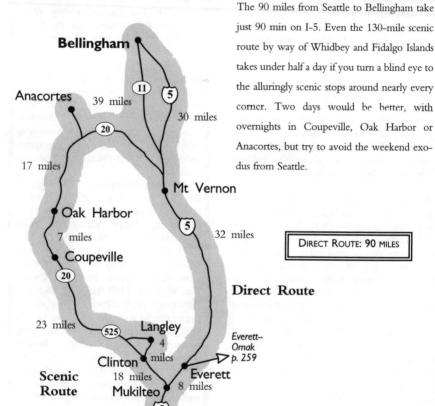

Bellingham

Anacortes 39 miles (11) (5)

30 miles

(20)

17 miles

Mt Vernon

Oak Harbor

7 miles (5)

Coupeville 32 miles

(20)

23 miles **Langley**

(525) 4

Clinton miles

18 miles **Everett**

Scenic **Mukilteo** 8 miles

Route (5)

12 miles

Edmonds

10 miles

Seattle

*Everett–
Omak
p. 259*

*Everett–
Omak
p. 259*

DIRECT ROUTE: **90** MILES

Direct Route

farming and dairy valleys north, with the Cascades growing ever rougher, ever more scenic and ever closer. Tulips carpet the Skagit Valley in spring; Mt Baker dominates the skyline east of Bellingham.

ROUTES

DIRECT ROUTE

The direct route follows I-5 north from Seattle to **Edmonds** and **Everett**, the northernmost extension of Greater Seattle. Towns become fewer and smaller in the

SCENIC ROUTE

The scenic route follows I-5 to Everett, then turns west on SR 526 past the Boeing Aircraft assembly plant to **Mukilteo**. Take the ferry to **Whidbey Island** and continue up island on SR 525 and SR 20. The highway runs through a succession of fields, forests and small valleys with frequent turnoffs to the ocean on each side. Continue 23 miles to **Coupeville** and another 28 miles passing **Oak Harbor**. Take the Deception Pass bridge onto **Fidalgo Island** and **Anacortes**.

From Anacortes, cross the Swinomish Channel bridge to the first traffic signal, *Bayview-Edison Rd.* Turn north (left) through 9 miles of gentle farming country to **Edison**. *Chuckanut Dr.*, Rte 11, winds between the steep sides of Chuckanut Mountain and Samish Bay into **Bellingham.**

EDMONDS

Tourist Information: Edmonds Visitor Bureau, *120 5th Ave, Edmonds, WA 98020; tel: (425) 776-6711; fax: (425) 712-1808,* open Mon–Fri 0900–1600, Sat (summer only) 1000–1400.

ACCOMMODATION AND FOOD

TL is the only chain. **Edmonds Harbor Inn**, *130 W. Dayton St, Edmonds, WA 98020; tel: (425) 771-5021* or *(800) 441-8033,* moderate, is the best independent.

Seattle weekenders keep restaurants busy. **The Eatery**, *The Landing Mall,* and **Chanterelle's**, *Main and Third Sts,* are favourites for budget breakfasts and lunches. **Brusseau's**, *Old Mill Town,* is a popular budget–moderate lunch spot. **Café Pinceau**, *5th Ave and Walnut St,* offers moderate continental cuisine.

SIGHTSEEING

Seattlites heading west to the northern Kitsap and Olympic Peninsula save time by driving to Edmonds and joining shorter queues to ferry to Kingston, **Washington State Ferries**; *tel: (206) 464-6400.* Frequent schedules and stunning views from Mt Rainier north to Mt Baker and west to the Olympic Peninsula make it a good ride for sightseers as well.

Edmonds was founded by George Brackett, a Maine lumberman, who washed ashore in 1870. Two years later, Brackett purchased what became the town centre and opened the first mill. As nearby forests were levelled, the lumbermen moved on. The last mill closed in 1951.

What was a squalid row of abandoned mills has become one of the more charming spots along Puget Sound, including a sparkling marina. Octopus, crabs, towering anemones and swarms of fish make **Edmonds Underwater Park**, *access from the foot of Main St; tel: (206) 771-0230,* a popular underwater park for scuba divers. The marine preserve began with a 300-ft dry dock scuttled to shield the ferry landing from fierce tidal currents. Other ships were sunk nearby more recently, none more than 40 ft deep.

Many historic buildings remain in the town centre, including a log cabin housing the Visitor Bureau and the **Edmonds Museum**, *118 Fifth Ave N.; tel: (206) 774-0900.* The Bureau publishes free self-guided walking maps. **Old Milltown**, *5th and Dayton Sts,* a busy shopping and restaurant complex, includes the Yost Garage, Edmonds' first automobile agency. Chanterelle's Restaurant occupies part of an 1890s grocery. A small wildlife refuge and salmon hatchery are south of the historic area.

EVERETT

Tourist Information: Everett Convention & Visitor Bureau, *1710 W. Marine Dr., Everett, WA 98206; tel: (206) 252-5181; fax: (206) 252-3105,* **Snohomish County Visitor Information Center**, *I-5 exit 186, 101-128th St SE., Suite 5000, Everett, WA 98208; tel: (206) 338-4437,* open 0900–1700 daily.

The site of one of the largest aircraft factories in the world, Everett has *BW, DI, hD, HJ, Rm* and *TL* plus many bed and breakfasts.

SIGHTSEEING

Everett is considerably smaller than Seattle as well as cleaner and more recently refurbished. The marina has expansive views of the Cascades and the Olympic Peninsula. Jetty Island, an artificial island, 2 miles long and 200 yds wide, supports 45 different species of birds and a herd of California sea lions Oct–June. Free ferry service from **Everett Marina Village**; *tel: (206) 259-0304.*

George Vancouver's visit interrupted several thousand years of settlement by Snoqualme, Stillaguamish, Snohomish and Skagit tribes in 1792. Everett's first sawmill commenced operations 60 years later. The town boomed with lumber railways from the Cascades, mills and

93

shipping lines, but working conditions created fertile ground for labour organisers.

A 1916 clash between the International Workers of the World (IWW), the 'Wobblies', and local police left two deputies and five unionists dead in what became known as the Everett Massacre. The last mills closed in the 1980s; the CVB occupies an ornately restored Weyerhaeuser office building.

The **Snohomish County Museum and Historical Association**, *2817 Rockefeller Ave, Everett, WA 98201; tel: (425) 259-2022*, explores local history in considerable detail. Pyrophiles might prefer the city's two **Fire Service Museums**, *Station No 4, 6530 Glenwood St* and *Station No 3, north end of city waterfront*, with early horse-drawn and motorised firefighting equipment.

Everett's economic mainstay in recent decades has been the **Boeing Aircraft Corp**, *off SR 526; tel: (425) 342-4801*, open Mon–Fri 0800–1600. Boeing welcomes visitors to the huge 747, 767 and 777 manufacturing facility all year, but the tours fill quickly in summer. Cameras and video equipment not allowed.

Baseball fans cheer the **Everett Aquasox**, *Everett Memorial Stadium, 38th and Broadway; tel: (206) 258-3673*, the Seattle Mariners' training team, playing mid June–Sept.

The **Mosquito Fleet**, *1724-F W. Marine View Dr., Everett, WA 98201; tel: (425) 252-6800 or (800) 325-6722; fax: (425) 252-6038*, named after the swarms of boats that once plied Puget Sound, offer whale watching tours May–Oct. **Naval Station Everett**, *just south of Marina Village Everett, WA 98201; tel: (425) 304-3000*, has periodic base tours.

MOUNT VERNON

Tourist Information: Mount Vernon Chamber of Commerce, *200 E. College Way, Mt Vernon, WA 98273; tel: (360) 428-8547*.

The Skagit Valley is one of the most productive bulb-growing areas in Washington. Daffodils bloom mid Mar–early Apr, tulips Apr, iris early May. The Chamber of Commerce publishes annual flower field maps. For recorded bloom information; *tel: (800) 478-5477*. **La Conner Flats Display Gardens**, *I-*

5 exit 226 or 230; tel: (360) 466-3190, open Mar–Oct, and **Roozengaarde**, *I-5 exit 226; tel: (360) 424-8531*, open all year, are the top public display gardens.

MUKILTEO

Native Americans from California to British Columbia and the Rocky Mountains once met at Mukilteo. Today's travellers meet **Washington State Ferries**; *tel: (206) 464-6400 or (800) 843-3798*, for the 20-min ride to Clinton, on Whidbey Island. Watch the ferries from the jetty, almost within touching distance of the huge ships, or from the park surrounding the **Mukileto Lighthouse**, *915 Second Ave; tel: (425) 359-9656*, an attractive 1905 lighthouse that is still active.

WHIDBEY ISLAND

Puget Sound is never more than 4 miles from the highway running 60 miles up Whidbey Island. Capt George Vancouver sighted the island in 1792 and named it after his sailing master, Lt Joseph Whidbey. Extensive parklands and scenic preserves have kept Whidbey rural despite its proximity to Seattle. Expect to pay $0.10 per gallon more for petrol than on the mainland.

CLINTON

Tourist Information: Clinton Chamber of Commerce, *6256 S. Central, Clinton, WA 98236; tel: (360) 341-4545*.

The town clusters around the ferry terminal and SR 525, *Whidbey Island Rd*.

LANGLEY

Tourist Information: Langley Chamber of Commerce, *Box 403, Langley, WA 98260; tel: (360) 221-6765*. Turn right onto Langley Rd 4.5 miles from the ferry landing.

Views east across Camano Island to the mainland and the Cascades are gorgeous. Whales and bald eagles are regular visitors. Return to SR 525 and continue straight onto *Cultus Bay Rd* toward **Possession Beach Waterfront Park**, an excellent spot to watch passing whales, eagles and ships. Return to SR 525 and turn north (left) for 16 miles through forests and small farms.

South Whidbey State Park; *tel: (360) 331-4559*, is a popular spot for camping and beachcombing. Even more popular is **Meerkerk Rhododendron Gardens**, *just north, 3531 S. Meerkerk Lane, Greenbank, WA 98253; tel: (360) 678-1912*, 10 acres of rhododendron and bulb gardens surrounded by 43 acres of forest laced with walking paths. Peak bloom is Apr–May. Wild rhododendrons, or rhodys, are common across the island.

Fort Casey State Park; *1280 S. Fort Casey Rd, Coupeville, WA 98239; tel: (360) 678-4519*, once guarded Puget Sound. Carry a torch to explore inside the battery. **Admiralty Head Lighthouse**; *tel: (360) 649-7391*, houses the interpretative centre.

Just south of the park is **Washington State Ferries**; *tel: (206) 464-6400* or *(800) 843-3779*, to Port Townsend.

COUPEVILLE

Tourist Information: Central Whidbey Chamber of Commerce, *5 S. Main St, Coupeville, WA 98239; tel: (360) 678-5434.*

ACCOMMODATION

There are a dozen bed and breakfasts and inns in the area and the moderate–expensive **Captain Whidbey Inn**, *2072 W. Capt Whidbey Inn Rd, Coupeville, WA 98239; tel; (360) 678-4097* or *(800) 366-4097*, one of Whidbey's oldest inns.

SIGHTSEEING

Coupeville was founded by ship captains lured to the protected anchorage that nearly cuts Whidbey in two. The Chamber of Commerce publishes a self-guided walking tour of the historic town. *Front St*, between *Alexander and Center Sts*, is lined with antique stores, handicraft shops and souvenir sellers. **Island County Historical Society Museum**, *902 NW Alexander; tel: (360) 678-3310*, open daily 1000–1700 May–Oct, Mon–Fri 1100–1600 Oct–May, concentrates on 19th-century farming.

Central Whidbey Island is protected in **Ebey's Landing National Historical Reserve**, *Box 774, Coupeville, WA 98239; tel: (360) 678-6084*, named for an early settler. The

Chamber of Commerce has an excellent 44-mile self-guided driving brochure of rambling farmland, deserted coves and historic sites.

OAK HARBOR

Tourist Information: Greater Oak Harbor Chamber of Commerce, *5506 Hwy 20, Oak Harbor, WA 98277; tel: (360) 675-3535.*

The nearby naval air station and seaplane base at the eastern end of Crescent Harbor keep local motels busy, including *BW*, the only chain on the island.

Deception Pass State Park, *5175 N. Hwy 20, Oak Harbor, WA 98277; tel: (360) 675-0990*, 14.5 miles north of Oak Harbor, encompasses the scenic beauty of Deception Pass. The sheer cliffs and jagged rocks of the passage are a stone's throw apart. Best view of the Pass is from the bridge to Fidalgo Island, just north of the park, or, tides permitting, from the beach just below the parking area at the south end of the bridge. Small boats trying to breast the tidal currents sometimes find themselves moving steadily backwards despite full throttle.

FIDALGO ISLAND

Named for Spanish explorer Salvador Fidalgo, the island is more rugged than Whidbey. Anacortes, Fidalgo's only town and the ferry terminal for the San Juan Islands, is 9.5 miles north of Deception Pass.

ANACORTES

Tourist Information: Anacortes Chamber of Commerce, *819 Commercial Ave, Anacortes, WA 98221; tel: (360) 293-3832.*

ACCOMMODATION AND FOOD

The French-Colonial **Majestic Hotel**, *419 Commercial Ave; tel: (360) 293-3355; fax: (360) 293-5214*, moderate–expensive, has the most coveted rooms in town. The Chamber of Commerce publishes a bed and breakfast guide.

A popular weekend destination and jumping-off point for the San Juan Islands, Anacortes has a good selection of eateries. The **Majestic Hotel**, moderate, is tops, followed closely by the budget–moderate **Anacortes Brewhouse**, *320 Commercial Ave; tel: (360) 293-3666*. **La Vie en Rose**, *416 Commercial Ave; tel: (360)*

95

Northwest Gold Rushes

Dozens of Hollywood epics have cast fur trappers, Oregon Trail pioneers and timber-men as the romantic heroes of the Pacific Northwest. It was gold miners, many of them failed prospectors from California's famous 1848 Gold Rush, who did more than any other single group to transform the region from a trackless frontier into a tempting land ripe for settlement.

Early Oregon Trail immigrants followed routes pioneered by fur trappers who linked Native American trails across the Rocky Mountains into the Pacific Northwest. Few ventured off what was already a well-beaten track until California gold strikes fired their own dreams of mineral wealth. Farming opportunities lured immigrants to lush valleys, but it was gold prospectors, blazing new trails through scorching deserts and virgin forests, who laid the economic and polit-ical foundation of today's Pacific Northwest. The discovery of gold was the catalyst that sparked development from Gold Hill to John Day and Baker City.

Gold discoveries in Canada had even greater impact. An 1856-57 find on the Fraser River led to the creation of British Columbia (see Background p.49). News of the Fraser River strike spread widely after the HBC shipped 800 ounces of raw gold to San Francisco, in Feb, 1858. Every craft that could float left San Francisco jammed with miners bound for Canada. Shipping on Puget Sound was paralysed as ships, rowboats and rafts made their way to Victoria, the sole source for mining licences, then up the Fraser River to Hope and Yale.

More than 30,000 gold seekers converged on Victoria between May and July of 1858 alone,

299-9546, is a local cheap–budget favourite for breakfast and lunch.

SIGHTSEEING

SR 20 comes to a T-junction on the outskirts of Anacortes. Turn left for **Washington State Ferries**; *tel: (360) 293-8166* or *(800) 843-3779*, to the San Juan Islands or Victoria, British Columbia.

Or go right onto *12th St* to *Commercial Ave*, then left to the town centre. *Commercial Ave* between *11th* and *2nd Sts* is lined with brightly restored 19th century buildings. **Marine Supply & Hardware Co.**, *202 Commercial Ave; tel: (360) 293-3014; fax: (360) 293-4014*, is bursting with marine supplies and hardware as well as purely practical clothing and useful travel supplies.

The **Anacortes Museum**, *1305 8th St; tel: (360) 293-1915*, covers local maritime history. So does the museum ship *W.T. Preston, 7th St and R Ave*, a sternwheel steamboat that col-lected floating snags on Puget Sound.

Padilla Bay Reserve, *1043 Bayview–Edison Rd, Mount Vernon, WA 98273; tel: (360) 428-1558*, protects more than 10,000 acres of Padilla Bay. The **Breazeale Interpretative**

Center explains the ecological and economic importance of the estuary; several miles of paths wind through shoreline and upland meadows for good birding.

Locals like **Samish Bay Shellfish Farm**, *188 Chuckanut Dr., Bow, WA 98232; tel: (360) 766-6002; fax: (360) 766-6812*, below the Oyster Creek Inn, for fresh oysters, mussels, clams and other seafood. Automobile makers like *Chuckanut Dr.* itself. Dramatic dropoffs and sharp curves make scenic backdrops for new car adverts. **Larrabee State Park**, *245 Chuckanut Dr.; tel: (360) 676-2093*, was Washington's first state park.

Tourist Information: Bellingham-Whatcom County Convention & Visitors Bureau, *904 Potter St, Bellingham, WA 98226; tel: (360) 671-3990; fax: (360) 647-7873.*

ACCOMMODATION

Chains include *BW, CI, DI, Ha, Hd, QI, Rm* and *TL*. Best bed and breakfast bets are **Schnauzer Crossing**, *4421 Lakeway Dr.; tel: (360) 733-0055* or *(800) 562-2808; fax: (360) 734-2808*, modern and expensive, or **Big**

almost all of them Americans. The business community prospered, but government was worried.

British authority was little more than a string of Hudson's Bay Company trading posts. Unruly Americans could annex HBC territory as they had taken California from Mexico and forced Britain north out of Oregon and Washington.

Britain replaced HBC commercial control with direct rule. The move consolidated political control but hastened the decline of the HBC. James Douglas, governor of Vancouver Island, became the first governor of the new colony of British Columbia in Nov 1858. He promptly requested British troops and British justices to enforce British law, measures that kept BC British through waves of immigrant miners rushing to gold strikes that lasted into the 20th century.

In Washington, farmers prospered by sending produce and cattle north along the Columbia River to the BC mines. Spokane grew rich on mines eastward in Idaho and west toward Republic. Gold prospectors explored the length of the Cascade Range, opening routes into the rugged mountains that were later used by loggers and farmers.

Prospectors also sparked their share of wars with Native Americans by ignoring reservation boundaries in their endless search for gold. It was a request for protection by trespassing gold prospectors that brought Col Edward Steptoe to a humiliating defeat by Native American forces on the Palouse in May, 1858. And it was repeated incursions by prospectors that helped ignite smouldering resentment into the Nez Perce War of 1878.

Trees, *4840 Fremont St; tel: (360) 647-2850* or *(800) 647-2850*, classic and expensive.

BABS, *Box 5025, Bellingham, WA 98227; tel: (360) 206-733-8642* and the **Bed & Breakfast Guild of Whatcom County**; *tel: (360) 676-4560*, list others.

EATING AND DRINKING

Wild Garlic, *114 Prospect; tel: (360) 671-1955*, adds generous touches of garlic to moderate Northwest classics. **Orchard Street Brewery**, *709 W. Orchard Dr.; tel: (360) 647-1614*, has great budget meals with the best town brews.

SIGHTSEEING

Bellingham has become a small-town alternative to Seattle. Joseph Whidbey named the bay Bellingham for the Admiralty comptroller who oversaw the outfitting of George Vancouver's expedition. About 3000 Native Americans lived along the bay and a creek called Whatcom, or 'noisy water'.

The area boomed with rail connections to the trans–Canada line in the 1880s and later links south to Seattle. **Fairhaven** developed as a port and red light district; many original brick buildings have survived to become a somewhat

more sedate historic and entertainment centre.

Old Fairhaven Association, *Box 4083 Fairhaven Stn; tel: (360) 647-0124*, publishes a self-guided walking map. The **Bellingham Cruise Terminal**, *355 Harris Ave; tel: (360) 676-8445*, serves the Alaska Marine Highway ferry system as well as ferries to the San Juan Islands and Victoria. **AMTRAK**, *401 Harris St; tel: (800) 872-7245*, handles rail traffic to Seattle and Vancouver. Both buildings match Fairhaven's distinctive style.

The ornate **Whatcom Museum of History and Art**, *121 Prospect St; tel: (360) 676-6981*, is one of the largest museums in Washington. Outdoor sculpture is displayed around the museum and at the **Western Washington University Outdoor Sculpture Museum**, *I-5 exit 252; tel: (360) 650-3963*. Bellingham's 1927 Moorish-style **Mt. Baker Theatre**, *106 N. Commercial St; tel: (360) 734-6080*, has been refurbished to its original splendour for live performances and cinema.

The waterfront along **Squalicum Harbor** has become a busy 2-mile promenade with sweeping views of the town and close-ups of commercial fishing boats and pleasure craft.

OLYMPIC PENINSULA

Olympic National Park, occupying most of the Olympic Peninsula, preserves legendary old-growth rain forest. Tall, moss-covered tree trunks are blanketed by ferns at ground level and a dense canopy above, creating an eternal greenish twilight. The best-known forests are the Hoh Rain Forest and Quinault Valley

Maple Glade; the Park also has craggy mountain ridges, hot springs, beaches and lakes. Explore for at least two days with side trips off perimeter highways before continuing to Aberdeen, on Grays Harbor. This route continues east to Olympia, Washington's capitol, or follow the Aberdeen to Astoria route south for more coastline. A scenic side track to Neah Bay skirts the south side of the Strait of Juan de Fuca to the Makah Nation's outstanding tribal museum.

98

Neah Bay
(112) 18 miles
Sekiu   Clallum Bay
Ozette   20 miles   57 miles
(113)   (112)
                                        Port Angeles
(101)
                        Lake
66 miles   20 miles   Crescent   25 miles
                Sol Duc
14 miles   Hurricane
La Push   (110)   Ridge
                        Hoh Rain
(101)   19 miles   Forest
Ruby Beach   OLYMPIC NATIONAL
                                PARK
42 miles
                Lake Quinault

39 miles
        (101)

Hoquiam   Satsop 5 miles   **Olympia**
4 miles   (12)   (8)
    Aberdeen   10 miles   Elma   20 miles

Aberdeen–
Astoria
p. 105

ROUTE

Take Hwy 101 west from Port Angeles to Beaver, then continue south through Forks to Queets, east to Amanda Park and south to **Hoquiam**. Go east on Hwy 12 through **Aberdeen** and continue east on SR 8 and Hwy 101 to Olympia.

For the scenic side track to **Neah Bay**, take Hwy 101 west, then turn right onto SR 112 to the **Makah Indian Reservation**.

Follow *Race St* south from Port Angeles to the **Olympic National Park Main Visitor Center** and **Hurricane Ridge**. Return to Port Angeles and turn left onto *Front St*, driving west on Hwy 101 past pulp mills and the long port industrial area. The SR 112 turnoff to Neah Bay is 8 miles from *Race St*. Two miles beyond, turn left to **Elwha** camping.

Lake Sutherland is on the left as Hwy 101 approaches **East Beach** picnic area along **Lake Crescent**. Follow the north shore 3 miles to **Log Cabin Resort**, or continue west on Hwy 101 around Lake Crescent to **Storm King Information Station**, **Lake Crescent Lodge** and **Mosquito Fleet Cruises**. There is another small watersports resort, petrol and ranger station at **Fairholm**, on Lake Crescent's south-west tip.

Two miles west, turn left to **Sol Duc** and **Sol Duc Hot Springs Resort**. Hwy 101 continues through the forested Sol Duc Valley, near the Sol Duc (Soleduck) River, habitat for beaver, mink, coho and chinook salmon, steelhead and cutthroat trout. To reach the scenic SR 112 side track to Neah Bay, turn right at Sappho, going 10 miles north on SR 113.

Highway 101 turns south after Sappho, through Beaver, past the SR 110 turn to **Mora**, **Rialto Beach** and **La Push** on the Pacific Coast. **Forks Chamber of Commerce Visitor Information**, *PO Box 1249, Forks, WA 98331; tel: (800) 443-6757 or (360) 374-2531*, has information on lodging, dining, seasonal steelhead fishing and an *Olympic West Arttrek* brochure of craftspeople and galleries welcoming visitors to the largest population centre west of the park. Timber at the junction of the Sol Duc, Bogachiel and Calawah Rivers is nearly gone, but the history is covered in the

Forks Timber Museum, *Hwy 101, Chamber of Commerce Building; tel: (360) 374-9663*, between two wooden lumberjacks. Less obvious, behind the museum, is a 0.4-mile path through magnificent forest.

There's camping, hiking through hemlock forest and steelhead fishing at **Bogachiel State Park**, *HC 80, Box 500, Forks, WA, 98331; tel: (360) 374-6356*. Turn right 8 miles south to **Hoh Rain Forest**. Back on Hwy 101, there's camping at **Hoh Oxbow** and **Cottonwood**. Cross the Hoh River into Hoh Clearwater State Forest. Seven miles west is budget **Rain Forest Hostel**, *169312 Hwy 101, Forks, WA 98331; tel: (360) 374-2270*.

Cormorants shelter on Sea Shelf Rocks off **Ruby Beach**. Parking areas near these popular beaches are congested. Take the 0.3-mile drive, then walk to the **Big Cedar Tree**, the gnarled roots of a red cedar nurse tree – 50 paces in circumference. The **Kalaloch Lodge**, restaurant, store, petrol and Visitor Center are 6 miles south.

Cross the Queets River. **Queets Elementary School**, 6½ miles south, has a tribal clan figure board above the portal as Hwy 101 passes eastward through the **Quinault Indian Reservation**. Watch for massive clear-cuts. Turn left at **Amanda Park** to Lake Quinault.

South of Amanda Park are forests, clearcuts and fish hatcheries. **Humptulips** has petrol and provisions. Continue on Hwy 101 to **Hoquiam** (pron: ho-kwe-um) and Aberdeen, then take SR 8 to Olympia.

TOURIST INFORMATION

North Olympic Peninsula Visitor & Convention Bureau, *338 W. First St, #104, PO Box 670, Port Angeles, WA 98362; tel: (360) 452-8552; fax: (360) 452-7383*. **Olympic Peninsula Travel Association**, *PO Box 625, Port Angeles, WA 98362-0112; tel: (360) 385-4938; fax: (360) 379-0151*. **Olympic National Park (Main) Visitor Center**, *600 E. Park Ave, Port Angeles WA 98362; tel: (360) 452-4501 or (360) 452-0330*, open 0900–1600 (later in summer), has general park information and exhibits. There are other park visitor centres at **Hurricane Ridge**, **Lake Crescent** (**Storm King** summer only) and the

Hoh Rain Forest. Ask for the free *Mount Rainier/Olympic National Parks Magazine* and *Bugler* newspaper.

GETTING THERE

While there is no public transportation in Olympic National Park, it is possible to reach some park entrances by bus or ferry. **Clallam Transit**; *tel: (360) 452-4511*, runs Mon–Sat between Sequim, Port Angeles, Joyce, Lake Crescent, Neah Bay, Forks and La Push, and to Hurricane Ridge during ski season. **Gray Line of Seattle**; *tel: (800) 426-7532*, offers summer Olympic Peninsula tours.

The *M.V. Coho* runs a 95-min, year-round passenger and vehicle ferry between Port Angeles and Victoria, BC: contact **Black Ball Transport, Inc. Victoria Express**, takes 55 mins; for address and telephone details for both, see under 'Port Angeles', p.81

ACCOMMODATION

As international visitors make pilgrimage to the temperate Olympic rain forest, book lodging well in advance, especially for summer. Most north side lodging is in Port Angeles and Sequim (see Seattle–Port Angeles, pp. 80–81). On the west side, **Forks** has motels and bed and breakfasts. North of Forks is the gorgeous **Eagle Point Inn**, *384 Stormin' Norman Rd, PO Box 546, Beaver, WA 98305; tel: (360) 327-3236*, three moderate rooms in a hand-built log house filled with antiques and stained-glass windows. **Amanda Park**, 17 miles south of Lake Quinault, and **Hoquiam** and **Aberdeen**, 40 miles south of the lake, have lodging.

Each chamber of commerce has local lodging information, included in *Lodging on the Olympic Peninsula*, from the **Peninsula Tourism Commission**, *PO Box F, Carlsborg, WA 98324*. **The Olympic Peninsula Bed & Breakfast Association**, *PO Box 1741, Port Angeles, WA 98362*, covers inns. **RV Parks of the North Olympic Peninsula**, *PO Box 3125, Port Angeles, WA 98362*, has RV campsite information. **Clallam County Parks and Fair Department**, *223 E. 4th St, Port Angeles, WA 98362; tel: (360) 417-2291*, administers four north peninsula recreation areas with camping.

Much of Olympic National Park is surrounded by the **Olympic National Forest, USFS**, *1835 Black Lake Blvd N.W., Olympia, WA 98512-5623; tel: (360) 956-2300*, with camping. Park campsites, including **Sol Duc** and **Hoh Rain Forest**, have no RV hook-ups, showers or laundry facilities. All campsites are first come, first served. Check for winter closures before venturing into the park.

There are five lodges in Olympic National Park: **Log Cabin Resort**, *Lake Crescent North Shore, 3183 E. Beach Rd, Port Angeles, WA 98363; tel: (360) 928-3325; fax: (360) 928-2088*, open Apr–Sept, popular with families, has moderate–expensive log cabins and motel rooms. On the south shore is **Lake Crescent Lodge**, *416 Lake Crescent Rd, Port Angeles, WA*

Olympic Wildlife

Roosevelt Elk were once common along the Pacific Coast from California to British Columbia, but overhunting and destruction of its open forest habitat nearly killed the species – when Olympic National Park was created in 1938, Roosevelt elk teeth were popular ornaments for watch chains. Today, the Park shelters the world's largest population of this largest North America elk. Bulls weigh up to 1000 lbs.

Elk are relatively common, but few visitors ever see the Park's other largest animals. Cougars, or mountain lions, are shy predators, preferring to slip away through the trees rather than face adult humans. Bears are more inquisitive and more opportunistic. They eat nearly anything, from wild berries and small animals to human garbage and toothpaste. They're occasionally sighted around campsites, where they have learned to scavange food.

The park is also home to one of the Pacific Northwest's least inquisitive creatures, the banana slug. Named for their bright yellow color, these slugs reach 10 inches long as they eat their way across the rain forest floor.

98363; tel: (360) 928-3211, open late Apr–Oct, with moderate–expensive rooms and fireplace cottages. **Sol Duc Hot Springs Resort**, *PO Box 2169, Port Angeles, WA 98362-0283; tel: (360) 327-3583*, open May–Sept, has moderate cabins. On the Pacific coast, **Kalaloch Lodge**, *157151 Hwy 101, Kalaloch, WA 98331; tel: (360) 962-2271; fax: (360) 962-3391*, open all year, has moderate–expensive cabins and rooms. **Lake Quinault Lodge**, *PO Box 7, Quinault, WA 98575-0007; tel: (800) 562-6672 or (360) 288-2900; fax: (360) 288-2901*, open year-round, moderate–pricey, is the quintessential stone and wood national park lodge.

EATING AND DRINKING

Port Angeles (see p.81), gateway to the Olympic Peninsula, National Park, and ferry terminals, is well-equipped with dining. **Forks** has an assortment from hearty hamburgers to well-prepared Chinese. **The Smokehouse Restaurant**, *Hwy 101, Forks; tel: (360) 374-6258*, is known for steaks and seafood; ambient smoke affirms the name. **In Place Restaurant**, *320 Hwy 101 and C St, Forks; tel: (360) 374-4004*, has cheerful service and fresh, budget seafood salads.

Within **Olympic National Park**, there are three cheap–budget self-service snack bars: **Hurricane Ridge**, open late Apr–Sept and snow season weekends and holidays; **Sol Duc**, summer only; and **Kalaloch Coffee Shop**, open year-round. In-park restaurants are casual dress, budget–pricey: **Log Cabin Resort**, *Lake Crescent N. Shore; tel: (360) 928-3245,* open June–Sept with lake views, serves seafood, including salmon, halibut and geoduck clams. **Lake Crescent Lodge**, *Lake Crescent S. Shore; tel: (360) 928-3211*, open late Apr–Oct, also serves seafood with lake views. **Sol Duc Restaurant**; *tel: (360) 327-3583*, open mid May–mid Sept, overlooks the hot springs pool with seafood, chicken and pasta. Sunset's time to dine at oceanfront **Kalaloch Lodge**; *tel: (360) 962-2271*. **Lake Quinault Lodge**; *tel: (360) 288-2900*, requires booking for its posh, Native American décor restaurant.

WEATHER

Fog is common all year, especially at coastal beaches. The average 70°sF summer temperature can plummet with sudden storms. Except in the mountains, winter hovers near 40°F. Always carry a jumper, rain gear, extra socks and easy-dry walking shoes or hiking boots.

OLYMPIC NATIONAL PARK

Seattlites look west toward the Olympic Peninsula with awe. Jagged mountaintops are silhouetted against salmon pink sunsets, the sun's last rays catching a glint of snow on the highest peaks, formed aeons ago by glaciers. Sixty glaciers remain. Ten miles of glaciers accost the flanks of Mt Olympus, reachable only by very experienced mountaineers and Nordic skiers.

The mystique of the Olympic Range does not change the reality of massive Pacific storms, which hurl an average of 200 inches of precipitation on the mountains' west side. Pacific Ocean sea stacks give way to sand and saltwater marshes, ancient rain forest growth in a temperate drizzle and swift rivers churning milky white with glacial silt. Officially, 95% is wilderness, accessible by permit to provide solitude despite half a million annual visitors.

Though native Roosevelt elk populations led to the area's conservation, virgin temperate rain forest is what draws people to this UNESCO International Biosphere Reserve and World Heritage Park. The world's other temperate rain forests are in New Zealand and Chile.

A long rainy season and summer fog create the Olympic Peninsula Rain Forest, defined by the presence of mosses, lichens and Sitka spruce. Nurse logs (huge logs upon which new seedlings germinate and use as protection) create rows of new trees sheltered along downed trunks. Seedlings grow on stilts as roots embrace decaying logs while big leaf maples create a colourful texture beneath the spruce behemoths. Native legends have warring dragons tossing boulders about, dropping moss and lichen scales and shedding tears to create Sol Duc hot springs.

The Park, surrounding national forest and the Native American tribes living in traditional lands along the Strait of Juan de Fuca and the Pacific Coast, is surprisingly varied. Stop at the

101

Main Visitor Center in Port Angeles, on the road to Hurricane Ridge, for maps, weather reports and information on specific attractions.

Hurricane Ridge is a 16.7-mile ascent from sea level, passing through three brief tunnels to the **Hurricane Ridge Visitor Center**, at 5230 ft. The drive traces the spine of a rough north–south mountain range, which meets other east–west ranges. Panoramic views of the Strait of Juan de Fuca, Dungeness Spit, San Juan Islands, Vancouver Island and peaks to the south make visitors gasp. Deer tolerate human shutterbugs on the half-wooded hillsides near the centre. Spring and summer wildflower blooms are spectacular, especially Olympic bluebells. Picnic tables beyond the centre, a favourite area for chipmunks and gray jays, have unobstructed alpine views. Paved 1½-mile Hurricane Hill Trail is at the end of the road, 1.3 miles from the centre.

In winter, *Hurricane Ridge Road* is usually open Sat–Mon and holidays 0900–dusk, weather permitting. For weather and road conditions; *tel: (360) 452-0329*, or take a shuttle bus from the Main Visitor Center. Winter sports include snowshoeing, and skiing.

Lake Crescent, with Mt Storm King on its south-east side, has hiking, swimming, water skiing, sailing, canoeing, fishing and a 1½-hr historical interpretative tour on a **Mosquito Fleet** vessel; *tel: (360) 452-4520*, June–Sept, adults $15, children 6–17 $7.50.

Sol Duc is a late spring–early fall hot springs resort, day use $6.25. A 1.6-mile return trail goes to beautiful **Sol Duc Falls**. Stop at the **Ancient Grove Nature Trail,** 9 miles from Hwy 101 towards Sol Duc, to hike a forest dominated by trees 175–750 years old, arrayed, like the road, along the Sol Duc River.

Ozette is south-west from SR 112, near the coast. **Lake Ozette** is 300 ft deep. Two trails to the **Olympic Coast National Marine Sanctuary**, *138 W. 1st St, Port Angeles WA 98362; tel: (360) 457-6622; fax: (360) 457-8496*, on the Pacific Ocean, begin at the **Ozette Ranger Station**. Trails can be combined into a loop by hiking 3 miles down the beach, watching for sea otters 'surfing' rough tides. **The Indian Village Nature Trail** goes 3.3 miles through lowland forest to Cape Alava.

Just north, a now-buried 1970s archaeological excavation yielded artefacts displayed at the **Makah Museum & Cultural Center** in Neah Bay. Another 3-mile trail goes to Sand Point.

Take SR 110 west from Hwy 101 just north of Forks to **Rialto Beach**, in the park. **La Push**, the **Quileute Indian Reservation** town, is on the south bank of the Quillayute River. Both are stunning spots for sea stacks surmounted by conifers, silhouetted against the sunset. Nineteen miles east from Hwy 101 is the astonishing **Hoh Rain Forest**, filled with huge western red cedar, Sitka spruce, western hemlock, mosses and thick ferns. Visitor centre exhibits introduce three forest trails. Plan an hour to walk 1¼-mile **Spruce Nature Trail** loop, passing the Hoh River and crossing beneath a trunk dwarfing a grown man. **Hall of Mosses Trail** is another ¾-mile loop. A paved ¼-mile trail hints at more panoramic reaches along the other trails.

Highway 101 returns to the **Pacific Coast National Marine Sanctuary** at a bluff above the fine, garnet-laced sands and white driftwood of **Ruby Beach**. Access the series of **six numbered beaches** by hiking down to the sand for winter whale-spotting, picnicking, walking and colourful sunsets. **Kalaloch Ranger Station** and **Kalaloch Lodge** are near Beach 2.

Lake Quinault, 26 miles east of Kalaloch, has swimming, canoeing, kayaking, sailing, bird-watching, horse riding, golfing and fishing. Quinault Native stories speak of a canoe-swallowing monster in the 180-ft deep lake. Hike or drive the 30-mile scenic loop around the lake, then shop and dine at the elegant **Lake Quinault Lodge**. Hiking trails abound. The exceptional north shore ½-mile **Maple Glade Rain Forest Trail** winds up and around old growth, with open areas to give dimension to the vibrant green flora.

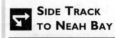

SIDE TRACK TO NEAH BAY

NEAH BAY

Take Hwy 101 8 miles west from Port Angeles, then turn right onto SR 112 for 70

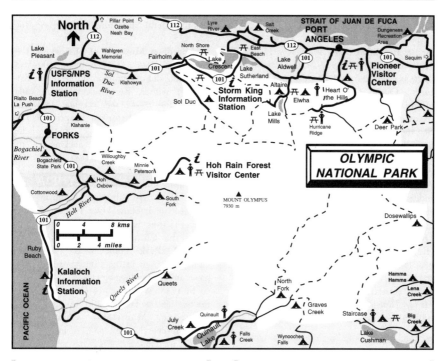

miles. The highway plays hide-and-seek with the shoreline along the Strait of Juan de Fuca. Vancouver Island is visible on clear days. Rocky outcroppings on the Washington side and dramatic tidal shifts provide rich habitat for shorebirds and bird-watching. The narrow, two-lane highway may be closed by mudslides in winter. The west side is forest, with occasional clear-cuts.

Fishing towns **Clallam Bay** and **Sekiu**, with services, RV parks and moderate bed and breakfast **Winters' Summer Inn**, *16651 Hwy 112, Clallam Bay, WA 98326; tel: (360) 963-2264*, are 50 miles from Port Angeles. **Clallam Bay-Sekiu Chamber of Commerce**, *PO Box 355, Clallam Bay, WA 98326; tel: (360) 963-2339*.

Neah Bay, at the end of Hwy 112, is the only town on the **Makah Reservation**, a salmon fishing port, where once there were longhouses sheltering tribespeople who hunted grey whales, fashioned fine canoes, carved intricate masks and formed ritual and decorative objects from local red cedar. For 500 years, the tribe kept the secret of Ozette Village, buried beneath a landslide. Artefacts began washing up in the 1960s, were excavated in the 1970s, and now form fine exhibits at the **Makah Museum**, *PO Box 160, Neah Bay, WA 98357; tel: (360) 645-2711*, open 1000–1700 daily June–Sept 15, Wed–Sun Sept 16–May, adults $4. Check with the **Makah Tribal Center**; *tel: (360) 645-2201*, or the museum for the condition of the road and hiking trail to **Cape Flattery**, Washington's wild north-west tip.

HOQUIAM/ABERDEEN

Tourist Information: Grays Harbor Chamber of Commerce, *506 Duffy St, Aberdeen, WA 98520; tel: (800) 321-1924 or (320) 532-1924*, covers Hoquiam and Aberdeen.

ACCOMMODATION AND FOOD

Hoquiam, and its larger neighbour Aberdeen, have moderate motels, including *RL* in

Aberdeen and **Timberline Inn**, *415 Perry Ave, Hoquiam; tel: (360) 533-8048.* **Lytle House Bed & Breakfast**, *509 Chenault Ave, Hoquiam, WA 98550; tel: (800) 677-2320 or (360) 533-2320*, is a beautiful moderate–expensive lumber baron's Queen Anne-style Victorian, next to Hoquiam's Castle. Moderate **Aberdeen Mansion Inn Bed and Breakfast**, *807 N. M St, Aberdeen; tel: (360) 533-7079*, was lumber baron Edward Hulbert's 1905 manse.

Grays Harbor dining includes Hoquiam, Aberdeen, Ocean Shores, and Westport (See Aberdeen–Astoria, pp. 109). Fast food and modest restaurants abound in this lumber area, alleged to harvest more trees than any other US county. Local seafood includes moderate **Duffy's Restaurant** *Number 3, 825 Simpson Ave, Hoquiam; tel: (360) 532-1519.* Try an excellent, casual breakfast or burger with a fresh strawberry milkshake at **Big Matt's Little Farm Ranch Kitchen**, *815 E. Heron, Grays Harbor Historical Seaport, Aberdeen; tel: (360) 532-1446.*

SIGHTSEEING

Hoquiam and Aberdeen, once prosperous timber towns on Grays Harbor, have grown together with urban sprawl. Capt Robert Gray sailed Columbia into the sheltered bay in 1792. Firewood-seeking Chehalis Native Americans called the north shore Hoquiam, 'hungry for wood'. White settlers further obeyed the mandate to cut the rich forests of Douglas-fir, spruce and hemlock.

Hoquiam's Castle, *515 Chenault Ave; tel: (360) 533-2005*, open 1100–1700, mid June–Labor Day and Sat–Sun Sept–Nov and Jan–mid June, adults $4, is the town jewel, a furnished, refurbished mansion built in 1897 by lumber baron Joseph Lytle. Another lumber baron house is the **Arnold Polson Museum**, *1611 Riverside Ave; tel: (360) 533-5862*, open 1100–1600 Wed–Sun (summer), adults $2, housing eclectic collections of old logging photographs, Quinault baskets, household artefacts and a massive 1870 Howard 60-beat clock in the foyer. Go west on SR 109 along Grays Harbor and turn left onto *Paulson Rd* to viewing areas and a trail to watch up to a million migrating shorebirds (in April) at **Bowerman**

Basin Federal Shorebird Refuge; *tel: (360) 532-6237.*

Aberdeen Museum of History, *111 E. 3rd St; tel: (360) 533-1976*, open 1100–1600 Wed–Sun during summer, 1200–1600 Sat–Sun in winter, has pioneer memorabilia, antique fire trucks and a canoe collection. **Grays Harbor Historical Seaport**, *813 E. Heron St, Aberdeen; tel: (360) 532-8611*, is being developed with shops and docking for the Gray-era replica *Lady Washington*.

ABERDEEN TO OLYMPIA

Take Hwy 101 through Hoquiam and Aberdeen and follow Hwy 12 east. A huge Weyerhaeuser lumberyard is visible south across the Chehalis River. Watch for the **Central Park** home with a 'Logging Consultant' sign in the front yard and enormous amounts of logging tack.

In 1941, Weyerhaeuser Company planted the first US tree farm on 130,000 acres around Montesano. **Montesano Chamber of Commerce**, *PO Box 688, Montesano, WA 98563; tel: (360) 249-5522*, has area information. In 1908, Sussex-born attorney William H. Abel built a nine-bedroom house, now moderate **Abel House Bed and Breakfast Inn**, *117 Fleet St S.; tel: (800) 235-2235 or (360) 249-6002*, with a lovely English garden.

Camp at **Lake Sylvia State Park**, *Box 701; tel: (360) 249-3621*, a mile north, with year-round canoeing, boating and swimming. **The Chehalis Valley Historical Museum**, *703 W. Pioneer Ave; tel: (360) 249-5800*, open 1200–1700 Wed–Sun June–Labor Day, 1200–1600 Sat–Sun Sept–May, housed in a former church, has logging and farming artefacts.

Satsop is a farming community outside **Elma**. Veer left onto SR 8 at Elma. McCleary's industry is a lumber mill which fabricates elaborate doors.

The McCleary Museum, *Carnell House, 314 2nd St*, open Memorial Day–Labor Day Sat–Sun 1200–1600, has excellent old photos of loggers and farmers. The 1912 **Old McCleary Hotel**, *42 Summit, McCleary, WA 98557; tel: (360) 495-3678*, has moderate lodging.

Drive east past the Summit Lake exit, and continue straight on Hwy 101 into Olympia.

ABERDEEN–ASTORIA

Rich fishing grounds, shellfish beds and thick forests lured entrepreneurs to Washington's south-west coast. This 145-mile route runs from the central Washington coast, famed until recent years for record timber production, through the prosperous seaport and tourist centre of Westport/Westhaven, past Willapa Bay oyster fleets and millions of birds in the Willapa National Wildlife Refuge.

A 30-mile return drive up the Long Beach Peninsula, included in this route, is a seaside holiday where ice-cream and fudge shops alternate with T-shirt emporia, seafood diners and tourist kitsch. The dunes are lovely and deserted; birds swoop over protected bay oyster beds. One very long day will accomplish this route; two days allows time to dine, shop and walk along lovely long white beaches.

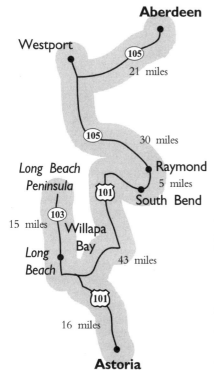

105

ROUTE: 145 MILES

ROUTE

From *Heron St* (Hwy 101) in Aberdeen, turn right onto *S. H St* and continue across the Chehalis River. Turn right onto SR 105 around the south side of Grays Harbor to **Westport**, then continue to the Hwy 101 junction, just north of **Raymond**.

Take Hwy 101 south around **Willapa Bay**, taking time to drive SR 103 and detour up the **Long Beach Peninsula**. Return to Hwy 101 and cross the Columbia River to Astoria, Oregon.

WEATHER

Coastal fogs are common year-round. Summer may seem balmy, but water temperature remains chilly. Winter brings magnificent storms, crashing surf, high waves and fierce winds that rearrange dunes and shoreline.

Cross the **Chehalis River** to **South Aberdeen**, then turn right onto *S. Boone St*, SR 105, which becomes *Westport Rd* as it skirts the south side of Grays Harbor. Pass an Ocean Spray Cranberry processing plant before crossing Johns River to **Markham** oysterbeds.

Cross South Bay at Bay City. **Twin Harbors State Park;** *Westport, WA 98595; tel: (360) 268-9717, camping; tel: (800) 452-5687*, is ahead. This popular park is congested in summer and during spring and fall razor clam season. It's dunes attract hikers to the **Shifting Sands Nature Trail.** **Westport** is right (north) on SR 105.

WESTPORT

Tourist Information: **Westport-Grayland Chamber of Commerce,** *2985 S. Montesano Ave, PO Box 306, Westport, WA 98595-0306; tel: (800) 345-6223 or (360) 268-9422; fax: (360) 268-1990*, has information on area lodging, dining and recreation.

ACCOMMODATION

The Chamber of Commerce has seaside resort information, from upmarket motels to RV parks. **Chateau Westport,** *710 Hancock Ave; tel: (800) 255-9101 or (360) 268-9101*, has moderate–pricey rooms. **Harbor Resort,** *871 Neddie Rose Dr., float 20; tel: (360) 268-0169*, offers moderate cottages with Grays Harbor views.

EATING AND DRINKING

Dine in Westhaven. **Totem Drive-In,** *2411 N. Nyhus; tel: (360) 268-0909*, serves a delicious, cheap, deep-fried oysterburger on a sesame bun.

Stroll along *Westhaven Dr.* to peruse the catch-of-the-day, or try a fresh shrimp or crab cocktail at **Merino's Seafoods, Inc.,** *1804 N. Nyhus St; tel: (360) 268-9286*, which offers shellfish, tuna and salmon.

SIGHTSEEING

Turn left on *W. Ocean Ave*. A viewing platform provides a good morning photography of 107-foot **Westport Light,** Washington's tallest lighthouse. Now automated, the lighthouse still has its 1895 Fresnel lens. **Westport Light State Park,** north and west, is a local favourite for picnicking, kite flying, surfing, clamming and fishing.

A 1.4-mile trail with viewing platforms and interpretative signs winds north from the lighthouse to **Westhaven State Park** at the Grays Harbor entrance. Dunes give character to the park where clamming and agate-hunting are popular along **Half Moon Bay.** Wetsuits are *de rigueur* at Washington's most popular surfing beach.

Follow SR 105 to Westhaven, turn right on *Dock Ave* to *Westhaven Dr.*, the main street for small seafood restaurants, souvenir shopping, motels, marinas and the summer-only **Westport/Ocean Shores Passenger Ferry,** *2453 Westhaven Dr., Float 10; tel: (360) 268-0047*. Whale-watching charters are popular Mar–May. There is jetty fishing by *Neddie Rose Dr.*, a 44-foot open-air observation tower and a fisherman's memorial, supervised by flocks of pelicans.

Only the museum-deprived venture into the **Westport Maritime Museum,** *2201 Westhaven Dr.; tel: (360) 268-0078,* open Wed–Sun, adults $2, formerly the Grays Harbor Coast Guard Station. Skeletons of gray and minke whales are well-displayed outside.

Feeding seals is the main attraction at **Westport Aquarium,** *321 Harbor St; tel: (360) 268-0471*, adults $2.50, with murky tanks and a large souvenir shop.

South on SR 105, **Grayland** is surrounded by 1000 acres of cranberry bogs, which turn a cheerful red near fall harvest time. Shop for cranberry preserves, candy, fudge, candles at local shops. **Wild Bird Garden,** *4986 SR 105; tel: (360) 268-0804*, has birding supplies. Turn right to **Grayland Beach State Park;** *tel: (360) 268-9717; camping; tel: (800) 452-5687*, a good spot for beachcombing or kite-flying. Bogs and a small section of the **Willapa National Wildlife Refuge** are south.

State Route 105 turns east at **North Cove** to the **Shoalwater Indian Reservation.** Follow signs to **Tokeland** on Willapa Bay and the lovely 1885 resort **Tokeland Hotel & Restaurant,** *100 Hotel Rd, Tokeland, WA 98590; tel: (360) 267-7006,* with moderate bayfront rooms and delicious budget–moderate meals, including cranberry pot roast.

WILLAPA BAY

Willapa Bay claims to be the continental USA's most pristine estuary. More than 65 square miles of water fill the bay. Seven and one-half million gallons of water per second cross the bar between the bay and Pacific Ocean with each tide. Among 250 species of birds are the black brant, great blue heron and wintering dunlin. Willapa Bay is one of the five most productive oyster areas in the world, providing 16% of oysters consumed at US tables.

State Route 105 follows Willapa Bay mudflats and grazing Holstein cows to the Hwy 101 junction at **Raymond.** Stop at **Raymond Chamber of Commerce & Visitor Information Center,** *524 N 3rd St, Raymond, WA 98577; tel: (360) 942-5419,* for information on lodging and the 200 iron statues of local animals and people in the **Raymond Wildlife-Heritage Sculpture Corridor.** In shadow, the sculptured silhouettes of cougars, deer, eagles and gulls look quite real. A **Willapa Seaport Museum** is being built to supplement the **Dennis Company logging history mural,** *5th and Blake Sts.*

Cross Skidmore Slough. The **South Bend Chamber of Commerce,** *W. 1st and Alder Sts, South Bend, WA 98586; tel: (360) 875-5231* has local information.

ACCOMMODATION AND FOOD

Maring's Courthouse Hill Bed & Breakfast, *602 W 2nd St; tel: (800) 875-6519* or *(360) 875-6519,* has moderate rooms in an historic, tree-shaded district. **Seaquest Motel,** *801 W. 1st St; tel: (360) 875-5349,* has cosy budget–moderate rooms.

Willapa Bay oysters are king in South Bend, scrumptious in cheap oyster chowder at **CJ's Dining,** *618 W. Robert Bush Dr.; tel: (360) 875-6155.* **Boondocks Restaurant,** *1015 W.*

Robert Bush Dr.; tel: (360) 875-5155, offers moderate dining, with a bay deck for sunset views.

SIGHTSEEING

The **Pacific County Courthouse,** *300 Memorial Dr.; tel: (360) 268-0891,* gleams white amidst elegant flower gardens, its art glass dome and foyer murals of Willapa Bay an elegant tribute to the 1893 kidnapping of the county seat from Oysterville on Long Beach Peninsula. One exterior wall of the **Pacific County Museum,** *1008 W. Robert Bush Dr.; tel: (360) 875-5224,* open 1100–1600, has a mural depicting South Bend in 1911. *Robert Bush Dr.,* Hwy 101, is the main road along the waterfront, dominated at the town's south end by **EH Bendiksen Co** cannery and seafood market; *tel: (800) 551-6239* or *(360) 665-6188.*

Highway 101 goes south through sloughs, over small rivers, past cattle and forests. **Willapa National Wildlife Refuge Headquarters,** *c/o HC 01, Box 910. Ilwaco, WA 98624, tel: (360) 484-3482,* is two miles beyond the Naselle River. No scheduled boat service reaches **Long Island** with its 0.75-mile **Ancient Cedars Trail,** eelgrass, marshes, tall trees and wildlife. The **Lewis Unit** freshwater marshes, six miles west along Hwy 101, are filled with waterfowl including trumpeter swans.

SIDE TRACK
TO LONG BEACH PENINSULA

Divert from Hwy 101, turning right onto SR 103 to Long Beach.

LONG BEACH PENINSULA

Tourist Information: Long Beach Peninsula Visitors Bureau, *junction Hwy 101 and SR 103, PO Box 562, Long Beach, WA 98631; tel: (800) 451-2542* or *(360) 642-2400,* has information on accommodation, dining, museums, shopping and parks.

ACCOMMODATION

Lodging ranges from moderate–expensive in this seaside resort area, including bed and breakfast inns, motels and RV facilities.

Prices are lower in the winter storm season, Jan–Mar. **Chick-a-Dee Inn at Ilwaco,** *120 Williams St NE., PO Box 922, WA 98624; tel· (360) 642-8686,* is an elegant, moderate–expensive wood-shingled former church, with a fine view of the town, and a 'third night free' scheme.

Seaview CoHo Motel, *3701 Pacific Hwy, Seaview, WA 98644; tel: (800) 681-8153* or *(360) 642-2531,* has moderate, basic rooms. The green and white **Shelburne Inn,** *4415 Pacific Way, PO Box 250, Seaview; tel: (800) 466-1896* or *(360) 642-2442,* is an expensive 1896 landmark country inn.

EATING AND DRINKING

The Shelburne Inn's renowned **Shoalwater Restaurant,** *tel: (360) 642-4142,* and the adjacent moderate **Heron and Beaver Pub,** have Northwest cuisine. **The Ark Restaurant and Bakery,** *270 3rd St, Nahcotta; tel: (360) 665-4133,* on Willapa Bay uses its own fresh grown or bay-harvested ingredients for outstanding moderate–pricey fare.

The Crab Pot, *1917 Pacific Hwy S., Long Beach; tel: (360) 642-8870,* serves extremely fresh budget–moderate seafood in a casual dining room.

SIGHTSEEING

Highway 101 touches the south end of the peninsula, self-proclaimed as the world's longest driving beach. Pacific Transit System; *tel: (360) 642-9418,* bus route No. 20, runs from Ilwaco north on SR 103 to Oysterville, $0.35.

FORT CANBY

Fort Canby State Park, *PO Box 488, Ilwaco, WA 98624; tel: (360) 642-3078; fax: (360) 642-4216;* for camping; *tel: (800) 452-5687,* is at the peninsula's south end, with camping, yurts and cabins, hiking, picnicking, lighthouses, fortifications and a Lewis & Clark interpretative centre. Washington's south-western tip was named **Cape Disappointment** in 1788 by Capt John Meares, an English explorer who

unhappily missed the Columbia River just beyond. Lewis & Clark's men looked 'with astonishment [at] the high waves dashing against the rock and this imence Ocian [sic]'.

Cliffs and the treacherous Columbia River bar have sent many ships to 'the Graveyard of the Pacific'. Two lighthouses, 1856 **Cape Disappointment** and 1898 **North Head,** still warn ships. Constant winds buffet the coast, making hiking to lighthouses a brisk challenge.

The US Army fortified Fort Canby, named after the general killed in the Modoc Indian War, to protect the Columbia River from 1862–World War II. A few gun emplacements remain. The **Lewis & Clark Interpretive Center,** *tel: (360) 642-3029,* open 1000–1700 unless closed due to windstorms, perches near one bunker. A spiral walkway 'up through time' follows the Corps of Discovery west with maps and interpretative exhibits.

Ilwaco is favoured by fishermen and boaters seeking a port base to explore the peninsula. **Ilwaco Heritage Museum.** *115 SE. Lake St; tel: (360) 642-3446,* open Mon–Sat 0900–1700 Sun 1200–1600, adults $2, children 6–12 $0.75, is a haphazard mixture of Chinook Native American artefacts, pioneer object, and railway equipment, with a fine working replica of a narrow-gauge railway. **Black Lake Park** has walking trails and picnicking. **Seaview's** best-known attraction is the elegant dining and lodging at the **Shelburne Inn.**

LONG BEACH

Long Beach boasts a half-mile long elevated beach boardwalk from the foot of Bolstad St. **Marsh's Free Museum,** *SR 103, Long Beach; tel: (360) 642-2188,* is easy to spot from the bizarre figures above the gift shop-cum-museum. Main attraction is 'Jake the Alligator Man', a blackened human skull on a baby alligator body, supplemented by antique arcade machines, critter skins and old crockery, glass, shells and small souvenirs for sale.

The **World Kite Museum and Hall**

of Fame, *3rd St NW.; tel: (360) 642-4020,* open 1100–1700 Fri–Mon June–Aug, Sat–Sun Sept–May, adults $1, children $.50, has kites from around the world on display and kite-fighting video exhibits. The **Washington State International Kite Festival**, *PO Box 387, Long Beach, WA 98631; tel: (800) 451-2542,* draws hundred of competitors and thousands of spectators each August.

The **Pacific Coast Cranberry Museum**, *Pioneer Rd; tel: (360) 642-4938,* open 1000–1500 Fri–Sun, is a free look at harvesting and processing the tangy red berry.

North of Long Beach, the peninsula becomes residential. **Loomis Lake State Park** has two sections. Dunes with sea grasses and pine trees separate the west side parking area from the beach. A right-hand turn just north goes to an undeveloped series of lakes, including Loomis Lake, a serene fishing area where birders spot trumpeter swans in winter. A mile north in **Ocean Park** is **Pacific Pines State Park** trail west to the beach.

Willapa Bay oysters have ruled the economy of towns on the east side of Long Beach Peninsula for 150 years. **Nahcotta,** named after Nahcati, a Chinook chief who showed Whites the bay's sheltered oyster beds, was once the terminus for the 'Clamshell Railroad' from Ilwaco and ferry service from Raymond and South Bend. A 1915 fire destroyed the town, but oystering is still important. **EH Bendiksen;** *tel: (800) 551-6239* or *(360) 665-6188,* has a cannery and store on the bay.

Stop at the **Willapa Bay Interpretive Center**, *on a pier east of SR 103; tel: (360) 665-4547,* open 1000–1500 May–Oct Fri–Sun, for exhibits on Native American oyster gathering, bay ecology and modern oystering. **Willapa Bay Excursions,** *270th and Sand Ridge Rds; tel: (360) 665-5557,* offer tours of the bay around Long Island.

In the late 19th century, San Francisco's insatiable demand for oysters depleted Willapa Bay. New stock was imported from Japan in the 1920s. Clutches of oyster larvae, spat, are laced onto shells called 'seed', and grown in mudflats, on lines stretched between poles, suspended on racks or in mesh bags. Spring–summer, larger oysters are moved; fall–winter, the molluscs are picked by hand or harvested by dredge, shucked, canned and shipped. **Nahcotta Tidelands Interpretive Site,** *Sand Ridge Rd,* has the only public oysterbeds on the bay.

OYSTERVILLE

Oysterville boomed with oyster production until the supply was exhausted. The town, which reputedly had as much gold hidden in mattresses as in San Francisco banks, lost most of its population in the 1880s.

National Historic District buildings like the 1892 **Oysterville Church**, are little-changed. Chief Nahcati is buried near the **Oysterville Cemetery** entrance.

Beach trails flood from Oct–May at low-lying **Leadbetter Point State Park,** south-west of **Willapa NWR Leadbetter Point Unit.** Peaceful dunes, marshes, and forest at the peninsula's north tip combine into a banquet area for birds resting and eating during migrating along the Pacific Flyway. ⬧

LONG BEACH PENINSULA TO ASTORIA

A wooden statue of the explorers marks Lewis & Clark's 1805 campsite, a pleasant shaded picnic spot near prime fishing on Baker Bay on Hwy 101.

Fort Columbia State Park, *Box 236, Chinook, WA 98614; tel: (360) 777-8221,* once a Columbia River artillery fortification, has a military museum in former enlisted men's barracks, complete with hospital and narration by the company cook. The former commandant's home and newspaper office are open for viewing.

Fort Columbia State Park HI, *Box 224, Chinook, WA 98614; tel: (360) 777-8755,* is open June–Sept.

Turn south onto the Astoria Bridge, crossing the Columbia River to Astoria, Oregon.

109

The Lewis and Clark Expedition

The Lewis and Clark expedition was the opening phrase in what America came to call Manifest Destiny. It was a notion that Americans had a divine destiny to rule the continent from Atlantic to Pacific and as far to the north and the south as Britain, Spain, France, Russia and Mexico could be coerced.

This brash expansionist imperative led President Thomas Jefferson to draft his confidante and personal secretary Meriwether Lewis to form a Corps of Discovery. Lewis tapped his former Army commander, William Clark, as co-leader.

The expedition's stated goal was to discover just what America got in the 1803 Louisiana Purchase, 827,000 square miles of French territory from the Mississippi River west to the Rocky Mountains and the Gulf of Mexico north to the vague border with British America. Lewis and Clark were to explore the Missouri River to its source and establish a land route to the mouth of the Columbia River, first charted by American Navy Capt. Robert Gray in 1792.

It was a scientific and geographic exploration with clear political overtones. The Corps was ordered to learn all they could of Native American tribes and impress them with the strength and authority of the United States, backed by gifts of oversized gold coins. Jefferson, chief author of America's 1776 Declaration of Independence from England, wanted local allies in his bid for 'Oregon Territory', claimed by both America and her former colonial master.

The 33-man expedition was a smashing success. Despite repeated brushes with death by accident, starvation and skirmish, the only fatality was due to appendicitis.

Sailing north up the Missouri River from St Louis in May, 1804, the group began treating with Native American tribes immediately, starting at Council Bluffs, Iowa, later part of the Oregon Trail. They wintered at Fort Mandan, near Washburn, North Dakota, and hired Toussaint Charbonneau, a French-Canadian fur trader, as interpreter-guide for the trek west. Fortunately, Charbonneau brought his Shoshone wife, Sacajawea, and their new-born son, Jean Baptiste.

In August, 1805, the Corps reached the source of the Missouri River and a Shoshone band led by Sacajawea's brother. They bought horses and headed west over the Rocky Mountains to the Snake River in Idaho. Crossing the Rockies, uncharted territory for the Americans, was an annual trading and hunting trek for many Native American bands. Sacajawea's diplomacy convinced the Nez Perce, long-time Shoshone trading partners, to help the Corps rather than kill them.

Trading horses for canoes, Lewis and Clark paddled down the Snake River and into Washington in October. After 17 months on the trail, they entered the Columbia River at present-day Sacajawea State Park. Clark and two men paddled upstream almost to the Yakima River, then rejoined the others and continued down the Columbia, amazed at scope of the autumn salmon harvest. They finally reached the Pacific Ocean in mid-November, camping at present-day Fort Canby State Park.

The north shore of the Columbia River estuary was too exposed to winter storms, so they moved to the wooded south shore at Fort Clatsop, near present Astoria. A smaller camp near present Seaside boiled seawater for salt. The Corps headed back up the Columbia in March, 1806 and arrived in St Louis in September, 28 months and 8000 miles after setting out. Although Great Britain would not relinquish its claims to Oregon and Washington until 1846, the successful expedition fired America's enthusiasm for expansion.

Before the 19th century expired, America had purchased Alaska from Russia; taken Texas, the Southwest and California from Mexico; captured Cuba and the Philippines from Spain; stolen Hawaii from its own monarch; and laid out a political doctrine that still affects politics and commerce throughout the Americas.

ASTORIA–BROOKINGS

At any moment, fog, rain, wind, a rare snow-fall or cloudless sunshine crowns the 360 miles of Oregon's spectacular coastline, dunes, forests and pastures along Hwy 101. Traffic slows behind logging trucks and RVs, and scenery-gawkers slow to pull onto lay-bys. It is possible to drive the route in one day, but one of the American West's most beautiful areas deserves a week, with time to explore Astoria, and overnights at least in Tillamook, Newport, Florence and the Coos Bay Area.

Summer warmth inland causes coastal fogs. Winter may bring constant pelting rain or days so clear that migrating whales can be seen 50 miles offshore. Oregon's Coast attracts fewer visitors during the winter and lodging prices plunge but many attractions and parks close

between Labor Day and Memorial Day. Water temperatures demand wetsuits for all but the most arctic-conditioned swimmer.

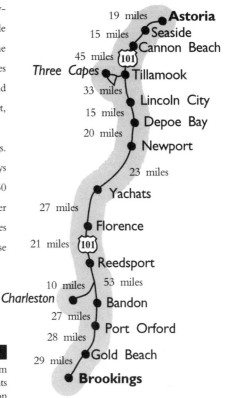

19 miles	**Astoria**
15 miles	Seaside
	Cannon Beach
45 miles	101
Three Capes	Tillamook
33 miles	
	Lincoln City
15 miles	
	Depoe Bay
20 miles	
	Newport
23 miles	
	Yachats
27 miles	
	Florence
21 miles	101
	Reedsport
10 miles	53 miles
Charleston	Bandon
27 miles	
	Port Orford
28 miles	
29 miles	Gold Beach
	Brookings

111

ROUTE: 360 MILES

ROUTE

The route follows Hwy 101 south from **Astoria** to **Brookings** (see Brookings–Grants Pass, p.129), all but 6 miles of the Oregon stretch of the 'Pacific Coast Highway' which loops from Olympia, Washington around the Olympic Peninsula and down the Washington State Coast through Oregon and California to the Mexican border just south of San Diego. From the Astoria Bridge linking Washington to Oregon, Hwy 101 runs 7 miles south-west, then continues south for 353 miles, occasionally winding around scenic bays. Two side tracks

enhance the route: **The Three Capes** (via Tillamook) and the **Charleston/Cape Arago Loop** (via Coos Bay).

Oregon Coast Tourist Information: Moderate lodging is widely available; enquire at a town's chamber of commerce, and be prepared for higher prices Memorial Day–Labor Day. **Oregon Coast Magazine**, *PO*

Box 18000, Florence, OR 97439-9970; tel: (541) 997-8401 or (800) 348-8401, publishes the free *Mile-by-Mile Guide to Hwy 101;* **Oregon Parks and Recreation Department**, *1115 Commercial St N.E., Salem, OR 97310-1001; tel: (800) 452-5687,* has information on lighthouses, tidepools and whalewatching sites. **US Fish and Wildlife Service**, *2030 S. Marine Science Dr., Newport, OR 97365-5296; tel: (503) 867-4550,* covers Oregon coastal wildlife refuges. **Oregon Department of Transportation**, *Bicycle/Pedestrian Program Manager, Room 210, Transportation Bldg, Salem, OR 97310; tel: (503) 378-3432,* has a free *Oregon Coast Bike Route* map.

ASTORIA

Tourist Information: Astoria-Warrenton Chamber of Commerce, *111 W. Marine Dr., Astoria, OR 97103; tel: (800) 535-3637 or (503) 325-6311; fax: (503) 325-976,* open 0800–1800 May–Oct, 0900–1700 Nov–Apr, or **Astoria-Warrenton Visitor Center**, *Young's Bay Plaza, off Hwy 101, Warrenton,* daily 0900–1700, have area information and book Astoria waterfront or Columbia River tours.

Accommodation

The Chamber of Commerce has a lodging list. Astoria's seaport never lost its *grande dame* Victorians, regally perched on the hills above the harbour. Many are bed and breakfasts, which cross-refer business. The moderate **Grandview Bed & Breakfast**, *1574 Grand Ave, Astoria, OR 97103; tel: (800) 488-3250 or (503) 325-0000,* is a cosy choice with 9 rooms and views of the Columbia River. The 1902 moderate–expensive 11 room **Rosebriar Hotel**, *636 14th St; tel: (800) 487-0224 or (503) 325-7427,* has bed and breakfast, phones and television.

Motels include the moderate *RL* and **Bayshore Motor Inn**, *555 Hamburg St; tel: (800) 621-0641 or (503) 325-2205,* the moderate–expensive **Shilo Inn**, *1609 E. Harbor Dr., Warrenton, OR 77146; tel: (800) 222-2244 or (503) 861-2181.* Warrenton camping includes the **KOA Kampground**, *1100 Ridge Rd, Hammond, OR 97121; tel:*

(503) 861-2606, and **Fort Stevens State Park**, *Ridge Rd; tel: (503) 861-1671.*

Eating and Drinking

Astorians are loyal dining patrons; some restaurants have a following even in south-west Washington. **Someplace Else**, *965 Commercial St; tel: (503) 325-3500,* supplements its map-and-postcard decor with generous portions of budget–moderate pasta and hearty home-made minestrone soup with French, Indian, Malaysian, Brazilian, Thai, Mexican, Greek or other ethnic specials nightly (except Tues). Strings of huge orange and red peppers adorn the window of the moderate and casual **Columbian Café**, *1114 Marine Dr., tel: (503) 325-2233.* **Pier 11**, *foot of 10th and 11th Sts; tel: (503) 325-0279,* has pricey–expensive seafood with Columbia River views. **Ira's**, *915 Commercial St; tel: (503) 338-6192,* has Northwest oysters or salmon for moderate dinners – avoid lunch. The **Labor Temple Café, & Bar**, *934 Duane; tel: (503) 325-0801,* the oldest purpose-built Union Hall in the Pacific Northwest, is a *very* basic cheap eatery, with burgers, hashbrowns with gravy, and a selection of fishermen, labourers and riffraff lending colour. A few blocks and a world apart is **Ricciardi Gallery and Café**, *108 10th St; tel: (503) 325-5450,* an expresso coffee-house with woodblocks, paintings and photographs on display.

Unique among North-west wineries is **Shallon**, *1598 Duane; tel: (503) 325-5978,* daily 1000–1800, with wines like Cran du Lait of cranberries, and Tillamook Cheese Factory whey; lemon and whey combined in Esther's Lemon Meringue Pie; peach or wild blackberry; and the startling Chocolate Orange Pots de Creme liqueur.

Sightseeing

A town at the mouth of the mighty Columbia River was inevitable, though the river bar is infamous among sailors as the 'Graveyard of the Pacific' for the more than 2000 shipwrecks that lie rotting under tremendous tides, shifting sand bars, waves and wind, seemingly coming from all directions at once. On a clear day from the top of 125-ft Astoria Column sitting on 600-ft

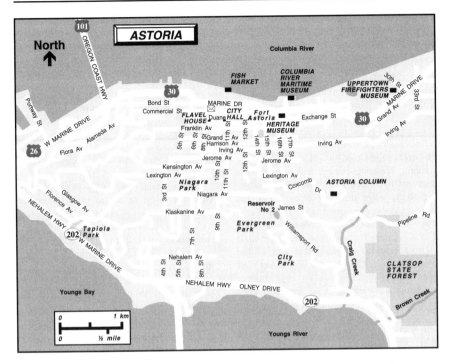

high Coxcomb Hill, 100 miles of the coastline of Oregon and Washington are visible, though Astoria often settles under fogs thick enough to have hidden America's second largest river from explorers like Captain James Cook, British trader Captain John Meares and Captain George Vancouver. Though Spanish explorer Bruno de Hezeta correctly surmised that he had found the mouth of a great river in 1775, it was two centuries before the river was claimed.

American trader Robert Gray sailed the *Columbia Rediva* over the bar in 1792, exchanged nails for salmon and beaver and otter skins with the Pacific Coast's own proficient Native American traders, the Chinook, then sailed for China where he made a golden killing on otter pelt sales. Lt William Broughton immediately sailed Vancouver's ship, the *Chatham*, upriver to chart the region and name several Cascade peaks.

The Lewis and Clark Corps of Discovery spent a few months during Winter 1805–6, a few miles from today's downtown Astoria, at the bare-bones Fort Clatsop stockade

constructed near a calm canoe pull-out on a Columbia River tributary. The Euro-American craving for beaver for fashionable men's hats mandated a trading post settlement at the point of beaver skin collection. American millionaire John Jacob Astor's lieutenants set up shop in **Fort Astoria**, now an unremarkable park at *15th and Exchange Sts,* in 1811. War and territorial disputes with Britain led to the fortress changing hands, ending with nominal American control under the British Hudson's Bay Company. Beaver were harvested almost to extinction, and fashionable silk hats dealt the last blow to a short-lived industry in the 1820s. Fishing at the mouth of a dangerous but species -abundant river was lucrative, as was timber which poured from every hillside like a green river. Scandinavians worked as lumberjacks and fishermen, building Astoria into a wealthy seaport of taverns, shanties, mansions, canneries and brothels. Fishing still drives Astoria's economy; timber exports ceased recently.

The Victorians lure Hollywood directors filming motion pictures like *Goonies,*

Kindergarten Cop and *Free Willy*. An assortment of museums draws cruise boat passengers May–Dec.

The **Columbia River Maritime Museum**, *1792 Marine Dr., Astoria, OR 97103; tel: (503) 325-2323; fax: (503) 325-2331;* open daily except Thanksgiving and Christmas, 0930–1700, adults $5, childr.en 6–18 $2, is a spacious well-lit paean to seafaring amidst the brutal conditions of the Columbia River Bar. Historic engravings of ships, exploration, whaling, lifesaving exhibits and boat artefacts augment the 30 'Life at Sea' photographs of listing ships, water smashing across decks and wives ensconced in live-aboard parlours. Look through the periscopes and conning gear of the *U.S.S. Rasher.* Docked near the museum is another exhibit – a self-guided tour of the retired lightship *Columbia*, the West Coast's last seagoing lighthouse.

Astoria's waterfront is no longer clogged with the salmon canneries which Rudyard Kipling chronicled in *American Notes* from a 20-min guts-and-gore visit in 1889. Commercial fishermen still sort the catch near the over-the-water piers of the *14th*, *12th* and *6th Sts* **Riverfront Park(s)**. The **Fergus McBarendse Lower Columbia River Fish Market**, *80 11th St at the pier; tel: (503) 325-9592,* is open daily. Sea lions lounge on piers at the **East Mooring Basin** marina, *Leif Erickson Blvd at 36th St.*

The **Heritage Museum**, *1618 Exchange St; tel: (503) 325-2203,* open 1000–1700 May–Sept, 1100–1600 Oct–Apr, (adults $5 for the Heritage Museum, Uppertown Firefighters Museum and Flavel House) housed in the 1904 neo-classical city hall building, covers cannery history from 1829 when barrels of salt-cured Chinook salmon were first shipped to Boston, to 1915 when a diminishing fish supply finished cannery activity. Many cannery workers were Chinese, famed for 'fast hands', and the museum has an elaborate Chinese altar from 1904. Another area covers the racially-prejudiced and anti-Semitic white-robed Ku Klux Klan members who influenced elections throughout Oregon in 1922.

Amidst the array of Victorians, the opulent mansion of the first professional Columbia River bar pilot, George Flavel, stands out. **Flavel House Museum**, *441 8th St; tel: (503) 325-2203,* open 1000–1700 May–Sept, 1100–1600 Oct–Apr, shows off the 1885 Queen Anne building and gardens.

Ghost stories haunt the red brick **Uppertown Firefighters Museum**, *2986 Marine Dr.; tel: (503) 325-2203,* open 1000–1700 May–Sept, 1100–1600 Oct–Apr. A horse-drawn, hand-crank 1884 La France wooden ladder tank truck, stars with a collection of fire extinguishers.

Follow scenic route signs to the **Astoria Column**, open sunrise to sunset. Towering over the city from *Coxcomb Hill*, the Astoria Column is a monument to Lewis and Clark's endeavours on behalf of the USA's 19th-century Manifest Destiny doctrine. The painted story flows in an umber, brown and gold mural up the exterior while 167 steps spiral up a circular staircase to the windy landing at the column's peak – and a 360° clear day vista.

Fort Clatsop National Memorial, *Rte # 3, Box 604-FC, Astoria, OR 97103, 5 miles south of Astoria following Bus. Hwy 101 south over the Old Youngs Bay Bridge; tel: (503) 861-2471; fax: (503) 861-2585,* open 0800–1800 mid June–Labor day, 0800–1700 Sept–mid June, is the evocative reconstruction of Lewis and Clark's 1805–6 winter quarters. In summer, living history includes flint-knapping, fire-making and muzzleloader care. A 200-yd stroll through the forest to the Lewis and Clark River canoe landing passes by an extraordinary number of trees and shrubs labelled with the explorers' journal commentary. Native American preparation and use of canoes, clothing, and arrows learned by expedition members is well-explained in the visitor centre with acknowledgement of the unique contributions of Sacajawea, the woman who acted as guide, interpreter and diplomat.

Fort Stevens State Park, *Ridge Rd, Hammond, OR 97121, 10 miles west of Astoria via Hwy 101 and Warrenton Dr.; tel: (503) 861-1671; 605-pitch campsite; tel: (800) 452-5687,* was the military guardian of the Columbia River mouth from the US Civil War through World War II. In June 1942, a Japanese submarine fired 17 shells near the fort, inflicting no damage. Though armament was removed long ago, a self-guided tour covers numerous batteries, bunkers and building foundations. A rose garden graces the entrance to the **Fort Stevens Military Museum**; *tel: (503) 861-2000, 1000–1800 Apr–Nov, 1000–1600 Dec–Mar,* which focuses on the Japanese submarine incident and US Civil War. A cannon is fired during summer Civil War re-enactments. Also in the park are wildlife viewing areas, Trestle Bay windsurfing, lake swimming, nature trails, clamming and the rusty 1906 wreck of the British schooner, the *Peter Iredale,* haunting at low tide. The **Oregon Coast Trail** begins at South Jetty. **Officer's Inn B&B**, *540 Russell Pl., Hammond, OR 97121; tel: (800) 377-2524* or *(503) 861-0884,* is a moderate, elegant converted quarters near the historic areas.

Follow *Ridge Rd* south from Fort Stevens to rejoin Hwy 101, watching for bicycles joining the southward traffic. On the right (west), at the edge of Camp Rilea Military Reservation are the spare hillside gravestones of the **Pioneer Cemetery** next to the white wood **Pioneer Presbyterian Church**.

Oregon State Parks and State Waysides dot the coast to the California border. Most have a parking area near beaches or a panoramic beach view. Elk roam grassy areas, sloughs bloom with lilypads. **Del Ray Beach Wayside**, 13 miles from Astoria, has beach access. **Gearhart** boasts Oregon's oldest golf course, and borders **Seaside.**

SEASIDE

Tourist Information: Seaside Chamber of Commerce, *Hwy 101 at Broadway, PO Box 7, Seaside, OR 97138-0007; tel: (800) 444-6740* or *(503) 738-6391, fax: (503) 738-5732.*

Seaside has ample lodging including *BW, CI* and *HI*. Moderate–expensive **Gilbert Inn Bed & Breakfast**, *341 Beach Dr.; tel: (800) 410-9770* or (503) 738-9770, is an elegant 10-room 1892 Queen Anne Victorian near where Lewis and Clark's men rendered sea salt following the 1805–6 expedition's successful quest to find a route to the Pacific Ocean. The explorers' statue overlooks the beach at the Seaside Turnaround at Broadway and Columbus, centred between North and South Promenades. A

carousel, souvenir shops, arcades and ice-cream parlours compete with hired motorised 3-wheel funcycles, surreys, skates and bicycles. **Seaside Aquarium**, *200 N. Promenade; tel: (503) 738-6211,* has seals to feed. The **Seaside Museum**, *570 Necanium Dr.; tel: (503) 738-7065,* open in summer, has Native American artefacts and old photographs of Oregon's first seaside resort town.

The J.C. Ranch's farmed emus move about their paddock on the right just before Hwy 101 ascends into forest. **Ecola State Park**; *tel: (503) 436-2844,* has a forest preserve with old-growth Sitka spruce, trails, surfing at Indian Beach and views of Haystack Rock and 'Terrible Tilly', Tillamook Rock lighthouse (now a columbarium) from Tillamook Head.

CANNON BEACH

Tourist Information: Cannon Beach Chamber of Commerce, *201 E 2nd St, PO Box 64, Cannon Beach OR, 97110; tel: (503) 436-2623; fax: (503) 436-0910.* Cannon Beach is well set with lodging for visitors who stroll the art galleries and the 7-mile-long beach. On the beach, expensive–pricey, and famed for relaxed posh atmosphere and some of the best 4-course dining on the Oregon Coast, is the **Stephanie Inn**, *2740 S. Pacific, PO Box 219, Cannon Beach, OR 97110; tel: (800) 633-3466* or *(503) 436-2221.* **Haystack Rock Marine Garden**, 236-ft high, is one of the largest volcanic formations amongst **Oregon Islands National Wildlife Refuge**'s 1400 islets and reefs. Spot tufted puffins from Apr–Aug.

Walk to Haystack rock's tidepools from **Tolovana Beach Wayside**. Follow a trail to **Arcadia State Park's** cove. Tidal caves and a waterfall lure hikers at **Hug Point State Park**; provisions are 2 miles south in **Arch Cape**. Just south is **Oswald West State Park**, with one trail through old growth cedar and spruce and others to beaches or up steep trails to **Neahkahnie Mountain** coastal vistas.

Nehalem Bay State Park, *9500 Sandpiper Lane, Nehalem, OR 97131,* is arrayed on a spit south of Bayshore junction just before Hwy 101 turns east at Nehalem to skirt **Nehalem Bay**. Try crabbing or clamming in season, ride a horse, hike a dune, or look for agates or glass floats; there are 291 pitches, 2 yurts and a small airstrip.

Nehalem Bay Area Chamber of Commerce, *13015 Hwy 101, Nehalem, PO Box 238, Wheeler, OR 97147; tel: (503) 368-5100,* has local information. The **Nehalem Bay Winery**, *34965 Hwy 53, Nehalem, OR 97131, 1 mile north-east of Hwy 101; tel: (503) 368-9463,* is open daily for tasting of pinot noir, white Riesling and Bay Blush.

Hwy 101 follows the bayshore back to the ocean and passes several state beaches. **Rockaway Beach Chamber of Commerce**, *103 1st St, PO Box 198, Rockaway Beach, OR 97136; tel: (800) 331-5928 or (503) 355-8108,* has specific information on local shopping, fishing, windsurfing and diving.

Barview guards the mouth of Tillamook Bay. **Garibaldi**'s boat basin is crammed with charter fishing boats. The **Garibaldi Chamber of Commerce**, *202 Garibaldi Ave, PO Box 915, Garibaldi, OR 97118; tel: (503) 322-0301,* has details on fishing, crabbing, clamming, where to buy fresh seafood, restaurants and lodging. Picnic in **Lumberman's Park**, *3rd and American Sts,* by a steam engine and rolling stock.

Lumber was king until a series of ferocious forest fires in 1933, 1939, 1945 and 1951, collectively the Tillamook Burn, created 500 sq miles of the worst timber loss in US history – and one of the best-organised reforestation efforts. Half a century later, the strange aspect of the hills to the east of Highway 101 is eerie. Tillamook, 'land of many waters' to Native Americans, is known for its dairies, cheeses, mink, oysters and holly.

TILLAMOOK

Tourist Information: Tillamook Chamber of Commerce, *3705 Hwy 1 across the parking area from the Tillamook Cheese Factory, Tillamook, OR 97141; tel: (503) 842-7525; fax: (503) 842-7526* has area-wide information; lodging is plentiful including the moderate **Mar Clair Inn**, *11 Main Ave, Tillamook, OR 97141; tel: (800) 331-6857 or (503) 842-7571,* in the centre of town.

Tillamook's cheese industry has inspired tourism for decades in the midst of a bucolic valley of rolling pastures and more bulging cows than citizens. **Tillamook Cheese Factory**, *4175 Hwy 101 N., Tillamook, OR 97141; tel: (503) 815-1325,* open summer 0800–2000, winter 0800–1800, annually produces 40 million pounds of cheddar cheese in a factory, offering self-guided tours above the hygienically-protected production floor, a deli, gift shop and packed double cones of creamy ice cream for $2. Dairy farm tours from the **Tillamook County Creamery Association**, *tel: (503) 815-1300,* mid June–Aug, adults $8, children 4–16 $6, depart from the Tillamook Cheese Factory.

Less theme park atmosphere prevails 1 mile south at **Blue Heron French Cheese Co**, *2001 Blue Heron Dr.; tel: (503) 842-8281, fax: (503) 842-8530,* which produces brie and camembert. Sample Oregon jams and condiments in the well-stocked deli; there is a small charge for tasting a good variety of Oregon wines; gentle barnyard animals reside in an outdoor petting zoo.

In town, the **Tillamook County Pioneer Museum**, *2106 2nd St; tel: (503) 842-4553,* is an old 3-storey courthouse filled with collections of Native American artefacts, Victoriana, and a full size fire lookout station. **Latimer Quilt and Textile Center**, *2105 Wilson River Loop; tel: (503) 842-8622,* open Tues–Sun, has five textile exhibits.

⊻ SIDE TRACK TO THREE CAPES SCENIC LOOP

Thirty-eight miles of driftwood-laced beaches, dunes, lakes, marshes, rocks, estuaries, cliffs and forests are divided between three capes. Two roads return to Hwy 101 from the coast along the route allowing an optional shorter visit to one or two of the cape parks.

From downtown Tillamook, drive west on *3rd St,* the *Netarts Hwy.* Cross the Tillamook River bridge, then veer right onto *Bayocean Road* along the south side of Tillamook Bay. The enclosed bay shelters numerous fishing boats, protected on the west side by the inaccessible Bay Ocean Spit, where 200 species of birds nest.

Continue on *Cape Meares Loop Rd* to the northernmost park, **Cape Meares State Park**. Only 9 miles from Tillamook's pastures and estuaries, the cape's forest-draped promontory has an outstanding view southwest to **Three Arches Rocks National Wildlife Refuge**, a staircase up to lens level at the 38-ft tall **Cape Meares Lighthouse**, a many-limbed Sitka spruce Octopus tree, seabirds and nearby sea lion preserves. South of the park, **Oceanside** has four moderate motels and several ocean-view restaurants. To return to Tillamook, turn east onto the *Netarts Hwy* at *Netarts*.

Follow the scenic loop south on *Whiskey Creek Rd*, past the **Whiskey Creek** [spring Chinook salmon] **Fish Hatchery**, open Dec–Aug. The narrow northward extension of **Cape Lookout State Park**; *tel: (503) 842-4981*, shelters the western side of Netarts Bay. Six miles south of Netarts, the park offers tent and RV pitches and yurts; *tel: (800) 452-5687*. Hike 2½ miles to the tip of 500-ft-high Cape Lookout for clear-weather views of Tillamook Head, 42 miles north, to Cape Foulweather, 39 miles south. To return to Hwy 101, continue south-east on *Cape Lookout Rd*, then continue east on *Sandlake Rd* to *Hemlock*.

Continue to Cape Kiwanda by going right, (south) on *Sandlake Rd*. **Sand Lake** is a recreation area. Pitches are available at the US Forest Service **Sandbeach Campground**, spring–autumn. Hangliders and surfers frequent Haystack Rock, just off-shore from **Cape Kiwanda State Park**. To return to Hwy 101, follow *Old Woods Rd*, just north of the park, to Cloverdale, or follow *Sandlake Rd* through Pacific City, then take *Brooten Rd* to the highway. ◣

TILLAMOOK TO LINCOLN CITY

Two miles south-east of Tillamook, a blimp hangar houses the **Tillamook Naval Air Station Museum**, *6030 Hangar Rd, Tillamook, OR 97141; tel: (503) 842-1130*, open daily, adults $5. One-fifth of a mile long and 15 stories high, the cavernous hangar was built of 2 million board foot of Douglas-fir to accommodate K-class blimps built to escort Allied

merchant vessels during World War II. Operational World War II aircraft, including a MK-8 Spitfire, are on display. Next to the hangar, **Tillamook Air Tours**, *PO Box 605; tel: (503) 842-1942*, operates *Spirit of Tillamook*, a 1942 Stinson Reliant V-77 gull wing, flying over the valley or over the coast during the winter whale watching season.

Dairy farms dot the landscape. Four miles from Tillamook, a rest area on the west (right) side has shaded picnicking by the Trask River. Two miles south, turn left and drive 1½ miles east to **Munson Creek Falls**. The 266-ft waterfall benefits from more than 100 ins of rain annually. Cliff-hugging walkways near the coast's highest fall are buffered by plenty of intensely green foliage or winter icicles.

Stop at **Hemlock**'s well-stocked Bear Creek Artichokes where *Sandlake Rd* (see Three Capes Scenic Loop, left) joins Hwy 101. The fruit stand claims to sell 800 kinds of herbs and offers samples of 30 Oregon jams. Another family sells fanciful wooden butterflies from a yard display. **Hebo Lake**'s lush forests, trails and campsites are several miles west of the **Hebo Ranger District Office**, *Siuslaw National Forest, Hebo, OR 97122; tel: (503) 392-3161*.

Cloverdale-Nestucca Valley Chamber of Commerce, *PO Box 75, Cloverdale, OR 97112; tel: (503) 392-3456*, is 3 miles north of the end of the Three Capes Scenic Loop. **Hudson House Bed & Breakfast**, *37700 Hwy 101 S., Cloverdale OR 97112; tel; (503) 392-3533*, has moderate countryside lodging.

Cross the **Little Nestucca River**, a protected refuge and favoured coho, Chinook and steelhead fishing spot. Pull over at the **Oretown Viewpoint** for views of Kiwanda Beach. The **Neskowin State Beach Wayside**, some distance from the beach, is next to the moderate **Proposal Rock Inn**; *tel: (503) 392-3115*. Hwy 101 ascends into the Siuslaw (pron:. see-ou-slaw) National Forest. Hiking trails west from *Cascade Head Rd* lead to headlands with good views of winter-migrating whales.

Cross the Salmon River. To the east is the Hwy 18 (Salem) junction; drive 3 miles to dine like a pilgrim at the unprepossessing **Otis Café**,

117

Otis Junction; tel: (541) 994-2813, where the faithful wait for the few tables for chowder, cinnamon rolls, omelettes, burgers, strawberry-rhubarb pie, in groaning lumberjack portions.

LINCOLN CITY

Tourist Information: Lincoln City Visitor & Convention Bureau, *801 S.W. Hwy 101, Lincoln City OR 97367; tel: (800) 452-2151 or (541) 994-2408; fax: (541) 994-240,* and the **Lincoln City Chamber of Commerce,** *4039 NW Logan Rd and Hwy 101, PO Box 787; tel: (541) 994-3070,* have information on the city and Lincoln County.

ACCOMMODATION

Lincoln City's 2500 rooms create the largest resort community between San Francisco and Seattle. Lodging includes *BW, KOA,* bed and breakfasts, and the pricey oceanfront views from the **Inn at Spanish Head,** *4009 S.W. Hwy 101 ; tel: (800) 452-8127, (800) 547-5235 (Canada)* or *(541) 996-2161.*

SIGHTSEEING

Lincoln City is a getaway for the urban denizens of Portland and Salem–expect weekend crowds. In Lincoln City, Hwy 101 is a 7.5-mile-long business strip of cloned fast food, lodging, service businesses, and the *SE 12th St* factory outlet stores. Collections of local family artefacts, dolls, and Abraham Lincoln memorabilia fill the **North Lincoln County Historical Museum,** *4907 S.W. Hwy 101; tel: (541) 996-6614.*

Lincoln City's current draw is **Chinook Winds,** *1777 N.W. 44th St; tel: (888) CHI-NOOK,* the Siletz tribal gaming centre heavily advertised in the Northwest as 'a bit of Las Vegas in Lincoln City, Oregon'. Present-day members of the Confederated Tribes of Siletz Indians are descendants of diverse Western Oregon tribespeople who in the 1850s were marched at gunpoint to a coast reservation. Most had to learn to fish, hunt, gather and build with coastal species and seasons; few shared any common language.

Reservation land was repeatedly appropriated by the US government, first for a railroad, then for White settlement. Siletz (inland via Hwy 229) is present-day tribal headquarters; the tribe's coastal enterprises include the Chinook Winds and Convention Center in Lincoln City and the Smokehouse in Depoe Bay (See p. 119).

Agate-hunting and kite flying are Lincoln City beach favourites, but the main attraction is Devil's Lake. The 120-ft-long **D River** claims to be the world's shortest, and connects **Devil's Lake** to the Pacific.

Devil's Lake State Recreation Area; *1452 N.E. 6th St; tel: (541) 994-2002,* includes **West Devil's Lake State Park's** tent and RV pitches; *tel: (800) 452-5687,* and **East Devil's Lake State Park's** picnic area, fishing spots, watersports, windsurfing, boat launch and short nature trail traversing a bog.

Wetlands surrounding the park lure the Oregon Coast's densest population of wintering geese and ducks, including mallards and canvasbacks.

The lake's placid appearance belies its name and legend: Siletz Chief Fleetwood sent canoe-paddling warriors across the lake, only to lose them to giant tentacles thrashing from the lake's depths (actually only 22 ft). Even today, boats tend to avoid moonlit passages across the chill-inducing 3-mile-long lake.

Highway 101 continues south through Nelscott and Taft. Three miles east, the faded red 1914 **Upper Drift Creek Covered Bridge,** Oregon's oldest, is but a shell.

Hwy 101 crosses Drift Creek at the north end of Siletz Bay, and skirts the bay. The south end of Siletz Bay is a wildlife refuge. **Salishan Lodge,** *7760 Hwy 101 N., PO Box 118, Gleneden Beach, OR 97388; tel: (541) 764-2371; fax: (541) 764-3681,* may be the priciest resort on the Oregon Coast. The posh style is California Pebble Beach; an 18-hole golf course and the appropriately pricey **Dining Room at Salishan Lodge;** *tel: (541)764-3635,* draw connoisseurs of both.

Gleneden Beach, Fogarty Creek, and **Boiler Bay State Parks** are excellent bird spotting and (in season) whale watching points. At low tide the boiler of the burned *SS J Marhoffer* is seen amongst Boiler Bay tidepools. Lay-bys overlook well-eroded golden rocks, mini-cliffs above sand pockets.

DEPOE BAY

Tourist Information: Depoe Bay Chamber of Commerce, *630 S.E. Hwy 101, PO Box 21, Depoe Bay, OR 97341; tel: (541) 765-2889,* Mon–Fri 1000-1500, claims to be the 'Whale Watch Capitol of the World', at least during the grey whale migration from Dec–May. Charter boats leave what may be the world's smallest navigable harbour by cruising through a passage in a narrow rock wall. A scenic bridge lets visitors watch boats passing from the safe harbour to open sea. Two blowholes, the 'spouting horns', propel spray 60 ft high.

Find delicious Native American-style fresh or tinned alder-smoked salmon, tuna and sturgeon at the **Siletz Tribal Smokehouse**, *272 Hwy 101 S., PO Box 1004, Depoe Bay; tel: (800) 828-4269* or *(541) 765-2286,* on the site where Siletz tribe member Charlie Depot, who later changed his surname to DePoe, lived. The **Oregon Coast Sports Museum**, *110 N.E. Hwy 101; tel (541) 765-2923,* open summer Thurs–Sun, has Olympic Games' memorabilia dating from 1896.

Picnic at scenic **Rocky Creek State Wayside** near **Cape Foulweather** named by Capt James Cook's reaction to storms he encountered in 1778. From the Cape Foulweather turnout, follow the **Otter Crest Loop** south for 2 miles along the coast to **Otter Rock** for the sensation of being on a cliff balancing above open water.

Walk to the beach at **Devil's Punchbowl State Park**, a sea cave whirling with high tide ocean foam. **Beverly Beach State Park**, *198 N.E. 123 St, Newport OR 97365; tel: (541) 265-9278,* with 279 pitches and yurts; for camping; *tel: (800) 452-5687,* is often crowded with holidaymakers at Beverly and Moolack Beaches. The moderate–expensive **Moolack Shores Motel**, *8835 N. Coast Hwy (101), Newport OR 97365; tel: (541) 265-2326,* has 14 theme rooms (Oregon, Whaling, Aviator), most with waterfront views.

Ninety-three feet up, and 262 ft above the ocean, **Yaquina Head Lighthouse**; *tel: (541) 265-2863,* is Oregon's tallest. Stark and white on the headland, it seems to brood over the

Quarry Cove tidepools below and Yaquina Bay to the south. **Yaquina Head Outstanding Natural Area** also has a stairway to the beach and excellent views of harbor seals. **Agate Beach State Wayside** draws picnickers and agate hunters just north of Newport.

NEWPORT

Tourist Information: Greater Newport Chamber of Commerce, *555 S.W. Coast Hwy, Newport OR 97365-4934; tel: (800) 262-7844* or *(541) 265-8801; fax: (541) 265-5589,* has visitor information.

ACCOMMODATION

Lodging includes *BI, BW, Hd* and *HI,* most along Hwy 101. The moderate–expensive **Sylvia Beach Hotel**, *267 N.W. Cliff, Nye Beach, Newport OR 97365; tel: (541) 265-5428,* is a unique combination of writer's retreat house, bed and breakfast, and beachside mansion. Two women, enamoured of the Shakespeare & Co. bookstore owner who encouraged many writers in Paris in the 1920s and 1930s, asked 20 friends to decorate an historic mansion's bedrooms in the manner of particular writers. The black-walled Edgar Allan Poe room, four-poster draped in red, has an axe blade 'suspended' above the bed as a raven watches. The Jane Austen room, plenty of volumes lying about, is lace and *Emma*-era cheer. Colette, the most popular room, Agatha Christie, and Mark Twain, all oceanfront rooms, have fireplaces and decks. Ernest Hemingway's African theme and Theodore 'Dr. Seuss' Geisel's' rooms are in perfect harmony with the authors. The upstairs library evokes a men's club; the public bookstore on the main floor is well-stocked with the room authors' books and literary gifts.

EATING AND DRINKING

The Sylvia Beach Hotel's **Tables of Content Restaurant**, *267 N.W. Cliff, Newport OR 97365; tel: (541) 265-5428,* serves tasty *prix fixe* family-style dinners. There are fast food and pizza choices along Hwy 101; most seafood restaurants are in the Bayfront District, east of Hwy 101 on the north side of Yaquina Bay.

Mo's Restaurant (separate from Mo's

119

Annex down the street), *622 S.W. Bay Blvd; tel: (541) 265-2979,* is the original of half a dozen chowder and seafood restaurants on the Oregon Coast. The charmless decor at this budget joint is early 1950s amateur oil paintings of harbour scenes. Service is poor, yet the cheap clam chowder is scrumptious. The moderate **Whale's Tale Restaurant**, *452 S.W. Bay Blvd; tel: (541) 265-8660,* includes grilled local Yaquina oysters on the seafood menu. The **Newport Candy Shoppe**, *440 S.W. Bay Blvd; tel: (541) 265-2580,* makes 57 flavours of salt-water taffy.

One of Oregon's best micro-breweries, **Rogue Ales**, began in Newport at the **Rogue Ales Public House**, *748 S.W. Bay Blvd; tel: (541) 265-3188.* A few blocks from the Oregon Coast Aquarium, **Rogue Ales Tasting Room**, *2320 OSU Dr.; tel: (541) 867-3660,* open 1100–1800, offers 9 samples for $4 and sells a diverse line of bottled brews.

SIGHTSEEING

Newport, once known for its canneries and fishing fleet, is now known to the world as the rehabilitation home of **Keiko**, the killer whale star of the film, *Free Willy.* Since he arrived in January, 1996, the orca has had his own 2 million gallon tank at the **Oregon Coast Aquarium**, *2820 S.E. Ferry Slip Rd, Newport OR 97365; tel: (541) 867-3474,* open 0900–1800 Memorial Day weekend–Labor Day weekend, other times 1000–1700; adults $8.50, children 4-13 yrs $4.25, 4-13, under 4 yrs free. Keiko can be seen from above, or through tankside view windows. While Keiko is one of Oregon's top three attractions, the aquarium's other creatures are splendid. Coastal jellies pulse and glide in a cylindrical tank; baby skates have faces like human babies; harbor seals and sea lions swim so close to children on the other side of a tank's glass window that startled parents tend to snatch the wee ones away. Close by, the **Mark O Hatfield Marine Science Center**, *2030 S. Marine Dr.; tel: (541) 867-0026,* has interactive displays of Oregon State University's coastal research.

Some cannery activity continues in the Bayfront area, now adorned with waterfront-theme murals. A barking colony of sea lions has

taken up residence on the piers near restaurants, pubs and art galleries. Three attractions share an address: *250 S.W. Bay Blvd, Newport OR 97365; tel: (541) 265-2206,* adults $5.75, 5-11 years $3 for each attraction or all three for $14.50, ($8.50 children). Walk through shell displays in **Undersea Gardens'** crowded gift shop to the lower level, in reality the below-deck area of a boat, with glass windows, Yaquina Bay fish and giant Pacific octopus feedings. **Ripley's Believe It or Not** and **The Wax Works** follow the style of others of their chains.

Newport's lighthouse is a cheerful red-roofed white building west of the Bayfront District above the **Yaquina Bay State Recreation Area**. The **Yaquina Bay Lighthouse**, *846 S.W. Government St; tel: (541) 265-5679,* open 1200–1700 summer, 1200–1600 winter weekends, is a historical museum and gift shop. The free **Lincoln County Historical Society Log Cabin Museum** and Victorian-era open 1000–1700 Tues–Sun June–Sept, 1100-1600 May–Oct, **Burrows House**, *545 S.W. 9th St; tel: (541) 265-7509,* cover local history, from pioneers, logging, fishing and the Siletz tribe in the log cabin with furnishings in the mansion.

The Yaquina Bay Bridge is a lovely set of curved green loops. Two miles south of the bridge, just beyond the exit to the Oregon Coast Aquarium, and Rogue Ales Tasting Room, is the **Mike Miller Park Educational Trail** walk through a Sitka spruce forest and wetlands. **South Beach State Park**, *5580 S. Coast Hwy (101), South Beach, OR 97366; tel: (541) 867-4715; for camping; tel: (800) 452-5687,* has 254 pitches, yurts, picnic areas and hiking.

A series of **state parks** borders the beach for 12 miles southward: **Lost Creek**, **Ona Beach**, **Seal Rock** and **Driftwood Beach**. The small town of **Seal Rock** has antique stores, wooden whirligigs and wooden carvings.

On the south side of the **Alsea Bay Bridge** is the **Alsea Bay Bridge Interpretative Center** and the **Waldport Chamber of Commerce and Visitors Center**, *620 N.W. Spring St (Hwy 101), Waldport, OR 97394; tel: (541) 563-2133.* The Interpretative Center

---

Oregon Lighthouses

The Pacific Northwest has been collecting shipwrecks for as long as people have sailed the coast. Early inhabitants built bonfires on prominent headlands to warn mariners; later arrivals created a string of lighthouses with beacons visible more than 20 miles out to sea.

The heyday of lighthouse construction was the 1840–1890s, an era when coastal towns were isolated and lighthouses even more so. The job of lightkeeper was no picnic when the only access might be on foot at low tide or by rowboat through fierce waves. Lightkeepers tended their lights around the clock: polishing lenses up to 9-ft across; winding clockwork mechanisms that controlled the sweep of the beacon every 4 hrs; ensuring that the light, be it an oil lamp or (in later years) an electric bulb, was never extinguished; repairing the damage the inevitably followed every storm that swept in from the Pacific Ocean.

Hwy 101 now provides easy access to Oregon's historic lighthouses, stretching from the Columbia River south to Cape Blanco, just north of Port Orford. Nine of the original dozen survive: Tilamook Rock; Cape Meares; Yaquina Head; Yaquina Bay; Heceta Head; Umpqua River; Cape Arago; Coquille River and Cape Blanco. The classic structures have been named to the National Register of Historic Places; most are in State Parks and open to the public at least in summer.

Several lighthouses are still in service, though lightkeepers were replaced by automated equipment in the 1960s. Yaquina Head, near Newport, is the tallest lighthouse at 93 ft; the shortest is Cape Meares, near Tillamook, 38 ft tall.

The most scenic lighthouse, Heceta Head, 12 miles north of Florence, has become a popular bed and breakfast. Umpqua River towers impressively above sand dunes south of Reedsport. Coquille River, north of Bandon, is a year-round park interpretive centre. Yaquina Bay, near Newport, is said to be haunted. Cape Blanco sits atop the westernmost point in the state overlooking a highly rated wildlife viewing area. Best guide to the nine lighthouses is Oregon Parks and Recreation Department's free *Oregon Coast Lighthouses* brochure.

121

---

chronicles north-central coastal development, transportation, Native American settlement, pioneer triumphs and the history of Conde B McCullough's innovative bridge engineering. Waldport is a centre for clamming and Dungeness crab; the Alsea River is famed for salmon and cutthroat angling. The **Siuslaw National Forest Waldport Ranger Station**; *tel: (541) 563-3211,* has upriver wilderness and hiking information.

Whitened driftwood covers long, flat beaches between Waldport and Yachats. **Patterson State Park** is day use; popular **Beachside State Park** and the US Forest Service's **Tillicum Beach Park** have camp pitches.

YACHATS

Tourist Information: Yachats Area

Chamber of Commerce, *441 Hwy 101, PO Box 728, Yachats, OR 97498; tel: (541) 547-3530,* has information on local attractions, lodging, bed and breakfasts and dining.

Motels line the road near **Smelt Sands State Park**. Silver sea smelt, resembling sardines, mate in Yachats' coves from Apr–Oct, and are scooped up by fishermen using triangular nets. Powerful winter storms, generally Dec–Feb, are touted as a reason to visit this prosperous town, named by Chinook peoples, 'dark waters at the foot of a mountain'. Yachats' (pron: yah-hots) indoor attraction is the **Little Log Church**, *328 W. 3rd St; tel: (541) 547-3976,* now a museum with Native American artefacts.

Yachats' rock-lined beach gives way to Hwy 101's twists and turns as the road rapidly rises toward 803-ft- high **Cape Perpetua.** No where else on the Oregon and Washington

Coast does the water meet the land with such spectacular violence. From the first **Cape Perpetua** parking area, there's a short, tree-lined path down to the **Devil's Churn.** Wave after mint-green froth-churned 20-ft wave hurtles at top speed towards a deep basaltic crevice. The impact is explosive, startling sea gulls listing almost horizontal with the force of wind on waves. Despite the waves' hypnotic effect, never turn your back on a wave!

On the east side of Hwy 101 from the **Marine Gardens Ocean Shore Preserve**, follow the autotour sign two miles up a road to the **Cape Perpetua Viewpoint**. The thickly-forested quarter-mile **Whispering Spruce Loop Trail** over-looks the coast's long lines of waves. For good winter whale-spotting, peer through openings in a stone hut built as a World War II observation post.

The **Cape Perpetua Visitors Center**, *Siuslaw National Forest, 2400 Hwy 101 S., Yachats, OR, 97498; tel: (541) 547-3289*, just south of the Marine Gardens tidepools, has information on hiking trails, camping, geology, whalewatching, wildflowers, mushrooms, the resident endangered populations of spotted owls and marbled murrelets.

Pause at the **Captain Cook's Chasm** lay-by for another water-wallops-land spectacle. Watch for elk for the next 10 miles while driving Hwy 101's rocky escarpments to Heceta Head Lighthouse. State parks and waysides abound, most offering only beach access and an occasional picnic table.

Pull over at **Strawberry Hill State Park** for an overlook spanning beaches to the north and south, sea lions and an occasional grey whale spouting offshore. Mussels cling to **Bob Creek**'s rocks. The US Forest Service has 16 sheltered pitches at **Rock Creek Campground**; **Carl G Washburne State Park** has pitches for RVs, tents, and hiker and bikers. Drive through a short tunnel and cross the Cape Creek Bridge.

Heceta Head Lighthouse State Scenic Viewpoint; *tel: (541) 997-3641*, 1200-1700 Mar–Oct, has information on tours Nov–Feb. Mist and dramatic rocks below lend the lighthouse lonely dignity. Heceta (pron:

heh-see-tuh) is named after Bruno de Hezeta, the Portugese captain who discover the Columbia River's entrance for Spain.

The path from the **Devil's Elbow Beach** parking area to the lighthouse takes 20 mins. The 56-ft tower, 205 ft above sea level, flashes warnings to ships 20 miles out. A short walk from the lightstation, the assistant lightkeeper's house is a bed and breakfast: **Heceta House**, *US Forest Service, Heceta Head Lightstation, PO Box 400, Waldport, OR 97394; tel: (541) 563-3211 or (541) 547-3696*, has three moderate refurbished rooms, enhanced by an eight-course breakfast.

For the classic photograph of Heceta Lighthouse on Heceta Head, stop at one of the Hwy 101 lay-bys just north of the Sea Lion Caves. The 1500-ft-long **Sea Lion Caves**, *91560 Hwy 101, Florence, OR 97439; tel: (541) 547-3111*, $6 adults, $4 children, naturally formed by volcanic flow, are reached via an elevator. Upon exiting to one of Oregon's classic attractions, the barking of the large colony of Steller sea lions is deafening, the smell equally overwhelming. Steller sea lions can be viewed free with binoculars or the eye at other open spots along the coast, most notably at Cape Arago (see p. 126).

Pull over one mile south to look at the long shoreline with lines of silvery waves framing Florence below. There are 22 pitches at **Alder Lake Campground** and lake swimming. Boats cruise **Sutton Lake. Darlingtonia Botanical Gardens**, a state wayside, has a boardwalk out to the bog which nurtures hundreds of *Darlingtonia californica*, the cobra lily or pitcher plant which attracts insects by the sickly-sweet odour emanating from its snake-like head. Just south,

Sutton Recreation Area offers camping facilities. Stop at **Spider Web Ranch**, *4465 Hwy 101; tel: (541) 997-2242*, to see a pricey shop where real webs decorate clock faces and picture frames.

FLORENCE

Tourist Information: Florence Area Chamber of Commerce, *270 Hwy 101, PO Box 26000, Florence, OR 97439; tel: (541) 997-3128; fax: (541) 997-4101*.

ACCOMMODATION AND FOOD

Chains include *BW* and *Hd*, but the largest lodging on the beach is the moderate–pricey **Driftwood Shores**, *88416 First Ave, Florence, OR 97439; tel: (541) 997-8263 or (800) 824-8774.* **Edwin K Bed & Breakfast**, *1155 Bay St, PO Box 2687; tel: (800) 833-9465 or (541) 997-8360,* in Old Town, has six elegant and expensive view rooms.

Most of the non-fast food eateries are in or near Old Town Florence, near the Siuslaw River. The cheap–budget **Oregon Coast Bakery and Coffee Café**, *327 Laurel St; tel: (541) 902-8901,* has good coffee, mouth-watering pastries, a lunch menu and local art on the walls of a cosy reading room. **Traveler's Cove**, *1362 Bay St; tel: (541) 997-6845,* has tables perched over the river, and budget–moderate meals. A moderate **Mo's Restaurant**, *1463 Bay St; tel: (541) 997-2185,* serves the chain's clam chowder and seafood. The moderate–pricey **International C-Food Market**, *1498 Bay St; tel: (541) 997-9646,* has Florence's largest fresh seafood menu.

SIGHTSEEING

At the centre of the Oregon Coast, Florence, known for its spring rhododendrons, functions as a hub for north-south traffic, and those accessing the coast via Hwy 126 (see p. 171). The Oregon Dunes National Recreation Area fills most of the Florence area's coast. The town is on the east side of the Siuslaw River. A popular 5-mile scenic drive begins near Old Town at Hwy 101 and *Rhododendron Dr.*, and continues north for 4.5 miles, then heads west (left) on Heceta Beach Rd.

The **Dolly Wares Doll Museum**, *Hwy 101 and 36th St; tel: (541) 997-3391,* open Tues–Sun 1000–1700, adults $5, children 5–12 years $3, displays 2500 dolls.

Explore **Old Town Florence** with a Merchants of Old Town map from the Chamber of Commerce. The **Fly Fishing Museum**, *280 Nopal St; tel: (541) 997-6349,* open 1000-1700, has a fine display of fish lures. Old Town has restaurants, gift shops like **Incredible & Edible Oregon**, *1350 Bay St; tel: (541) 997-7018,* art galleries, artisan-crafted

women's natural fibre clothing at **Bonjour!**, *1336 Bay St; tel (541) 997-8194,* and a cheerful modern gazebo giving way to a riverside viewing pier. *Westward Ho!; tel: (541) 997-9691,* a sternwheeler, leaves from Old Town to explore the river.

After crossing the graceful Siuslaw River Bridge, Hwy 101 enters the surreal country of the **Oregon Dunes National Recreation Area.**

Tourist Information: Oregon Dunes National Recreation Area, *Siuslaw National Forest, 855 Highway Ave, Reedsport OR 97467; tel: (541) 271-3611,* vehicle entry charged, has a visitor centre, open Sat–Thurs 0800–1630 Fri 0800–1800 Memorial Day–Sept 30, Mon–Fri 0800–1630 Oct 1–Memorial Day. Ask for *Sand Tracks*, a newspaper with current Dunes information, and brochures covering geology, hiking trails, camping, plants, bird watching, digging for Eastern soft shell clams and an off-highway vehicle guide. Book well in advance for camping; *tel: (800) 280-2267.*

Mixed use of public lands was never so obvious. Major sections of the 41-mile-long Oregon Dunes are open to use of vehicles, particularly OHV (off highway vehicles). Non-destructive sightseeing on paved roads is possible by driving the *South Jetty Dune & Beach Access Rd* (Siuslaw River) to a favourite wind-surfer launch site; *Siltcoos Beach Access Rd;* to the Oregon Dunes Overlook; *Umpqua Beach Parking Lots;* or stop at the *Sandtrack Picnic Area.*

Avoid hiking in OHV areas for safety. Several operators have dune buggy (an open-air lorry) tours and hire one–four person smaller buggies. Though permitted by Forest Service use regulations, the vehicles displace sand, upset small animals and bird habitat, rip up stabilising grasses, are noisy and render hideous the naturally beautiful dune formations. Unfortunately, most areas seen from Hwy 101 are depredated dunes.

The vehicle-prohibited areas are for hiking, walking, horse riding and photography. In places, dunes up to 500 ft tall stretch from the ocean beach to several miles inland, with forests of conifers and sea grasses and wetlands for punctuation. Fog may hide the coastal dunes from hikers, yet skies may be blue above. Wind

123

rearranges the grains of sand, mostly lightweight quartz and feldspar, into constantly-changing patterns. Be cautious hiking in winter when standing water creates quicksand between dunes. For excellent dune hiking, park at the **Eel Creek Campground** (Umpqua Dunes area) and walk up a ¼ path to the dunes. Hiking trails wander towards the beach; from dune ridges, the sands glide elegantly into shifting rows. Hiking trails in the **Siltcoos River** area or on **Horsfall Dunes** are also near camping.

Just south of *South Jetty Rd*, the **Siuslaw Pioneer Museum**, *85294 Hwy 101 S.; tel (541) 997-7884*, is open 1000–1600 Jan–Nov, Tues–Sun, with Native American and settler household artefacts. Though abutting the Dunes on the west side, **Jessie M Honeyman State Park**; *tel: (541) 997-3641*, with numerous camp pitches; *tel: (800) 452-5687*, near **Cleawox** and **Woahink Lakes**, gives little hint of sand or ocean. Evergreens hug the lakesides where swimming, boating and fishing are favourite pastimes.

Hwy 101 passes **Dunes City**; **Siltcoos Lake** is east; the **Siltcoos River** dune hiking is west. The **Oregon Dunes Overlook** is south of **Carter Lake Campground**. The Tahkenitch area has a trailhead, a campsite and angling on the lake. **Gardiner**, proud of its historic white homes near the Umpqua River is blighted by foul fumes emitted from the International Paper Company plant. Cross the Umpqua River bridge to Reedsport.

REEDSPORT

Tourist Information: Lower Umpqua, Reedsport/Winchester Bay Chamber of Commerce, *PO Box 11, Reedsport, OR 97467; tel: (541) 271-3495* or *(800) 247-2155*, has local lodging, dining and activities information. **Oregon Dunes National Recreation Area Visitor Center**, *Siuslaw National Forest, 855 Highway Ave, Reedsport OR 97467; tel: (541) 271-3611*, is open Sat–Thurs 0800–1630 Fri 0800–1800 Memorial Day–Sept, Mon–Fri 0800–1630 Oct 1–Memorial Day. In-town lodging includes *BW*; the Dunes have numerous campsites.

The **Umpqua Discovery Center**, *409 Riverfront Way, Reedsport OR 97467; tel: (541)*

271-4816, covers local history. Three miles east of Hwy 101 via SR 38 is the 3-mile long **Dean Creek Elk Viewing Area**; *US Dep't of the Interior, Bureau of Land Management, Coos Bay District, 1300 Airport Lane, North Bend, OR 97459; tel: (541) 756-0100*. The combined wetland, woodland and pasture is a lush home for a permanent herd of 100 Roosevelt Elk, sometimes visible from the Hinsdale Interpretative Center kiosk.

Three miles south on Hwy 101 and turn right onto *Salmon Harbor Dr*. The **Salmon Harbor Belle Bed & Breakfast**, *PO Box 1208, Winchester Bay, OR 97467; tel: (800) 348-1922* or *(541) 271-1137*, is a refurbished 6-bedroom sternwheel paddleboat. Expensive.

Salmon Harbor Dr. veers south; almost half a mile later, take the left-hand uphill road, *Umpqua Lighthouse Rd* (signs are gone), to the **Coastal Visitors Center** and the operational **Umpqua Lighthouse**; *tel: (541) 271-4631*, open May–Sept. Directly opposite, the **Umpqua River Whale Watching Station** overlooks the sandy bar framing the river's mouth. **Umpqua Lighthouse State Park** has picnic facilities and camping; *tel: (800) 452-5687* to book pitches.

Winchester Bay Wayfinding Point on Hwy 101 has a panoramic Pacific Ocean view. The Oregon Dunes NRA continues on the west side of Hwy 101. Base activities and camping at **William M. Tugman State Park**; *tel: (800) 452-5687*; or **North Eel Creek Campground**, **Spinreel Campground**, or the three camping areas at **Horsfall Dunes (Horsfall** for OHVs, **Bluebill**, or **Wild Mare Horse Camp)**; *tel: (800) 280-2267*.

Leave the Oregon Dunes NRA and cross McCullough Memorial Bridge to North Bend and the **Bay Cities**. **North Bend** and its contiguous neighbour, **Coos Bay**, offer lodging and services. **Tourist Information: Bay Area Chamber of Commerce and Visitor Information Center**; *50 E. Central, PO Box 210, Coos Bay, OR 97420; tel: (800) 824-8486* or *(541) 269-0215; fax: (541) 269-2861*, open Mon–Fri 0830–1900 Sat 1000–1600 Sun 1100–1600 summer; Mon–Fri 0900–1700 Sat 1000–1600 winter, has regional information on attractions, lodging, dining and services.

ACCOMMODATION AND FOOD

Chains include *BW, M6,* and *RL* in Coos Bay. North Bend's largest lodging is centrally-located, moderate **Pony Village Motor Lodge**, *Virginia Ave, North Bend, OR 97459; tel: (541) 756-3191; fax:(541) 756-5818.* Among the area's pleasant bed and breakfasts is the quiet, budget **2310 Lombard B & B**, *2310 Lombard St, North Bend, OR 97459; tel: (541) 756-3857.* RV parks provide most Charleston area lodging.

The Bay Area has plenty of fast food and restaurants. Seafood abounds at Charleston's fishing harbour. The modest **Basin Café**, *4555 Kingfisher Dr., Charleston; tel: (541) 888-5227,* serves delicious budget meals like grilled ling-cod fillet, salad, potatoes and vegetables for half the price usually found on the coast. **Portside Restaurant and Lounge**, *8001 Kingfisher Rd; tel: (541) 888-5544,* has live crab or lobster, and karaoke. The **Timber Inn Restaurant and Lounge**, *1001 N. Bayshore Dr., Coos Bay; tel: (541) 267-4622,* boasts lumberjack breakfasts and live music Wed–Sat. Fishermen like **Carolyn's Breakfast Barn**, *8062 Cape Arago Hwy, Charleston; tel: (541) 888-4512.*

NORTH BEND SIGHTSEEING

Tourist Information: North Bend Information Center, *1380 Sherman, North Bend, OR 97459; tel: (541) 756-4613; fax: (541) 756-8527.* For local history and a steam locomotive engine, hie to the **Coos County Historical Society Museum**, *1220 Sherman Ave (Simpson Park); tel: (541) 756-6320,* open Tues–Sat 1000–1600. Native Americans operate slots and gaming at **The Mill Casino,** *3201 Tremont (Hwy 101); tel: (800) 953-4800;* for events and concerts, *tel: (541) 756-8800.* North Bend's **Pony Village Mall**, *Virginia Ave,* has over 100 stores, shops and restaurants.

COOS BAY SIGHTSEEING

The Bay Area Chamber of Commerce has a self-guided walking tour of the old-fashioned but well-preserved downtown. Coos Bay's waterfront east of downtown is filled with big seagoing ships and wood chips, testimony to Coos Bay's long-standing claim to be the world's largest lumber port, a port through which much of the lumber to build San Francisco flowed. The covered **Boardwalk**, *Bayshore* (Hwy 101, N. direction) along the riverfront has interpretative signs on local timber history and the many tree species processed through the port. The **Marshfield Sun Printing Museum**, *1049 N. Front St (Hwy 101); tel: (541) 756-6418,* open Memorial Day–Labor Day, Tues–Sat 1300–1600, displays artefacts from 1891-1944 when the local paper was published by hand. The **Coos Art Museum**, *235 Anderson Ave; tel: (541) 267-3901,* presents varied art exhibits. Myrtlewood logs are milled, then crafted into household items like bowls and candlesticks at the **Oregon Connection**, *1125 S. 1st St; tel: (800) 255-5318* or *(541) 267-7804.* The Bay Area Chamber of Commerce has information on professional forester-guided summer tours through a local forest.

 SIDE TRACK TO CHARLESTON

This scenic loop leaves Hwy 101 in North Bend to access the coast, an ecologically rich slough, a magnificent sunset spot, sea lions and a formal flower garden before heading east on a country road to Millington. To see all of the Hwy 101 route, backtrack north on Hwy 101 to North Bend, then go south through North Bend and Coos Bay.

From Hwy 101 in North Bend, turn right onto *Virginia Ave,* the *Cape Arago Hwy.* Turn left on Broadway, then right on *Newmark Ave,* following it to the west arm of Coos Bay. Go left on *Empire Blvd,* still the *Cape Arago Hwy,* to Charleston. Cross the South Slough; the Charleston Boat Basin is on the right (west). Continue south-west to Sunset Bay, Shore Acres and Cape Arago State Parks. Return, and cross South Slough. Turn right at *McLain-Libby Dr.,* then go right on *Shinglehouse Slough Rd* to join Hwy 101 south of Millington.

CHARLESTON

Tourist Information: Charleston Visitors Center, *north-east of the South*

Slough Bridge, PO Box 5735, Charleston, OR 97420; tel: (541) 888-2311; or (800) 824-8486; fax: (541) 269-2861; open May–Sept.

Commercial fishing and pleasure boats fill Charleston's marina while expert windsurfers skim the harbour. Local residents rely upon Charleston restaurants for excellent seafood. The **Oregon Institute of Marine Biology**, *4619 Boat Basin Dr.; tel: (541) 888-2581,* is a good spot to learn about local fish species.

South Slough National Estuarine Research Reserve, *4 miles south of Charleston on Seven Devils Rd, PO Box 5417, Charleston, OR 97420; tel: (541) 888-5558,* is open daily June–Aug, Mon–Fri Sept–May 0830–1630. South Slough, a 19,000-acre watershed where fresh water meets salt water, is one of the most pristine estuaries on the planet though the drive up *Seven Devils Rd* is marred by numerous clearcuts to the west. South Slough's paths, from a quarter-mile loop path near the Visitors Center to a long descent to the sea-level slough, are surrounded by natural, wild vegetation. Upland forests give way to wetlands, saltmarshes, tideflats and open water, with habitat for creatures as varied as bald eagles, blue herons, bobcats, bears, shrimp and worms. Plan a day to canoe the South Slough for a close encounter with tides and wildlife. Return to Cape Arago Hwy.

NORTH BEND TO BANDON

Sunset Beach State Park cove is a perfect place to watch a sunset sheltered by rocky cliffs, to surf, scuba dive, or to watch mists rise off the water. Legend holds that fog hid pirate smuggling. **Cape Arago Lighthouse**, closed to the public, is visible only from a trail from **Sunset Beach State Park**; *tel: (541) 888-4902.* The park's east side has camping; *tel: (800) 452-5687.*

Shore Acres State Park; *tel: (541) 888-3732,* open daily 0800–dusk, $3 per car, is one mile south. Lumber magnate Louis B Simpson, North Bend's founder, laid out formal gardens around his mansion almost a century ago. An enclosed shoreline observatory has replaced his home's crumbling ruins, and sea

lions bark lustily from perches on rocks pocked like Swiss cheese. The Japanese Garden surrounding a lilypond, a rose garden, a begonia greenhouse and European-style formal gardens with a Garden House remain. March daffodils are followed by tulips in Apr, rhododendrons and azaleas in May, annuals, perennials, and roses, dahlias from Aug–Oct, and a glittering display of Dec holiday lights.

Cape Arago State Park, 1½ miles south at the end of the *Cape Arago Hwy*, is a prime spot for watching harbor seals, elephant seals and Steller sea lions ensconced offshore on Simpson Reef and Shell Island, part of the **Oregon Islands National Wildlife Refuge.** Black oystercatchers and pelagic cormorants add cries to the din. Gray whales swim past Dec–June, and a few youngsters stay to cavort in the area during summer.

Highway 101 swoops inland through forest for 20 miles. There's a cranberry bog viewpoint at *Randolph Rd.* Yurts and camp pitches are near **Bullards Beach State Park** entrance; *tel: (541) 347-2209;* for camping, *tel: (800) 452-5687,* on the north side of the Coquille River. Once in the park, drive 3 miles past the boat ramp and horse camp south to the **Coquille River Lighthouse**; *tel: (541) 347-2209* for tours. **Bandon Marsh National Wildlife Refuge** straddles the river. Hwy 101 veers west in **Bandon.**

BANDON

Tourist Information: Bandon-by-the-Sea Chamber of Commerce, *300 SE 2nd St, PO Box 1515, Bandon, OR 97411; tel: (541) 347-9616,* has information on Old Town, the *Scenic Beach Loop Dr.,* lodging and dining. Ask for directions to the **Coquille River** and **Driftwood Museums.** From Nov–Apr, the **Bandon Storm-Watchers**, *Box 1693, Bandon, OR 97411; tel: (541) 347-2779,* organise natural history programs around Bandon's spectacular storms.

Bandon has six moderate–expensive motels and a bed and breakfast on Scenic *Beach Loop Dr.,* several motels along Hwy 101, and HI. Moderate **Andrea's Old Town Café,** *160 Baltimore Ave; tel: (541) 347-3022,* with lamb dishes and home-made bread, is the best.

Old Town Bandon's gift shops and restaurants are on the south side of the Coquille River. Thirty million pounds of cranberries are grown and harvested in Oct near Bandon, Oregon's 'Cranberry Capital.' Cranberries, tourism, artisans and cheese support the economy. Watch cheddar cheese being made into half-pound chunks through a window before sampling at the **Bandon Cheese Factory**, *680 E. 2nd St (Hwy 101); tel: (800) 548-8961 or (541) 347-2456.*

South Jetty County Park has a fine view of the Coquille River Lighthouse across the river. Take *Scenic Beach Loop Dr.* south for dramatic rock formations. Beaches are favoured by agate and jasper hunters. Off **Coquille Point**, tufted puffins, Western gulls and Brandt's cormorants are spotted on **Elephant Rock**. Picnic at **Bandon State Park**.

Though no tours are offered, the large Ocean Spray Cranberry processing plant is a landmark on Hwy 101. **West Coast Game Park**, *7 miles south of Bandon on Hwy 101; tel: (541) 347-3106*, adults $6.50, children $4-5.25, has 450 animals, and some walk-through encounter areas.

South of Langlois, windsurfers go west on the loop road to **Floras Lake** for mild 'beginner' winds. There are pastures and rolling hills to the east and sheep around **Sixes**.

Go west on the Cape Blanco Hwy to **Cape Blanco State Park**; *tel: (541) 332-6774; for camping; tel: (800) 452-5687.* The **Hughes House**, open May–Sept, is a Victorian on a bluff overlooking the Sixes River. Runners and hikers enjoy the park's extensive trail system, but the jewel, 10 miles from Hwy 101, is its **Cape Blanco Lighthouse**, open Thurs–Mon 1000–1530 May–Oct. Historic photos line the ground floor walls; tours proceed into the lightkeeper's workroom, then climb 64 steps to the light, Oregon's oldest.

PORT ORFORD

Tourist Information: Port Orford Chamber of Commerce, *Battle Rock Park parking lot, PO Box 637, Port Orford OR 97465; tel: (541) 332-8055; fax: (541) 332-656,* has information on the handful of motels and a bed

and breakfast, the port and area recreation. George Vancouver named the point after George Walpole, third Earl of Orford. Port Orford claims to be the oldest townsite on the Oregon coast, and may be the westernmost incorporated city in the USA. An annual average of 108 ins of rain make it Oregon's rainiest town.

Follow the arrow painted on the pavement to **Port Orford Viewpoint** west of downtown to overlook the deepwater port where boats are routinely hoisted out of the water and stored against buffeting by southerly winter storms. Autos, but not RVs, may drive up *Coast Guard Rd* past the flower-festooned **Port Orford Heads State Park** ranger's residence and other buildings to a small parking area. Take the short loop path through forest to a breathtaking southward view of the rocks arrayed offshore. Deer wander freely, squirrels chirp and dance on tree limbs and bells toll in the distance.

Battle Rock Wayside along Hwy 101 marks an 1851 conflict. Intending to settle, a Capt Kirkpatrick brought a party ashore, and trained a cannon inland from the spot. When friendly Native Americans stood in front of the weapon, he fired at close range, killing natives. A fortnight later, Kirkpatrick having failed to return as promised to pick up the settlement party, the Native Americans attacked but their chief was killed.

Watch for wind gusts six miles south on Hwy 101 at **Humbug Mountain State Park**, *tel: (541) 332-6774; for camping; tel: (800) 452-5687.* Canyon walls form a narrow defile by the campsite entrance, made even more spectacular in maples' and alders' golden fall colours. A 3-mile trail goes to the top of 1756-ft Humbug Mountain for coastal views and seasonal whale spotting. Hwy 101 turns inland, a winding section best driven at 30 mph. It's impossible to miss the huge, painted dinosaur statue marking **Prehistoric Gardens**, *36848 Hwy 101 S., Port Orford; tel: (541) 332-4463,* where cheerful-looking statues look like rainforest dino heaven.

GOLD BEACH

Tourist Information: Gold Beach

127

Chamber of Commerce Visitors Center, *29279 Ellensburg Ave (Hwy 101), # 3, Gold Beach, OR 97444; tel: (800) 525-2334 or (541) 247-7526; fax: (541) 247-0188*, open Mon–Fri 0800–1700 Sat-Sun 0900–1600 Memorial Day–Labor Day, Mon–Fri 0800–1700 Labor Day–Memorial Day. The Chamber of Commerce shares offices with the **Siskiyou National Forest**, *Gold Beach Ranger District, 1225 S. Ellensburg (Hwy 101), Gold Beach OR 97444; tel (541) 247-3600*, which has information on forest drives and hiking trails.

ACCOMMODATION AND FOOD

The Chamber of Commerce and **Jerry's Rogue Jets**; *tel: (800) 451-3645 or (541) 247-4571; fax: (541) 247-7601*, have lists of lodges, motels, Bed and Breakfasts and RV parks. The moderate **Inn at Gold Beach**, *1435 S. Ellensburg (Hwy 101); tel: (800) 503-0833 or (541) 247-6606* is quiet and comfortable. There is a BW. **Tu Tu' Tun Lodge**, *96550 N. Bank Rogue, Gold Beach OR 97444; tel: (541) 247-6664; fax: (541) 247-0672*, is an expensive-pricey modern wooden inn on the Rogue River, open May–Oct. Its *prix fixe* dinners are pricey, served family-style.

SIGHTSEEING

Black sand laced with gold lured 19th-century miners. At the Rogue River's mouth, Gold Beach now serves as a stopover for those going up or down the Rogue, salmon and steelhead fishermen, or for visitors pausing before driving by the Samuel H. Boardman State Park's spectacular scenery.

The largest of four tour operators, **Jerry's Rogue Jets**; *Box 1011, Gold Beach, OR 97444; tel: (800) 451-3645 or (541) 247-4571; fax: (541) 247-7601*, run trips up the Rogue River May–Oct with a choice of 64-, 80-, or 104-mile round trips. The 80- and 104-mile trips navigate a series of rapids.

Jerry's Rogue River Museum & Gift Shop has photographs of early river runs hauling freight and passengers. **Rogue River Mailboats**, *PO Box 1165; tel: (800) 458-3511 or (541) 247-7033*, hauls both post and passengers. For more local history, June–Sept Tues–Sat, there's the **Curry County**

Historical Museum, *920 S. Ellensburg (Hwy 101); tel: (541) 247-6113*.

On a clear day, **Cape Sebastian State Park** south parking area has a clear view south to Arch Rocks and the curving coves and astounding cliffs and rocks of Boardman State Park. Spring wildflowers carpet the cape, while tidepools below draw clam diggers. A few miles east of **Pistol River State Park**'s sand dunes and windsurfers is **Hawk's Rest Ranch Stables and Trail Rides**, *PO Box 6048, Pistol River, OR 97444; tel/fax: (541) 247-6423*, which conduct beach or ranch horserides.

The eight miles of coastline which comprise **Samuel H Boardman State Park** are stunning, each pull-out and turn offering a different aspect of towering stacks, dune grasses, wildflowers, arches, natural bridges, sea-bleached driftwood, shore birds, and endless waves of crashing tides. The **Pacific Coast Trail** wends between main parking areas, through vibrant green forests and hazy fog clinging to the bluffs.

Particularly splendid are **Arch Rock Viewpoint**; the collapsed sea cave which forms a **Natural Bridge** over crashing waves; **Whalehead Trail Viewpoint** of the blow hole near **Whalehead Beach** and coastal panoramas from 250-ft high **Cape Ferrelo Viewpoint**. Arch Rock Viewpoint, **Indian Sands Trail**, **Whalehead Beach**, and **Lone Ranch** have picnic tables.

Harris Beach State Park, *1655 Hwy 101 N., Brookings OR 97415; tel: (541) 469-2021*, just south of Boardman Park on the west side of Hwy 101, has 151 camp pitches and yurts; book in advance; *tel: (800) 452-5687*. An **Oregon State Welcome Center/Rest Area**, *1630 Hwy 101; tel: (541) 469-4117*, is on the east side, open May–Nov.

Continue on Hwy 101 to Brookings.

Colour section (i): Rialto Beach Rocks at Olympic National Park (p.102); Samuel H Boardman State Park (p.128)
(ii): Astoria Column (see p.114)
(iii): Sea lions on Newport Pier; marine life at Oregon Coast Aquarium, Newport (p.120)
(iv): Trolley tours in Portland's Skidmore Historic District (pp.134–141)

BROOKINGS–GRANTS PASS

In striking contrast to the cliffs, beaches, wildlife and fogs of the Oregon Coast, this 90-mile route dips briefly into Northern California redwood forest to follow the narrow, winding Smith River Canyon and connect with Interstate 5 at Grants Pass, Oregon. A 40-mile return scenic side track to Oregon Caves National Monument will add an additional day to this 3-hr drive.

From Grants Pass, the interstate goes north to the Willamette Valley towards Portland, and east towards Medford, the base for highway access to Crater Lake National Park and the vast natural beauty of Eastern Oregon.

ROUTE: 90 MILES

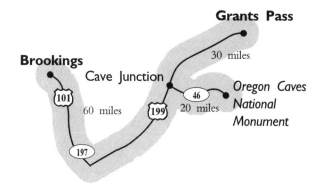

series. See advertisement, p. 14 for more information about *On the Road around California.*

ROUTE

From Brookings, take Hwy 101 south 6 miles to the California border. Continue 9½ miles on Hwy 101, then turn left (east) onto SR 197 for 6½ miles. Turn left (north-east) onto Hwy 199, 68 miles to Grants Pass. Turn off onto SR 46 for a scenic side track to Oregon Caves National Monument.

For those venturing further south, California is covered in another volume in this

BROOKINGS

Tourist Information: Brookings-Harbor Chamber of Commerce, *16330 Lower Harbor Rd (Port of Brookings-Harbor), PO Box 940, Brookings, OR 97415; tel: (800) 535-9469 or (541) 469-3181; fax: (541) 469-4094,* has brochures on lodging, dining, sights, shopping, whale watching, birds, trees and hiking trails from Brookings south to California. The **US Forest Service Chetco Ranger District,**

555 5th St; tel: (541) 469-2196, has detailed wilderness, forest and hiking information.

ACCOMMODATION AND FOOD

Lodging includes 3 *BW,* moderate **'Stay on a Yacht' Bed and Breakfast,** *C Dock # 38, Port of Brookings-Harbor; tel (707) 465-6203,* 10 RV parks and various state park campsites.

Mexican, Chinese and Italian restaurants compete with fast food. Go to any place in Brookings Harbor, peruse the menu and choose the fresh seafood, especially ling cod or another species of whitefish. The **Wharfside Restaurant,** *16362 Lower Harbor Rd; tel: (541) 469-7316,* serves budget–moderate seafood.

SIGHTSEEING

Brookings claims the sobriquet 'Banana Belt' to describe its mild temperatures and ability to cultivate palm trees, roses, citrus and raise Easter lilies. Ninety percent of the USA's Easter lilies are grown from Brookings south to Crescent City, California.

Strahm's Lily Farms, *15723 Oceanview Dr., Brookings, OR 97415; tel: (541) 469-3885,* open from June–Labor Day, show off the local crop.

Even trees associated with the coast hundreds of miles south thrive: the USA's largest Monterey cypress (on museum grounds) is the 99-ft-tall star of the **Chetco Valley Historical Museum,** *15461 Museum Rd; tel: (541) 469-6651,* open mid Mar–Oct. The trunk's 27-ft circumference makes an interesting comparison to the huge coastal redwoods less than 20 miles south along the route. In July, look for bulbs in riotous bloom before flowers are removed to strengthen the bulbs.

Azalea Park, *N. Bank Chetco River Rd,* is in spectacular bloom, Apr–June.

Brandy Peak Distillery, *PO Box 4078, Tetley Rd; tel: (541) 469-0194,* open Mar–Dec, employ wood-fired pot stills to craft brandies from Pinot Noir, Muscat and Gewürztraminer grapes and pears.

Brookings' many stores, 6 miles north of the California border, cater to Californians driving across the border to shop in a sales tax-free haven. Brookings prices are higher than most Oregon Coast towns. Petrol prices are comparable to California's, but the attendant petrol-pumping service, required by Oregon law, is a pampering well worth paying for before crossing the border.

BROOKINGS TO JED SMITH

Drive south on Hwy 101 from Brookings' Banana Belt climate.

Six miles south of Brookings, the crossing to California is marked by a significant timber clear-cut. Bulb nurseries and dairy farms spread on both sides of the highway.

Smith River, 6 miles from the border, is on the northern side of the eponymous river. Huge rocks are visible offshore. **Ship Ashore,** *12370 Hwy 101; tel: (707) 487-3141,* is a *BW* with a budget restaurant and gift shop in a real boat perched on land. A gangplank flanked by wooden statues reinforces the surreal feeling of a ship run aground. Watch for Roosevelt elk wandering across the road.

Turn east (left) at Hwy 197. The pungent sweet smell of the California laurel along the banks of the Smith River wafts through the redwood forest. A series of federal (Redwood National Park), State of California and local parks in Humboldt and Del Norte Counties are combined as **Redwood National and State Parks**; information requests for all park entities are answered centrally; for camping, *tel: (707) 464-6101.* **DESTINET;** *tel: (800) 444-7275.* **Ruby Van Deventer County Park** has camp pitches, swimming, picnic tables and fishing.

Turn left (east) onto Hwy 199, which for 27 miles east and north-east is a National Scenic Byway. On the right is **Jedediah Smith Redwoods State Park,** *1111 2nd St, Crescent City, CA 95531; tel: (707) 464-6101;* for camping information, *tel:* **DESTINET,** *(800) 444-7275* or *(619) 452-0150.* **Jed Smith,** as the park is known, is arrayed along the banks of the Smith River, the largest undammed river in California.

Jedediah Strong Smith, a mountain man, was the first American known to have reached California overland from the US East Coast. Competing with the Hudson's Bay Company for beaver and furs, he wound his way through Mexican/Spanish settlements in San Diego and Monterey, Native American areas, and in 1828 trekked up the North California Coast and redwood regions. The first 'European' to travel the length of California, Smith provided the first detailed information about Western resources, albeit as a wild fighter and explorer in buckskins, a devout Methodist who seldom drank.

One hundred inches annual rainfall swells the Smith River into a wild, raging torrent. In 24 hrs the chalky-white gravel riverbed is overwhelmed with a ten-ft surge of water. Jed Smith Park and the other parks on this route have significantly less fog than in Crescent City, 10 miles west on the Pacific Coast. Snow is rare.

Jed Smith summer campers enjoy sun, swimming and sandy beach. Walking tracks visit quiet redwood groves. The 30-min **Stout Grove Trail** combines fine swimming and the area's tallest trees. The **Hiouchi Trail** is best for rhododendrons and huckleberries (wild blueberries); the **Simpson** and **Peterson Trails** combine into an easy 2-mile loop through ferns and redwoods. Protect food from bears which wander campsites amongst the lush ferns, rhododendrons and azaleas which cushion the floor of the redwood forest.

Hiouchi Redwood National and State Parks Ranger Station, *across from Jed Smith Park; tel: (707) 464-6101,* spring–autumn, has books, maps, and information on Smith River activities including kayak and float trips.

Hiouchi has petrol and **Hiouchi Hamlet RV Resort,** *2000 Hwy 199, Crescent City, CA, 75531; tel: (800) 722-9468 or (707) 458-3321,* with 120 pitches, a market and restaurant. Redwood burls, tree tumours carved into figures, are for sale.

JED SMITH TO CAVE JUNCTION

Smith River National Recreation Area (NRA) is a huge, 303,337-acre expanse of wilderness, **Six Rivers National Forest,** and several forks of the Smith River. The scenic byway twists to repeatedly criss-cross the river.

Gasquet, a miniature oasis of civilisation in the thick forest, has a petrol station, a deli, and a budget flamingo-coloured café, **She-She's,** *9900 Hwy 199; tel: (707) 457-3434,* is reminiscent of a Los Angeles diner. French sailor Horace Gasquet settled in 1852 and conducted a lucrative toll road operation for stage coaches travelling between Crescent City and Grants Pass. Other Frenchmen followed, and the settlement's grape vines and gold panning became well-known.

For NRA information, stop at **Smith River NRA** headquarters, **Gasquet Ranger Station,** *Box 228, 10600 Hwy 199, N. Gasquet, CA 95543-0228; tel: (707) 457-3131;* for camping *tel: (800) 280-2267.* Carry snow chains in winter.

The scenic byway serpentines through a narrow canyon following the Smith River Middle Fork. From late spring–early autumn, this Wild and Scenic River section draws canoeists, kayakers, floaters, boats, swimmers, and steelhead fishermen. Book in advance; *tel: (800) 280-2267,* for one of 108 camp pitches amongst **Big Flat, Panther Flat** (recently burned over), **Grassy Flat** and **Patrick's Creek** campsites. 'Pack in, pack-out' low impact primitive camping is permitted, free, in the NRA. **Patrick Creek Lodge and Historical Inn;** *13950 Hwy 199, Gasquet; tel: (707) 457-3323,* provides standard moderate accommodations and a full restaurant and lounge.

Hwy 199 winds for 11 miles with speed limits posted for 35–45mph. After leaving the Smith River NRA, **Collier Tunnel Safety Rest Area** has restrooms and picnicking. Bicyclists are required to push a button before entering **Randolph Collier Tunnel,** to make lights within the 0.3-mile tunnel flash to warn vehicles. This is a favourite California Highway Patrol spot to catch cars speeding two miles north to cross the **Oregon Border.**

Oregon's speed limit is 55 mph. Hwy 199 crosses the West Fork of the Illinois River, and passes through **O'Brien** at the entrance to **Illinois Valley,** a small town with a store, RV park and restaurant. **Out'n'About Treehouse Treesort,** *300 Page Creek Rd, Cave Junction; tel: (800) 200-5484 or (541) 592-2208,* east of O'Brien in Takilma, sells $75–$125 silk-screened T-shirts, then (may) invite purchasing friends to lodge in a treehouse. Wildflowers at **Rough and Ready Botanical Wayside** include Howell's mariposa lily and the Siskiyou butterwort. **Kathy's Blackberry Patch Café,**

131

27893 Redwood Hwy (Hwy 199); tel: (541) 592-4918, serves home-made pie. **Illinois River Forks State Park** has picnicking and fishing.

CAVE JUNCTION

Tourist Information: Illinois Valley Chamber of Commerce, PO Box 312, Cave Junction, OR 97523; tel: (541) 592-3326.

The **Illinois Valley Visitor Center,** 201 Oregon Caves Hwy (Hwy 46), Cave Junction; tel: (541) 592-2631; fax: (541) 592-6545, provides area information, with the National Park Service, Forest Service, and Bureau of Land Management operating from one location to facilitate visits to sights, local wilderness areas and the Oregon Caves National Monument.

ACCOMMODATION AND FOOD

Cave Junction has plenty of RV parks, several motels and **HI-Fordson Home Hostel.** Moderate **Oregon Caves Lodge;** tel: (541) 592-3400, is an historic landmark, open all year at the national monument.

A Chinese restaurant, **Dragon Gate,** 240 Redwood Hwy; tel: (541) 592-3113, **Art's Red Garter Steak House,** 125 S. Redwood Hwy; tel: (541) 592-2892, and **Wild River Brewing & Pizza Co.,** 249 N. Redwood Hwy; tel: (541) 592-3556, are dining possibilities. From June–Sept, the **Illinois Valley Saturday Market & Country Fair,** Redwood Hwy and Laurel Rd, has fresh produce and food. **Taylor's Sausage,** 525 W. Watkins St; tel: (541) 592-4185, sells 25 kinds of sausage.

SIGHTSEEING

To taste fine **Rogue River appellation** wine, drive 2 miles east on Hwy 46 and turn right onto Holland Loop Rd. **Bridgeview Vineyard and Winery,** 4210 Holland Loop Rd; tel: (541) 592-4688, is famed for Blue Moon Riesling in a blue bottle. Taste the exceptional Pinot Noir and a wide range of varietals in the tasting room; a relaxed picnic area is just outside.

Continue on Holland Loop Rd, then turn right onto Kendall Rd for the rich and complex wines of **Foris Vineyards Winery,** 654 Kendall Rd; tel: (800) 84-FORIS, open daily 1100–1700.

⤴ SIDE TRACK FROM CAVE JUNCTION

Cave Junction is the starting point for a visit to the caves, 20 miles east, a 45 min-drive along SR 46. As the last 8 miles of highway are steep and winding, RVs over 28 ft are not permitted to drive to the caves.

OREGON CAVES NATIONAL MONUMENT

Tourist Information: The **Oregon Caves Company,** 20000 Caves Hwy, Cave Junction, OR 97523; tel (541) 592-3400, conduct tours, except on Thanksgiving and Christmas, and operate the monument's lodge and food operations. Tours, adults $6, children to age 11, at least 42 ins tall, $3.75, quickly fill up to a 16-person maximum in summer. The caves are chilly; practical walking shoes are a must.

The Oregon Caves are the only limestone caverns in the state, limestone recrystallised into marble with 'living', or growing, stalactites and stalagmites. Access is by a strenuous 75-min guided tour, not for visitors with heart, breathing, walking or claustrophobia problems. Six-tenths of a mile of passages seems easy until traversing 218 vertical ft, 550 stair steps, and uneven, dripping, wet and muddy terrain without a cane or staff. The largest accessible cavern, the **Ghost Room,** is completely darkened during the tour. Bats, giant Pacific salamanders, crickets, spiders and packrats live in the caves. Trails for hikers, open to snowshoers in winter and spring, loop into the Siskiyou National Forest from the Caves. At **US Forest Service, Siskiyou National Forest, Illinois Valley Ranger District,** 26568 Redwood Hwy, Cave Junction, OR 97523; tel (541) 592-2166, you can find information on hiking. ▣

CAVE JUNCTION TO GRANTS PASS

North of Cave Junction, the **Kerbyville Museum,** Hwy 199, Kerby; tel: (541) 592-2076, is open Mon–Sat 1000–1700 Sun 1330–1700 May 15–Sept 15, adults $2, has a legendary hanging tree outside the 1870s Stith

132

House, with rooms in period furnishings. To the side is the 'collections' museum, which has a display of Grants Pass Cavemen (tourism booster) paraphernalia.

Kerbyville is virtually a ghost town, with a few buildings and **Kerbyville Inn Bed & Breakfast,** *24304 Redwood Hwy, Kerby; tel: (541) 592-4689.* Expect winter snow. Left (west) is the **Kalmiopsis Wilderness Area.** **Lake Selmac** is a few miles east of Hwy 199 from **Selma's** petrol and market. There is a **KOA Campground** 13 miles north of Kerbyville. An antiques/trading post/junk store fills tiny **Wonder.**

Twelve miles beyond is **Grants Pass.** Grants Pass is a hub between freeways: I-5 skirts the north-east side of town, Hwy 99, as *6th* (going south from I-5, Exit 58) and *7th* (going north) *Sts*, is the main north-south artery through town, and Hwy 199 connects to both.

GRANTS PASS

Tourist Information: Grants Pass Visitors and Convention Bureau, *1501 NE. 6th St, PO Box 1787, Grants Pass, OR 97526; tel: (541) 476-5510,* has lodging and dining lists and information on Rogue River watersports.

ACCOMMODATION AND FOOD

Grants Pass has abundant lodging, including *BW, Hd, M6,* and *S8.* Most clusters around the I-5/Hwy 99 and I-5/Hwy 199 junctions. The comfortable **Holiday Inn Express,** *105 NE Agness Ave; tel: (800) 838-7666 or (541) 471-6144,* has magnificent views south to the Siskiyou Mountains.

Grants Pass is well-equipped with fast food outlets. The **Victorian Rose Restaurant and Tea Room,** *147 SW G St, in the Keinlen-Harbeck Bldg, G St Historic District; tel: (541) 471-9290;* is open Mon–Sat 1000–1700, for budget 'British' tea, snacks and strawberry and caramel pecan fudge pies. The **Laughing Clam,** *121 SW. G St,* has a long wooden bar, brick walls, and budget–moderate Pacific Northwest-style food.

SIGHTSEEING

Grants Pass, on the north side of the Rogue

River, once a logging centre, is now a highway hub and May–Sept recreation centre for tourists wanting to jetboat, float, raft, kayak, or fish for steelhead. Water trips may be from several hours to a week long, and traverse sheer rock passages (Hellgate Canyon), whitewater rapids, and smooth stretches of lazy-flowing river.

The **Caveman Statue,** by the Chamber of Commerce Building near the I-5/Hwy 99 junction of the north side of town, is a silly but famous symbol of a civic booster club, whose members while dressed in animal skins, have ceremoniously 'kidnapped' visiting dignitaries and movie stars in order to garner press coverage. More authentic history remains in the **G St Historic District,** one block once known as *Front St,* between *S.W. 5th and S.W. 6th Sts.* Old buildings, some red brick, are all that remain of the once-lucrative timber industry's prosperous showing.

The 1900 **Keinlen-Harbeck Bldg,** *on the corner at 147 SW. G St,* is a 2-storey model of Victorian architecture. **Cat & the Fiddle,** *147 SW. G St, downstairs; tel:(541) 479-1579,* has nice toys; *upstairs* is the **Victorian Rose Tea Room.** The **Oregon Outpost,** *137 SW. G St; tel: (541) 474-2918,* has a fine selection of Oregon-made goods, myrtlewood, and micro-brew beers.

Never a Bum Steer, *125 SW G St; tel: (541) 474-0726,* has good quality leather goods and Birkenstocks. Try the ale at the long bar at the **Laughing Clam,** *121 SW. G St.* **Blind George's News Stand,** *117 SW. G St; tel: (541) 476-3463,* the local gossip spot for a century, has current magazines, newspapers, popcorn, Keno (lottery) and old photos of Grant's Pass.

The 1901 **Schmidt House,** *508 SW. 5th St; tel: (541) 479-7827,* open Tues–Fri 1300–1600, the Josephine County Historical Museum, has restored the family's rooms. The **South Oregon Public Market/Growers Market,** *F St,* open 0900–1300 Sat mid Mar–Nov, Tues June–Sept, is a cornucopia of local produce, preserves, honey, trees, plants, crafts, and hand-made clothing, in the best selection south of Portland. **Riverside Park** on the south bank of the Rogue River is a pleasant place for a picnic.

133

PORTLAND

Roses, Mt Hood, the Willamette River, commerce, high-tech, planned growth and an independent spirit combine in Portland, a city worlds apart from West Coast neighbours Seattle and San Francisco. Portland's port, technology industry and go-our-own-way attitude is in tandem with the other two, but Portlanders' ability to relax in comfortable, still somewhat old-fashioned surroundings is unequalled. That business person rushing to a meeting might as well be the CEO as a free-lance consultant – riding a bicycle, coffee in hand, portable computer tucked in a back-pack, a book in a pocket.

TOURIST INFORMATION

Portland Oregon Visitors Association (POVA), *Three World Trade Center, 26 S.W. Salmon St, Portland, OR 97204-3299; tel: (800) 345-3214 or (503) 222-2223; fax: (503) 275-3299;* open Mon–Fri 0900–1700, Sat 0900–1600, for visitor information and 10-day regional weather forecasts. Tickets for local events are also on sale.

The **Oregon Welcome Center at Jantzen Beach**, *12348 N. Center St, Portland OR 97217; tel: (503) 285-1631; fax: (503) 289-0455,* has information on Portland and the state for drivers approaching Portland on I-5. *Powell's Books Walking Map of Downtown Portland,* from **Powell's City of Books**, *1005 W. Burnside St; tel: (503) 228-4651,* is a free, lightweight map with each sight, park, car park, shopping area, ATM and MAX light rail station clearly marked.

WEATHER

Though 78 miles from the Pacific Ocean,

Portland still gets 37 inches of precipitation, rain or fog, yearly. Be prepared for occasional snow and ice from late fall–winter.

Weather is reported almost minute-by-minute on local radio and television stations, as a combination of conditions from the Pacific Ocean, Columbia River, and Mt Hood and other Cascade Range peaks can quickly change the weather. Temperatures range from 33°F in winter to 80°F in July. POVA has recorded 10-day forecasts; *tel: (800) 345-3214.* For current information; *tel: (503) 275-9792 or (503) 225-5555, code 4101.*

ARRIVING AND DEPARTING

By Air
Portland International Airport (PDX), *700 N.E. Multnomah St, Portland, OR 97232-2131; tel: (800) 547-8411 or (503) 231-5000; fax: (503) 731-7080,* is an airy airport 20 miles north-east of downtown Portland. **Oregon Market** shops, centred between the concourses, include quality local food products at **Made in Oregon**, a **Nike** store, **Dogs & Cats**, glassware and Native American art at **The Real Mother Goose**. A children's play area between D and E concourses simulates a jetliner flight deck.

Massive construction will disrupt terminals and facilities through to mid-1999 as PDX expands concourses and parking. Car hire areas and car parks will shift several times during construction. Call PDX parking; *tel: (503) 288-7275,* for updated parking information.

PDX has information booths in the ticket lobby, open 0600–1900, and in baggage claim, open 0930–2330, supplemented with interactive video kiosks. Luggage carts are $1.00.

The main highway from PDX to downtown is I-5, but during rush hour it may be faster to take I-205 south to Tualatin, then continue north to Portland on I-5 against the commute. The **Port of Portland Ground Transportation Office**; *tel: (503) 335-1272,*

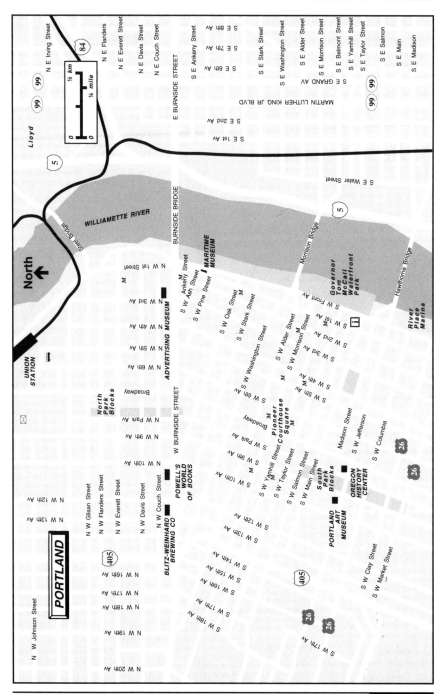

135

has information on transportation options to downtown including shuttles, buses, taxis and limousines.

Tri-Met; *tel: (503) 238-7433, bus no. 12*, gets to downtown Portland in 30 min for $1.05. Private **Airport buses**; *tel: (503) 246-4676*, run every half hour, 0500–midnight, adults $8.50, children 6–12 $2.

By Train

AMTRAK arrives at **Union Station,** *800 N.W. 6th Ave; tel: (800) 872-7245* or *(503) 273-4866*, with services from Seattle and Vancouver, BC, Emeryville/San Francisco (originating in Los Angeles) and two routes from Chicago. Union Station's 1886 marble and wooden waiting benches shine.

By Bus

Greyhound-Trailways Bus Lines, *550 N.W 6th Ave; tel: (800) 231-2222* or *(503) 243-2357*, has bus connections.

Driving is complicated by one-way streets and the partially blocked Portland Transit Mall. Streets run east–west, avenues north–south, divided at *Burnside St*, with five direction-delineated areas: N., N.W., N.E., S.W. and S.E.

136

Public Transport

Portland's well-connected public transportation system is easy to use, clean, cheap and bicycle-friendly. **Tri-Met,** *Pioneer Square, 701 SW. 6th Ave; tel: (503) 238-7433*, open Mon–Fri 0900–1700, and *4012 S.E. 17th Ave*, open Mon–Fri 0800–1700, sells tickets and has information and schedules for the 87-line bus system.

Most bus routes transit through the **Portland Transit Mall,** *by Pioneer Courthouse Square, along brick-lined S.W. 5th and SW. 6th Aves*. Tri-Met uses a 3-zone system, $1.05 for 1–2 zones, $1.35 for 3 zones, $3.25 all-day ticket for adults. Transfers are time-limited, but free. All buses except shuttles have exterior bike racks.

Fareless Square is a 300-block free area, bounded by the Willamette River, *N.W. Irving* and I-405, and includes most sights and

attractions. Blue and white Tri-Met signs indicate bus line number, fare zone, Max (streetcar) connections, and the service area, Red Fish, Purple Raindrop, Blue Snowflake, Brown Beaver, Green Leaf, Yellow Rose or Orange Deer. Present a pre-paid ticket or pay as you board. In bad weather, check the **Tri-Met Snow & Ice Line**; *tel: (503) 231-3197*, for re-routing information.

Tri-Met connects to **MAX** (Metropolitan Area Express) light rail line which goes north of downtown, crosses the Steel Bridge and continues 15 miles to Gresham. In late 1998, MAX will extend south-west to Beaverton and Hillsboro. The same inexpensive fares apply on MAX – no more than $1.35 to the furthest point; purchase tickets at MAX stop machines. Trains run every 7 mins during the commute; at 15 min intervals otherwise.

Four red and cream-coloured **Vintage Trolley** cars, liven the MAX system scene, May–Jan 1, Mon–Fri 0930–1500, weekends 1000–1800; Mar–Apr weekends 1000–1800. Modelled after Portland's Council Crest trolleys, the 40-min return route passes through scenic areas of downtown, stops at the Portland Saturday (and Sunday) Market, then crosses the Willamette River to the **Oregon Convention Center** and **Lloyd Center** shopping.

Driving in Portland

Smart Park have six downtown car parks, convenient to shopping and Portland Saturday Market: *1st Ave* and *Jefferson St, 4th Ave* and *Yamhill St, 3rd Ave* and *Alder St, 10th Ave* and *Yamhill St, O'Bryant Sq. on Stark St*, and *Front Ave and Davis St*, $0.75 per hour, $1.50 per night, $3 all day on weekends. Downtown merchants validate 2 hours of free parking for each $15 purchase.

Beware of driving during weekday rush hour, 0700–0830 and 1600–1800, as most bridges and arterial roads slow to a crawl. Hotel parking averages $15 per night at downtown hotels. Hotels, tourism officials and residents recommend car parks, especially at night, to prevent vehicle vandalism or theft.

Meters are strictly enforced, Mon–Sat, and tickets are dear. For **area road conditions**; *tel: (503) 222-6721*.

Accommodation

Conventions are big business in Portland and fill hotels year-round. Most major hotel and motel chains are represented. A wide selection of moderate chain motels is in the **Lloyd District**, between the Oregon Convention Center and the Lloyd Center, including the lively **Red Lion Hotel Lloyd Center**, *1000 N.E. Multnomah; tel: (800) 547-8010 or (503) 281-6111.*

Staying downtown is moderate–pricey. The pricey **Governor Hotel**, *611 S.W. 10th at Alder St; tel: (800) 554-3456 or (503) 224-3400,* combines two historic buildings, one modelled after Rome's Farnese Palace. The warmly-lit lobby has a dramatic Lewis and Clark wall mural. **Fifth Avenue Suites Hotel**, *506 S.W. Washington St; tel: (800) 711-2971 or (503) 222-00001; fax: (503) 222-0004,* also pricey, has light, airy, colourful rooms with a late afternoon wine hour for guests. The **Benson Hotel**, *309 S.W. Broadway; tel: (503) 228-2000,* and the **Heathman Hotel**, *1001 S.W. Broadway; tel: (800) 551-0011 or (503) 241-4100,* are other pricey historic hotels. **Riverplace Hotel**, *1510 S.W. Harbor Way; tel: (503) 228-3233,* has pricey rooms with river views.

John Palmer House, *4314 N. Mississippi Ave, Portland, OR 97217; tel: (503) 284-5893,* is a moderate–expensive bed and breakfast in a stunning corner 1890 Victorian, in the Northeast section of Portland. **HI-Portland**, *3031 S.E. Hawthorne Blvd, Portland, OR 97214; tel: (503) 236-3380; fax: (503) 236-7940,* is a budget alternative.

Be cautious about personal and vehicle safety in Portland's north-east Lloyd neighbourhood and the north-west industrial area.

Eating and Drinking

Ingredients are fresh, coffee is strong, residents are savvy diners and Portland claims the most microbreweries in the land. **Cadillac Café**, *914 N.E. Broadway; tel: (503) 287-4750,* serves great budget breakfasts, including pancakes laced with local hazelnut sauce.

Ron Paul Broadway, *1441 N.E. Broadway; tel: (503) 284-5347,* has moderate, ultra-fresh food like salad with greens, Oregon pears, hazelnuts and blue cheese, served in a charcuterie dining room.

Pazzo Ristorante, *627 S.W. Washington St; tel: (503) 228-1515,* moderate–pricey, bustles with business people socialising over an Italian menu, including grilled radicchio appetisers. Moderate–pricey **Zefiro**, *500 N.W. 21st Ave; tel: (503) 226-3394,* is spare of décor, with subtle lighting, brilliant flower arrangements and scrumptious catch-of-the-day – best grilled. **Jake's Famous Crawfish**, *401 S.W. 12th Ave; tel: (503) 226-1419,* atmospherically dark for a century, is a local landmark for moderate shellfish specials.

For soup, salads, sandwiches and quiche, the **Gate Lodge** at **Pittock Mansion**; *tel: (503) 823-3627,* has budget lunch. **Powell's City of Books**, *1005 W. Burnside St,* has **Anne Hughes Coffee Room**; *tel: (503) 228-0540 ext. 234,* a budget café with delicious soups, sandwiches and snacks. **Portland Saturday Market**, *Ankeny Park under Burnside Bridge; tel: (503) 222-6072,* food stalls have cheap international cuisine ranging from Tibetan to Mexican to vegan, Sat 1000–1700 Sun 1100–1630 Mar–24 Dec.

For moderate tea, the **Heathman Hotel**, *1001 S.W. Broadway; tel: (503) 241-4100,* serves daily, 1400–1600, and **John Palmer House**, *4314 N. Mississippi Ave, Portland, OR 97217; tel: (503) 284-5893,* where waiters in Victorian-era dress offer Sun high tea at 1300.

Portland boasts 37 brewery outlets, with beers and ales enhanced by local hops and Mt Hood water. Beer is ubiquitous. **Blitz–Weinhard Brewing Co**, *1133 W. Burnside St; tel: (503) 222-4351,* occupies several blocks north of downtown, with tours Mon–Fri at 1200, 1330 and 1500. Unfermented beer wort crust pizzas compliment the top-fermenting ales at Oregon's oldest microbrewery, **BridgePort Brewing Co, Inc.**, *1313 N.W. Marshall St; tel: (503) 241-7179.* **Oregon Brewers Guild**, *510 N.W. 3rd Ave, Portland, OR 97209; tel: (503) 295-1862; fax: (503) 226-4895,* has an extensive list of breweries and brewpubs. **Portland BrewBus**, *319 S.W. Washington,*

137

Suite 812; tel: (888) 244-2739, conducts 5-hr guided Sat tours of five breweries with sampling and lunch.

Oregon Wines on Broadway, 515 S.W. Broadway; tel: (503) 228-4655, conducts public wine tastings Thur 1700–1900, Oct–May.

Communications

Mail and faxes can be sent to or from any hotel. The **Central Post Office**, 204 S.W. 5th Ave, Portland, OR 97240: tel: (503) 294-2419, has all services. The **Airport Mail Facility**, 7640 N.E. Airport Way, Portland OR; tel: (503) 335-7921, is a convenient stop for posting souvenirs home.

Money

Thomas Cook Currency Services, 701 S.W. 6th Ave; tel: (503) 222-2665, is in the heart of Pioneer Courthouse Sq., located within **Powell's Travel Book Store**.

Dress

Portlanders tend to be casual for most occasions; business wear is well-tailored and conservative in colour. Individual style is expressed in footwear, sometimes Birkenstocks or sandals or light-coloured stockings and highly-patterned ties and scarves. Dressing up is optional for fine dining and the performing arts, otherwise dress in lightweight layers, with a heavy coat for fall–winter, and a ready umbrella – always.

Current club, music and DJ (live dance club) offerings are listed each Tues in free *Willamette Week* and on Fri in *The Oregonian* A&E (Arts and Entertainment) Guide. Blues, jazz, rock and country music are all popular genres. Hot groups and venues change frequently. Many musicians start careers in the Greater Portland area, then go on to greater fame performing and recording in New York or Los Angeles. **La Luna**, 215 S.E. 9th Ave; tel: (503) 241-5862, features up-and-coming Northwest blues, jazz, and rock and roll bands.

Brasserie Montmartre, 626 S.W. Park Ave; tel: (503) 224-5552, features jazz combos nightly. Arrive early to stake out a table for Portland's best jazz at **Jazz de Opus**, 33 N.W.

2nd Ave; tel: (503) 222-6077. **Berbati's Pan**, 231 S.W. Ankeny St; tel: (503) 226-2122, and **Key Largo**, 31 N.W. 1st Ave; tel: (503) 223-9919, have a variety of rock band offerings. **Darcelle XV**, 208 N.W. 3rd Ave; tel: (503) 222-5338, has cheerful female impersonators.

From spring through Christmas, Portland's best quality shopping is on weekends at the **Portland Saturday Market**, Ankeny Park under Burnside Bridge; tel: (503) 222-6072, open Mar–24 Dec Sat 1000–1700 Sun 1100–1630. Ceramics, glassware, handmade and ethnic clothing, wood carvings and masses of fresh flowers fill more than 300 hundred open-air booths in Ankeny Park, while musicians and buskers perform and shoppers munch their way through food stall savouries.

Get the local mascot on clothing at the **University of Oregon–Duck Shop at Portland Center**, 734 S.W. 2nd Ave; tel: (503) 725-3057. **Made in Oregon**, 5 N.W. Front Ave; tel: (800) 828-9673 or (503) 273-8498, has good-quality local products. **NIKE-TOWN Portland**, 930 S.W 6th Ave; tel: (503) 221-6453, sells the nearby Fortune 500 company's products, with life-size superstar figures 'flying' in space, and sound effects of shoes screeching, skidding and crunching on playing courts and fields.

Public transportation, cheap parking and a downtown cleaning programme draw Portlanders to fine downtown shopping. **Pioneer Place**, 700 S.W. 5th Ave; tel: (503) 228-5800, has 55 shops, including Saks Fifth Avenue, and a food court. **Meier & Frank**, 621 S.W. 5th Ave; tel: (503) 223-0512, is a venerable department store with frequent sales on fine quality clothing. **Nordstrom**, 701 S.W. Broadway; tel: (503) 224-6666, faces the west side of Pioneer Courthouse Square. **The Galleria**, 921 S.W. Morrison St; tel: (503) 228-2748, has 125 shops. **Northwest 23rd District**, also called **Nob Hill**, is filled with upmarket boutiques and galleries around N.W. 23rd Ave. East of the Willamette River, the **Lloyd Center**, 2201 Lloyd Center; tel: (503) 282-2511, is another major 200-shop complex with cinemas and an ice-skating rink.

Portland was crumbling 25 years ago. Today, its lifestyle and ambience are a US example of how to re-make urban areas. Roughly half a million people live in Portland, which drew an Urban Growth Boundary around its expanse in 1979. Though its dormitory communities are booming even across the Columbia River in Greater Vancouver, Washington, Portland's city limits can't expand.

Downtown buildings have retail shops on ground level; merchants contribute to a 212-block area sidewalk and graffiti clean-up scheme with housing built on small plots in the inner city. The once-decrepit riverfront is now **Tom McCall Waterfront Park**; the Saturday Market stimulates an empty downtown area on weekends. Public transportation makes it cheap and easy to sightsee and explore restaurants, brew pubs and clubs. Pairs of strolling **Portland Guides** wear green jackets and act as information sources and informal security, as does the equestrian **Portland Mounted Patrol**.

Portland obliquely claims Lewis and Clark as first discoverers, as the Corps of Discovery stopped at a Native American village on the Columbia River near today's airport in 1805. In 1825, the Hudson's Bay Company built Fort Vancouver as its headquarters, bringing trappers and traders to the region. Within 20 years, Oregon Trail pioneers claimed the Willamette River area just south of the Columbia River. Portland was named for Portland, Maine, the result of an 1845 penny toss by its founders, a Portland, Maine businessman and a Boston lawyer, each of whom favoured his native city.

The Willamette's confluence with the Columbia and long, straight stretch at Portland made it a desirable port to load wheat coming from the east and timber from the Cascades and coastal ranges of Oregon and Southern Washington. The Willamette Valley, just south, turned out to be agriculturally productive. By the late 19th century, railroads connected north and south, and eastward along the Columbia River.

In 1905, Portland hosted the Lewis and Clark Centennial Exposition, a chance for the city to show a sophisticated face to the world. Public works philanthropy has long been a Portland and Northwest tradition. In Portland, parkland was preserved in the 1850s. In the 1870s, Stephen Skidmore bequeathed graceful **Skidmore Fountain**, supported by classical maidens, 'for the horses, men, and dogs' of Portland. Downtown drinking fountains are bronze, four-basin Benson Bubblers, named for the lumber baron who decreed that his lumberjacks might imbibe less beer if they had running water to drink – the scheme worked. Fountains, statues and public art adorn the modern downtown, including 36-ft high, 6½-ton hammered copper **Portlandia**, *S.W. 5th Ave between Main and Madison Sts,* holding a trident over the **Portland Building** entrance.

Downtown

The history of Portland lives in artefacts like the name-determining **Portland Penny** and multimedia presentations at the **Oregon History Center,** *1200 S.W. Park Ave; tel: (503) 222-1741,* open Tues–Sat 1000–1700 Sun 1200–1700, adults $6, students $3, children 6–12 $1.50. Above the museum, on the exterior of the old Sovereign Hotel, are two **Oregon History Murals**, showing Lewis and Clark's Corps of Discovery and Native American, early settler and Oregon Trail pioneers.

Portland Art Museum, *1219 S.W. Park Ave; tel: (503) 226-2811,* open Tues–Sat 1100–1700 Sun 1300–1700, adults $7.50, children 6–12 $2.50, claims 35 centuries of art and has a fine collection of Native American artefacts.

Between the **Oregon History Center** and **Portland Art Museum**, centre of the **Cultural District**, are some of the 12 **South Park Blocks** donated by prominent citizens in 1852 as a permanent greensward with trees, statue and benches. South Park Blocks are popular with students who attend Portland State University at the south end of the blocks. **Portlandia** is two blocks east of the museums.

Colourfully-painted **ARTBus**, Tri-Met line no. 63, makes stops at museums and cultural spots, including Washington Park. The **First Thursday**, *PO Box 29138, Portland, OR*

97209, of each month, from 1800–2100, downtown art galleries are open for browsing, shopping for art and chatting with artists. Coffee-houses, bookstores and brew pubs accommodate the thousands of Portlanders who use the evening to go downtown to relax and learn about art.

Pioneer Courthouse Square, *S.W. 6th Ave and S.W. Broadway, S.W. Yamhill St and S.W. Morrison St,* in the heart of department store shopping, is called 'Portland's living room'. The **Portland Transit Mall** is at its north side. **Thomas Cook Foreign Exchange** within **Powell's Travel Store** are in the plaza. **Starbuck's** on the corner is always under siege by coffee fanatics. **Tri-Met** offices and restrooms are below ground level under a waterfall graced with gargoyles. The square is a red brick-lined plaza to relax, read, have a coffee, or peruse the **Weather Machine,** which indicates the weather while trumpeting, spraying water, blinking and playing a noon-time musical fanfare.

Waterfront

Tear down an expressway and find a long-lost riverfront, adored by joggers, cyclists, rollerbladers, skaters, skateboarders and strollers. Urban redevelopment created 23-acre **Tom McCall Waterfront Park** along the Willamette River, paralleling *Naito Blvd* (formerly *Front St*). **POVA,** *26 S.W. Salmon St,* is across from **Salmon Street Springs,** a fountain which arches in all directions from the ground. **Mill Ends Park,** *in the traffic median at Front and Taylor Sts,* 24 inches in diameter, claims to be the world's smallest city park, donated by a businessman who wanted a park near his window.

The **Portland Spirit,** *842 S.W. 1st Ave; tel: (800) 224-3901* or *(503) 224-3900,* has sightseeing and dining along the Willamette River. The Sternwheeler *Cascade Queen, 1200 N.W. Front Ave, Suite 110, Portland, OR 97209; tel: (503) 223-3928,* departs from RiverPlace Marina North Dock for 2-hr narrated excursion cruises daily Fri–Mon June–Aug, May and Sept.

Oregon Maritime Center and Museum, *113 S.W. Front Ave; tel: (503) 224-*

7724, open 1100–1600 June–Aug Wed–Sun, Sept–May Fri–Sun, adults $4, has a good model ship collection. Museum admission includes a tour of the restored sternwheeler *Portland,* anchored on the Willamette River, the last working steam powered sternwheel tug boat which operated in a US harbour.

Portland Saturday Market, *Ankeny Park under the Burnside Bridge,* operates spring through Christmas Eve weekends. The **American Advertising Museum,** *50 S.W. 2nd Ave; tel: (503) 226-0000; fax: (503) 226-2635,* open Wed–Sun 1100–1700, adults $3, children $1.50, has excellent special exhibits of posters, print and television advertisements. The *Advertising Timeline* covers 300 years of dubious to inspired product promotion; the clever *All-Time Best Advertising Campaigns* provoke chuckles.

On weekends, cross *Front St* from the Saturday Market to watch bongo drummers, skateboarders, old hippies and punk-grunge youth 'rumble' amiably together on sunny weekends. Continue along the park north of Burnside Bridge to the **Japanese American Historic Plaza,** sculptures and rock-carved memoirs of the discrimination and internment suffered by this prominent ethnic group.

Washington Park

Perched in rolling hills west of downtown, **Washington Park** is 145 acres of walking and hiking trails laced with formal gardens, trees, an arboretum and a zoo.

The **International Rose Test Garden,** *400 S.W. Kingston; tel: (503) 823-3636,* may be the most-visited spot in Portland – the classic camera view of Mt Hood hovering above buildings is here, but so are 10,000 rose buses representing 400 varieties, their terraces stunning May–summer. The first test gardens still put new varieties on trial – be prepared for occasional failures.

The **Japanese Garden,** *611 S.W. Kingston Ave; tel: (503) 223-1321,* hours vary by season, adults $5, children 6–17 $2.50, offers daily tours at 1045 and 1430 Apr–Oct. The peaceful year-round garden, known for spring iris, fall colour and winter icicles lacing pagodas, is a very authentic creation of five traditional gardens, including a tea garden, weathered sand and stones, flat, raked sand, a strolling pond and a natural garden.

Metro Washington Park Zoo, *4001 S.W. Canyon Rd; tel: (506) 226-1561*, open 0930–dusk, adults $5.50, children $3.50, has a wide range of animals, and is renowned for its success at breeding Asian elephants in captivity. **ZooTrain**; *tel: (503) 226-1561*, runs spring–fall, $2.75, for zoo visitors to easily access the Japanese Garden and International Rose Test Gardens.

Joggers enjoy **Hoyt Arboretum**, *4033 S.W. Canyon Rd; tel: (503) 228-8733*, open 0600–2200, with 10 miles of trails through the nation's largest collection of conifers.

World Forestry Center, *4033 S.W. Canyon Rd; tel: (503) 228-1367*, open summer 0900–1700, winter 1000–1700, adults $3, children 6–18 $2, is housed in a building resembling a wooden cathedral. The worship of wood and its industries is strong, the 70-ft 'talking tree' booms narrative in a Biblical tone. Old growth forests and tropical rain forests are excellently interpreted in separate exhibits. The **James Burnett Collection of Petrified Wood**, justifies a centre visit.

North of the park, the **Pittock Mansion**, *3229 N.W. Pittock Dr.; tel: (503) 823-3624*, open late Jan–Dec 1200–1600, adults $4, children 6–18 $1.50, was the residence of *The Oregonian* newspaper magnate, English-born Henry Pittock and wife Georgiana, both Oregon Trail Pioneers. Château-style turrets accent the bright and comfortably-decorated mansion. The elaborate bathrooms rival any modern spa. Visit on a clear, sunny day when the Drawing Room windows show a 180° vista of the city, Willamette and Columbia Rivers and five Cascade peaks. Take a picnic or have lunch at the **Gate Lodge**; *tel: (503) 823-3627*.

East of the Willamette River

The twin metal-trussed towers of the **Oregon Convention Center** dominate the view east of downtown. Across the Willamette River by the Hawthorne Bridge, **OMSI**, the **Oregon Museum of Science & Industry**, *1945 S.E. Water Ave; tel: (503) 797-4000*, open 0930–seasonal closing hours, adults $6, children 4–13

$4.50, has six halls with interactive exhibits, including a simulated earthquake, the internal design of a computer, and a walk-through house designed with handicapped access components and an astronomy show. An **OMNI-MAX ® Theatre**; *tel: (503) 797-4640*, adults $5.50, children 4–13 $4, and the 219-foot diesel electric *U.S.S. Blueback Submarine*, Tues–Sun 1300–1800, $3.50, are in the facility. Combined tickets are $12 for adults, $10 for children 4–13. **Laser light shows**; *tel: (503) 797-4646*, are $2 and $6.50.

The Grotto, *N.E. 85th Ave and Sandy Blvd; tel: (503) 254-7371*, 0900–2000 May–Sept, 0900–1730 Oct–Apr, the National Sanctuary of Our Sorrowful Mother, is a Roman Catholic shrine with magnificent rhododendron gardens and views of the Columbia River from the Upper Level cliff, 110 ft above the grotto.

Unique Attractions

Find Portland's independent streak in three museums: the **Portland Police Historical Museum**, *1111 S.W. 2nd Ave, 16th Floor; tel: (503) 823-0019*, open Mon–Thur 1000–1500, runs the range from a holding cell to badges, wanted posters, vehicles, uniforms, and guns. The **Church of Elvis**, *720 S.W. Ankeny; tel: (503) 226-3671*, open most afternoons, reveres 'The King' through coin-operated shrines, said to reassure worshippers who could not expiate guilt without paying to do so. Knock on the blue door – hours are erratic. The **UFO Museum**, *1637 S.W. Alder St; tel: (503) 227-2975*, $1, also open erratically is an offbeat collection of sci-fi and literally far out extraterrestrial posters, photos and 'artefacts'.

Portland's most popular draw may be **Powell's City of Books**, *1005 W. Burnside St; tel: (503) 228-4651*, open Mon–Sat 0900–2300 Sun 0900–2100. With one million books, it claims to be the largest new and used bookstore in the USA, able to find any book in print. It may be. Shopping baskets brim with books. Students, workers, business people, pensioners, all seem to meet, read, have coffee and socialise here, where parking is free for patrons, service is friendly, and the rain never follows browsers inside.

PORTLAND CIRCUIT

Portland's sights are within an easy, two-hour driving circuit from the **Portland Oregon Visitors Association (POVA)**, *26 S.W. Salmon St*, but stops in Washington Park, downtown and along the waterfront can easily extend the ride to a full day – or two. One-way streets and traffic flow suggest following the route in the direction indicated. *Front Ave* was recently renamed *Naito Blvd*, and both names are used.

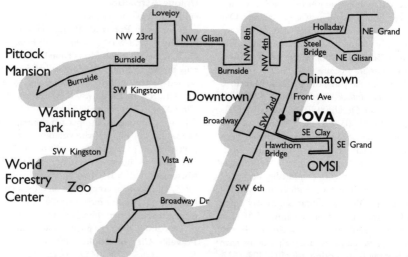

Begin on *S.W. Salmon St* facing the Willamette River with **POVA** on the left. **Tom McCall Waterfront Park** is across *Front Ave (Naito Blvd)*. In warm weather, children frisk through the **Salmon Street Springs Fountain** and the (summertime) *Portland Spirit* boarding dock is nearby.

WATERFRONT

Turn left onto *Front Ave*. One block ahead at *Taylor St* is tiny **Mill Ends Park**, marked with two black posts in the meridian.

Straight ahead on *Front Ave* is the **Skidmore/Old Town Historic District**, Portland's first settled area and commercial centre. Brick buildings have graceful arched windows and are trimmed with cast iron fashioned to look like fine plaster. The sternwheeler *Portland,* part of the **Oregon Maritime Center and Museum** is docked north of the Morrison Bridge. The battleship *U.S.S. Oregon*'s mast, a war memorial, is near the *Portland*'s gangplank. The museum is on the left between *Pine* and *Ash Sts.*

One block ahead on the left is the **Central Fire Station**. Look through the glass at **Jeff Morris Fire Museum**, *55 S. Ash,* to see horse-drawn hand-pump fire engines. **Ankeny Park**, site of the **Portland Saturday Market**, is behind the ruined Roman pillars on the left. **Skidmore Fountain** is at *Ash St* and *1st Ave*, behind Ankeny Park. Across *1st Ave* is the **American Advertising Museum** in the **New Market Theatre Building**.

Back on *Front Ave*, north of the Burnside Bridge, the **Japanese American Historic Plaza**'s stone sculpture and rocks are on the right, at the north end of Tom McCall Waterfront Park. Follow *Front Ave* onto the **Steel Bridge**, following signs for 'Coliseum, Convention Center'.

EAST OF STEEL BRIDGE

The **Oregon Convention Center** twin spires are ahead, with the **Rose Garden Arena**, home to the **Portland Trailblazers** NBA basketball team, on the left.

Leaving the bridge, turn right onto *N.E. Interstate Ave/NE. Lloyd Blvd* to *N.E. Grand Ave* and turn left. Stay in the left lane to *N.E. Multnomah St.* Turn right on *N.E. Multnomah St* for **Lloyd Center** shopping mall, ice rink and cinemas. Or, turn left onto *N.E. Multnomah* for one block, left on *Martin Luther King Jr Blvd* for two blocks, then right onto *Holladay St* to cross the **Steel Bridge**, also used by MAX light rail.

CHINATOWN

From the left lane, turn left onto *N.W. 3rd Ave* for four blocks. Turn right onto *Burnside St* for one block, then right again onto *N.W. 4th Ave* through **Chinatown Gate** to the red lamp posts along **Chinatown**'s few blocks. Continue six blocks on *N.W. 4th Ave*, then veer left through the *Hoyt St* stop sign to **Union Station**. Some streets have still have cobblestones, ballast from sailing ships.

Turn left on *Broadway* for two blocks, then turn right onto *N.W. Glisan St* for one block, turning left on *N.W. 8th Ave* to drive by the **North Park Blocks**, an 1852 greenway lined with elms. Drive south on *N.W. 8th Ave* to *Burnside St.* The **Church of Elvis** is directly ahead, but requires a several block diversion to return to this circuit.

NORTH PARK BLOCKS TO NOB HILL

Go right two blocks on *Burnside St*, right for one block on *N.W. 10th Ave*, then left on *N.W. Couch* (pron: cooch) for one block. **Powell's City of Books** car park is one-half block left on *N.W. 11th Ave*. The **Blitz-Weinhard Brewery** is across *N.W. 11th Ave.*

Turn right on *Burnside St* for one block, then right on *N.W. 12th Ave* to the **Pearl District** lofts, galleries and boutiques. Turn left onto *N.W. Glisan St.* **McMenamin's Mission Theatre and Pub**, *1624 N.W. Glisan St* at *N.W. 17th Ave; tel: (503) 223-4031,* shows $1 movies for diners and microbrew drinkers. Turn right onto *N.W. 21st Ave* for the **Nob Hill Shopping District**. Turn left on *Lovejoy St*, and left again on *N.W. 23rd Ave*. Turn right onto *Burnside St*, going one mile to a flashing yellow light before turning right onto *N.W. Barnes Rd* to follow signs to the **Pittock Mansion**.

WASHINGTON PARK

Return to *Burnside St*, turn left, then drive half a mile to turn right onto *S.W. Tichner Dr.* into **Washington Park**. Go right on *S.W. Kingston Ave.* The **Japanese Garden** is on the right; the **International Rose Test Garden** is on the left, below the tennis courts. Continue on *S.W.*

143

Kingston Dr. following signs to **Metro Washington Park Zoo**. *S.W. Kingston Dr.* winds through the park; turn left on *S.W. Knights Blvd* to the **World Forestry Center** or turn right to **Hoyt Arboretum Visitors Center**. Retrace your drive to the Rose Garden parking area, and continue on *S.W. Sherwood Blvd* down the slope past **Rose Garden Children's Park** and the **Portland Reservoir**. Turn right onto *Park Place*, circling around the **Sacajawea statue** to leave Washington Park.

COUNCIL CREST

Go right on *Vista* past fine mansions to *Broadway* and turn right. Immediately turn left onto *Greenway Ave* for one mile, veering right onto *Council Crest Dr.* to access **Council Crest Park**, with good weather views of Mts Jefferson, Hood, Adams, St Helens and Rainier. To return, turn left on *Greenway* to *Patton Rd*, then turn right. *Patton Rd* becomes *Broadway Dr.*

DOWNTOWN

Mt Hood is ahead as *Broadway Dr.* descends toward downtown. Veer left at the bottom of the hill, heading towards the city centre. Go

---

Skid Rows

The term 'Skid Row' originally applied to the logging industry before it became used to describe an area frequented by down-and-outs.

To move cut logs through the forest, lumberjacks used to yoke oxen or horses and 'skid' (pull) logs to a river or other collection point. This path, which might have been a stream, a salmon-grease oiled dirt road or a dirt trench, was called the skid road.

Methods of moving logs today include hooking logs to portable spars on an overhead tram system, avoiding the need to install a skid road and ruin even more forest land. However, skid roads are still used in some places.

---

right at the stop sign, getting immediately into the left lane to turn left onto *S.W. 6th Ave*. Drive eight blocks north on *S.W. 6th Ave* through the **Portland State University** campus area, then turn left onto *S.W. Clay St* for two blocks to the **South Park Blocks**. Turn left on *W. Park/S.W. 9th Ave* for one block, then go left onto *Market St*. **Ira Keller Fountain** cascades are five blocks along on the left.

Turn left onto *S.W. 2nd Ave* for seven blocks, then go left again for two blocks on *S.W. Taylor St*. Turn right onto *S.W. 4th Ave*. **Saks Fifth Avenue** and **Pioneer Place** shopping mall are on the left.

Go left on *S.W. Morrison St*, following MAX light rail lines to the **Portland Transit Mall** adjacent to **Pioneer Courthouse Square**. Cross the MAX tracks to turn left onto *S.W. Broadway Ave*. **Arlene Schnitzer Concert Hall**, the 'Schnitz', marked with the bright 'Portland' marquee, houses the Oregon Symphony and a huge electronic organ.

Turn right on *S.W. Jefferson St* to the **South Park Blocks**. Turn right on *S.W. Park Ave* at the **Teddy Roosevelt Statue**. The **Oregon History Center** is on the right. Turn left onto *S.W. Main St*, then left onto *S.W. Park Ave* to pass the **Portland Art Museum**.

Go left three blocks on *S.W. Columbia St*, then left onto *S.W. 6th Ave*. Turn right on *S.W. Madison St*. One block east on the left is **Portlandia**, looming over *S.W. 5th Ave*. **Portland City Hall** is right.

EAST OF THE WILLAMETTE

Continue in the right lane on *S.W. Madison St* and cross the Hawthorne Bridge. **RiverPlace Marina** is to the right. Leaving the bridge, stay right and take the McLoughlin Blvd Exit. Immediately turn right onto *S.E. Clay St*, and continue to *Water Ave*. Turn left to **OMSI, Oregon Museum of Science and Industry**.

Take *Water Ave* to leave OMSI, turning right onto *S.E. Clay St*; left on *S.E. Grand Ave*, and staying left to cross the Willamette River via the Hawthorne Bridge. As you exit from the bridge into downtown, **POVA** offices in the **World Trade Center** building are to the right.

PORTLAND–EUGENE

Oregon Trail pioneers settled in the fertile Willamette Valley between the snow-capped Cascade Mountains and the Coast Range. The 110-mile drive between Portland and Eugene along Interstate 5 takes two hours. Salem, Oregon's capital, and Albany, with three historic districts, are convenient spots to stop.

Willamette Valley farmlands, wetlands, vineyards, hills and refuges are criss-crossed by scenic country roads. Scenic loop possibilities are endless; sights and stretches of particular interest are mentioned as sightseeing from the city where it is most convenient for a visitor to be based. The 100-mile-long valley is named after the Willamette River, which meanders through its western side.

Spring sees the blossoming of orchards, the greening of vineyards and migratory birds flying north. Summer is warm, bustling with field husbandry, grazing cows and sheep. Fall harvest and the wine crush arrives with morning mists and the honking arrival of Canada geese. Winter rains average 40 ins, startling in comparison to 100 ins of annual rainfall on the south-west Oregon Coast or the more than 250 ins of snow that pours on Crater Lake.

SR 99 is a rural artery through some scenic parts of the Willamette Valley. Take several days to explore the countryside, taste the wine, peruse farm antiques, dine on local produce, hike to forest waterfalls and watch rural life unfold.

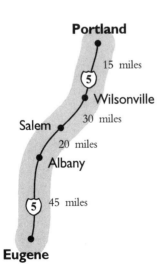

Portland

15 miles

5

Wilsonville

Salem

30 miles

20 miles

Albany

45 miles

5

Eugene

ROUTE: 110 MILES

ROUTE

From the Portland Oregon Visitors Association office at *S.W. Salmon St* and *S.W. Front Ave*, take *S.W. Front Ave* five blocks south and turn left onto *S.W. Market St*, I-5. For the direct route, take I-5 110 miles south to Eugene. Willamette Valley sights are scattered on zigzagging country roads and SR 99 E. and SR 99 W., and are described in 'Sightseeing' under a major town or city located along I-5.

Tourist Information: Willamette Valley Visitors Association/Albany Visitors Association, *300 2nd Ave S.W., PO Box 965, Albany, OR 97321; tel: (800) 526-*

2256 or (541) 928-0911; fax: (541) 926-1500, has information on scenic driving routes, bicycling, accommodation including bed and breakfast, dining, wineries and valley history. Chambers of Commerce have information for cities and towns. Major motel chains are well represented along I-5; watch for blue exit signs with lodging, dining and petrol company logos.

Greater Portland residential areas extend 11 miles south along I-5 to **Tualatin**. **Tualatin Chamber of Commerce,** *8611 SW. Tualatin Rd, PO Box 701, Tualatin, OR 97062; tel: (503) 692-0780; fax: (503) 692-6955,* has local information. An excellent lodging choice is moderate–expensive **Sweetbrier Inn,** *7125 S.W. Nyberg Rd, Tualatin, OR 97062-9231; tel: (800) 551-9167 or (503) 692-5800.* Also moderate is **Stafford Road Country Inn,** *22262 S.W. Stafford Rd; tel: (503) 638-0402,* a farmhouse bed and breakfast. South of Tualatin, the land opens into agriculture.

WILSONVILLE

Tourist Information: Wilsonville Chamber of Commerce, *8880 S.W. Wilsonville Rd, Wilsonville, OR 97070; tel: (503) 682-0411,* has lodging, dining and scenic driving tour information. Motel chains include *BW, Hd* and *S8.* Civilisation is invading Wilsonville's herb nursery and rose growing farms in the form of high technology companies.

SIGHTSEEING

The **Canby Ferry**; *tel: (503) 650-3030,* $1, transports autos and RVs across the Willamette River south-east of Wilsonville. **Swan Island Dahlias,** *995 NW. 22nd Ave, Canby, OR 97013; tel: (503) 266-7711,* 40 acres of public gardens open Aug–first frost Mon–Fri 0900–1630, is the USA's largest dahlia grower. The **Phoenix & Holly Miniature Railroad;** *at the Flower Farmer Nursery, 2512 N. Holly; tel: (503) 266-3581,* operates weekends, May–Oct. **Canby Depot Museum,** *888 NE. 4th Ave; tel; (503) 266-9421,* open Thur–Sun 1300–1600 Mar–Dec, is the former Oregon & California Railroad's oldest surviving station.

For two decades from 1855, **Aurora** flourished south of Canby as a German Christian communal settlement resembling Harmony,

Amana and the Shaker Colony further east. The **Aurora Chamber of Commerce,** *PO Box 86, Aurora, OR 97002; tel: (503) 678-2288,* has information on the town's history and more than 200 antique shops. **Old Aurora Colony Museum,** *15008 2nd St; tel: (503) 678-5754,* offers guided tours of five buildings Feb–Dec. As 97% of US hazelnuts (filberts) are grown in the North Willamette Valley, **Pacific Hazelnut Candy Factory,** *14673 Ottaway Ave; tel: (503) 678-2755,* is a fine place to indulge in toffee, chocolate and confections laced with Oregon hazelnuts

Wilsonville Rd goes west along the Willamette River to **Newberg,** boyhood home US President Herbert Hoover, the **Hoover Minthorn House Museum,** *115 S. River St, Newberg, OR 97132; tel: (503) 538-6629,* open Wed–Sun 1300–1600 Mar–Dec, Sat–Sun Feb and Dec. **Newberg Chamber of Commerce,** *115 N. Washington; tel: (503) 538-2014; fax: (503) 538-2463,* has information on lodging, dining, llama ranches and numerous wineries in Yamhill County.

Cross the river via SR 219 to *Champoeg* (pron: sham-pooh-ee) *Rd.* Go right (west) to **Heirloom Old Garden Roses,** *24062 Riverside Dr. N.E., St Paul, OR 97137; tel: (503) 538-1576,* open 0800–1600, for displays of antique and rare roses. Left (east) on *Champoeg Rd* is **Champoeg State Heritage Area,** *8239 Champoeg Rd N.E., St Paul, OR 97137; tel: (503) 633-8170,* for camping; *tel: (800) 452-5687.* Earliest settlers were French-Canadian trappers. With the influx of American Oregon Trail migrants in 1843, settlers met at Champoeg and voted to establish the Northwest's first provisional government – to replace the Hudson's Bay Company regime. A visitor centre, open daily 0900–1700, explains Calapooia Native American habitation, fur trapping and settlement history. Manson Barn next door survived a disastrous 1861 flood. Next to the park is reconstructed **Newell House Museum;** *tel: (503) 678-5537,* a pioneer Victorian with a quilt collection and basketry. Though the first winery was planted in Champoeg in 1862, it was wiped out during Prohibition.

Not far from I-5 north of Woodburn is **Wooden Shoe Bulb Company,** *33814 S.*

Meridian Rd; tel: (503) 634-2243, 60 acres of tulips and daffodils in full bloom Mar–Apr. **Woodburn Area Chamber of Commerce,** *2233 Country Club Rd, PO Box 194, Woodburn, OR 97071; tel: (503) 982-8221,* has local information.

Brooks, a quarter-mile west from I-5 Exit 263, is home to the **Antique Powerland Museum,** *3995 Brooklake Road N.E., Brooks, OR 97303; tel: (503) 393-2424,* open 1000–1800 Apr–Oct, 1000–1600 Nov–Mar, filled with restored farm equipment powered by steam and petrol engines. The **Pacific Northwest Truck Museum;** *tel: (503) 678-5108,* open weekends Memorial Day–Labor Day 1000–1630, is on the Antique Powerland grounds. The eastern side of Salem is 7 miles south on I-5.

SALEM

Tourist Information: Salem Convention & Visitors Association, *1313 Mill St S.E., Mission Mill Village, Salem, OR 97301; tel: (800) 874-7012 or (503) 581-4325; fax: (503) 581-4540,* has information on Salem, Marion and Polk Counties and general Oregon literature.

GETTING THERE

AMTRAK, *13th and Oak Sts S.E.; tel: (503) 588-1551,* is located downtown. **Greyhound,** *450 Church NE; tel: (503) 362-2428,* serves Oregon's capital. For downtown parking, there's **Marion Parkade,** between *Marion, Union, Liberty* and *High Sts;* **Chemeketa Parkade,** *Commercial between Chemeketa and Court Sts;* and a car park, *High and Mill Sts.*

ACCOMMODATION

Oregon's state capital is well-supplied with lodging, including *BW, M6, QI, RM, S8* and *TL.* The **VISIT Group, Salem Convention & Visitors Association,** *1313 Mill St S.E., Salem, OR 97301; tel: (800) 998-4748 or (503) 399-7199,* has a brochure of 20 Marion & Polk Counties bed and breakfasts in the Willamette Valley, including Salem. **Marquee House,** *333 Wyatt Ct N.E., Salem, OR 97301; tel: (503) 391-0837,* near the capital on Mill Creek, is a moderate, cheerful mini-mansion with antiques and cinema-theme rooms.

EATING AND DRINKING

Locals' favourite is moderate–pricey **Morton's Bistro,** *1128 Edgewater St N.W.; tel: (503) 585-1113,* with French country inn décor and delicious scallops and Northwest fare. Willamette University students create a cheerful sports bar with burgers, fajitas and pizza at budget **Ram Border Café & Big Horn Brewery,** *515 12th St S.E.; tel: (503) 363-1904.* **Karma's Café,** *1313 Mill Creek S.E.; tel: (503) 370-8855,* is a convenient budget place for soup and lunch while touring Mission Mill Village. Satisfy craving for afternoon tea at **Tudor Rose Tea Room,** *480 Liberty St S.E.; tel: (503) 588-2345.*

SHOPPING

Major department stores like Nordstrom, Meier & Frank and Penney's are downtown between *Commercial* and *High Sts.* Find fine quality Oregon-crafted ceramics, jewellery and paintings at **Bush Barn Art Center,** *600 Mission St S.E.; tel: (503) 581-2228.* Stroll through artists' studios at **Leonardo's Loft,** *142 High St S.E.; tel: (503) 581-4642.* **Mission Mill Village Wool Warehouse** shops, *1313 Mill St S.E.; tel: (503) 585-7012 or (800) 874-7012,* include a museum store with Pendleton Woolens, a braid shop, fabric store and Victoriana gift shop.

SIGHTSEEING

While Portland is Oregon's commercial centre and Eugene its university town, Salem, the state capital, is its bureaucratic heart. Most Oregonians look upon Salem as necessary, but otherwise not of interest. It's a fallacy. Salem's tree-lined downtown is gracious, its historical buildings interesting. Salem is also an ideal centre for touring Willamette Valley wineries, parks, nurseries and well-preserved farm towns.

Jason Lee, a Methodist missionary, established a mission on the Oregon Coast, was dissatisfied with poor results, and in 1840, started a new mission headquarters at Chemeketa, 'place of peace', where the Willamette River meets Mill Creek. Missionary success was not overwhelming, so the renamed Salem became the centre for Methodist learning at Willamette University. A town grew, the missionaries became businessmen, and by 1851 Salem was the territorial capital.

The **Oregon State Capitol Building**, *900 Court St N.E., between Court and State Sts; tel: (503) 986-1383;* open Mon–Fri 0800–1700, Sat 0900–1600, Sun 1200–1600, the third on this site since 1876, is made of white Vermont marble with a gold leaf-covered statue of an Oregon Pioneer at the peak of the dome. The 1938 capitol is flanked on its west side by tree-filled **Willson Park**. An indoor **visitors information kiosk** is directly opposite the *Court St* entry. On the inside walls surrounding the rotunda and up the staircases are Oregon history murals depicting Capt. Robert Gray at the mouth of the Columbia River, Lewis and Clark's expedition, Dr. John McLoughlin greeting the first women to traverse the Oregon Trail, settlement, lumber, wheat and fish. The legislative chambers of the House of Representatives and State Senate and the ceremonial governor's office are open. Most surprising are the unabashed natural poses of recent governors' official portraits.

Across from the capitol are the red brick buildings of **Willamette University,** *900 State St; tel: (503) 370-6300.* Founded in 1842, the Methodist institution is the oldest University in the Western USA.

East of the campus across *12th St* is the **Mission Mill Village** complex, *1313 Mill Creek S.E.,* with the Salem CVA, Wool Warehouse shops, **Karma Café,** and town founder Jason Lee's 1841 wood frame house**.**

Thomas Kay Woolen Mill Museum; *tel: (503) 585-7012;* adults $5, children 6–18 $2, has a self-guided or 1-hr interpretative tour. A Samson Leffel turbine powered the 1889 mill for 70 years, a bright but cavernous, two-storey building where signs guide the visitor from picking and carding to spinning, weaving, washing and the many finishing steps. The **Museum Store** sells Pendleton blankets like those formerly fabricated in the mill.

At the north-west corner of Mission Mill Village is the **Marion County Historical Society Museum**, *260 12th St SE.; tel: (503) 364-2128,* open Tues–Sat 0930–1630, for local history and Calapooian Native artefacts, notably a dugout canoe.

North of Mission Mill Village is the **Court-Chemeketa Residential Historic District.** Ask the CVA for an excellent walking tour brochure of the area between *Court, Chemeketa, 13th* and *19th Sts,* where Methodist missionaries and state supreme court justices lived side-by-side with owners of tanneries and furniture factories.

South of downtown and south-west of Willamette University is **Gaiety Hill/Bush's Pasture Park Historic District.** The Salem CVA has a brochure on elegant district architecture and gardens. **Bush's Pasture Park,** *Mission and High Sts,* once orchards and cow pasture, is 100 acres of grass, trees and gardens.

Bush House, *600 Mission St SE., Salem, OR 97302; tel: (503) 363-4714,* open Tues–Sun 1200–1700 June–Sept, 1400–1700 Oct–May, adults $2.50, children 6-12 $1, is the great house from which *Oregon Statesman* publisher Asahel Bush II guided state politics, Ladd & Bush Bank, Salem social affairs and his family from 1878–1913. Tours take in 10 marble fireplaces, electrified gas light fixtures and many original furnishings. Just outside is a greenhouse and small sitting garden. A white gazebo was recently added to the well-kept rose garden at the corner of *Mission* and *High Sts.* Bush House's rebuilt barn is **Bush Barn Art Center,** *600 Mission St SE., Salem, OR 97302; tel: (503) 581-2228,* open Tues–Fri 1000–1700, Sat–Sun 1300–1700, an art gallery with the best of Oregon's contemporary artwork and handicrafts.

Deepwood Estate, *1116 Mission St S.E., on the eastern side of Bush's Pasture Park; tel: (503) 363-1825,* is open Sun–Fri 1200–1630 (May–Sept), Sun–Mon Wed–Fri 1300–1600 (Oct–Apr), adults $2.50, children 6–12 $1. Deepwood Estate's gracious veranda, stained-glass windows and golden oak interior panelling reflect its 1894 Queen Anne heritage. The formal English-style gardens, with a gazebo, were designed by the Northwest's first female landscape architecture firm, Lord and Schryver. Look for weddings on Sats. A large public greenhouse of hothouse specimens is near the parking area. **Rita Steiner Fry Nature Trail** follows Pringle Creek's native vegetation.

Honeywood Winery, *1350 Hines St SE.;*

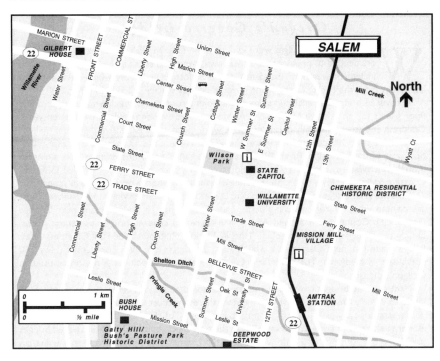

SALEM

North ↑

MARION STREET
GILBERT HOUSE (22)
COMMERCIAL ST
FRONT STREET
Water Street
Willamette River
Commercial Street
Liberty Street
High Street
Marion Street
Union Street
Center Street
Chemeketa Street
Court Street
State Street
Church Street
Cottage Street
Winter Street
W Summer St
E Summer St
Summer Street
Capitol Street
Mill Creek
Wyatt Ct
12th Street
13th Street
(22) FERRY STREET
(22) TRADE STREET
Wilson Park [i]
STATE CAPITOL
WILLAMETTE UNIVERSITY
CHEMEKETA RESIDENTIAL HISTORIC DISTRICT
State Street
Ferry Street
MISSION MILL VILLAGE [i]
Commercial Street
Liberty Street
High Street
Church Street
Winter Street
Trade Street
Mill Street
Shelton Ditch
BELLEVUE STREET
Leslie Street
Pringle Creek
Oak St
University St
Summer Street
Leslie St
12TH STREET
AMTRAK STATION
Mill Street
(22)
BUSH HOUSE
Mission Street
Galty Hill/ Bush's Pasture Park Historic District
DEEPWOOD ESTATE

0 — 1 km
0 — ½ mile

149

tel: (503) 362-4111, open Mon–Fri 0900–1700, Sat 1000–1700, Sun 1300–1700, is Oregon's oldest producing winery. Loganberry joins cranberry for unusual fruit wines; taste peach, blueberry, blackberry and raspberry along with grape varietals.

Salem's modern downtown retains many older buildings in the **Commercial Street Business District,** *between Chemeketa and Ferry, Commercial and Liberty Sts.* Named after A.C. Gilbert, inventor of the Erector Set, **Gilbert House Children's Museum,** *116 Marion St NE., Salem, OR 97301-3427; tel: (503) 371-3631,* open Tues–Sat 1000–1700 Sun 1200–1600, admission $4, is ensconced in two Victorian buildings. Boise-Cascade's paper-finishing operation is south along the Willamette. **Salem Riverfront Park,** *Front St between the Marion St Bridge and Boise-Cascade,* is a new greenspace with views of **Minto-Brown Island** birdlife. **Schreiner's Iris Gardens,** *3625 Quinaby Rd NE., Salem, OR 97303; tel: (503) 393-3232,* has 250 acres in bloom, mid May–early June 0800–dusk.

Out of Town
East of Salem are spectacular waterfalls, iris, and a religious town.

Silver Falls State Park, *on SR 214, 26 miles east of Salem; tel: (503) 873-8681,* is Oregon's largest state park. The 7-mile hiking **Trail of 10 Falls** passes behind South, Lower South and North Falls, along Silver Creek Canyon past falls 27–178 ft high. Other trails are for bicyclists, horse and llama riding. Tents and RV pitches are open year-round, but book early, as this is Salem's mountain holiday spot. Even visitors driving through the park must pay a fee, but a brief free stop is possible at the spectacular **North Falls Viewpoint.**

Silverton has an old-fashioned downtown and historic district, easily self-guided with a brochure from the **Silverton Chamber of Commerce,** *421 S. Water St, Silverton, OR 97381; tel: (503) 873-5615.* The Norman Rockwell murals on downtown buildings are outstanding. **Cooley's Gardens,** *11553 Silverton Rd N.E., Silverton; tel: (503) 873-5463; fax: (503) 873-5812,* largest grower of bearded

Oregon's Covered Bridges

Wooden covered bridges were known in the Eastern USA and Canada, where farmers needed to protect road access over rivers and streams during heavy snow and inclement weather. Abundant Douglas-fir forests and heavy winter rains and salty air wafting from the Pacific Ocean made covered bridges equally practical in Oregon.

A covered bridge has enclosed sides and a sloping roof that protect wooden trusses and floor planks for an average of 40 years. An unprotected wooden bridge may last ten years. Concrete and steel, especially during wartime, were much more expensive than local timber.

Of more than 300 covered bridges in the 1930s, Oregon has 53 today, the largest collection west of the Mississippi River. (Request the 'Oregon's Covered Bridges' map from **Oregon Tourism Division**.) Not all are used and some have been moved from original locations. Crossing traffic still slows to 5 mph, a nostalgic reminder of horse-drawn carriage speed.

Each covered bridge has a unique design. Some have interior carvings and windows. Most are painted white or red, matching barns. Lane County has 19 bridges, many near Cottage Grove. Linn County has 9 around Albany, and there are covered bridges in Benton, Coos, Deschutes, Douglas, Jackson, Josephine, Lincoln, Marion, Multnomah and Polk Counties. Office Bridge (Lane Co. near Oakridge) is 180 ft long; the shortest is 39-ft Lost Creek (Hwy 140 north-east of Medford). The 1914 Drift Creek Bridge near Lincoln City, no longer used, in Oregon's oldest.

Most covered bridges have name and construction date plaques below the roof peak. Step inside to admire the strong Howe truss system shared by most Oregon covered bridges: half 'A' timbers slope towards the roof's centre to make an 'X' using vertical tie rods. Though heavy modern vehicles and faster speed limits make them an anachronism, Oregon's covered bridges still evoke the romance of a time when life in the country was slower and even a utilitarian bridge was built of fine wood to last for decades.

150

iris in the world, has millions of flowers in bloom for public viewing mid May–June.

Mt Angel is indeed religious. Benedictine Mt Angel Abbey overlooks the town, famed for celebrations of German heritage and the gardens of **Queen of Angels Monastery,** *840 S. Main St, Mt Angel, OR 97362-9527; tel: (503) 845-6141.* **Mt Angel Chamber of Commerce,** *PO Box 221, Mt Angel, OR 97362; tel: (503) 845-6882.*

West of Salem are an old-fashioned ferry, spectacular wineries, and fudge. Take the *Marion Street* bridge west over the Willamette River. **Wallace Marine Park** on the riverbank, is to the right. SR 221 parallels the river north, with several small signs marking hiking and **Willamette River Greenway Access**. Turn right at **Maud Williamson State Park** to reach the historic **Wheatland Ferry**, cars $1, motorcycles $.75, which takes about 3 mins to make the Willamette River crossing. On the

east bank 8 miles north of Salem is **Willamette Mission State Park,** *Wheatland Rd; tel: (503) 393-1172,* where Methodist missionary Jason Lee established Oregon's first Mission house in 1834. A monument marks the mission site not far from the USA's largest black cottonwood, which spreads 110 ft from a height of 156 ft. Jogging, hiking, bicycling, horse riding and fishing are daily activities.

Among several fine wineries north-west of Salem is **Redhawk Vineyard & Winery,** *2995 Michigan City Ave N.W., Salem, OR 97304; tel: (503) 362-1596,* open 1200–1700 May–Nov. The tasting room looks over the vineyards planted on a slope. Chardonnays are flavourful and intense. Fine quality wines masquerade under humourous cartoon labels like Rat Race Red. A terrified surfer on a shark graces Great White. Bigfoot Blend has two Sasquatch chatting over glasses of wine, and Chateau Mootom Cabernet Sauvignon has two bovines remarking on how curious it is that humans drink milk.

Turn left (west) from SR 221 onto *Zena Rd,* then right (north) on Hwy 99W to **Amity. Amity Vineyards,** *18150 Amity Vineyards Rd, Amity, OR 97101-9603; tel: (503) 835-2362,* open 1200–1700 Feb–Dec 23, has picnic tables perched on a hill above the farming town. One of Oregon's early wineries, Amity was the first US producer of Gamay Noir and makes organic, sulphite-free ECO Pinot Noir. Try the wide range of varietal wines offered in the tasting room for a good sampling of Oregon-style Pinot Noir, Gewürztraminer and Riesling. Monks at the **Brigittine Monastery,** *23300 Walker Lane, Amity, OR 97101; tel: (503) 835-8080,* open 0930–1730, sell home-made fudge and truffles for $8 per box.

For the best introduction to Oregon wine, visit the **Oregon Wine Tasting Room,** *19700 Hwy 18, Sheridan, OR, 97378; tel: (503) 843-3787,* open 1130–1730, west of Amity in space shared with **Lawrence Gallery;** *tel: (800) 894-4278,* a venue for fine arts by 150 Northwest artists.

South-west of Salem, the **Monmouth/ Independence Chamber of Commerce,** *110 N. Atwater, Monmouth, OR 97361; tel: (503) 838-4268,* has information on both towns. The disappearance of Eskimo culture and the need to preserve its artefacts led Paul Jensen to establish **Jensen Arctic Museum,** *Western Oregon State College, 590 W. Church St, Monmouth, OR 97361; tel: (503) 838-8468,* open Tues–Sat 1000–1600. The 1888 First Baptist Church building houses Independence's **Heritage Museum,** *112 S. 3rd St, Independence, OR 97351; tel: (503) 838-4989,* open Wed, Sat 1300–1700, Thurs–Fri 1300–1600.

Two miles south of Salem overlooking I-5 (from Exit 247) is **Willamette Valley Vineyards,** *8800 Enchanted Way S.E., Turner, OR 97392; tel: (800) 344-9463 or (503) 588-9463,* open 1100–1800, Oregon's largest wine producer with a huge range of wines to sample. Don't miss the Chardonnays and pinot noir. **Enchanted Forest,** *8462 Enchanted Way S.E;* tel: *(503) 371-4242,* open mid Mar–Sept 0930–1800, is a children's theme park based on figures formed from trees.

Take Exit 243 *(Ankeny Hill Rd)* west .25 mile, then turn right for 1½ miles to access **Ankeny National Wildlife Refuge**'s viewing area above Willamette River bottomlands. The three Willamette Valley refuges protect dusky Canada geese during fall and winter after their migration from spring nesting sites in Alaska's Copper River Delta. Ankeny, William L. Finley and Baskett Slough National Wildlife Refuges are closed when 'duskies' winter over.

ALBANY

Tourist Information: Albany Visitors Association, *300 2nd Ave SW., PO Box 965, Albany, OR 97321; tel: (800) 526-2256 or (541) 928-0911; fax: (541) 926-1500,* has literature for the Willamette Valley, Albany lodging, dining and shopping, covered bridges, and a *Historic Albany* newspaper describing its 3 historic districts.

ACCOMMODATION AND FOOD

The **Albany Visitors Association** has lodging and dining information. Chains include *BW, CI* and *Hd.* There are several RV parks in town and a **KOA Campsite. Brier Rose Inn Bed & Breakfast,** *206 7th Ave S.W., Albany, OR 97321; tel: (541) 926-0345,* a moderate 1886 Queen Anne Victorian, is in the centre of the 3 historic districts. Saturday high tea and dinner theatre is the fare at **Flinn's Parlour,** *222 1st Ave S.W., downtown historic district; tel: (541) 928-9638.*

SIGHTSEEING

Albany's 350 Victorian buildings – businesses, homes and churches in more than 10 architectural styles – were bypassed when freeways were built. The somewhat shabby **Downtown Historic District,** *from Washington to Baker Sts and Water St to 3rd Ave,* includes 20 antique shops amidst buildings which were once at the heart of the confluence of the Calapooia and Willamette Rivers. It's easy to imagine the steamboat landing, blacksmithy, opera house, livery stables, banks, a theatre, general store and cigar store. The **Flinn Block,** *222 1st Ave SW.,* still preserves a rakish French Second Empire décor. **Flinn's Parlour, Flinn's Living History Theatre** and **Flinn's Tours;**

151

tel: (800) 636-5008 or (503) 928-5008, still make use of the premises.

The two residential historic districts were rivals. The **Hackleman District,** *between Ellsworth and Madison Sts, 2nd to 8th Aves,* housed the working class which toiled in the furniture factory and foundry, or on the railway. The houses were practical, but laced with Victorian decoration which still rivals the wealthier mansions in the adjoining **Monteith District,** *Elm to Ellsworth Sts, 2nd to 12th Aves.* Monteith District residents were Republican party advocates, merchants and businessmen who sided with the Union (North) in the US Civil War. Hackleman residents were Democrats and Confederate (South) sympathisers. The **Albany Regional Museum,** *303 Ferry St SW.; tel: (541) 967-6540,* open 1200–1600 summer Wed–Sun, winter Wed–Sat, in the basement below the library, has a reconstructed 1939 shoe-shine shop once owned by the Albany's only Black couple; trunks, pictures and posters of the Harlin-Talbert vaudeville act; a doctor's office; a mercantile shop and a photography studio. The 1849 **Monteith House,** *518 2nd Ave SW; tel: (541) 967-8699,* open 1200–1600 summer Wed–Sun, has collections from the pioneer era when Albany's first frame house was built.

Eleven miles south-west of Albany on Hwy 20, **Corvallis** hosts a major Oregon University Campus. **Corvallis Oregon Convention & Visitors Bureau,** *420 NW. 2nd, Corvallis, OR 97330; tel: (800) 334-8118 or (503) 757-1544; fax: (503) 753-2664,* open Mon–Fri 0800–1700, has area information. As Oregon is the country's largest mint oil producer, the US Department of Agriculture's Agricultural Research Service keeps a 500-species **mint collection,** the USA's largest, in Corvallis. **Irish Bend Covered Bridge,** *on the OSU campus,* for walking and bicycling, is a good example of a Willamette Valley covered bridge.

Wet prairie, a homestead and barn, grazing cows and hay mark **William L. Finley National Wildlife Refuge;** *26208 Finley Refuge Rd; tel: (503) 757-7326,* open May–Oct. One of three Willamette Valley dusky Canada geese wintering spots, Finley, 12 miles south of Corvallis, with oak and Douglas-fir forests,

savannah, ash swale woodlands and marsh, is the headquarters for all three refuges. Roosevelt elk roam the pastures. The Fiechter homestead shows the style of well-to-do pioneer ranchers. Local grasses are so high that birdwatchers are well-hidden when walking the Woodpecker Loop Trail.

Continue south on I-5 to **Coburg,** a tree-lined town with antique shops in the midst of historic homes. South of Coburg, I-5 crosses the McKenzie River; **Springfield** (see p. 174) is on the east (left) side and Eugene is on the western (right) side of the interstate.

EUGENE

Tourist Information: Convention & Visitors Association of Lane County Oregon (CVALCO), *115 W. 8th Ave, Suite 190, PO Box 10286, Eugene, OR 97440; tel: (800) 547-5445 or (541) 484-5307; fax: (541) 343-6335,* open Mon–Fri 0830–1700; Sat in summer, has information on Eugene lodging, dining and attractions. The **Eugene Area Chamber of Commerce,** *1401 Willamette St; tel: (541) 484-1314; fax: (541) 484-4942,* open Mon–Fri, also has a visitors centre.

GETTING THERE

Eugene Airport, *28855 Lockheed Dr, Eugene, OR 97402; tel: (541) 687-5544,* north-west of downtown Eugene, is served by major airlines. **AMTRAK**'s main station is at *433 Willamette St; tel: (800) 872-7245.* **Greyhound**'s depot is at *987 Pearl St; tel: (800) 231-2222.* Local bus service for Eugene and Springfield is **Lane Transit District (LTD),** *Eugene Station Customer Service Center, 10th Ave and Willamette St; (800) 248-3861 or (541) 687-5555,* open Mon–Fri 0600–2325, Sat–Sun 0900–1725.

ACCOMMODATION

Eugene's prominence as home of the University of Oregon means lots of lodging for relatives visiting students. **CVALCO** has a *Lane County Restaurant & Lodging Guide.* BW, CI, Hd, and Hn are among the chains in Eugene. The expensive–pricey **Eugene Hilton Hotel,** *66 E. 6th Ave, Eugene, OR 97401; tel: (541) 342-2000,* is in the heart of downtown adjacent to the Hult Center. The **Phoenix Inn,** *850*

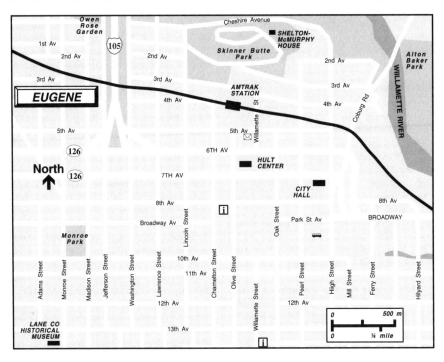

Franklin Blvd; tel: (541) 344-0001, is moderate–expensive comfort within a block of the UO campus. Most of the dozen bed and breakfasts are in the moderate range. Rooms in Springfield, just east of Eugene and in Cottage Grove, south on I-5, may be cheaper, if not as convenient as staying near the centre of Eugene.

EATING AND DRINKING

CVALCO has a restaurant list. **Fifth Street Public Market,** 5th Ave between Pearl and High Sts, has a food court with good ethnic, bakery and expresso selections. **Mekala's Thai Restaurant,** 296 E. 5th Ave; tel; (541) 342-4872, moderate, is one of the restaurants in the complex. Across the street, moderate **Jo Federigo's Café, & Jazz Bar,** 295 E. 5th Ave; tel; (541) 343-8488, serves Italian/Continental fare with nightly jazz. Posh, pricey **Chanterelle,** 207 E. 5th Ave, Suite 109; tel: (541) 484-4065, is a place to be elegant. Try feasting on prime rib in classic railway cars at moderate **Oregon Electric Station,** 27 E. 5th

Ave; tel: (541) 485-4444, with music on weekends. Vegetarians and vegans eat well at budget **Downtown Garden Café, and Juice Bar,** 120 W. Broadway; tel: (541) 484-2993. Closer to the UO campus, **Studio One Café,** 1473 E. 19th Ave; tel: (541) 342-8596, serves budget food, and is known for breakfast French toast with berry compote and almond custard. For entertainment venues, check the free Eugene Weekly newspaper.

SHOPPING

Fifth Street Public Market, 296 5th Ave between Pearl and High Sts; tel: (541) 484-0383, shopping ranges from the **Nike Store;** tel: (541) 342-5155, a solid wall of shoes displayed in the town where the company began, to **Southwest Journey, Ltd.;** tel: (541) 484-6804, with outstanding objets d'art and jewellery made by Native Americans from the Southwest and Northwest. The **Oregon Cotton Mill;** tel: (541) 687-2420 has natural fibre clothing. A braid store and scent shop fill the other space around a Spanish-style courtyard. **Real Goods,**

77 W. Broadway St, Eugene; tel: (541) 334-6960, has a wide selection of environmentally friendly kitchen objects and garden tools made of non-native wood.

SIGHTSEEING

Oregonians are fond of Eugene, the state's prime university town. On Eugene's east side, Springfield, an industrial and agricultural centre, adjoins Oregon's second most populous city. Eugene's two activity centres are downtown, near the Willamette River (*4th to 11th Aves* and *High to Lincoln Sts*), and the University of Oregon (*south of Broadway/Franklin Blvd*). Four self-guided *Trees of Eugene* tour brochures, *Eugene Tree Commission, City of Eugene Public Works, 1820 Roosevelt Blvd; tel: (541) 687-5220,* cover pre-statehood, west downtown, and the west and south university neighbourhoods.

Hult Center for the Performing Arts, *faces Willamette St, between 5th and 6th Aves; tel: (541) 342-5746,* or for tours, *(541) 687-5087,* is the non-governmental downtown hub. In the centre, **Silva Concert Hall** hosts Eugene's ballet, symphony and opera companies and visiting artists. **Soreng Theatre** stages smaller productions and plays.

Skinner Butte offers views of the Cascades. At the base of the butte is **Shelton-McMurphey House,** *303 Willamette St.* There are occasional tours, but it's possible to view the building's exterior amidst a tree-filled park, the beginning of a self-guided walking tour round the **East Skinner Butte Historic Landmark Area,** *Eugene Planning Dept; tel: (541) 687-5481.* Drive on *Cheshire Ave* by **Skinner Butte Park,** set along the banks of the Willamette River below the butte. A replica of Applegate (Oregon) Trail pioneer Eugene Skinner's 1846 one-room log cabin is at the park's west end. Skinner platted and settled Oregon Donation land in 1851 to establish the largest town in the upper Willamette Valley, and gave his first name to Eugene. North-west on *Cheshire Ave* is **G. Owen Memorial Rose Gardens,** a magnificent floral display with numerous picnic tables.

The **Lane County Historical Museum,** *740 W. 13th Ave; tel: (541) 687-4239;* open Wed–Fri 1000–1600, Sat 1200–1600, adults $2, children 3–17 $.75, has a pristine 1890 hearse, 1920s–30s flapper and jazz-era clothing and artefacts, sheet music and Depression-era necessities in a better-than-average collection of local memorabilia.

Near Eugene Airport, the **Oregon Air & Space Museum,** *90377 Boeing Dr.; tel: (541) 461-1101,* open Thur–Sun 1200–1700, adults $3, children 6–11 $1, has aeroplanes and more than 600 small models tracing aviation history.

More than 17,000 students attend the **University of Oregon at Eugene,** *1585 E. 13th Ave; tel: (541) 346-3111.* Many are runners, in the tradition of several US Olympic gold medallists and local hero Steve 'Pre' Prefontaine, killed in a car accident at the moment he held all USA running records. One of Pre's track coaches founded Nike. Three loops connect bark chip-padded **Pre's Trail,** (free map from **Prefontaine Foundation,** *PO Box 693, Eugene, OR 97440*) 3.87 miles long, from UO's **Autzen Stadium** to a jog over the Willamette River. Hire a canine from **Working Dogs;** *tel: (541) 345-8086,* to go with you. Or hire a reconstructed reclining (recumbent) bicycle from **Eugene Bicycle Works,** *Center for Appropriate Transport, 455 W. 1st Ave; tel: (541) 683-3397,* Tues–Sun, $5 per hr to tackle the Willamette River Bike Path.

On the UO campus, 1876 Deady Hall is an ivy-covered Victorian house, reminiscent of the Addams Family. The **Museum of Natural History,** *1680 E. 15th Ave; tel: (541) 346-3024,* open Wed–Sun 1200-1700, calls itself 'The 13,000 year old tourist trap', with a collection of ancient fibre sandals excavated on the Columbia River's banks and a displays of Oregon animal species. Asian, Russian and African artefacts are displayed at the **Museum of Art,** *1430 Johnson Lane; tel: (541) 346-3027,* open Wed–Sun 1200–1700. Just off campus, **Maude Kerns Art Center,** *1910 E. 15th Ave; tel: (541) 345-1571,* open Tues–Fri 1000–1700 Sat–Sun 1300–1700, has galleries filled with fine art by local painters, and artists. A few blocks south on a ridgeline is **Hendricks Park,** *Summit Dr.,* with 5000 May-blooming rhododendrons and azaleas planted amidst magnolias and Douglas-fir.

EUGENE-MEDFORD

The agricultural southern stretches of the Willamette Valley along Interstate 5 give way to forests and well-preserved Victorian-era farm towns. South of Eugene's sprawling university town atmosphere, farming, lumbering, fishing and hunting have been the mode of life for generations. Innate conservatism lends a rough and ready look to the less-developed landscape, a studied wildness just off the interstate.

Allot four hours non-stop driving. If time permits, take at least two days to explore this 170-mile route, part of the mid-19th century Portland to Sacramento, California stagecoach run. Roseburg and Grants Pass have extensive lodging and services. Wildlife Safari near Roseburg can easily occupy half a day; historic Jacksonville, west of Medford, another half day. The Umpqua River is a short drive east from Roseburg. Interstate 5 follows the Rogue River Valley east from Grants Pass. Medford, the regional hub at the end of this route, has few in-town attractions but is an ideal base for Jacksonville, Ashland's Shakespeare Festival and Highway 62, the only year-round road to Crater Lake.

155

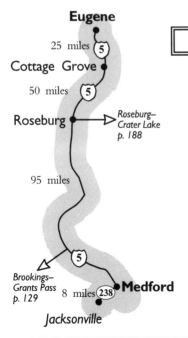

ROUTE: 170 MILES

ROUTE

Take I-5 south from Eugene for 138 miles to Grants Pass. Interstate 5 turns east for 30 miles to Medford. As with the Portland to Eugene Route, the side roads off I-5 can be very scenic.

From Exit 182, the **Creswell Chamber of Commerce**, *55 N. 5th St, PO Box 577, Creswell OR 97426; tel: (541) 895-5161,* shares space with the **Creswell Historical Museum** in an 1889 white church decked in Victorian gingerbread and tapering steeple. Four miles south is a **rest area.** Exit 174 to Dorena Lake winds through countryside and strip malls to **Cottage Grove.**

COTTAGE GROVE

Tourist Information: Cottage Grove Chamber of Commerce, *710 Row River Rd, PO Box 587, Cottage Grove, OR 97424; tel: (541) 942-2411; fax: (541) 942-7625,* has information on the well-preserved historic residential neighbourhoods, downtown and covered bridges. Accommodation in the self-proclaimed 'Covered Bridge Capital of Oregon' include *BW, CI* and **US Forest Service campgrounds, Cottage Grove Ranger District**, *78405 Cedar Park Rd; tel; (541) 942-5591.*

Riverfront Park, *south-west of Main St and the historic district*, is a lovely, tree-lined walk along the Willamette River. **Cottage Grove Museum**, *Birch & H Sts; tel: (541) 942-3963,* open 1300–1600 Wed–Sun mid June–Labor Day, Sat–Sun Sept–June, has historic Bohemia Mines gold mining and timber industry artefacts in an old octagonal-shaped church.

Territorial Seed Company, *20 Palmer Ave; tel: (541) 942-9547,* tests and sells seeds from around the world which grow well in the Northwest. **Georgia-Pacific Corp Research Center & Tree Seedling Nursery**, *76928 Mosby Creek Rd; tel; (541) 942-5516; fax: (541) 942-5681,* has tours of this major timber company laboratory, arboretum and greenhouse nursery. **Weyerhaeuser Lumber Mill**, *Hwy 995; tel: (541) 942-3301,* takes advance tour bookings.

COTTAGE GROVE TO ROSEBURG

There's a rest area at mile 140. Take Exit 138 right (east) to **Oakland**, several well-preserved blocks of red brick storefronts. The town put all its buildings on rollers in 1872, and moved the structures 2 miles to the new railway depot. Stop at the **Oakland Museum**, *136 Locust St, Oakland, OR, 97479; tel: (541) 459-3087,* open daily 1300–1630, for tourist and lodging information. Ask for the free self-guided *History & Walking Tour* brochure, also available at **City Hall**, *117 3rd St; tel: (541) 459-4531.*

The first settled town in the area, Oakland served as a stage-coach stop, central post office, plum and hops centre, and claims to have

developed broad-breasted turkeys. Today, the draw is tourism.

Tolly's, *115 Locust St; tel; (541) 459-3796,* draws prime rib connoisseurs and old-fashioned soda fountain fans from miles around. **Tollefson's Antiques**, adjacent to the restaurant, has an eclectic mix of collectable art.

Rural scenery predominates north of Roseburg. A large collection of older wooden barns remains, many in the outskirts around Oakland, Sutherlin, and Roseburg. The **Sutherlin Visitor Center**, *1470 W. Central, Sutherlin, OR 97479; tel: (800) 371-5829,* has information on Douglas County barns, covered bridges and gold mining.

ROSEBURG

Tourist Information: Roseburg Visitors & Convention Bureau, *410 SE. Spruce St, PO Box 1262, Roseburg, OR, 97470; tel: (800) 444-8584 or (541) 672-9731; fax: (541) 673-7868.*

ACCOMMODATION AND FOOD

The Roseburg VCB *Umpqua Valley Bed & Breakfast Association* brochure covers seven inns. Chains include *BW, CI, Hd, HJ* and *TL*. The **Windmill Inn**, *1450 N.W. Mulholland; tel: (800) 547-4747 or (541) 673-0901* is a motel conveniently situated next to I-5. Moderate.

Fast food is abundant, especially on Garden Valley Blvd and Hwy 99. **Umpqua Brewing Co.**, *328 SE. Jackson; tel: (541) 672-0453,* open Tues–Sun, supplements 16 on-tap microbrews with pesto and artichoke pizzas and live jazz, reggae and blues music Thur–Sat. Try UPA (Umpqua Pale Ale), Downtown Brown and No Doubt Stout.

SIGHTSEEING

Roseburg is a jumping-off point for Umpqua River recreation (Hwy 138, see p.188) and Umpqua Valley winery touring. Two of the eight **Umpqua Region Appellation Wineries** are west of Roseburg via, *Garden Valley Rd*, Exit 125. **Callahan Ridge Winery**, *340 Busenbark Lane, Roseburg; tel· (800) 695-4946 or (541) 673-7901,* open 1130–1700 Apr–Oct, the largest Pacific Northwest zinfandel producer, is in a 110-year old hay barn. Picnic tables have good vineyard views; tasting room

156

staff tell Oregon wine history while pouring a large varietal selection.

Ten miles from Roseburg, **HillCrest Vineyard**, *240 Vineyard Lane, Roseburg; tel: (800) 736-3709,* open 1100–1700, pioneered grape wine production in Oregon 30 years ago and is famed for Riesling and Cabernet Sauvignon. With November's harvest blessing is the valley winemakers' Whole Roast Pig Dinner.

Wine is the area's most recent attraction. Roseburg was an 1850 Donation Land Claim, which prospered as a county seat, then thrived between 1872 and 1927 as an important railway hub. Railway workers' homes, many quite grand, survive in the **Downtown Roseburg** and **Mill-Pine Historic District**. Ask the RVCB for excellent historic district and downtown mural tour brochures.

The **Douglas County Museum of History and Natural History**, *97470 I-5, Exit 123, Roseburg; tel: (541) 957-7007,* open 0900–1700, adults $3.50, children $1, has an exceptional collection of farm family photographs from nearby Glendale, Applegate Trail pioneer history and sound recordings of local owl cries.

ROSEBURG TO JACKSONVILLE

The Pacific Northwest's best drive-through wild animal park is south of Roseburg in **Winston**. **Wildlife Safari**, follow signs from I-5, *Exit 119, PO Box 1600, Winston, OR 97496-0231; tel: (800) 355-4848* or *(541) 679-6761,* open daily, core hours 0900–1600, open earlier and later in summer, adults $9.95, children 4–12 $ 6.75, $1 car fee, has large herds of animals from Africa, Asia and North America. Plan on several hours to drive through 600 acres twice *very slowly,* as 600 resident animals and birds amble by car windows or block the road. Bears and Bengal tigers are in separate areas, and other animals like elephants are electrically restrained from contact with humans. Thundering groups of giraffes, bison, moufflon sheep, emus and antelope wheel through rolling hills in an extremely evocative safari experience.

Find a rest area off Exit 112. Take Exit 108 for a short detour to **Myrtle Creek** where a

covered bridge, no longer used, spans Horse Creek.

At Exit 99, near Christmas tree farms, the Cow Creek Band of Umpqua Tribe of Indians operates the moderate **Seven Feathers Hotel & Gaming Resort**, *146 Chief Miwaleta Lane, Canyonville, OR 97417; tel: (888) 677-7771* (hotel), *(800) 548-8461* (casino), open 24 hrs, with an RV park.

For information on Cow Creek Band history, contact the **Canyonville Chamber of Commerce**, *250 N. Main St, tel: (541) 839-4258.* Canyonville's **Pioneer Park** has a 110-inch diameter stump of a Douglas-fir tree. **Herbert's Pond** is a lovely wetland for geese, Canada geese and ducks.

Forested canyon walls flank I-5 which crosses over 2020-ft Canyon Creek Pass. From Exit 88, take *Azalea Glen Rd* to the old-fashioned **Azalea General Store** and delicious hearty breakfasts at **Cow Creek Station Café.** Country roads parallel the interstate to **Glendale.** Six miles south of Azalea on the east side of I-5 is another rest area. I-5 leaves the Cow Creek Valley at 1830-ft Stage Road Pass just beyond Exit 80, Glendale.

Wolf Creek, Exit 76, is a hamlet kept on the map by the **Wolf Creek Tavern**, *Oregon State Parks; tel: (541) 866-2474,* a moderate eight-room inn and restaurant built 1868–1873 as a way station for Portland–Sacramento stagecoach line travellers. Wolf Creek also has a general store, petrol station and RV park.

Three miles east is 1890-era **Golden**, a gold mining ghost town with a wooden church and store. Sinners were sent elsewhere, as evidenced by two churches, but no saloons in its heyday. Golden yielded $1½ million in gold.

Sunny Valley KOA is on the west side of I-5 at Exit 71. On the east side, **White Grave Creek** Covered Bridge gleams brightly amidst farms. Interstate 5 crosses the 1960-ft Sexton Mountain Pass, then descends. Two miles north of Merlin is a rest area with shaded picnic tables.

Exit 58 is at the junction of I-5 and Hwy 99, at north **Grants Pass**. (see p. 133). Exit 55, south Grants Pass, is the I-5/Hwy 199 junction. The interstate turns east, roughly following the course of the **Rogue River**, favoured in the

157

1930s by Western novelist Zane Grey. The Rogue, named after a rough translation of a local Native American group name by unkind French fur trappers, is born in the forests around **Prospect** (see p. 194) to the west of Crater Lake.

It reaches the Oregon Coast at **Gold Beach** 215 miles later. Kayakers and May–Oct white water rafting operators use Grants Pass as a staging centre. Rafting and steelhead fishing are superb in the 32-mile wild and scenic river wilderness north-west and downriver from Grants Pass, starting from Grave Creek. The **Grants Pass Visitors and Convention Bureau**, *1501 N.E. 6th St, PO Box 1787, Grants Pass, OR 97526; tel: (541) 476-5510,* and the **Bureau of Land Management**, *3040 Biddle Rd, Medford, OR 97504; tel: (541) 770-2200,* have information on outfitters, guides, jetboats and wilderness hiking on the Rogue River.

Not far east of Grants Pass is **Savage Rapids Dam**, a local watersport recreation area, which has so blocked river water flow that authorities are proposing fish ladders to save fish mangled in dam turbines. The town of **Rogue River** is at Exit 48. **Tourist Information: Rogue River Chamber of Commerce**, *Main St; tel: (541) 582-0242.* Lumber is processed at a huge plant near town, most famous for the annual June Rooster Crow Contest. **Palmerton Arboretum**; *tel: (541) 582-4401,* conserves a tree collection gathered from around the world and is spectacular with spring-blooming azaleas and rhododendrons. The arboretum is connected to Anna Classick Park by a swaying suspension bridge. Take Exit 45B to the lovely riverside **Valley of the Rogue State Park**; *tel: (541) 582-1118,* with 178 pitches.

A winding country road parallels I-5 to **Gold Hill**. **Oregon Vortex**, *4303 Sardine Creek Rd, Gold Hill, OR 97525; tel: (541) 855-1543,* open Mar–Oct 15, adults $6.50, allegedly has proof that nature can defy gravity. Balls roll uphill and height and shape are reversed.

Gold Hill, at Exit 40, has a few older buildings and antique shops. Approaching Medford on I-5, the **Bear Creek Greenway** is on the left (north) side. A hikers' favourite, the **Table Rocks**, *Bureau of Land Management, 3040 Biddle Rd, Medford, OR 97504; tel: (541) 770-2200,* rise from the valley floor in two 800-ft high mesas just beyond the greenway. Wildflowers bloom in the grasslands below Table Rocks Mar–June. A unique meadowfoam species blooms on top.

Stop at **Crater Rock Museum**, *2002 Scenic Ave, Central Point, OR 97502; tel: (541) 664-1355,* opening hrs 0900–1700, for a good look at Oregon's geology and Rogue area tribal artefacts.

◤ SIDE TRACK TO JACKSONVILLE

Although Jacksonville is easily reached from Medford via Rte 238, for an ultra-scenic country drive to **Jacksonville**, take Exit 40, *Old Stage Road,* south for 10½ miles to where it becomes *Oregon St.* The Siskiyou Mountain foothills are south (right); Mt McLoughlin, a Cascade peak, rises regally to the north (left).

On the outskirts of town, the **Nunan Catalog House**, once a museum, is being refurbished in Victorian mail order catalogue style.

JACKSONVILLE

Tourist Information: Jacksonville Chamber of Commerce, *185 N. Oregon St (in the Rogue River Railway Depot), PO Box 33, Jacksonville, OR 97530; tel: (541) 899-8118; fax: (541) 899-4462,* open 1000–1600 Thur–Mon, closed winter, has complete information and a keyed walking tour map of Jacksonville, entirely preserved as a national historic district.

ACCOMMODATION

Jacksonville Bed & Breakfast Association, *PO Box 787, Jacksonville, OR, 97530,* represents six fine inns. The 1861 **Jacksonville Inn**, *175 E. California St, PO Box 359, Jacksonville OR 97530; tel: (800) 321-9344* or *(541) 899-1900,* has eight expensive antique-furnished rooms above the **Jacksonville Inn Dinner House**, one of Oregon's best restaurants.

Sixty rosebushes flank the walkway to the white Colonial **McCully House Inn & Gardens**, *240 E. California St, PO Box 13; tel: (800) 367-1942 or (541) 899-1942*, also built in 1861, with three expensive rooms. Dinners and Sunday brunch are famous, using fresh garden herbs for dishes like Chinook salmon cakes and Hoisen BBQ sauce baby back ribs with garlic mashed potatoes. Pricey. The moderate **Stage Lodge**, *830 N. 5th St; tel: (800) 253-8254 or (541) 899-3953*, is the motel alternative.

EATING AND DRINKING

The **Bella Union,** *170 W. California St; tel: (541) 899-1770*, is Jacksonville's third historic fine dining establishment. Cheap–budget **Liberty Foods & Bakery,** *150 W. California St; tel: (541) 899-1851*, has delicious roasted vegetable sandwiches, muffins and breads. Ice-cream shops do great business in summer.

For wine tasting, there's **Gary West Tasting Room,** *690 N. 5th St; tel: (541) 899-1829* and **Anne Marie Tasting Room,** *130 W. California St; tel: (541) 899-1001*.

SIGHTSEEING

Jacksonville's main road is *California Street,* three blocks of brick and wooden buildings, many with overhanging balconies to shade passers-by. The town began as an 1851 gold mining camp following a rush to the Rogue River Valley, and was the county seat until 1884 when the railway chose Middle Ford (later, Medford) as its stop. Miners become farmers, but Jacksonville's buildings remained.

In summer, motorised trolley cars conduct 50-min narrated town tours, *from 3rd and California Sts; tel: (541) 535-5617*, adults $4, under 12, $2. Horse-drawn carriages can be hailed, **Keens Cross J Carriage Service,** *tel: (541) 846-8972.* Though street parking is free, park only in marked areas.

The **Jackson County Courthouse** is now used for the **Jacksonville Museum of Southern Oregon History,** *206 N. 5th St; tel: (541) 773-6536*, open Memorial Day–Labor Day 1000–1700, Tues–Sun Sept–May, adults $3, with a large rifle collection, a good display of baskets by Native Americans from the central Oregon Coast to Northern California and a film documenting forcible removal of Takelma natives to the coast on Oregon's Trail of Tears. **C.C. Beekman House,** *352 E. California St; tel: (541) 773-6536*, open Memorial Day–Labor Day, 1300–1700, adults $3, children 6-12 $2, has living history tours through the mansion guided by the maid, piano students, and banker Beekman himself.

Jacksonville Cemetery, *E. St rise*, is 30 acres of wildflowers and graceful trees encircling beautiful old gravestones, many from the 1860s. The mid June–Aug **Britt Festivals,** *517 W. 10th St, PO Box 1124, Medford, OR, 97501; tel: (800) 882-7488 or (541) 773-6077; fax: (541) 776-3712*, named after a gold rush-era miner-turned-photographer, Peter Britt, feature an eclectic range of concerts, from John Mayall's blues to Helen Reddy, Harry Belafonte and Hugh Masekela.

MEDFORD

Tourist Information: Medford Visitors & Convention Bureau, *101 E. 8th St, Medford, OR 97501; tel: (800) 469-6307; (541) 779-4847; fax: (541) 776-4808;* **Medford Information Center,** *1314 Center Dr.*, next to *Harry & David's/Jackson & Perkins stores, tel: (541) 776-4021*, open Mon–Fri 0900–1700, and **Southern Oregon Visitors Association,** *304 S. Central Ave; tel; (541) 779-4691*, have Jackson County information. The Fri *Medford Mail Tribune* Tempo section list events.

GETTING THERE

Jackson County Airport, *I-5 Exit 30, via Biddle Rd to Airport Rd,* with several car hire facilities, serves as a quick starting point for Ashland's Shakespeare Festival, Klamath Lakes, Eastern Oregon, or the Southern Oregon Coast. Baggage trolleys are $1.

Greyhound, *212 Barnett Rd; tel: (541) 779-2103,* is supplemented by the local system,

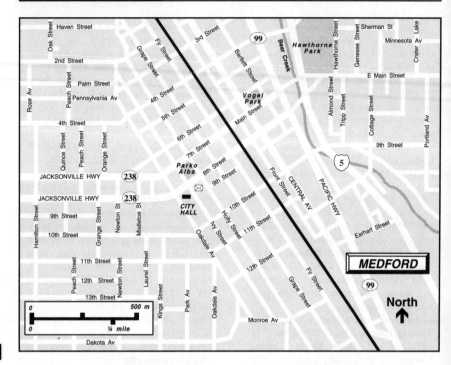

Map of Medford showing street layout, parks, and landmarks including Hawthorne Park, Vogel Park, Parko Alba, City Hall, and highways 99, 5, and 238.

Rogue Valley Transportation, *3200 Crater Lake Ave; tel: (541) 799-2988.*

ACCOMMODATION AND FOOD

As a regional shopping hub, Medford is well-equipped with lodging. **Medford VCB** has a lodging list.

Chains include *BW, CI, DI* and *M6.* The **Horizon Inn,** *1154 E. Barnett Rd; tel: (800) 452-2255* or *(541) 779-5085,* is a comfortable, moderate choice.

McGrath's Fishhouse, *68 E. Stewart Ave; tel: (541) 732-1732,* is budget–moderate, with daily fresh fish specials. **Samovar Family Restaurant & Bakery,** *101 E. Main; tel: (541) 779-4967,* serve Russian delicacies like blinis, knishes and hot fresh breads. **Streams,** an Oregon Eatery, *1841 Barnett Rd; tel: (541) 776-9090,* uses local ingredients. Moderate.

SIGHTSEEING

Medford sprawls for three miles along I-5 (Exits 30–27), a plethora of fast food, motels, supermarkets, discount stores shopping malls and medical services. **Rogue Valley Mall,** *1600 N. Riverside; tel: (541) 776-3255,* pulls shoppers from Northern California, south-central–eastern Oregon, and the Rogue River and Crater Lake recreation areas. Mt Mc-Loughlin's white cap dominates the north-east horizon.

The **Southern Oregon History Center,** *106 N. Central; tel; (541) 773-6536,* adults \$3, children 6-12 \$2, has excellent exhibits on pioneer history, Oregon Trail and Applegate Trail journeys, and an excellent prairie schooner mock-up.

Harry & David's, *1314 Center Dr.; tel: (541) 776-2277,* is a produce store and gift shop. This Medford institution has been shipping local pears and other fruit for 60 years. No longer selling from a farm wagon, Harry & David's South Gateway Center includes deli dining and the **Jackson & Perkins** rose garden and store; *tel: (541) 776-2388,* outlet for the world's largest private rose grower and major catalogue-order operations. The **Medford Information Center** is between the two.

MEDFORD–
KLAMATH FALLS

Forested summits and lakes vie for attention along this winding 80-mile route between Medford's shopping hub and Klamath Falls' surrounding lake wetlands and bird refuges. Oregon's prime summer attraction is the Shakespeare Festival in college-town Ashland, with three theatres including a Globe Theatre replica. Plan on two hours, direct; all day if stopping for a play and dinner in Ashland.

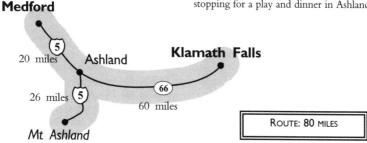

Medford

Ashland

Klamath Falls

20 miles

26 miles

60 miles

Mt Ashland

ROUTE: 80 MILES

161

Take I-5 20 miles through the Bear Creek Valley from Medford to Ashland, then follow Hwy 66, the Green Springs Highway, to Klamath Falls.

Pear Tree Factory Stores, *205 Fern Valley Rd; Medford/Phoenix, OR 97501; tel: (541) 535-1194,* at Exit 24, has designer label bargains. **Phoenix**, once filled with pear orchards, is now a Medford dormitory community with RV parks and a truck stop. The **Phoenix Chamber of Commerce,** *PO Box 998, Phoenix, OR 97535; tel: (541) 535-6956,* has a list of historical sites.

Tourist Information: Ashland Visitors and Convention Bureau, *110 E. Main St (next to Black Swan Theatre), PO Box 1360, Ashland, OR 97520; tel: (541) 482-3486.* **Downtown**

Plaza Information Booth, open Memorial Day–Labor Day 1000–2000. Both have information on lodging, dining, attractions and the Oregon Shakespeare Festival.

The **Ashland VCB** has an extensive list of lodging, including *BW, QI* and *S8* motels. The moderate 1925 **Mark Anthony Hotel,** *212 E. Main St; tel: (800) 926-8669* or *(541) 482-1721,* is a good place to people watch during theatre season.

To book one of Ashland's forty moderate–expensive bed and breakfasts, contact **Ashland Area Assn of Oregon B & B Guild**, *PO Box 3187; tel: (800) 983-4667;* **Ashland B & B Clearinghouse**; *tel: (800) 588-0338* or *(541) 488-0338;* **Ashland's B & B Reservation Network**, *PO Box 1051; tel: (800) 944-0329* or *(541) 482-2337;* or **Southern Oregon Reservation Center**, *PO*

Box 477; tel: (800) 547-8052 or (541) 488-1011. **Ashland Hostel**, 150 N. Main St; tel; (541) 482-9217, has 40 budget rooms.

EATING AND DRINKING

Ashland is a college town (Southern Oregon State College) and a summer mecca for theatre fanatics. Restaurants cater to both crowds, with a variety of price and ethnic choices. Pricey **Chateaulin**, 50 E. Main St; tel: (541) 482-2264, is French and atmospheric, à la pâté and escargot; a recent excellent bistro menu features meals at half the price. **Oregon Cabaret Theatre**, 1st St and Hargadine, PO Box 1149; tel: (541) 488-2902, open Feb–Dec, $11–$18, also has dinner performances inspired by Patsy Cline, Stephen Sondheim and other classic musicians.

SIGHTSEEING

Though Rogue River Valley residents talk wistfully about carving the (USA's 51st) State of Jefferson from Northern California and Southern Oregon, the real Ashland action is theatrical make-believe. Founded in 1935, the **Oregon Shakespeare Festival**, 15 S. Pioneer St, PO Box 158, Ashland, OR 97520; tel: (541) 482-4331; fax: (541) 482-8045, presents high quality repertory productions of works by playwrights from the Bard to Tom Stoppard. The 11-play season is mid Feb–Oct at the intimate **Black Swan** and **Agnus Bowmer Theatre.**

The **Elizabethean Theatre,** a faithful reproduction of London's Globe Theatre, has June–Oct performances of Shakespearean classics. Adult prices are $19–$42; no children under 5 admitted. Elizabethean Theatre standing room, $10 on performance day, has great sight lines, and is one of Oregon's finest bargains. Backstage tours, 1000–1145 most days of the season, are $8–$9. Classes, lectures, discussions, new play readings and Festival museum admission are scheduled throughout the season. In summer, Elizabethean music and dance is performed in the free **Green Show** in the courtyard by the Elizabethean Theatre. The **Tudor Guild Gift Shop**; tel: (541) 482-0940, just off the courtyard, has scripts, play summaries and Bard-related souvenirs.

Lithia Park's 100 acres settle against the

Festival theatres' flanks. White swans swim on a pond while secluded paths wander amongst small groves of trees in a park designed by John McLaren, responsible for San Francisco's Golden Gate Park. A public fountain offers medicinal tastes of the natural Lithia Springs.

The **Pacific Northwest Museum of Natural History**, 1500 E. Main St; tel: (800) 637-8581 or (541) 488-1084, open Apr–Oct 0900–1700, Nov–Mar 1000–1600, adults $6, children 5–15 $4.50, uses computers and sights, sounds, and smells of the ocean, forests and desert to create an out-of-doors being there atmosphere.

Sample Rogue Valley wines at **Ashland Vineyards**, 2775 E. Main St; tel: (541) 488-0088, open Mar–Dec Tues–Sun 1100-1700 and at **Weisinger's of Ashland**, 3150 Siskiyou Blvd; tel: (800) 551-9463 or (541) 488-5989.

SIDE TRACK TO MT ASHLAND

Winter alpine and Nordic skiers and snowboarders will drive 18 miles south of Ashland (to I-5 Exit 5, then 8 miles west) to 7500-ft **Mt Ashland**, PO Box 220, Ashland, OR 97520; tel: (800) 547-8052 or (541) 482-2897, highest peak in the Siskiyou Mountain Range. Half of the 23-run terrain, normally open Thanksgiving–Apr, is classified 'expert'. Vistas are superb. **Mt Ashland Inn**, 550 Mt Ashland Rd, Ashland, OR 97520; tel; (800) 830-8707, has moderate bed and breakfast lodging in the forest two miles from the ski centre.

ASHLAND TO KLAMATH FALLS

Few of Ashland's thousands of summer visitors venture east. For the first 18 miles, Hwy 66 follows the historic route of the 1846 Applegate Trail offshoot (see box, p.163) into southwestern Oregon from the Oregon Trail. The highway serpentines, rising quickly into Douglas-fir forest. Watch for deer along the Hwy 66's tree-shaded curves.

Glenyan KOA, 5310 Hwy 66, Ashland; tel: (541) 482-4138, is conveniently near Ashland. Five miles east of Ashland is the U-shaped

The Applegate Trail

In 1843, two ten-year-old Applegate boys drowned in the Columbia River, the Oregon Trail's final challenge. Vowing to find a less perilous way for others, Jesse and Lindsay Applegate, the boys' fathers, blazed a trail in reverse starting from Corvallis in the Willamette Valley in 1846. Travelling south through unknown Native American areas, the brothers' party forded the Umpqua River, walked the Rogue River/Bear Creek Valley (Ashland), crossed the Cascade Mountains to Upper Klamath Lake (Klamath Falls), moved south-east to the Tule Lake area (California), then followed the Humboldt River east across Northern Nevada to Fort Hall, Idaho.

While less prone to devastation by water, to many the Applegate Trail deserts and harsh mountain ascents seemed equally brutal and perilous. The 1850 Donation Land Claim Act spurred mass interest in free Oregon land for permanent settlers. The best Willamette Valley agricultural land was claimed, so settlers hauled prairie schooners over the Applegate Trail to south-west Oregon valleys. Today's two-hour drive between Medford and Klamath Falls on I-5 and Hwy 66 barely hints at the stoic strength of Applegate Trail pioneers 150 years ago.

We arrive here in the Rogue Valley Oct 26th in company with a train of 87 persons, 23 wagons, 334 head of cattle, 1700 sheep and 29 horses and mules—all right, save the 'ordinary wear and tear' of wagons and teams, and some wear and tear of heart, esp. for going hungry now and then...
– Correspondence of Samuel Hobart Taylor, Oregon Bound, 185.

Emigrant Lake Recreation Area, *Hwy 66; tel: (541) 776-7001,* with boating, fishing, swimming and camping. Eighteen miles from Ashland near the 4550-ft summit of Green Springs Mountain is **Green Springs Inn Restaurant and Lodge,** *11470 Hwy 66, Ashland OR 97520; tel: (541) 482-0614; fax: (541) 488-3942,* across from the E. Hyatt Rd turnoff leading to **Hyatt Lake;** *tel; (541) 482-3331,* and **Howard Prairie Lake;** *tel: (541) 773-3619,* both recreation resort areas. Green Springs Inn looks like a roadhouse with moderate rooms, moderate–pricey dinners, budget nightly specials, and scrumptious home-made marionberry and apple pies. **Tub Springs State Wayside** along Hwy 66 has shaded picnic tables in pleasant Ponderosa pine forest.

The **Pinehurst Inn at Jenny Creek,** *17250 Hwy 66, Ashland; tel: (541) 488-1002,* is a moderate–expensive bed and breakfast and restaurant in a lovingly-restored 1923 roadhouse. **Green Springs Box R Ranch,** *16799 Hwy 66, Ashland; tel; (541) 482-1873,* is a working cattle ranch with nine rooms. Expensive.

Weyerhaeuser has extensive logging activity and some reforestation projects along the 12 miles to **John Boyle Reservoir,** which stores Klamath River flow. Pioneers followed this route along the South Fork of the Applegate Trail 150 years ago. Gulls, white pelicans and swifts dip and fish in the reservoir, competing with humans fishing from shore and the Hwy 66 bridge. Swimming and waterskiing are local favourites. Dragonflies dart lazily around a pleasant picnic ground.

Camp at **Topsy Campground,** *Bureau of Land Management, Klamath Falls Resource Area, 2795 Anderson Ave, # 25, Klamath Falls, OR 997603; tel: (541) 883-6916.*

Sportsman's Park, a few miles east on Hwy 66, is a good picnic spot. Cross the Klamath River at **Keno. Mount Shasta's** white cap rises dramatically from California to the right (south). Lorry traffic picks up, and a big Weyerhaeuser plant marks the outskirts of **Klamath Falls.**

KLAMATH FALLS

Tourist Information: Klamath County Department of Tourism, *1451 Main St, Klamath County Museum, PO Box 1867, Klamath Falls, OR 97601; tel: (800) 445-6728* or *tel/fax: (541) 884-0666,* has information on lodging and activities in Klamath County or Modoc County, California.

163

GETTING THERE

Klamath Falls International Airport, *Kingsley Field, Rand Way; tel: (541) 883-5372,* has flights from Portland and Redding, CA. **AMTRAK**, *S. Spring St; tel: (800) 872-7245* or *(541) 884-2822,* has rail service and **Greyhound**, *1200 Klamath Ave; tel; (541) 882-4616,* has bus service. **BTS, Basin Transit Service**, *1130 Adams St; tel: (541) 883-2877,* operates buses Mon–Sat, including routes between *S. 6th St* and **Reed Transit Center**, downtown.

ACCOMMODATION AND FOOD

The Klamath County Dept of Tourism *Visitor Guide* has a lodging list. Chains include *BW, CI, EL, M6, S8* and *RL*. Most accommodation is east from downtown along *S. 6th St,* including the moderate **Cimarron Motel**, *3060 S. 6th; tel: (800) 742-2648* or *(541) 882-4601,* and **Red Lion Inn**, *3612 S. 6th St; tel: (541) 882-8864.* **KOA Kampgrounds of Klamath Falls**, *3435 Shasta Way; tel: (541) 884-4644,* is for the camping set.

Klamath Falls may have more pizza restaurants per capita – nine – than elsewhere in Oregon. Tons of fast food joints fill *S. 6th St/Hwys 39* (to Reno, Nevada) and 140 to Eastern Oregon and the Hwy 97 corridor to remote Modoc County, California. There are modest coffee shops and delis on *Main St* in Old Downtown.

SIGHTSEEING

Falls? Never were any, say local residents. Well, perhaps they were small, on the Link River which gave Klamath Falls its original Linksville name, but they're gone now, say others. Oregon's lack of sales tax draws out-of-staters to Klamath Falls to shop where petrol is also cheaper. Eastern Oregonians pause to refresh before heading to Medford's shopping malls, to Upper Klamath Lake recreation or to Crater Lake National Park. Compared to the Cascade Range and Western Oregon, Klamath Falls' 14 ins of annual precipitation are like a dry spell.

In summer, a 1906 trolley rolls through Old Town, little changed from the modest storefronts of decades ago. The Klamath County Dept of Tourism has an *Old Town Historic Walking Tour* brochure. **Baldwin Hotel Museum**, *31 Main St; tel: (541) 883-4208,* open Tues–Sat 1000–1600 June–Sept, adults $2–4, has 1906-era furnishings.

Klamath Falls is proud of Cell Tech, producer of Super Blue Green™, an ingestible health food product. In striking contrast to the rest of Old Town, its headquarters building, *1300 Main St; tel: (541) 882-5406,* resembles an ancient Egyptian temple facade.

Klamath County Museum, *1451 Main St; (541) 883-4208,* open Mon–Sat 0900–1730 June–Sept, 0800–1630 Oct–May, in a warehouse-size building, introduces the bird life and Native American history of the Klamath Basin. Six national wildlife refuges, **Klamath Basin National Wildlife Refuges**, *Rte 1, Box 74, Tulelake, CA 96134; tel: (916) 667-2231,* from Upper Klamath Lake (See Crater Lake to Klamath Falls, p.196) to Tule Lake and Clear Lake Refuges in California, protect 400 animal and bird species. Millions of birds call the refuges home from April–Nov, in a land once roamed by the giant grand sloth, mastodons, bison and giant camels. Excellent captions explain the Klamath tribe's distinctive two-horn grinding rocks, woven gambling mats and a beautiful collection of Klamath and Modoc baskets. The 1872-3 Modoc Indian War, where US Army clashes with displaced Native Americans ended with the hanging of Modoc Chief Kentipoos, 'Captain Jack', is sympathetically explained.

The private **Favell Museum**, *125 W. Main St; tel: (541) 882-9996,* open Mon–Sat 0930–1730, adults $4, children 6–16 $2, has extensive collections of Native American ceremonial stone knives, boomerang-like weapons, arrowheads, pottery, paintings and Western and cowboy art. The **Link River Trail** begins behind the museum north of downtown. Close by and parallel to Hwy 97, **Lake Ewauna Trail** has good waterfowl viewing along the 1.1-mile path. Underground activity is explained during **Geothermal Tours** of the **Oregon Institute of Technology**, *3201 Campus Dr.; tel: (541) 885-1750,* where building environmental systems are run by harnessing this natural resource.

PORTLAND–OLYMPIA

From Oregon's largest city to Washington's capital city is a direct two-hour, 120-mile drive. Add a day to visit Mount St Helens National Volcanic Monument, and the drive becomes a dramatic introduction to the force and power of the Pacific Northwest's most recent change in geography.

ROUTE: 120 MILES

Olympia

Tumwater 6 miles

60 miles

(5)

Castle Rock
10 miles

(504)
70 miles

Longview/Kelso
10 miles

Kalama
10 miles (5)

50 miles
(503)

Mount St Helens National Volcanic Monument

24 miles **Woodland**

Portland

165

ROUTE

Take I-5 120 miles north from Portland to Olympia. State Route 503 east of Woodland follows the Lewis River to **Mt St Helens National Volcanic Monument**, one of two scenic side tracks to the most recently-explosive Cascade mountain. SR 504 from **Castle Rock**, the main route to the monument, follows the Toutle River.

TOURIST INFORMATION

Tourist Information: **Southwest Washington Tourism Council,** *PO Box 876, Longview, WA 98632; tel: (360) 425-1211,* has information for attractions along much of this route, including Mt St Helens.

PORTLAND TO WOODLAND

Interstate 5 crosses the Columbia River north of Portland; Vancouver, Washington, is just east (See Portland–Yakima, p.236).

Seven miles north is a brief glimpse of Mt St Helens. Tree-shaded **Gee Creek Rest Area**, *Exit 11,* has an information centre, phones, picnicking and at the restrooms, weather reports for Vancouver, Portland–Pacific Coast and Eastern Washington.

Take Exit 14 west to **Ridgefield National Wildlife Refuge,** *PO Box 457, Ridgefield, WA 98642; tel: (360) 887-4106.* The 2-mile **Oaks to Wetlands Wildlife Trail** in the north section, open all year, is spectacular in spring foliage and late autumn–winter waterfowl migration. The refuge was established after south-eastern Alaska's 1964 earthquake destroyed dusky Canada geese nesting grounds in the Copper River Delta. Dusky Canada geese and sandhill cranes are numerous on the Ridgefield refuge. The tawny brown lumps near wetland grasses are nutria, a greenery and dike-destroying introduced South American rodent. From Apr 16–Sept 30, there is a short drive through the **River S unit** wetlands south of downtown Ridgefield, with stops at observation blinds.

Paradise Point State Park, *33914 NW. Paradise Pt Rd, Ridgefield, WA 98642; tel: (360) 263-2350,* Exit 16, east of I-5, has spring–fall camping. Swimming at a beach below the interstate is popular in summer. RV parks alternate with wetlands. Cross a green bridge over the green waters of the Lewis River to **Woodland.**

WOODLAND

Tourist Information: Woodland Chamber of Commerce, *1225 Lewis River Rd, Box 1012, Woodland, WA 98674; tel: (360) 225-9552,* has information on accommodation and dining for Woodland and along SR 503, *Lewis River Hwy,* to Mt St Helens.

Woodland is an excellent spot to get petrol and picnic provisions before taking the SR 503 to the volcanic monument.

On the west side of town, where rich bottomland farms and flower bulb nurseries nestle near the Columbia River, is **Hulda Klager Lilac Gardens,** *S. Pekin Rd; tel: (360) 225-8996.* Klager cross-bred plants in the early 20th century. Her house, a small museum, is open by appointment; the beautiful gardens, with pleasant shaded sitting areas and 50 species of lilacs and other flowers are always open. Nearby is tiny **Horseshoe Lake.**

SIDE TRACK VIA SR 503 TO MT ST HELENS NATIONAL VOLCANIC MONUMENT

Drive 34 miles east from Woodland, following the fisherman-favoured Lewis River, past lakes and dams to views of the south side of Mt St Helens across a lunar-like lava field. Check for winter road closure; *tel: (360) 750-3900.*

Agriculture mixes with riverbank fishing east of Woodland. Two miles from town is **Lewis River Bed & Breakfast,** *2339 Lewis River Rd, Woodland, WA 98674; tel: (800) 517-3200* or *(360) 225-8630,* an expensive, but comfortable house overlooking the water.

Six miles beyond is moderate **Grandma's House Bed & Breakfast,** *4551 Old Lewis River Rd, Woodland, WA 98674; tel: (360) 225-7002,* in a farmhouse close to the local golf course and salmon hatchery.

A Native American family specialising in North Coast Indian art presents members' and other native artists' carved wooden masks, sculpture, dolls, and silver bone and shell jewellery at **Lelooska Gallery,** *165 Merwin Village Rd, Ariel, WA 98603; tel: (360) 225-9735* or *(360) 225-8828,* open Thur–Sun, 11 miles from Woodland.

Turn right and follow signs to the grassy park at the base of **Merwin Dam** and a swimming area. **Merwin Fish Hatchery** has a short, self-guided tour. The next ten miles of SR 503 are forest alternating with clear-cuts. **Merwin Reservoir,** on the right (south) 23 miles from Woodland, has a good swimming beach and shaded picnic tables at **Speelyai Bay Park.** Climbers must sign in at the **Climbers Register,** a wooden building on the left at 27 miles.

The first view of the top of Mt St Helens is one mile east. On the right is **Yale Reservoir** with picnic tables and a beach. Mushroom gathering is popular in this area, though fungi hunters may be hostile to outsiders. Gathering permits are required. **Merrill Lake** campground and boating is 4 miles left.

Cougar has a few stores, petrol, **Blue**

166

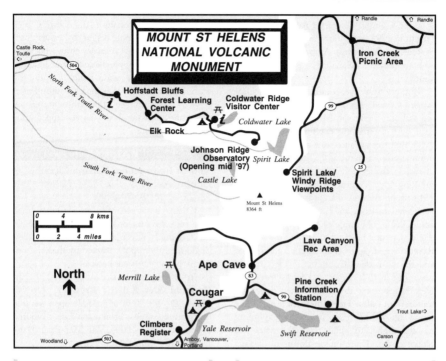

MOUNT ST HELENS NATIONAL VOLCANIC MONUMENT

Castle Rock, Toutle

504

North Fork Toutle River

Hoffstadt Bluffs Forest Learning Center

Coldwater Ridge Visitor Center

i

Coldwater Lake

Elk Rock

Johnson Ridge Observatory (Opening mid '97)

Spirit Lake

Castle Lake

South Fork Toutle River

Spirit Lake/ Windy Ridge Viewpoints

Mount St Helens 8364 ft

Iron Creek Picnic Area

Randle   Randle

99

25

Lava Canyon Rec Area

North ↑

Merrill Lake

Ape Cave

83

Cougar

Pine Creek Information Station

90

Trout Lake ➤

Climbers Register

Yale Reservoir

Amboy, Vancouver, Portland

Swift Reservoir

Carson

Woodland ⇩   503

0   4   8 kms

0   2   4 miles

Bird Helicopters; *tel: (360) 238-5326,* **Wildwood Bar & Grill,** and moderate **Lone Fir Resort RV Park & Motel,** *16806 Lewis River Rd, Cougar, WA 98616; tel: (360) 238-5210.*

At **Swift Dam,** turn left (north) onto FR 83 for the 3 miles to **Ape Cave,** a 12,810-ft lava tube, which divides at the entrance into an (easier) lower cave downslope and an experienced climber's upper cave on the upslope. The cave has nothing to do with apes, and everything to do with good shoes, good cave-exploring skills, three light sources (lantern and flashlights/torches) per person, and warm clothing against 42°–47°F temperatures and constant 7 mph breezes.

Continue north-east on FR 83 to **Lava Canyon Recreation Area,** where pebbly pumice creates a lunar landscape, with a fine view of Mt St Helens to the north and Mt Adams to the east. Several trails begin at the road's end. Storm damage and construction permitting, return to Swift Dam and go

east on FR 90, left (north) on FR 25, and south-west on FR 99 to **Windy Ridge Viewpoint**, a stunning view of Mt St Helen's east slopes.

MOUNT ST HELENS NATIONAL VOLCANIC MONUMENT

Tourist Information: There are several visitors centres on SR 504. **Mount St Helens National Volcanic Monument Headquarters;** *42218 NE. Yale Bridge Rd, Amboy, WA, 98601; tel: (360) 750-3900* or *(360) 750-5003* (recording); *fax: (360) 750-3901,* has information, and issues permits for volcano climbing, mushroom and berry gathering, or Christmas tree and firewood cutting. Camping is prohibited in the monument.

The **Cowlitz County Department of Tourism,** *207 4th Ave N., Kelso, WA 98626; tel: (360) 577-3137; fax: (360) 423-9987,* has area information and excellent free maps of the SR 503 and SR 504 routes to the volcanic monument.

Capt. George Vancouver named Mount St Helens in 1792 after Alleyne Fitzherbert, Baron St Helens, the British Ambassador to Spain. The mountain's behaviour was anything but saintly.

If there was ever doubt that the white-capped Cascade Range was formed by shattering volcanic upheaval, Mt St Helens restored faith with a terrifying explosion on May 18, 1980. Pumice, ash and gasses spewed out of the mountaintop, a pyroclastic (non-magma) flow of rocks, ash, ice and pumice forming a hazy, smoking grey vertical plume 11 miles high. 1314 ft of summit disappeared, lopping the peak's height from 9677 ft to 8383 ft in minutes. Half a cubic mile of rock and glacial ice slid down the north face. West, the Toutle River clogged, Spirit Lake emptied and refilled and the 40-ft-deep Columbia River Channel was mired in 15 ft of rock and debris. Interstates were blocked for days. Ash rained down for hundreds of miles. Trees 150 ft tall toppled like straws up to 17 miles from the explosion; enough timber to build 160,000 homes was blown down. Three billion dollars of damage resulted. Fifty-seven people died in an act of nature viewed on television by millions around the world.

The Sunday morning blast was the latest in a series of Mt St Helens eruptions viewed by Northwest explorers, 19th century painters and Native Americans.

Lawelatla, *'The One from whom Smoke Comes'*, was the Cowlitz' name. Klickitat called it *Tah-One-Lat-Claw*, *'Fire Mountain'*. Native American legends evoke the mountain's stunning white-capped beauty before May 1980. A husband (Mt Hood) had a contrary wife (Mt St Helens). They threw fire at one another, the wife winning and causing her husband to be afraid. The wife 'having a stout heart, still burned'. Klickitat legend tells of the lovely Loowit, keeper of the sacred fire, who was rewarded by the Great Spirit with the answer to her wish to be eternally young and beautiful. She was transformed into a shining maiden (Mt St Helens).

The world remembers pictures of stripped tree trunks strewn down slopes, blocking nearby lakes and rivers. Visitors today see few areas where reforestation or nature's own regeneration has not begun to cover bare slopes. Insects, small animals, birds, and seeds survived under the pyroclastic flow or in caves, surprising scientists with their reappearance within a few months after the explosion. Forest service rangers struggle to explain why areas are green and what that lovely snow-capped cone looked like 'before'.

KALAMA

Tourist Information: Kalama Chamber of Commerce, *PO Box 824, Kalama, WA 98625; tel: (360) 673-6299.*

Kalama is named after an Hawaiian man who collected furs for HBC in the 1830s. Near the Columbia River stands the world's tallest single-tree totem pole, flanked by three others. A few picnic tables are nearby.

In 1984, Hart Brewing, Inc., began **Pyramid Ales Kalama Brewery,** *110 W. Marine Dr; tel: (360) 673-2121,* open for free tours/tasting of ales, brown and fruit-flavoured beers, Mon–Sat 1000–1600 Memorial Day–Labor Day ; winter, Mon–Fri.

LONGVIEW/KELSO

Longview, Exit 36, is the odiferous industrial section of these adjoining cities. The **Longview Chamber of Commerce,** *1563 Olympia Way, Longview, WA 98632; tel: (360) 423-8400,* has information on accommodation, dining and Washington's third deep-water port. Cheerful, helpful staff and clean facilities overcome the air pollution near moderate **Holiday Inn Express of Longview,** *723 7th Ave, Longview, WA 98632-2106; tel: (800) 465-1329 or (360) 414-1000.*

The **Kelso Chamber of Commerce/ Mount St Helens Volcano Information Center,** *105 Minor Rd, Kelso, WA 98626; tel: (360) 577-8058,* open 0800–1800 May–Oct, Wed–Sun 0900–1700 Nov–Apr, covers this much-pleasanter community at Exit 39, a timber-based economy with a Mt St Helens tourism sideline. Accommodation include *BW, CI, M6* and *RL.* The **Cowlitz County Department of Tourism,** *207 4th Ave N., Kelso, WA 98626; tel: (360) 577-3137; fax: (360) 423-9987,* also has area information.

The best food and steaks in town are found in a red-flocked wallpaper and 1890's atmosphere at moderate **Peter's Restaurant,** *310 S. Pacific Ave; tel: (360) 423-9620.* The free **Cowlitz County Historical Museum,** *405 Allen St, Kelso; tel: (360) 577-3119;* open Tues–Sat 0900–1700, Sun 1300–1700, has excellent displays on historic logging from the area west to the Columbia River bar and well-preserved Cowlitz Native American artefacts. The Museum store has a good selection of Northwest books and locally made reproduction Victorian ornaments.

CASTLE ROCK

Tourist Information: Castle Rock Chamber of Commerce/Exhibit Hall, *147 Front Ave NW, Castle Rock, WA 98611; tel:(360) 274-6603,* open summer, 0900–1800, winter Wed–Sat 1000–1400, is a local historical museum and Mt St Helens visitor centre. The chamber has information on motels, RV parks, restaurants and Mt St Helens tours.

Free visitors centres along SR 504 have short films covering the eruption. The *Eruption of Mount St. Helens is* a 30-min, giant screen version, **Eruption Cinedome,** *1239 Mt St Helens Way NE.; tel: (360) 274-8000,* open May–Oct, adults $5, children $4. Fill up on petrol before driving to the mountain.

⤷ SIDE TRACK VIA SR 504 TO MT ST HELENS NATIONAL VOLCANIC MONUMENT

Take I-5, Exit 49 to Castle Rock, and continue east on SR 504, the Spirit Lake Memorial Highway. **Mount St Helens Visitor Center at Silver Lake,** *milepost 5, 3029 Spirit Lake Hwy; tel: (360) 274-2100* or *(360) 274-2103 (recording); fax: (360) 274-2101,* open 0900–1700, is an excellent introduction to the mountain's dramatic geology, exploration, flora, wildlife, and the 1980 event. **Seaquest State Park;** *tel: (360) 274-8633,* across the highway has 92 pitches and a tree-filled picnic area. **Silver Lake,** *milepost 8,* has boating and fishing.

Cross the Toutle River at **Toutle,** *milepost 10,* a small town with services and RV parks. **Kid Valley Store,** *milepost 18,* is the last chance for petrol. **19 Mile House,** touts fruit cobblers and an ash remnants museum. Close by is **Maple Flats,** marked by a huge, crumbling statue of Bigfoot, whose footprints are alleged to have been discovered in the area. Displayed in the gift shop are hand-blown Mt St Helens ash art ornaments and decorative glassware, along with a video whose entire soundtrack can be heard while browsing. A half-buried, decrepit A-frame house remains from May, 1980.

At Milepost 22, walk 300 ft to view the **Sediment Retention Structure** where the US Army Corps of Engineers traps ash-laden water that could clog the Toutle, Cowlitz and Columbia Rivers. There is a short nature trail and a gift shop with more ash glass and a counter filled with Bigfoot foot impressions, mostly from alleged Oregon finds. **Eco Park,** *430 Spirit Lake Hwy, milepost 25, Castle Rock; tel: (360) 274-6542,* has moderate yurt, tent, cabin and RV camping.

Hoffstadt Bluffs Visitor Center; *milepost 27; tel: (360) 577-3137,* open 1000–2000 May–Oct, 1000–1700 Nov–Apr, has the first dramatic view up the Toutle River Valley towards the mountain, plus gift shops and dining. **Hillsboro Helicopters;** *tel: (800) 752-8439* or *(360) 274-7750,* take off from the centre for narrated tours of the monument May–Sept, weather permitting.

Stop at the **Hoffstadt Creek Bridge Overlook,** *mile 30,* to see the edge of the Blast Zone, and the 18.4-million tree reforestation undertaken by the Weyerhauser Company which lost 68,000 acres of timber. Weyerhauser operates the **Forest Learning Center,** *milepost 33; tel: (360) 414-3439,* open May–Oct 1000–1800. It's worth a stop if only to see a four-min film in the Eruption Chamber, mixing shockingly close footage with a local TV station's coverage by an stranded, endangered reporter. Pre-explosion forest dioramas are excellent; check your weight against a grizzly bear's and your 'eagle eyes'. Outside, volunteers from the Rocky Mountain Elk Foundation

169

help visitors spot the roving Roosevelt elk herd in the distance.

Enter **Mount St Helens National Volcanic Monument** at milepost 37, **Elk Rock Viewpoint**, where 'matchstick' trees are still visible.

Coldwater Ridge Visitor Center, *US Forest Service, 3029 Spirit Lake Hwy, Castle Rock, WA 98611; tel: (360) 274-2131; fax: (360) 274-2129,* open May–Sept 1000–1800, Oct–Apr 0900–1700, is the main interpretative centre, with exhibits, ranger lectures, a gift shop and snack bar. Free audio tours interpret the eruptions in German, French, Spanish and Japanese.

The view from Coldwater Ridge, eight miles from the volcano, takes in the crater, lava dome, Toutle River Valley, Coldwater and Castle Lakes. Walk the quarter-mile **Winds of Change loop trail** just below the centre to see wildflowers and small plants thriving amidst lava-scoured tree limbs. Watch fishing from the quarter-mile **Birth of a Lake Trail** boardwalk at **Coldwater Lake.**

Johnston Ridge Observatory, *milepost 52,* opened in mid-1997 at 4313-ft, with volcanism exhibits where a researcher who correctly predicted the eruption perished in the blast.

Lewis & Clark State Park; *east from I-5, Exit 68; tel: (206) 864-2643,* has 25 pitches and a ½-mile **Old Growth Forest Trail.**Take the **Chehalis–Centralia Railroad steam train**, *Exit 77, tel: (360) 748-9593,* from Memorial Day–Labor Day.

Twin Cities/Lewis County Visitors and Convention Bureau, *500 NW Chamber of Commerce Way, PO Box 1263, Chehalis, WA 98532; tel: (800) 525-3323* or *(360) 748-8885,* covers **Chehalis** and **Centralia.** The area produces record quantities of milk. Cheese, hay, blueberries, frozen peas, mint oil and tulip bulbs round out agricultural production.The **Lewis County Historical Museum,** *599 NW. Front Way, Chehalis; tel: (360) 748-0831,* open Tues–Sat 0900–1700, Sun 1300–1700, housed in a former railway depot,

covers the founding of Centralia by Black pioneer George Washington in the 1880s and Chehalis tribal history. **Centralia Factory Outlets,** *Exit 82; tel: (800) 831-5334* or *(360) 736-3327,* is halfway between Portland and Seattle. **Centralia Square Antique Mall,** *201 S. Pearl St; tel: (360) 736-6406,* occupies two venerable downtown buildings. ⏏

TUMWATER

Tourist Information: Tumwater Chamber of Commerce, *488 Tyee Dr., Tumwater, WA 98512; tel: (360) 357-5153,* has information on the historical district and brewery history of the town which perches just south of Olympia at Exit 103.

Thirty Missouri pioneers settled government-grant land in 1845, establishing a sawmill and gristmill by a Deschutes River waterfall, to become the first American community north of Fort Vancouver. Oregon Trail migrants followed; a railway boosted the economy in 1878. The stage was set for brewmaster Leopold Schmidt's arrival from Germany via Montana in 1895, and the founding of Olympia Brewing Co. using artesian water, the following year.

Olympia Brewery, *PO Box 947; tel; (360) 754-5177,* open 0900–1630, with tours Apr–Sept, still brews its pale, weak beer with the slogan, 'It's the Water'. Avoid midday summertime tours when lack of air can cause dizziness. The cool tasting room is festooned with beer steins and awards.

Next to the brewery is **Tumwater Falls Park;** *tel: (360) 943-2550,* a fine spot for viewing 82-ft falls falling through a narrow gorge, walking trails, and watching salmon ascend a fish ladder Sept–Oct to spawn upriver. Above the park is the Centennial Rose Garden around the Schmidt family mansion, all part of **Tumwater Historic District. Henderson House Museum,** *602 Deschutes Way; tel: (360) 753-8583,* is the district interpretative centre, including a replica log cabin. **Crosby House,** built in 1858 by seafaring settlers at Grant and Deschutes, is singer Bing Crosby's ancestral home. Continue north on I-5 to Olympia.

EUGENE–FLORENCE

Amongst the several routes from Interstate 5 to the Oregon Coast, SR 126 is one of the most scenic. The 60 miles from the Willamette River in Eugene to the northern end of the Oregon Dunes National Recreation Area in Florence allow coastal access through the centre of the state. Heavy lorry traffic and congestion in Eugene may slow the two-hour non-stop drive to three hours, especially on summer weekends. There are few lay-bys, but one-store hamlets and local fishing spots are a chance to pull off the road for a short hike, a picnic, or to pause within a lush deep green forest by a rushing river and sun-dappled creeks.

```
ROUTE: 60 MILES
```

South Willamette

30 miles

Florence (126)

Eugene

Walton

30 miles

Valley Vineyards

ROUTE

From Eugene's *Fifth Street* Public Market (*5th Ave* and *Pearl Sts*), drive one block south to *6th Ave* and turn right, going east on SR 126. Turn left on *Garfield St*, then right onto *11th Ave*, again SR 126. Drive 55 miles east, through Veneta, **Walton** and Mapleton, to the junction of SR 126/Hwy 101.

TOURIST INFORMATION

Tourist Information: Lane County Convention & Visitors Association (CVALCO), *115 W. 8th Ave, Suite 190, PO Box 10286, Eugene, OR 97740; tel: (800) 547-5445 or (541) 484-5307; fax: (541) 343-6335,* has information on the route which falls completely within Lane County.

Lane County Parks, *3040 N. Delta Hwy, Eugene, OR 97408; tel: (541) 431-6940,* operates some of the campsites en route. For motels, hotels or bed and breakfast, plan on staying in Eugene or Florence.

EUGENE TO WALTON

SR 126 winds through Eugene's town centre. *Eleventh Ave* is a solid strip of small malls, petrol stations, fast food and visual blight.

After 5 miles, the countryside begins at the city limits. The land opens up, and at **Fisher Butte Wildlife Area** on the north side of SR 126 it's easy to spot birds resting on wooden posts.

One of **Fern Ridge Lake's** six parks, **Perkins Peninsula Park,** *north across from Crow Rd,* has a picnic area, swimming beach and boat ramp, but no camping.

Fern Ridge Chamber of Commerce, *Territorial Rd, PO Box 335, Veneta, OR 97487; tel: (541) 935-1504,* open Memorial Day–Labor Day, has area information. **Fern Ridge Wildlife Area** parking is also on the north side of SR 126. White egrets and osprey are resident in the protected area.

SR 126 approaches the Coast Range at **Noti** and alder forest appears to replace the rolling wetlands, farms and oak-studded hills.

SIDE TRACK FROM EUGENE

SOUTH WILLAMETTE VALLEY VINEYARDS

About 15 miles from Eugene are three excellent South Willamette Valley vineyards. **La Velle Vineyards**, *89679 Sheffler Rd,* turn north at *Territorial Rd* in Veneta to *Elmira, OR 97437; tel: (541) 935-9406,* open 1200–1800, is where one of Oregon's first vineyards started production. Recently renovated, the elegant tasting room offers the winery's own Riesling, chardonnay, pinot noir and blush (rosé), and a co-operatively produced Oregon Vineyards marque for premium varietals.

Upstairs, an art gallery curated by Eugene's Maude Kearns Art Center offers superb rotating exhibits. Outside, a picnic area overlooks a gazebo, often used for weddings.

Back on SR 126, turn south at *Territorial Rd* to **Hinman Vineyards**, *27012 Briggs Hill Rd, Eugene, OR 97405; tel: (541) 345-1945,* open daily 1200–1700. One unusual offering is Muscat-Huxelrebe.

Secret House Vineyards Winery, *88324 Vineyard Lane, Veneta, OR 97487; tel: (541) 935-3774,* open Wed–Mon 1100–1700 mid Feb–Dec 24, is up a dirt road from SR 126, and a world away. Friendly dogs lounge near the tasting room, attesting to the winery's cheerful style and the excellent quality of the pinot noir and sparkling wine.

McGillivray's Log Home Bed & Breakfast, *88680 Evers Rd, Elmira, OR 97437; tel: (541) 935-3564,* has two moderate rooms in the woods.

WALTON TO FLORENCE

Walton has a provisioning store. Just west of Walton, SR 126 begins to follow the Siuslaw River. The highway narrows, twining around huge Douglas-fir and thick forest underbrush. **Austa**, **Linslaw**, **Turner Creek** and **Archie Knowles** are parks between Walton and Mapleton.

Look for Wildcat (covered) Bridge near the Austa boat launch area; another boat ramp at Linslaw; hopeful trout anglers fishing at Turner Creek, and after passing through a 0.2 mile long tunnel, hiking at Siuslaw National Forest's Archie Knowles.

East of Mapleton is the **Gingerbread Village Restaurant**; *tel: (541) 268-4713,* serving budget American food in a German chalet decor.

Mapleton serves as a recreation headquarters for **Siuslaw National Forest**, **Mapelton Ranger Station**, *10692 SR 126, PO Box 67, Mapleton, OR 97453; tel: (541) 268-4473.* Rangers have information on hiking trails, camping and fishing in the forest lands bordering the Oregon Dunes. If desperate for petrol, there's a station in Mapleton.

The Siuslaw River widens with a southward jog at Mapleton. Tidal estuaries and sand bars appear, marking the mouth of the river 14 miles ahead in Florence. Timber clear-cuts appear, giving steelhead and sturgeon fishermen in small boats the look of paper dolls plastered against nicked scenery.

Three miles east of the SR 126 junction with Hwy 101, the wooden **Cushman Railroad Bridge** crosses the river. There is a major shopping centre at the junction. **Heceta Lighthouse** and the **Sea Lion Caves** are north. The Oregon Dunes are south.

For speedy beach access, continue straight west in Florence on *9th St* beyond the junction, then turn north (right) on *Rhododendron Dr.* (see Florence, p. 122).

EUGENE–BAKER CITY

For steady drivers with manoeuvrable vehicles, this 354-mile route has much of Oregon's least-seen but most spectacular scenery, with rivers, mountains, lakes, lava, farms, forests, painted hills, mesas striated with colours, barns, ranches and mining towns. The route finishes at the begining of the end of the Oregon Trail.

Lorry drivers love the open, winding roads, and tolerate speed limits as slow as 20 mph. In perfect driving conditions, plan on 10 hours to reach Eastern Oregon. This route has many mountain passes where snow falls unexpectedly Oct–April. Check weather conditions in advance; a 37-mile stretch on Hwy 242 from Harris Wayside to Sisters closes in winter, Nov–June.

The breathtaking scenery of John Day Fossil Beds National Monument Sheep Rock Unit is a microcosm of vistas and geological formations usually associated with the American Southwest. The Painted Hills Unit is a thick rust-red dusting across golden sandstone with feathery black accents. Lush forests show little sign of logging.

Except for Sisters, purpose-built for tourism, the scattered towns and residents along this route are a real taste of the West, from cowboys and ranchers to loggers, outdoorsmen and the West's most perfectly preserved Chinese general store and apothecary. Take at least three days to stop and raft or fish the McKenzie River, walk to lava flows and waterfalls near McKenzie Pass and hike the John Day Fossil Beds National Monument.

173

ROUTE: **354** MILES

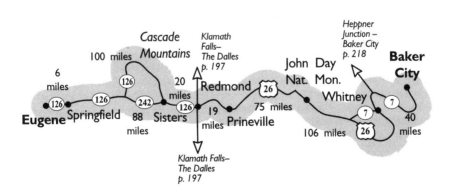

ROUTE

Take SR 126 east from Eugene to **Harris Wayside**, then follow SR 242 to **Sisters**.

As a winter (Nov–June) alternative, follow SR 126 north for 20 miles, then turn east on Hwy 20/SR 126 by **Hoodoo Ski Bowl** and cross **Santiam Pass** to Sisters.

Continue east from Sisters on SR 126 to **Prineville**, then east 163 miles on Hwy 26 to **Unity Lake State Park**, then turn left on *Big Flat Rd* 18 miles to **Whitney**. Turn right on SR 7 for 40 miles to Baker City.

To avoid the scenic detour, head left off Hwy 26 just east of Dixie Pass onto SR 7 to Baker City.

There are two routes leaving Eugene in the South Willamette Valley, following SR 126 east to **Springfield**. To bypass downtown Springfield and quickly reach the McKenzie River, take Hwy 105/SR 126 north across the Willamette River and immediately turn east. Business SR 126 goes east from the University of Oregon campus on *Franklin Blvd* across the river to *Main St*, Springfield. Eugene revolves around the University of Oregon and the performing arts. Springfield is industrial.

SPRINGFIELD

Tourist Information: Springfield Chamber of Commerce, *101 S. A St, in the 1891 Southern Pacific Railroad Depot, PO Box 155, Springfield, OR 97477; tel: (541) 746-1651; fax: (541) 726-4727* or **Convention & Visitors Association of Lane County, Oregon,** *115 W. 8th, Suite 190, PO Box 10286, Eugene, OR 97440; tel: (800) 547-5445* or *(541) 484-5307; fax: (541) 343-6335.*

ACCOMMODATION

Springfield has its share of lodging, including *BW, M6,* and *RL.* Most is found on *Gateway Blvd.*

SIGHTSEEING

Sandwiched between the Middle Fork of the Willamette River and the McKenzie River, forest products dominate Springfield industry. **Weyerhaeuser Container Mill,** *785 N. 42nd St; tel: (541) 741-5478,* has tours 0900

Mon–Fri. South of town, the **Dorris Ranch,** *220 S. 2nd St; tel; (541) 726-4325; fax: (541) 726-2751,* open Mon–Fri, has self-guided and guided tours of the USA's first commercial hazelnut (filbert) orchard.

'Native Americans and the Oregon Trail' is the theme of one of Springfield's 10 outstanding downtown murals, next to City Hall at *Main* and *5th Sts.* The **Springfield Museum,** *590 Main St; tel: (541) 726-2300,* open Wed–Fri 1000–1600, Sat 1200–1600, covers local history.

Just beyond Springfield, SR 126 rises through a broad floodplain. **Hendrick's Bridge State Wayside** near **Cedar Flat** has boating and a picnic area. The river is on the right, south of McKenzie Bridge. Rafting and floating (drifting) is a summer activity while the waters are high.

For information on riverside accommodations, hiking, fishing, rafting the river and a list of outfitters, stop at the **McKenzie River Chamber of Commerce,** *Hwy 126, Old McKenzie Trout Hatchery Tourist Information Center, PO Box 1117, Leaburg, OR 97489; tel: (541) 896-3330.*

Whitewater upstream justifies the McKenzie's designation as a National Wild and Scenic River. Sheer terrain and heavy winter snows saved it from human encroachment for decades after 1812, when Donald MacKenzie's exploring party left Fort Astoria to search the river unsuccessfully for fur-bearing animals. A mining supply trail to Idaho was blazed in 1862. Autos braved rugged excursions to the river and lava beds until a Depression-era road, present day Hwy 126, was built by the Civilian Conservation Corps.

On the right, 25 miles from Springfield, is 165-ft **Goodpasture Covered Bridge**, Oregon's second longest, in use since 1938. Small hamlets like **Vida** and **Nimrod** were stage coach stops and today provision for picnics at **Ben and Kay Dorris State Park** (33 miles east of Eugene) or **Howard J. Morton Memorial State Park** (40 miles from Eugene), near **Finn Rock**. Local folklore holds that Finn claimed to be Mark Twain's model for Huck Finn. True or not, the canyon narrows along this stretch of river. **Martens**

Rapids between the two parks is some of the wildest whitewater on the McKenzie. Thick stands of Douglas-fir darken the road.

Blue River Rd turns left at **Blue River** winding north to the May–Sept **Blue River Reservoir** recreation area and campsite, **Willamette National Forest, Blue River Ranger District,** *51668 Blue River Dr., Blue River, OR 97413; tel: (541) 822-3317; fax: (541) 822-3783.* H J Andrews Experimental Forest, Lookout Creek Old-Growth Trail and huge **Wolf Rock** are other Blue River attractions. There is also camping to the right (south) along Aufderheide Scenic Byway.

Belknap Covered Bridge is 0.8 mile right on *McKenzie River Dr.* near **Rainbow.** Eighteen-hole public **Tokatee Golf Course;** *54947 Hwy 125, Blue River, OR, 97413; tel: (800) 452-6376 or (541) 822-3220,* offers scenic forest play with Cascade peaks as background.

McKenzie Bridge is the largest of the tiny roadside towns which cater to tourists and salmon and steelhead fishermen, and one of the few with petrol. A stage-coach stop that hosted Clark Gable, US President Hoover and the Duke of Windsor, the **Log Cabin Inn,** *56483 McKenzie Hwy, Hwy 126, McKenzie Bridge, OR 97413; tel: (800) 355-3432 or (541) 822-3432,* has six moderate riverside guest cottages, tepees and moderate dining on buffalo and wild boar in a wood-panelled dining room. Three nearby Apr–Oct campsites are administered by the **US Forest Service, McKenzie Ranger District,** *McKenzie Bridge, OR 97413; tel: (541) 822-3381.* **Jenny B. Harris State Park** has picnicking.

In winter, Nov–Mar, enquire at the ranger station for weather conditions ahead. If SR 242 over McKenzie Pass is closed, check weather and road conditions for the loop around Santiam Pass to **Sisters.** It is 4½ miles from McKenzie Bridge to the SR 242 junction.

SR 242 is no 37-mile easy jaunt to Sisters. The road is slow (posted 20 mph near McKenzie Pass), narrow (16 ft wide, not recommended for large RVs) and winding, one of the few roads in Oregon where there are frequent, well-used lay-bys.

The highway snakes upwards around sharp turns. **Proxy Falls** is 8.7 miles from the junction. The half-mile falls loop trail is a 40 min hike on rocky paths through forest spongy with moss and ferns. **Upper Proxy Falls** hides around a curve, then plunges under lava rock. The **Lower Falls** crashes, then meanders over rocky plateaux.

Alder Springs Campground *(Willamette National Forest),* 1½ miles east, is near Linton Lake. Five miles beyond, the **Obsidian Trail** goes south across shiny black volcanic glass through **Three Sisters Wilderness. Scott Lake Campground,** ½ mile east, has convenient access to the **Scott Trailhead.**

Wilderness stretches on both sides of SR 242 as huge boulders left by *a'a* (chunky) lava flows fill the landscape. **Dee Wright Observatory,** 21 miles from the junction, is a lava-stone tower overlooking the lava fields and Cascade Peaks. Inside, wind-blown tourists seek shelter, only to discover that each Cascade (Mt Hood, Mt Jefferson, Three Fingered Jack, Mt Washington, North sister, Middle Sister) has a window framing it, complete with nameplate. On a landing outside the entrance, a round brass orientation marker shows the name, direction and elevation of each peak.

A paved **Lava River Trail** meanders below over a 2600–2900 year old lava flow through an almost treeless landscape of pressure ridges, gutters and crevasses. Trees are deprived of rain and soil, whipped by wind, and snowed under Nov–June.

McKenzie Pass Summit, 5324 ft, offers another panoramic view of the Cascades. On the eastern side of the pass, forest buries the lava. Arabian horses and more than 500 llamas graze at **Patterson Llamas,** *15425 Hwy 126; tel: (541) 549-3831,* just outside Sisters.

SISTERS

Tourist Information: Sisters Area Visitoir Information Center, *231 E. Hood St, Suite D, PO Box 430, Sisters, OR 97759; tel: (541) 549-0251; fax: (541) 549-4253,* has llama trekking information.

ACCOMMODATION

Oregonians who don't get east of Sisters think of the tourist town as that 'little ol' Western

Town' getaway. Sisters has *BW* and *CI*, moderate **Sisters Motor Lodge,** *600 W. Cascade, McKenzie Hwy, PO Box 28; tel: (541) 549-2551,* a **Sisters KOA,** *tel. (541) 549-3021,* RV and nearby camping in **Deschutes National Forest, Sisters Ranger District,** *PO Box 249; tel: (541) 549-2111.* **Camp Sherman,** west on Hwy 20/SR 126, also has resort lodges and camping.

EATING AND DRINKING

Sisters is well-supplied with ice-cream and sweet shops. **Hotel Sisters Restaurant & Bronco Billy's Saloon,** *101 Cascade St; tel: (541) 549-7427,* has moderate barbecue rib specialities, with chicken and dumplings with country gravy for Sunday supper. Walk in the 1912 former hotel's foyer to see one of Sisters' few truly old buildings.

SIGHTSEEING

Sawmills followed the shepherds into traditional Native American grazing lands around Sisters, named after the Cascade's North, Middle and South Sister peaks (originally Faith, Hope and Charity).

When Black Butte Ranch (10 miles northwest on Hwy 20/SR 126 towards Santiam Pass) wanted a place for its dude ranch visitors to dine and shop, 1970s-era Sisters obliged with 'new' 1880s store fronts. The Old West replica town has ice-cream shops, galleries, souvenirs and an outstanding bookstore, **Paulina Springs Book Co.,** *367 W. Hood St; tel: (800) 397-0867* or *(541) 549-0866,* carrying a wide range of books on the Pacific Northwest and Native Americans.

> ## ◤ SIDE TRACKS
> ## FROM SISTERS
>
> Ten miles north-west of Sisters, turn north from Hwy 20/SR 126 onto USFS Rd 1419. Turn right (east) onto Rd 14 to the **Head of the Metolius,** a raging torrent that emerges at the base of Black Butte (volcanic cinder cone), with white-capped Mt Jefferson gleaming to the north.
>
> Six miles east of Sisters is a lay-by with a panoramic view of **Cascade Mountains.**

Weather permitting, peaks visible from south to north are: Broken Top, South Sister, Middle Sister, North Sister, Black Crater, Mt Washington, Three-Finger Jack, Black Butte and Mt Jefferson.

Just west of Redmond, **Operation Santa Claus,** *4355 W. Hwy 126, Redmond, OR 97756; tel: (541) 548-8910,* have more than 100 reindeer to entice gift shop visitors. **Cline Falls State Scenic Viewpoint** overlooks the Deschutes River, 4 miles west of **Redmond.** ◤

REDMOND

Redmond Chamber of Commerce, *446 SW. 7th St, Redmond, OR 97756; tel: (800) 574-1325* or *(541) 923-5191; fax: (541) 923-6442,* open Mon–Fri 0800–1700, Sat–Sun (lobby) 0800–1700, has area-wide information on Central Oregon accommodation, dining and attractions.

ACCOMMODATION

Bend, south on I-97 has a huge lodging selection (see Eugene to Bend p.186), but prices and availability are better in Redmond.

The 1927 **New Redmond Hotel,** *521 S.W. 6th St; tel: (800) 228-5151* or *(541) 923-7378,* is a well-restored downtown Quality Hotel. **Best Western Rama Inn,** *2630 SW. 17th Place; tel: (800) 821-0543* or *(541) 548-8080,* in south Redmond, is convenient for quick access south or east.

Eagle Crest Resort, *1522 Cline Falls Rd; tel: (800) 682-4786 or (541) 923-2543,* moderate–pricey, is luxury on a golf course near the west end of town.

Moderate **Llast Camp Llamas B & B,** *4555 NW. Pershall Way; tel: (541) 548-6828,* has mountain views and critters in the yard, available for hire for guided or self-conducted wilderness treks.

EATING AND DRINKING

Decorated with 1300 cattle brands, moderate **Brand Dinner House,** *5876 S. Hwy 97; tel: (541) 548-3168,* serves family style.

Weekends are for music with Northwest cuisine, downtown at the **Paradise Grille,** *404 SW. 6th St; tel: (541) 548-0844.*

SIGHTSEEING

Redmond was established in 1905, but is best known as the regional training and operations base for smoke jumpers and fire fighting air tanker craft. Call a day in advance for tours of the **US Forest Service Redmond Air Center**, *1740 S.E. Ochoco Way, Roberts Field; tel: (541) 548-5071.* Be prepared to watch the take-off scramble during summer wildfire season.

At **Petersen's Rock Gardens**, *7930 S.W. 77th St; tel: (541) 382-5574,* adults $2, children 12–17 $1, screaming peacocks wander amongst such rock creations as a miniature Statue of Liberty. **Crooked River Railroad Company,** *5252 S.W. 6th St; tel: (541) 548-8630; fax: (541) 548-8702,* runs a summertime theme-based trains (murder mysteries, Sat night dinners, cowboy breakfasts, and train robberies) on a 38-mile return journey.

East of Redmond, SR 126 rises through grasslands for 20 miles, passing through the tiny town of **Powell Butte**. Mint, alfalfa, wheat, barley, oats, garlic and carrot seed grow near Prineville. Pause at **Ochoco** ('willows') **State Viewpoint** for a 180° view from the bluff just west of Prineville, then take Hwy 26 east into town.

PRINEVILLE

Tourist Information: Prineville-Crook County Chamber of Commerce, *390 N. Fairview, Prineville, OR 97754; tel: (541) 447-6304.*

Prineville has *BW* and other motel lodging, and is the last petrol supply before Mitchell, 48 miles east, where prices are much higher.

Settled in the 1860s, Prineville benefited from an 1871 gold discovery in the Ochoco Mountains (east on this route). Ranching, then lumbering, became the main industry. To move harvests and lumber, the town voted to build and operate a railway in 1918; the **City of Prineville Railway,** *185 E. 10th St; tel: (541) 447-6251,* still operates, with summer excursions in conjunction with Redmond's Crooked River Railway Company.

In the 1950s, **agates** and **thunder eggs** (see *Travel Essentials p.29*), were found nearby.

Rockhounds can prospect at ten Prineville Chamber of Commerce sites; *tel: (541) 447-6304.*

The **A R Bowman Museum**, *246 N. Main St; tel: (541) 447-3715,* open Mon–Fri 1000–1700, Sat 1100–1600 Mar–Dec, $1, covers that history in two floors of excellent displays in a former bank building, complete ornate high ceilings and teller cages. **Jasper Wright Log Cabin** in **Pioneer Park,** *3rd and Elm Sts,* is a one-room 1878 furnished pioneer home, visible behind glass. The **Crook County Courthouse** in Pioneer Park has an imposing white clocktower.

Ochoco Lake State Recreation Site; *tel: (541) 447-4363;* camping, *tel: (800) 452-5687,* open year-round has 22 primitive campsites 7 miles east of Prineville. Sno-park permits are required from mid Nov–Apr in the **Ochoco National Forest,** *3160 N.E. 3rd St, PO Box 490, Prineville, OR 97754; tel: (541) 416-6500* (headquarters).

Pine forest thickens as Hwy 26 ascends 24 miles to 4720-ft **Ochoco Pass**, and 28 pitches at **Ochoco Divide Campground**. **Painted Hills Unit** of **John Day Fossil Beds National Monument** is 9 miles north of **Mitchell's** petrol and services (see p.178).

Tourist Information: Eastern Oregon Visitors Association, *PO Box 1087, Baker City, OR 97814; tel: (800) 332-1843; fax: (541) 523-9187,* is a good information resource for this route eastward.

JOHN DAY FOSSIL BEDS NATIONAL MONUMENT

Tourist Information: John Day Fossil Beds National Monument, *HCR 82, Box 126, Kimberly, OR 97848; tel: (541) 987-2333; fax: (541) 987-2336.* The **Sheep Rock Unit** has the **Fossil Museum/Visitors Center**, open 0830–1700 daily Mar–May, Sept–Thanksgiving, and 0830–1800 Mon–Fri Dec–Feb, Memorial Day–Labor Day. There is no lodging or food within the monument.

Named after a Virginian who joined an Astor Columbia River fur scouting expedition in 1812, the fossil beds owe their discovery to minister and amateur palaeontologist Thomas Condon.

Five years after Charles Darwin published the 'Origin of Species', Condon followed US Army gold prospectors to the area, and recognised fossilised tortoise shell. Scientists seconded by Yale, the University of Pennsylvania, Princeton and the University of California, Berkeley, competed for specimens of shell and bone in what turned out to be one of the world's richest fossil beds from the Cainozoic (Cenozoic) Period, the Age of Mammals.

The monument's 14,000 acres are divided into three units: **Clarno** (palisade formations, not on this route), **Painted Hills** and **Sheep Rock**, all with wildly different scenery. Trails are well-marked; to venture off is dangerous because of sediment slippage and damage to ancient fossils. It is illegal to touch or remove anything in the monument. Take precautions for heat, especially when hiking on open trails, and watch for rattlesnakes.

Painted Hills Unit

The Painted Hills Unit, most dramatic in late afternoon, is unreal splashes of rust, yellow and black across golden claystone, iron oxide, magnesium oxide and other chemicals produced from air oxidation and ground water leaching of the soil of Cascade Mountain ash eruptions 30 million years ago. After rain, the same compounds turn burgundy, sage green and ebony on folded layers of land where the only marks are deer and antelope prints.

Drive to overlook parking to walk the ¼-mile **Overlook Trail**, or take the more strenuous ¾-mile **Carroll Rim Trail** from the viewpoint road entrance. To walk amongst the hills, follow signs to the ¼-mile **Painted Cove Trail**. If visiting Apr–May; *tel: (541) 462-3961*, for information on wildflower bloom in the Painted Hills.

It is 30 slow winding miles through a steep canyon from Mitchell to **Picture Gorge**, a narrow defile through wildly formed red rock pinnacles with pictographs.

Sheep Rock Unit

Turn left (north) on SR 19 into the Sheep Rock Unit. The state road follows the John Day River through a patchwork of ranching and farming mixed with protected land

formations. Five formations, in best light at mid-day and the Visitors Center/Museum are attractions.

The Visitors Center is in the two-storey 1918 white Cant Ranch house. To preserve the charm, the National Park Service tends a small collection of farm animals outside. Inside, rangers have information and orientation videos.

A small museum gives an overview of fossil discoveries, some slightly resembling horses or cats. The 'touch me' table allows the hands-on that is legally forbidden outside. A ranching-era front parlour has been preserved.

A short way south of the Visitor Center is **Sheep Rock Overlook** and a striking craggy peak that dominates the landscape. Two miles north is **Goose Rock**, nestled against the river canyon flanks.

BLUE BASIN AREA TO JOHN DAY

Three miles north of the centre is the **Blue Basin Area**, named for the blue-green glow of its hills. The gentle, 1-mile **Island in Time Trail** with interpretative signs wanders between the light mint-green coloured hills. Plan 3½ hours for a strenuous 3-mile loop up the 600-ft rise of the **Blue Basin Overlook Trail** for awesome views of the colourful badlands below.

With an astounding variety of colourful horizontal striations, **Cathedral Rock** towers above the John Day River at a bend in the road. It is best photographed without shadows at mid-day.

The **Foree Area** is fossil central. A ¼-mile **Flood of Fire** Trail gently ascends for views of the valley, but the fine and easy ¼-mile **Story in Stone Trail** has interpretative signs with fossil replicas, like the *oreodont* plant browser which resembled pigs and deer, evoking both the age of the blue-green formation and its natural past.

Drive south through Picture Gorge and Sheep Gulch. **Dayville** has petrol, a grocery store, café, the moderate **Fish House Inn Bed & Breakfast & RV Park**, *Hwy 126, PO Box 143, Dayville, OR 97825; tel: (541) 987-2124,* and excellent coffee and hand-made crafts and

The Oregon Trail

Three hundred thousand pioneers set out from Missouri and Iowa between 1843 and the 1860s, willing to brave 2000 harrowing miles across plains, deserts, mountains, rapids and rivers, along trails lined with graves every 80 yards. The trek took 120–180 days in wide-wheeled, ox-drawn prairie schooners covered with canvas, hauling a ton of household goods and food.

The lure? New land and a new start.

Lewis and Clark's Corps of Discovery (1804–6) and Astor's Pacific Fur Company had established the value of furs and other natural resources, where Native American salmon fishermen prospered in Oregon's mild climate. French-Canadian trappers and retired HBC and American traders settled in the Willamette Valley

Charles Wilkes' 1841 US Exploring Expedition and John C Frémont's 1843 diary and map were guidebooks for future travellers. Missionaries like Jason Lee, Marcus and Narcissa Whitman, and Henry and Eliza Spaulding wrote glowing descriptions of good land for the taking, part of 'America's Second Great Awakening'.

The economic Panic of 1837 was fresh in the minds of would-be pioneers who remembered plague in the lower Mississippi Valley, 30,000 cholera victims in 1850, endless hot summers, cyclones, floods and icy winters.

The United States was imbued with a territorial imperative to expand West. James K Polk's 1844 presidential campaign slogan was '54°40′ or Fight!', a reference to the dispute with Great Britain over a northern boundary. Within two years, Polk had the 49th Parallel Canadian border sealed in the Oregon Treaty. In 1850, the Donation Land Act gave free land to all homesteaders in Oregon. For women, it was the first place in America where they could own their own land.

Oregon Trail settlers were not refugees. Many were self-sufficient farmers from Missouri, Iowa, Arkansas, Illinois, Indiana, Ohio, Kentucky and Tennessee. Others were professionals, lawyers, doctors, ministers and accountants.

After outfitting a wagon with food, clothing, stoves, mementoes and a host of impractical goods, they set out in caravans from Westport, Independence, Fort Leavenworth, St Joseph, Missouri or Council Bluffs, Iowa. They encountered flash floods, lightning storms, dust, prairie fires, rattlesnakes, buffalo stampedes, quicksand – and ironically feared Native Americans whose help and friendship made the journey possible. The trail was soon littered with stoves and anything too heavy for the iron-shod, wooden wheels to bear over well-worn trail ruts.

Men stood guard, hunted, managed the livestock, made repairs and dealt with the generally friendly Native Americans en route. They also rode horses, fired guns, took off their clothes to swim and got drunk. The reason, someone said, was to be 'strong, it's expected of them'. Women, the image of piety, purity and submissiveness, laboured from dawn to dark, driving, loading and unloading wagons, setting up camp, making the campfire, cooking, cleaning, tending the sick, caring for children, giving birth, yet finding time to write stoic, descriptive journals. Children were miniature adults.

Oregon Trail travellers crossed the Plains, the Rocky Mountains and the Blue Mountains west of Baker City, to face deadly rapids in the Columbia River Gorge or a horrific trek on an Oregon Trail offshoot, the southerly Applegate Trail. Some went north into Washington, while the 1849 California Gold Rush drew a steady trickle south to the Sierra Nevada Mountains, Sacramento and San Francisco.

Why go through six months of hell? Oregon Country, the Oregon Territory, the legendary Willamette Valley apple orchards, the contented cows, the mild climate – all must have seemed like heaven.

birdhouses at **Juniper Connection**, *217 W. Franklin; tel: (541) 987-2355.* Just east on Hwy 26 at **Murderer's Creek Wildlife Area** is the **Old Red Barn** interpretative site, a superb 1883 structure with wood pins, dowels and louvered windows.

Mount Vernon, named in the 1870s after a trapper or local racehorse, is surrounded by scenic barns and ranchland. Mid-way between Mount Vernon and John Day, **Clyde Holliday State Park**, *PO Box 9, Canyon City, OR 97820; tel: (541) 575-2773,* camping Mar–Nov; *tel: (800) 452-5687,* open year-round, has picnic tables under large, shady trees.

JOHN DAY TO BAKER CITY

John Day is a major population centre, with lodging, petrol and other amenities in a mountainous setting surrounded by the Malheur National Forest.

Tourist Information: Grant County Chamber of Commerce, *281 W. Main, John Day, OR 97845; tel: (800) 769-5664 or (541) 575-0547.*

Accommodations in **John Day** and nearby **Canyon City** range from *BI* and *BW* to *RV* parks and campsites.

After an 1862 strike, claims around **Canyon City**, south of John Day, produced gold valued at $26 million. Chinese miners flocked to the Canyon City-John Day area, willing to sift through the tailings Whites had left. Mining declined after a decade and today's ranch and agriculture economy took over.

Ancient grizzled cowboys volunteer at the interesting **Grant County Historical Museum,** *Hwy 395, Canyon City, OR 97820; tel: (542) 575-0362,* open Mon–Sat 0930–1630, Sun 1300–1700 June–Sept, adults $2, children 13–18 $1, 6–12 $0.50, with photos of cattle drives through John Day, agate collections, two-headed calves, a 1910 jailhouse and a log cabin built by Joaquin Miller, the 'poet of the Sierras', a Grant County judge 1866–1870. There's also quaint **St Thomas Episcopal Church** along the main street, one block from Hwy 395.

Area residents remark on the lack of ethnicity in John Day, in direct contrast to the mid-1880s. **Kam Wah Chung & Co.**

Museum, *N.W. Canton in John Day City Park; tel: (541) 575-0028,* is open Mon–Thur 0900–1200 1300–1700, Sat–Sun 1300–1700 May–Oct, adults $2, children 13-18 $1, under 12 $0.50. Chinese gold miners were run out of Canyon City by jealous locals and moved to John Day where they were well-served by 'Doc' Ing Hay, a practising Chinese herbalist who ran a general store in the wood frame and stonework 'Golden Flower of Opportunity' building.

Many artefacts remain to bring the excellent tour to life. An opium room is across from a kitchen full of hand-made tools and implements. The bedroom is papered with advertisements for men's suits. Doc Hay was famed for his pulse diagnosis, apothecary preparations, mail order business and horse and buggy house calls.

A large lumber plant sits on the western side of **Prairie City;** the wild-appearing Strawberry Mountains are south. **DeWitt Depot Museum**, *S. Main St by the RV park; tel: (541) 820-3598,* open May 15–Oct 15, Thur–Sat 1000–1500, was the terminus for the narrow-gauge Sumpter Valley Railroad in 1910. It now has rooms of railway and lumbering memorabilia. East of town is moderate **Strawberry Mountain Inn,** *HCR 77 # 940 on Hwy 26 E., Prairie City, OR 97869; tel: (800) 545-6913.*

Stop at the covered wagon kiosk at **Strawberry Mountain Overlook** as Hwy 26 ascends from the John Day Valley towards forested 5240-ft **Dixie Mountain Summit.** Stop at the **Austin Junction Store/ Restaurant** to rub shoulders with locals drinking coffee at the old-time lunch counter. Take Hwy 26 for 20 miles through Malheur National Forest and over 5098-ft **Blue Mountain Summit**. Turn left on SR 245 to **Unity Lake State Park,** a reservoir-recreational area with watersports and camping; *tel: (800) 452-5687.* After passing towering hoodoos (east), turn left on *Big Flat Road,* and follow the winding North Fork of the Burnt River to **Whitney,** a crumbling agglomeration of 1911-era wooden houses and a huge abandoned sawmill. A few denizens hold out to defy Whitney's ghost town reputation.

Turn right onto SR 7, then right on *Dredge*

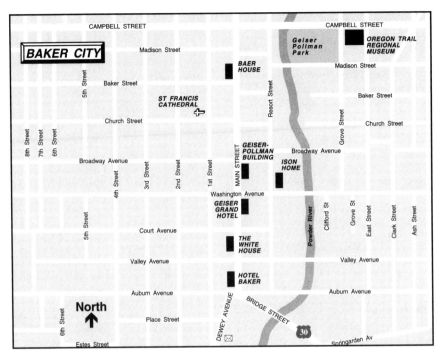

BAKER CITY

CAMPBELL STREET
CAMPBELL STREET

Madison Street

5th Street

Baker Street

ST FRANCIS CATHEDRAL ✛

Church Street

8th Street
7th Street
6th Street

Broadway Avenue

4th Street
3rd Street
2nd Street
1st Street

MAIN STREET

GEISER-POLLMAN BUILDING

BAER HOUSE

Geiser Pollman Park

OREGON TRAIL REGIONAL MUSEUM

Madison Street

Resort Street

Baker Street

Grove Street

Church Street

Broadway Avenue

ISON HOME

Washington Avenue

GEISER GRAND HOTEL

5th Street

Court Avenue

THE WHITE HOUSE

Valley Avenue

HOTEL BAKER

Auburn Avenue

Powder River

Clifford St

Grove St

East Street

Clark Street

Ash Street

Valley Avenue

Auburn Avenue

North ↑

6th Street

Place Street

DEWEY AVENUE

BRIDGE STREET

30

Estes Street

Springarden Av

Loop Rd to the **Sumpter Valley Railroad;** *tel: (541) 894-2268,* a 5-mile steam locomotive excursion on summer weekends between Sumpter and McEwen. **Baker County Railroad Park** next to the depot has a bird refuge, trails and picnicking.

State Route 7 crosses the Powder River. **Sumpter;** *tel: (541) 894-2362* or *(541) 894-2568,* an expanding 1862 gold mining and timber town, is three miles left. The unrestored **Sumpter Valley Dredge** (State Heritage Area) is a decaying monolith five storeys above the 1600 acres of placer gold tailings it created. Several motels and antique shops are open in summer; in winter, restaurants do a good business with refugees from the snow. A bank vault sits on the main road through town; only the door is still standing.

Return to SR 7. **McEwen**'s weathered wooden buildings include a church, country store and antlers mounted on the side of a barn. The Whitman-Wallowa National forest is left (north); wetlands and a picnic ground are south towards Phillips Lake. Recreation areas abound

on the south side: **Union Creek, Mason Dam Viewpoint** (trailhead, boat launch, toilets), **Powder River Recreation Area** (riverside trails, view of back of the dam), and **Mason Dam Picnic Area** (tables, toilets). Forest becomes cattle pastures, good for wildlife viewing, as SR 7 approaches **Baker City**.

BAKER CITY

Tourist Information: Baker County Visitors & Convention Bureau, *490 Campbell St, Baker City, OR 97814; tel: (800) 523-1235 or (541) 523-3356; fax: (541) 523-9187,* open Memorial Day–Labor Day Mon–Fri 0800–1800, Sat 0800–1600, winter Mon–Fri 0800–1700, has a wealth of information on Eastern Oregon and the Oregon Trail, lodging and dining lists.

ACCOMMODATION

The Baker County VCB has an extensive lodging list including four bed and breakfasts and *BW, QI, S8.* Biggest in town and close to I-84 is **Best Western Sunridge Inn**, *1 Sunridge*

Lane; tel: (800) 233-2368 or (541) 523-6444. **Quality Inn,** *810 Campbell St; tel: (800) 228-5151 or (541) 523-2242,* includes a terrific breakfast in the comfortable lobby. The 1889 **Geiser Grand Hotel,** *1996 Main St; tel: (541) 523-1889,* an imposing downtown building, is reopening in 1997 as a moderate–expensive inn.

EATING AND DRINKING

Baker City's dining ranges widely, from Chinese to Mexican and steakhouses. At **Front Street Cafe and Coffee House,** *1840 Main St; tel: (541) 523-7536,* families and tourists mix to enjoy budget–moderate ultra-tasty salads, pizza and beer in an historic building. **Brass Parrot,** *2190 Main St; tel: (541) 523-4266,* has budget–moderate steaks and good burritos in an old brick bakery building. **Klondike's Pizza,** *1726 Campbell St; tel: (541) 523-7105,* serves an excellent budget salad bar.

SIGHTSEEING

Oregon Trail pioneers approaching what would become Baker City saw a beautiful but daunting barrier, the Blue Mountains. In summer's wilting heat or winter's white-cap, the Blues are an eerie, if magnificent, deep blue. Gold rushes in the 1860s and 1890–1910 made centrally located Baker City the 'Queen City of the Mines', with the cultural attractions, saloons, dance halls, brothels and hopeful Salvation Army corpsmen which denote civilisation.

State Route 7 enters Baker City on the south-west side, then runs through the historic downtown along *Main Street.* **Historic Baker City, Inc.;** *tel: (541) 523-5442,* and **Baker City VCB** have a free 100-building historic district walking tour brochure; a more detailed booklet is for sale. The horse-drawn **Oregon Trail Trolley;** *tel: (541) 856-3356,* tours the historic downtown in summer.

US Bank, *2000 Main St,* open Mon–Fri 1000–1700 Fri 1000–1800, has the 80.4-oz Armstrong gold nugget on display. The red brick Queen Anne **Ison House,** *179 Washington,* open Mon–Thur 0900–1700, Fri 0900–1800, Sat 0900– 1300, now a Bank of America, is open to the public for free viewing

of the well-preserved interior. **Betty's Books,** *1813 Main St; tel: (541) 593-7551,* has an excellent selection of Western books in the 1888 gold brick Bamberger Building. **Goose Creek Gallery,** *2022 Resort; tel: (541) 523-6299,* has excellent coffee amongst plants, sleeping cats, quality quilts and art, in a Victorian interior painted in bold colours. Birds are the mania at **Powder River Wild Birds,** *2040 Resort St; tel: (541) 523-5494,* with bird and butterfly houses and feeders.

Go right on *Campbell Rd* past the gracious **Geiser-Pollman City Park** to the **Oregon Trail Regional Museum,** *2490 Grove St; tel: (541) 523-9308,* open daily May–Oct 0900–1600, adults $2. The museum in a restored natorium has very little Oregon Trail history, but does have the outstanding Cavin Warfel Rock Collection, including local petrified wood, Oregon plume agate and bubble agate nodules, thunder eggs, Oregon fire obsidian, an ultra-violet display and fossils.

Campbell Rd has petrol stations, most lodging, dining and provisions, and continues east to I-84, Exit 304. Take the interstate north to Exit 302, and go east on SR 86 to the **National Historic Oregon Trail Interpretive Center at Flagstaff Hill,** *PO Box 987, Baker City, OR 97814; tel: (541) 523-1843,* open May–Sept 0900–1800, Oct–Apr 0900–1600, one of the West's finest museums, with dramatic view windows to the Blue Mountains from the same point where covered wagon occupants paused to gaze at the barrier ahead.

A corridor of life-size sound-narrated dioramas provides an introduction to the types of Oregon Trail pioneers, their equipment, routes, deaths, disasters, and Native American encounters. A second area has covered wagon equipment and provisions with background on national rivalries, motivations, and trail preparations well-explained around the walls. A third area tracks the pioneers from Midwest staging towns to the Blue Mountains with narratives, journal excerpts printed on the wall, prints, artefacts and a video re-enactment. A 4.2-mile trail system runs through sagebrush and wildflowers to a wagon sitting a few feet from original wagon ruts. And, as always, the Blue Mountains loom.

EUGENE–BEND

This 165-mile route, open June–October, leaves the agricultural South Willamette Valley for dramatic fir forests, deep blue alpine lakes, skiing at Mount Bachelor and stunning vistas from the heart of the Cascade Mountains. Upon arrival in Bend, you enter the drier landscape of Central Oregon and a town with a prosperous young-urban-professional-with-family mindset. Bend's pleasant setting on the Deschutes River only hints at the world-class whitewater rivers, mountain peaks and high desert scenery that awaits at its doorstep.

DIRECT ROUTE: 165 MILES

Eugene

40 miles

58

Mount Bachelor

30 miles

Bend

372

Oakridge/Westfir

95 miles

Cascade Lakes Highway

46

183

ROUTE

Drive south from Eugene/Springfield on I-5, then take Exit 188A south-east onto SR 58. South of **Odell** and **Crescent Lakes**, 80 miles from Eugene, turn left (north) onto SR 46, the **Cascade Lakes Hwy**, and drive the 100-mile loop past alpine lakes and **Mt Bachelor** before descending to Bend via *Century Dr.* Part of the Cascades Lake Hwy closes in winter, but SR 58 and the road from Bend to Mt Bachelor remain open. Allow a day to drive slowly through the astounding scenery along this 180-mile route, or stop at Mount Bachelor to ski or hike the mountain.

TOURIST INFORMATION

Convention & Visitors Association of **Lane County, Oregon (CVALCO)**, *118 W. 8th St, Suite 190, PO Box 10286, Eugene, OR 97440; tel: (800) 547-5445* or *(541) 484-5307; fax: (541) 343-6335*, and the **Central Oregon Welcome Center, Central Oregon Visitors Association**, *63085 N. Hwy 97, Suite 104, Bend, OR 97701; tel: (800) 800-8334, (541) 382-8334* or *(541) 389-8799; fax: (541) 385-9487*, open Mon–Sat 0900–1700, Sun 1100–1500. Ask for the *Cascade Lakes Tour* brochure.

EUGENE TO OAKRIDGE/WESTFIR

College-town atmosphere is replaced by agriculture along I-5. Four miles south of downtown Eugene, take Exit 188A (Goshen), and head south-east on SR 58, the two-lane

Willamette Hwy. Elijah Bristow was Lane County's first settler in 1846, near **Pleasant Valley.** Amidst oaks and conifers, **Elijah Bristow State Park,** 15 miles south-east of Eugene, has a large lawn, picnic tables, equestrian paths, bicycling and hiking paths.

There is camping and picnic tables above the water at **Dexter Park,** *Lane County Parks; tel: (541) 341-6940,* at the west end of **Dexter Reservoir.**

HI-Lost Valley Center, *81868 Lost Valley Lane, Dexter, OR 97431; tel; (541) 937-3351,* offers environmental programmes and budget lodging. State Route 58 is on the south shore of the 17-mile stretch along the **Dexter** and **Lookout Point Reservoirs.** Deer, bald eagles, osprey and elk live in the lush forest below power lines surrounding the reservoirs, as fishermen, sailors, water skiers and picnickers seek recreation.

Two miles east of Dexter Park, turn north across Dexter Reservoir to **Lowell,** and the 1945 **Lowell Covered Bridge. Cannon Street Covered Bridge** in downtown Lowell was built in 1988 for pedestrians. The **Lane County Public Works Department,** *3040 N. Delta Hwy, Eugene, OR 97408; tel: (541) 341-6911,* publishes a Lane County covered bridges guide which includes three other covered bridges in the area.

There are several trailheads to the right (south) and additional camping at the east end of Lookout Point Reservoir, near **Hampton Public Boat Landing.**

State Road 58 follows the Middle Fork of the Willamette River. The turn north to **Aufderheide National Scenic Byway** (closed Nov–Mar) is 9 miles from Hampton and 45 miles from Eugene.

Borrow a free cassette tour tape from **USDA Forest Service, Oakridge Ranger District,** *46375 SR 58, Oakridge, OR 97492; tel: (541) 782-2291.* **Westfir,** which has grown to adjoin **Oakridge,** is one mile beyond on SR 58.

OAKRIDGE/WESTFIR

Tourist Information: Oakridge Chamber of Commerce, *47811 Hwy 58, PO Box 217, Oakridge, OR 97463; tel: (541) 782-4146.*

ACCOMMODATION AND FOOD

This resort area is well-equipped with moderate lodging, including *BW* and *RV.* **Westfir Lodge,** *Westfir, OR 97492; tel: (541) 782-3103,* is a moderate, eight-room bed and breakfast in a remodelled lumber mill. The **Ridgeview Motel,** *47465 Hwy 58, Oakridge, OR 97463; tel: (800) 500-3430 or (541) 782-3430* is a budget choice.

Salmon Creek Falls Campground, *Oakridge Ranger District, 46375 Hwy 58, Westfir, tel: (541) 782-2291,* is in old growth forest near the falls. There is an assortment of fast food outlets.

SIGHTSEEING

Westfir and Oakridge began in the 1920s as lumber milltowns, processing local Douglas-fir. The economies of the two waxed and waned until tourism became the economic force. Mountain biking is popular enough to generate an annual **Fat tire Festival competition.**

The 180-ft **Office Covered Bridge** in Westfir, Oregon's longest, has a covered pedestrian walkway separate from the bridge roadway. **Hills Creek (Lake) Reservoir,** *US Forest Service, Rigdon Ranger District, 49098 Salmon Creek Rd, Oakridge, OR 97463; tel: (541) 782-2283,* south-east of Oakridge, has camping, fishing, swimming, boating, water skiing, and a wetlands area below the dam.

OAKRIDGE/WESTFIR TO CASCADE LAKES HIGHWAY

For 20 miles, SR 58 follows Salt Creek, as the Cascade foothills loom closer. Go through a short tunnel, then stop to view 286-ft **Salt Creek Falls** from a platform, or see the water plunge standing on a trail below. There are picnic tables and toilets.

Turn left to large and clear **Waldo Lake,** or right to the **Diamond Peak Wilderness.** Four miles east of Salt Creek Falls, the view from **Forest Vista** lay-by is magnificent. Enter **Willamette National Forest,** *211 E. 7th Ave, Eugene, OR 97401; tel: (541) 465-6521.*

Cross 5280-ft **Willamette Pass. Willamette Pass Ski Area,** *PO Box 5509, Eugene, OR 97405; tel: (541) 484-5030;* for snow

184

conditions; *tel: (541) 345-7669,* open late Dec–Mar, has downhill and Nordic skiing, snowmobiles, and snowshoeing. Buy a Sno-Park permit from National Forest rangers to park and enjoy the area from Nov 15–April 30. **Willamette Pass Inn;** *tel: (800)30l-2218* or *(541) 433 2211* is moderate–expensive. Chalet-style **Summit House Restaurant** is open in winter and summer.

State Route 58 descends to **Odell Lake,** a favourite spot for windsurfing and Nordic skiing. Several resorts, campsites, stores and modest restaurants service tourism to **Odell and Crescent Lakes,** including, **Odell Lake Lodge,** *PO Box 72, Crescent Lake, OR 97425; tel: (541) 433-2540,* with moderate hotel rooms and cabins.

Twelve miles from Willamette Summit, turn left onto SR 46, the **Cascade Lakes Hwy,** sometimes called **Century Drive,** only open June–Oct.

CASCADE LAKES HIGHWAY

The scenic drive is characterised by reservoirs and lakes, most at 4300-ft elevation, girdled by Ponderosa pine forest. Cascade Mountains loom north. The route curves around Mount Bachelor's north side with the magnificent white-capped peak dominating the landscape. Beyond the ski area, the highway descends through forest past posh resorts and golf courses to Bend.

The lakes are popular for watersports and camping. Tents are permitted; most of the major lakes also have cabins, lodge rooms and RV pitches. Fishing requires a licence, available from resort operators. Birders spot protected osprey nests, bald eagles, cormorants and terns, while deer roam freely at all hours.

Hwy 46, *Lava Bed Odell Rd,* passes on the right side of **Davis Lake.** Just north is a lava flow. **Wikiup Reservoir** on the right (east) is named after the permanently fixed tepee poles used by Native Americans, covered when the east side was dammed and flooded in 1949.

Take SR 42 right (east) around the north side of Wikiup Reservoir to 60-ft-deep **North** and **South Twin Lakes,** formed from volcanic craters. **Twin Lakes Resort,** *11200 S. Century Dr, Sunriver, OR 97707; tel: (541)*

593-6526, moderate, serves visitors to South Twin Lake.

At **Crane Prairie Reservoir,** SR 46 becomes *Lava Lake Rd* and passes on the left (west) side of the water. **Crane Prairie Resort RV Park,** *PO Box 1171, Bend, OR 97709; tel: (541) 383-3939,* is open late Apr–mid Oct for boating, fishing and wildlife spotting. **Osprey Point,** a well-populated Apr–Oct fish hawk observation area is on the reservoir's west side.

Little Cultus Lake and **Cultus Lake** are west, with Cultus Mountain in-between. **Cultus Lake Resort,** *PO Box 262, Bend, OR 97709; tel; (541) 389-3230,* open mid May–mid Oct, has 23 moderate cabins, on the larger lake north of its eponymous mountain. Sandy beaches, good windsurfing and varied conifers make Cultus Lake a popular spot.

Lava Lake and **Little Lava Lake** are tiny by comparison, yet unlikely Little Lava Lake is the Deschutes River headwater. Mount Bachelor begins to fill the landscape in photographs of the lakes. **Hosmer Lake** is stocked with Atlantic Salmon for barbless hook, catch-and-release fly fishing.

Elk Lake Resort, *PO Box 789, Bend, OR 97709; tel: (541) 317-2994,* caters to windsurfers at Sunset Cove, and wintertime Nordic skiers and snowmobilers heading to the lake, lodge, cabins and dining area. South Sister and Mt Bachelor appear to be very close to **Elk Lake.**

SR 46 turns south-east by **Devil's Lake** and fly fishing-only **Sparks Lake.** Rugged lava flows to the north (left) in the **Three Sisters Wilderness,** a hikers-only area of past volcanic activity and active glaciers where Native Americans etched pictographs and US astronauts trained for lunar walks. (See Eugene–Baker City, pp.173–182, for information on the McKenzie Hwy and Dee Wright Observatory, north of the wilderness.)

Just south-east of **Todd Lake, Dutchman Flat,** which accommodated the filming of *How the West Was Won,* is a virtually treeless pumice desert.

MOUNT BACHELOR

Tourist Information: Mt Bachelor Ski & Summer Resort; *tel: (800) 829-2442* or *(541)*

382-2442, is open year-round, with skiing Nov–July. For ski condition reports; *tel: (541) 382-7888.* There is no overnight lodging on the mountain. Parking is free. Six day lodges have dining, snacks, bars, telephones, ATMs, restrooms, video arcades, child care, gift shops, lockers, information desks, ticket sales, and ski and snowboarding equipment rental. Sunrise Lodge is open in summer.

From mid Dec–Easter, a free Bend–Mt Bachelor Super Shuttle provides morning and afternoon service between Colorado and Simpson Aves Park-and-Ride lot and Mt Bachelor's West Village. A free inter-lodge bus runs frequently.

Downhill and Nordic skiing lessons are offered in winter, divided into Christmas Holiday–Easter and the reduced-hour Summit Season, Easter–July 4. Seven of 11 chairlifts are high speed. Nordic skiers have 56 km of track. **Dog Sled Rides** and snowmobiles leave from Sunrise Lodge.

From Memorial Day–Labor Day, the **Summit Express Chairlift,** adults $9, children 7–12 $4.50, under 6 years free, runs on two connecting lifts from Sunrise Lodge to the top of Mt Bachelor, weather permitting, one of Oregon's most stunning views.

Take sunscreen, sunglasses, warm, layered clothing, and shoes suitable for hiking across glacial ice. US Forest Service rangers conduct free interpretative walks daily at 1130 and 1430, hiking to three separate areas on the summit.

At the top is a small alpine-blue lake. Below to the west is panorama of Cascades Hwy Lakes. Cascade peaks march south from Mt Adams in Washington to Mt Shasta in Northern California. Eastward is the black and brown volcanic detritus of Newberry Crater and the Lava Cast Forest. Lower forest is Ponderosa Pine; mid-level yields lodgepole pine, and the highest trees are mountain hemlock.

Like the other Cascades, Mt Bachelor is volcanic, one of many proving grounds for the Ring of Fire which makes the Pacific Rim the most geologically active area on earth.

Tectonic plate shifts are the cause: the Juan de Fuca Plate is sliding beneath the North American Plate, causing friction and magma

build-up. Bachelor's eruption 12,000 years ago met nearby Ice Age glaciers, forming not only the mountain's flanks, but the lava flows, domes and craters visible from the 360° summit vista. The porous quality of Mt Bachelor's soil makes it the only Cascade volcano with no runoff.

Mount Bachelor, 9065 ft, gets over 300 ins of snow annually, the result of the Cascade Range's barrier trapping moisture blown east from the Pacific Ocean. The mountain's rain shadow causes Bend and areas to the east to have less than 30 ins yearly.

Two miles east on the Cascade Lakes Hwy is the right-hand (east) turn to Sunriver–La Pine (see Klamath Falls–The Dalles, p. 198). There are several sno-parks (permit required Nov 15–Apr) as the highway descends. Four miles from Mt Bachelor, stop to look backwards at a magnificent morning view of the white peak gleaming above green forest. Three miles east at 5600 ft is **Swampy Lakes,** a skiing, hiking and mountain biking staging area.

The Inn of the Seventh Mountain, *18575 S.W. Century Dr., Bend, OR 97702; tel: (800) 452-6810* or *(541) 382-8711,* is the closest resort to Mt Bachelor with overnight lodging. **Mount Bachelor Village Resort,** *19717 Mount Bachelor Dr, Bend, OR 97702; tel: (800) 452-9846* or *(541) 389-5900,* has luxurious condominiums overlooking the rushing Deschutes River and a 2-mile nature trail. Both are moderate–pricey.

BEND

Tourist Information: Bend Chamber Convention and Visitors Bureau, (same location as **Central Oregon Welcome Center/Central Oregon Visitors Association-COVA***), 63085 N. Hwy 97, Bend, OR 97701-5765; tel: (800) 905-2363* or *(541) 382-3221; fax: (541) 385-9929.*

ACCOMMODATION

COVA makes lodging referrals. Well-equipped with lodging, Bend fills on winter weekends and holidays with skiers and snowboarders bound for Mt Bachelor.

Chains include *BW, CI, EL, RL, S8* and *HI-***Alpine Hostel***, 19 S.W. Century Dr., Bend, OR 97702; tel: (800) 299-3813* or *(541)*

389-3813. **Sleep Inn**, *600 N.E. Bellevue (Hwy 20); tel: (541) 330-0050; fax (541) 383-8109,* is moderate at the edge of town. Several moderate–expensive bed and breakfasts are downtown.

EATING AND DRINKING

Dining out is a way to be seen by friends, neighbours and business contacts. Downtown has many eateries, amongst them the moderate **Pine Tavern Restaurant**, *967 N.W. Brooks St; tel: (541) 382-5581,* well-known for its food, location overlooking Mirror Pond and Ponderosa pines growing in the dining area. **Deschutes Brewery & Public House**, *1044 N.W. Bond St; tel: (541) 382-9242,* has fine microbrewery beers like Bachelor Bitter and Obsidian Stout, also available, bottled, in super-markets.

An ostrich burger is a novel offering in the **Hot Rod Grill**, *917 Wall St; tel: (541) 385-7098,* sandwich, salad and Tex-Mex menu. The Bend Area Chamber of Commerce has a *Dining Guide*.

SIGHTSEEING

Early pioneers who crossed the Deschutes River called it Farewell Bend when they said goodbye at a bend in the river. Grazing was good in high desert, and later irrigation attracted farmers. The railway presence in 1911 drew lumber mills in 1914 to process Ponderosa pine in Bend. Timber production is still an economic mainstay.

If not Oregon's exact geographical centre (Prineville, about 25 miles north-east claims that honour), Bend is Central Oregon's recreation centre and shopping hub.

Mount Bachelor and the Cascade Highway lakes are west, high desert and lava formations are south. North-west is the McKenzie River's whitewater rafting and fishing; Oregon's version of a Grand Canyon, north of Redmond, are the canyon walls sheltering Lake Billy Chinook.

Bend is in the throes of a population explosion of urbanites who have fled to the pseudo-country, a boom that makes the Hwy 97 corridor from Bend to Redmond a strip of service businesses and new housing. High tech entrepreneurs are setting up shop from home in the high desert, and bringing their urban demands for goods and good life services with them.

The lifestyle starts in **Downtown Bend**, between *Bond* and *Wall Sts* and *Greenwood* and *Franklin Aves*. **Pioneer Park** and **Drake Park** provide a greenway walk along the Deschutes riverbank. **Bend Downtowners;** *tel: (541) 385-6570,* has a brochure and information about downtown activities, art shows and concerts.

The **Deschutes County Historical Society,** *129 N.W. Idaho Ave; tel: (541) 389-1813* and the Bend Area Chamber of Commerce, sell an excellent downtown *Heritage Walk* brochure. In good weather, the downtown area is outdoor tables and casually-dressed café society. Summertime Thursday evenings, for 'Munch and Music' in Drake Park, families patronise local restaurant food booths, browse handicrafts and listen to free concerts.

Painted Pony Trading Co, *933 N.W. Wall St; tel: (541) 317-1190,* has Southwestern *objets d'art* and gifts, typical of the up-market merchandise preferred by newer residents.

Deschutes County Historical Museum, *129 N.W. Idaho St, PO Box 5252; tel; (541) 389-1813,* open Tues–Sat 1000–1630, in a 1914 school building, has photographs of lumbering and local artefacts, including a mysterious stone thought to have been left by an early 1800s trapper or explorer.

Residents flock from all over the region to shop at department and discount stores and bargain factory outlets. The malls are strung along Hwy 97: **Mountain View Mall, River Bend Mall, Wagner's Mall, Bend Town Center, Fred Meyer Mall,** the **Bend Factory Outlets,** and **Wagner's Pinebrook Mall**.

Morning or afternoon is the best time to join joggers, walkers, pram pushers and bicyclists trekking one mile up a spiralling road, 500 ft up a volcanic cinder cone, to **Pilot Butte State Park,** *Greenwood Ave.* Cars have a 15 mph speed limit.

The stunning 360° vista from the top takes in Bend below and nine Cascades Mountains, Mt Hood to Mt Bachelor.

ROSEBURG–CRATER LAKE

The North Umpqua River may be the most beautiful amongst Oregon's Wild and Scenic Rivers. This 95-mile route follows the river east from Roseburg, through moss-covered canyons resembling Chinese water-colours of Guilin, whitewater rapids, past magnificent waterfalls cascading through basalt crevices and ravines to Diamond Lake Resort and, via State Route 62, the north entrance to Crater Lake National Park.

Plan at least a half day to drive this route; a full day if stopping to raft, kayak, fish or walk to the waterfalls. There is abundant camping en route. Crater Lake National Park north entrance is closed in winter, except to authorised snowmobile excursions. As a winter alternative, continue east on State Route 138 to Highway 97.

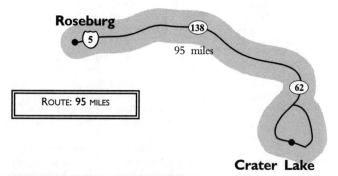

Roseburg
138
95 miles
62
Crater Lake

188

ROUTE: **95** MILES

ROUTE

Take I-5, Exit 124, east on SR 138, *Oak Ave*, across the Umpqua River. Turn left at *Stephens St*, then right onto *Diamond Lake Blvd*, the continuation of SR 138 east. Follow SR 138 85 miles, then continue south, except in winter, 10 miles on SR 62 into Crater Lake National Park.

TOURIST INFORMATION

Tourist Information: Bureau of Land Management, *777 Garden Valley Blvd, Roseburg, OR 97470; tel: (541) 440-4930;* **Umpqua National Forest,** *Supervisor's Office, PO Box 1008, Roseburg, OR 97470; tel: (541) 672-6601;* **North Umpqua Ranger Station,** *18782 N. Umpqua Hwy, Glide, OR 97443; tel:*

(541) 496-3532. **Douglas County Parks;** *PO Box 800, Roseburg, OR 97470; tel: (541) 440-4500.*

ROSEBURG TO CRATER LAKE

The outskirts of Roseburg have a log pond for P & M Cedar Products lumber mill. Eastward, the countryside quickly changes to rolling agricultural hills and pastures. **Whistlers Bend Park** is 8 miles from town on the right.

Oft-photographed **Cavitt Creek Covered Bridge** is 16 miles east of Roseburg. Turn right on *Little River Rd*, County Roads 17A and 17C, for 8 miles.

Glide, 17 miles from Roseburg, is home to

the Glide Lumber Products mill. **Colliding Rivers Wayside Area,** *visitor centre; tel: (541) 496-0157,* open 0900–1700 May–Sept, is named after the dramatic head-on meeting of the North Umpqua and Little Rivers. There is a short **Glide Loop Scenic Drive** from Colliding Rivers through lush forest to SR 138. **Steelhead Run Bed & Breakfast,** *20349 N. Umpqua Hwy, PO Box 639, Glide, OR 97443; tel: (800) 348-0563 or (541) 496-0563; fax: (541) 496-3200,* has moderate rooms and one cabin on the river.

Idleyld Park has several lodges, including budget–moderate **North Umpqua Resort,** *23885 N. Umpqua Hwy, PO Box 177, Idleyld Park, OR 97447; tel: (541) 496-0149.* Whitewater at a curve in the river marks the road to the **Rock Creek Fish Hatchery** on the opposite (north) side. Cross **Swiftwater Bridge** to **Swiftwater County Park** for picnicking. On Hwy 138's north side, **Swiftwater Day-Use Area** also has picnic facilities, with information on the 23-mile dedicated fly-fishing section of river, the **North Umpqua River Trail**, which parallels the river for 79 miles, and the quarter-mile **Deadline Falls Trail**, to a viewing area where fish jump, June–Oct, on their way to spawn.

There are frequent waysides along the river, most with picnic tables and fine views of fly fishing, including **Hill Creek Wayside, Baker Wayside** and **Smith Springs Wayside**. Summer is native (wild) and hatchery-raised steelhead fishing season on the river which Western writer Zane Grey considered among the world's finest. The North Umpqua River also has winter steelhead, coho salmon, fall and spring chinook salmon and a declining population of sea-run cutthroat trout. **Dogwood Motel;** *tel: (541) 496-3403,* moderate, is one of the few motels on the route.

Picnic at **Susan Creek (BLM) Rest Site** before hiking one mile to **Susan Creek Falls,** and a quarter-mile further to **Susan Creek Indian Mounds.** Susan Creek is the last boat, kayak, canoe, or raft take-out point along the stretch of Wild and Scenic River (others are **Wright Creek, Bogus Creek, Gravel Bin, Apple Creek, Horseshoe**, and **Boulder Flat**). Five miles east in the **Umpqua**

National Forest is **Fall Creek Falls,** accessed by a scenic one-mile trail. The 6 miles from Bogus Creek to Gravel Bin are closed to boating July 15–Oct.

Around a dramatic bend in the river, **Steamboat** has 26 fly-fishing pools; Steamboat Creek is permanently closed to fishing to protect wild summer steelhead spawning. **Steamboat Inn,** *42705 N. Umpqua Hwy, Steamboat, OR 97447-9703; tel; (541) 498-2411,* expensive–pricey, is the poshest lodging on the river, with an elegant, pricey evening dinner.

The sides of the river canyon narrow gradually for the next 13 miles with camp pitches only at **Island, Apple Creek, Horseshoe Bend, Eagle Rock** and **Boulder Flat campgrounds.** Stark basalt columns on the right are covered with mossy-looking green lichen.

Small signs for three stunning waterfalls, **Toketee,** 272-ft **Watson, Whitehorse,** and **Clearwater Falls,** appear in rapid succession. From each parking area, it is a short walk to the falls viewpoint, each surrounded by huge rocks, ferns, huge firs and mist.

Highway 138 turns south on *Windigo Pass Rd,* a section of the Cascade Lakes Hwy. **Diamond Lake Resort & Convention Center,** *Diamond Lake, OR 97731, tel: (800) 733-7593,* has moderate–expensive motel rooms and cabins, and is the concessionaire for snow-mobiling, snowboarding, Nordic skiing, sail and motor boating, canoeing, trout fishing and horses. Snow-capped 8363-ft **Mt Bailey**, is the backdrop for deep blue Diamond Lake, carved by glaciers during the last Ice Age. Daily snowcat skiing to Crater Lake National Park for 12 intermediate–expert skiers is offered by Diamond Lake Resort; *tel: (541) 793-3333.* **Diamond Lake RV Park;** *tel: (541) 793-3318,* has 140-pitches at the south end of Diamond Lake, mid May–mid Oct.

As the route continues south to **Crater Lake National Park,** 9182-ft **Mt Thielsen**, the frequently-struck 'Lightning Rod of the Cascades', is left (east). If continuing east on SR 138 to Hwy 97 because of winter park closure, prepare to cross a near-lunar landscape of pumice exploded from Mt Mazama, Crater Lake's original peak, 7000 years ago.

189

CRATER LAKE NATIONAL PARK

Crater Lake is bluer than blue, surreal, a view of the edge of the world before creation. Mount Mazama's explosion 7700 years ago spewed debris as far away as Saskatchewan, Canada. The collapsed mountain formed a caldera which trapped precipitation.

Oregon's only national park and the USA's deepest lake is closed by colossal snowfall for many months of the year, half-open on the Western Rim Drive for a third of the year and fully open at the Rim two–three months.

190

The full 33-mile circuit around the caldera rim can be driven in 2 hours, though speed limits, traffic and many scenic viewpoints demand at least a half day. Sunrise is opalescent pink. Sunset may have streaks of purple and green.

Access varies by snowfall: West Rim Drive opens roughly May–Oct; East Rim Drive opens July–Sept. Dress warmly for variable conditions and dramatic temperature shifts.

TOURIST INFORMATION

Crater Lake National Park, Box 7, Crater Lake, OR 97604; tel: (541) 594-2211. **Steel Information Center,** the park headquarters, 2¾ miles from the Rim, open year-round 0900–1700, has exhibits, weather forecasts and back-country permits. **Rim Village Visitor Center,** in a log building near Crater Lake Lodge, is open June–Sept. Rangers give geology talks hourly, 1000–1600, a Rim Village History Walk at 1300, and a 1¾-mile guided hike up

Mt Garfield at 1400. Though both visitor centres sell books and maps, **Rim Village gift-shop** (summer only) has the best selection of books on Crater Lake, vulcanism, geology, Native Americans and Pacific Northwest subjects. Rangers conduct programs at Mazama Campground at 2100.

ACCOMMODATION

Weather permitting, park lodging is open mid May–mid Oct. The shingle and stone, well-appointed **Crater Lake Lodge** at the Rim is expensive. **Mazama Village Motor Inn,** moderate, is south near the Annie Spring Entrance Station. Book well in advance for either lodging; **Crater Lake Company,** 1211 Avenue C, White City, OR 97503; tel: (541) 830-8700; fax: (541) 830-8514. Plan on first-come, first served at the 198-pitch tent and RV **Mazama Village Campground,** which opens when the snow melts. **Lost Creek Campground** on East Rim Drive, open mid July–mid Sept, has 12 tent pitches.

EATING AND DRINKING

Dining with fine lake views include moderate-pricey casual dress **Crater Lake Lodge Dining Room,** and cheap–moderate **Watchman Restaurant and Lounge** above the Rim Village giftshop. Arrive for dinner an hour before sunset to see the odd colours playing over the lake. A cheap–budget **cafeteria** is adjacent to the giftshop; buy sodas and snack food in the shop. **Mazama Village** has a well-provisioned grocery store. An alternative is to eat or get picnic provisions in Medford.

Native American traditions, probably from marsh-dwelling Klamaths, explain the explosion of 11,000–12000-ft Mt Mazama as a violent conflict between Skell (Mazama), lord of the beautiful marsh lands of the world above and Llao (Shasta), lord of the underworld. Both

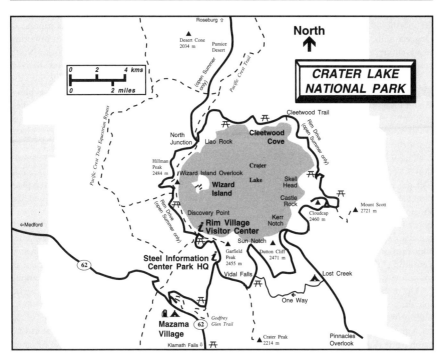

North ↑

CRATER LAKE
NATIONAL PARK

Roseburg

Desert Cone
2034 m

Pumice
Desert

Pacific Crest Trail (open Summer only)

0   2   4 kms
0   2 miles

Pacific Crest Trail Equestrian Bypass

Cleetwood Trail

Rim Drive (open Summer only)

North
Junction   Llao Rock

Cleetwood
Cove

Hillman
Peak
2484 m   Wizard Island Overlook

Crater

Lake

Skell
Head

Wizard
Island

Castle
Rock

Mount Scott
2721 m

Discovery Point

Rim Drive (open Summer only)

Kerr
Notch

Cloudcap
2460 m

←Medford

Rim Village
Visitor Center

Sun Notch

Steel Information
Center Park HQ

Garfield
Peak
2455 m

Dutton Cliff
2471 m

Lost Creek

Vidal Falls

Godfrey
Glen Trail

One Way

Mazama
Village   62

Crater Peak
2214 m

Pinnacles
Overlook

Klamath Falls ↓

spirits fell in love with Loha, the mortal daughter of a Native chief. Loha rejected Llao's promise of eternal life in return for marriage. Scorned, Llao was furious and jealously stomped on Skell's peak, ruining the handsome god's good looks and blowing most of him hundred of miles in all directions.

Science has confirmed Mazama's distinctive and unique mineral 'fingerprint'. Thick, slow-moving andesite lava, rich in silica dioxide, began creating Mazama's steep slopes 500,000 years ago, trapping gas as it moved. The dome was so thick 7700 years ago that the pressurised gasses escaped in a megablast 42 times the force of Mt St Helens' explosion in 1980. A **caldera**, or crater, remained. Eons of rain and snow covered all but Phantom Ship and Wizard Island to a depth of 1932 ft. The deep lake absorbs the colour spectrum, leaving only blue to show on the surface. In 1988–89, the Deep Rover submersible descended to check thermal activity on the bottom of a lake which averages 64°F on the surface. The crew found earthworms and a flea-like mite.

SIGHTSEEING

Summer at Crater Lake

There is only one way to explore the lake's surface. Arrive early to get a seat on the guided 1.¾-hr 60-passenger boat tour of Crater Lake. Weather conditions may cancel or delay boat departures during the season, mid June–mid Sept. Passengers on pre-noon boat departures can get off at unshaded Wizard Island to hike or fish with artificial lures, and are picked up at 1630 ($2 more). Most boat tourists are shocked by the unshaded 1.1-mile Cleetwood Trail, to lakeside Cleetwood Cove, to board the cruise. The 'moderately steep' trail is as hard and thirsty as they come, requiring water, sunscreen, a hat, and protective shoes for volcanic rock. The **Crater Lake Company,** (details on p.190), has information but no advance bookings, adults $12, children $6.50.

Unpredictable weather and precipitous slopes make bicycling viable only July–early Sept. Helmets must be worn. Other challenges are shortness of breath at altitude, narrow roads clogged with autos and RVs, no verges and blind curves. There are two mountain bike roads. Hiking is always popular.

Winter at Crater Lake

Crater Lake's summertime royal blue yields to a subtler Navy blue in winter. An average of 45 ft of snow falls annually; half that remains in avalanche-prone snowpack.

The Rim Drive connecting Steel Information Center/Park Headquarters to the Rim Village remains open in winter but unploughed, opening up Nordic skiing and snowshoeing on 140 miles of unploughed and ungroomed trails. Hire skis and snowshoes at the Rim Village cafeteria; *tel: (541) 830-8700.* Blue diamonds mark popular ski trails. Weather permitting, rangers conduct guided weekend snowshoe walks; *tel: (541) 594-2211.*

Up to eight campers may ski or snowshoe together to camp pitches well away from ski trails or water sources. Each person must register with the park service for a free backcountry camping permit after completing a skills and equipment checklist, before setting off carrying all provisions, including firewood.

Skiing or snowshoeing the 30 mile unploughed Rim Drive around the lake is popular, but requires 3–5 days for skiers, and longer for those on snowshoes. Complete backcountry permit checkout, park in the Rim Village parking lot, and take the circuit clockwise to Steel Information Center/Park Headquarters. There is also snowmobiling from Diamond Lake.

Crater Lake Rim Drive

Over 30 overlooks relieve traffic congestion on the lake circuit and offer vistas, stand-up picnicking and photo opportunities. The circuit traditionally runs clockwise from the south side Rim Village. **West Rim Drive** is open from Rim Village to Cleetwood Trail. **East Rim Drive,** from just east of Cleetwood Trail past the Phantom Ship Overlook and Sun Notch, is open July–Aug. From **Rim Village** landmarks are visible six miles across the lake, including cone-shaped Wizard Island, the crater's most recently formed land mass. Mileage is from the Rim Village starting point.

Discovery Point, 1.3 miles, is panoramic amidst aggressive chipmunks scampering around drooping mountain hemlock. North are Wizard Island and, between 8151-ft Hillman Peak and 8094-ft Llao Rock, the solidified magma dike called Devil's Backbone.

At **Wizard Island Overlook,** 4 miles, 8031-ft Watchman Peak is on the right side of the parking area; plan 30 mins up and 15 back to hike the sheer path to a fire tower 'aerial' view near the summit. Wizard Island is directly below. Hillman Peak is left. Look west to a fine sunset line-up of Cascade Peaks . A barren plain to the north-west forms the Pumice Desert and Red Cone in front of Mt Thielsen.

North Junction cuts off to the park's north entrance and SR 138 (See Roseburg–Crater Lake, pp. 188–189). **Llao Rock,** 9.5 miles, is on the right as the road rises through forest to the **Cleetwood Cove Trailhead** and parking lot. The **East Rim Drive** begins at this point, and turns south.

Skell Head, 15 miles, has good morning views of the lake's west side. Turn right at 17.5 miles onto a 1-mile road to the lake's highest viewpoint near 8070-ft Cloudcap. The wizened and misshapen trees are whitebark pines, half dead from cold winds.

The 5-mile return hike to 8929-ft **Mt Scott's** fire tower has a view of the entire lake. **Castle Rock** or **Pumice Castle,** 21 miles, is the name given to glowing pink and orange striated rock formed about 70,000 yrs ago on the caldera wall.

Kerr Notch, 23 miles, is the traditional **Phantom Ship** overlook. Take Pinnacles Rd east 6 miles past the **Lost Creek Campground** to spectacular **Pinnacles.**

Sun Notch, at 27 miles, looks directly out upon **Phantom Ship.** It's a short walk from the parking area across a flower-filled meadow dotted with wind-dwarfed trees. The vantage point has the picture-perfect view of the aptly named **Phantom Ship** – what's left of a 160-ft tall, 400,000-yr old volcanic dike.

Vidae Falls mist makes a refreshing summer stop at 29 miles. Stop at 0.4-mile **Castle Crest Wildflower Trail,** 31 miles, for a forest-to-meadow summer carpet. Turn right at Steel Information Center to return to Rim Village.

CRATER LAKE– MEDFORD

This route descends 70 miles from Crater Lake National Park on the Crater Lake highway, through pine forests, past the source of the Rogue River, mountain towns and through farmland to Southern Oregon's industrial and retail centre. Plan on a two-hour drive, or three allowing for weekend and holiday traffic.

DIRECT ROUTE: 70 MILES

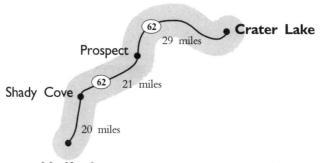

Crater Lake

62 — 29 miles

Prospect

62 — 21 miles

Shady Cove

20 miles

Medford

ROUTE

Take SR 62 70 miles west and south from Crater Lake National Park Annie Spring Entrance Station to Medford.

TOURIST INFORMATION

Tourist Information: Nearly the entire route is within Jackson County. **The Chamber of Medford/Jackson County**, *101 E. 8th St, Medford, OR 97501; tel: (541) 779-4847; fax: (541) 776-4808,* and **Rogue River National Forest**, *333 W. 8th St, PO Box 520, Medford, OR 97501; tel: (541) 858-2200,* have information. SR 62 generally remains open in winter,

but sno-park permits are required Nov 15–Apr. **Prospect Ranger District**, *Prospect, OR 97536; tel: (541) 560-3400,* can advise of weather, facilities, activities and camping for Rogue River Gorge–Prospect on this route.

CRATER LAKE TO PROSPECT

Flanked by tall, thick pine forests, the **Crater Lake Highway** descends west across the Cascade (Range) divide, out of the national park and into the **Rogue River National Forest**.

Rogue River Gorge, as SR 62 meets SR 230 and turns south, is not far from the river's birthplace at **Boundary Springs** in Crater Lake National Park. The Upper Rogue is a US Wild and Scenic River, appearing from below a rocky overhang to form a chasm 500 ft long which quickly narrows to 25 ft wide after the initial surge. Every minute 410,000 gallons of 44°F water flow through a 45 ft deep channel. A rocky path lined with ferns and green undergrowth winds along the lip of the chasm.

Civilisation intrudes with **Union Creek** historic district's brown shingle buildings. **Union Creek Resort**, *56484 Hwy 62, Prospect, OR, 97536; tel: (541) 560-3565* or *(541) 560-3339*, has moderate lodge rooms, sleeping and housekeeping cabins. **Beckie's Cafe** berry or apple pie makes a good snack in a log cabin-style dining room, and there's an ice-cream shop. **Crazy Cayuse Ranch & Pack Station**; *tel: (541) 779-9121*, has horse riding from **Union Creek Stables**. **Union Creek** is a centre for hiking, rafting, fishing, horse riding, swimming, Nordic skiing and snowmobiling. There are picnic tables and 78 camping pitches.

When the Rogue River disappears into a basaltic lava cave for 200 ft, a **Natural Bridge** is formed. There is a short, fenced-off walk to see the gently-curving bridge from several angles.

Walk a pleasant, quarter-mile loop around the **Mammoth Pines**, old growth and huge overgrown fallen stumps which shelter many birds.

PROSPECT TO SHADY COVE

Five miles south, usually just below the snow-line, is **Prospect**, an old-fashioned town with a saloon-diner and the moderate **Prospect Historical Hotel and Dinnerhouse**, *391 Mill Creek Dr., Prospect, OR 97536; tel: (800) 944-6490* or *(541) 560-3664; fax: (541) 560-3825*. Bed and breakfast is provided for guests staying in the 8 hotel rooms; there are adjacent moderate motel rooms. The moderate dinnerhouse is open Wed–Sun. The 1889 hotel was a convenient roadhouse stop for Zane Grey and other Upper Rogue River fishermen, as well as notables visiting Crater Lake like Jack London and US President Teddy Roosevelt. The well appointed turn-of-the-century rooms are a way to stay near, but not in, the national park. Follow *Mill Creek Dr.* one mile south of town to **Prospect State Scenic Viewpoint** and a trail to **Pearsoney Falls**.

Below Prospect, llama, sheep and cattle ranches appear. Half way along the route, SR 62 crosses **Lost Creek Lake/Reservoir**, where a Rogue River dam provides flood control and blocks salmon access to spawning areas. Swimming, waterskiing, rainbow trout fishing, hiking and biking are based at popular lakeside **Joseph H. Stewart State Park**, *35251 Hwy 62, Trail, OR 97541; tel: (800) 452-5687* or *(541) 560-3334*, with 151 RV and 50 tent pitches and a modest café.

Continue on SR 62. **Lost Creek Dam powerhouse**; *tel: (541) 878-2255*, has daily tours at 1300, Memorial Day–Labor Day.

Turn right (north) on *Takelma Rd* to **Cole M Rivers Fish Hatchery**. There is fishing and boating at **Casey State Recreational Site** along the river. **Rogue Elk County Park**, *tel: (541) 776-7001* or *(541) 826-8101*, is a few miles west with swimming, fishing, rafting and camping. Budget–moderate **Rogue Elk Hotel**, *27395 Hwy 62, Trail, OR 97541; tel: (541) 878-2768*, built in 1916, is an alternative campsite.

SHADY COVE TO MEDFORD

Veer left at the SR 227 junction and continue south on SR 62 to **Shady Cove**, a main centre for Upper Rogue River fishing, rafting and float companies. **Upper Rogue Regional Park**; *tel: (541) 776-7001* or *(541) 826-8101*, has picnicking and river access. **Shady Cove** businesses have a free *Catch the Spirit* brochure with local information and advertisements. **Royal Coachman Motel**, *PO Box 509, Shady Cove, OR 97539; tel: (541) 878-2481*, has moderate rooms.

Eagle Point, once a farming town is now best known for **Butte Creek Mill**, *402 Royal Ave N., Box 561, Eagle Point, OR 97524; tel: (541) 826-3531*, an old wooden grist mill which sells stone-ground grains, cornmeal, pancake mix, dried herbs and preserves. Down the street is a small museum, open in summer. The 1922 **Antelope Creek Covered Bridge**, one of the prettiest in Oregon, is at the end of *Main St.* An 18-hole golf course is an attraction.

Six miles north of Medford, surrounded by pastures, **White City** is an industrial centre with chemical companies and wood product manufacturers.

CRATER LAKE– KLAMATH FALLS

South-east of Crater Lake National Park are the northern reaches of the vast Klamath River and Klamath Lakes system, one of the world's richest migratory bird and waterfowl resting areas. Native American Klamath tribespeople live, farm, hunt and fish along much of this 55-mile route, which passes a pinnacle overlook, rich grassy pastures, an historic fort where the US Army watched for signs of native attack, and vast stretches of water where bald eagles soar and white pelicans and herons feed. Take two hours to allow for wildlife viewing stops.

195

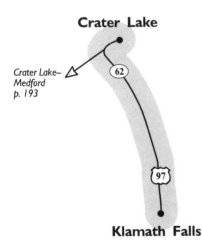

Crater Lake

Crater Lake–
Medford
p. 193

62

97

Klamath Falls

ROUTE: 55 MILES

ROUTE

Take SR 62 south-east from the Crater Lake National Park Annie Spring Entrance, turn right on Hwy 97 south to Klamath Falls. The entire route is in Klamath County.

TOURIST INFORMATION

Tourist Information: Klamath County Department of Tourism, *1451 Main St, PO Box 1867, Klamath Falls, OR 97601; tel: (800) 445-6728 or (541) 884-0666; fax: (541) 884-0666*, has area information.

For **Klamath Basin Refuges** information: Refuge Manager, **Klamath Basin National**

Wildlife Refuges, *Rte 1, Box 74, Tulelake, CA 96134; tel: (916) 667-2231.*

For tribal and cultural information and guided tours, contact the **Klamath Tribe**, *Hwy 97, S. of Chiloquin, PO Box 436, Chiloquin, OR 97424; tel: (541) 783-2095*, well in advance.

Fly fishing, Nordic skiing and snowmobiling are easily accessible from Fort Klamath.

ACCOMMODATION AND FOOD

Aspen Inn, *52250 Hwy 62, Fort Klamath, OR*

97626; tel: (541) 381-2321, **Wilson's Cottages and Camp,** *Hwy 62, PO Box 488; tel: (541) 381-2209* and **Crater Lake Resort,** *50711 Hwy 62; tel: (541) 381-2349,* have limited moderate lodging.

Crater Lake Campground, *57575 Hwy 62; tel: (541) 381-2275,* has cabins and RV pitches. **Cattle Crossing Cafe;** *tel: (541) 381-9081,* open 0600–2100, is the town's only eatery.

CRATER LAKE TO KLAMATH FALLS

As SR 62 descends from Crater Lake National Park Annie Spring Entrance, through regal stands of trees, there are hints of a dramatic canyon to the left (north).

An interpretive sign at the **Godfrey Glen** pull-out explains the mystery. Pinnacle shafts formed from fumaroles – underground steam tubes – are visible as Annie Creek flows noisily below. The pinnacles form the wind, ice and water-eroded sides of a twisting canyon that winds within a few miles of Crater Lake's Rim. If the National Park East Rim Drive is closed, Sept–June, this may be the only view of the hoodoo-shaped Pinnacles. Annie Creek waters may not be visible, but a bright greensward marks the waterway path.

Suddenly, forest gives way to pastures and grazing cattle, with steep-roofed silvery metal or red painted barns in the distance. Ranches are vast enough to supplement cowboys riding horses for cattle round-up with motorised carts zipping across country. Summer wildflowers are abundant in these high meadows.

Jackson F Kimball State Recreation Site; *3 miles east of SR 62 on Dixon Rd; tel: (541) 783-2471,* has a short marshy path to the stunning alpine green Wood River headwaters, a haven for mosquitoes. There are 10 tree-shaded camping pitches.

Fort Klamath town's two-block-long main street cries out for cowboys driving cows through town. A few weathered wooden buildings and the steel-door white clapboard Fort Klamath Community Methodist Church are among the few older buildings in the 200-person town. A snowy peak depicted in the

stained-glass window above the church door mimics the peaks north-west towards Crater Lake.

SR 62 turns right (east) briefly, east of town. **Fort Klamath Museum,** *Hwy 62; tel: (541) 883-4208,* open Thur–Mon 1000–1800 June–Labor Day, is a heavily refurbished wooden building on the spot where the 1863 fort was constructed. A model shows the fort configuration and explains the history which led from US Army wagon train protection to the 1870 forced movement of Modoc Native Americans from Tule Lake in the south to the nearby **Klamath Reservation**.

The Modocs and Klamaths, traditional enemies, were not consulted, and force applied by fort troops exacerbated the problems. Modoc villages were torched by soldiers. Modocs took to the lava beds (now North California). Under the leadership of Kentipoos' 'Captain Jack', 60 braves held off 1200 US troops for four months. In the end, Captain Jack and other Modocs were executed in an aspen grove south of the fort, and are buried a hundred yards from the museum building.

Seven miles south is **Klamath Agency** Native American facilities, closed to the public.

Agency Lake adjoins soft blue **Upper Klamath Lake,** part of the **Upper Klamath National Wildlife Refuge**. Bald eagles and osprey are numerous in the 14,400-acre refuge.

Turn right, south onto Hwy 97. The highway hugs the shore of Upper Klamath Lake, though railway tracks prevent lakeside pull-outs. **Hanks Marsh** is a small freshwater area giving way to the open water of the lake. Looking west across the lake, the snowy peak of **Mt McLoughlin** shimmers above placid Canada geese, mallards and ruddy ducks.

Hire a canoe from a refuge-recommended concessionaire to experience the lake at waterfowl level along self-guided canoe trails. Silky white pelicans breed in spring; ducklings and goslings fledge June–Aug; fall flyover is an awesome display of over a million geese, ducks, swans, herons, grebes, terns, gulls and white pelicans resting briefly before heading south; and winter is left to eagles and hawks to soar above the frosty marshlands.

KLAMATH FALLS– THE DALLES

The 275 miles north along Oregon's central corridor pass from Klamath Refuge lakes and wetlands, through high desert lava flows, southwest-type gorges and rock formations to cattle range and wheat farms, before descending to the Columbia River at The Dalles. One or more Cascade peaks rise white-capped to the west. Allow six hours for the drive on excellent highways. Bend is a perfect multi-day stop. A side track from Madras goes to the Warm Springs Indian Reservation.

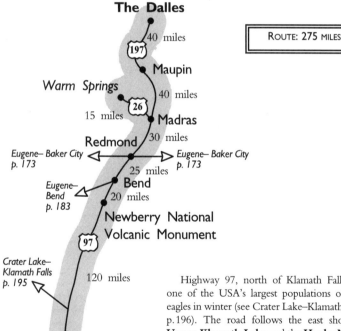

The Dalles

40 miles

197

Maupin

Warm Springs

40 miles

26

15 miles

Madras

30 miles

Redmond

Eugene– Baker City p. 173

Eugene– Baker City p. 173

25 miles

Eugene– Bend p. 183

Bend

20 miles

Newberry National Volcanic Monument

97

Crater Lake– Klamath Falls p. 195

120 miles

Klamath Falls

ROUTE: 275 MILES

197

Highway 97, north of Klamath Falls, has one of the USA's largest populations of bald eagles in winter (see Crater Lake–Klamath Falls, p.196). The road follows the east shore of **Upper Klamath Lake** and the **Hanks Marsh** unit of **Upper Klamath Refuge**. The year-round waterfowl haven is one of a series of freshwater lakes and marshy wetlands which extend south along the Klamath Basin towards Tule Lake in California. **Klamath Basin National Wildlife Refuges**, *Rte 1, Box 74, Tulelake, CA 96134; tel: (916) 667-2231,* and the **Klamath Wildlife Area**, *Oregon*

ROUTE

Take Hwy 97 to 25 miles north of Madras. Continue straight north on Hwy 197 to The Dalles on the Columbia River.

Department of Fish and Wildlife, 1800 Miller Island Rd W., Klamath Falls, OR 97603; tel: (541) 883-5734, have information on birds and recreation around both **Klamath Refuge** and the **Klamath Marsh National Wildlife Refuge** about 60 miles north. The route enters **Winema National Forest.**

Chiloquin is just east of Hwy 97 beyond the SR 62/Hwy 97 junction. **Klamath Tribe,** *PO Box 436, Chiloquin, OR 97624; tel: (800) 524-9787* or *(541) 783-2095,* has information about the Native American tribe, its' facilities and institutions and can arrange Klamath-led tours of marshes, rivers, a mullet hatchery and Modoc War-related sites (see also p.196).

The Klamath Reservation land onto which Klamaths, Modocs and Yahooskins were forced in the 1860s–70s by the US Government was dissolved by White politicians in the 1950s. Landless, many Klamaths moved to the cities; a core remains to perform traditional ceremonies and carry on modern businesses. Chiloquin has many White residents, readily in evidence at **Kirchner's Coast to Coast,** *117 S. 1st St; tel: (541) 783-2239,* a well-stocked hardware store with over 100 trophy animal heads, including Oregon antelope, mule deer, elk and Canadian caribou taken by the store owners, and 400 local ranch branding irons mounted above the wares.

Collier State Logging Museum, at **Collier Memorial State Park,** *Hwy 97, 30 miles north of Klamath Falls; tel: (541) 783-2471;* camping; *tel: (800) 452-5687,* includes huge stumps and a large outdoor collection of manual and motorised heavy equipment. Log skidders and steam engines are notable. Furnished log cabins are in a tree-shaded **Pioneer Village** section. The state park has two separate picnic areas and 18 tent and 50 RV camping pitches.

Thunderbeast Park, a former dinosaur model theme park, left a few menacing creatures facing Hwy 97. Wildfires damaged the forest a few miles north. Fake dinosaurs are bested by the stunning drive east (right) on paved *Silver Lake Rd* into **Klamath Forest National Wildlife Refuge.** The road forms a small levee separating grazing land from numerous birds living, mating or resting in the marsh. Six miles east, the marsh abuts an oak and pine

forest at the mouth of Wocus Bay, named for the numerous yellow water lilies growing there. Klamaths harvested wocus seeds, dried them in the sun, then roasted and ground the kernels as a nutty-flavoured food. Raptors, blackbirds and ducks coexist in the rich wetlands.

Fifteen miles north on the left is SR 138, **East Diamond Lake Hwy,** passing through forest and pumice fields to SR 62 and Crater Lake National Park north entrance (closed in winter), and the North Umpqua River (see Roseburg–Crater Lake, p.189). There is budget lodging near **Beaver Marsh State Airport,** a rest area 3 miles north, services and two moderate motels in **Chemult.**

Mt Thielsen's craggy peak is on the left. SR 58 goes west to Eugene (see Eugene–Bend, pp.183–187). **Crescent** is another small town with two moderate motels and services. **Gilchrist,** owned by Pacific Mill, is one of the Northwest's few remaining company-owned lumber towns.

The corridor of trees lining Hwy 97 becomes sparser as the highway ascends into Central Oregon's high desert. For tourist information, contact **Central Oregon Visitors Association (COVA),** *Central Oregon Welcome Center, 63085 N. Hwy 97, Suite 104, Bend, OR 97701; tel: (800) 800-8334* or *(541) 389-8799; fax: (541) 385-9487.*

La Pine and Sunriver recreation areas depend upon summer visitors to Mt Bachelor and the **Cascade Lakes Hwy** route a few miles west (see p.187).

La Pine Tourist Information: La Pine Chamber, *51636 Huntington Rd, PO Box 616, La Pine, OR 97739; tel: (541) 536-9771* has information on lodging and the area. Take *State Park Rd* west to **La Pine State Park,** *on the Deschutes River; tel: (541) 382-3586,* with 145 pitches amidst large Ponderosa pines. Float through untouched forest 16 miles north to **Sunriver.**

Tourist Information: Sunriver Area Chamber of Commerce, *Sunriver Village, Bldg 15, PO Box 3246, Sunriver, OR 97707; tel: (541) 593-8149; fax: (541) 593-3581.* **Sunriver Resort,** *PO Box 3609; tel: (800) 547-3922* or *(541) 593-1221; fax: (541) 593-5458,* with expensive–pricey rooms, homes and condominiums, is a mecca for golfers. **Sunriver Nature Center**; *tel: (541) 593-4394*, is an excellent way for children to encounter animals.

NEWBERRY NATIONAL VOLCANIC MONUMENT

Five hundred square miles of lava formations north to Bend are a graphic illustration of the outward flow of ash and pumice from Newberry Crater, a caldera which now holds Paulina Lake and East Lake. Just south of Paulina Lake are **Paulina Falls**, 7985-ft **Paulina Peak** with a view of the Cascades and Central Oregon and a black obsidian flow. North are **Lava Cast Forest**, **Lava River Cave**, **Lava Butte** and the monument visitor centre.

Lava Lands Visitor Center, *58201 Hwy 97 S., Bend, OR 97707; tel: (541) 593-2421*, open May–Oct, has national monument information, brochures and geological exhibits. A narrated shuttle runs to Lava Butte Memorial Day–Labor Day, adults $1.75, children 6–12 $1. **Deschutes National Forest**, *1230 N.E. 3rd St, Suite A-262, Bend, OR 97701; tel: (541) 593-2421; fax: (541) 383-4700*, has year-round information.

Follow *East Paulina Lake Rd*, Road 21, right off Hwy 97 just north of La Pine, to two lakes in **Newberry Crater** stocked with Kokanee salmon and rainbow and German brown trout. Moderate–expensive **Paulina Lake Resort**, *PO Box 7, La Pine, OR 97739 tel: (541) 536-2240*, and moderate **East Lake Resort**, *PO Box 95, La Pine, OR 97739; tel: (541) 536-2230*, service lakes of the same names with housekeeping cabins, boat rentals, modest restaurants, general stores and fishing. The area is snowbound in winter, but Paulina Lake Resort encourages snowmobiling visitors mid Dec–mid Mar, and cross-country skiing is popular. East Lake is fed by hot springs. Be warned if not purchasing services, vehicles may be ticketed! Motorhomes are prohibited up *Paulina Peak Rd*.

Paulina Falls and **Big Obsidian Flow** are at the south end of Paulina Lake. Take a half-hour to hike the ¾-mile trail up through the stunning shiny black glass obsidian boulders formed 1300 years ago during Central Oregon's last eruption period. Northwest Native Americans traded obsidian from this 6000-ft high flow for knives, arrowheads and tools. Hard as it looks, obsidian is not rock, but glass made of silicon and oxygen, or silica. Traces of iron oxide turned the 150-ft-deep mass black. Taking rocks for souvenirs is illegal, and take caution of frogs from Lost Lake which move to the flow in Aug.

Turn right from Hwy 97 onto bumpy, unpaved Road 9720 for 9 miles to **Lava Cast Forest**. *Pahoehoe* ('creeping paw') lava flowed over a Ponderosa pine forest about 6000 years ago, forming a casing or mould around trees. The dead trees decayed, leaving visible fissures and lava tubes. A one-mile loop trail winds by a few wind-scored tree trunks over a lunar landscape with lava spreading to the horizon. In summer, purple penstemon and red paintbrush bloom over the slate-coloured lava.

One mile south of the visitor centre on the right is **Lava River Cave**, open mid May–mid Sept, adults $2.50, lantern hire $1.50. A 2.4-mile return self-guiding walk through an uncollapsed lava tube descends about 200 ft. The walk traverses a corridor of ice stalagmites and stalactites, an echoing hall, a smooth-walled chamber, pendant and soda straw stalactites and a section of pinnacles amidst sand. Wear sturdy shoes and dress warmly for the year-round 42°F temperature.

Reddish **Lava Butte** rises 500 ft behind **Lava Lands Visitor Center**. In summer, take a shuttle up the cinder cone, or drive your own vehicle the rest of the year for a spectacular view of South Sister, Broken Top, Middle and North Sisters, and a close-up look at the mixture of red and black cinders flung out during a Northwest Rift Zone eruption 6200 years ago.

A few miles north is the **High Desert Museum**, *59800 S. Hwy 97, Bend, OR 97702-7963; tel: (541) 382-4754; fax: (541) 382-5256*, open 0900–1700, adults $6.25, children 13–18 yrs $5.75, 5–12 $3. Art, river otters, fish, an operating sawmill, a desertarium with touchable snakes, Western history exhibits and cheap–budget **Rimrock Cafe** make an eclectic mix of indoor and outdoor desert experiences. Time a visit for an interpretative talk on

199

birds of prey, complete with fierce raptors. **Silver Sage Trading** gift shop is expensive.

BEND

Tourist Information: Bend Chamber/ Visitor & Convention Bureau, *Central Oregon Visitor Center, 63085 N. Hwy 97, Bend, OR 97701; tel: (541) 382-3221.* See Eugene–Bend, p. 186.

REDMOND

Redmond Chamber of Commerce, *446 SW. 7th St, Redmond, OR 97756; tel: (800) 574-1325* or *(541) 923-5191; fax: (541) 923-6442,* open Mon–Fri 0800–1700 Sat–Sun (lobby) 0800–1700, has area-wide information on Central Oregon lodging, dining and attractions (See Eugene–Baker City, p.176).

Six miles north of Redmond is **Smith Rock State Park**, *in Terrebonne; tel: (541) 548-7501*, a golden gorge rising above the Crooked River. Ragged rocks on the north face oppose a rimrock plateau. A summer 1996 wildfire badly burned rim vegetation. Smith Rock is known for world-class rock-climbing, except when prohibited during bird-of-prey nesting season. **Juniper Junction** store at the park boundary has climbing gear, clothing and huckleberry ice cream. Rangers are vigilant in enforcing paid parking.

Peter Skene Ogden Scenic Wayside is a large rest area on the west side of Hwy 97. Cross a deep chasm over the Crooked River and enter the 105,000-acre **Crooked River National Grasslands**, *tel: (541) 475-9272*, one of the few place in the USA to see wide expanses of native grasses.

Go left on *Jericho Lane*, then north on *Elbe Dr.* to **Culver**, a seed and garlic growing town. Have a tasty, cheap burger at **Beetle Bailey Burgers**, *406 1st Ave, Culver, OR 97334; tel: (541) 546-8749*, in the centre of town. Follow signs to **The Cove Palisades State Park**.

The meeting of the **Crooked** and **Deschutes Rivers** resembles the Grand Canyon. **Lake Billy Chinook**, named after explorer John Fremont's **Warm Springs** native guide, extends to the west, created when Portland General Electric's Round Butte hydroelectric dam flooded the Crooked,

Deschutes and Metolius Rivers canyons in 1963. **Warm Springs Indian Reservation** is north. **The Cove Palisades State Park**; *tel: (541) 546-3412;* with camping, seasonal houseboat and cabin hire, *tel: (800) 452-5687*, has picnicking, boating, water skiing, swimming and fishing. It is a hugely popular local summer fishing and recreation area. A six-mile drive along the rim to Round Butte Dam Viewpoint has many pull-outs overlooking the lake canyon walls, and a summer-only **Round Butte Dam Observatory**, *Portland General Electric, 121 SW. Salmon St, Portland, OR 97204; tel: (541) 475-1332.*

MADRAS

Tourist Information: Madras/Jefferson County Chamber of Commerce; *197 S.E. 5th St, PO Box 770, Madras, OR 97741; tel: (800) 967-3564,(541) 475-2350* or *(541) 475-6975; fax: (541) 475-4341,* has information on the area, Lake Billy Chinook recreation, the Warm Springs Indian Reservation, rafting the Deschutes River between Madras and Maupin and thunder egg collecting. Madras (pron: Mad-dress) is the regional population centre with 3000 people and all services. Lodging includes *BW* and *BI*.

> ## ▧ SIDE TRACK
> ## FROM MADRAS
>
> Tune the radio to 91.9 FM for Native American chanting, music, tribal news and political discussions. Three tribes, Wasco, Warm Springs and Northern Paiute form the **Confederated Tribes of Warm Springs**, *PO Box C, Warm Springs, OR 97761; tel: (541) 553-1161,* inhabitants of a 600,000-acre reservation from south of Mt Hood to north-central Oregon. Take Hwy 26 north-west for 14 miles, crossing the Deschutes River, entering the reservation through rimrock canyon and mesas reminiscent of the American Southwest. Pass the Warm Springs Forest Products Industries plant and a textile mill, both owned by the tribe.
>
> **The Museum at Warm Springs**, *Hwy 26, PO Box C, Warm Springs, OR 97761;*

tel: (541) 553-3333, open 1000–1700, adults $5, children 5–12 $2.50, is a coherent look at a rich tribal culture that still fishes with nets (as Warm Springs and Wasco ancestors did on the Columbia River before falls were dammed and flooded at The Dalles), and still crafts intricate beadwork in the fashion of Plains Paiutes. A narrated wedding trade ceremony tableau has mannequins, including horses, fitted out with beaded clothing and accessories, complete with carrying bags, belts and footwear. Traditional dwelling reconstruction and photographs evoke ancestral life. A small gift shop has lovely beadwork and well illustrated Native American theme children's books for sale.

Turn right on *Agency Hot Springs Rd* 11 miles north to **Kah-Nee-Ta**, *PO Box K, Warm Springs, OR 97761; tel: (800) 554-4786* or *(541) 553-1112,* an expensive–pricey lodge with native themes carved into the building's stone supports. A huge fireplace burns merrily in the resort lobby. Sat nights are a salmon bake with tribal dancers adding to the standard golf and tennis atmosphere of a posh resort. **Kah-Nee-Ta Village**, damaged by floods and fires in 1996, is being rebuilt with tepees, camping and RV facilities and a hot springs-fed swimming pool. **Indian Head Gaming Center**, *PO Box 1240; tel: (800) 554-4786* or *(541) 553-6122,* has tribal-run gambling. The tribe can arrange kayaking, rafting or horse riding on the reservation and suggest hiking trails. 🔺

MADRAS TO MAUPIN

Eleven miles north of Madras is the turnoff to the agate and thunder egg beds at **Richardson's Ranch**, *Gateway Route Box 440, Madras, OR 97741; tel: (541) 475-2680.* Cows, pastures and scenic barns replace the crops filling the horizon since Redmond. **Antelope**, east on the Antelope Hwy near the Jefferson–Wasco County border was the early 1980s site for the Rajneeshpuram ashram. There is a grassy, pine-studded rest stop on the west (left) side of Hwy 97, 2 miles before the sudden curve left onto Hwy 197.

An unmarked 'snow cap identifier' 5 miles north on Hwy 197 names major Cascade peaks. Conifers alternate with large ranches and Mt Hood and Mt Adams play hide-and-seek as the highway traverses the rolling landscape 24 miles from the Hwy 97/197 junction.

MAUPIN

Tourist Information: Greater Maupin Area Chamber of Commerce, *PO Box 220, Maupin, OR 97037; tel: (541) 395-2599,* has information, including Deschutes River rafting operators. Maupin straddles the river. From 1909–1911, Maupin was the site of a bitter rivalry between railway companies, each one favouring a different side of the river. The east side track is still used. Turn right just before the crossing the river onto *Deschutes River Rd*, and drive north through the **Deschutes River Recreation Area**. Rapids and clear, leaf-green waters hailed by fly fishermen are on the left. Native Americans use traditional dip nets to fish at **Sherar's Falls**.

Return to Hwy 197. At the Deschutes River is moderate **C & J Lodge Bed & Breakfast**, *304 Bakeoven Co Rd, Maupin, OR 97037; tel: (800) 395-3903* or *395-2404,* a whitewater rafting centre with barbecue specialities for lunch and dinner. Cross the river and drive to (upper) Maupin, with good views of the river, city services, and several budget cafés.

Power lines parallel the winding road. To the south and east stretches parched land, bluffs and mesas; Mt Hood's white peak is to the west. **Tygh Valley** has a petrol station and store. Turn from Tygh Valley in summer to hike to the falls in **White River Falls State Park (Tygh Valley Wayside)**, also an Oregon State Game Refuge.

Cross Tygh Ridge Summit and continue north to **Dufur**, a pretty town with excellent views of Mt Hood across wheat fields. **Dufur Chamber of Commerce**, *PO Box 402, Dufur, OR 97021.* Fifteenmile Creek, protecting the easternmost run of wild winter steelhead, is alongside Schreiber Log House, inhabited from 1900–1974. The 1907 red brick Balch Hotel is now **Nansene Dining Room**. In summer, **Dufur City Park**; *tel: (541) 467-*

2832, has RV camping, a picnic area, baseball field, swimming pool and volleyball court next to Fifteenmile Creek.

Ten miles north through rolling wheat fields, enter the **Columbia River Gorge Scenic Recreation Area**.

THE DALLES

Tourist Information: The Dalles Convention and Visitors Bureau, *901 E. 2nd St, The Dalles, OR 97058; tel: (800) 255-3385,* has a *Vacation Planner* brochure with a map and information on The Dalles, as well as regional information for Wasco County and North Central Oregon. See Portland–The Dalles, pp. 207–213, for the Columbia River Gorge Route and The Dalles Lock and Dam.

ACCOMMODATION

A main Columbia River Gorge town, The Dalles has plenty of lodging, including *BW, DI,* and **The Dalles Quality Inn**, *2114 W. 6th St; tel: (800) 848-9378* or *(541) 298-5161,* moderate. Nine bed and breakfasts are conveniently located in the historic downtown district.

EATING AND DRINKING

There are plenty of fast food eateries, plus the locally-patronised budget–moderate **Cousins' Restaurant & Saloon**, *2116 W. 6th St; tel: (541) 298-2771,* with cow and horse statues outside the large red building at the QI. The **Baldwin Saloon**, *1st and Court Sts; tel: (541) 296-5666,* is a restored moderate restaurant and pub in a building which served as a steamboat navigation office, mortuary coffin storage spot and government employment office.

SIGHTSEEING

The Dalles (pron: The Dalz) is never abbreviated, and is always found in indices under 'T', not 'D'. The Dalles were the official 'End of the Oregon Trail', the point of rough passage over treacherous Celilo Falls for those who ventured the Columbia River route.

The Dalles have had a long-standing rivalry with Hood River, 20 miles west, a battle that the latter has won with gentrification as one of the windsurfing capitals of the planet. The Dalles cultivates tourism to supplement

aluminium plant output, wheat, and bing and Queen Anne cherry cultivation. The **Columbia Gorge Discovery Center**; *tel: (541) 296-8600,* with three museums, the **Discovery Center**, **Wasco County Historical Museum** and **Oregon Trail Living History Park**, opens mid 1997.

Start a driving tour from I-84, Exit 83, going north on *Weber St* to the Industrial Area. Turn right on *1st Trail* for several blocks to **Rock Fort**, the Lewis and Clark Corps of Discovery riverside camping site in 1805, 'a calmer spot with rocky formations which would make a good defense.'

Return on I-84 to Exit 84, and go right into downtown. The Dalles' symbol is the weathervane rooster on the steeple cross on 1898 **Old St Peter's Landmark**, *3rd and Lincoln Sts; tel: (541) 296-5686;* open 1100–1500 Tues–Fri, 1300–1500 Sat–Sun, for tours of the former church's architecture, stained-glass windows and pipe organ. The Chamber of Commerce has a good historic walking tour brochure for the commercial district and Trevitt residential areas of downtown.

Fort Dalles Museum, *500 W. 15th; tel: (541) 296-4547,* adults $3, was the Chief Surgeon's Quarters for the 1850 fort, built to protect Oregon Trail pioneers. The museum building is all that remains. An old surrey, hearse and Buick are part of an excellent, but poorly displayed, vehicle collection. **Anderson House**, built by a Swedish immigrant farmer using squared-off logs, is part of the museum.

Take *Scenic Dr.* to an overlook (by the Vietnam Memorial flagpole) for sweeping views of Dallesport, WA, The Dalles Bridge eastward and Mt Hood to the west. Tree-shaded **Sorosis Park**, behind, is open 0600–1800. Drive east to the restful **Pioneer Cemetery**, *E. 15th Place and Terrace Dr.*

Descend to **Pulpit Rock**, *12th and Court Sts behind the high school,* a boulder where Methodist Missionaries preached to Native Americans in 1838. **Rorick House**, *300 W. 13th St,* the Fort Dalles Sergeant's Quarters, is The Dalles' oldest residence. **City Park**, *Union St between W. 5th and W. 7th Sts,* with the restored Victor Trevitt House, claims to be the true 'End of the Oregon Trail'.

PORTLAND–HOOD RIVER

Mt Hood's proximity to Portland makes going to the mountain a pleasant three-hour, 105-mile drive. Mt Hood's lovely, gracefully contoured 11,235-ft peak dominates views east of Portland and the centre of the Columbia River Gorge National Scenic Area. This route runs from Portland to Hood River; complete a full circuit of Mt Hood by returning to Portland from Hood River via I-84 (see p. 207).

Windsurfers glide in summer winds beneath its snowy white shape. Farms embrace the plains below its slopes, orchards and tree farms scattering like a chequer-board accented with bright red and silver barns. Skiers from Portland crowd Mt Hood ski areas, notably the sheer slope at Timberline.

Across the Columbia River in Washington, Mt Adams forms almost a mirror image of one of the Cascades' most accessible peaks. Pahto, Mt Adams, Wy'east and Mt Hood, said Native Americans, vied for the affections of a maiden, Mt St Helens, throwing stones and fire at each other, breaking the natural Bridge of the Gods over the Columbia River. The Great Spirit turned Pahto and Wy'east into the river guardians, and cloaked St Helens in a white mantle of eternal youth.

Lt William Broughton, exploring the Columbia River for Britain in 1792, spotted 'a very distant high snowy mountain' east of the mouth of the Willamette River. Broughton named it for Rear Admiral Hood, who had signed Capt George Vancouver's orders for the voyage of exploration. Oregon's highest mountain was a symbol for weary Oregon Trail pioneers that their goal, the fertile Willamette Valley, was finally within reach.

203

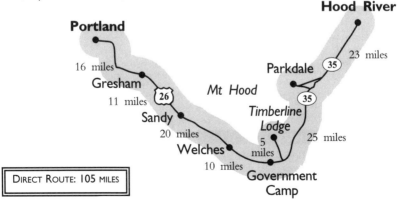

ROUTE

Drive east of Portland on I-84, and take Exit 16A to **Gresham**. Go south on *N.E. 238th Dr.*, jog left onto *242nd Dr.*, which becomes *N.E. Hogan Dr.* Turn left onto *E. Powell Blvd*, 3½ miles from Exit 16A, and go east on Hwy 26 via **Sandy** to **Mt Hood**.

Continue east, then north-east on SR 35 through the **Hood River Valley** to Hood River on the Columbia River.

TOURIST INFORMATION

Tourist Information Columbia River Gorge National Scenic Area, *USDA Forest Service, 902 Wasco Ave, Suite 200, Hood River, OR 97031; tel: (541) 386-2333; fax: (541) 386-1916,* has brochures and information on the **Mt Hood Columbia Gorge Loop**, covered in this route. Route information is available at **Mt Hood National Forest Headquarters**, *2955 N.W. Division St, Gresham, OR 97030; tel: (503) 666-0771.* En route, **Mt Hood Information Center**, *65000 E. Hwy 26, Welches, OR 97067; tel: (503) 622-4822; fax: (503) 622-6163,* open 0800–1630, is an excellent source of hiking, lodging and recreation information. Lodging is plentiful everywhere along this route, ranging from RV parks to bed and breakfasts, rustic cottages, posh tennis resorts and ski lodges.

GRESHAM

If getting an early start and avoiding Portland rush hour or heavy weekend traffic to the slopes appeals; Gresham has basic lodging including *BW, Ha* and *QI* and services. **Gresham Area Chamber of Commerce/Visitors Information Center**, *150 W. Powell St, PO Box 1768, Gresham, OR 97030; tel: (503) 665-1131.*

Highway 26 ascends 9 miles through orchards, vineyards and berry fields to **Sandy**.

SANDY

Tourist Information: Sandy Area Chamber of Commerce/City Hall, *39260 Pioneer Blvd, PO Box 536, Sandy, OR 97055; tel: (503) 668-4006,* open Mon–Fri 0900–1700, has brochures for local attractions. **Sandy**

Historical Museum, with local artefacts, shares the City Hall building.

Go left (north) ½-mile on *N. Bluff Rd* to **Johnsrud Viewpoint**, a panoramic vista of Mt Hood across the Sandy River Valley. Lewis and Clark called it the Quicksand River, a name quickly corrupted. Sandy's plant nurseries, berries and tree farms have replaced the lumbering and sawmills of the past. In fall, the Cascade foothills are bathed in colour; many nurseries cultivate red maples which blaze across the farms.

For many, Sandy is an outlying dormitory community of Portland. **Wasson Brothers**, *41901 Hwy 26; tel: (503) 668-3124,* open 0900–1700, has a winery tasting room with Chardonnay and Pinot Noir, berry wines and carbonated rhubarb bubbly. **Oregon Candy Farm Factory**, *48620 S.E. Hwy 26; tel: (503) 668-5066,* open Mon–Fri 0900–1700, Sat–Sun 1200–1700, 5½ miles east, tempts visitors with mouth-watering glimpses of chocolate and toffee candy-making.

Beyond Sandy, the beginning of the snow zone, Hwy 26 enters forest, with numerous bed and breakfasts and small lodges lining the road to **Government Camp**. Beware of deer feeding on roadside foliage. Cross the Salmon River at **Brightwood**. **Wildwood Recreation Area**; *tel: (541) 467-2291 or (541) 622-3936,* has traces of wagon wheel ruts from Oregon Trail pioneers using the *Barlow Road* around Mt Hood.

WELCHES

Mt Hood Information Center, *65000 E. Hwy 26, Welches, OR, 97067; tel: (503) 622-4822; fax: (503) 622-6163,* open 0800–1630, with clean restrooms and picnic tables outside; a necessity for obtaining permits for hiking any of Mt Hood's 11 glaciers, for local trail maps, Nordic skiing terrain and Mt Hood National Forest campsite information. **Mt Hood Village**, *same address; tel: (800) 255-3069 or (503) 622-4011,* has 420 pitches, cabin rentals, a small café, pool, spa and most services. **The Resort at the Mountain**, *68010 E. Fairway Ave, Welches, OR 97067; tel: (800) 669-7666 or (503) 622-3101; fax: (503) 622-0567,* is expensive, but offers tennis and golf and

Scottish shops and décor. Grill you own moderate steaks and listen to live music at weekends at **The Inn Between Restaurant and Lounge**, *67858 E. Hwy 26; tel: (503) 622-5400.*
Zigzag is just down the road, with **Zigzag Ranger District**, *70220 E. Hwy 26, Zigzag, OR 97049; tel: (503) 666-0704.* **Barlow Trail Inn Restaurant and Lounge**, *69580 E. Hwy 26; tel: (503) 622-3112,* and **Zig Zag Inn**, *70162 E. Hwy 26; tel; (503) 622-4779,* both budget to moderate pizza, sandwiches and dinners are in 1920s-era log buildings. Hwy 26 enters Mt Hood National Forest, narrowing to a single lane in each direction at **Rhododendron**, named after the many varieties which bloom near the Ranger Station in spring.

GOVERNMENT CAMP

Ascend through forests and 18 miles of scenic vistas to **Government Camp**, a small village with lodging, restaurants and provisions arranged around a loop road. One mile west of the village where an army troop stayed in 1849, a trail goes to Laurel Hill wagon ruts, testimony to one of the highest and most awkward Oregon Trail passes. Look for the log cabin in Government Camp for the area's history and Oregon Trail travails.

Mt Hood Brewing Company; *tel: (503) 272-3724,* a popular Government Camp gathering spot, has made-on-premises beer and budget–moderate food. Berry pie is renowned at **The Huckleberry Inn**, *PO Box 249; tel: (503) 272-3325,* a moderate–expensive lodging with budget bunk rooms. **Summit** is a small ski area at the east end of Government Camp, with Nordic track on the slope.

Mt Hood Skibowl, *PO Box 280, Skibowl, OR 97028; tel: (503) 222-2695 or (503) 272-3206,* is just south of Government Camp, with dining and drinking establishments, night skiing and a summer **Sky Chair** up to hiking or mountain biking.

SIDE TRACK
TO TIMBERLINE LODGE

Turn left just east of Government Camp; it's a 6-mile, 2000-ft drive up to **Timberline**

Lodge, *OR 97028; tel: (800) 547-1406 or (503) 231-5400.* The lodge, primary focus of the ski area, is renowned for its architecture, its setting against the slopes of Mt Hood, the local beer selection at **Ram's Head Bar**, the views from the **Blue Ox Bar** informal restaurant and fine gourmet Northwest cuisine in the **Cascade Dining Room**. *The Shining*, a film made in 1983, used the lodge as the building with horrifying effects. The 1937 chalet-style lodge with French château flourishes *is* beautiful, inside and out, with moderate–expensive rooms, always in demand.

Timberline Lodge lower level has a ski museum with heavy wooden skis, bindings, posters, photographs and memorabilia from skiing legends. A massive wooden staircase with animals and birds topping 12 newel posts, gives onto the hexagonal lobby, with a famed picture window looking straight up the spine of the mountain. Lobby centrepiece is the 92-ft high grey stone fireplace carved with reliefs of local animals, including coyotes and mountain lions. Huge timbers provide support; hand-hooked rugs, weavings and upholstery follow bold Native-American themes.

Wy-East Day Lodge next door accommodates skiers and snowboarders with equipment rental, ski school including telemark; *tel: (503) 231-5402,* **Wy'east Kitchen** restaurant, a lounge and a small historical exhibit of pioneer settlers and skiers in the Mt Hood area.

Timberline Ski Area; *tel: (503) 231-7979 or (503) 272-3311; fax: (503) 272-3710,* has skiing information. For Timberline conditions, call **SNO-phone**; *tel: (503) 222-2211.* Summertime chair lifts take hikers 1000 or 2000 feet up to moderate **Silcox Hut** bunkroom accommodations and light meals. The snow never melts, and skiing is usually possible year-round from the Palmer Express lift.

Turn south 2 miles to **Trillium Lake** camping, picnicking and a breathtaking reflection of Mt Hood. The view is also stunning from

205

Snowbunny Sno-Park, which has a hill to slide down in winter.

Continue straight on SR 35 to the **Pioneer Woman's Grave** marker, a heap of stones marking a simple wooden coffin found when the highway was constructed in 1924. Wagon ruts are close by.

Barlow Pass, at 4161 ft, is named for Kentucky native Samuel K Barlow, who blazed a road around Mt Hood from The Dalles to near Oregon City in 1845, completing the last major offshoot of the Oregon Trail. For his efforts, he charged subsequent travellers a toll to traverse his road.

Cross the White River, with Mt Hood rising majestically on the left. Sno-parks at **White River** and 4647-ft **Bennett Pass** access winter sports 'play' areas. **Mt Hood Meadows Ski Resort**, *Hwy 35, PO Box 470, Mt Hood, OR 97041-0470; tel: (503) 337-2222 or (503) 246-1810*, is 2 miles to the left, with skiing and snowboarding but no accommodation. A loop road opposite Mt Hood Meadows has trailheads to **Sahalie Falls** and **Umbrella Falls**.

As SR 35 curves north along the Hood River, Mt Hood's volcanic slopes yield to rocky gorges, mimicking the Columbia River's own land formations 40 miles ahead. **Robinhood** and **Sherwood Campgrounds**, open Memorial Day–Labor Day, have riverside pitches.

There's summer camping near **Cooper Spur Ski Acres**, *11000 Cloud Cap Rd; tel: (541) 352-7803*, the modest ski area which was the first ski resort on Mt Hood. **Cooper Spur Inn**, *10755 Cooper Spur Rd, Parkdale, OR 97041; tel: (541) 352-6692*, offers year-round moderate lodging and Wed–Sun dining; *tel: (541) 352-6037*.

PARKDALE

Follow the Hood River Canyon, with large rocks and a sheer wall on the left, to the turn west (left) to **Parkdale**.

Hood River Ranger District, *6780 Hwy 35, Mt Hood-Parkdale, OR 97041; tel: (541) 352-6002*, has recreation and camping information for the mountain, but the **Hutson Museum**, *Baseline and Clear Creek Rds, PO Box 501; tel: (541) 352-6808*, open Tues–Sun

1100–1800 Apr–Oct, adults $1, children 6-18 $0.50, has rock collections and Native American grinding stones, mortars and basalt slave-killer weapons from the Columbia River Gorge. The Parkdale station for **Mt Hood Scenic Railroad**, *110 Railroad Ave, Hood River, OR 97031; tel: (800) 872-4661 or (541) 386-3556*, adults $21.95, children 2–12 $13.95, is next door. The 44-mile, 4-hour excursion train, built in 1906, runs most days from mid April–Oct, offering views of Mt Hood and Mt Adams from restored 1910–1926 Pullman coaches pulling up a steep grade through the Hood River Valley. Book well in advance for Spring Blossom excursions when miles of fruit trees are in full bloom.

Gravenstein and Newtown Pippin apples, Bartlett, Bosc and Anjou pears, Red Haven and Alberta peaches, Hood River cherries, berries, plump cows, alpacas and red barns replace forest scenery as the highway approaches the Columbia River. The super-productive Hood River Valley benefits from volcanic soil and runoff from Mt Hood. **Hood River Shipper-Grower Association**, *PO Box 168, Odell, OR 97044; tel: (541) 354-2565*, publishes *Hood River County's Fruit Loop*, a guide to 20 local farms, all within a few miles of SR 35.

River Bend Farm & Country Store, *2363 Tucker Rd, Hood River; tel: (800) 755-7568 or (541) 386-8766*, open 0900–1700 July–24 Dec, Tues–Sun Mar–June, offers free samples of outstanding preserves. Some, like pumpkin butter, are seasonal. Arrive early for a giant slice of berry pie, a huckleberry milkshake, or to cut fresh flowers from beds outside the historic old building. Unique in the Northwest, **Eve Atkins Distilling Company/Marichelle Brandy Tasting Room**, *4420 Summit Dr., Odell; tel: (541) 354-2550*, open 1100–1700 May–Oct, produces apple brandy and fruit *eaux de vie* from local pears, cherries, blueberries and marionberries.

Go right following signs to **Panorama Point** for a morning view of Mt Hood and the valley, or watch a backlit sunset glow deep pink behind the mountain. Descend between the last set of hills to Hood River, in the heart of the Columbia Gorge (See Portland–The Dalles, p.209).

PORTLAND–THE DALLES

Moss-flanked waterfalls, river vistas, powerful' dams, windsurfers, white-peaked Cascade Mountains – this 85-mile route, east from the Sandy River to the Deschutes River along the Oregon side of the Columbia River Gorge, has surprising variety. Allow three hours for the direct route on Interstate 84, five hours to explore Historic Columbia River Highway waterfalls and views along Highway 30 between Troutdale and Ainsworth State Park.

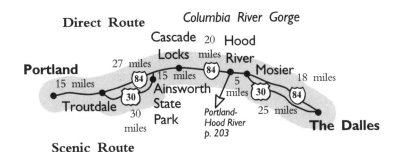

Direct Route

Columbia River Gorge

Scenic Route

207

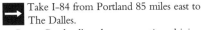

DIRECT ROUTE: 85 MILES

ROUTES

DIRECT ROUTE

Take I-84 from Portland 85 miles east to The Dalles.

Leave Portland's urban congestion driving east on I-84, crossing the Sandy River to the Columbia River at mile 20. The direct route remains close to the water with high cliffs and bluffs on the right (south) side. Trees signal changing geology. Portland's Interior Valley zone gives way to Western hemlock near Bonneville, Douglas-fir at **Cascade Locks**, and Ponderosa pine near The Dalles, with sagebrush steppes to the east.

Railway structures occasionally obstruct views, but in one of the most historic and scenic areas of the Northwest, even the railways give literal colour. On the Washington shore, **Burlington Northern**'s green locomotive engines and red container stock is called the *Green Machine*. The *Yellow Peril*, **Union Pacific**, is the goldenrod-coloured equipment on the Oregon side. Fifty daily trains ply each side, causing an illusion of colour speeding by like a streaking superhero. It's a railway rivalry that has existed for a century, Maryhill builder Sam Hill's dream of freight hauling to Portland.

Rooster Rock State Park, *Exit 25*, has picnicking and a popular swimming beach with good windsurfing winds in early and late summer. Picnic near the river at **Benson State Park**, *Exit 30*.

Take Exit 40 to **Bonneville Lock and Dam**, *US Army Corps of Engineers, Cascade Locks, OR 97014-0150; tel: (541) 374-8820, (south side)*, open 0900–1700. Bonneville Lock and Dam, finished in 1938, was the first of eight Columbia-Snake River dams and still draws scientists, tourists and fishermen.

Stop at the **Bonneville Fish Hatchery**, open 0730–1700, then drive to the Navigation Lock and cross the **First Powerhouse** Dam to **Bradford Island Visitor Center**, an excellent source of information and dam views. On the bottom level, from Mar–Oct, watchers count *each* Chinook and Sockeye salmon, shad and steelhead climbing the fish ladder Apr–Sept. The leaping fish are visible through illuminated viewing windows. Walk to the **First Powerhouse** to feel the turbines vibrate with a forceful *thrum*.

Two miles east on the Bonneville complex is **Eagle Creek Trail**, *FS Trail # 440, cliffside*, which goes 6 miles south past waterfalls. Exit 44 provides access to the **Bridge of the Gods** (See Portland–Yakima, p.238) and **Cascade Locks**.

SCENIC ROUTE

Take I-84 east to Exit 18, **Troutdale**. Follow Hwy 30, the Columbia River Scenic Highway, 24 miles to **Ainsworth State Park** and onto I-84 at Exit 35. Frequent short roads connect Hwy 30 and I-84. Follow I-84 to Exit 69 at **Mosier** onto Hwy 30, the Mosier–The Dalles Highway, then rejoin I-84 at Exit 82, 2 miles from The Dalles.

TOURIST INFORMATION

Columbia River Gorge National Scenic Area, *USDA Forest Service, 902 Wasco Ave, Suite 200, Hood River, OR 97031; tel: (541) 386-2333; fax: (541) 386-1916*, has brochures, including the **CRGNSA** *Lodging and Activities Guide* map, *Forest Trails of the Columbia Gorge* map and other information. **Gorge Visitor Association**, *404 W. 2nd St, The Dalles, OR 97058; tel: (800) 984-6743 or (541) 296-2231; fax: (541) 296-1688*, also has information on

the mid-Gorge. Summer brings thousands of board sailors from around the world to cruise perfect winds near Hood River; for windsurfing safety regulations, write to the **Oregon State Marine Board**, *435 Commercial St N.E., Salem, OR 97310* or **Columbia Gorge Windsurfing Association**, *PO Box 182, Hood River, OR 97031; tel: (541) 386-9225; fax: (541) 386-2108*.

CASCADE LOCKS

Tourist Information: Port of Cascade Locks Visitors Center, *Marine Park Dr., PO Box 307, Cascade Locks, OR 97014; tel: (541) 374-8619; fax: (541) 374-8428*.

ACCOMMODATION AND FOOD

There are six moderate motels, including moderate–expensive riverview rooms at *BW* **Columbia River Inn**, *735 Wanapa St; tel: 800) 595-7108* or *(541) 374-8777*, an RV park and **KOA Kampground**.

There is lodging and dining in Stevenson, WA, a few miles east of the Bridge of the Gods. Cascade Locks has two restaurants, a drive-in and a grocery store along *Wanapa St*.

SIGHTSEEING

There are no longer locks in Cascade Locks because Bonneville Dam waters overwhelmed the navigation locks which had helped ships negotiate major falls. Most visitors stop to gaze at the Bridge of the Gods, drive ($0.75 each way) or walk ($0.50) to the Washington shore.

Cascade Locks Historical Museum, *Marine Park; tel: (541) 374-8619* or *(541) 374-8427*, is open May–Oct. The *Oregon Pony*, a locomotive engine once used to portage between Cascade Locks and The Dalles, sits in front. The sternwheeler *Columbia Gorge*, **Cascade Sternwheelers**, *1200 N.W. Front Ave, Suite 110, Portland, OR 97209; tel: (541) 374-8427*, has several daily narrated cruises with stops at Bonneville Dam Visitors Center and Stevenson, WA, from mid June–mid Oct.

Exit 51, **Wyeth Campground**, and Exit 56, **Viento State Park**; *tel; (541) 374-8811*, have camping, though Viento is closed in winter. **Starvation Creek State Park** on the south side is only accessible going east.

Starvation Creek Trail leads to a lovely waterfall and a Gorge viewpoint at 4960 ft. Mitchell Point looks north over Exit 58 to Washington, while Wygant State Natural Area trails also lead to river views.

HOOD RIVER

Tourist Information: Hood River County Chamber of Commerce, *Exit 63, 405 Portway Ave, Hood River, OR 97031; tel: (800) 366-3530 or (541) 386-2000; fax: (541) 386-2057,* has information on lodging, dining, attractions, activities and windsurfing.

Gorge Central Reservation Service, *1220 Eugene St; tel: (541) 386-6109,* books lodging, cars, airlines, windsurfing lessons, child day-care and event entries.

ACCOMMODATION

Book far in advance for summer. Not all lodging is open out of (windsurfing) season; some impose higher season rates, some don't. There are 15 bed and breakfasts, most moderate. Best Western Hood River Inn, *1108 E. Marina Way; tel: (800) 828-7873 or (541) 386-2200,* moderate–pricey, along the water, is good value.

The pricey 1921 Columbia Gorge Hotel, *4000 Westcliff Dr.; tel: (800) 345-1921 or (541) 386-5566,* is uniquely situated on a rock above the river, over a cascading 180-ft waterfall. Large rooms are furnished with 1920s pieces. The lobby and bar feel Victorian; the dining room serves a nibble-as-you-go five course breakfast included in room rates, or very pricey for non-guests. The gardens allow guests to wander over rocks and through flowerbeds. Resident cats purr for attention.

EATING AND DRINKING

Most restaurants close early – some as early as 2000, possibly in deference to the active schedule of summertime windsurfers. Hood River Bagel Co, *1769 12th St; tel: (541) 386-2123,* prepares a cheap warm bagel breakfast. Wy'east Naturals, *110 5th St; tel: (541) 386-6181,* stocks food, sandwiches, soup and snacks.

Full Sail Tasting Room, *506 Columbia St; tel: (541) 386-2281,* open 1200–2000, has river views from a deck, and serves its local

brews, sausages and limited menu. Full Sail Brewing Company, which operate the 9-beers-on-draught tasting room, offer tours of the brewery and bottling line 1200–1600 on the hour, daily May–Oct, Thur–Sun Nov–Apr.

SHOPPING

Hood River designers create state-of-the-art windsurfing gear and equipment. Kerrits, *316 Oak St; tel: (541) 386-4187,* has fine-quality, attractive outdoor clothing for swimmers, climbers, windsurfers and equestrians. Chukar Cherries, *315 Oak St; tel: (541) 386-3299,* has excellent dried and preserved cherry and berry treats.

SIGHTSEEING

Hood River was a quiet fruit farming town until someone noticed about 15 years ago that the strong, steady winds, blowing up to 45 mph against the current through this section of the Gorge, create a heaven of 8-ft swells without reefs or sharks. Local spots to watch or try the windsurfing are the protected Hook lagoon for beginners and Hood River Marina, Exit 64 and Event Site, Exit 63, for intermediates skilled in water starts. Experts find challenges from Washington side launch points.

In summer, the relaxed but hip boardsailors and followers create a resort atmosphere not unlike other seasonal ski or sun capitals. Blossoming fruit trees south of town fill lodging and eateries for a few weeks in April; fall foliage colour and crisp skies draw in autumn. Mt Hood is several hours south (See Portland–Hood River, p.204). Hood River benefits from year-round skiers willing to sleep some distance from the slopes.

Hood River Vineyards, *4693 Westwood Dr.; tel: (541) 386-3772,* open 1100–1700 Mar–Nov, is known for red wines and dessert wines like Zinfandel Port and heavenly marionberry. Try the local Anjou pear wine. Flerchinger Vineyards and Winery, *4200 Post Canyon Dr.; tel: (541) 386-2882,* open daily 1100–1700, has a variety of good Riesling, from dry to sweet, and is known for Cabernet and Merlot.

Explore local history, particularly the

extensive collection of local fruit-crate labels and Schonhut Circus figures at **Hood River County Museum**, *Port Marina Park, PO Box 781, tel. (541) 386 6772,* open Mon–Sat 1000–1600 Sun 1200–1600 Apr–Aug, daily 1200–1600 Sept–Oct.

Mt Hood Scenic Railroad, *110 Railroad Ave, Hood River, OR 97031; tel: (800) 872-4661* or *(541) 386-3556,* adults $21.95, children 2–12 $13.95, makes a 44-mile, 4-hr excursion to the **Hood River Valley** most days mid Apr–Oct. Restored 1910–1926 Pullman coaches load at Hood River's historic railway depot. Springtime blossom tours book early. Columbia River Gorge glider rides operate June–Sept, **Flightline Services,** *3608 Airport Dr.; tel: (541) 386-1133,* $35–$100.

HOOD RIVER TO THE DALLES

At mile 66 on I-84, **Koberg Beach State Park** (westward direction, I-84), has another windsurfing launch site.

Mosier has services and cherry orchards. **Memaloose State Park,** *from westbound I-84;* tel: (503) 731-3411; camping, tel: (800) 452-5687, closed in winter, has RV and tent pitches. An interpretative board at the rest area explains Oregon Trail migrations.

Cliffs rise sheer on the right. **East Mayer State Park** has water access all year. **Rowena,** *Exit 76,* is another popular windsurfing spot. Leave the interstate at Exit 81 for the new **Columbia Gorge Discovery Center/Wasco County Museum;** *tel: (541) 296-8600* (see Klamath Falls–The Dalles, p.202). Take Exit 84 to **The Dalles** (see also p.202).

COLUMBIA RIVER HIGHWAY

Before Interstate 84 was built in the late 1950s, Highway 30 was the only driving route along the Oregon shore of the Columbia River. Called the **Historic Columbia River Highway,** Hwy 30 followed the ups, downs and contours of the cliffs, providing a slow ride with awesome views and magnificent waterfalls. The 1916 road was designed for views while low, golden stone retaining walls, viaducts and decorous signs added elegance and harmony to the splendour.

Two short sections remain, from Troutdale

east to Ainsworth State Park and from Mosier to The Dalles. Speed limits vary from 15–40 mph along the narrow, one-lane highway. Congestion is extreme in summer and on fine-weather weekends. **Multnomah Falls,** the best-known attraction, gets more visitors than most other Northwest attractions combined.

TROUTDALE TO BRIDAL VEIL FALLS

Take Exit 18 off I-84 at **Troutdale**. **Troutdale Area Chamber of Commerce,** *338 E. Historic Columbia River Hwy (Hwy 30), Troutdale, OR 97060; tel: (503) 669-7473,* has information on **Harlow House** farmhouse, *726 E. Hwy 30,* open Wed–Sat 1000–1600 Sun 1300–1600 June–Oct, Sat–Sun 1300–1600 Nov–May.

Portlanders have made **McMenamins Edgefield,** *2126 S.W. Halsey; tel: (800) 669-8610* or *(503) 669-8610,* exceedingly popular. The 1911 **Multnomah County Poorhouse** has 100 moderate–expensive shared-facility bed and breakfast rooms, suites, family rooms and a budget hostel; Northwest cuisine in the **Rabbit Restaurant;** *tel: (503) 492-3086;* **Power Station Pub,** one of a chain of McMenamins brewpubs; **Edgefield Brewery** ales; **Edgefield Winery** tasting room; a summertime beer garden; flower and herb gardens; **Corcoran Glassworks** glassblowers; and **Power Station Theatre** cinema; *tel: (503) 669-8754.* **Lewis & Clark State Park** has picnicking, hiking and fishing at the mouth of the Sandy River, a shortening of the river's name from Lewis and Clark's 1805 name, Quick Sand River. For Gorge information, stop at **Columbia Gorge Ranger Station,** *31520 S.E. Woodard Rd; tel: (503) 695-2276.*

Highway 30 skirts bottomlands and farms for 10 miles east to **Portland Women's Forum State Park** at **Chanticleer Point**, the first river vista point. From the overlook, gaze eastwards at the winding river and rounded hills forming the shoreline on the Washington side of the river. The point was named after a popular 1915–1930 roadhouse; the Portland Women's Forum bought the neglected property in honour of the Historic Highway builders, (Maryhill) railway attorney Sam Hill,

Columbia River Gorge

Roads, railways, barges, power pylons, dams, locks and bridges hide evidence of earth-shattering eruptions, lava flows, and glacier ebb and flow that formed the Gorge. The Columbia River Gorge National Scenic Area could have been a national park. Its 60,000 inhabitants might have developed everything in sight outside existing state parks. The 1986 'NSA' represented an uneasy compromise between environmental and entrepreneurial.

Spectacular scenery, failing fish stocks and traditional Native American fishing balance against the need to keep timber and wheat flowing downriver aboard huge barges. Several million annual visitors add to the pressure on this 85-mile stretch of the Columbia River as dormitory communities serving Portland Oregon, and Vancouver, Washington push steadily eastward.

Driving by misty waterfalls, golden cliffs and sparkling blue water, it's hard to remember that massive cascades blocked the waters before the Columbia and Snake Rivers were charted and dammed for hydroelectric power. Warm Springs, Wasco, Umatilla, Yakama and Nez Perce wandered and fished for salmon so plentiful that early White explorers were stunned by shore-to-shore roiling during spawning.

Native commerce thrived long before Whites arrived, before the HBC and rivals set up stockades to sell goods shipped around South America from England or New England. The vast Northwest trading system reached from California to Alaska and eastward through the Great Plains. Captains Cook and Vancouver searched in vain for the fabled Northwest Passage across upper North America. A Yankee trader, Robert Gray, explored and charted 10 miles up the Columbia from its mouth in 1792, beating Vancouver's efforts by a few months. If any river was the route to the Far East, they thought, surely this was it.

Meriwether Lewis and William Clark's 1804–1806 Corps of Discovery finally verified what Native Americans had known for centuries, that the Great River of the West was huge, powerful, and chock-full with natural resources. Fur trappers, missionaries, then middle-class settlers lured by their reports raced to the region; most feared the river and its difficult portages.

As railways spread through the Northwest in the latter 19th century, timber, grain and cattle could be shipped to hungry markets in the Eastern US. Steamboats plied the middle Columbia River using a series of locks, transporting settlers, businessmen, farmers and workers along the bustling transportation corridor. The railways won eventually, providing fast and efficient freight and passenger service over thousands of miles.

A few *bona fide* tourists made their way West too, gasping at the Gorge's sheer natural beauty, so unlike the rolling hills lining Eastern US rivers or the flat Midwestern plains.

As population grew, government noted that an efficient energy source was needed to provide power to the cities. The Columbia River Dam System was a barely-disguised Great Depression makeshift scheme that transformed the region economically and prepared aeroplane production and shipbuilding when the USA entered World War II, less than three years after the completion of Bonneville Dam's First Powerhouse.

Dams tamed the Columbia's kinks, whitewater and cascades forever. No Gorge resident is without a stand on development. The Columbia River Gorge only seems a tame cross-roads of dams, locks and fish ladders. Occasional signs on bridges or farm fences protest past invocation of eminent domain when the NSA was formed. Newspapers carry running commentary along the lines of, 'we need to preserve the traditional lifestyles and industries, but need to make sure the trees, fish, and recreational areas are there, too...'

A few remaining vestiges of the river-that-was are treaty-guaranteed spots where Native Americans standing on simple wooden platforms above the river still dip long-handled nets, just feet from some of the world's best windsurfing.

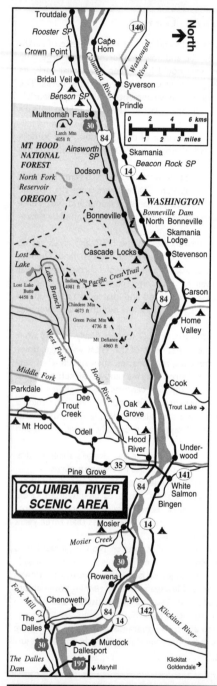

highway engineer Samuel Lancaster, Portland lumber baron Simon Benson and others.

Continue one mile east to **Vista House** at **Crown Point State Park**. Vista House, open 0800–1800 in summer, is a visitor centre with Gorge interpretative exhibits. The round stone observatory follows 1910s German architectural styles. The stone looks grey, pink or golden, depending on the light. The building honours pioneers and politicians, but the real attraction, 733 ft above the river, is the panoramic west–east view.

Crown Point was originally Thor's Point. There are frequent strong winds, a boon to windsurfers. Golden light standards switch on at dusk, glowing against a lustrous deep pink sky.

The Historic Highway engineers designed hairpin turns to drop 600 ft in one mile to 249-ft **Latourell Falls**. Though the cascade is visible from Hwy 30, the view is even more stunning from the viewpoint a short walk from the car park or the trail beneath the arching Latourell Bridge. **Guy W Talbot State Park**'s pleasant picnic tables beneath ancient trees are nearby.

Park in the lay-by one mile east of Shepperd's Dell Bridge. Cross to the south side of the highway, then follow a curving, moss-lined misty path to the face of **Shepperd's Dell Falls**, and views back towards the golden stone bridge.

Walk a mile to view **Bridal Veil Falls**, where a large mill once produced lumber for Hood River fruit crates, cheese boxes, and later, for World War II ammunition boxes and cedar fencing. **Bridal Veil Falls State Park** has picnicking and the falls hike. **Bridal Veil Lodge**, *at the falls, PO Box 87, Bridal Veil, OR 97010; tel: (503) 695-2333*, is a moderate bed and breakfast in a rustic 1926 roadhouse. Translated from Yakama as 'most beautiful', **Wahkeena Falls**, 2½ miles east, appear to flow on the diagonal. A popular picnic area is nearby.

BRIDAL VEIL FALLS TO AINSWORTH

Multnomah Falls, half a mile east and accessible from an I-84 parking area, has long been Oregon's most visited attraction. Its easy proximity to Portland makes Multnomah accessible to those making short stopovers in the area. It's worth the drive and the occasional wait in the summer-congested car park.

Spectacular year-round, the 620-ft falls plummets in two sections, visible through heavy mist and framed by ferns. Multnomah Falls is at its most forceful from Larch Mountain spring runoff. Fall foliage lines the cliffs with gold and red around plunging waters.

The elegant two-storey grey stone **Multnomah Falls Lodge**; *tel: (503) 695-2376*, just south of the highway, gives scale to the thunderous water flowing from above. View dining rooms, open Mon–Sat 0800–1000, offer budget–moderate breakfast, lunch and dinner; a summer snack bar sells drinks and sandwiches. The lodge also has a gift shop and summer US Forest Service Interpretive Center with maps and hiking information.

Simon Benson Bridge, named after the lumberman-philanthropist who donated the land for many parks and preserved areas on the Historic Highway, gracefully spans the pool above the lower fall. The bridge looks suspended partway up the cliff. It's a quarter-mile, 5-min uphill walk to the footbridge from an excellent viewpoint behind the lodge at the base of the falls. Thick mist drizzles from above like constant cool rain from the eternally-shady cliff face.

The switchback trail (# 441) to the top of the upper portion of Multnomah Falls gains 550 ft in less than one mile. Despite the uphill haul, it's a favourite jog for many Portlanders through old Douglas-fir and ferns, with superb views of the river. At the top, there's a quick turn to the right to reach the falls viewing platform. The water roars here, more a sound than a sight, a sensation of unchained power plunging downward.

Oneonta Gorge is narrow, green and protected, perfect framing for the exceeding straight falls dropping into a clear pool. The flow has eroded back from the Columbia River's perpendicular Gorge, creating a subtle micro-climate that is perfect for delicate plants seeking half-light. Hiking to the base of the falls is popular, but be prepared to wade through the pool to see the best views.

Driving past **Horsetail Falls**, the closest falls to the Historic Highway, is like driving though a rain shower. The 175 ft of water twist like a twitching horse's mane. Pull off to the parking area to see the pulsating 'tail'.

AINSWORTH PARK TO MOSIER

Highway 30 veers southward around **Horsetail Marsh**; a rich wetlands. **Ainsworth Park**; *tel: (503) 695-2301*, has 45 RV pitches for large vehicles and space for hikers and bikers. Continue east from Exit 35 on I-85 to Exit 69, **Mosier**.

MOSIER TO THE DALLES

The Gorge cliffs soften as the route extends eastward. Though much of Hwy 30 was neglected after I-84 provided more direct, riverside transportation, this short section survives. Horse farms and barns alternate with stands of Oregon white oak. Carpets of spring wildflowers cover the grassy hillsides.

From Mosier, Hwy 30 ascends to a barn-studded landscape. Colonial-style white buildings mark **Columbia View Orchards** (cherry). Look west (behind) for a spectacular river vista.

The **Tom McCall Preserve**, *Nature Conservancy, OR; tel: (503) 230-1221*, at the top of a slope overlooking the Gorge, offers Mar–May hiking through a sea of wildflowers. Pink Columbia desert parley, broad-leaf lupine, grasswidow, and shooting star with yellow bell and balsam root, produce vibrant pastel swaths. A fairly flat 1-mile **Plateau Trail** and steep, 4-mile **Upper Trail** provide access. Take precautions for ticks.

Across from Tom McCall Preserve at the same height as Washington's clifftops, **Rowena Crest** viewpoint overlooks the **Rowena Plateau** at Lyle, Washington near the Klickitat River.

Highway 30 winds away from the river through huge rocks and cherry orchards which bloom riotously in spring. Drive slowly on this blind-curve winding section to **Mayer State Park**, back at the river, with boat and windsurfer launch sites. Continue through a pine and oak-lined narrow road that seems to cling to the hillside 6 miles to *W. 6th St*, The Dalles.

THE DALLES–ONTARIO

Tens of thousands of immigrants once struggled and starved their way through weeks of travel between the water and rich forage of the Snake River near Ontario, over parched deserts and across the towering Blue Mountains to The Dalles, the end of the Oregon Trail on the Columbia River. Today, it takes six hours to drive approximately the same route in reverse, but the 285-mile journey is better enjoyed with frequent side trips to Oregon Trail sites off the freeway and overnight stops in Pendleton, La Grande and Baker City.

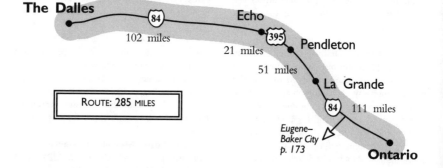

The Dalles

84

102 miles

Echo

395

21 miles

Pendleton

51 miles

La Grande

84   111 miles

ROUTE: 285 MILES

Eugene–Baker City p. 173

Ontario

ROUTE

Take I-84 east from The Dalles at Exit 87 to Ontario.

THE DALLES TO ECHO

Begin at the End of the Oregon Trail in The Dalles, former site of dangerous Columbia River rapids and waterfalls. I-84 follows the south bank of the river to Boardman, views frequently interrupted by railways tracks and power lines. Sheer cliffs rise on the right (south) side of the road, an escarpment that makes the mesas ahead more dramatic.

At Exit 87, **The Dalles (Dam) Visitors Center**, *Bret Clodfelter Way; tel: (541) 296-9887,* open Apr–Sept, has train tours of the dam, lock, powerhouse and fish ladder for this major Columbia River dam. **The Dalles Bridge** spans the Columbia River.

Take Exit 97 to riverside **Celilo Park** picnicking, where Oregon Trail pioneers encountered the 20-ft vertical drop of Celilo Falls. **The Dalles Dam** inundated the falls and the rapids below in the 1930s. Across the interstate are tepees and houses of **Celilo Indian Village**. Cross the mouth of the Deschutes River at the end of the Columbia River Gorge National Scenic Area.

Biggs, at the Hwy 97 junction and bridge to the Washington shore, is a popular lorry stop, with services, *BW* and other motels. Follow signs to the **Deschutes River State Recreational Area**; *tel: (541) 739-2322.* There is a fine view across the river to **Maryhill** (see p. 239), perched in the Washington hills.

John Day Lock and Dam visitor facilities, including fishwatching, are off Exit 109. **Giles French Park**, with camping, has an excellent view of the lower face of the dam and Native

American pole and net fishing platforms on shore. Take Exit 114 to **LePage Park** for picnicking and camping with views across the river to Washington's mountains, serrated like lions' paws in golden afternoon light.

For 5 miles after Exit 131, I-84 rises to the height of Washington's cliffs, then descends to **Arlington**, Exit 137, with services, riverside **Arlington Recreation Area** and **Arlington City Park** miniature stage-coach and Oregon Trail interpretative kiosk.

Cross the Columbia Plateau to a sandy, rocky landscape where sheep graze. **Umatilla National Wildlife Refuge** wetlands appear outside **Boardman**, Exit 159, with services. The empty scrub south-east of Boardman is a military bombing range. Rows of low white concrete structures, on the north side of I-84 about 12 miles north of Boardman, are military ammunition bunkers at the **Umatilla Ordinance Depot**. The nearby bunkers are empty, but thousands of artillery shells and missiles loaded with nerve gas, awaiting destruction, are stored a few miles from the freeway. Oregon Trail buffs should take Exit 193 and backtrack 4 miles through open farmland to Echo.

ECHO

Tourist Information: City of Echo, 20 S. Bonanza St, Box 9, Echo, OR 97826; tel: (541) 376-8411, open 0800–1600 Mon–Fri.

This small town on the Umatilla River was once a major Oregon Trail stopping point, then one of the busiest agricultural railway towns in Oregon. The city publishes an excellent self-guided walking tour brochure for the town and a detailed driving guide to Oregon Trail sites in the region. **Echo Historical Museum**, Main and Bonanza Sts; tel: (541) 376-8154, open Sat–Sun 1300–1700 Apr–Oct or by appointment, occupies the neo-classical Bank of Echo building, clad in white tile to simulate marble. Displays include local Native American artefacts as well as Oregon Trail and early settlement collections. **Fort Henrietta Park**, Main St, includes a replica blockhouse (the original fort was across the Umatilla River), local history displays and a picnic area.

Lush meadows provided the only good pasturage between Pendleton and The Dalles. The first Indian Agency, the federal agency which dealt with Native Americans, in the area was opened in 1851, the only frame building Oregon Trail immigrants had seen in months. The Agency was burned during the Yakima Indian War in 1855 (see p.90), most probably by the Agent himself, and immediately replaced by Fort Henrietta.

The town sprang up when the area was opened to settlement in 1860, fuelled by farms and river transport down the Umatilla to the Columbia River. When the railway arrived in 1881, Echo boomed as a transportation centre for grain, cattle, sheep and more. The town declined as agricultural employment shrank after World War II, but is slowly growing again. Intensive agriculture has spread with irrigation, but high winds can raise enormous dust storms when fields are empty.

PENDLETON

Tourist Information: Pendleton Chamber of Commerce, 25 S.E. Dorion St, Pendleton, OR 97801; tel: (800) 547-8911 or (541) 276-7411, has area and Oregon Trail information.

ACCOMMODATION

Pendleton has the best supply of accommodation in the area, including BW, RL, S8 and VI. The moderate **Parker House Inn**, 311 N. Main St; tel: (800) 700-8581 or (541) 276-8581, is the most pleasant bed and breakfast. **Raphael's**, 233 S.E. 4th St; tel: (541) 276-8500, moderate, the best restaurant in the area, specialises in salmon, beef, lamb, venison and an excellent Oregon wine list. **Cimmiyotti's**, 137 S. Main St; tel: (541) 276-4314, has the best budget–moderate steaks and Italian dishes.

SIGHTSEEING

Pendleton revels in its' reputation as one of the wildest towns in the Northwest, a booming market town that mixed farmers, merchants, cattlemen, sheep ranchers, Native Americans, soldiers, barkeepers, gamblers and prostitutes. Changing demographics and an unforgiving clergyman brought the good times to an end in 1953, but many fine old buildings remain. The Chamber of Commerce publishes a free self-guided walking tour brochure for the **South**

215

Main Street Commercial Historic District. Many of the same buildings are visible in photographs at the 1909 Union Pacific Railroad Depot, now the **Umatilla County Historical Society Museum**, *108 S.W. Frazer; tel: (541) 276-0012*.

Pendleton Underground Tours, *37 S.W. Emigrant St; tel: (800) 226-6398 or (541) 276-0730*, daily 1000–1600, adults $10, children $5, winds through a succession of city cellars and back rooms that once served as laundries, meat markets, saloons, gambling halls, ice-cream parlours, living quarters for the city's important Chinese community and a brothel furnished as the day it closed in 1953. The 90-min walking tour is an excellent introduction to the realities of life in the Pacific Northwest from the 1880s through to the 1950s. **Living Heritage Tours**, *351 S. Main St; tel: (541) 278-2446*, offers heritage tours of the region, including the **Confederated Tribe of the Umatilla Indian Reservation**. Cowboys and cattle ranching skills are the centrepieces at the **Pendleton Round-Up Hall of Fame**, *I-84 Exit 207, Box 609; tel: (800) 457-6336 or (541) 276-2553*, bulging with memorabilia from one of the largest rodeos in the West. The Round-Up is held in early Sept. **Pendleton Woolen Mills**, *1307 S.E. Court Place; tel: (503) 276-6911*, offers free guided tours of the manufacturing facility Mon–Fri. The sales shop is open Mon–Sat 0800–1700, with prices as high as any department store.

Just north of town is **Wildhorse Gaming Resort**, *I-84 Exit 216; tel: (800) 654-9453 or (541) 278-2274*, a casino operated by the Cayuse, Umatilla and Walla Walla tribes. For information on tribal lands, contact the **Confederated Tribes of the Umatilla Indian Reservation**, *Box 638; tel: (541) 276-3165*. **Wind Song Gallery**, *7 S.E. Court St; tel: (541) 276-7995*, specialises in Native American arts.

PENDLETON TO LA GRANDE

One of the more scenic stretches of I-84 begins at Pendleton, running 93 miles south-east over the Blue Mountains to Baker City, closely following the Oregon Trail route. The mountains begin at **Cabbage Hill**, just south of

Wildhorse. Lorry and RV traffic slows to a crawl as the freeway winds grandly up the hill for 6 miles. A rest area accessible from the northbound lanes offers expansive views. For a sample of what driving over the Blue Mountains used to entail, take *Old Emigrant Hill Rd* south from Pendleton up the steep, serpentine grade. A petrol station, 'The Boiling Point', is the state in which most ascending vehicles found themselves at the summit. The old highway joins I-84 just south at Exit 224.

Emigrant Springs State Park, *I-84 Exit 234; tel: (541) 983-2277*, is a former Oregon Trail camping and rest area after the arduous trek through the Blue Mountains. The park has 33 tent and 18 RV pitches and excellent interpretative displays. **Blue Mountain Summit**, 4316 ft, is 6 miles south.

The US Forest Service **Oregon Trail Interpretative Park**, *3 miles off I-84 at Exit 248, on SR 30 and FR 600; tel: (541) 963-7186*, open May–Sept, protects some of the most easily accessible Oregon Trail wagon ruts in the state. Paved ¼-mile and ¾-mile loop paths connect the wagon ruts, the remains of an 1861 stage-coach road and a replica prairie schooner, surrounded by stunning Blue Mountain peaks. The trails are marked with detailed interpretative signs and Oregon Trail diary excerpts.

Hilgard Junction State Park, *I-84 Exit 252; tel: (541) 523-2499*, was the traditional Oregon Trail stopping point after the first day of climbing into the Blue Mountains from Grande Ronde Valley. The park offers camping, picnicking and hiking.

LA GRANDE

Tourist Information: La Grande/Union County Chamber of Commerce, *1912 Fourth St #200, La Grande, OR 97850; tel: (800) 848-9969 or (541) 963-8588*, has information on the entire area.

ACCOMMODATION AND FOOD

Chain motels include *BW*, *CI* and *S8*. Best choice for Northwest cuisine is **Ten Depot Street**, *10 Depot St; tel: (541) 963-8466*. **Mamacita's**, *110 Depot St; tel: (541) 963-6223*, specialises in Mexican; **Golden Crown**,

1116 Adams St; tel: (541) 963-5907, in Cantonese; and **Wrangler Steak House**, 1914 Adams St; tel: (541) 963-3131, in steaks and seafood; all budget–moderate.

SIGHTSEEING

The Grande Ronde Valley was a welcome respite along the Oregon Trail, a calm, fertile basin between the deserts of Baker City and the daunting heights of the Blue Mountains. La Grande, a small wheat and cattle town, is the commercial hub of the valley. The downtown is a prosperous mix of old brick and newer buildings that concentrate more on local needs than the tourist trade. The Chamber of Commerce publishes a self-guided walking brochure of the turn-of-the-century commercial district.

LA GRANDE TO ONTARIO

From La Grande, the freeway climbs out of the valley to the south and into increasingly dry hills and valleys leading to Baker City. Go left from Exit 302 on SR 86 to the **National Historic Oregon Trail Interpretative Center** at **Flagstaff Hill** (See Eugene–Baker City, p.182). Turn right at Exit 304 to **Baker City** (see p.181).

The 70 miles from Baker City to Ontario wind through mountains as rough-looking as when traversed by Oregon Trail pioneers. Enter the Mountain Standard Time Zone at mile 350. Where **Farewell Bend State Park** now stands, new arrivals in Oregon Territory sadly bade farewell to travelling companions. Not far from present-day I-84 Exit 353, they tearfully left camp areas along the tree-lined Snake River. **Farewell Bend State Park**; tel: (541) 869-2365, marked by two life-sized covered wagons at the entrance, has watersports and swimming on the river, picnicking and RV, tent, covered camper wagons and tepees; tel: (800) 452-5687. One mile north of Ontario, **Ontario State Park** has a restful picnic area along the Snake River, with views east to Idaho.

217

HEPPNER JUNCTION– BAKER CITY

This journey into the heartland of north-eastern Oregon, via the Blue Mountain and Elkhorn Scenic Byways, is a scenic alternative to the Interstate 84 route from The Dalles to Ontario. Loop through sheep farms and grass-lands little changed in the 150 years since ranchers and wheat farmers arrived over the Oregon Trail. As the land rises, a few trees become many, thickening into forests.

Traverse high Elkhorn Mountain passes to old gold-mining towns now close to becoming ghost towns. For the last 30 miles of this 180-mile route, drive past cows grazing in serene pastures.

Baker City waits on the eastern side of the formidable Blue Mountains. A section of this route is closed in winter between Heppner and Ukiah, and fires have reduced sections of forest to blackened spikes. Plan on a five-hour drive in excellent weather.

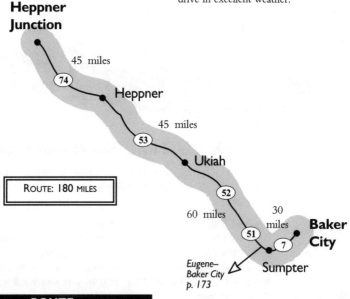

Heppner
Junction

45 miles

74

Heppner

45 miles

53

Ukiah

ROUTE: 180 MILES

52

60 miles

30 miles

51

7

Baker
City

Eugene–
Baker City
p. 173

Sumpter

ROUTE

Take I-84, Exit 147 onto SR 74 at Heppner Junction and drive 45 miles to **Heppner**. Go south on SR 207 for one mile, then turn left onto Forest Service (FS) Road 53 to **Ukiah**.

Turn right (south) onto FS 52, turn right again onto FS 51 at **North Fork John Day Campground** and continue to **Sumpter**. Follow SR 7 to Baker City.

TOURIST INFORMATION

Information for the Umatilla National Forest and the Blue Mountain and Elkhorn National Scenic Byways is provided by **Umatilla National Forest**, *2517 S.W. Hailey Ave, Pendleton, OR 97801; tel: (541) 278-3716,* with a field office in Heppner.

HEPPNER JUNCTION TO HEPPNER

Heppner Junction is not on any road sign, but its name is shown on maps at I-84, Exit 147. Leave the east end of the Columbia River Gorge and head south on SR 74 through Willow Creek Valley, past occasional ranch houses, bee hives and cows grazing amidst rocky outcroppings.

Fourteen miles south, William Y. Cecil stopped along the way to repair a wagon, found his services in demand, and built the first store, still in operation in the ranching hamlet along Willow Creek that bears his name, **Cecil**.

To retrace a short portion of the Oregon Trail, go left (east) for 14 miles to **Wells Springs**, looking closely to see the well-worn wagon ruts.

Pheasants wander near **Morgan,** a grain shipment centre from 1888–1994. A game refuge spreads on both sides of the road outside **Ione**; *tel: (541) 422-7122,* notable for the grain elevators which rise above the town. Nearby wheatfields sustain 1883-era Ione with a bank, store, petrol station, coffee shop, restaurant, a majestic old Masonic Lodge building and city park.

Four miles beyond is a distant view of the Blue Mountains. **Lexington,** Morrow County's agricultural centre, has petrol, a market and a steak restaurant.

HEPPNER

Tourist Information: **Morrow County Tourism Committee/Heppner Chamber of Commerce**, *289 N. Main St, PO Box 1232, Heppner, OR 97836; tel: (541) 676-5336,* has information for the area.

A huge lumber mill looms outside Heppner, Morrow County's government centre. Best known for the disastrous 1903 Heppner Flood,

Heppner residents still talk about the Sunday afternoon when a cloudburst formed a 200-yard wide wall of water in Willow Creek, pushing debris before it and taking 247 lives as it gushed over the town. Only the **Roberts Building** on *Main St* survived.

The **Morrow County Courthouse**, *Court St*, open 0800–1700, is built of locally-quarried blue basalt rock. Its clock tower chimes sonorously on the hour. Inside the Courthouse, a photograph shows the town transformed by snow in 1929. The white **United Methodist Church**, *N.W. Gate and N.W. Church Sts,* has a steeple bell suspended in a frame and a lovely round stained-glass window.

Find most of the action on *Main St*, including the **Umatilla National Forest Ranger Station**; *tel: (541) 676-9187,* two restaurants and two saloons.

HEPPNER TO UKIAH

Follow SR 207 for one mile, then turn left and follow FS 53 as it rises into the hills above Heppner.

On the left, **Willow Creek Lake and Dam**, the world's first roller-compacted concrete dam which prevents another Heppner Flood disaster, offers a viewpoint, campsite, picnicking and year-long swimming, fishing and boating.

Cattle graze as the road continues its gradual rise through rounded, rock-strewn hills. Western larches (tamarack) appear, dramatically yellow in autumn, and the only Northwestern conifer to shed its needles in winter. Pines nestle in clefts between rolling hills. The road serpentines.

Cutsforth County Park, marked with a totem pole and huge wheel, is 20 miles from Heppner. Camping, fishing, hiking and picnicking are popular in summer, but only Nordic skiers, snowmobilers or four-wheel drive vehicles can make their way through the 4000-ft-high park in winter.

The narrow road rises quickly into the **Umatilla National Forest**, but driving is slow. Trees are old, but badly burned, many dripping with light-coloured moss. There are many trails and primitive backcountry camp pitches around the forested mountains.

Stop two miles after entering the forest at the **Coalmine Hill Day Use Area** for self-service brochures.

Twenty-three miles from Heppner, veer left to follow FS 53, *Western Route Rd*, up the Blue Mountain National Scenic Byway. This section closes in winter; check in advance with National Forest Rangers for conditions. Begin the descent a few miles later.

On the right, **Kelly Meadow** is a frost pocket, lower, wetter and colder than surrounding forest, and unable to sustain trees. Mule deer, marmots, pikas, voles, kestrels, meadowlarks and hummingbirds call the verdant meadow home.

A sign at FS 5327 indicates a 32-mile return drive to **Potamus Point**, a vista over the Wild and Scenic North Fork John Day River canyon. Continue on FS 53, and gradually descend to cross Hwy 395 at Owens Creek. The mountains flatten to a valley plain at Ukiah.

UKIAH

Tourist Information: **North Fork John Day Ranger District**, *PO Box 158, Ukiah, OR 97880; tel: (541) 427-3231.*

Ukiah, named after the first postmaster's hometown in California, was Camas Prairie to Native Americans, who in early summer collected the prized blue-blossoming camas bulbs. They told stories of a turbulent sea which suddenly disappeared. The turn of the century centre for loggers, ranchers and farmers now gets by on recreational tourism through the area.

Ukiah has services, several places to get a quick snack, and the **Antlers Inn**, *Hwy 395, PO Box 97, Ukiah, OR 97880; tel: (503) 427-3492,* a modest hotel named for the many racks of horns mounted on the two-storey wood and log post building.

Fill up with petrol at the **North Fork John Day Ranger District** (see above) before continuing. Turn right at the Granite/Scenic Byway sign and continue south-east on FS 52.

UKIAH TO ELKHORN MOUNTAIN RANGE

Watch for wintering Rocky Mountain elk,

spring wildflowers and the view of Bridge Creek Falls from Umatilla National Forest's ½-mile long **Bridge Creek Interpretative Trail**, 5 miles from Ukiah. Adjacent **Bridge Creek Wildlife Area** is only accessible on a rutted road barely suitable for 4WD vehicles.

The forest recently burned below the usually panoramic wilderness vista from **North Fork John Day Overlook**.

North Fork John Day River, designated 'Wild and Scenic', was mined for gold in the late 1800s; the fine-quality rock was used for building foundations. In the dry season, blue-black haze and smoke show off the intense hue of the Blue Mountains. Fire damage to the forest continues for 10 miles along the route.

Thirty-seven miles from Ukiah, FS 52 becomes FS 73, joining the Elkhorn Drive National Scenic Byway at **North Fork John Day Campground**. Facilities include camping, fishing and areas for horses – but no horses are for hire and there is no drinking water.

ELKHORN MOUNTAIN RANGE TO BAKER CITY

'Walls' along the side of the roadway were built by Chinese miners. Cross a series of summits. Alp-like **Elkhorn Mountain Range** on the left (east) was formed by glaciers carving volcanic basalt, granite and remnants of an ancient sea.

Enter **Wallowa-Whitman National Forest**, *1550 Dewey Ave, PO Box 907, Baker City, OR 97814; tel: (541) 523-6391,* and descend to gold country. Sluices and ruined wooden huts dot the roadside, mute testimony to those who hoped to make fortunes from ore they sluiced, shook through mesh pans or pick-axed from boulders. Piles of tailings, the rubble that remained after their mining efforts, are visible on all sides.

The Granite Store and Café, a Mexican restaurant, cabins, an RV park and a petrol station, are what remains of **Granite**, site of an 1862 gold strike and continuing profits until gold mining was discontinued during World War II. Now, it barely escapes the ghost town label.

Continue to **Sumpter**, then follow SR 7 to Baker City (See Eugene to Baker City, p.181).

KLAMATH FALLS– ONTARIO

Nowhere in Oregon is as vast or as distant from the urban rush as the little-known southeast Wetlands, a high desert antelope refuge and a bird refuge nestled amidst dark volcanic craters that lie along this long, but visually stunning, 415-mile route. Several roads are roughly paved, extremely narrow and require slow driving to ensure safety. This route is not recommended for RVs. Plan on a minimum of two days with an overnight in Burns, or three nights with an additional stopover in Lakeview.

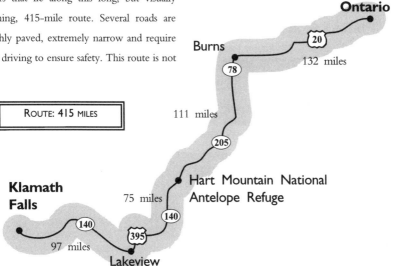

ROUTE: 415 MILES

221

ROUTE

Take SR 39 south-east through Klamath Falls, then go left (east) on SR 140 for 90 miles to **Lakeview**. Turn left (north) for 5 miles on Hwy 395, go 27 miles right on SR 140 to Adel, and go left (north) 18 miles to Plush. Follow signs to the right up a poorly paved road to **Hart Mountain National Antelope Refuge** and **Frenchglen**. Turn left (north) 60 miles on SR 205 through **Malheur National Wildlife Refuge**, then turn left 2 miles on SR 78 to **Burns**. Drive north 2 miles on Hwy 395, then turn right (east) 130 miles on Hwy 20 to Ontario. Keep the petrol tank as full as possible, and prepare for sudden weather changes.

KLAMATH FALLS TO LAKEVIEW

Five miles east of Klamath Falls at **Olene** is a scenic view of mountains rising above cattle grazing on the banks of the Lost River. Birds fly over marshes near picnic tables at **Stevenson County Park**. As pastures give way to forest near 5087-ft Bly Mountain Summit, logging lorries fill the road. Pass briefly through a badly-burned area of Winema National Forest, then enter **Fremont National Forest**, *524 N. G St, Lakeview, OR 97630; tel: (541) 947-2151.* **Beatty**, 37 miles from Klamath Falls, has petrol, a small café, convenience store and tiny motel. RJR Ranch's sign matches the vertical white stripe and curly black hair of its cows.

'A man, a miss/A car, a curve/He missed the miss/And missed the curve', announce four signs preceding a 'Welcome to Bly, Oregon, Population 700 more or less, elev. 4340'. Huge cattle ranches with horses and hay bales surround **Bly**'s humorous citizenry. **Gearhart Mountain Wilderness** is north-east of Bly. **Quartz Mountain Pass**, 5504 ft, is in an area originally worked for obsidian by Native Americans and later mined by Whites for gold and uranium. Nordic skiing is popular in this section of Fremont National Forest. Cross 5306-ft **Drew's Gap**. **Booth State Park** has a pleasant picnic area.

LAKEVIEW

Tourist Information: Lake County Chamber of Commerce, *126 N. E St, Lakeview, CA 97630; tel: (541) 947-6040; fax: (541) 947-4892*, has local information and becomes the logistics centre for an international Hang Gliding Festival in July.

WEATHER

The climate is pleasant with 250 days of sun annually. Rain and snow fall in every month, however, so be prepared for bright sunshine to snowy conditions anytime, anywhere along this route.

ACCOMMODATION AND FOOD

Lakeview has several RV parks and six motels including *BW* and the moderate, basic rooms at **Hunter's Hot Springs Resort**, *1 mile north on Hwy 395; tel: (541) 947-2127,* with a mineral water pool and **Old Perpetual Geyser**'s 60-ft-high eruption near a duck pond. Dining is informal, with a small selection of coffee shops, pizza parlours and steakhouses.

SIGHTSEEING

Lakeview's moniker is the 'Tallest Town in Oregon', marked with a gun-slinging cowboy sign at the edge of town. Just south extending into California is blue **Goose Lake**. Hangliders launching off **Black Cap Hill**, 2000 ft above the east side of Lakeview during the May–Oct

season have excellent soaring near Goose Lake, appreciated during an international meeting staged from Lakeview in early July.

Cattle production and six lumber mills, including large Fremont Sawmill, sustain the economy. The Chamber of Commerce has an historic buildings walking tour brochure covering the Western-looking downtown.

Lake County Museum, *118 S. E St; tel: (541) 947-2220,* open 1000–1600 Wed–Sun, has excellent Native American beadwork and other artefacts, including a 9200-year-old reed sandal. Next door, **Schminck Memorial Museum**, *128 S. E St; tel: (541) 947-3134,* open Tues–Sat 1300–1700 (Feb–Nov), displays extensive collections of American pressed glass, quilts, clothing, furniture, and Paiute and Pitt River Native American baskets in a beautiful, painstakingly preserved bungalow.

LAKEVIEW TO HART MOUNTAIN NATIONAL ANTELOPE REFUGE

North on Hwy 395, on the left, is **Morisette Holstein House**, a private owners' rendition of the cow theme where everything on the property is painted in black and white spots.

One mile north, turn right onto SR 140, a National Backcountry Byway, continuing through Fremont National Forest over 5846-ft **Warner Pass** with colourful riparian areas ahead.

The scenery changes again as cows graze below waterfalls streaming over rock mesas near **Adel**, which has a petrol station, a small store and an RV park. Turn left at the petrol station to continue north to **Plush**. Smell Indian sagebrush while driving by lakes which swell or shrink depending on precipitation. Butterflies, birds and dragonflies are thick over lakeside grasses. **Egan Park** in Plush has a shaded picnic area with toilets.

Turn right (east) one mile north of Plush onto *County Rd 312*; the road resembles a levee through the wetlands around **Hart Lake**, with a small swimming area on the right side.

Warner Wetland Area of Critical Environmental Concern, a major stopping point on the Pacific Flyway migration route, is 51 acres of former agricultural land restored to meadows, lakes, ponds, marshes and uplands. Park at the information board and take a short path to the observation blind. Canoes can manoeuvre in spring when water is high.

Meadow grasses provide covered forage for curlews, sandhill cranes, northern harriers and short-eared owls. Lake and ponds have fisheries and waterfowl nesting habitat. Diving ducks are half-hidden in marshland bulrushes and cattails. Greasewood and other salt-tolerant plants mark the uplands, habitat for small mammals, mule deer and pronghorn antelope. White pelicans fill a creek just east of the wetland.

The high desert of the Great Basin looms ahead. Lakes, some alkaline, shine under occasional sand-ridden funnel clouds. Fifteen miles of gravel road lie ahead.

HART MOUNTAIN NATIONAL ANTELOPE REFUGE

Tourist Information: Hart Mountain National Antelope Refuge, *PO Box 111, Lakeview, OR 97630; tel: (541) 947-3315,* or the self-service visitor centre on Hart Mountain, have information.

Turn right at the large refuge sign and drive *very* slowly 3 miles up a steep, narrow dirt road, which affords magnificent views of lakes amidst the Warner Valley rangeland 3600 ft below. The protected antelope prefer the south-eastern corner of the 275,000-acre refuge, but mule deer, bighorn sheep, sage grouse and golden eagles may be seen on this route.

Hart Mountain levels off at 8065 ft high sparse landscape, formed from a seismic fault block. Well-hidden springs provide an oasis for animals. Campers using the all-year **Hot Springs Camp** 4 miles south of the visitor centre must carry water and provisions for all weather conditions. Hiking, rockhounding, fishing and photography are also popular May–Oct.

FRENCHGLEN TO BURNS

Frenchglen is 49 miles from Hart Mountain Refuge visitor centre on the unpaved, but graded road. Sage and a few ranch buildings break up the monotonous drive across the high desert. Strong wind gusts can blow cars quickly out of control.

Frenchglen is a half-year town, that is, the 1914 **Frenchglen Hotel State Heritage Site**, *Frenchglen, OR 97736; tel: (541) 493-2825,* is open mid Mar–mid Nov with moderate rooms, no television, phones and bathrooms are down the hall. Breakfast and lunch is cheap–budget. Book ahead for delicious moderate family-style dining at 1830. **Frenchglen Mercantile** is an old-fashioned wooden country store, well-stocked with food, drinks, tin ware, books and Southwest Native American jewellery. The adjoining **Buckaroo Bar** could be lifted from a Western film set.

Petrol, a corral, post office, telephone booth and Bureau of Land Management information kiosk complete the facilities, named after local ranchers. Frenchglen is the jumping off point for a summer-only drive over very rough road to 9773-ft **Steens Mountain**, *Bureau of Land Management; tel: (541) 573-5241,* a 30-mile long fault block carved by seismic shifts and glaciers. The drop-off is like a view off the edge of the earth.

Take SR 205 north following a corridor of power lines between widely-spaced tablerock mesas coloured with orange and yellow lichen. **Malheur National Wildlife Refuge**, (pron: mowl-year or molly-yur), *HC-72, Box 245, Princeton, OR 97721; tel: (541) 493-2612,* extends 60 miles north to Burns. **Refuge Headquarters/Visitor Center**, *halfway, 6 miles east on Sodhouse Lane,* open 0700–1630 Mon–Thur, 0700–1530 Fri, overlooks **Malheur Lake**, and provides information and waterfowl exhibits. The **George M Benson Memorial Museum** collection of 200 birds and their eggs, including a huge trumpeter swan, is part of the complex.

Stop at **Buena Vista Ponds and Overlook**, 18 miles from Frenchglen, facing Steens Mountain. Hundreds of birds flit though the pond grasses. Look for nesting trumpeter swans in spring–summer. A few miles east are a dramatic series of volcanic craters.

Turn right on *Diamond Lane* 13 miles to **Diamond** where the less-than-friendly reception belies the moderate **Hotel Diamond**; *tel: (541) 493-1898,* history as a welcome spot for lonely turn-of-the-century shepherds. The moderate **McCoy Creek Inn**, *HC 72 Box 11,*

223

Diamond, OR 97722; tel: (541) 493-2131, 2 miles south is a pleasant alternative, complete with hot tub.

Sixteen miles north is Peter French's circa 1880 **Round Barn**, a major cattle rancher's innovative idea to exercise winter-confined horses confined by running them around an indoor track in a stone building.

Of most interest is the **Diamond Craters Outstanding Natural Area**, *Bureau of Land Management, Burns District Office, HC 74-12553 Hwy 20 W., Hines, OR 97738; tel: (541) 573-5241*. A detailed self-guided auto tour brochure covers red and black cinder cones, lava flows, craters and ridges formed by a volcanic explosion 9.2 million years ago. Park at **Lava Pit Crater**, formed by the repeated welling and retreat of magma, and walk over sharp pumice to the crater rim. Return to SR 205 and go north, turning left on SR 78 to Burns.

BURNS

Tourist Information: Harney County Chamber of Commerce, *18 W. D St, Burns, OR 97720; tel: (531) 573-2636*, has information on area lodging, dining and attractions, including a one-mile historical walking tour.

ACCOMMODATION AND FOOD

Sage Country Inn, *351 1/2 W. Monroe, PO Box 227; tel: (541) 573-7243*, is a beautiful, moderate bed and breakfast in a mansion in the centre of town. Two of the women owners are Burns cattle ranch owners with extensive knowledge of ranch culture, the forests and recreational areas north and south and Oregon pioneer traditions.There are five motels including *BW*. **Pine Room Cafe**, *Monroe and Egan Sts; tel: (541) 573-6631*, the local favourite, serves moderate dinners.

BURNS TO ONTARIO

Burns and the adjacent dormitory community, **Hines**, are the commercial, transportation and government base for ranchers and those charged with conserving forest resources to the north and the wetlands and volcanic areas to the south. **Harney County Historical Museum**, *18 W. D St; tel: (541) 573-2636*, open

0900–1700 Tues–Fri (May–mid Oct), 0900–1200 Sat, has a varied collection of pioneer artefacts.

Drive 2 miles north on Hwy 395, then turn right (east) onto Hwy 20. Drive 24 miles past grazing cows to **Buchanan**. **OARD'S**, *SR 20-1604 Buchanan, Burns, OR 97720; tel: (800) 637-0252* or *(531) 493-2535*, is a huge gift shop with Native American jewellery, rugs and handicrafts with a small free museum. Beautiful thunder eggs are taken from the store owner's own land a few miles off the road. A mile beyond is a rest area.

Highway 20 ascends quickly to a view over the Malheur River and Warm Springs Reservoir. Set watches one hour ahead shortly after traversing 4212-ft Drinkwater Pass, to reflect Mountain Standard Time. **Juntura**, 58 miles from Burns, is a tiny town. Book a budget–moderate room or park an RV next to the **Oasis Restaurant**. Pies and mugs of coffee accompany the speciality: budget buffalo meat burgers with thick fries.

Cross the North Fork of the Malheur River to enter a narrow, winding canyon; the riverbank is covered with grass and sparse sage. An occasional pumice flow glows like a golden brocade tapestry streaked with red.

The road rises with a view of hay, wheat, cattle, onions and peppers growing in the agricultural valley to the east, near **Vale**, a stopping point on the **Oregon Trail**. **Vale Chamber of Commerce**, *275 N. Main St, Vale, OR 97918; tel: (541) 473-3800*, has information on the trail, the poignant Oregon Trail murals on downtown buildings and a walking tour brochure of Vale's historic downtown. Stone **Rinehart House**, *S. Main St; tel: (541)*

Colour section (i): A view of Mount Bachelor (p.185); Painted Hills at John Day Fossil Beds National Monument (see p.178).

(ii): Crater Lake National Park: Wizard Island; Pinnacles at Annie Creek (pp. 190–192).

(iii): Columbia River Gorge: Sunset at Crown Point; Native American Fishing Platforms (pp.211–212).

(iv): An early schoolhouse, Pendleton (p.215); A mural at Toppenish (p.240).

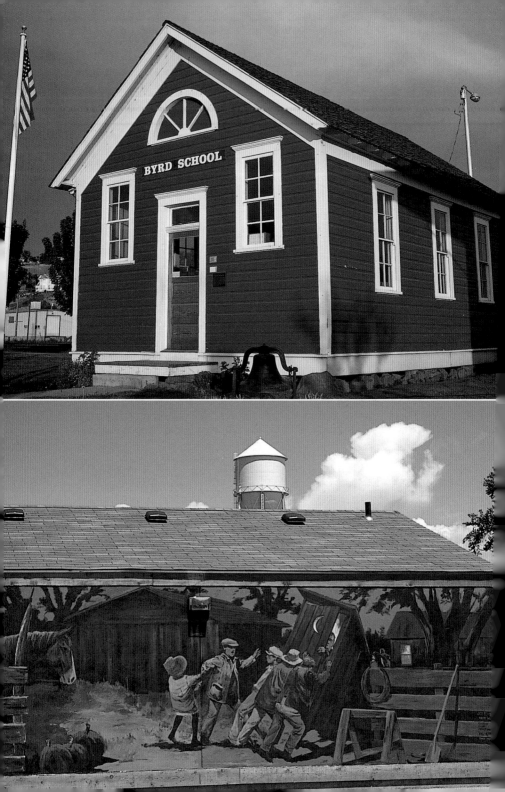

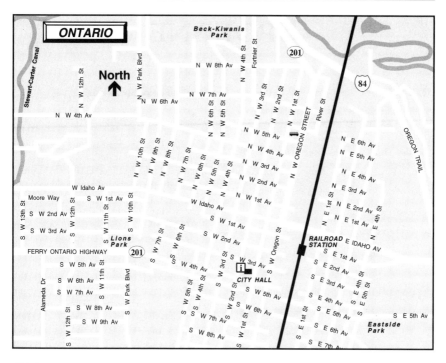

473-2070, open 1200–1600 Tues–Sat (Mar–Nov), was Vales's first permanent building. Wagon wheel ruts are visible in the desolate hills at **Keeney Pass**.

ONTARIO

Tourist Information: Ontario Visitors & Convention Bureau, *88 SW. 3rd Ave, Ontario, OR 97914; tel: (541) 889-8012; fax: (541) 889-8331,* open 0800–1700 Mon–Fri, and **Ontario (Oregon State) Welcome Center**, *I-84, ½ mile from the Idaho border,* open daily, have area information.

Ontario serves traffic crossing the Snake River from Boise, Idaho, 55 miles south-east on I-84. Most lodging serves visitors heading to the Columbia Gorge via I-84 or to Central Oregon. Accommodations include *BW, BI, Hd, HJ* and **Super 8**, *266 Goodfellow St; tel: (541) 889-8282,* conveniently located near I-84. **Casa Jaramillo**, *157 S.E. 2nd St; tel: (541) 889-9258,* has hearty, budget Mexican food. **Alexander's on the River**, *1930 S.E 5th Ave; tel: (541) 889-8070,* has moderate

seafood and steaks. **Oregano's**, *West Park Plaza Mall, N.W. 4th Ave; tel: (541) 889-7444,* has tasty pizzas and sandwiches. There is an assortment of fast food.

Ontario is above all a cross-roads, an early stop in Oregon for Oregon Trail pioneers. Contrary to its namesake in Canada, Oregon's Ontario receives 9.6 in of rain annually, a desert climate along the Snake River. Agriculture replaced cattle transportation as Ontario's main industry in the 1930s. The magnificent Snake River is now heavily dammed upstream (Hell's Canyon) to irrigate the potatoes, mint and produce growing in nearby fields. Descendants of Basque sheepherders join the descendants of Oregon Trail pioneers, Japanese-Americans resettled in the area after World War II internment nearby and Hispanics who came to toil in the fields, helping build Ontario's prosperity. The **Four Rivers Cultural Center**, *676 S.W. 5th Ave, Ontario; tel: (888) 2111-1222* or *(541) 889-8191,* open 0900–1700, has exhibits covering Northern Paiute Native Americans, Basques and a Japanese Garden.

SPOKANE

Home to the first non-Native settlement in the Pacific Northwest, Spokane has become the only genuine city in Washington east of the Cascades. Built at the largest falls on the Spokane River, it's the commercial and cultural capital of the Inland Empire, a vast area stretching north into British Columbia, east to the Rocky Mountains, south to the Columbia River and west to Cascades. Abandoned by fur traders and missionaries, Spokane was imagined into existence by land speculators, nourished by railroads and reinvented by the first World's Fair to carry an environmental theme. It remains one of the most pleasant cities in the region, big enough to provide urban amenities, small enough that the commute hour seldom lasts 30 mins, and rife with outdoor recreation opportunities.

TOURIST INFORMATION

Tourist Information: Spokane Regional Convention & Visitors Bureau, *W. 926 Sprague St, Suite 180, Spokane, WA 99204; tel: (800) 248-3230 or (509) 624-1341; fax (509) 623-1297;* **Visitor Information Center**, *201 W. Main Ave (at Browne St); tel: (509) 747-3230,* open 0830–1700 Mon–Fri, (Sat–Sun in summer). Ask for the excellent *Spokane Daytours* brochure with inclusive driving tours of Spokane and the region.

WEATHER

Spokane lies just east of the arid Columbia Plateau. Summers are dry and warm, to the high 80°s F, winters are rainy to snowy with temperatures dropping to the mid 20°s F.

ARRIVING AND DEPARTING

Spokane International Airport, *just west between Hwy 2 and I-90,* has frequent flights from other US and Canadian cities. A large fleet of rental cars is based at the airport, but advance booking is essential, especially in spring, autumn, the meetings and convention season, and summer. **Airport Shuttle***; tel: (509) 535-6979,* provides convenient airport transport.

AMTRAK, *221 W. First St; tel: (800) 872-7245 or (509) 624-5144,* has regular train services west to Seattle, east to Chicago and Minneapolis and south-west to Portland. **Greyhound***; tel: (509) 624-5251,* and **Northern Trailways***; tel: (509) 838-5262,* provide long distance coach services. The primary auto routes are **I-90** east and west, **Hwy 2** and **Hwy 395** north and **Hwy 195** south. In the city centre, **Streets** run east–west, **Avenues** run north–south.

STAYING IN SPOKANE

Accommodation

As a regional commercial centre, Spokane is well-supplied with hotel, motel and bed and breakfast rooms, but demand is growing. Advance booking is essential in summer and at holidays, and strongly recommended the rest of the year. Chains include *BW, CI, CM, DI, Ha, Hd, QI, RL, Rm* and *S8.* Best motel bargains are along Hwy 2, *Division St,* on the north side of the city toward Newport.

Fotheringham House, *2121 W. 2nd Ave; tel: (509) 838-1891; fax: (509) 838-1807,* moderate–expensive, is easily the city's most comfortable bed and tastiest breakfast. The 1891 house has been scrupulously restored by Graham and Jackie Johnson, who verge on the fanatical in their knowledge of the city.

Campsites include **Riverside State Park***; tel: (509) 456-3964,* **Ponderosa Hill**, *S. 7520 Thomas Mallen Rd; tel: (800) 464-7275 or (509) 747-9415; fax: (509) 459-0148,* **KOA** of

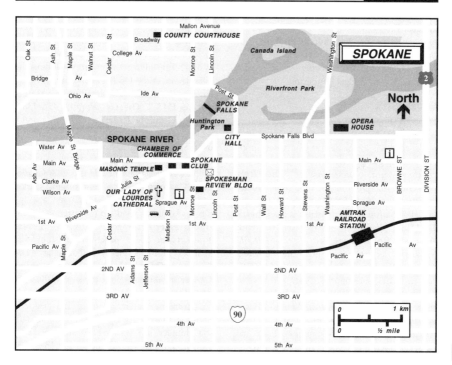

Spokane, N. 3025 Barker Rd, Otis Orchards, WA; tel: (509) 924-4722, and **Park Lane Motel & RV Park**, E. 4412 Sprague; tel: (800) 533-1626 or (509) 535-1626.

Eating and Drinking

The pleasant climate and recreational opportunities make Spokane as popular with top chefs as it is with their customers. One of the top choices is pricey **Patsy Clark's Mansion Restaurant**, W. 2208 2nd Ave; tel: (509) 838-8300, which serves elegant Northwest dishes. Mining magnate Patrick Clark built the ochre sandstone mansion in 1898, ordering the architect to spare no expense. The result is Tiffany glass, plush oriental carpets, hand-carved wood and, as the entry hall centrepiece, a flashy lamp set with coloured glass jewels that Clark reportedly won in a whorehouse poker game.

Most of the better restaurants are near the Spokane River in the city centre. Two exceptions worth searching out: **Birkenbeiner Brewery**, 35 W. Main Ave; tel: (509) 458-0854, budget, the best brewery in town with a lively international menu that mixes Thailand, Mexico, Germany, Italy and Louisiana Cajun. **Two Moon Cafe**, in the Mars Hotel, 300 W. Sprague Ave; tel: (509) 747-6277, budget–moderate, is a trendy Northwest choice with one of the best wine lists in town. The popular **Ugly Rumors** night-club downstairs includes a small casino.

Don't be put off by the lunch-counter exterior of **Something Else Restaurant & Pub**, W. 518 Sprague St; tel: (509) 757-3946, cheap–moderate. Northwest dishes with heavy influences from Asia and Mexico make it one of the most popular lunch and dinner spots in the city centre. **The Mustard Seed Oriental Cafe**, W. 245 Spokane Falls Blvd; tel: (509) 747-2689, is a popular budget–moderate Japanese choice. **Arizona Steakhouse**, W. 333 Spokane Falls Blvd; tel: (509) 455-8206, moderate, serves Spokane's best steaks. Top Greek choice is **Niko's**, W. 725 Riverside Ave; tel: (509) 624-7444; Italian lovers head for **Cucina Cucina Italian Café**, W. 707 Main Ave; tel: (509) 838-3388, both budget–moderate. **Milford's Fish**

House, *719 N. Monroe St; tel: (509) 326-7251*, moderate, has the best fish in Spokane, but **Salty's At the Falls**, *N. 510 Lincoln St; tel: (509) 327-8888*, has a better view of the Spokane River. Budget–moderate.

SHOPPING

Devoted shoppers blithely ignore the weather in Spokane. A system of air-conditioned sky-walks connects major department stores, shops and parking garages across 15 blocks in the city centre. Major outlets include **The Bon Marché**; *tel: (509) 747-5111*, and **Nordstrom**; *tel: (509) 455-6111*, both at *Main Ave and Wall St*. Just down the street is the **Liberty Building**, *Washington St and Main Ave*, with **Auntie's Book Store**; *tel: (509) 838-0206*, Spokane's largest book shop, and **Uncle's Games, Puzzles & Etc**; *tel: (509) 456-4607*, the city's best selection of games and toys to occupy children of all ages during long driving trips. On the north side of the Spokane River and Riverfront Park is the **Flour Mill**, *621 W. Mallon Ave*, an 1895 brick flour mill that has been remodelled into shops and restaurants.

SIGHTSEEING

Riverfront Park; *tel: (509) 625-6621*, is Spokane's defining feature. **Spokane Falls**, in the centre of the park, were an important Native American fishery and settlement. The same falls attracted a Salem apple seller named James Glover. In 1872, Glover bought out the only settlers, a pair of cattlemen who were more likely rustlers than ranchers, and a minuscule saw mill near the corner of *Spokane Falls Blvd* and *Howard St*, and began selling a dream. In 1878, he laid out a town on the south side of the river near the falls. In 1881, the first Northern Pacific train steamed along *Railroad Ave*, and Glover's dream become a real city.

The Spokane River became Spokane's industrial centre, dammed for electricity and hidden by the growing squalor of one of Washington's busiest rail centres. The polluted rail yards were demolished for the 1974 World's Fair. The Fairgrounds became 50-acre Riverfront Park. All that remains is a graceful 1902 clock tower that was part of the late and unlamented train depot.

Miles of paths wind through the shady park, attracting walkers and cyclists in all but the most inclement weather. Several of the original World's Fair attractions remain, including the open lattice of the US Pavilion, now an entertainment complex and wintertime ice skating rink, an **IMAX Theatre**; *tel: (509) 456-4386*, and the **Gondola Ride**; *tel: (509) 625-6600*, which runs from the west side of the park out over Spokane Falls and beneath the graceful **Monroe Street Bridge**.

Newer attractions include the 1909 Charles Looff **Carrousel**, restored to its original sparkle and colour, and *The Childhood Express*, a sculpture and children's slide in the shape of a giant **Radio Flyer** red wagon. The CVB's *Spokane Visitor Guide* has a park walking tour that includes 11 major pieces of public art. The **Spokane Opera House** and **Convention Center** are also part of the park; *tel: (509) 747-3230* for performance information.

Upstream water diversion has reduced Spokane Falls to a seasonal sight, but the falls still thunder late spring–early summer. Best viewing spots are the Gondola Ride (closed in winter and during inclement weather) or the **footbridge** directly over the falls (spray is drenching). Other prime spots are the second floor viewing deck at **Spokane City Hall**, *W. 808 Spokane Falls Blvd*, and **Washington Power's Huntington Park**, *accessible by a walkway from the S.W. corner of City Hall*, and the Monroe Street Bridge.

Miners, lumbermen, farmers, barkeepers, prostitutes, preachers and teachers followed the railroad to Spokane. A restaurant fire turned 32 square blocks to ash in 1889, but the city rebuilt within a year, fuelled by rich mining strikes in nearby Idaho and Kootennay, BC. Many fine brick and stone buildings from those ebullient years survive in the city centre, *Jefferson–Bernard Sts* and *First Ave–Mellon Ave,* north of the Spokane River.

One of the most scenic commercial streets is **Riverside Ave**, *Jefferson–Post Sts*. The red brick **Spokesman Review Building**, *W. 927 Riverside Ave*, completed in 1891, is a revered landmark with its five-storey tower. To the west are the Georgian Revival **Spokane Club** (1910), originally a male-only retreat, the romantic **Chamber of Commerce** (1933), the grand colonnade of the **Masonic Temple** (1905), the copper-roofed **Elks Club** (1919) and the French Empire **Smith Funeral Home** (now closed).

Local government buildings benefited from the same sense of optimism that fuelled commercial construction. **City Hall**, *W. 808 Spokane Falls Blvd*, is a recycled 1929 Montgomery Ward department store, the hand-painted art deco floral motifs disguising its stock design. Across the river, the 1895 château-style **Spokane County Courthouse**, *W. 1116 Broadway*, is the product of a local architect whose only training was a correspondence course.

Spokane's urge to beautify also produced more than 90 municipal parks and recreation areas. The largest is the 39-mile long Centennial Trail, a paved walking and cycling path that wanders through parks, forests and meadows along the Spokane River from Spokane east to the Idaho border, where it continues to Coeur d'Alene.

Coeur d'Alene Park, *across 2nd Ave from Fotheringham House*, with its towering oaks and lacy white gazebo, is Spokane's oldest public park. **Manito Park**, *S. Grand Blvd and 18th Ave; tel: (509) 625-6622*, offers an exquisite Japanese garden, a showy rose garden, tropical conservatory (especially popular in winter) and vast walking areas. Formal and perennial gardens flower May–Oct, the rose garden blooms June–Sept. **Finch Arboretum**, *3404 W. Woodland Blvd; tel: (509) 624-4832*, has 65 acres set with more than 2000 labelled ornamental trees, shrubs and flowers.

Calling Spokane the first White settlement in the Pacific Northwest stretches the truth only slightly. In 1810, Canadian-controlled North West Fur Company established **Spokane House** at the confluence of the Spokane and Little Spokane Rivers, now part of **Riverside Park**, *tel: (509) 456-3964*. **Spokane House Interpretive Center**; *tel: (509) 466-4747*, is open Wed–Sun mid May–Sept. The Spokane House site, with trading post walls marked by concrete posts, is open all year.

James Glover, like many of the city's first

nouveau riche, built a mansion on the hillsides south of town, *W. 321 Eighth Ave*, now a private building. Most of the city's élite preferred **Browne's Addition**, *5 miles W. of the city centre around W. Second Ave*. Patsy Clark's Mansion is open for diners and bar patrons, but anyone can visit **Cheney Cowles Museum & Historic Campbell House**, *2316 W. First Ave; tel: (509) 456-3931*, open Tues–Sat 1000–1700, Wed to 2100, Sun 1300–1700, $4 adults, $2.50 children. The 1898 mansion and original furnishings have been a museum since 1925. The dimly lit, richly carpeted and heavily draped upper-class world of the last century is a striking contrast to today's obsession with windows, light and natural ventilation. The museum has excellent displays on the history of the Inland Empire, particularly mining, timber and farming.

The **Crosby Student Center Library**, *Gonzaga University, E. 502 Boone Ave; tel: (509) 328-4220*, open daily Sept–Apr and Mon–Fri the rest of the year, celebrates local son Harry Lillis Crosby, who found fame, fortune and an Academy Award as baritone crooner Bing Crosby. Spokane's newest museum is the **Broadview Dairy Museum**, *W. 411 Cataldo at Washington St; tel: (509) 324-0910*. The 1897 building is packed with historical dairy equipment and a birdseye view down into one of the oldest continuously operating dairies in the Washington.

The dairy also houses **Caterina Winery**, *905 N. Washington; tel: (509) 328-5069*, Spokane's only in-town winery, on the ground floor. **Arbor Crest Wine Cellars**, *4705 N. Fruithill Rd; tel: (509) 927-9463*, has settled in its own historic building, the clifftop **Eagle's Nest**. The 1920s estate was created by Royal Riblet, inventor of the aerial tramway used by ski resorts around the world. The winery and broad picnic grounds overlooking the Spokane Valley far below are worth visiting even without the excellent red wines. **Latah Creek Winery**, *I-90 exit 289, 13030 E. Indiana; tel: (509) 926-0164; fax: (509) 926-0710*, sits in a charmless strip mall, but the Spanish-style winery produces the richest chardonnay, merlot and cabernet sauvignons in the region. The wineries are open daily for tours and tastings.

229

SPOKANE–BAKER CITY

The 325 miles between Spokane and Baker City cover some of the most unexpected scenery in the Pacific Northwest. Views run from urban Spokane through the sensuous hills of the Palouse, one of the richest agricultural areas in North America, down isolated mountain valleys to Hells Canyon, the deepest gorge on the continent, across remote ranches and arid mountains into the eastern Oregon desert. Drivers in a rush can accomplish the route in two mind-bending days with a stop near Enterprise, Oregon, missing scenery that has become enshrined in the American West. A more realistic timetable allows at least five days with overnights in Colfax, Clarkston, Enterprise/Joseph and Halfway.

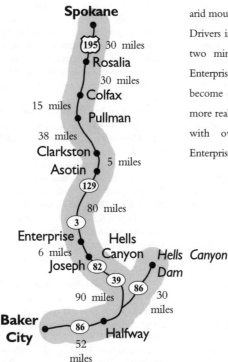

Spokane
195 — 30 miles
Rosalia
30 miles
Colfax
15 miles
Pullman
38 miles
Clarkston
5 miles
Asotin
129
80 miles
3
Enterprise **Hells**
6 miles **Canyon** *Hells Canyon*
Joseph 82 *Dam*
39
90 miles 86 30 miles
Baker 86
City 52 **Halfway**
miles

ROUTE: 325 MILES

ROUTE

Follow I-90 eastbound to Exit 279 and take Hwy 195 south. Forest slowly gives way to the undulating hills of the Palouse, dunes of wind-blown topsoil covered with an endlessly changing patchwork of wheat, barley, lentils and fallow fields.

The highway follows natural valleys past Spangle, **Rosalia** and Steptoe Butte to **Colfax**, Colton and Uniontown, then drops precipitously into the Snake River Canyon and on to **Clarkston**.

Take SR 129 south from Clarkston, following the Snake River to **Asotin**, then winding back up to plateau farmlands and Anatone. The highway climbs south of Anatone, crosses into Oregon to become SR 3 and drops into the

Wallowa Valley and the town of **Enterprise**. Take SR 82 six miles south to **Joseph** and 8 miles east to Forest Service Road 39, **Hells Canyon National Scenic Byway,** closed in winter.

The narrow road clings to 55 miles of near-vertical slopes, twisting through two major passes and a glimpse into **Hells Canyon** before reaching.SR 86. A 60-mile return sidetrack leads north to **Hells Canyon Dam**.

SR 86 continues south to the farming towns of **Halfway** and Richland, turns east to follow the Powder River through increasingly arid mountains and drops past the **Oregon Trail Interpretative Center** at **Flagstaff Hill** into Baker City.

SPOKANE TO ROSALIA

Hwy 195 runs through farms and forests in the **Hangman Valley**, named for the drumhead justice meted out to Native Americans during the close of the 1858 US Army campaign. The indefinable boundary between the forests of Spokane and the nearly treeless Palouse lies just south of **Spangle**, east of Hwy 195 on old SR 195.

From road level, the Palouse is a sea of low hills, flowing to the horizon in all directions. Even roads and fences undulate with the landscape, disappearing into *breaks,* valleys between hills, and reappearing in an entirely different direction.

The hills are dunes of *loess* – rich, wind-blown soil that accumulated up to 200 ft deep during the last Ice Age. The ancient dunes, too dry for forests but ideal for grass, stretch from the Spokane Valley south to the Snake River and from the Channeled Scablands east to the mountain pine forests of Idaho.

Native Americans prized the Palouse for its fine horse grazing and sheltered valleys. Fur trappers named the Nez Perce's spotted war horses *Appaloosa* for their home range.

Later settlers discovered that the same range grows some of the most bountiful crops of wheat, barley and lentils in North America. Fields are emerald green in spring, turning to gold as summer advances. Newly ploughed fields are black to tan, depending on rainfall, while winter drops a blanket of white.

ROSALIA

Tourist Information: Rosalia City Hall, *W. 106 5th St, Rosalia, WA 99170.*

Whitman St, the main street and old SR 195, is lined with prosperous houses, elegant Victorians and brick commercial buildings the better part of a century old. The **Rosalia Museum**, *106 5th St, Box 277; tel: (509) 523-5991,* open when the neighbouring · public library or city hall are open, has an eclectic collection of local memorabilia.

Rosalia is better known for the most resounding defeat of Army troops by Native Americans in the Northwest (see p.232). In May 1858, Lt Col Edward Steptoe left Fort Walla Walla headed for Colville with 158 dragoons. The force met 600–1200 Native Americans determined to teach the Army to stay out of territory guaranteed by the 1855 treaty. After a day of running skirmishes and steady casualties, Steptoe took refuge on a hill near Rosalia.

Realising his force couldn't survive another battle, Steptoe ordered a night-time retreat to the Snake River. The Native Americans, whose traditional warfare called for defeat, not annihilation, allowed the survivors to flee in disgrace. *Seventh St* leads east to the grey granite **Steptoe Monument**.

COLFAX

Tourist Information: Colfax Chamber of Commerce, *N. 612 Main St, Colfax, WA 99111; tel: (509) 397-3712.*

Siesta Motel, *S. Main and Thorn Sts; tel: (509) 397-3417,* budget, is the most comfortable motel in town.

SIGHTSEEING

Colfax is a bustling commercial hub with the first traffic signals south of Spokane. Vintage commercial buildings in brick and stone line *Main St.* The 1884 **Perkins Mansion**, open 1300–1700 Thur and Sun (June–Sept), or by appointment, has been refurbished by the **Whitman County Historical Society**, *N. 623 Perkins; tel: (509) 397-2555.*

The **Codger Pole**, *off N. Main St,* is a monument to the utter seriousness of high

Washington Indian Wars

Native Americans have lived throughout the Pacific Northwest for at least the last 10,000–13,000 years. Most were hunters and gatherers, moving with the seasons through well-defined territories that included fishing areas, hunting grounds, berry patches and bulb fields.

Some tribes travelled as far east as the Great Plains to hunt buffalo, trading hunting rights with Plains tribes for rights to harvest bulbs and berries west of the Rocky Mountains. Ownership of the land was irrelevant, but long-term use of its resources was life itself.

The White settlers, who began appearing in large numbers from the 1840s, had different ideas. They wanted absolute property rights for farming, timbering and mining, uses which usurped and destroyed the resources upon which Native Americans depended for their existence.

'We have no fear of Whites carrying rifles and swords', a Palouse chief reportedly told government officials in the 1850s, 'but we live in terror of your people who come with axes, shovels and plows'.

Washington Governor Isaac Stevens attempted to settle growing tensions with treaty negotiations at Walla Walla, near the Oregon border, in 1855. Stevens tried to force the chiefs into signing treaties relegating tribes to reservations far too small for their needs. A few chiefs refused to sign, but most accepted Stevens' terms in return for promises of cash payments and delays of at least two years to prepare for the move. Twelve days later, Stevens declared Indian Territory open for White settlement.

His deception turned simmering tensions into open revolt. The Yakima killed trespassing miners after a rash of horse thefts and rapes left unpunished by White authorities. Yakima Chief Kamiakin attempted to organise a Native American confederation to stop the invasions. To the North, Chilcotin warriors killed White surveyors laying a road from Bella Coola to the Cariboo. Haida, Tlingit and Tsimshian chiefs stepped up raids on the Puget Sound area. To the south, armed resistance sprang up along the Rogue River.

The US Navy sent a gunboat, the *Decatur*, and marines to Seattle in the autumn of 1855. After several pitched battles, Native American forces retreated east over the Cascades, ending most fighting west of the mountains. Sporadic fighting continued east of the Cascades, promoting the establishment of Forts Simcoe and Walla Walla.

Col George Wright built a temporary 'basket fort' of wicker baskets filled with earth and rocks near present-day Yakima, then marched up and down the eastern side of the Columbia Plateau in pursuit of Chief Kamiakin and hostages. Wright eventually marched his hostages to Fort Simcoe and declared the war over. It wasn't that simple.

In May 1858, miners near Colville demanded Army protection to prospect Native American lands, a clear violation of the 1855 treaty.

Col Edward Steptoe led a troop north through Yakima territory, another violation and provocation. Steptoe gave his name to a lone butte thrusting above the Palouse plain near Colfax (see p. 233), then marched to a crushing defeat at the hands of a combined force of Spokane, Coeur d'Alene, Palouse and other tribes near Rosalia (see p. 231).

Col Wright stormed out from Fort Dalles, on the Columbia River, to avenge Steptoe's loss. Armed with more modern rifles than either Steptoe or his foes, Wright defeated Native American forces near Four Lakes, west of Spokane, and again a few days later near the present Fairchild Air Force Base. He stunned Plateau Natives by capturing about 900 horses, then ordering his troops to choose 200 for their own use and slaughter the rest. A few brutally efficient drumhead hearings and summary executions later, Wright tersely, and correctly, declared the war to be closed.

school football. In 1938, the Colfax Bulldogs lost a crucial game to the St John Eagles, rivals from a smaller town. The loss so rankled that Colfax demanded a rematch on the same pitch – exactly fifty years later. The memorial pole, claimed to be the tallest chainsaw carving in the world, carries the 1968 likenesses of both teams, complete with spectacles, wattles and broken veins. The Bulldogs won the rematch.

Steptoe Butte, *9 miles north of Colfax off Hume Rd*, is the highpoint of the Palouse at 3192 ft. Named for Lt Col Steptoe, who climbed the hill to scout out the territory (as did his opponents), the butte is the tallest peak of an ancient mountain range. Lower peaks were buried by later eruptions of basalt lava that formed the Columbia Plateau. *Steptoe* has become the geological term for an older rock formation that protrudes through younger layers.

The road to the summit cuts through rippling fields of wheat to a small picnic area, then winds corkscrew fashion around the peak. The spectacular view from the top extends from Mica Peak south to the Blue Mountains in Oregon, west to the Rocky Mountains in Idaho and east across the Columbia Plateau. The long shadows of sunset and sunrise create panoramas that look too perfect to be real.

PULLMAN

Tourist Information: Pullman Chamber of Commerce, *N. 415 Grand Ave, Pullman, WA 99163; tel: (800) 365-6948 or (509) 334-3565; fax: (509) 374-5061, open Mon–Sat;* **Washington State University Cougar Center**, *in the former railway depot, N. 225 Grand Ave; tel: (509) 332-3232, open Mon–Fri.*

ACCOMMODATION

Pullman has the best lodging supply between Clarkston and Spokane. Chains include *BW, QI, Hd* and *S8*. Advance bookings are wise as University business and sport events attract crowds in every season.

SIGHTSEEING

Located just east of Hwy 195 on SR 270, Pullman spreads across five hills separated by three rivers. The city was named for George Pullman, inventor of the eponymous sleeping carriage, who gave city fathers his heartfelt thanks and $50 instead of a hoped-for endowment. A Pullman and caboose are on display at *N. 300 Grand Ave.*

Fine brick buildings line downtown streets, but the most important sight is **Washington State University**, **WSU** (pronounced WA-zoo), *Pullman, WA 99164; tel: (509) 335-3564*, which began as an agricultural college in 1892.

Several striking brick buildings remain, particularly **Bryan Auditorium and Thompson Hall**. Fifteen campus museums include one of the state's best collections of Columbia Basin artefacts and the largest fine arts collection east of the Cascades. *Cougar spoor,* emblems of WSU sport teams, the Cougars, are prominent all over town.

Campus tours are offered at 1300 Mon–Fri, *442 French Administration Bldg; tel: (509) 335-3581.*

Ferdnand's, *101 Food Quality Bldg; tel: (509) 335-2141*, operated by the WSU Creamery, may have the best ice-cream in the state.

Colton and **Uniontown**, twin farming communities near the southern edge of the Palouse, are notable mostly for their church steeples.

Civic rivalry was so fierce that the adjoining congregations of German-speaking Roman Catholics refused to co-operate in church-building. Colton even poached a convent from Uniontown to open a new school for the Colton faithful.

Don't miss the fine farming mural covering a building facing south on the way out of Uniontown. Hwy 195 joins I-95 just south of Uniontown and crosses into Idaho.

CLARKSTON

Tourist Information: Clarkston Chamber of Commerce, *502 Bridge St, Clarkston, WA 99403; tel: (800) 933-2128 or (509) 758-7712.*

ACCOMMODATION

Best value for money is the **Best Western Rivertree Inn**, *1257 Bridge St; tel: (800) 528-1234 or (509) 758-9551.* Other chains include *M6* and *QI.*

233

SIGHTSEEING

Clarkston, and its larger neighbour Lewiston, across the Snake River in Idaho, are major grain and timber ports 465 river miles from the Pacific Ocean. Both are named after the Lewis and Clark Expedition, which camped nearby. The most scenic approach is down *Lewiston Grade*, a 1917 auto road that drops 1700 ft in 10 miles of hairpin curves. The views from the frequent lay-bys are stunning. The easier but more boring approach is to follow I-95 into Lewiston, then turn west to Clarkston. Petrol is considerably cheaper in Clarkston than either Lewiston or Pullman.

Alpowai Interpretative Center, Chief Timothy State Park, *8 miles west on Hwy 12; tel: (509) 758-9112*, has an excellent museum and multimedia presentation on the Lewis and Clark Expedition, as well as pleasant camping and picnicking facilities. **Nez Perce National Historical Park**, *11 miles east on Hwy 95 S.; tel: (208) 843-2261*, concentrates on the Nez Perce, the major Native American tribe in the region. **Luna House Museum**, *3rd and C Sts, Lewiston, ID 83501; tel: (208) 743-2535*, covers local history from early days as a steamboat port for Idaho milesners.

Hells Canyon is just up the Snake River. Several operators offer boat trips into the canyon lasting from a few hours to several days. **Beamers Hells Canyon**, *1451 Bridge St; tel: (800) 522-6966 or (509) 758-4800*, is one of the largest canyon tour operators.

ASOTIN

Tourist Information: Asotin Chamber of Commerce, *Box 574, Asotin, WA 99402; tel: (509) 243-4411*.

The **Asotin County Museum**, *3rd and Fillmore Sts, Box 367; tel: (509) 243-4659*, is a fascinating local museum with historic buildings moved to the site and filled with a century's worth of bric-à-brac. The main building is a former funeral parlour, complete with embalming implements.

Chief Looking Glass Park, *on the river-front*, is home to the *Jean*, a 1938 sternwheel steamboat. Check the petrol tank: next fillup is Enterprise, 77 miles south.

Anatone is so small it passes in a blink, but watch for **Rattlesnake Summit**, 3965 ft, 4 miles south, and **Fields Spring State Park**, *Box 37, Anatone, WA 99401, 7 miles beyond*. Highlight of the park is **Puffer Butte**, a 4450-ft ridge rising 3000 ft above the Grande Ronde River. The 45-min walk up is steep in places, but the forest, meadow and canyon scenery are worth the effort. SR 126 twists down to river level south of the park, then climbs into Oregon to become SR 3.

ENTERPRISE

Tourist Information: Wallowa County Chamber of Commerce, *Wallowa Valley Mall, Box 427, Enterprise, OR 97828; tel: (800) 585-4121 or (541) 426-4622*.

The Chamber of Commerce publishes an all-inclusive *Lodging Guide* listing two dozen possibilities.

Enterprise is the commercial hub of Wallowa County, an area quiet enough and remote enough that it has neither traffic signals nor cellular telephone service. The Chamber publishes a walking guide to the town's many historic buildings, including the **County Courthouse, Enterprise Hotel, Oddfellows Hall** and several private homes.

The **Bookloft–Skylight Gallery**, *107 E. Main St; tel: (541) 426-3351*, across the street from the courthouse, is the best bet for local history, art and coffee.

JOSEPH

Tourist Information: Joseph Chamber of Commerce, *Box 13, Joseph, OR 97848; tel: (541) 432-6095*.

ACCOMMODATION AND FOOD

Most lodging is near Wallowa Lake, just south of town. **Wallowa Lake Lodge**, *60060 Wallowa Lake Hwy, Joseph, OR 97846; tel: (541) 432-9821; fax: (541) 432-4885*, moderate, an elegantly restored 1920s resort hotel, is the most comfortable choice. **Wallowa Lake State Park**; *tel: (541) 432-4185*, has 90 camping pitches and 121 RV sites.

Vali's Alpine Deli & Restaurant, *Wallowa Lake; tel: (541) 432-5691*, has exquisite Hungarian dishes, advance booking required. Top American choice is the **Wagon Wheel**, *500 N. Main St; tel: (541) 432-9300*, both budget–moderate.

SIGHTSEEING

The Wallowa Valley was the ancestral home of the Nez Perce, known for their fine horses, fierce independence and fighting skills.

White usurpation of the valley, guaranteed to the tribe by treaty, sparked the Nez Perce War in 1877 (see p.256). The town is named for Chief Joseph, the Nez Perce chief whose 1700 mile fighting retreat toward Canada is required study at war colleges around the world.

The scenic valley, hemmed in by mountains on all sides, is largely open rangeland, fields and scenic barns. Joseph has become an artistic centre, fuelled by 200 working artists and four bronze foundries. **Valley Bronze**, *307 W. Alder; tel: (541) 432-7551; fax: (541) 432-0255*, has regular tours. **Bronze Gallery of Joseph**, *603 N. Main St; tel: (541) 432-3106; fax: (541) 432-3789*, has an excellent selection of local bronzes and other art.

Manuel Museum, *Main St, in the centre of town, Box 905; tel: (541) 432-7235*, concentrates on John Wayne memorabilia and Native American history. The **Wallowa County Museum**, *W. 2nd and S. Main Sts; tel: (541) 432-6095*, an 1888 bank building, concentrates on White settlement days.

Wallowa Lake is a textbook example of a glacial lake, 280-plus-ft of mountain runoff trapped between the terminal and lateral moraines left by glaciers grinding down from the 10,000-ft Wallowa Mountains. **Old Chief Joseph**, father of the Nez Perce War chief, is buried just off SR 82 in the **National Indian Cemetery**, a traditional Nez Perce burial ground open to the public.

The lake is popular for swimming, fishing, boating, camping, hiking and horse riding. For the best view of the region, take the **Wallowa Lake Tramway**; *tel: 541-432-5331*, open May–Sept, 3200 ft up to 8150-ft Mt Howard. The panorama covers four states, 26 mountain peaks, glaciers, alpine rivers and the Snake River gorge.

HELLS CANYON

Tourist Information: Hells Canyon National Recreation Area, *88401 Hwy 82, Enterprise, OR 97828; tel: (541) 426-4978*, and **Hells Canyon Recreation Chamber of Commerce**, *Box 192, Oxbow, OR 97840*.

There are several campsites in the Hells Canyon NRA and the surrounding Wallowa-Whitman National Forest. Joseph, Oxbow, Halfway and Baker City offer motels and bed and breakfasts.

Hells Canyon is the deepest gorge in North America, more than 8000 ft from rimrock to river along the east side. **Hells Canyon Adventures**, *Box 159, Oxbow, OR 97840; tel: (800) 422-3568 or (541) 785-3352; fax: (541) 785-3353*, is one of many commercial operators touring the canyon by jet boat between Clarkston or Asotin and the Hells Canyon Dam at the south end of the gorge. There are no roads into the gorge, but a viewpoint 42 miles south of Joseph looks across to the Seven Devils Mountains in Idaho and 5400 ft down into the Canyon.

235

SIDE TRACK FROM HELLS CANYON

For a hint of the rugged splendour lying deep in the gorge, follow SR 86 north from the junction with FR 39 past Oxbow Dam to **Hells Canyon Dam**, built by Idaho Power in 1955. A visitor centre at the end of the road one mile downstream from the dam is open in summer. Picnicking and camping are available at parks adjacent to both dams.

HALFWAY

Tourist Information: Hells Canyon Chamber of Commerce, *S. Main St, Box 841, Halfway, OR 97834; tel: (541) 742-5722*.

The **Halfway Motel**, *Box 740; tel: (541) 742-5722*, is the best on the route east of Baker City. The top bed and breakfast is **Clear Creek Farm**, *Box 737; tel: (541) 742-2238*, a working buffalo and fruit ranch with a bucolic view across the well-watered valley and the surrounding mountains. Both are moderate.

PORTLAND–YAKIMA

The Washington side of the Columbia River Gorge is less-visited than the Oregon shore, but is equally scenic eastbound as great cliffs give way to golden crags and tableland mesas. The twists and turns of the Great River of the West are visible from high points along early sections of this 190-mile route. At Maryhill, the route leaves the river for rolling farmland to Goldendale, then through increasingly dry mountains and desert to Toppenish and Yakima. Allow a full day for the route, or pause at White Salmon, Goldendale or Toppenish.

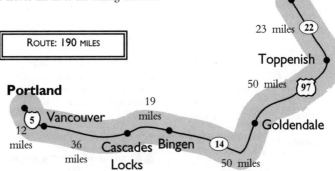

ROUTE: 190 MILES

ROUTE

Take I-5 from Portland north across the Columbia River to Exit 1B, Vancouver, Washington. Go east on SR 14, the **Lewis & Clark Hwy**, then north on US 97 to **Toppenish**. Follow SR 22 north-west to Yakima.

   Tourist Information: Columbia River Gorge National Scenic Area, USDA Forest Service, *902 Wasco Ave, Suite 200, Hood River, OR 97301; tel: (541) 386-2333; fax: (541) 386-1916.*

VANCOUVER

Tourist Information: Greater Vancouver Chamber of Commerce, *404 E. 15th St, Suite 11, Vancouver, WA 98663; tel; (800) 377-7084 or (360) 693-1313,* covers Vancouver, one of Washington's fastest-growing areas.

ACCOMMODATION AND FOOD

Chains include *BW, Hd, RI, TL* and riverside views at **Red Lion Inn at the Quay**, *100 Columbia St; tel: (800) 733-5466.* The 1903 **Vintage Inn**, *310 W. 11th St; tel: (360) 693-6635,* in downtown Vancouver, has bed and breakfast. **Sheldon's Cafe**, *1101 Officers Row, Grant House; tel: (360) 699-1213,* has budget–moderate lunch and dinner in a cheerful dining room. Budget **Little Italys Trattoria**, *901 Washington St; tel: (360) 737-2363,* has excellent pizza and lasagne.

SIGHTSEEING

Fort Vancouver National Historic Site, *from I-5 Exit 1C, east on Mill Plain Blvd, south on Fort Vancouver Way; tel: (360) 696-7655,* free, open 0900–1600, later in summer. Hudson's

Bay Company Fort Vancouver was once *the* British presence in the Northwest overseeing trade, diplomacy, defence and social life for more than 20 outposts in Washington, British Columbia, Oregon and Idaho. When the US-British boundary was fixed at the 49th Parallel in 1846, the shrewd, American-leaning chief factor, John McLoughlin, retired and moved to Oregon City, taking American citizenship.

A lush vegetable and flower garden marks the entrance to the reconstructed palisade and buildings. Rangers, sometimes in costume, guide visitors through the trading post, black-smithy and Chief Factor's Residence. Queen Victoria's birthday is still celebrated in May. Visit a fur trappers' encampment in mid June or the fort by candlelight in early Oct. Check with the visitor centre just north of the site for tour hours and special presentations.

The US Army eventually inherited Fort Vancouver. Twenty-one **Officers Row** buildings north-west of the HBC fort, built between 1850–1906, comprise **Fort Vancouver National Historic District**. Most of the balconied two-storey white buildings are legal or business offices. Stroll the tree-lined street to **Grant House Folk Art Center**, *1101 Officers Row; tel: (360) 694-5252,* named after US President Ulysses S Grant who was once the fort's quartermaster. Quilts decorate **Sheldon's Cafe** walls. Walk upstairs to see an exposed patch of original log construction and 19th-century wallpaper. The 1886 **Marshall House**, *1301 Officers Row; tel: (360) 693-3103,* housed Gen. George C Marshall of Marshall Plan fame.

East of the HBC Fort, **Pearson Air Museum**, *1105 E. 5th St; tel: (360) 694-7026,* open 1200–1700 Wed–Sun, has changing displays of vintage aircraft. In 1937, Soviet pilots completed the first non-stop transpolar flight in 63 hrs, 16 mins, landing at Pearson Airpark. **Chkalov Soviet Transpolar Monument**, *1109 E. 5th St,* commemorates the event.

Begin exploring a 4-mile **Waterfront Trail** along the Columbia River's north bank at the **Captain Vancouver Monument**, *foot of Columbia St,* which recalls his 1792 expedition. A pedestrian underpass leads to **Old Apple Tree Park** picnicking. A **Water Resources Education Center**; *tel: (360) 696-8478,* a

grassy marsh favoured by ducks, is east. Close by is **Kaiser Shipyard Memorial & Viewing Center**, a river overlook on the former site of Vanport, a housing and factory area flooded just after World War II.

VANCOUVER TO CASCADES LOCKS

From downtown Vancouver, turn east onto SR 14 from *Washington and W. 5th Sts.* Pass Fort Vancouver and the Pearson Air Museum. Cross I-205. The odour of Washington's first paper mill hovers heavy over **Camas**. **Camas-Washougal Chamber of Commerce**, *422 N.E. 4th, Camas, WA; tel: (360) 834-2472,* has information on the area. **Washougal** may be best-known for tours and discounts at the **Pendleton Woolen Mill**, *2 17th St, Washougal, WA 98671; tel: (360) 835-1118.* **Steamboat Landing Park**, on the right (south) side of SR 14, has excellent river views.

As the road ascends 3 miles east, enter the **Columbia River Gorge National Scenic Area**. Wooden signs mark main sights. Freight trains run regularly along both sides of the river. Just south on Reed Island, Lt William Broughton claimed the Columbia River for Great Britain in 1792, and naming Mt Hood (Oregon) for the Lord of the Admiralty; see p.203.

Eight miles from Washougal is spectacular **Cape Horn** overlook, green fields stretching east on a plateau above the twisting river. Five miles beyond, at milepost 30, turn right at **St Cloud**, cross the railway tracks and walk a pretty figure-eight trail through apple orchards and Himalayan blackberry brambles planted by a French-American family in 1909. Colourful wood ducks, osprey, tundra swans and beaver are found in **Franz Lake National Wildlife Refuge**, *milepost 31; tel: (509) 427-5208.*

Pass the white Skamania General Store and Beacon Rock Trailer and RV Park to **Beacon Rock State Park**, *milepost 35, SR 14, Skamania, WA 98648; tel: (509) 427-8265,* with camping. Hike an 0.8-mile multiple-switchback trail to the 848-ft basalt summit for wonderful Gorge vistas.

North Bonneville, *milepost 37,* is a residential area. **Bonneville Dam and Lock**, *US Army Corps of Engineers, Cascade Locks, OR*

237

97014-0150; tel: (541) 374-8820, (north side) is at milepost 39, marked by huge red and white high-tension towers along both sides of the river. The **North Shore Recreational Area** offers good views. A 1.4-mile drive leads to **Hamilton Island Recreation Area**, favoured by fishermen.

Bonneville Dam's two powerhouses, spillway and navigation lock span the river. Both shores have good visitor centres. The Washington shore 1982 **Second Powerhouse**, rated capacity 558,000 KW, routes visitors down to generator level. View a thrumming turbine shaft straight on, possibly the closest view of this sort of machinery to be had. Salmon and other species, most numerous in June and Sept, navigate fish ladders in the adjacent **Fish Viewing Building**.

Dam Access Rd goes to **Fort Cascades Historic Site and Trail**. In 1100 AD, a landslide created three rapids along 5 miles of the Columbia River. Oregon Trail pioneers portaged around the cascades. In the 1850s, the US Army built a portage road to supply its forts. In 1856, Lt Philip Sheridan's troops converged on Fort Cascades to bloodily quell a native attack on settlers and build additional forts.

Traditional native net fishing for salmon and sturgeon was eliminated by fish wheels which, by the late 19th century, had almost obliterated those species and were finally outlawed.

Steamboats plied the river using portage facilities to negotiate the fierce rapids. Muledrawn 'railways' were replaced by steam locomotives in 1863. Washington-side railways remained important until 1880, when the Oregon Railway & Navigation Company opened a route between The Dalles and the major north-western river city, Portland. Bonneville Dam's construction inundated the rapids and the last vestiges of Fort Cascades. East is the **Bridge of the Gods**, *Box 307, Cascade Locks, OR 97014; tel: (541) 374-8619,* a graceful 1928 span to Cascades Locks, ($0.75 toll). Park east of the bridge for a superb view of the place named after a natural stone arch that native legends say once spanned the river at the Upper Cascades. A suitors battle between Mt Hood and Mt Adams destroyed the bride, now 'collapsed in grief' at Adams' base.

CASCADES LOCKS TO BINGEN

Turn left at milepost 43 for **Skamania Lodge**, *1131 S.W. Skamania Lodge Dr., Stevenson, WA 98648; tel: (800) 424-4777 or (509) 427-7700,* cosy, expensive–pricey rooms and budget–pricey dining in a stone and wooden building with fine lobby views and a US Forest Service information centre. Golf and horse riding are popular. At the base of the hill, the **Columbia Gorge Interpretative Center**, *PO Box 396; tel: (509) 427-8211,* open 1000–1700, adults $6, children 6-12 $4, is an expensive museum featuring machinery and settler artefacts in a lovely wood beam and glass building.

Stevenson perches on SR 14 with services, an *EL*, delis, pizza and Mexican food. The **Skamania County Chamber of Commerce**, *PO Box 1037, Stevenson, WA 98648; tel: (800) 989-9178 or (509) 427-8911,* has area information. Narrated **Cascade Sternwheeler Riverboat** tours of the mid-Columbia River Gorge area, *1200 N.W. Front Ave, Suite 110, Portland, OR 97209; tel: (503) 223-3928,* depart from Cascade Locks, stopping at Stevenson mid June–Oct, adults $11.95, children 4–12 $5.95. **Carson** is 4 miles east on SR 14 at the mouth of the Wind River. To the north is the Gifford Pinchot National Forest and Mt St Helens. The **Columbia Gorge Motel**, *1261 Wind River Rd, Carson, WA 98610; tel; (509) 427-7777,* has moderate rooms. Book in advance for 1920's clawfooted bathtub luxury at **Carson Mineral Hot Springs Resort**, *# 1 St Martine Rd; tel: (800) 607-3678,* moderate–expensive.

Though much of the Columbia River Gorge's summertime world-class windsurfing is staged from Hood River, Oregon, Washington devotees swear by the 10 miles from **Home Valley** to Bingen. Cliffs are golden, craggy, with a few pinnacles. Spring wildflowers carpet **Dog Mountain Trail**. Windsurfers often launch from **Little White Salmon National Hatchery**; *tel: (509) 538-2755,* where the public can see chinook and coho salmon spawning May–Nov. Wooden remnants of **Broughton Lumber Co flume** remain at **Drano Lake**.

A series of five short tunnels gives onto

238

Spring Creek National Fish Hatchery, *61552 SR 14, Underwood, WA 98651; tel: (509) 493-1730*, a fine spot to see Tule autumn chinook ('white') salmon spawn in Sept. Golden hills and flattened tablelands await on the east side of the tunnels. **Underwood** is at the mouth of the White Salmon River. Hood River, Oregon, flanked by Mt Hood, is across a toll bridge. **Bingen**'s windsurfing equipment manufacturers attest to this windsurfing mecca. Named by early German settlers for a Rhennish city, Bingen retains a touch of alpine chalet architecture, mixed with restaurants. **Mont Elise Winery**, *SR 14; tel: (509) 493-3001*, has a tasting room in **Bingen Brewpub**. The **Gorge Heritage Museum**, *202 E. Humboldt; tel: (509) 493-3228*, open weekends May–Sept in a former church, has a replica country store and Klickitat Native American basketry.

BINGEN TO GOLDENDALE

White Salmon is just north on SR 141, the route to Mt Adams Wilderness. Riverview Savings Bank's 14-bell glockenspiels match the Rhine River settler tradition, but are controlled by computer. **Inn of the White Salmon**, *172 W. Jewett, White Salmon, WA 98672; tel: (800) 972-5226 or (509) 493-2335*, is a moderate–expensive historic bed and breakfast.

Chamberlain Lake Safety Rest Area, *milepost 7*, has a good overlook to the Eastern Gorge's stair-step formation. Cross the Klickitat River to **Lyle**, a small town with outstanding vegetarian sandwiches and rich coffee at **Mother's Marketplace**, *SR 14 in an old petrol station; tel: (509) 365-5600*, open Wed–Sat. Watch for raptors flying above the cliffs near **Doug's Beach (State Park)** a challenging windsurfing and kayaking area south of the railway tracks. Emus are sold at **Schreiner Farms**, near the **Dallesport** sign. The hamlet has an airport with cherry orchards surrounding a small dormitory community. To reach **The Dalles Dam**, follow the road south at milepost 83 to Oregon.

Basalt cliffs topped by grasses mark the entrance to **Horsethief Lake State Park**, *Box 734, Dallesport, WA 98617; tel: (509) 767-1159*, open Mar–Nov. Horsethief Butte rises above a Columbia River dam reservoir. Lewis and Clark's force portaged around the 'Great Falls' near this site, finding a place where tribes traded and socialised. Native American vestiges remain: a fenced cemetery with statues of braves and regalia adorning graves. The most famous symbol of the gorge, the petroglyph of big-eyed Tsagaglalal, 'She Who Watches', is up a trail that has been vandalised. For ranger-led rock art tours; *tel: (509) 787-1159*. There is picnicking and a few camping pitches.

Cattle graze the rangeland ahead. At milepost 93, Celilo Falls once cascaded dramatically, witnessed by Oregon Trail pioneers trying to go west down the river. The Dalles Dam inundated this fabled Native American gathering point and fishing spot in 1957. The railway town of **Wishram** nestles below.

Leave the **Columbia River Gorge National Scenic Area** at milepost 98. Turn right at milepost 99 to **Maryhill Museum of Art**, *35 Maryhill Dr., Goldendale, WA 98620; tel: (509) 773-3733*, open daily 0900–1700 Mar–Nov, adults $5, children $1.50. The museum began as the palatial home of Sam Hill, an ambitious highway engineer who founded a nearby Quaker colony in 1907. When the colony failed and Hill lost interest in living in Maryhill, friend Loie Fuller, an acclaimed Folies Bergère dancer, suggested turning it into a museum. Fuller's Parisian art contacts enabled Hill to purchase a fine collection of original Rodin sculptures. Queen Marie of Roumania and Alma Spreckels became Maryhill's chief benefactors. The museum also has an extensive collection of Native American art and artefacts.

Continue 2 miles east to US 97 and turn south (right) nearly to the Columbia River. Turn left toward **Maryhill State Park**, *50 Hwy 97, Goldendale, WA 98620; tel: (509) 773-5007*, with swimming, picnicking and 50 pitches, and the **Klickitat County Visitor Information Center**, *just outside the park; tel: (509) 773-4395*. Follow the river road 1 mile east through verdant fruit trees to the 1888 **Maryhill Community Church**, with its brilliant white steeple rising above the orchards. Turn left (uphill) through the farming village of Maryhill and up the canyon wall to **Stonehenge**, overlooking the Columbia River. Sam Hill built the concrete replica of Britain's

239

original stone calendar as a World War I monument. His own tomb lies just below. Continue uphill to SR 14, turn left (west) to US 97 and continue north toward Goldendale. A lay-by on the left, just beyond the crest of the road, offers a vivid panorama of the Cascades rising above verdant farmland. Mt Hood and Mt Adams, 50 and 45 miles distant, are visible most days; Mt St Helens and Mt Rainier, 75 and 80 miles away, are visible on clear days.

GOLDENDALE

Tourist Information: Goldendale Chamber of Commerce, *131 W. Court St, Goldendale, WA 98620; tel: (800) 648-5462 or (509) 773-3400; fax: (509) 773-4521.*

The budget–moderate **Far Vue Motel**, *Hwy 97 and Simcoe Dr.; tel: (800) 358-5881 or (509) 773-5881; fax: (509) 773-6216*, is excellent value. The budget **Main Street Cafe**, *120 W. Main St; tel: (509) 773-6919*, has solid American fare.

Goldendale Observatory State Park, *1602 Observatory Dr.; tel: (509) 773-3141*, open daily, has America's largest amateur-built telescope open for public use, a 24½-in reflecting Cassegrain. The observatory is open for tours during the day with slide shows and celestial viewing on clear nights. **Presby Museum**, *127 W. Broadway; tel: (509) 773-4303*, open May–Sept or by appointment, is a turn-of-the-century mansion fully furnished by the Klickitat County Historical Society.

Hwy 97 enters the Simcoe Mountains almost immediately north of Goldendale, climbing into conifer forests toward Satus Pass, 3104 ft, the boundary of the **Yakima Indian Reservation**. The land is noticeably drier on the north side of the pass, descending through increasingly sparse forest to sagebrush-covered hills and the Yakima Valley. **Toppenish National Wildlife Refuge**, *Pumphouse Rd, south of Toppenish*, offers good birding spring and autumn.

TOPPENISH

Tourist Information: Toppenish Chamber of Commerce, *A-11 S. Toppenish Ave, Toppenish, WA 98948; tel: (509) 865-3262*, has local information.

ACCOMMODATION AND FOOD

Moderate **Toppenish Inn Motel**, *515 S. Elm St; tel: (800) 222-3161 or (509) 865-7444; fax: (509) 865-7719*, has the best facilities. **Yakama Nation Resort RV Park**, *280 Buster Rd; tel: (800) 874-3087 or (509) 865-2000*, is among the better RV parks in the Yakima Valley. **Cattlemen's Restaurant**, *2 S. Division St; tel: (509) 865-5885*, specialises in steaks; **Villa Senor's**, *225 S. Toppenish Ave; tel: (509) 865-4707*, is Mexican, both budget–moderate.

SIGHTSEEING

Toppenish's dual claims to fame are three dozen fine **murals** depicting Native American and pioneer life in the area and the Yakama Nation. Self-guided mural tour brochures are available from the Chamber of Commerce; walking and horse-drawn tours are available; *tel: (509) 865-6516.*

Yakama Nation Museum, *280 Buster Rd; tel: (509) 865-2800*, is one of the country's few Native American museums created by Native Americans. **Toppenish Museum**, *1 S. Elm St; tel: (509) 865-4510*, open Tues–Sat, has its own Native American collections as well as cattle industry and other local history exhibits. The **American Hop Museum**, *22 S. B St; tel: (509) 865-4677*, open daily, traces the development of the hop industry in North America, focusing on the Yakima Valley, where hops remain a major crop. The **Yakima Valley Rail & Steam Museum**, *10 Asotin Ave; tel: (509) 865-1911*, occupies the historic brick railway depot. The museum operates weekend rail excursions to White Swan, 20 miles west, June–Oct. Seven miles beyond White Swan is **Fort Simcoe State Park Heritage Site**, *5150 Fort Simcoe Rd, White Swan, WA 98952; tel: (509) 874-2372*, open Wed–Sun (Apr–Oct) or by appointment, a restoration of the 1856 US Army Fort that played a key role in the Yakima Indian Wars.

Continue north on SR 22 to **Union Gap**, the original site of Yakima, and the **Central Washington Agricultural Museum**, *4508 Main St; tel: (509) 457-8735*, open daily 0900–1700, a hodgepodge of well-used agricultural equipment. Continue into Yakima.

YAKIMA–SPOKANE

It is possible to cruise across the Columbia Plateau in half a day, but the 200 miles of scenery and history deserve more. Beyond the fertile farming valleys surrounding Yakima and Ellensburg, Interstate 90 runs straight through endless wheat fields to bypass the heart of Washington. Side roads wander past cathedral-like cliffs down to the Columbia River, through the other-worldly Channeled Scablands and into farming towns that look more like 1900 than 2000. Allow a night in Ellensburg and another in Moses Lake before the final trek across flat fields to Spokane.

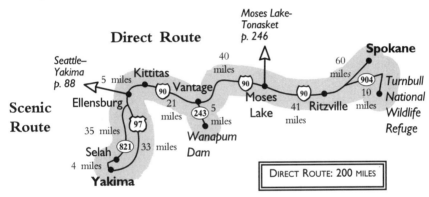

ROUTES

DIRECT ROUTE

Take I-82/Hwy 97 north from Yakima to **Ellensburg**. Follow I-90 east from the lush **Kittitas Valley** into the arid hills surrounding **Ryegrass Pass**, 2535 ft, to **Vantage**, on the Columbia River. Cross the river just above **Wanapum Dam**, then turn north past a striking ridge top sculpture and Columbia River vista points to **Moses Lake**. Continue east across the treeless plain to **Ritzville** and turn north-east. The first trees begin to appear near Sprague, growing thicker toward Spokane.

SCENIC ROUTE

From Yakima, follow I-82/Hwy 97 north to Exit 30A (a left-hand exit) to SR

823 N. and the town of **Selah**. Go 23 miles north on SR 821, following the Yakima River Canyon back to I-82/Hwy 97 to rejoin the direct route. Side-tracks near **Vantage**, George, **Moses Lake** and Cheney explore the dramatic countryside.

SELAH

Tourist Information: Selah Chamber of Commerce, *108 W. Naches Ave, Selah, WA 98942; tel: (509) 697-5545,* open Mon–Fri.

A Yakima name, Selah means 'calm and peaceful' for the gentle river current flowing south from the canyon above. The Yakima Nation once had a major salmon fishery in this quiet valley. Apples and apple juice are the mainstay today.

The **Yakima River Canyon**, *Bureau of Land Management, Wenatchee Resource Area*

Office, 1133 N. Western Ave, Wenatchee, WA 98801; tel: (509) 662-4223, is one of the most peaceful scenic areas in Washington. The Yakima River winds between arid basalt cliffs with rich meadows bordering the deep, swiftly flowing waterway. The river follows an ancient meandering course older than the cliffs. As the land was slowly lifted up by geologic forces, the river cut its way down, forming vertical drops. Try to make the drive in early morning or late afternoon when long shadows enhance the scenery.

The canyon is best known for trophy rainbow and cutthroat trout and the birds of prey that nest in the cliffs. Twenty-one types of raptors use the canyon, from resident golden eagles to migratory bald eagles which patrol the shallows in fall and winter for salmon. Yakima-born US Supreme Court Justice William O Douglas was largely responsible for turning the canyon into a recreation preserve. Rafting the calm waters is especially popular in the heat of summer.

The **Roza Dam** stores water to irrigate Yakima Valley fields. An adjacent recreation area offers easy river access as well as shaded picnic grounds. Other major access points are the **Squaw Creek Recreation Site** and **Umtanum Recreation Site**, both with picnicking, camping and river activities. The Cascades are visible through the north end of the Canyon 7 miles north of Umtanum.

ELLENSBURG

Tourist Information: Ellensburg Chamber of Commerce, *436 N. Sprague St, Ellensburg, WA 98926; tel: (509) 925-3137*, has extensive lists of lodging, restaurants, shopping, bookstores and other tourist resources.

ACCOMMODATION

The Chamber of Commerce has an inclusive list of local motels and bed and breakfasts. Most establishments are clustered around I-90 Exits 109 and 106. Best values for money are **Nites Inn Motel**, E*xit 109, 1200 S. Ruby; tel: (509) 962-9600*, and **Thunderbird Motel**, *Exit 106, 403 W. 8th Ave; tel: (800) 843-3492 or (509) 962-9856*, both budget–moderate. Chains include *BW* and *S8*.

EATING AND DRINKING

Fast food outlets are congregated near Exit 109, as are the cheapest petrol stations. In the historic city centre, **Palace Restaurant**, *323 N. Main St; tel: (509) 925-2327*, budget–moderate, serves traditional pancakes, sandwiches and steaks in a historic building. **Billy Mac's Juice Bar and Gallery**, *115 W. 4th Ave; tel: (509) 962-6620*, has the best local selection of juices and bagels. **Sweet Memories**, *310 N. Pearl St; tel: (509) 925-4783*, may be the best bakery for breakfast and lunch.

SIGHTSEEING

A failed contender for the state capitol (against Olympia and Yakima) in 1889, the busy farming and transportation hub of Ellensburg burned to the ground that July 4. The city promptly rebuilt in brick, creating the **National Historic District** that covers nearly the entire city centre, *3rd–6th Aves* and *Ruby–Main Sts*. The Chamber of Commerce has an outstanding self-guided walking tour brochure.

The splendidly turreted **Davidson Building**, *Pearl St and 4th Ave*, carries a 3-ft phoenix in bas relief commemorating the rebuilding. A former furniture store has become the **Kittitas County Historical Museum**, *114 E. Third St; tel: (509) 925-3778*, free, with extensive collections of petrified wood, blue agates and local artefacts. A Chamber of Commerce guide lists the best areas to search for blue agates, unique to the area.

The **Clymer Museum & Gallery**, *416 N. Pearl St; tel: (509) 962-6416*, open 1000–1700 Mon–Fri 1200–1700 Sat and Sun, $2, exhibits works of Western artist and native son John Clymer. The collection includes dozens of illustrations from the *Saturday Evening Post* and other magazines as well as oil paintings and changing exhibits of current north-western artists. Ellensburg's other gallery is **Dick and Jane's Spot**, *101 N. Pearl St*, across from the police station. The garden of the private home is filled with kinetic sculptures made of bicycle wheels and safety reflectors that move with the breeze, phantasmagorical mannequins, wild fountains and more 'yard art' by a changing group of about 35 Northwest artists.

In 1891, Ellensburg was awarded the Central Washington Normal School as a consolation for losing the capitol. The school has grown into **Central Washington University**; *tel: (509) 963-1111*, while retaining many of its original red brick buildings. The hottest ticket on campus is **Chimposiums**; *tel: (509) 963-2244*, $10, 1-hr public workshops with chimpanzees which have learned to use American Sign Language (ASL) to communicate with each other and with humans.

KITTITAS VALLEY

To reach **Olmstead Place Park**, *Rte 5, Box 2580, Ellensburg, WA 98926; tel: (800) 562-0990 or (509) 925-1943*, take I-90 north to Exit 115. Follow *Main St* to the end and turn left onto *Patrick Ave*. Follow signs for the park 2½ miles to *N. Ferguson Rd* and turn left again. The park, an 1875 homestead and farm built by the Olmstead family, is at the end of the road.

The original Olmstead cabin is furnished as an 1875–1890s home. A second cabin is furnished as a frontier school, one of its many uses. The bright red barn and the Olmstead's five-bedroom house date from 1908. Their 200-acre farm is still used primarily as a demonstration for period farming techniques.

VANTAGE

The tiny town, at I-90 Exit 136, on the east side of the Columbia River, has overpriced petrol and one of Washington's unique attractions, **Gingko Petrified Forest State Park**; *tel: (509) 856-2700*. The park protects an estimated 7500 petrified logs about 10 million years old. Included in the park are the only known examples of petrified gingko trees, which are cultivated widely in Asia but have disappeared from the wild.

The visitor centre, overlooking the river one mile north of the Vantage petrol stations, has excellent examples of petrified wood as well as a film and written explanation of the Ice Age floods that created today's Columbia Basin (see p.249). Just below the centre is a collection of petroglyphs rescued from the rising Columbia after it was dammed.

Follow the Vantage Hwy 2 miles east to the petrified forest section of the park, and a series

of walking paths through the dry hills. Nearly all of the visible logs have been encased in stone and steel cages, but the ¾-mile interpretative loop trail makes a pleasant walk. A 3-mile loop leads to more petroglyphs.

SIDE TRACK FROM VANTAGE

Wanapum Dam Recreation Area is just south of Vantage, with picnicking, camping and boating facilities.

Wanapum Dam and Heritage Center, *I-90 Exit 137* (west side of the Columbia River), *5 miles south on SR 243; tel: (509) 754-3541*, offers self-guided tours of the fish ladders, a fish viewing room to watch migrating salmon and a good Native American exhibit centred on the nearly-extinct Wanapum band for whom the dam was named. The Heritage Center also features the long history of steamboats on the Columbia River.

Grandfather Cuts Loose the Horses, a monumental steel sculpture, stands atop the Frenchman Hills on the west side of the Columbia just north of the crossing from Vantage. The outsized herd of rampant horses, spilling from an overturned basket and galloping down the ridge, depicts the origin of horses from local Native American legend.

Descendants of horses that escaped from early Spanish explorers in the Southwest actually came into the Pacific Northwest by trade from other Native Americans around 1700. The sculpture is best viewed from a lay-by on the east side of I-90, 3 miles east of Vantage. A steep path leads to the base of the installation.

Frenchman Coulee, *I-90 Exit 143*, leads to the old Vantage Hwy, now called *Silica Rd*, which disappears abruptly into the Columbia River 5 miles later. The scenic drive twists down a long-dry flood channel to the Columbia River, skirting soaring basalt cliffs and columns carved by raging Ice Age flood waters. Dozens of the basalt layers that form the Columbia Plateau are clearly visible, stark against the sagebrush

243

and greasewood that dot the dry coulee. The scenery is particularly stark and scenic in the deep shadows and rich light of late afternoon. Summer concerts are presented at a nearby outdoor amphitheatre. ▄

MOSES LAKE

Tourist Information: Moses Lake Chamber of Commerce, *324 S. Pioneer Way, Moses Lake, WA 98837; tel: (800) 992-6234* or *(509) 765-7888*, open Mon–Fri 0800–1200 and 1300–1600.

ACCOMMODATION

A recreational magnet, Moses Lake is well-supplied with motels and campsites. Chains include *BW, HI, M6, S8* and *TL.* The most comfortable choice is **Best Western Hallmark Resort**, *3000 Marina Dr.; tel: (800) 235-4255* or *(509) 765-9211; fax: (509) 766-0493*, moderate.

SIGHTSEEING

The biggest sight is **Moses Lake** itself, with three main arms more than 18 miles long and a mile wide, but just 30 ft deep. The lake lures boaters, birders and fishermen, who also flock to the **Channeled Scablands**, south of Moses Lake. The Scablands, irregular patches of basalt exposed by Ice Age floods sweeping west and south from Montana, look like rough scabs. In a sense, they are.

About 12,000 years ago, glaciers creeping down from Canada dammed the mouth of the Clark Fork River in Montana. More than 500 cubic miles of water, dubbed **Lake Missoula**, backed up behind the 2000-ft ice dam. When rising waters finally broke through, the entire lake drained in days.

Floods of Biblical proportions, repeated dozens of times until the ice sheets finally retreated north, thundered across the Columbia Plateau, ripping away topsoil and cutting deep canyons, called *coulees* by the French-Canadian trappers who first reported them, into the bedrock.

The torrents washed west to the Cascades near Wenatchee and into the Yakima Valley, then crashed against the Horse Heaven Hills and rebounded east through the Wallula Gap.

Something of the order of ten times the volume of all the rivers of the world raged down the Columbia River, laden with soil, gravel and icebergs carrying building-sized boulders. The floods turned south into the Willamette Valley near Portland, dropping rich loads of topsoil as the speed abated and the water flowed back to the Columbia and out to sea.

These days, thunder is more likely to be Boeing 747s and other jumbo jets practising at **Grant County Airport**, *SR 17 north of downtown*. Built as a World War II Air Force base, the airport is a training facility for Boeing aircraft pilots from around the world and Japan Air Lines' flight school.

Adam East Museum & Art Center, *122 W. Third Ave; tel: (509) 766-9695*, open 1200–1700 Tue–Sat, free, is the town's official history museum. Its unofficial counterpart, **The House of Poverty**, *Moses Lake Iron and Metal, Box 448; tel: (509) 765-6342*, open 0900–1700 Mon–Fri, free, is an eclectic collection of memorabilia by a former hobo who founded the hugely successful **Moses Lake Iron and Metal**. The collection includes several major railway carriages, including a 1915 private carriage used by US presidents.

> ↻ **SIDE TRACK**
> **FROM MOSES LAKE**
>
> The Scablands south of Moses Lake have turned to lakes and marsh, much of it protected in the **Columbia Basin National Wildlife Refuge**, *735 E. Main St, Othello, WA 99344; tel: (509) 488-2668*. An excellent driving tour by the Central Basin Audubon Society and the Grant County Tourism Commission includes velvety green irrigated farmlands, a desert wildlife area and a Scablands section called Potholes Reservoir. Best map for the self-guiding tour is *Grant County Day Tours*, free at area tourist offices.
>
> The full 80-mile route runs from Moses Lake west on I-90, south on *Dodson Rd* to *Frenchman Hills Rd*, east to SR 262 and *Road M*, and north to I-90. Allow at least 2 hrs. A short section of the route is unpaved, but the gravel road is in excellent condition.

Scenery and wildlife are at their best early–mid morning and mid–late afternoon.

RITZVILLE

Tourist Information: Ritzville Chamber of Commerce, *Box 122, Ritzville, WA 99169; tel: (509) 659-1930.*

Once the largest wheat shipper in Washington, Ritzville is now a living time capsule from the early years of the 20th century. Wheat remains the chief crop, but modern farming requires only a fraction of the labour force once needed. Cattle graze the poorer, rocky soil of the Channeled Scablands nearby.

Take Exit 220 or 221 to the old downtown, near the railroad tracks. Formerly busy streets are still lined with graceful brick commercial buildings and gracious homes. The 1889 **Dr Frank Burroughs Home**, *408 W. Main St; tel: (509) 659-1936*, built by a prosperous physician, is now a historical museum. The 1907 **Carnegie Library** is next door. The salmon pink brick **Leonard Mansion**, *Fifth*

and Adams Sts, a private residence, is one of the most imposing homes in the area.

SIDE TRACK TO TURNBULL NATIONAL WILDLIFE REFUGE

Take Exit 257, SR 904, 10 miles toward Cheney. Turn right onto *Cheney-Plaza Rd* and then onto *Smith Rd* and the **Turnbull National Wildlife Refuge**, *S. 26010 Smith Rd, Cheney, WA 99004; tel: (509) 235-4723*. A 5-mile auto tour and several miles of walking paths explore the rich mosaic of small ponds, wet meadows, basalt outcroppings and dry uplands typical of the Channeled Scablands. The area is a transition zone between Ponderosa pine savannah and bunch grass plains typical of the dryer Columbia Plateau farther west. Two hundred different bird species are regular visitors, primarily during spring and autumn migrations.

245

MOSES LAKE–TONASKET

Visual changes between Moses Lake and Tonasket are dramatic, from Columbia Plateau tableland to the cliff-sided string of canyon lakes that was once the Columbia River, densely forested mountains and Okanogan Valley apple orchards. But more travellers are fascinated by the engineering magic of Grand Coulee Dam and the graves of Chiefs Moses and Joseph than the splendid scenery. Both chiefs are buried on the Colville Indian Reservation, the largest timber stand under Native American ownership in America. The 170-mile drive can be accomplished in three hours, but deserves at least two days with an overnight near Grand Coulee Dam.

246

ROUTE: 170 MILES

Tonasket

97 16 miles

Omak

Everett–
Omak
p. 259

155 63 miles

Grand Coulee Dam

36 miles

155

30 miles   **Coulee City**

17

Soap Lake

6 miles 28

Ephrata

19 miles 17

Moses Lake

Everett–
Omak
p. 259

ROUTE

Follow SR 17 north 14 miles from Moses Lake, past the Grant County Airport to SR 282. Continue 5 miles to **Ephrata** and SR 28. Take SR 28 6 miles north-east to SR 17 at **Soap Lake**. Follow Grand Coulee, an Ice Age channel of the Columbia River, north past a series of small lakes to **Dry Falls**, once the largest waterfall on earth. Just north of Sun Lakes State Park, take Hwy 2 east to **Coulee City**, then turn north and follow SR 155 for 26 miles along the shores of Banks Lake, past Steamboat Rock, to the tri-towns of Electric City, Grand

Coulee and Coulee Dam, surrounding **Grand Coulee Dam** itself.

Follow SR 155 north into the Colville Indian Reservation, passing the graves of Chief Moses (near the Colville Indian Agency) and Chief Joseph (in Nespelem). The highway climbs through farmland and forest to Disautel Summit, then drops into the Okanogan Valley at **Omak**. Turn north on Hwy 97/SR 20 for the final 16 miles to Tonasket.

EPHRATA

Tourist Information: Ephrata Chamber of Commerce, *Box 275, Ephrata, WA 98823; tel: (800) 345-4656 or (509) 754-4656.*

According to Native American legend, Ephrata and the surrounding Quincy Basin was once a lake. The legends are correct: repeated Ice Age floods deposited 25 cubic miles of Columbia Plateau earth in the valley, leaving rich, deep soil. Vast herds of wild horses grazed the area when White settlers arrived in the 1880s. Later arrivals fenced the open grassland for farming.

Competition between farmers and horses for water and land prompted Washington's final wild horse roundup in 1906 near Ephrata. Three hundred cowboys roped 5000 horses and drove them to the south end of the valley. Most of the horses died along the way from lack of food and water; many of the survivors were sold to glue and tinned beef factories; some were shipped by rail to new ranges in Montana. The **Last Roundup** is a source of local pride, but a persistent legend tells of a fiery white-maned stallion that kicked his way from a box-car and led a tiny band of horses back into the wild, where their descendants still roam the back country. The rearing stallion statue at the **Grant County Pioneer Village & Museum**, *742 Basin St N.; tel: (509) 754-3334*, open 1000–1700 Mon–Sat, 1300–1600 Sun, closed Wed (May–Sept), $2, is a tribute to the myth. The museum also has extensive collections of artefacts and photographs from prehistoric times to the 1930s. A 28-building village includes authentic saloons, blacksmithy, barbers shop and a bank; admission includes a village tour.

SOAP LAKE

Tourist Information: Soap Lake Chamber of Commerce, *Box 433, Soap Lake, WA 98851; tel: (509) 246-1821.*

Soap Lake was a favourite camping, healing and recreation spot for Native Americans, who valued the shallow 2-mile long lake for its healing waters. High concentrations of minerals cause the water to form a white soap-like lather in high winds, an effect much diminished since the advent of large scale agricultural irrigation.

Early White explorers, cattle drovers and settlers sampled the waters and liked the results. The salty waters gained local fame for curing everything from lice and ticks on cattle to human scrofula and stomach upsets. The water *does* soothe many irritating skin conditions and stomach ulcers, but it is also a powerful laxative. Fortunately, the salty, bicarbonate of soda taste discourages more than casual tasting from the public fountain downtown.

Soap Lake is the southern-most of a chain of lakes lining **Grand Coulee**, a deep 25-mile gorge cut by the Columbia River during the last Ice Age. The canyon road is scenic but slow. Towering cliffs of basalt columns widen to form **Lake Lenore**, 6 miles north of Soap Lake.

Lake Lenore Caves Historical Area, *north side of SR 17*, protects caves ripped high in the canyon walls by ancient floods and later used by Native Americans. The caves, at the end of a ¼-mile walking path, are now home to bats and swallows.

Just north of Lake Lenore is aptly-named **Alkali Lake**. **Blue Lake** is famed for the lava cast of an ancient rhinoceros found nearby in 1935. **Sun Lakes State Park**, *7 miles south-west of Coulee City; tel: (509) 632-5583*, has 193 pitches as well as extensive water recreation facilities. SR 17 climbs from lake level near the park to the head of Grand Coulee and **Dry Falls Visitor Center**; *tel: (509) 632-5214.*

Dry Falls separates upper and lower Grand Coulee. The great plunge, 400 ft deep and 3½ miles wide, was probably the greatest waterfall on earth. During the Ice Age, glaciers advancing south from Canada blocked the Columbia River, forcing it into what is now Grand Coulee. Other glaciers formed **Lake Spokane** and **Lake Missoula**. When the ice dams broke – every 55 years on average – flood waters poured west into the Columbia, turning the river into a torrent raging south toward a massive waterfall at Soap Lake.

The repetitive floods gouged the river course into Grand Coulee, 900 ft deep and up to 6 miles wide, as the cataract retreated up-stream. When the glaciers finally retreated, the Columbia returned to its present channel, the flooding ceased and Dry Falls remained. Rough

247

roads, passable by passenger vehicles but not recommended for RVs, lead upstream from Sun Lakes to smaller lakes near the base of the falls. The falls are also visible from the Visitor Center, which houses an excellent geological museum. A shaded picnic area is crowded in summer. The gleaming grain elevators of Coulee City are visible to the north.

COULEE CITY

Tourist Information: Coulee City Chamber of Commerce, *Box 896, Coulee City, WA 99115; tel: (509) 632-5713.*

This former junction for railway and stagecoach lines across the Columbia Plateau flourished by deliberately mismatching timetables, forcing travellers to spend the night in local hotels. It became a thriving construction town during the building of the Columbia Basin Project (see p.249). Hwy 2 crosses Banks Lake atop the Dry Falls Dam shortly before the SR 155 junction.

Steamboat Rock State Park, *Box 370, Electric City, WA 99123; tel: (509) 633-1304,* sits at the base of Steamboat Rock, an ancient Columbia River island that now rises from Banks Lake. Steamboat Rock was a landmark for Native American travellers; today it's a landmark for pilots in training at Moses Lake and other airports. The park has 100 pitches, extensive picnic areas, swimming and boat ramps. The setting is spectacular, with towering basalt columns and treeless canyon rims reflected in the waters below. There are numerous lay-bys, all on the west (left) side of the road. A steep trail leads to the flat top of the 700-ft rock and expansive views in all directions.

GRAND COULEE DAM

Tourist Information: Grand Coulee Dam Area Chamber of Commerce, *306 Midway* (next to Safeway), *Box 760, Grand Coulee, WA 99133; tel: (800) 268-5332 or (509) 633-3074,* has information on Grand Coulee Dam, and Coulee Dam, Electric City and Grand Coulee.

Because most visitors come to the dam on day trips, there is relatively little lodging in the area. **Four Winds Guest House**, *301 Lincoln St, Coulee Dam, WA 99116; tel: (800) 786-3146 or (509) 633-3146,* is an excellent bed and breakfast in a restored dam engineers' residence. The area's few motels are on SR 155.

Grand Coulee Dam harnesses the Columbia River for irrigation, electrical power and flood control. Claimed to be the largest concrete structure on earth, the dam is 550 ft high, 500 ft wide at its base and 5223 ft long. A road atop the dam is open to the public.

An irrigation dam at Grand Coulee was proposed as early as 1918. When the US government decided to build the project in 1930 electrical power demand in the Northwest was negligible. The three towns surrounding the dam were born as construction camps. An immense sand pile north-east of Coulee Dam is left over from the construction project, which began in 1933 and ended in Sept 1941, three months before the US entered World War II. Nearly the entire power output of the dam was directed to aluminium smelters, Boeing aircraft plants, shipyards and other wartime projects around Puget Sound. The Chamber of Commerce publishes a self-guided walking tour of Coulee Dam. The dam itself is open for tours daily. A free **Visitor Center**; *west bank below the dam; tel: (509) 633-9265* is open daily 0830–2200 May–Sept, 0900–1700 the rest of the year. The most impressive vistas are from atop the dam looking down the spillways and from the viewing balcony of Powerhouse #3 on the east side of the river. The Powerhouse #3 tour offers the best look at how the dam was built and how electrical power is generated.

A narrated **laser light show** plays on the face of the dam nightly May–Sept. Music, narration and moving images from Native American legend and dam building explain the purpose, construction and impact of the dam. The closest viewpoint is the seating area and lawns around the Visitor Center, which has an outdoor sound system. Other popular spots are across the river below the **Coulee House Motel** and from the clifftop **Crown Point State Park**, *SR 174 west of the river.* The soundtrack is broadcast on radio at 89.9.

Coulee Dam Casino, *515 Birch St; tel: (800) 556-7492,* is run by the Colville Confederated Tribes, an amalgamation of the remnants of eleven Native American groups from the region. The **Colville Confederated**

The Columbia Basin Project

Grand Coulee Dam is the centrepiece in a vast and confusing irrigation scheme called the Columbia Basin Project, or CBP. The confusing part: the scheme involves two great reservoirs, Banks Lake and Lake Roosevelt. But Lake Roosevelt, which stretches 150 miles up the Columbia River to Canada, doesn't water a single CBP field.

CBP irrigation water flows south from Banks Lake, created by damming Dry Coulee, the Columbia River channel, during the last Ice Age. Once the Columbia resumed its normal looping course, Dry Coulee became an empty canyon stretching 25 miles south to Dry Falls and Soap Lake. Dry Coulee was sealed by the Dry Falls Dam at Coulee City. Electricity from Grand Coulee Dam pumps water from Lake Roosevelt into Banks Lake via six enormous pipes. From Banks Lake, water is piped to fields lying to the south.

The scheme was born in the 1880s and 1890s, when railroads lured thousands of farmers to the Columbia Plateau with promises of rich soil and bumper crops. The promises were half-met. The soil is rich. In wet years, crops prospered in the long, sunny growing season. But when rainfall dropped below the 6–10 ins annual average, crops withered and farmers went bankrupt. Farmers, bankers and local newspapers began pushing for a grand irrigation scheme following World War I. In the 1930s, the US government signed on, both to create jobs badly needed during the Great Depression and to boost farming in the region.

Grand Coulee Dam began producing power and pumping water up to Banks Lake in 1941. A decade later, irrigation water began flowing south across the Columbia Plateau through 2300 miles of canals. What had been rich, if unreliable, farmland has blossomed into spreading fields of wheat, maize, mint and more than 50 other crops stretching for more than 100 miles. Plans call for the irrigated area to double to 1.2 million acres sometime in the next century.

Tribes Museum, *512 Mead Way; tel: (509) 633-0751; fax: (509) 633-2320*, has an excellent collection of tribal artefacts and a poignant rendition of local history from the Native American perspective. The Confederation is based at the **Colville Indian Reservation**, with headquarters at the **Colville Indian Agency**, just south of **Nespelem**, 19 miles north on SR 155. Chief Moses, chief of the Sinkiuse band who resisted White settlement of the Columbia Plateau, is buried beneath a plain grey marble headstone in a cemetery just south of the Agency offices. Nez Perce Chief Joseph (see p.256) lies in a hilltop cemetery at the north end of Nespelem, with a single tree shading his grave and white marble obelisk. The only ornamentation is a bas relief of the Chief looking south-east toward the Wallowa Valley. Both graves are surrounded by beads, flowers, feathers and other offerings.

SR 155 continues through the dense forests of the reservation over the **Disautel Summit**, 3252 ft, and down to the Okanogan Valley and Omak (see p.262).

TONASKET

Tourist Information: Tonasket Chamber of Commerce, *Box 523, Tonasket, WA 99955; tel: (509) 486-2154.*

The best lodging selection is just south in Omak/Okanogan (see Everett–Omak route pp.262–263). Local choices include the **Red Apple Inn**; *tel: (509) 486-2119*, and **The Bunkhouse Motel**; *tel: (509) 486-4500*, both budget–moderate.

Tonasket is named after a Native American chief who gave up rights to land where the town stands in return for cash and a school on the Colville Reservation.

This tiny town is an apple growing centre as well as headquarters for the **Okanogan National Forest Tonasket Ranger District**, *1 W. Winesap; tel: (509) 486-4429*. The 1.7-million acre National Forest includes several wilderness areas. There are more than 200 miles of hiking trails within the Tonasket District alone, which was once part of the Colville Indian Reservation.

SPOKANE–OSOYOOS

The northern tier of Washington, often called *Panorama Country* for the vast mountaintop vistas, is the most isolated section of the state. Three river valleys, the Pend Oreille,

ROUTE: 275 MILES

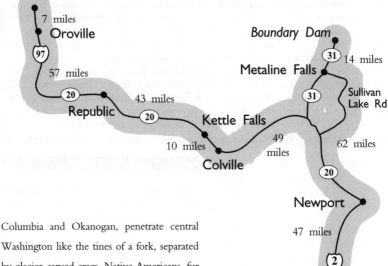

Columbia and Okanogan, penetrate central Washington like the tines of a fork, separated by glacier-carved crags. Native Americans, fur trappers, gold miners and cattle drovers used the valleys as highways, but seldom braved the rugged mountain ranges that still defeat most east–west roads.

This twisting 275-mile itinerary is the northern-most route spanning all three valleys. The drive can be accomplished in two days, but allow at least three days to sample the splendid vistas, dense forests and historic towns that few Washingtonians ever see.

Newport on the Pend Oreille River, Colville near the Columbia River, and the mountain mining town of Republic are convenient stopping points. There are numerous campsites en route.

ROUTE

From central Spokane, take *Division St* north, which becomes Hwy 2 as it runs up the Spokane Valley, past **Mt Spokane State Park** on the way to **Newport**, on the Pend Oreille River. Cross the river into Idaho and immediately turn north (left) onto *Leclerc Creek Rd,* which crosses back into Oregon.

Follow the Pend Oreille east shore of the 33 miles north through the **Kalispell Indian Reservation**, squeezed between the river and the trackless mountains of the Pend Oreille National Forest, to *Sullivan Lake Rd.*

Turn east (right) past the scenic shoreline of **Sullivan Lake** and down to the almost-ghost town of **Metaline Falls**. A side-track leads north to **Boundary Dam** and the **Gardner Caves** on the Canadian border.

Follow SR 31 south along the Pend Oreille through **Ione** to **Tiger**. Turn west (right) onto SR 20 through the **Selkirk Mountains** to **Colville**, **Kettle Falls** and the **Columbia River** (flooded by Grand Coulee Dam to form Lake Roosevelt).

The highway climbs into the Kettle River Range and through **Sherman Pass**, the highest pass open all year in Washington, to **Republic**, in a narrow valley.

Climb back up to **Wauconda Summit**, then drop down to **Tonasket**, in the **Okanogan Valley**. Follow Hwy 97 north along the Okanogan River through rich fruit orchards to **Oroville**, the **US-Canadian border** and **Osoyoos**.

SPOKANE TO NEWPORT

Follow *Division St*, Hwy 2/395, north from downtown Spokane through ever-expanding shopping malls and housing estates into the more rural **Spokane Valley**. At the division of Hwys 2 and 395, keep right to follow Hwy 2 north 4 miles to **Mt Spokane State Park**, *Box 336, Mead, WA 99021; tel: (509) 456-4169,* 20 miles east on SR 206. The 16,000-acre park includes Mt Spokane, 5851 ft, and Mt Kit Carson, 5306 ft. There are only 12 camping pitches, but the park is enormously popular in winter and summer.

A twisting summit road ends near **Vista**

House, a former fire lookout, with 360° views from the Selkirk Mountains in British Columbia and Washington to the Bitterroot Range in Idaho and south to Oregon. The road up passes from semi-arid prairie and Ponderosa pine into wetter alpine zones laced with walking trails, picnic areas and lay-bys at almost every turn. Alpine and Nordic ski areas are open in winter.

The final 7½ miles from the campsite to the summit are steep and winding, not advised for large RVs.

Hwy 2 continues north through gentle lodgepole pine forests and open farmland. **Pend Oreille County Park** (pron: pend o-ray), *22 miles north of SR 206,* and **Diamond Lake**, *4 miles beyond,* are popular spring–autumn getaway spots for Spokanites with walking, picnicking, camping and fishing.

NEWPORT

Tourist Information: Newport-Oldtown Chamber of Commerce, *322 S. Washington Ave, Box 1795, Newport, WA 99156; tel: (509) 447-5812,* open 0900–1700 Mon–Sat.

ACCOMMODATION

The Chamber of Commerce has a list of accommodation in the area. **Golden Spur Motel**, *924 W. Hwy 2; tel: (509) 447-3823,* budget–moderate, is the best value.

SIGHTSEEING

Newport began life in the 1880s as Newport, Idaho, on the Pend Oreille River. When the Great Northern Railway set up an ore and timber depot 3175 ft away in Washington, the post office and most other buildings moved west. The smaller Idaho section is now called Oldtown.

Hwy 2, *Washington Ave*, is the main street, lined with graceful brick commercial buildings. **Centennial Plaza Park**, *south end of Washington Ave*, has the Chamber of Commerce, a fine old steam engine and a pair of historic railway depots.

The 1910 **Great Northern Depot** is now a lumber company office. The 1908 **Idaho Washington Northern Depot** has become the **Pend Oreille County Historical**

251

Museum, *402 S. Washington Ave; tel: (509)* 447-5388, open daily 1000–1600 May–Sept.

Hwy 2 continues east into Idaho. Immediately past the river, turn left onto *Leclerc Creek Rd*, a scenic, seldom-travelled road along the east bank of the river. Parts of the road are gravel, but in excellent condition.

There are many pleasant views west across the river, lined with rotting pilings once used to moor log rafts and now favourite nesting sites for ospreys. The largest concentration of pilings lies between **Dalkena**, **Usk** and **Cusick**, former railroad and logging towns on the west side of the river. Mills specialised in turning forest giants into matchsticks.

Tours of the **Kallispel Indian Reservation**, Box 39, *Usk, WA 99187; tel: (509) 445-1147*, can be booked in advance; the tribe's free 37-page book, *The Kallispels: People of the Pend Oreille*, explains local history.

The band has its own commercial buffalo herd, often visible from *Leclerc Rd*. Native to the plains east of the Rocky Mountains, buffalo are increasingly popular in the Northwest. North America's largest grazing animal is much hardier than cattle, needs fewer expensive feed supplements and produces leaner, tastier meat.

The **Manresa Grotto**, a natural cave near the 1914 blue-and-white **Our Lady of Sorrows** chapel, has been a place of worship since Father Pierre-Jean DeSmet celebrated mass there in 1844. Easter Mass is still held in the cave, named after a famous grotto near Barcelona, Spain. The car park is just beyond the chapel on the east (right) side of the road.

Sullivan Lake, 3½ miles long and 275 ft deep, fills a glacial canyon. The 6222-ft slopes of Hall Mountain are reflected in the still waters of the lake. Look for mule deer and Rocky Mountain Big Horn sheep on the steep slopes opposite the road.

METALINE FALLS

Tourist Information: Metalines Community Library, *302 Park, Metaline Falls, WA 99153; tel: (509) 446-3232.*

Leclerc Valley Rd passes a 1910 **Mill Pond** two miles north of Sullivan Lake. The pond fed a flume that dropped 470 ft to a hydroelectric powerhouse that supplied Metaline Falls and

the town's *raison d'être*, a now-closed cement factory. The flume washed out in an April, 1956 storm, but the millpond remains. A flat 0.6-mile interpretative loop recounts early area history.

The town of Metaline Falls stands at the foot of the hill. The cement plant remains, as do most of the brick buildings from the once-busy town.

Residents were once known for having the cleanest cars in Washington. They had to wash their cars every few days to prevent dust from the plant building up and turning into an impenetrable coat of cement at the next rain.

Katie's Oven, *in the Washington Hotel, 225 E. 5th St; tel: (509) 446-4806*, is the best bakery in the area.

⚡ SIDE TRACK FROM METALINE FALLS

Follow SR 31 10 miles north from Metaline Falls and turn west (left) onto *East Side Access Rd* for **Z Canyon** and **Boundary Dam**.

The canyon, 18 ft wide and 400 ft deep, squeezes the Pend Oreille into a foaming torrent. The dam, proposed by Seattle Light and Power in 1914 but not built until 1967, matches every stereotype of a mountain canyon dam, 340 ft tall and spanning a narrow, twisting canyon.

The rest of the installation could be a James Bond film set, a rough-hewn tunnel that dives nearly 500 ft into the canyon wall ending in a glassed-in viewing area overlooking the throbbing powerhouse.

The viewing area is open most days; free dam tours are offered 1030–1630 Thur–Mon May–Sept.

Crawford State Park and **Gardner Cave**, *Metaline Falls, WA 99153; tel: (509) 446-4065*, are 1½ miles beyond the dam. The limestone cave, discovered in 1899 by a bootlegger, is over 1000 ft long. Guided tours explore the upper 494 ft of the cave, festooned with stalactites, stalagmites and other natural ornaments.

Return via SR 31 or continue south on the west bank of the Pend Oreille on *Boundary Dam Rd*, which is unpaved but

252

First Nations, Native Americans and the Pacific Northwest

Descriptions of Juan de Fuca, Vitus Bering, James Cook, Lewis and Clark and other explorers from Europe and eastern North America 'discovering' the Pacific Northwest are highly exaggerated. Those early explorers themselves noted the great variety of Native peoples they encountered in the Northwest, peoples with a bewildering variety of languages, cultures and ways of survival.

Call them Native Americans, First Nations, Indians, aboriginal inhabitants or some other name, archaeological evidence indicates that humans have been living in the Pacific Northwest for at least the last 10,000 to 15,000 years and possibly longer. The earliest inhabitants migrated into the region from Asia during successive Ice Ages, when the sea level was about 300 ft lower than today. What is now the Bering Sea was a broad land bridge leading from Asia to North America, a land bridge cut with rivers, mountain valleys and plains offering natural travel routes.

Bands of nomadic hunters and gatherers slowly followed game and plant foods into North America. Once here, the new inhabitants spread widely, retreating south as ice sheets advanced, moving north as the glaciers retreated and learning how to survive in the new land.

Bands that settled on the west side of the Cascades thrived on salmon, whale, shellfish, game and berries. The Haida, Tlingit and others sailed the coastal and ocean waters in great canoes, travelling regularly from Alaska up the Columbia River to The Dalles in search of trade and slaves. Relieved of the need to spend most of their time searching for food by a rich natural harvest, coastal tribes developed some of the most intricate, richly ornamented artistic traditions ever seen around the Pacific Rim.

Inland bands also depended on the salmon migration for nourishment, but remained semi-nomadic in a seasonal search for other sources of food. Many became adept traders, ranging from the coast to the Great Plains east of the Rocky Mountains. When trade routes from the Southwest introduced horses around 1700, Nez Perce and other interior tribes began to range even farther, trading buffalo hunting rights on the Plains for bulb and root harvests in the Wallowa and other Northwest valleys.

The arrival of White explorers in the late 18th and early 19th centuries disrupted a long-established way of life. There was little hesitation at adopting metal cooking utensils, firearms and other trappings of Western civilisation. And there was no choice about unanticipated gifts such as smallpox and measles. Every tribe and village was struck sooner or later. Some lost up to 90% of their inhabitants. Some simply disappeared. When White settlers arrived, they appropriated land and resources almost at will, forcing the original inhabitants of the region onto ever-shrinking reservations. As gold, potential farmland and other resources were found on reservation land, Whites conveniently rewrote treaties or ignored them altogether, usually with the open connivance of government officials.

Two centuries later, more than 60 different tribes still live in the Pacific Northwest. Most have learned to use the legal system so long ranged against them to go on the offensive. Bands in British Columbia have used treaties and proclamations signed in the name of Queen Victoria to gain a large measure of self-government. Bands in Washington and Oregon have used treaty language to reassert rights to salmon, water and other resources. Other groups have used treaty protections to shelter enormously profitable casinos and other business operations.

There are still enormous tensions between the original inhabitants of the Pacific Northwest and its later settlers, but there is also a growing realisation that the two groups have more in common that not.

Barely 20 years after the last survivor of the Nez Perce War died, farmers and ranchers in the Wallowa Valley are offering overtures aimed at bringing the Nez Perce home again.

well-maintained, back to Metaline Falls and SR 31 southbound.

METALINE FALLS TO COLVILLE

Box Canyon Dam, *tel: (509) 447-3137*, open Mon and Tue 0700–1530, Wed–Sun 0900–1700 in summer, Mon–Fri 0700–1500 the rest of the year, is 6 miles south of Metaline. The small dam has a pleasant picnic area, a very informal visitor centre and free dam tours.

Best view of the dam, river and an imposing railway trestle are from a lay-by on the east side of the road 1 mile above the visitor centre.

Ione and **Tiger**, once important river towns, are now little more than highway hamlets. Ione is the larger of the pair; all that remains of Tiger is the **Tiger Historical Museum**, *junction of SR 31 and 20; tel: (509) 442-3737*, in the former post office.

Take SR 20 west (right) as it climbs into the Selkirk Mountains. **Beaver Lodge Resort**, *Little Pend Oreille Lakes, 2430 Hwy 20 E., Colville, WA 99114; tel: (509) 684-5657*, budget, has rustic cabins beneath the trees as well as tent and RV pitches, a restaurant, grocery store and launderette.

A sign on the south (left) side of the highway less than a mile east of Beaver Lodge masquerades as the **Colville National Forest Information Center**; *tel: (509) 684-3711*. Headquarters for the 1.1-million acre forest is at *765 S. Main St, Colville.*

Much of the forest west of the National Forest is protected as the Washington Department of Natural Resources' **Little Pend Oreille**, *225 S. Silke Rd, Colville, WA 99114; tel: (800) 527-3305* or *(509) 684-7474*, which has trail maps and facilities guides.

The DNR also administers **Douglas Falls Grange Park**, *4 miles north of SR 20 on Douglas Falls Rd*, a 20-acre state park surrounding a 60-ft waterfall. The park has picnicking and pleasant forest walks around Douglas Falls. SR 20 continues east into rich valley farmland sloping toward the Columbia River.

COLVILLE

Tourist Information: Colville Chamber of Commerce, *121 E. Astor (at Main St), Box 267, Colville, WA 99114; tel: (509) 684-5973; fax: (509) 684-1344.*

Accommodation and Food

Colville has the best selection of lodging in the region, including *CI.*

Most comfortable and best value is the budget–moderate **Colville Inn**, *915 S. Main St; tel: (509) 684-2517; fax: (509) 684-2546.* The adjoining **Ruffed Grouse**; *tel: (509) 685-1308*, budget–moderate, is easily the finest restaurant in the valley. Best bet for ice-cream or a sandwich is **Barman's Country Store**, *230 S. Main St; tel: (509) 684-9710*, an imposing brick building that has been restored as a retail antique and tourist shop.

Sightseeing

Colville got its start in 1883 when the US Army abandoned Fort Colville, 3 miles north-east on *Colville-Aladdin-Northpoint Rd*, for Fort Spokane. Civilians who had lived near Fort Colville promptly scavenged the Army structures and moved to today's location, nearer the Columbia River and a planned railway line. Fort Colville is now an empty hayfield.

The US Army fort, like the Hudson's Bay Company's Fort Colvile, the Colville Confederated Tribes, and the town of Colville, were named for Andrew Colvile, HBC director when the English fur post was opened in 1826.

The new town of Colville boomed as the regional farming, timber and transportation centre. The boom has long since faded, but farming and timber have kept Colville prosperous. Many early commercial and residential buildings remain.

Barman's Country Store (see above), a former bank with gleaming white columns at *Main* and *Astor Sts* and the **Oddfellows Hall** on *W. First St* are the most impressive. *N. Main* and *E. First Sts* have a number of elegant Victorian-style residences. The Chamber of Commerce publishes a self-guided tour of historic buildings.

Keller Heritage Center and Museum, *700 N. Wynne St; tel: (509) 684-5968*, open May–Sept, is far and away the best White settlement-era museum in the region. The

254

modern museum building houses a chronology of the region from pre-history to modern times. The elegant Keller family mansion, rebuilt in 1912, has been lovingly restored and furnished. Other museum buildings include a fully restored 1930s forest lookout tower, a miner's log cabin, a trapper's cabin, blacksmith shop, sawmill and an extensive collection of antique farm implements, all set on a 7½-acre landscaped estate.

SR 20 winds 10 miles west across a series of broad terraces leading to the Columbia River. The plain was once heavily forested, but a century of lumbering has left local forests much diminished. The terraces, as well as smaller side valleys, have become rich grain farms and pastures. Hwy 395 joins SR 20 as far as the Columbia.

KETTLE FALLS

Tourist Information: **Kettle Falls Area Chamber of Commerce**, *265 W. 3rd St (at Hwy 395), Kettle Falls, WA 99141; tel: (509) 738-2300*, has lodging lists and a self-service brochure rack.

There is no obvious reason for the existence of Kettle Falls, and no sign of any waterfalls. Until 1940–1941, there was a thunderous set of falls where the present-day highway bridge spans the Columbia River. When the spillways of Grand Coulee Dam were closed in 1939, the river backed up to form Lake Roosevelt, leaving the falls 90 ft beneath the surface. The new lake destroyed the riverside town of Kettle Falls, 2½ miles south of the bridge near the present-day marina. It also destroyed one of the most important Native American salmon fisheries on the Columbia River.

When North West Company explorer David Thompson arrived at Kettle Falls in 1811, he noted thousands of Native Americans catching salmon so numerous they were more like flocks of birds than individual fish. Most of the million pounds or so of fish caught at the falls each year were dried for storage. Some were cooked immediately in the natural, water-filled holes in the rocks around the falls, which Thompson called kettles. Hot rocks were dropped into the kettles, boiling the water and cooking the salmon.

It took 14 years for the North West Company, and later the Hudson's Bay Company, to convince local chiefs to allow Fort Colvile to be built just above the falls. The chiefs permitted the HBC to settle and farm the rich land around the river, but reserved salmon fishing rights for themselves.

Washington and Fort Colvile, passed into American hands when the US-Canada boundary was fixed in 1846, but the boundary treaty was vague about compensation for British assets. Fort Colvile remained firmly under HBC control until financial arrangements were settled in 1871.

When Lake Roosevelt began to back up the 100-plus miles to Kettle Falls, most residents put their homes and businesses on wheels and moved 4 miles inland to Meyers Falls, which they renamed Kettle Falls.

Foundations and residential gardens are still visible, but Fort Colvile disappeared beneath a quiet bay in the Lake, now marked by a plaque on a hillside. Outlines of the fort's major buildings and fields are sometimes visible in the mud below during the spring and early summer draw-down of the lake.

The **Kettle Falls Historical Center**, *last right (north) turn before the Columbia River bridge, Box KFHC; tel: (509) 738-6964,* provides the best recounting of the history and death of both the falls and Kettle City. Don't miss the video of the final Native American fishing season at the falls and the hurried efforts to excavate Native American cemeteries and archaeological sites along the river before the inundation.

Just behind the museum is **St Paul's Mission**, a rebuilt 1845 mission established by Father Pierre-Jean DeSmet. A short walking path passes an old cemetery, the Fort Colvile marker and a boulder deeply grooved by generations of Native Americans honing fishing implements.

Visitors to modern Kettle City are welcomed by a sign proclaiming '1324 Friendly People and 1 Grouch'. The official Town Grouch is elected annually as a fund-raising event. Both residents and visitors are encouraged to vote early and often at $0.25 per vote.

Much of the surrounding forest is part of the **Colville National Forest**, *255 W. 11th St; tel:*

'I Will Fight No More Forever' – Chief Joseph and the Nez Perce

Of all the injustices visited on the original inhabitants of North America, few are as wantonly rapacious as the war against the Nez Perce. The name means pierced noses, given by French-speaking trappers even though those who called themselves Nee-Me-Poo, 'The People,' didn't pierce noses or anything else.

Nomadic masters of the rugged river gorges and mountain valleys where Oregon, Washington and Idaho meet, the Nez Perce lived a stable life trapping salmon, digging roots and hunting as far east as the Great Plains. Their fatal mistake was rescuing the starving Lewis and Clark expedition as they staggered out of Idaho's Bitterroot Range in the winter of 1805. Those who followed would be the Nez Perce's undoing.

For 50 years, the Nez Perce gained a solid reputation as friends of the White Man. Secure in the Grande Ronde, Wallowa and other remote valleys, they willingly aided travellers in their rugged territory.

By the time of the Walla Walla Treaty of 1855, the Nez Perce could proudly boast that their people had never killed a White. They even signed Washington Territorial Governor Isaac Stevens' treaty, exchanging most of their traditional territory for 5000 square miles extending eastward from the Grande Ronde and Wallowa Valleys.

Trouble began when prospectors discovered gold on Nez Perce land in 1860. Miners, merchants and settlers overran much of the reservation, then demanded protection from the US Army when the Nez Perce objected. The federal government convened another treaty council in 1863, demanding most of the reservation. Many of the chiefs walked out. The few who remained, later called 'treaty' bands, signed, ceding the lands of the absent, or 'nontreaty' bands.

Among the nontreaty Nez Perce was a band based in the Wallowa Valley near present-day Joseph. Pressed by settlers, the band appealed to the Bureau of Indian Affairs. In 1863, President US Grant formally reserved the Wallowa Valley 'as a reservation for the roaming Nez Perce Indians' and ordered White settlers out.

The settlers objected and forced the government to reverse its position in 1875. When band leader Chief Joseph appealed to federal authorities, Major Clay Wood surveyed the conflicting claims. His report, supported by Civil War hero Gen. Otis Howard, backed the Nez Perce.

Settlers threatened to go on the warpath themselves unless the Nez Perce were evicted.

(509) 738-6111; fax: (509) 738-7780, which administers an extensive network of trails, campsites and recreation facilities.

The other major forest user is **Boise Cascade Corp**; tel: (509) 738-3211, with mills on Hwy 395 west of town and on Lake Roosevelt just south of the bridge. Plant tours are usually available by prior arrangement.

Lake Roosevelt is the largest lake in Washington. **Grand Coulee Dam National Recreation Area Kettle City Campground**, 2½ miles south of Hwy 395; tel: (509) 738-6266, has an extremely pleasant picnic ground and campsite with 12 pitches and a small visitor centre. **Lake Roosevelt Marina**;

tel: (800) 635-7585 or (509) 738-6121, has full marina facilities, including house boat rentals. Rainbow trout and kokanee salmon are raised in net pens at the north end of the marina. There is no fishing near the pens, but the public are welcome to watch and feed the fish, reared at **Sherman Creek Hatchery**, 4 miles east off SR 20; tel: (509) 738-6971.

KETTLE FALLS TO REPUBLIC

SR 20 eastbound is the Sherman Pass National Forest Scenic Byway. **Kettle Falls Ranger District**; tel: (509) 738-6111, and **Republic Ranger District**; tel: (509) 775-3305, have self-guiding brochures.

In late 1876, Wood, Howard and three civilians were assigned to settle the issue. They voted for eviction, by force if need be. Chief Joseph's band had until the middle of 1877 to join treaty bands in Idaho.

Five hundred people, including 150 warriors and 2000 horses forded the flooding Snake River, then paused in Idaho to rest. Two bands of young warriors, smouldering at the eviction and the unprosecuted murders of Nez Perce by Whites, attacked two small settlements, killing about 20. The war was on.

The Nez Perce fled into the mountains, knowing that the Army would pursue them. The consequences were disastrous. Fighting to protect their families, the heavily outgunned and outnumbered Nez Perce won more than 20 battles. Unprovoked Army attacks on neutral bands swelled the revolt. The Nez Perce force, led by *Looking Glass*, the War Chief, grew to 250 warriors and 500 old men, women and children. Faced with the reality that the US Army would never accept peace, the band retreated into Yellowstone National Park and turned north into Montana. Their goal was 'Old Lady Country', Canada, ruled by Queen Victoria, which had offered refuge to the Sioux after the 1876 massacre at Wounded Knee, South Dakota.

They never made it. After 1200 miles of running battles with more than 2000 Army troops plus civilian militias, the Nez Perce were surrounded less than 40 miles south of the border in the Bears Paw Mountains in October, 1877.

Chief Joseph has been credited as the band's war chief, but he was actually charged with safeguarding noncombatants. He was also the Nez Perce spokesman who delivered the surrender:

'My people have no blankets, no food. No one knows where they are, perhaps freezing to death. Hear me, my chiefs. I am tired; my heart is sick and sad. From where the sun now stands, I will fight no more forever'.

The ordeal continued. Chief Joseph had been promised return to his homeland in return for surrender. Instead, the survivors were banished to Oklahoma, where many died of disease and malnutrition. They were eventually allowed to return to Washington, but only as far as the Colville Reservation. Chief Joseph died in 1904 without ever seeing Wallowa again. He is buried at Nespelem, on the reservation.

'I think that, in his long career', wrote Major Wood, *'Joseph cannot accuse the government of the United States of one single act of justice'.*

257

Log Flume Heritage Site, *4 miles east of the Sherman Creek Hatchery turnoff*, is an excellent comparison of turn-of-the-century timber technology.

The Headlund Lumber Co. laid narrow gauge rails along the banks of Sherman Creek to haul logs from the dense Ponderosa pine forests. Competitor Klopp Lumber Co. built a flume along the same route to float logs downstream. Both companies were put out of business by a lightning-caused fire that burned 120 square miles of forest in 1929.

A short forest loop trail passes both flume and rail routes as well as wild roses, berries, flowers and Sherman Creek.

The byway climbs west through 16 miles of dense forest to **Sherman Pass**, 5575 ft, the state's highest all-year pass. **Sherman Pass Overlook**, *just east of the pass*, offers broad vistas into the Kettle Mountain Range, a patchwork of different shades of greens resulting from different stages of regrowth following forest fires and decades of logging.

Just west of Sherman pass is the **White Mountain Fire and Forest Interpretative Site**, overlooking a 1988 forest fire that burned more than 20,000 acres. A charred skeleton forest towers above the brilliant green of new growth.

Tin-Na-Tit Kin-Ne-Ki Tee-Ga Indian

Arts & Gallery, *7 miles west of Sherman Pass, 993 Hwy 20 E., Republic, WA 99166; tel: (509) 775-3077*, may be the largest Native American gallery in the region. Stock includes dead pawn jewellery (items left as security for loans and never reclaimed), new jewellery, stone and wood carvings, masks and other items from tribes across North America.

REPUBLIC

Tourist Information: Visitor Information Center, *61 N. Kean St, Box 1024, Republic, WA 99166; tel: (509) 775-3387*, and **Republic Chamber of Commerce**, *Box 502; tel: (509) 775-2704*.

ACCOMMODATION

The Chamber of Commerce publishes a complete list of lodgings in the area, including the **Cottonwood Motel**, *852 S. Clark Ave; tel: (509) 775-3371*, **Frontier Inn**, *797 S. Clark Ave; tel: (509) 775-3361*, **Klondike Motel**, *150 N. Clark Ave; tel: (509) 775-2555*, and **Triangle J Ranch Youth Hostel**, *423 Old Kettle Falls Rd; tel: (509) 775-3933*.

SIGHTSEEING

Republic exploded into life when the northern tier of the Colville Reservation was opened for mining in 1896. It looks much as it did in the early 1900s, with authentic looking (but new) false fronts and scattered pines dotting the steep hillsides.

The main street, *Clark Ave*, was named for Patsy Clark, president of the Republic Gold Mining and Milling Company and builder of Patsy Clarks Mansion in Spokane (see p.227).

The mines and mills are memories, but the Ferry County Historical Society publishes an excellent *Historic Republic Walking Tour*, 3.1 miles long, and a 200-plus mile driving *Ferry County Historical Tour*.

The **Ferry County Museum**, *15 N. Kean St*, shares a site on the west side of town with **Stonerose Interpretative Center**; *tel: (509) 775-2295*, open 1000–1700 Tues–Sat May–Oct, which provides a look at life in the region 50 million years ago through maps and fossils. Visitors are encouraged to visit the fossil bed,

quarter of a mile north, to prospect for their own fossils of plants, fish and insects, $2 per person. Hammer, chisel and safety goggles can be hired at the Center.

SR 20 climbs back into the mountains toward **Wauconda Pass**, 4310 ft, and 15 miles west of Republic. The town of Wauconda, 2 miles below the pass, is little more than a café and grocery store.

The highway follows Bonaparte Creek down through the Okanogan Highlands, a region of rolling farmlands and scattered trees along the hilltops. The land becomes drier as the elevation drops to irrigated apple orchards dotting the desert-like Okanogan Valley at Tonasket (see p.249). Turn north (right) onto Hwy 97 toward the Canadian border and Osoyoos.

OROVILLE

Tourist Information: Oroville Chamber of Commerce, *1730 Main St, Box 536, Oroville, WA 98844*.

Gold finds on the Fraser River in 1858 finally necessitated a proper survey of the border between America and Canada. A British surveyor supposedly made the Similkameen River gold discovery that created Oroville. The camp boomed as a mining supply centre, then a centre for cattle drovers taking herds to BC gold camps.

Miners and drovers discovered the relatively mild winters and good grazing along the shore of **Lake Osoyoos**, at the north end of town. When gold fever subsided, many returned as merchants and farmers. Apples, recreation and cross-border traffic rule the economy today. The **Old Oroville Depot**, *1210 Ironwood St, tel: (509) 476-3693*, has become a local history museum and community hall.

A point of land jutting into Lake Osoyoos was the site of the first orchard in the region. Some of the original trees still bear fruit. The lowest petrol prices in the area are at stations just south of the Canadian border, 7 miles north.

The best view of the area is from a lay-by at the top of the hill east of Osoyoos on BC 3 (see p.290).

EVERETT–OMAK

The 240-mile route between Everett and Omak covers some of the most spectacular mountain scenery in Washington. Geography and climate defeated every attempt at road-building until the 1970s, but the engineering victory is only partial. Roads through this glacier-carved wilderness of granite peaks and forested canyons remain closed from the first snows until winter storm damage can be repaired after the spring thaw. Secondary routes occasionally remain impassable until late summer. Allow a full day for the journey, or camp overnight en route. Accommodation in Darrington, Winthrop and Twisp are heavily booked in summer.

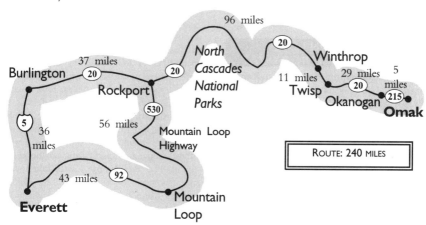

96 miles
North Cascades National Parks
Winthrop
Burlington — 37 miles — 20 — 20
Rockport
11 miles — Twisp — 29 miles — 20 — 5 miles — 215
Okanogan — Omak
530
5 — 36 miles — 56 miles — Mountain Loop Highway
ROUTE: 240 MILES
43 miles — 92
Everett
Mountain Loop

ROUTES

North Cascade passes are generally closed mid Nov–May, depending on the weather. For reports on snow closures; *tel: (888) 766-4636, (800) 695-7623* or *(206) 368-4499*. I-90 and BC 3 are less scenic but remain open all year.

Take Hwy 2 east from Everett across the Snohomish River wetlands to SR 9. Turn north (left) to SR 92. Go east (right), following signs for **Granite Falls**, 8 miles east, and the Mountain Loop Highway. Continue east 31 miles along the Stillaguamish River through the tiny towns of **Robe** and **Silverton** to **Barlow Pass**. The road becomes gravel for 14 miles at the pass, but closes in winter. Follow the Mountain Loop Highway north to **Darrington** and SR 530. Continue north on SR 530 to **Rockport** and SR 20, the North Cascades Highway. Turn east (right) to **North Cascades National Park**. Winter storm damage occasionally keeps the gravel section closed into summer. Before setting out, contact the **Darrington Ranger Station**, *1405 Emmens St, Darrington, WA 98241; tel: (360) 436-1155*, to check road conditions.

The 90 miles from Rockport to Winthrop are the slowest and most scenic section of the route. Snow-capped peaks begin to tower above the forest near **Newhalem** and the **North Cascades National Park Visitors**

Center. Best views are lay-bys at Diablo and Ross Lakes and Washington Pass. The road drops into the Methow Valley, following the Methow River to **Winthrop**, a rebuilt Western frontier town. Continue 11 miles to **Twisp** and drop down the eastern slope of the Cascades into the irrigated desert of the Okanogan Valley to **Okanogan** and Omak.

ALTERNATE ROUTE

If the Mountain Loop Highway is closed, or for drivers who prefer paved roads, follow I-5 36 miles north from Everett to **Burlington**. Turn east (right) onto SR20, the North Cascades Highway, following signs for Sedro Woolley and North Cascades National Park to Rockport and into the park. The alternate is slightly shorter but saves about two hours of driving.

MOUNTAIN LOOP NATIONAL SCENIC BYWAY

Tourist Information: Darrington Ranger Station, *1405 Emmens St, Darrington, WA 98241; tel: (360) 436-1155*, and the **Verlot Public Service Center**, *Mountain Loop Highway, Granite Falls, WA 98252; tel: (360) 691-7791*, open May–Sept. Lodging is extremely limited except for campsites in the Mt Baker-Snoqualmie National Forest. For campsite bookings; *tel: (800) 280-2267*.

This rugged mountain route was created by miners in the early 1890s. Most headed north to the Klondike Gold Rush in 1898. Mine trails became a railway, which grew into a logging road that was eventually paved. The miners and most of the loggers are long gone. Forest has returned, although the immense stands of red cedar that originally lured lumbermen to these slopes may never reappear.

Storm damage can be severe, especially beyond Barlow Pass. A Nov 1897 storm washed out so many bridges that the train from Monte Cristo was officially delayed 3 years, 8 hrs. The best guide is *The Mountain Loop National Scenic Byway*, a Northwest Interpretative Association booklet sold throughout the area.

Granite Falls was once a vital rail link between the mines to the east and the ore smelter in Everett. Turn north (left) at the four-way stop in the centre of town to the Mountain

Loop Hwy. **Robe** blossomed in 1891 with a busy shingle mill but soon withered. Just north is the Forest Service summer-only **Verlot Public Service Center**, *Mountain Loop Highway, Granite Falls, WA 98252; tel: (360) 691-7791*. The centre was created by the Civilian Conservation Corps, a federal makeshift programme during the 1930s.

Silverton was a boomtown of 3000 people in 1897, but the boom collapsed when the railway washed out. A few residents have returned. **Big Four Ice Caves**, 3 miles east, was a posh mountain resort for the rich and famous of Seattle. The resort burned in 1949, but a large meadow, beaver ponds and picnic areas remain. An easy 1-mile trail leads to the caves, actually the melting remnants of winter avalanches.

Sunrise Mine Trailhead is a 2½-mile detour south onto FSR 4065. Views from the trailhead parking area up the U-shaped Stillaguamish Valley are magnificent. **Barlow Pass** marks the end of the paved road and the divide between the Stillaguamish and the Sauk Rivers. A 4-mile walking and cycling road leads to **Monte Cristo**, where a small 1889 gold strike sparked the Cascades Gold Rush. The town numbers a handful of hardy souls today. Expect summer congestion, particularly on the gravel section. The three **Monte Cristo lakes** were once favourite campsites for Sauk Indian hunters. Mine tailings washing down from Monte Cristo are quickly choking the waters into marshland and meadow.

Beaver Lake Trailhead opens onto a 3.2-mile trail along the old railway grade past decaying, moss-covered trestles and immense red cedar stumps. One of the few survivors of the original forest is near a 1916 Ranger Station. The tree, 48 ft in circumference, was spared to serve as a fire lookout.

A clear-cut near the road 2 miles from the trailhead has opened views of **White Chuck Mountain** and a good spot for birding. The surrounding forest was thinned in 1985 and 1992. The White Chuck River, milky white from glacial flour, or silt, is a stunning contrast to the blue-green water of the Sauk River. The **Old Sauk Trail**, 5 miles from the White Chuck junction, traces what remains of old growth forest along the river.

DARRINGTON

Tourist Information: Darrington Chamber of Commerce, *Box 351, Darrington, WA 98241; tel: (360) 436-1177.*

Hemlock Hills Bed & Breakfast, *612 Stillaguamish; tel: (800) 520-1584*; **Sauk River Farm B&B**, *32629 SR 530 N.E.; tel: (360) 436-1794*, both moderate, are the best choices.

This timber and recreation town lies just beyond the National Forest. The lumber industry is alive and defiant, if not as healthy as it once was. **Michelle's Country Coffee & Deli**, *1015 Sauk, Darrington, WA 98241; tel: (360) 436-0213*, is the best place in town to eat.

Marble Mount, 8 miles north of the SR 20/530 junction, has the last petrol station and some of the least appealing scenery on the western side of the Cascades. High tension lines march along SR 20 and mountainsides above are raw with clear-cuts. Logging and development continues 5 more miles to the edge of North Cascades National Park. **Newhalem** and the park Visitor Center are 8 miles east of the park boundary.

NORTH CASCADES NATIONAL PARK

Tourist Information: North Cascades NPS Complex, *2105 SR 20, Sedro Woolley, WA 98282; tel: (360) 856-5700.*

NCNP was created in 1968 to protect 505,000 acres of some of America's most breathtaking scenery: tall, jagged peaks; fishbone ridges; deep valleys; uncounted waterfalls and more than 300 glaciers. The park was first proposed in 1892 by nearby residents incensed at the wholesale slaughter of mountain goats and grizzly bears by hunters from Europe and the Eastern USA.

Park proposals surfaced almost every decade thereafter, slowly wearing down opposition from timber, mining, hydroelectric and real estate interests. The final compromise is called the North Cascades National Park Service Complex: Ross Lake National Recreation Area; the SR 20 corridor; North and South NCNP on each side of the road; and Lake Chelan National Recreation Area, just south of NCNP. The complex is surrounded by millions of acres of National Forest, National Wilderness and other public lands.

SR 20 is the only highway through the North Cascades. The roadway is well maintained with frequent lay-bys at scenic points, but expect steep grades and slow traffic. In midsummer, allow half a day to drive the 90 miles between Marble Mount and Mazama without stopping; half as long in spring or autumn. *North Cascades Highway Guide*, by Fred T. Darvill, Jr., is an excellent pocket guide to the sights, history, geology, flora and activities along the highway. The brochure is sold at most area ranger stations and tourist shops.

The **North Cascades Visitor Center**, *Newhalem; tel: (360) 386-4495*, 0830–1800 daily in summer, weekends in winter, shares a building with the Seattle City Light visitor facility. The locomotive engine nearby was used to build dams just upstream. The **Skagit General Store** is the last spot for snacks and souvenirs until Winthrop. Even if you're not hungry, hire a copy of *North Cascades Scenic Highway*, a 60-min cassette tape, using local legend and history to explain the Cascades. Leave the $2 tape at the **Okanogan National Forest Methow Valley Visitor Center**, *Winthrop*. Eastbound travellers can hire the tape in Winthrop and return it in Newhalem.

Water hunters invaded the Cascades around 1900 in search of drinking water and hydroelectric power. Seattle City Light proposed tapping the Skagit River gorge above Marble Mount. The original **Gorge Dam** was completed in 1924, 3 miles north of Newhalem, a construction camp. The current Gorge Dam was completed in 1960. **Diablo Dam**, finished in 1930, is 3 miles upstream from Gorge Dam. The dam is open daily for 90-min tours summer–autumn with no advance bookings. Seattle City Light also offers half-day boat tours of scenic Diablo Lake to Ross Dam, advance booking required. **Skagit Tours**, *500 Newhalem St, Rockport, WA 98283; tel: (360) 233-2709*, has information on both tours.

The most popular lay-bys are 6 miles east of Diablo Dam, overlooking Diablo Lake, and 2 miles beyond, overlooking both Diablo and Ross Lakes.

Refrain from feeding the chipmunks

261

scampering around the parking lots – they carry bubonic plague and other diseases. Glacial flour washing into Diablo Lake has turned the waters a striking emerald green. Ross Lake, not fed by glacial rivers, is azure blue.

Rainy Pass, at 4855 ft the Cascade crest, is 22 miles east of Ross Dam. Creeks on the west side of the pass drain into the Skagit River, those on the east side into the Columbia River. Weather and vegetation also change at Rainy Pass. Newhalem gets 80 ins of precipitation annually, which feeds the dense coastal forests and frequent avalanches. **Winthrop**, on the eastern slope, gets just 20 ins of moisture, supporting Ponderosa pine forests. A side road (east side of the road) leads to a parking area with picnic facilities and the Pacific Coast Trailhead.

Washington Pass, 5477 ft, the high point of SR 20, is 5 miles east of Rainy Pass. A side road 0.1 mile west of the pass leads to a summer visitor centre and the best views on the entire route. The treeless channels running down the mountainsides are avalanche chutes formed by tonnes of snow cascading down the slope at speeds of 100 mph. The immense piles of snow at the base of the chutes last well into summer.

WINTHROP

Tourist Information: Winthrop Chamber of Commerce, *Box 39, Winthrop, WA 98862; tel: (509) 996-2125*, and **Okanogan National Forest Methow Valley Visitor Center**, just west on SR 20; *tel: (509) 996-4000*.

Methow Valley Central Reservations, *Box 505; tel: (800) 422-3048*, or **The Methow Valley Lodging Association**, *Box 237, Winthrop, WA 98862* have accommodation details. Most choices are moderate–expensive.

Winthrop is a Western theme park with genuine roots. It was founded as a wilderness trading post in 1891 by a young Harvard University graduate, Guy Waring. Waring's university roommate, Owen Wister, wrote America's first Western novel, *The Virginian*, after honeymooning in his friend's town. Several original buildings survive, including the **Shafer Museum**, *off Main St*, a log cabin built by Waring in 1897. Waring, who disapproved of alcohol, also opened the **Duck Brand Saloon**, *Main St*, to keep competitors out.

Anyone who became drunk was thrown into the street, to the great consternation of first-time patrons. Today it's a community centre.

When the North Cascades Hwy was nearing completion, Winthrop was remodelled on a Western theme to attract tourists. The scheme worked. *Main St* is lined with what look like genuine period buildings, but the interiors are thoroughly modern and busy – restaurants, souvenir shops and espresso stands. The town is also a centre for outdoor recreation, especially fishing, hiking and Nordic skiing. **Winthrop National Fish Hatchery**, *1 mile south off SR 20; tel: (509) 996-2424*, raises more than 1 million salmon and trout yearly for the Methow and other rivers.

TWISP

Tourist Information: Twisp Chamber of Commerce, *Box 565, Twisp, WA 98856; tel: (509) 997-2926; fax: (509) 997-5423*.

Twisp is a more affordable and decidedly untrendy alternative to Winthrop. **The Idle-A-While**, *N. Hwy 20; tel: (509) 997-3222*, budget–moderate, is the largest motel in town, the **Sportsman Motel**, *1010 E. Hwy 20; tel: (509) 997-2911*, budget, the least expensive.

Twisp is best known as the birthplace of airborne forest fire fighters known as smokejumpers, who parachute into inaccessible areas. **North Cascade Smokejumper Base**, *5 miles north on E. County Rd; tel: (509) 997-2031*, has tours June–Oct. The town names comes from the local Native American word for the buzzing sound of yellowjacket wasps.

OKANOGAN

Tourist Information: Okanogan Chamber of Commerce, *Box 1125, Okanogan, WA 98840; tel: (509) 422-1541*, **Visitor Center**, *1030 2nd Ave*.

Although the Okanogan Valley is part of a desert running from Mexico into Canada, irrigation schemes have fostered vast fruit orchards from Okanogan northward. The **Okanogan County Historical Museum**, *1410 2nd Ave; tel: (509) 422-4272*, has excellent displays on early settlement, ranching and agriculture. The **Okanogan National Forest Headquarters**, *1240 S. Second Ave; tel: (509) 826-3275*, open

Logging

The cutting and processing of trees was a major part of Pacific Northwest life long before the first Europeans arrived. Native peoples turned trees into an enormous variety of products. So did later immigrants from Europe and Eastern North America, who saw the seemingly endless forests as a treasure trove waiting to be tapped.

Loggers call Capt. George Vancouver the region's first non-Native timberman. He was probably not the first passing sailor to replace masts and spars, but his journal records the first detailed search for the straightest trees (Douglas-fir) and the effort involved in cutting and dragging them from the forest to the shore. Two centuries of technology have changed the scale of logging, but Vancouver's carpenters would likely recognise today's forest industry.

A **logger** works in the forest, usually called the **woods**. **Fallers** fell, or cut, trees, a process now called **harvesting**. Felled trees are collected in a yard, from where they are hauled away by truck, train or helicopter to be sorted by size, quality and species at inland mills, where they are turned into pulp, paper or lumber. When possible, logs are sorted at a **dryland sort** on the shores of a river, lake or estuary, then dumped into the water. The floating logs are **boomed**, or bound into bundles, and tied into **rafts** to be towed to a mill for processing.

Work that was once done by hand is now largely mechanised. Axes and saws have been replaced by chain saws, themselves giving way to mechanical harvesters that can grasp and clip a tree a metre in diameter as neatly as a gardener prunes a rose – and almost as quickly. Teams of oxen replaced rope and windlass, to be replaced in turn by steam engines and diesel power, resulting in fewer workers needed in the woods and mills. Because machinery is most efficient in open areas, **clear-cutting**, cutting every tree on a parcel, has become the norm. With no trees left to hold soil during the heavy rains, entire mountainsides turn into churning masses of sliding mud and rock. The fish habitat in streams and rivers are smothered. Logging is a major cause of the decline in salmon and other fish populations throughout the Northwest.

Milling can be equally destructive. Pulp and paper mills traditionally dumped tonnes of poisonous wastes into the nearest waterway. Public pressure has forced changes, but the cloying stench of pulp and paper production still hangs heavy over many coastal regions. Producers call it the 'smell of money'. Timber has fuelled much of the region's economic development, providing wood to lay railway tracks across the US and lumber for today's towns and cities.

Reforestation is the industry solution: clear cut, replant with the most profitable tree species, fertilise, thin and harvest every 30–80 years, depending on species and locale. In practice, clear-cutting destroys the old growth forest that deer, elk, bear, many smaller species and birds need for survival. Timber companies on both sides of the border are cutting trees far faster than they are replanting. The fate of what remains of the Pacific Northwest's vast forests is still being decided in courtrooms, legislatures and on logging roads throughout the region.

263

0745–1630 Mon–Fri, has complete information on the 1,706,000-acre recreation area.

OMAK

Tourist Information: Omak Visitor Information, Rte 2, Box 5200, Omak, WA 98841; tel: (509) 826-4218 or (800) 225-6625.

Omak has more lodging choices in nearby Okanogan. **Thriftlodge**, 122 N. Main St; tel: (509) 826-0400, budget, is central and excellent value for money. **The Breadline Cafe**, 102 Ash St; tel: (509) 826-5836, cheap–budget, is the best eating choice in the region. Sunday brunch is crowded and worth the wait. **Our Place Cafe**, 19 E. Apple St; tel: (509) 826-4811, budget, has the best omelettes.

Omak has been the regional commercial hub for decades. The brick town centre is a well-preserved example of early 20th-century architecture. More modern shopping centres near the junction of SR 20 and US 97 draw trade from 100 miles in every direction.

BELLINGHAM– MOUNT BAKER

The 110-mile return trip to Mt Baker is one of the shortest drives into the Northern Cascades, and one of the few open all winter. Highway views of Mt Baker (10,778 ft) and Mt Shuksan (9127 ft) are nearly as stunning as the panoramic views from 200 miles of walking paths that wind through the mosaic of national park, national forest and national wilderness. The highway is kept cleared to Heather Meadows and the Mt Baker Ski Area

despite an average snowfall of nearly 50 ft. Another four miles of road is open in summer, providing access to some of the most-photographed vistas in North America.

ROUTE: 55 MILES

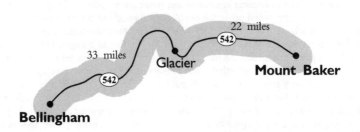

ROUTE

Take **SR 542**, *Mt Baker Rd*, east from I-5 at Exit 255 (Bellis Fair mall) across the **Nooksak Valley** to **Nugent's Corner** and up the narrowing valley through the village of **Glacier**. The last 10 miles of highway beyond is a series of steep hairpin turns across the tree line into **Heather Meadows**. The road to **Artist Point** is usually open mid July–Oct.

NOOKSAK VALLEY

Nooksak Valley is a broad agricultural plain stretching north toward Canada and west toward the Pacific. Farmed since the mid-19th century, the valley still has immense dairy herds, horse farms and neat fields of black-, rasp- and other berries, all framed by the looming peaks and glistening glaciers of Mt Baker and Mt Shuksan. A brief gold rush interrupted farming in the 1890s, but only two of the five thousand claims staked along the Nooksak River ever turned a profit.

The valley begins to narrow after crossing the Nooksak River, 10 miles east of I-5. In spring, flower lovers flock to **Iris to See**, *4288*

Deming Rd, Everson, WA 98247; tel: (360) 592-5800, an iris nursery with more than 500 named varieties. Peak iris bloom is Mar–April; the wildflower bloom advances with the retreating snows. Spring doesn't arrive until late July–early Aug at higher elevations.

The only winery in the region, **Mount Baker Vineyards**, 4298 Mt Baker Hwy, Deming, WA 98244; tel: (360) 592-2300, is 1½ miles east of the Nooksak River. Specialities are chasselas, a white grape from Switzerland, and siegerrebe, a German white grape, both rare in US vineyards, but the best reason to stop is the shady picnic ground looking across the vineyards to Mt Baker. Nooksak Indians have staked their financial future on a casino on the south side of the highway 2 miles beyond the winery.

The valley narrows sharply above the casino, with farmland giving way to increasingly dense forest. The slopes of Mt Baker and the surrounding peaks have been feeding local lumber mills for more than a century, leaving a ragged patchwork of different shades of green as trees regrow. Traditional logging in the area was by clearcutting – stripping hillsides of every tree in parcels marked for harvest. A particularly graphic clearcut stretches north from the highway, 2½ miles beyond the tiny town of Maple Falls.

The **Mt Baker Overlook**, Forest Road 39, 1½ miles beyond the clearcut, offers the best roadside view of the mountain. The volcanic peak is named after Lt Joseph Baker, a member of Capt. George Vancouver's expedition, who sighted the peak from Puget Sound in 1792. The Indian name of the mountain 'Kulshan', means steep, an apt description for the crags and glaciers that feed the Nooksak and other rivers. What looks like a small cloud near the summit could be steam from a volcanic vent that opened in 1975. The last eruption was an ashfall in the mid-19th century, but volcanologists are monitoring the mountain.

GLACIER

Tourist Information: The **Glacier Public Service Center**, a rustic-looking collection of stone buildings and spreading shade trees on the south side of the highway, is open in summer for National Park Service and US Forest Service information. For information the rest of the year, contact the **Mt Baker Ranger Station**, 2105 Hwy 20, Sedro Woolley, WA 98284; tel: (360) 856-5700.

Glacier, 3½ miles beyond the overlook, is the last town before the summit. Best restaurants are **Innisfree**; tel: (360) 599-2373 and **Milano's**; tel: (360) 599-2863, both moderate.

GLACIER TO MOUNT BAKER

The upper 24 miles of SR 542, a **National Forest Scenic Byway**, hugs the north fork of the Nooksak River. **Nooksak Falls** is 9 miles beyond Glacier. The 100-ft waterfall is thunderous in spring but considerably less impressive the rest of the year. A walking path to the falls leaves from the lower corner of the parking area.

Following a series of breathtaking hairpin turns, **Heather Meadow** and **Mt Baker Ski Area**, 1017 Iowa St, Bellingham, WA 98226; tel: (360) 734-6771; fax: (360) 734-5332, are 13 miles beyond the falls. A visitor centre is open mid July–Sept.

In winter, the area is extremely popular with local skiers and snowboarders who revel in the deepest snow of any resort in North America (595 in, just shy of 50 ft, on average) and some of the toughest, steepest runs in the region.

Food is available during the ski season, but the nearest accommodation is in Glacier. Most visitors sleep in Bellingham (see p. 96) and drive up.

In summer, the road continues another 4 miles over Austin Pass by a picturesque picnic area to **Artist Point** and 360° of unrestricted grandeur across the Cascades. A number of easy (and some quite strenuous) walks to nearby alpine lakes leave from Artist Point.

Trail maps are available at Heather Meadows. Photographer's Guide to Mount Baker, a small pamphlet by Norm and Diane Perreault, offers detailed walking directions as well as photographic tips.

THE SAN JUAN ISLANDS

It takes a high tolerance for tranquillity to enjoy the San Juan Islands between September and May, and an equally high tolerance for queues in summer. Some seven hundred islands dot the sparkling blue waters of Puget Sound – the precise number depends on the height of the tide and the amount of dry land needed to qualify as an island. Just 172 of the San Juans are named and 60 inhabited (some by one person), but only Lopez, Orcas and San Juan Islands are developed enough for significant tourism. Each of the trio has a distinct character, but all three retain a genuine sense of *away*. The ferry ride from Anacortes takes just 90 mins, but the ferry pulls out from the dock with all the finality of great ship setting out to cross some uncharted ocean.

TOURIST INFORMATION

San Juan Island Visitor Information Services, *Box 65, Lopez Island, WA 98261; tel: (360) 468-3663.*

GETTING AROUND

The main link and only car ferry is **Washington State Ferries**; *801 Alaskan Way, Seattle, WA 98104; tel: (206) 464-6400; (800) 843-3779 (US); or (604) 381-1551 (British Columbia)* from Anacortes and Sidney, BC. Schedules change quarterly.

Fares for domestic passage are collected west-bound only; the return trip and inter-island rides are free. Selected sailings continue on to Sidney, with single fares only in both directions. All-day waits are not uncommon in summer or at weekends and holidays year-round.

In other seasons, be at the dock at least 1–2 hours before the scheduled departure time. Advance bookings are generally not accepted, except to and from Sidney.

Victoria Clipper, *2701 Alaskan Way, Pier 69, Seattle, WA 98121; tel: (206) 448-5000, (800) 888-2535, or (604) 382-8100*, take passengers between Seattle, Friday Harbor (San Juan Island) and Victoria, BC. Advance booking required in summer and suggested all year.

Spring–autumn, **San Juan Island Shuttle Express**, *Bellingham Cruise Terminal, 355 Harris St, Bellingham, WA 98225; tel: (360) 671-1137*, provides daily service between Bellingham and Orcas Island/San Juan Island, as well as narrated whale-watching and nature cruises.

Puget Sound Express, *431 Water St, Port Townsend, WA 98368; tel: (360) 385-5288*, has daily service between Port Townsend and San Juan Island as well as day trips through the islands. Schedules change seasonally; advance bookings required.

Air service is also available from Seattle, Bellingham, Victoria and Port Townsend. **Kenmore Air**, *Box 80264, Seattle, WA 98028; tel: (206) 486-1257; (800) 543-9595; fax: (206) 485-4774*, operates seaplanes throughout Puget Sound and the Inside Passage. Advance booking required.

SIGHTSEEING

Nature is the big draw in the San Juans, from orcas leaping just offshore from Lime Kiln State Park on San Juan Island to sightseeing amidst hundreds of islets with whales, bald eagles and seals for company.

Nestled in the rain shadow of the Olympic Mountains, the San Juan Islands get 40% less rain than Seattle. Most days are sunny May–Oct and even the worst winter storms blow through quickly.

Victoria, BC, which shares similar weather patterns, provides more accurate weather forecasts than Seattle or Bellingham newspapers and radio/TV stations.

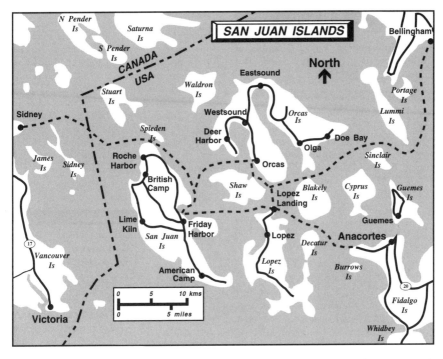

Many of the San Juans were farmed in past decades, but forest has reclaimed most fields. From ground or water level, the San Juans could be a quiet mountain lake dotted with dozens of tree-clad islands, albeit a lake that has the largest concentration of bald eagles in America and the largest population of orcas in the world. Wildflowers carpet forest meadows in spring while orchards gone wild still produce apples, pears and cherries each autumn. Residents devote even more time to boating, hiking, bicycling, camping and kayaking than visitors.

Tranquillity and recreational activities have attracted large numbers of artists and artisans, particularly to quieter Lopez and Orcas Islands. The same isolation that drew artists to the San Juans has helped to keep art prices relatively low, even though the cost of living on the islands is higher than on the mainland.

For the ultimate in tranquillity combined with public transportation, take the ferry to **Shaw Island**, just south of Orcas. Aside from the Franciscan nuns who operate the ferry dock

and the **Little Portion** general store, non residents are rare. Shaw has eight pitches in a county campsite but no restaurants, motels or bed and breakfasts.

Another 17 islands are **state marine parks**; *tel: (360) 755-9231*, accessible only by boat and largely untouched. Sea kayaks are the most popular way to island hop, but even experienced kayakers should consider starting out with an organised group. Local knowledge is crucial when tidal currents run up to 10 knots and reverse themselves a few hours later.

Tranquillity reigns nine months of the year, but expect crowds June–Aug. Car ferry queues can stretch all day while foot and bicycle passengers walk aboard the next sailing. Advance planning is crucial for car hire. Cars and rooms are booked up to a year in advance for summer and 4–6 months early for holidays and weekends. Midweek and off-season bookings can be made a few weeks early. If you do drive in the Islands, allow for speed limits of 45 mph or slower and petrol costs up to 50% over mainland prices.

LOPEZ ISLAND

Tourist Information: Lopez Chamber of Commerce, *Box 102, Lopez Island, WA 98261; tel: (360) 468-3663.*

ACCOMMODATION AND FOOD

Inn at Swifts Bay, *Port Stanley Rd; tel: (360) 468-3636; fax: (360) 468-3637*, moderate–expensive, may be the most luxurious bed and breakfast in the San Juans. Other choices include **Edenwild Inn**, *Box 271; tel: (360) 468-3238*, **MacKaye Harbor Inn**; *Rt 1, Box 1940; tel: (360) 468-2253*, and **Lopez Lodge**; *Box 117; tel: (360) 468-2500.*

Locals like the cheap lunches at **Lopez Island Soda Fountain**, *Village Rd; tel: (360) 468-3711*, and budget–moderate lunch or dinner at **Gail's**, *Village Rd; tel: (360) 468-2150.* **The Bay Cafe**, *Lopez Village; tel: (360) 468-3700*, moderate, has the best food and wine list on the island.

SIGHTSEEING

The flattest and least visited of the three main islands, Lopez has become a favourite with cyclists. **Cycle San Juans**, *Rte 1, Box 1744; tel: (360) 468-3251*, hire bicycles and publish an excellent pocket map. There are about 70 miles of paved road on the island, used mostly by the 2200 residents who habitually wave to every passing vehicle, cyclist and pedestrian. **Lopez Kayak**, *Fisherman Bay Rd; tel: (360) 468-2847*, hires sea kayaks and leads water tours around the island.

Lopez' rolling landscape and sunny summers encouraged farming from the early days of settlement in the 1850s. The island supplied grain, fruit and dairy products to Western Washington until the Columbia River irrigation project turned eastern deserts into rich farms with lower transportation costs. A few farms remain, but most have been sold or returned to forest.

The most notable exception is **Lopez Island Vineyards**, *Fisherman Bay Rd; tel: (360) 468-3644*, open weekends all year for tasting and Wed–Sun Jun–Sept. Varietal specialities include Madeleine Angevine, Siegerrebe and several excellent fruit wines.

Island history began with Samish and Lummi Native Americans who visited in summer to collect salmon, deer, clams and camas bulbs. Briefly charted as Chauncey Island by an American expedition in 1841, the British reasserted their authority by renaming it Lopez for the pilot of Spain's 1790 explorations in Puget Sound. **Lopez Historical Museum**, *Box 163; tel: (360) 468-2049*, concentrates on settlement, farming and fishing. Exhibits include what was probably the first car on the island. The museum also publishes a useful self-guided driving tour map that visits three dozen vintage buildings.

ORCAS ISLAND

Tourist Information: Orcas Island Chamber of Commerce, *Box 252, Eastsound, WA 98245; tel: (360) 376-2273.*

ACCOMMODATION

Rosario Resort, *One Rosario Way, Eastsound, WA 98245; tel: (360) 376-2222 or (800) 562-8820; fax: (360) 376-2289*, expensive, is the most luxurious resort in the San Juans. Built early in the century as the private estate of Seattle shipbuilder Robert Moran, the main building and grounds have been gloriously restored as a nationally known resort. Since Moran had less than the normal quota of musical ability, he 'played' the 1972-pipe organ like a piano player with none of his guests the wiser. The daily hotel/museum tour and organ concert are well worth taking in.

Most of the alternatives to Rosario are bed and breakfasts. **Spring Bay Inn**; *tel: (360) 376-5331*, expensive, has stunning bay views from every room and private sea kayak tours. **Orcas Hotel**, *Box 155, Orcas, WA 98280; tel: (360) 376-4300*, moderate, overlooks the ferry landing.

Deep Meadow Farm, *Box 321, Deer Harbor, WA 98243; tel: (360) 376-5866*, caters to cyclists. **Deer Harbor Inn**; *tel: (360) 376-4110*, moderate–expensive, overlooks the harbour named after the local black-tailed inhabitants; deer still swim between the many islands.

The **Outlook Inn**; *tel: (360) 376-2200*, moderate–pricey, is well-located in Eastsound.

The Pig War

America was a 150-year headache for Britain. Matters went from war with the French to skirmishes with colonists, revolution in 1776 and yet another war in 1812. It took the death of a pig to bring hostilities to a close.

The first European who might have seen the San Juan Archipelago was a Greek explorer sailing for Spain under the name Juan de Fuca in 1592. By the time Spain got around to exploring in greater detail in 1790, the British had arrived in force. It took Capt. George Vancouver four years to talk the Spanish into relinquishing their claims to the Pacific Northwest, but convince them he did. The United States was more obdurate.

American explorers Lewis and Clark paddled down the Columbia River in 1805, followed by Capt. Charles Wilkes who charted much of Puget Sound in 1841.

Reinforced by growing emigration from eastern America, the US claimed the entire Pacific Northwest from California north to Alaska. '54°40'' or Fight!' was the rallying cry in the US presidential election of 1844.

Both countries breathed a sigh of relief when diplomats set the US-Canada border at the 49th Parallel in 1846. England got Vancouver Island, with the sea boundary running along the main channel between the islands and the mainland. Unfortunately, there are two main channels, Haro Strait, west of the San Juans, and Rosario Strait, to the east.

The ambiguity may have been an oversight. It may also have been a strategic move. James Douglas, governor of Vancouver Island and former head of the Hudson's Bay Company in the Northwest, knew the strategic importance of San Juan Island, which controlled the Haro Strait and the approaches to Victoria. America had already won the Columbia River and forced him to move HBC operations from Vancouver, Washington, to Victoria. He was determined to hold the new border.

Once the border treaty was signed, Douglas moved a small garrison force to a pretty cove midway down the west coast of San Juan Island. The Americans built their own fort at the barren southern end of the island. A few dozen settlers from both nations trickled in.

An amiable stand-off ensued until June, 1859. A prickly American, Lyman Cutlar, planted potatoes in the middle of an HBC sheep pasture. Cutlar's potato patch was visited repeatedly by a British hog, so the American shot the trespasser.

The HBC demanded damages and, when Cutlar refused, demanded trial in Victoria. American officials insisted that US courts had jurisdiction.

Douglas dispatched warships to enforce British sovereignty. The American commander dispatched his own ship, ostensibly to defend against 'Indian attack'. The British flotilla could easily have flattened the feeble American defences, but Americans vastly outnumbered the British throughout the Northwest. The battle could have spread to Vancouver Island itself, which counted four Americans for every British subject.

Cooler heads decided on a joint occupation by 100 men from each nation until the matter could be settled. Both governments immediately turned their attentions to domestic matters and ignored the Pig War. So did the soldiers, who replaced the earthworks and tents of English Camp and American Camp with comfortable wooden buildings, parade grounds and formal gardens. The two commanders took turns hosting monthly balls while other ranks openly traded beer, spirits and other supplies across what was supposed to be a line of hostilities.

Britain and America eventually submitted the matter to Germany's Kaiser Wilhelm I for arbitration. By the time Wilhelm decided for America in 1872, San Juan Island had become an extremely comfortable, if somewhat boring, posting.

British Marines lowered their colours for the last time on 25 Nov, 1872, finally ending more than a century of colonial hostilities in North America.

269

For last-minute bookings, try the **Chamber of Commerce Innkeepers Hotline**; *tel: (360) 376-8888.*

EATING AND DRINKING

The **Rosario Resort**, pricey, is one of the best restaurants in the San Juan Islands as well as the fanciest. In Doe Bay, try the **Doe Bay Café**; *tel: (360) 376-2291*, for budget vegetarian. **Vern's Bayside;** *tel: (360) 376-2231*, gets most of the local traffic for budget omelettes, burgers, sandwiches and pizzas. **Chimayo**; *tel: (360) 376-6394*, is one of Orcas' few Mexican choices.

In Olga, **Café Olga**; *(360) 376-5098*, is often crowded, but worth the wait for budget meals. In Westsound, the **Westsound Store & Deli**; *tel: (360) 376-4440*, offers solid budget food with great views.

SIGHTSEEING

At 57 square miles, Orcas is the largest, and arguably the most beautiful, of the San Juan Islands. Cyclists have no doubt about it being the roughest. There are little hills, big hills and 2409-ft Mt Constitution, the tallest point in the archipelago. **Dolphin Bay Bicycles**, *Orcas Ferry Landing; tel: (360) 376-4157*, and **Wildlife Cycles**, *Eastsound; tel: (360) 376-4708*, have the best selection of hire cycles.

It's 5 grinding miles up the twisting road through **Moran State Park**, *Star Rte Box 22, Eastsound, WA 98245; tel: (360) 376-2326*, a route not recommended for RVs or sometime cyclists. The view from the top of Mt Constitution is stunning. A stone observation tower adds an additional 50 ft and 360° views to Bellingham, Victoria, the Olympic Peninsula and Mt Rainier. The 5175-acre park has more than 30 miles of walking paths, including a 1½ mile trail almost straight down to the appropriately named **Twin Lakes**, directly below the Mt. Constitution summit overlook.

It's comforting to believe that 18th-century Spanish explorers were so taken with the immense pods of killer whales that they named the island in their honour, but not true. The real namesake was the Viceroy of Mexico, one Don Juan Vincente de Guemes Pacheco y Padilla Orcasitees y Aguayo Conde de Revilla

Gigedo, who underwrote a 1792 voyage by Francisco Eliza.

Recognising the value of publicity as much as any Russian, British or American explorer, Eliza also named Guemes Island, Padilla Bay, and the entire *Archipelago de San Juan* for his patron.

Orcas' geography never welcomed agriculture, but the island has a long history as a holiday destination. Mainlanders began flocking to Orcas with the first ferries in the 1890s. Washington State Ferries now dock at Orcas Village on the southern end of the U-shaped island, which is split by Westsound and the much larger Eastsound.

The main settlement is **Eastsound**, at the head of the deep inlet that separates Orcas' two lobes. Several historic buildings have become modern tourist businesses, including the **Outlook Inn**, which incorporates part of an 1838 fur trapper's cottage. **Orcas Island Historical Museum**, *just up North Beach Rd; tel: (360) 376-4849*, has Lummi and Samish artefacts as well as original documents and pioneer articles from six 1880s island homesteads.

A number of artists have studios and galleries on Orcas. **The Orcas Island Artworks**, *Box 125, Olga, WA 98279; tel: (360) 376-4408*, is a co-operative gallery with about 70 local artists that shares a converted farm building with the Olga Café. **Howe Art**, *on the Horseshoe Hwy, Box 362, Eastsound, WA 98245; tel: (360) 376-2945*, is the source of the oversized kinetic sculptures along the *Horseshoe Hwy* between Orcas and Eastsound.

The miles of protected shoreline along Eastsound, Westsound and Deer Harbor make Orcas a favourite with sailors and kayakers. **Shearwater Adventures**, *Box 787, Eastsound, WA 98245; tel: (360) 376-4699*, hire kayaks and organise tours from three hours to several days. For the less adventurous, the **Morning Star**, *Rosario Resort; tel: (360) 376-2222* or *(800) 562-8820; fax: (360) 376-2289*, a 56-ft working sailboat, provides cruises in nearby waters. And for a close-up look at Orcas and nearby islands from above, **Magic Air Tours**, *Box 223; Eastsound, WA 98245; tel: (360) 376-2733*, offer daily flightseeing in an open biplane during good weather.

SAN JUAN ISLAND

Tourist Information: San Juan Island Chamber of Commerce, *Box 98, Friday Harbor, WA 98250; tel: (360) 378-5240*, and **Visitor Information Services**, *East St, next to ferry lanes; tel: (360) 378-6977*.

ACCOMMODATION

San Juan Central Reservations, *Cannery Landing, Ste 26, Friday Harbor, WA 98250; tel: (360) 378-6675*, handles bookings for the entire island.

Inns at Friday Harbor, *680 Spring St, Friday Harbor, WA 98250; tel: (360) 378-3031 or (800) 752-5752; fax: (360) 378-4228*, moderate, is the island's largest collection of motel rooms. **Olympic Lights**, *4531-A Cattle Point Rd, Friday Harbor, WA 98250; tel: (360) 378-3186*, moderate–expensive, has spectacular views of mountains and straits. **Orcinus Inn**, *3580 Beaverton Valley Rd, Friday Harbor, WA 98250; tel: (360) 378-4060*, budget–moderate, is more basic. **Roche Harbor Resort**, *Box 4001, Roche Harbor, WA 98250; tel: (360) 378-2155 or (800) 451-8910; fax: (360) 378-6809*, moderate–expensive, is a scenic and historic inn on the north-west tip of the island.

EATING AND DRINKING

The **San Juan Brewing Company**, *1 Front St, Friday Harbor, WA 98250; tel: (360) 378-2337; fax: (360) 378-5555*, cheap–budget, the only brewery in the islands, has live music most weekends and in summer. **Springtree Café**, *310-C Spring St, Friday Harbor, WA 98250; tel: (360) 378-4848*, moderate, has the best seafood on San Juan. **San Juan Coffee Roasting Company**, *18 Cannery Landing, Friday Harbor, WA 98250; tel: (360) 378-4443*, makes the best espresso west of Seattle.

SIGHTSEEING

San Juan is the most varied of the islands. Look for 55 square miles of forest, cliffs and miniature mountains to the north, farmland in the middle and windswept grasslands to the south. 'The City' is **Friday Harbor**, the seat of government and the only incorporated town in the Islands. Named after a Hawaiian labourer called Joe Friday (employers declined to learn the melodious syllables of his real name), Friday Harbor has gone from a rough and ready frontier town to a bustling tourist and government port. Most ferries and day trips to the San Juans stop here, as do thousands of pleasure sailors.

Cycling is an ideal way to see San Juan. **Island Bicycles**, *380 Argyle, Friday Harbor, WA 98250; tel: (360) 378-4941; fax (360) 378-4706*, have the best hire selection. **Susie's Moped Rentals**, *Nichols and A Sts, Friday Harbor, WA 98250; tel: (360) 378-5244 or (800) 532-0087*, offer a less strenuous alternative for the carless.

Afoot or on wheels, don't skip the **San Juan Island National Historic Park** headquarters, *125 Spring St, Friday Harbor, WA 98250; tel: (360) 378-2240*, for island history. The **Whale Museum**, *62 First St, Friday Harbor; tel: (360) 378-4710*, explores the biology, behaviour and sounds of whales.

The easiest way to see real whales is to cross the island west to **Lime Kiln Point State Park**; *tel: (360) 755-9231*, surrounding Lime Kiln Lighthouse. The name comes from the lime that was once mined nearby. Lime Kiln is *the* place to spot orcas May–Aug. The waters just off the park are also popular for whale watching cruises from Friday Harbor, other San Juan islands, Seattle, Port Townsend, Bellingham and Victoria. Expect to see everything from one-person sea kayaks to open pontoon boats and luxury cruisers jockeying for the best view of black-and-white orcas who are determinedly charting their own course along the coast.

At the south end of the island is **American Camp**, site of the American camp during the Pig War (see p.269). Officers' quarters and other buildings have been rebuilt. North of Lime Kiln is **English Camp**, above Garrison Bay. The blockhouse, commissary, hospital, barracks and formal garden are restored. Both sites are laced with walking trails, but English Camp is by far the more attractive with forested hills and views across Garrison Bay to Haro Strait. American Camp is noted more for relentless wind and swarms of rabbits inhabiting the rolling grassland. Hungry eagles and owls are frequent visitors.

271

BELLINGHAM–VANCOUVER

This route crosses the USA-Canada border at Blaine, the busiest border crossing east of Detroit, Michigan-Windsor, Ontario.

The 75-mile drive can take less than two hours mid-week, or half a day on holiday weekends, when heavy traffic clogs both sides of the Peace Arch crossing and Vancouver city streets. Whichever direction you're headed, allow time to fill up on petrol in Blaine. US petrol prices can be 40% lower than a few hundred metres north.

Vancouver
20 miles
Richmond
99
20 miles
White Rock
10 miles
Blaine
99
15 miles
Lynden
Ferndale
539
10 miles
5
12 miles
Bellingham

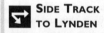
ROUTE: 75 MILES

ROUTE

Follow I-5 north past exits for Ferndale, Lynden and Semiahmoo to **Blaine** and the 24–hr **international border crossing** (see p.273 and p.19). Continue north on BC Hwy 99, also a motorway, past the resort town of **White Rock** and exits for BC Ferries (at Tsawwassen), **Richmond**, Vancouver International Airport and across the Fraser River into **Vancouver**, where traffic drops onto city streets. Follow *Oak St* north to *W. King Edward Ave*, turn left, continue to *Granville St* and turn right. *Granville St* crosses Granville Island and False Creek into central Vancouver.

FERNDALE

Tourist Information: Ferndale Chamber of Commerce, *5640 Riverside Dr., Ferndale, WA 98248; tel: (360) 384-3042.*

Originally a teeming steamboat port for the Nooksak River, Ferndale now depends on oil refining, aluminium smelting and tourism.

Hovander Homestead Park, *5299 Nielsen Rd; tel: (360) 384-3444*, a National Historic Site, is a painstakingly restored turn-of-the-century farm, complete with a Victorian farm house, an enormous red barn and period farm equipment. **Pioneer Park**, *2 blocks south of Main St on First Ave; tel: (360) 384-6461*, has a fine collection of log cabins, early buildings and artefacts from around Whatcom County. **Tennant Lake Natural Interpretative Center**, *5236 Nielsen Rd; tel: (360) 384-3444*, is housed in an early homestead. Boardwalks and a lookout tower offer access to a 200-acre marsh for bird watching.

SIDE TRACK TO LYNDEN

LYNDEN

Tourist Information: Lynden Chamber of Commerce, *444 Front St, Lynden, WA*

98264; tel: (360) 354-5995. Originally settled by Dutch immigrants, this farm town has rebuilt its central district as a Dutch theme park, complete with windmill, Dutch pastries, children dancing in wooden shoes and Sunday closing. The **Lynden Pioneer Museum**, *217 W. Front St; tel: (360) 354-3675*, is among the biggest and most complete regional history collections in Washington. 🚶

BLAINE

Tourist Information: Blaine Visitor Information Center, *900 Peace Portal Dr., Blaine, WA 98230; tel: (360) 332-4544.* Once a major salmon and canning centre, Blaine now lives on tourism and Canadian shopping dollars. **Peace Arch Factory Outlets**, *I-5 Exit 270; tel: (360) 366-3127*, is the largest shopping complex between Bellingham and the border.

Edric's, *8394 Harborview Rd; tel: (360) 371-3838*, expensive, has the best steaks and seafood in the area. **The Inn at Semi-ah-moo**, *9565 Semiahmoo Hwy; tel: (360) 371-2000; fax: (360) 371-5490*, is a posh and pricey resort on the site of an abandoned salmon cannery looking across Drayton Harbor into Canada. Afternoon views of Mt Baker across Semi-ah-moo's 1000-acre wildlife preserve are superb.

The **Peace Arch**, a 67-ft neoclassical arch astride the border, sports a pair of iron gates that are bolted open on each side of the longest undefended border in the world. The arch is set in a landscaped park that can be entered from either side of the border on foot. An average of 70,000 people cross the border at Blaine each day. For the best petrol prices, take Exit 276 off I-5 to check prices at competing stations. Cheese is another favourite buy for Canadians.

WHITE ROCK

Tourist Information: White Rock & South Surrey Chamber of Commerce, *15150 Russell Ave, White Rock, BC V4B 2P5; tel: (604) 536-6844; fax: (604) 536-4994.* Once an isolated farming and fishing town, White Rock has become a holiday destination. US teenagers like the BC drinking age, 19, versus 21 in Washington. Canadians head for the 3-km promenade and broad beaches on Semiah-

Border Formalities

US and Canadian citizens need a passport or other proof of citizenship to cross the border in either direction; a driving licence is not sufficient. Citizens of other countries may need passports and visas to enter either the US or Canada. Check with the nearest US and Canadian consulates for current requirements. Hired vehicles may cross the border if the hire company permits. Ask when booking the car, and again when picking it up. Some contracts and insurance policies restrict driving to a specific area.

The usual customs allowances apply (see p.23), although vehicle searches are infrequent. Canadian officials zealously enforce restrictions on handguns and other weapons. The crossing is open 24 hours a day, but traffic can back up badly at peak holiday weekends. **Tourism British Columbia** has a walk-in visitor centre on the right just opposite the customs and immigration offices, open 0800–2000 daily. The **Blaine Information Center** serves southbound travellers.

moo Bay. The holiday scene is centred around the historic pier, 460m long. The white boulder (colour-enhanced with a coat of white paint) that gave the town its name is just east of the pier. **White Rock Museum**, *14970 Marine Dr.; tel: (604) 541-2222; fax: (604) 541-2223*; was built as the Great Northern Railway station. It now houses local exhibits.

RICHMOND

Tourist Information: Travel InfoCentre, *7888 Alderbridge Way, Richmond, BC V6X 2A5; tel: (604) 278-9333.* Richmond is the favourite district for up-market Hong Kong emigrants establishing an alternative residence against the Chinese takeover of their home city on July 1, 1997. The **International Buddhist Society temple**, *9160 Steveston Highway; tel: (604) 274-2822*, the second largest Buddhist temple in North America, is also a traditional Chinese art and culture centre.

VANCOUVER

Big-city Vancouver carries the trappings of a small town. Immigration from around the world has given it more foreign-born citizens than any other city in the world, yet it remains essentially Canadian, a polite, tidy place where everyone seems to know everyone else and quite likes it that way. Canada's third largest city is an overgrown village sitting on the edge of a rainforest with some very serious mountains rising almost within walking distance from City Hall. It's the home of Greenpeace but equally at home with a government voted into office on promises to cut down every tree in sight to create jobs – a regime that was promptly voted out again at the next election.

TOURIST INFORMATION

Tourism Vancouver and the **Greater Vancouver Convention and Visitors Bureau**, *Suite 210 Waterfront Centre, 200 Burrard St, Vancouver, BC V6C 3L6; tel: (604) 682-2222; fax: (604) 682-1717;* **Visitor Information Centres** are located at *Vancouver International Airport arrivals terminals,* open daily, and at *Pacific Centre,* open daily in summer.

Downtown Ambassadors; *tel: (604) 685-7811,* wearing blue walking shorts, crested white shirts and Downtown Ambassadors logo, proffer help on city centre streets 1000–1800 in summer from *Canada Place* south to *Robson St* and along *Robson* from the West End to BC Place Stadium. The **Georgia Straight**, *1770 Burrard, Vancouver, BC; tel: (604) 730-7000,* a free weekly newspaper, has the most complete listing of local events, cultural attractions, performances, cinemas and other happenings, with reviews and opinion from a decidedly independent perspective.

WEATHER

The Pacific Ocean buffers the extremes of winter and summer. Daytime temperatures occasionally hit 33°C, but 20–25°C is more common. Summer is usually sunny, with the most reliable sunshine in May and mid Sept–early Oct.

While the rest of Canada shivers beneath winter white, Vancouver temperatures can climb to a balmy 15°C. Snow is heavy on the ski slopes of Grouse Mountain just across the harbour but rare in the city centre. Rain, however, is no stranger.

Downtown Vancouver receives more than 1400 mm (55 in) of rain yearly, most of it in winter. It rained for a memorable 40 days and 40 nights in 1966. More often, rain falls from skies the colour of wet wool blankets for 2–3 days, then clears temporarily to reveal crystal clear vistas of snow-capped peaks before low clouds, fog and rain return.

ARRIVING AND DEPARTING

By Air

Vancouver International Airport, (YVR), *Box 23750, Airport Postal Outlet, Richmond, BC V7B 1Y7; tel: (604) 276-6101; fax: (604) 276-6516,* is 30 min south of the city centre by car. Airport-area hotels have free shuttles.

YVR Airporter; *tel: (604) 244-9888* or *(800) 668-3141,* travel between the airport and major city hotels, $9 single, $15 return. Taxi is about $15. **BC Transit**; *tel: (604) 521-0400,* stops at the domestic terminal. Car access is via BC 99. Use Exit 39 if travelling northbound, Exit 39A if southbound, and follow the airport signs.

International flights arrive and depart from the International Terminal Building (ITB), opened in 1996. Domestic flights use the adjoining Domestic Terminal Building. The complex surrounds a central parkade (car park) and hire car pick-up area.

North Vancouver

WELSH STREET

BC RAIL
NORTH
VANCOUVER
STATION

LIONS GATE BRIDGE

BURRARD
INLET

VANCOUVER

0   ½ km
0   ¼ mile

LIONS GATE BRIDGE ROAD

Stanley Park

■ AQUARIUM

North
⇧

SEABUS

Coal Harbour

English Bay

DENMAN STREET

Robson Street

GEORGIA STREET

PENDER STREET

West End

Canada Place

WATERFRONT
STATION

NELSON STREET

◆ BARCLAY
HERITAGE
SQUARE

● BURRARD
STATION

DUNSMUIR STREET

HASTINGS
CENTRE

Gastown

WATER STREET

DAVIE STREET

THURLOW STREET

BURRARD STREET

Hornby Street

HOWE STREET

Granville Mall

SEYMOUR STREET

● GRANVILLE
STATION HASTINGS ST

ℹ

Pender St

Chinatown

STADIUM
STATION

DUNSMUIR STREET

MAIN STREET

BEACH AVENUE

MARITIME
MUSEUM ■

Vanier Park

VANCOUVER
MUSEUM ■

PACIFIC STREET

BURRARD STREET BRIDGE

RICHARDS STREET

ORPHEUM
THEATRE ◆

Yaletown

GEORGIA STREET

BC PLACE
STADIUM ◆

VIA/AMTRAK
VANCOUVER
STATION

CAMBIE ST BRIDGE

SCIENCE
WORLD ■

MAIN ST
STATION

GRANVILLE ST BRIDGE

Granville
Island

Pacific Blvd

False
Creek

STAMPS
LANDING

CORNWALL AVE

Kitsilano

2ND AVENUE

4TH AVENUE

6TH AVENUE

ARBUTUS STREET

BURRARD STREET

Fir Street

GRANVILLE STREET

Hemlock Street

BROADWAY

7th Avenue

MAIN STREET

BROADWAY

BROADWAY

Kingsway

12TH AVENUE

OAK STREET

12TH AVENUE

CAMBIE STREET

16TH AVENUE

16TH AVENUE

⇨ AIRPORT 13 km

Free luggage trolleys are available in the baggage claim areas. Avis, Alamo, Budget, Hertz, Thrifty and Tilden car hire check-in counters are immediately outside the customs area. Follow the walkway through the parkade and down luggage trolley ramps leading to the hire car park.

Coaches load and unload at kerb-side bays outside the arrivals level. Taxis, hotel courtesy shuttles and other transport services alight at marked stops on the centre roadway. There are small shops and food outlets in the gate areas, but the selection is far better in the central hall near check-in counters. Tastiest airport meals are at the ITB food court.

Once checked in, international passengers clear Canadian Immigration and Security on the way to duty-free shopping and boarding gates. US-bound passengers also clear US Customs and Immigration in Vancouver.

By Car

Primary access from the US is **BC 99**, from the border at the Peace Arch past White Rock, Delta, Richmond (and YVR) into the city centre. From Vancouver Island, **BC Ferries**; *tel: (604) 277-0277*, dock in Tsawwassen, south of the city centre, and Horseshoe Bay, on the north shore of Burrard Inlet. From the north, the *Sea to Sky Highway*, BC 99, follows Howe Sound past Horseshoe Bay to the Lions Gate Bridge and into the city centre. From the east, **Canada 1**, the TransCanada Highway, runs down the Fraser River Valley to **Port Moody**, where it becomes BC 7A and continues into the city centre.

By Train

AMTRAK; *tel: (800) 872-7245*, has daily service between Seattle and Vancouver. **VIA Rail**; *tel: (800) 561-8630*, serves Canadian points east. Both routes use **Pacific Central Station**, *Main & Terminal Sts, Vancouver, BC V6A 2X7*. **BC Rail**; *tel: (604) 631-3500*, has daily service between Whistler and the **BC Rail Station**, *1311 W. 1st St, North Vancouver*.

By Bus

The **Pacific Central Station**, *Main & Terminal Sts*, is also the long distance bus

terminal. **Pacific Coach Lines**; *tel: (604) 662-8074*, **Maverick Coach Lines**; *(604) 662-8051*, and **Greyhound Lines**; *tel: (604) 662-3222*, provide services.

GETTING AROUND

Greater Vancouver spreads from the US border north to Horseshoe Bay and east into the Fraser Valley. The compact central city is well-served by public transport and is a very practical option when sightseeing, but driving to the University of British Columbia, the North Shore, Capilano and Grouse Mountain will save time. Parking is often scarce, particularly in Yaletown, Gastown and Chinatown. Try to avoid commuter routes at rush hour, 0730–0900 and 1600–1800, especially roads leading to Lions Gate Bridge and *Granville St*. Bicycling is a popular alternative to driving in all but the wettest winter weather.

Visiting Americans breathe a sigh of relief in Vancouver, which is quite safe compared to cities on the US side of the border. Canadians generally take law and order much more seriously than do Americans, who sometimes exalt violence to a degree that is not accepted in Canada. Canada's tight restrictions on firearms also contribute greatly to lower crime rates.

Vancouver is not, however, immune to drug-related crimes, which *are* far less common than in comparable US cities. It's not wise to wander east beyond the crowds of Gastown at night without company, or to explore the narrow alleys around *E. Hastings, Granville or Seymour Sts*.

Public Transport

Vancouver has the most extensive public transport system in Canada. **BC Transport**, *13401 108th Ave, Surrey (Gateway SkyTrain Station, Lower Plaza level), BC V3T 5T4; tel: (604) 521-0400 or (604) 985-7777*, schedules and routes are timed for quick connections. A free brochure, *Discover Vancouver on Transit*, available at most tourist information centres and brochure racks, gives detailed route information for most popular destinations. A full-colour *Transit Guide* showing complete routes for all three systems costs $1.50.

Fares are exact change only, based on three

zones and time of day. Maximum fare, crossing three zones during rush hours (Mon–Fri before 0930 and 1500–1830) is $3 adults, $1.50 for children and seniors. Off peak fares are $1.50 and $0.75. Day passes, valid outside rush hours, are $4.50 and $2.25. One fare covers bus, trolley, rail and ferry. Transfers are valid for 90 min. **Waterfront Station** is the nexus for all three systems.

Bus and **trolley** routes serve more than 1800 sq km, and every major visitor attraction. Buses run daily but the frequency varies.

The **SkyTrain** light rail system covers the 28 km between Burnaby, New Westminster and Surrey in 39 mins. Four downtown stations are underground and clearly marked at street level, 16 others are elevated. Trains run every 2–5 mins daily.

SeaBus harbour ferries cross between Vancouver and the North Shore in 12 mins. Service operates daily every 15–30 mins. Main transfer points to ground transport are Waterfront Station in Vancouver and Lonsdale Quay in North Vancouver.

False Creek Ferries

Aquabus; *tel: (604) 689-5858*, is a fleet of small boats serving False Creek from Science World to Concord Presentation Centre, Stamps Landing, Granville Island and the Hornby Street Dock. Competing **False Creek Ferries**; *tel: (604) 684-7781*, runs from Science World to Stamps Landing, Granville Island, the Aquatic Centre and the Maritime Museum. Fares are $1.75 to $5 depending on distance.

Driving in Vancouver

Traffic flows smoothly outside commuting hours, but roadways are narrow. Residential streets are often choked to a single lane by parked vehicles while larger multi-lane thoroughfares can suddenly shrink to a single line of traffic. If possible, plan driving routes to avoid left turns. Left turn lanes and left turn traffic signals are rare. *Granville St,* the main north–south artery, is a particular problem. With few left turn signals, traffic can back up in seconds when a single car attempts to turn left.

Parking meters are common except in residential districts. Car parks cost $1.25 per hour to $15 per day. Parking regulations are strictly enforced. Parked cars which impede traffic flow are quickly towed away.

STAYING IN VANCOUVER

Accommodation

Tourism BC; *tel: (800) 663-6000*, can book most Vancouver-area accommodations, but advance booking is essential Apr–Oct and wise the rest of the year. A steady stream of Alaska cruise ship passengers, Vancouver-bound tourists, conventions and business travellers keeps hotels busy all year. Chains include *BW, CI, CP, CS, FS, Hd, HI, Hy, PP, Rn, Sh, TL* and *WT*. Best sources for bed and breakfasts are the **Tourism BC** booking service and **British Columbia Bed and Breakfast Directory**, *1609 Blanshard St, Victoria, BC V8W 2J5; tel: (604) 382-6188 or (800) 661-6188; fax: (604) 382-9172.*

There are more than 16,000 rooms in Greater Vancouver, 10,000 of them in the downtown core. The average room rate is just over $100 per night, dipping mid Oct–end May and soaring summer–autumn. Highest rates are in the city centre. Least expensive are the airport area and outlying towns such as Richmond, Burnaby and Langley. Best balance of price and convenience is south of False Creek from *Main St* west to UBC.

Grande Dame of Vancouver hotels is Canadian Pacific's **Hotel Vancouver**, *900 W. Georgia St, Vancouver, BC V6C 2W6; tel: (604) 684-3131 or (800) 441-1414; fax: (604) 662-1929,* restored to its early 20th-century elegance in late 1996. Next door is the somewhat stuffy **Hotel Georgia**, *801 W. Georgia St., Vancouver, BC V6C 2W6; tel: (604)682-5566 or (800) 663-1111; fax: (604) 682-8192.* The **Wedgewood Hotel**, *845 Hornby St, Vancouver, BC V6Z 1V1; tel: (604) 689-7777 or (800) 663-0666; fax: (604) 688-3074,* is a modern version of the same luxury with better food than its two competitors. All are expensive–pricey.

Best budget–moderate rooms are the **Hostelling International Vancouver Jericho Beach**, *1515 Discovery St, Vancouver, BC V6R 4K5; tel: (604) 224-3208; fax: (604)*

224-4852, **Hostelling International Vancouver Downtown**, *1114 Burnaby St, Vancouver, BC V6E 1P1; tel: (604) 684-4565; fax: (604) 684-4540,* the **University of British Columbia Conference Centre**, *5961 Student Union Blvd, Vancouver, BC V6T 2C9; tel: (604) 822-1010; fax: (604) 822-1001,* and the **YMCA Hotel/Residence**, *733 Beatty St, Vancouver, BC V6B 2M4; tel: (604) 895-5830; fax: (604) 681-2550.*

Not long ago, bed and breakfast meant a spartan spare room, but luxury has become the norm. **Heather Cottage**, *5425 Trafalgar St, Vancouver, BC V6N 1C1; tel/fax: (604) 261-1442,* is a prime example. Heritage homes are also emerging as guest houses. **The Manor**, *345 W. 13th Ave, Vancouver, BC V5Y 1W2; tel: (604) 876-8494; fax: (604) 876-5763,* is among the best. Both are moderate–expensive.

Eating and Drinking

Vancouver is becoming one of North America's hottest food cities. Credit the lucky confluence of rising incomes, a steady tide of immigration, demands by a growing cinema and television industry and a young population. Trendy Vancouver restaurants are more international than their counterparts in Seattle, San Francisco or Los Angeles, a bit less expensive and far friendlier. Wine lists are extensive, if somewhat expensive, thanks to BC sin taxes (excise taxes levied on alcohol and tobacco products). Vancouver claims the highest per capita wine consumption in North America.

Northwest or **New American cuisine** implies fresh local ingredients (especially seafood) with varying combinations of Asian and Mediterranean flavours and cooking methods. **Canadian cuisine** typically brings 1950s fare: fried steaks drowned in sauce; mystery-meat scaloppini or egg foo yung. The *Georgia Strait* has the most straightforward food reviews and reliable restaurant descriptions.

Bishop's, *2182 4th Ave; tel: (604) 738-2025,* pricey, is reputedly the most polished New American restaurant in Vancouver. **Bacchus Ristorante**, *Wedgewood Hotel, 845 Hornby St; tel: (604) 689-7777,* pricey, has the best blend of Northern Italian and Northwest. **900 West**, *Hotel Vancouver, 900 W. Georgia St;* *tel; (604) 684-3131,* pricey, is an unabashed knockoff of San Francisco megachef Jeremiah Tower by Tower himself.

Stanley Park has food to match its views. The pricey **Fish House**, *8901 Stanley Park Dr.; tel: (604) 681-7275,* is the best fish restaurant in the city. **The Teahouse Restaurant**, *7501 Stanley Park Dr. (at Ferguson Pt); tel: (604) 669-3281,* moderate–pricey, specialises in Northwest cuisine. **Prospect Point Café**, *Prospect Point, Stanley Park; tel: (604) 669-2737,* budget–moderate, is a casual version of The Teahouse, complete with take-away hot-dogs and hamburgers.

Star Anise, *1485 W. 12 St; tel: (604) 737-1485,* moderate, is a fine Asian-Northwest fusion with shockingly good service. **Tang's Noodle House**, *2807 W. Broadway; tel: (604) 737-1278,* cheap–budget, is one of the city's favourite Chinese restaurants. Best bet for dim sum, Chinese dumplings, is **Pink Pearl**, *1132 E. Hastings; tel: (604) 253-4316,* in Chinatown. The best sushi bargain is the **Japanese Deli House**, *381 Powell St; tel: (604) 681-6484,* for budget all-you-can-eat sushi or tempura at lunch. **Thai House**, *1116 Robson St; tel: (604) 683-3383,* budget–moderate, is crowded at lunch and nearly as popular for dinner at locations in Kitsilano, Richmond and Metrotown as well as downtown.

Surat Sweet, *1938 W. 4th Ave; tel: (604) 733-7363,* budget–moderate, is a good vegetarian Indian choice. **The Sitar Indian Restaurant**, *308 Water St; tel: (604) 681-3678,* moderate, has a good selection of meat and fish as well as fine veg. **A Taste of Jamaica**, *941 Davie St; tel: (604) 683-3464,* budget, serves some of the best goat curry and ackee north of Porto Antonio.

Any of Vancouver's ethnic enclaves, Chinatown, Japantown, Little India, Little Italy or Greektown, are good choices for cheap–moderate ethnic restaurants, or sample them all at **Granville Island Public Market**, *Granville Isl; tel: (604) 666-6477.* Dozens of stalls sell everything from local breads and goat cheese to imports from around the globe. Harbour-side tables inside and out offer pleasant views in any weather. **Granville Island Brewery**, *Granville Island; tel: (694) 687-2739,* has daily tours at 1500 with free samples. Best place to drink in peace, if not quiet, is **Mulvaney's Restaurant**, *Granville Isl; tel: (604) 685-6571*, cheap–moderate, with great beer, good food and loud music.

Coffee has become as much an institution in Vancouver as it has in Seattle. With 170 officially rainy days each year, frequent doses of caffeine help keep grey-sky depression at bay. Starbucks is Canada's reigning coffee chain, but Vancouver has no lack of independent coffee roasteries or coffee bars. **Murchie's Tea & Coffee**, *970 Robson St; tel: (604) 662-3776, and branch locations*, has been roasting and serving coffee since 1908. The Yaletown branch, above, has an interesting coffee museum.

Ciao Espresso Bar, *1074 Denman St; tel: (604) 682-0112*, is a prized hangout for writers who thrive on steady diets of caffeine and tobacco. Singles mingle on comfortable sofas at **Dakoda's**, *1602 Yew St; tel: (604) 730-9266*, then stop next door for designer condoms at Willi Wear before retiring to more private pursuits. **Joe's Cafe**, *1150 Commercial Dr.*, is a vigorous mix of poolhall hustlers, bohemian philosophers, poets, feminists, political agitators and the occasional politician.

ENTERTAINMENT

Forget the days when Vancouver rolled up the sidewalks at 2200. The city has 32 professional theatre groups and two dozen performance venues, plus 18 professional dance companies and music venues specialising in *taiko* (Japanese drumming), jazz, blues, rock, classical, opera and more. Best information: *The Georgia Strait*; the Thurs *Vancouver Sun* or the Fri *Province* newspapers. **Arts Hotline**; *tel: (604) 684-ARTS (2787)*, has pre-recorded information.

Granville Mall, *Granville St, Hastings–Georgia Sts*, a slightly seedy section of town, is **Theatre Row** with the cheapest cinemas in Vancouver. All films are half-price on Tuesdays. Nearby are the **Orphium Theatre**; *tel: (604) 280-4444*, home of the **Vancouver Symphony**, and the **Commodore Ballroom**, *870 Granville St; tel: (604) 681-7838*, Vancouver's other top concert venue, the **Yale Hotel**, *1300 Granville St; tel: (604)681-9253*, is the pre-eminent blues house despite a

questionable neighbourhood; safest parking is at the hotel or the equally raucous strip club next door.

Yaletown is the current night-time hotspot. Even the **Yaletown Brewing Co**, *1111 Mainland St; tel: (604) 688-0064*, is likely to have a queue Fri–Sat nights. **Bar None**, *1222 Hamilton St; tel: (604) 689-7000*, has queues more nights than not for live blues, rock and soul. Hotter still are pool halls, starting with the original **Soho Cafe**, *1144 Homer St; tel: (604) 688-1180*, and **Automotive Club**, *1095 Homer St; tel: (604) 682-0040*, a former automobile dealership.

Acts as diverse as the Three Tenors and Aerosmith play **BC Place**, *777 Pacific Blvd S.; tel: (604) 661-7373*. The **Ford Centre for the Performing Arts**, *777 Homer St; tel: (604) 606-0616*, hosts touring Broadway and other stage shows. The **Vancouver Opera**, *845 Cambie St; tel: (604) 682-2871; fax: (604) 682-3981*, plays Oct–May.

Communications
There are dozens of post offices in Vancouver. Mail can be addressed to hotels.

Money
Thomas Cook Foreign Exchange branches are located at *Eaton's Dept Store, 701 Granville St; tel: (604) 687-6111; Pan Pacific Hotel, 999 Canada Place; tel: (604) 641-1229; Eaton Centre, 2139A 4700 Kingsway, Burnaby; tel: (604) 430-3990; Marlin Travel, Park Royal Shopping Centre, 2009 Park Royal South; tel: (604) 922-9301*, and *Guildford Town Centre, 1111 Guildford Town Centre, Surrey; tel: (604) 584-3338*. Traveller's cheque refunds are available at all the above and most offer Money Gram services.

SHOPPING

The major department stores are **Eaton's**, *701 Granville St; tel: (604) 685-7112*, plus other locations, and **The Bay**, *674 Granville; tel: (604) 681-6211*. BC's largest shopping centre is **Metrotown Centre**, *4800 Kingsway, Burnaby; tel: (604) 438-2444*, 15 min by SkyTrain from the city centre. **Pacific Centre**, *Georgia & Howe Sts; tel: (604) 688-7236*, is the leading inner city mall. Other major shopping areas include **Granville Island**, *West 4th Ave*, Kitsilano, and *Robson St*, Vancouver's less-studied answer to Beverly Hills' *Rodeo Dr*.

Top shops for First Nations items are **Hill's Indian Crafts**, *165 Water St; tel: (604) 685-4249; fax: (604) 682-4197*, and **Inuit Gallery of Vancouver**, *345 Water St; tel: (604) 688-7323*, both in Gastown. Best source for books is **Duthie Books**, *919 Robson St; tel: (604) 684-4496*, and other locations. For guidebooks and travel-related items, try **The Travel Bug**, *2667 W. Broadway; tel: (604) 737-1122*, in Kitsilano.

SIGHTSEEING

Vancouver got its start in 1791 when Spanish Captain Jose Maria Narvaez anchored west of **Point Grey**, now home to the **University of British Columbia**. Capt George Vancouver anchored nearby the next year and rowed into Burrard Inlet, which he named after a naval friend. The UBC **Museum of Anthropology** (MOA), *6393 NW. Marine Dr., Vancouver, BC V6T 1Z2; tel: (604) 822-5087; fax: (604) 822-2974*, has one of the world's finest collections of First Nations art with modern and antique totems, feast dishes and carvings in gold, stone and wood. Tens of thousands of additional artefacts are visible in storage cases. Don't miss the outdoor totems behind the museum building. The **Nitobe Memorial Garden**, *200m north on S.W. Marine Dr.*, is one of the most authentic Japanese Gardens in North America. UBC's **Botanical Garden**, *6804 N.W. Marine Dr.; tel: (604) 822-9666*, is one of the finest in BC.

The city of Vancouver began in 1862 when 'three greenhorns' decided to make bricks on the wild shore of Coal Harbour instead of scrabbling for gold in nearby mountains. John Morton, Samuel Brighouse and William Hailstone paid $550.75 for what would become the **West End**, stretching from sea to sea, Coal Harbour to English Bay. Home to the rich and powerful during the Edwardian era, the West End has become a mix of tree-lined streets, modern flats, a few surviving mansions and trendy restaurants sandwiched between Stanley Park and downtown. *Denman St* is the West End's high street, a 7-block strip of restaurants and coffee bars.

The **Roedde House Museum**, *1415 Barclay St, Vancouver, BC V6G 1J6; tel: (604) 684-7040*, open weekends, is one of the few surviving Victorians in the West End. The museum is part of **Barclay Heritage Square**, *Barclay, Nicola, Haro and Broughton Sts*, a collection of nine period homes in their original settings.

Stanley Park; *tel: (604) 257-8400*, is one of North America's finest urban parks, 400 hectares of forest laced with 80 km of walking and cycling paths. The most popular path is a 10-km shoreline loop around the peninsula. Highlights include totem poles, sweeping vistas across Vancouver and the North Shore, three fine restaurants (see p.278), picnic grounds, a rose garden and beaches. **Vancouver Aquarium**, *Stanley Park; tel: (604) 268-9900; fax: (604) 631-2529*, which specialises in the Pacific Northwest, is one of the best aquaria in the region.

Yaletown is a former warehouse district on the north shore of **False Creek**, a shallow inlet stretching east from English Bay. Architects, designers, TV producers and filmmakers are cheek-to-jowl with trendy restaurants, nightspots and pool halls. Parking is at a premium, especially as development burgeons on the 83 hectares along False Creek that was the site of EXPO 86. The **BC Sports Hall of Fame**, *777 Pacific Blvd, Gate A, BC Place Stadium; tel: (604) 687-5520*, showcases the history of sports in the province. **Science World**, *1455 Quebec St, Vancouver, BC V6A 3Z7; tel: (604) 268-6363*, uses hands-on exhibits to explain science. An OMNIMAX theatre beneath the silver geodesic dome has one of the world's largest screens.

One million cubic metres of mud dredged from False Creek early in the century transformed a sandbar into a metal bashing haven called Industrial Island. Island factories produced 50 years worth of rivets, chain, nails, cement and industrial pollutants. When the public finally revolted in the 1960s, industry was eased out and the site cleaned up. The rundown eyesore has become **Granville Island**, one of North America's most successful urban makeovers and a busy refuge for artists, casual shoppers and entertainers.

First Arts

Vancouver has long been a cultural centre for Canada's First Nations artists and artisans. Spurred by academic interest at the University of British Columbia, totem pole carving was revived in 1949 after generations of federal laws forbidding many traditional cultural practices.

The new totems, in turn, helped fuel a cultural renaissance and a resurgence of artistic forms which had all but disappeared except in museum collections.

By the 1990s, modern interpretations of the bold, stylised images of raven, bear, beaver, killer whale and other traditional First Nation themes has become as much a part of BC as European, Chinese and East Indian motifs.

The Burrard, Capilano, Musqueam and Twawwassen are the principal First Nations bands in the Vancouver area, but groups from around the province are well-represented in area galleries, museums, studios and displays. Vancouver International Airport has one of the finest public collections.

Gitksan carvers created the three totems rising outside the international terminal. Banners, prints, thunderbirds, model totem poles and traditional welcoming figures are displayed throughout the arrival and departure areas.

The artistic focus is *The Spirit of Haida Gwaii, the Jade Canoe*, a 6-m bronze by carver Bill Reid incorporating traditional Haida themes and images. The first casting was commissioned for the Canadian Chancery in Washington, DC.

Reid is also well-represented at UBC's Museum of Anthropology, which has a display of jewellery and other small works as well as several larger wood sculptures. He also helped create the Haida houses and totem poles standing behind the MOA overlooking the Georgia Strait. An even large collection of modern poles by other caravers are on display in Stanley Park.

The commercial and artistic success of Reid, Mungo Martin and others has helped create a worldwide market in First Nations arts and crafts. The MOA gift shop has an excellent collection of affordable prints and copies of display pieces.

Commercial gallery prices are higher, but so are selection and quality. Vancouver Island gallery prices, particularly in Campbell River, Port Hardy, Tofino and Ucluelet, are slightly lower than in Vancouver.

As with other original works of art, look for the artist's signature on each piece and a certificate of authentication. 'Indian-style', 'in the tradition of ' 'Indian heritage' and similar phrases are usually attempts to circumvent laws prohibiting the promotion and sale of art made by non-Natives as Native-made pieces.

Several of the best galleries are owned by First Nations artists. **Potlatch Arts Ltd**, *8161 Main St, Suite 100; tel: (604) 321-5888*, is a collector's gallery that sells only the best First Nations wood carvings, glass sculptures and other art.

Totem pole carver and jeweller Norman Tait has his own gallery, **Wilp's Ts Ak Gallery, 'The House of the Mischievous Man'**, *2426 Marine Dr.; tel: (604) 925-5771*, where he welcomes visitors who want to watch carvers working wood, gold and silver.

Wickaninnish Gallery, *The Net Loft, Granville Island*, is one of Vancouver's best sources for traditional and contemporary Native jewellery from throughout BC.

The Cedar Root Gallery, *1607 E. Hastings St; tel: (604) 251-6244*, is a small, community-based gallery that specialises in new artists and more experimental works.

Traditional ceremonies are also being revived, including potlaches and pow-wows. Potlaches are generally private affairs, but the non-Natives are generally welcome at pow-wows, general gatherings that focus on dances and other public events, including art sales. Check with the CVB and local newspapers for dates, time and locations.

Gastown, *Water St between Alexander and Richards Sts*, was settled in 1870 by a saloon-keeper called Gassy Jack for his ability to maintain a running conversation with no outside help. Once a rowdy red light district handy to the docklands, Gastown has become a tamer, if no less popular, entertainment venue. Hanging flower baskets adorn lamp standards spring–autumn.

Chinatown, *E. Pender and Keefer Sts, Carrall–Gore Sts*, began as a ghetto for Vancouver's Chinese immigrants. Reviled for their race and despised for their willingness to accept absurdly low wages, thousands of Chinese labourers were imported in the 1880s to build Canada's railroads. Most eventually drifted into Vancouver and other major cities, settling in Chinatowns for mutual protection against periodic rampages by Whites.

Anti-Chinese violence has disappeared, but the sentiment remains. Thousands of well-to-do Hong Kong Chinese moved to Vancouver during the runup to the June, 1997 handover of the British colony to China. There is occasional talk of Vancouver's transformation into 'Hongcouver', even though most new arrivals settled in Richmond, near the airport.

Parking is a challenge in Chinatown. Best bet is near **Dr Sun Yat-Sen Classical Garden**, *578 Carrall St, Vancouver, BC V6B 2J8; tel: (604) 689-7133*, calling itself the only authentic classical Chinese garden outside China. The **Sam Kee Building**, *8 W. Pender St*, is the narrowest commercial building in the world, less than 2 m wide after the city expropriated most of the building to widen *Pender St*.

Kitsilano, *Burrard to Alma Sts, English Bay south to 16th Ave*, is one of Vancouver's liveliest neighbourhoods, a mix of left-over hippies, young families and UBC students. Classic views of Vancouver, the city centre and Stanley Park with North Shore mountains rising behind, are everyday sights from ever-popular **Vanier Park** and **Kitsilano Park**, on English Bay. *Fourth Ave* is one of the city's premier shopping districts, known more for individual shops than chain outlets. **Broadway**, sometimes called **Greektown**, is a secondary shopping area.

Vancouver Maritime Museum, *1905 Ogden Ave, Vancouver, BC V6J 1A3; tel: (604)*
257-8300, has model ships, naval uniforms and other maritime artefacts. Highlight is the *St Roch* **National Historic Site**, a 1928 ship built for arctic patrol by the Royal Canadian Mounted Police and now open for exploration inside the museum. *St Roch* was the first vessel to sail the Northwest Passage from Pacific to Atlantic Oceans, the first to make the return voyage and, after sailing through the Panama Canal, the first to circumnavigate North America.

The **Vancouver Museum**, *1100 Chestnut St, Vancouver, BC V6J 3J9; tel: (604) 736-4431; fax: (604) 736-5417*, has one of the most extensive collections of BC First Nations' art, relics and costumes as well as city history exhibits. In the same building, the **Pacific Space Centre**; *tel: (604) 738-7827*, offers planetarium and laser-light shows.

Gordon Southam Observatory; *tel: (604) 738-2855*, is open 1900–2300 Fri–Sun, weather permitting, for viewing through a 500mm Cassegrain telescope.

The best overall view of Vancouver is from **The Lookout!**, *atop Harbour Centre, 555 W. Hastings St, Vancouver, BC V6B 4N4; tel: (604) 689-0421; fax: (604) 685-7329*, 167m above the pavement. The white sails to the west are the roof of **Canada Place**, Vancouver's cruise ship terminal and **IMAX Theatre**; *tel: (604) 682-4629*. Directly across Burrard Inlet is **Capilano Suspension Bridge**, *3735 Capilano Rd, North Vancouver, BC V7R 4J1; tel: (604) 985-7474*, a scenic pedestrian suspension bridge over Capilano Canyon. **Grouse Mountain**, *6400 Nancy Greene Wy, North Vancouver, BC V7R 4K9; tel: (604) 984-0661; fax: (604) 984-6360*, rises in the background. At 4100 ft, Grouse Mtn is a winter ski area and a summer walking retreat. Access is by aerial tramway.

Vancouver's mild climate encourages gardens. **Van Dusen Botanical Garden**, *5251 Oak St, Vancouver, BC V6M 4H1; tel: (604) 266-7194*, is one of Canada's most comprehensive collections of ornamental plants. The **Bloedel Floral Conservatory**, *Queen Elizabeth Park, 33rd and Cambie Sts, Vancouver, BC; tel: (604) 872-5513*, is a lush tropical garden within a triodetic dome, surrounded by 53 hectares of arboretum.

VANCOUVER CIRCUIT

The route begins and ends at *W. 4th Ave* and *Burrard St* for convenience, but you can pick it up at any point. The circuit can be taken in either direction (except for the Stanley Park and Gastown sections, which are one-way), but the directions given reduce left turns and take advantage of one-way streets. Avoid the downtown and Lions Gate Bridge sections during commuting hours, 0730–0900 and 1600–1800.

Allow at least half a day for this 100-km driving circuit. Visiting all of the museums and attractions could stretch to the better part of a week.

KITSILANO

The *4th Ave* shopping district begins at *Burrard St,* but shops are busier and trendier west of *Maple St.* During the 1970s, Kitsilano was Canada's hippie haven, a past that is fondly remembered but almost invisible beneath a veneer of 1990s prosperity. The shopping ends abruptly at *Balsam St,* where *4th Ave* becomes a residential street. The next major shopping area is *MacDonald–Alma Sts.* One block west of Alma on the left is the Jerico Barracks,

Vancouver Detachment, Canadian Forces Base Chilliwack. **Jerico Beach Park** is on the right.

Watch for cyclists as the road veers to the right and becomes *N.W. Marine Dr.* toward **Locarno Park**, **Locarno Beach** and **Spanish Banks Beach**, all fronting on **English Bay**. The three parks merge imperceptibly, with expansive vistas north to West Vancouver and east to the inner city and Stanley Park. The beachfront walkway is extremely popular with walkers, runners, cyclists, and dog walkers – watch where you step. There is ample parking, particularly near Locarno Park, as well as picnic and recreational facilities.

POINT GREY

Capt. George Vancouver anchored just off Point Grey in 1792, only to find that two Spanish ships had preceded him. Vancouver led the way north up the Georgia Strait, around the north tip of Vancouver Island and south to Nootka Sound, the first step in a successful campaign to convince Spain of British superiority in the region.

Pacific Spirit Regional Park begins at the city limits just west of Spanish Banks. The 770-hectare park surrounds the **University of British Columbia** campus on **Point Grey**, providing a buffer against urban expansion as well as one of Vancouver's most expansive parks. Wild parklands lie between road and ocean. The expensive, well-protected homes on the other side of the road are on UBC Endowment Lands.

UBC is built in grey concrete and red brick. At the first stop sign, the junction with *Chancellor Dr.*, turn right. Just after the turn is the entrance to the parking lot for the UBC **Museum of Anthropology** (MOA), on the right. The main UBC parkade is to the left, but the museum lot is more convenient. Parking regulations are strictly enforced on the campus. Parking is by permit only except in scattered locations, including MOA. Buy parking tickets from the yellow boxes in the MOA lot, which accept both coins and credit cards. MOA's main entrance is at the far end of the parking lot. The outdoor totem exhibition area is over a small rise behind the lot and left behind the museum building. Walk the 200m west along *Marine Dr.* to **Nitobe Japanese Tea Gardens**, on the left.

Marine Dr. curves south around Point Grey. The **Botanical Garden** is on the right, 2 km beyond the MOA parking lot.

SHAUGHNESSY HEIGHTS

When leaving the Botanical Garden, turn right onto *Marine Dr.* and immediately move to the left-hand lane. At the first traffic signal, turn left onto *16th Ave*. Follow *16th Ave* east through the campus and Pacific Spirit Park back into Vancouver and the pleasant, tree-shaded residential neighbourhoods of Shaughnessy

Heights. The road is a broad parkway, but residential parking frequently blocks the kerb lane.

Follow *16th Ave* to *Granville St* and turn south (right), toward the airport. The street is lined with grand houses, most of them well-screened by tall hedges and trees. Rather than trying to turn left across heavy traffic, continue to *34th Ave*, turn east (right) and right again (north) onto *Connaught Dr.*, then right (west) again onto *33rd Ave*.

Follow *33rd Ave* across Granville to the next traffic signal and turn south (right) onto *Oak St,* following signs for **Van Dusen Botanical Gardens**. Take *Oak* to *37th Ave* and turn west (right) at the sign for Sprinkles Restaurant and turn into the first drive for the Van Dusen parking lot.

KITSILANO MUSEUMS

After leaving Van Dusen, turn north (left) onto *Oak St* 1 km to *W. 12th Ave*, at Vancouver Hospital. Turn east (left) onto *W. 12th* at the left turn lane. The imposing red brick building at *Hemlock St* was originally a Presbyterian church, now Holy Trinity Anglican Church. Continue east across *Granville St* through more shady residential areas to *Arbutus St* and turn north (right) into a light industrial area that is quickly being overrun by private homes. Several blocks north of *W. 4th Ave* are still paved with brick and become slippery in rain. Continue downhill toward **Kitsilano Pool**, **Hutton Park** and **Vanier Park,** with English Bay in the distance.

Follow signs for the **Maritime Museum** and **Vancouver Museum**, skirting the edge of Vanier Park. The entrance for the Maritime Museum is to the north (left), just beyond the tall totem pole, also on the left. Parking is extremely limited near Vanier Park; the Maritime Museum is handy for museum parking as well as the heritage ships moored just behind and Vanier Park itself.

WEST END

After leaving the Maritime Museum, go straight on *Chestnut St* to *Whyte Ave* and turn east (left) for the **Vancouver Museum** and observatory. From the museum, turn south (left) onto *Chestnut* for 1 block, then go west (right) on

Greer Ave, following signs for the bicycle route to the Burrard Bridge. Turn south (left) onto Cypress Ave, then east (left) onto Cornwall Ave. Keep in the left-hand lanes and veer left onto the **Burrard Bridge** at the Molson Brewery (not open to the public). There is a good view south-east to Granville Island from mid-span, but no place to stop on the bridge.

After crossing the bridge, continue straight on Burrard St for 10 blocks to Georgia St. Turn east (right) for 1 block to Hornby St and turn south (right). The **Victoria Art Gallery**, 750 Hornby St; tel: (604) 682-668, is on the left. To the right is the **BC Provincial Courts** building, with an urban park and waterfalls rising above street level. Turn south (right) onto Howe St at **Eaton's** department store and west (right) onto Smythe St. Follow Smythe across Burrard to Thurlow and turn south (left) for 2 blocks to Nelson St. Turn west (right) onto Nelson for 4 blocks to Nicola St, then turn north (right) 1 block to Barclay. Turn east (right) on Barclay to **Barclay Heritage Square** and the **Roedde House Museum**.

STANLEY PARK

Take the first left turn after the museum. Continue north to Robson St. and turn west (left), passing the **Robson Public Market** (on the south (left) side of the street) on the way to Denman St. Turn north (right) on Denman, following signs for ferries to Nanaimo and the Sunshine Coast. Stay in the right-hand lane to avoid delays by cars turning left. At Georgia St, turn north (left) toward **Stanley Park**. Stay in the right-hand lanes and curve right into the park.

Park roads are one-way in a clockwise direction. Parking regulations are enforced all year; buy parking coupons at the yellow dispensers, which accept coins and credit cards. Parking tickets are valid throughout the park. Best bet is to buy all-day parking at the first convenient stop and concentrate on enjoying the park. The first parking lot on the left is convenient for visits to the **Aquarium** and **horse tram tours** of the park. One kilometre beyond is the main parking area and **totem pole** display. Just ahead and on the right are broad views back to the inner city and the sail-like

roofline of **Canada Place**, Vancouver's cruise ship terminal. Expect to see cruise ships docked at Canada place during the day May–Oct. Ships returning from Alaska dock around 0800 and depart about 1800 the same day. The **Nine O'clock Gun**, on the waterfront just past a bronze statue of a runner, is fired at 2100 each evening. The cannon was originally sounded at 1800 to signal the close of commercial fishing each day.

A convenient lay-by is 1 km ahead, with good views across to docks on the North Shore. The bright yellow piles are sulphur waiting to be loaded aboard ships; the tan-coloured piles are wood pulp, also waiting to be loaded. The suspension bridge to the left is **Lions Gate Bridge**, the main artery to the North Shore. Just beyond **Brockton Point** is Vancouver's answer to Copenhagen's Little Mermaid, **Girl in a Wetsuit**, a bronze statue of a woman diver in a wet suit. A left-hand exit 1 km ahead leads out of the park and back to Georgia St. Continue straight to continue the park tour. The entrance to Lions Gate Bridge, 1 km ahead, is closed 1530–1830 to minimise traffic in the park.

Prospect Point is the best view down on Lions Gate. The informal restaurant has good views of harbour traffic; garbage bins are popular with racoons and other park residents. Continue around the point past parking areas for **Third Beach** and **Teahouse Restaurant** at **Ferguson Point**, **Second Beach** and the start of two-way traffic near the **Fish House Restaurant**. Watch for geese and small children on the road. The **Seawall Promenade**, leading south to the Burrard Bridge, is an extremely popular beach and walkway.

NORTH VAN(COUVER)

Just after leaving the park, Beach Ave curves to the right, following the Seawall Promenade. Instead, go straight one short block to Denman St and turn north (left) back to Georgia St. Turn left onto Georgia, this time staying in the left-hand lanes to pass **Lost Lagoon** and join BC 99 through the park to Lions Gate Bridge.

Cross the bridge and then turn east (right) onto Marine Dr., following signs for North Vancouver, Capilano Canyon and Grouse

Mountain. Move to the left-hand lane and turn north (left) at the first traffic signal, *Capilano Road*. Petrol is slightly cheaper in North Vancouver.

Capilano Rd climbs through 3 km of housing estates to **Capilano Suspension Bridge**. The bridge is on the left, parking is on the right. The swaying pedestrian bridge, built a century ago for fishing and logging access, was Vancouver's first tourist attraction. Continue 4 km north on *Capilano Rd,* which becomes *Nancy Greene Way,* to **Grouse Mountain** and the tramway, open all year.

Return to *Marine Dr.* and turn east (left) through North Vancouver. Veer right onto *Third St,* following the Scenic Drive signs, to *Forbes Ave* and right again to *Esplanade,* past **Lonsdale Quay** and **Public Market**, just to the right at the end of *Lonsdale Rd.* Continue east along Esplanade and veer right onto *Low-level Rd* to follow the railway tracks east. There are excellent views south (right) to Vancouver unless trains are parked on the sidings.

INNER CITY

Road signs for Vancouver begin appearing about 3 km east. Move into the right-hand lane and cross Burrard Inlet on the **Second Narrows Bridge**, often called **Ironworkers Memorial Bridge**, on Canada 1. The right-hand lanes offer good views west over the Vancouver docklands. Take the first exit after the bridge, following signs for the bicycle route onto *McGill St.* Follow *McGill* past **Exposition Park** and along the waterfront for 3 km. Turn north (right) onto *Wall St* and continue through residential areas above the docks for another 2 km, then go north (right) again onto *Dundes St.* Pass the **BC Sugar Museum**, *at the foot of Roger St; tel: (604) 253-1131,* with photos, videos and artefacts of sugar production in BC to *Heatley St.*

Turn south (left) onto *Heatley* and cross *E. Cordova St* one block to Hastings. Go east (left) on *Hastings* to *Hawks St* and turn north (left) to *Powell St.* Turn west (left) to pass **Oppenheimer Park** and **Japantown**, which never recovered from the forced relocation of Japanese-Canadians during World War II.

Continue 2 blocks to *Gore St* and turn south

(left) along the edge of **Chinatown** to *E. Pender.* Turn west (right) through the heart of Chinatown, past the Chinese Cultural Centre behind the large gate on the south (left) side of the street with the **Dr Sun-Yat Sen Chinese Gardens** behind.

GASTOWN

Turn north (right) onto *Abbott St* to *E. Cordova St* and turn east (right) along the edge of **Gastown** 2 blocks to *Columbia St.* Go 2 blocks north (left) on *Columbia* to the dead-end and turn west (left) onto *Alexander St.* At the first stop sign, where the brick pavement begins, turn north (right) onto *Water St.* A flamboyant statue of **Gassy Jack**, who built the first bar in Gastown, is on the left. The Gastown **steam clock** is on the north (right) at *Canby St.* Traffic slows to a crawl through Gastown with pedestrians wandering the streets as though it is a pedestrian mall.

At the end of *Water St,* turn south (left) into *Richards St,* immediately west (right) onto *W. Hastings St,* then south (left) onto *Howe St.* The **Four Seasons Hotel** is on the east (left) and the **Hotel Georgia** on the west (right) at *Georgia St.* Cross *Georgia.* West (right) is the **Vancouver Art Gallery**, on the east (left) is **Eaton's**. Turn (left) onto *Robson St.* **Cinema Row** and *Granville St* are to the south (left) one block ahead.

Continue on *Robson* across *Home St,* with the new **Vancouver Public Library** on the north (left), looking like a modernistic Roman Coliseum. Go south (right) onto *Hamilton,* which jogs right and left to become *Maitland St* and run through the narrow streets of warehouses-become-trendy **Yaletown** to a dead end at *Davie St.* Turn north (right) for 5 blocks to *Granville St* and turn south (left). The **Yale Hotel** is on the left just before the **Granville Bridge**.

Stay in the right-hand lane and follow signs for *4th Ave W.,* turning onto *Pine St,* then north (right) following signs for **Granville Island**. Turn east (right) onto *W. 3rd Ave* to drive beneath the bridge and onto **Granville Island**. When leaving Granville Island, follow signs for *4th Ave W.* Follow *4th Ave* one block back to *Burrard St.*

VANCOUVER–WHISTLER

The Sea to Sky Highway is aptly named, snaking from West Vancouver along the cliffs lining Howe Sound as far as Squamish, then twisting up mountain canyons to the resort development of Whistler. The 120-km drive can zip past in two hours if traffic co-operates, but allow three hours midweek and closer to four hours at the weekend. In winter, the return trip to Vancouver can take most of the day if snow snarls going home traffic on Sunday. No matter how good the weather, drive cautiously. The roadway can be narrow and steep, the scenery spectacular and the verges absent.

DIRECT ROUTE: 120 KM

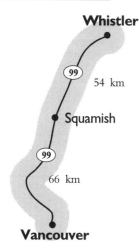

Whistler

54 km

Squamish

66 km

Vancouver

287

ROUTE

From the *Burrard St Bridge*, turn onto *Pacific St* and immediately go left onto *Howe St*. Follow Howe to *Georgia St* and turn left into the middle lanes. At the edge of Stanley Park, follow the overhead signs for Lions Gate Bridge. Georgia becomes BC 1A and 99 in the park. At the north end of Lions Gate Bridge, stay in the middle lane, following traffic signs for West Vancouver and Squamish to veer right, pass beneath the bridge and immediately cross the Capilano River headed west.

One kilometre beyond Lions Gate, turn right at the first traffic signal onto *Taylor Way* and drive uphill in the middle lane. Follow signs for BC 99 north onto the expressway toward Horseshoe Bay, Squamish and Whistler. The expressway has good views north to the mountains and south across Vancouver Harbour. Follow the expressway 11 km to Exit 1 for Squamish and Whistler. (The expressway continues to the BC Ferries dock at Horseshoe

Bay). Take Exit 1 onto BC 99, the *Sea to Sky Highway*. The road follows the edge of Howe Sound past Porteau Cove and the abandoned copper mine at Britannia Beach to **Shannon Falls**, **Provincial Park** and **Squamish**. Occasional views up the Sound reveal the pulp mills belching the blue-grey haze that obscures mountain views and the queasy chemical stench that sometimes fouls the air.

From Squamish, the highway turns into the mountains and narrows. A marked scenic viewpoint to the right, 15 km beyond Squamish, has the best view back to Howe Sound. There are occasional overtaking lanes, but expect slow going behind motorcoaches and lorries as far as **Brandywine Falls Provincial Park**. On the return trip, lumber trucks speed down the highway loaded with logs for the Squamish mills. Whistler development begins 12 km north of **Brandywine**; Whistler Village is 4 km beyond the travel infocentre at Whistler Creekside.

SIDE TRACK
FROM VANCOUVER

The Royal Hudson, *1782 W Georgia St, Vancouver, BC V6G 2V7; tel: (800) 663-1500 or (604) 688-7246*, a beautifully restored steam locomotive, provides daily rail service in summer between North Vancouver and Squamish along the edge of Howe Sound. The day tour includes boat passage in one direction.

VANCOUVER TO SQUAMISH

The Sea to Sky Highway, BC 99, was carved into the cliffs forming the eastern side of Howe Sound, the most southerly fjord in North America. The 1958 highway follows the route of the Pacific Great Eastern Railway, completed to Squamish in 1956. Before the rail line and highway, the only transport along Howe Sound was a daily steamer between Vancouver and Squamish. The frequent lay-bys have stunning views across the water, but nearly all are on the Sound side of the road. Left turns are generally prohibited on Sea to Sky, so northbound traffic misses the best views.

One of the first good northbound views is at **Porteau Cove Provincial Park**; *tel: (205) 898-3678*, 25 km north of Exit 1. The cove served as a sand and gravel quarry early in the century. The pits and surrounding community became a regular stop for the Howe Sound Steamer, but the community evaporated after the pits and nearby Britannia Mine were closed. Beachcombers haunt the rocky beach while scuba divers explore four ships that were sunk just off shore. Everyone tries to ignore the pulp mill visible across the Sound, difficult when southerly winds blow the haze and stench down the Sound. A second mill at the head of the Sound also contributes to the pollution.

It's impossible to miss **Britannia Beach**, 8 km north of Porteau Cove. On the Sound side sits the rusting hulk of the *SS Prince George*, once the largest ship on Howe Sound. The ship, which had been slated to become a floating museum, burned at dock in 1994 and remains the centre of continuing litigation.

Almost directly across the highway is **Britannia Mine**, once the largest copper mine in the British Empire. The abandoned mine climbs the mountainside east of the road, its broken windows glinting in the setting sun. Mine and site have become the **B.C. Museum of Mining**, *PO Box 188, Britannia Beach, BC V0N 1J0; tel: (604) 688-8735*, open May–Oct.

Copper was discovered at Britannia Beach in 1888. Oliver Furry, a trapper who gave his name to a creek and a golf course just south of Britannia Beach, staked the first claims in 1897. The mine ran continuously from 1899 until rising costs and falling copper prices forced it to close in 1974. The surviving mine buildings are being converted to museum use. The interpretative centre, in what was once the Engineering Building, traces local mining history. A mine tour includes a train ride 400m into the old shafts for a look at the early days of hard rock mining, complete with hard hats. The mine site is a National Historic Site as well as a popular cinema and TV set. **Murrin Provincial Park**, 5 km north of Britannia Beach, offers spectacular views of the nearly vertical mountains surrounding Howe Sound. The horizontal scratches in the rock faces are evidence of the immense glaciers, which carved an ordinary river valley into today's granite-lined fjord.

Howe Sound also claims the third highest waterfall in BC in **Shannon Falls Provincial Park**. The 335-m cascade is an easy 5-min walk through a dense patch of forest from the parking area. The park is also popular for a strenuous climb up 652-m **Stawmus Chief**, the massive peak north of the falls overlooking the Sound. The trail up the second largest granite monolith in the world (after Gibraltar) gains 550m in just 2½ km. The rock is a favourite with technical climbers from around the world. Best spot to watch climbers worming their way skyward is a lay-by on the eastern side of the

---

Colour section (i): Grand Coulee Dam (p. 248); Looking across to the San Juan Islands (pp.266–271)
(ii): The Steam Clock in Vancouver (p.286)
(iii): A view of Downtown Vancouver; travelling by Aquabus on False Creek, Vancouver (see pp.274–282)
(iv): The Empress Hotel, Victoria (p.304); the end of the road at Tofino (p.342)

road 1 km north of the park entrance. Almost directly across from the park is the dock for BC Ferries' route across Howe Sound to the **Western Pulp Squamish Operation**, *PO Box 5000, Squamish, BC V0N 3G0; tel: (604) 892-6644*, the largest pulp mill on the Sound. Tours of the mill can be booked in advance 1000–1400 Thur, May–Sept. Western Pulp maintains an extensive network of walking trails around the mill. Walkers must obtain permission in advance; *tel: (604) 892-6611*, and sign in at the first aid station at the mill before setting out. Squamish is 3 km north.

SQUAMISH

Tourist Information: Squamish & Howe Sound Chamber of Commerce, *PO Box 1009, Squamish, BC V0N 3G0; tel: 604-892-9244; fax: (604) 892-2034*, at the west end of *Cleveland Ave*, open 0900–1700 Mon–Fri.

Squamish is schizophrenic. A pair of massive pulp mills, out of sight if seldom out of smell, make Squamish the largest deep sea woodpulp port on the west coast of North America and a hotbed of forest industry partisans. But the number of recreational outfitters, companies selling sea kayaking, fishing, rock climbing, scuba diving and walking trips, is growing yearly.

The entrepreneurs who depend on uncut forests, clean air and healthy waters are only too happy to point out the environmental havoc wreaked on Howe Sound by the timber industry. The **Soo Coalition for Sustainable Forests**, *PO Box 1759, Squamish, BC V0N 3G0; tel: (604) 892-9766*, promotes the timber side with the kind of smooth arguments and colourful literature North Americans have come to expect from well-financed political campaigns. The **Coalition visitor centre**, *Cleveland Ave and Victoria St*, also arranges tours of nearby dryland sort and sawmill operations Mon–Fri at 1300.

Despite decades of intensive logging and pollution, Squamish remains the winter home for about 3000 bald eagles, possibly the largest concentration of bald eagles in North America south of Alaska. The town is also the gateway to recreational activities on Howe Sound and throughout **Garibaldi Provincial Park**,

which covers much of the mountainous area north-east of town. Squamish also offers the only fast food fix between Vancouver and Whistler. Rail buffs from around the world make pilgrimage to the **West Coast Railway Heritage Park**, *Box 2790 Stn Terminal, Vancouver, BC V6B 3X2; tel: (604) 898-9336, 3 km north of McDonald's on BC 99 in Squamish, then west 1 km on Centennial Way*. The park has more than 50 vintage railway carriages and locomotive engines, including a superb 1890 Executive Business Carriage finished in hand-rubbed teak, a restored colonist car that once carried settlers across Canada on hard benches, Pacific Great Eastern's only surviving steam locomotive engine and an enormous orange snowplough.

Brohm Lake and **Brohm Lake Interpretative Forest** are 13 km beyond the Railway Park. The shallow lake offers fishing and, for those immune to icy temperatures, swimming. The 400-hectare forest area has 11 km of connecting trails with spectacular views of the Tantalus Mountain Range and one of the largest icefields in North America.

The best view back to Howe Sound is 3 km beyond Brohm Lake. Follow the scenic view signs onto a short section of the old highway. The southbound lanes have a similar scenic layby, but the view is better from the northbound side. The road narrows and winds another 27 kms to **Brandywine Falls Provincial Park**, *on the east side of the highway*, named for an early bet on the height of the falls by railroad surveyors who were short of cash but well-stocked with brandy and wine. In early summer, when snow melt is at its peak, 600 cubic metres of water shoot over the edge of the cliff each minute, but the 66-m falls are worth the 10-min walk through the forest in any season.

The first evidence of Whistler appears 9 kms later. **Whistler Interpretative Forest**, *Municipal Hall, 4325 Blackcomb Wy, Whistler, BC V0N 1B4; tel: (604) 932-5555; fax: (604) 932-6636*, extends to the right with an extensive network of walking and mountain biking trails. All of the trails are open for walkers but some are closed to mountain bikers. To the left is **Function Junction**, a cluster of businesses that supply Whistler with beer, bread,

289

masseuses and other essentials. Whistler's ever-expanding condominium complexes have spread to within 3 kms of Function Junction. The first travel infocentre is the **Whistler Chamber of Commerce**, *Box 181, Whistler, BC V0N 1B0; tel: (604) 932-5528, east on Lake Placid Rd in Whistler Creekside,* open daily 0900–1700. **Whistler Village** is 4 kms north.

WHISTLER

Tourist Information: Whistler Chamber of Commerce, *Box 181, Whistler, BC V0N 1B0; tel: (604) 932-5528, at the Whistler Gondola base;* **Whistler Resort Association**, *4010 Whistler Wy, Whistler, BC V0N 1B0; tel: (604) 932-3928; fax: (604) 932-7231.*

ACCOMMODATION

Whistler Resort Association, *4010 Whistler Wy, Whistler, BC V0N 1B0; tel: (604) 932-4222 or (800) 944-7853; fax: (604) 932-7231,* co-ordinates lodging for the entire resort. **Whistler Bed & Breakfast Inns**, *(604) 932-3282 or (800) 665-1892,* books local Bed and Breakfasts. **The Fireplace Inns**, *4250 Village Stroll, Whistler, BC V0N 1B4; tel: (604) 932-3200 or (800) 663-6416; fax: (604) 932-2566,* is solid value in Whistler Village, with fireplaces in all rooms. Top choice is the pricey **Chateau Whistler**, *4599 Chateau Blvd, Whistler BC V0N 1B0; tel: (604) 938-8000 or (800) 268-9411 (Canada), (800) 828-7447 (US); fax: (604) 938-2020,* at the foot of Blackcomb Mountain.

EATING AND DRINKING

Whistler has all the usual chains as well as sidewalk cafés, snack shops, and elegance. **Caramba!**, *12-4314 Main St Town Plaza; tel: (604) 938-1879,* is a lively, moderate choice for Italian. Pricey **Ristorante Araxi**, *4222 Village Square; tel: (604) 932-3348,* is more staid. **Zeuski's Tavern**, *Town Plaza; tel: (604) 932-6009,* is moderate, lively and Greek. **Cows**, *Whistler Village Centre; tel: (604) 938-9822,* budget, has Whistler's best ice-cream. **Ingrid's Village Café**, *4305 Skiers Approach; tel: (604) 932-7000,* has out-the-door lines for budget vegetarian fare. **Whistler Cookie Co.**, *7-4433 Sundial Pl; tel: (604) 932-2962,* is a local budget favourite for breakfast.

ENTERTAINMENT

Whistler exists to entertain, and entertain it does, with the emphasis on skiing, mountain biking, walking and other outdoor activities. The resort also offers just about every form of aprés-sport activity imagination can create, from a **Hard Rock Café** to hot tubs and hotel discos. The hotel front desk can point out the current hot spots.

SIGHTSEEING

Whistler was envisaged as a site for Winter Olympic Games, but the International Olympic Committee's lack of co-operation hasn't slowed what has become one of North America's most successful resort developments. What began as a ski resort has become equally busy in summer. The European-style village (nearly all a pedestrian zone) is a mountain theme park for adults, its steep roof lines and pastel colours an alluring contrast against the snow-capped mountains and deep blue sky. Lifts whisk skiers, snowboarders, mountain bikers and the merely curious up the resort's two mountains, Whistler (2287 m) and Blackcomb (2182 m) from the village centre. Five lakes loop through the valley like blue-green beads on a necklace, set off against forests, golf courses and an extensive network of walking and biking routes that become cross-country skiing trails in winter.

A resort that began as a garbage dump for an unruly collection of weekend cabins in the 1970s is short on history, but the **Whistler Museum and Archives**; *tel: (604) 932-2019,* open daily, does what it can with logging, early fishing resorts and archaic skiing gear. In winter, downhill skiing and snowboarding on more than 200 named runs is exceptional with the continent's longest fall line drops. In summer, the mountains offer spectacular walking, with trails circling upper slopes, alpine lakes and flower-filled meadows as well as the valley below. Most mountain skiing trails are opened to mountain biking, which has become the dominant summer sport. **Whistler Backroads**, *Box 643, Whistler, BC V0N 1B0; tel: (604) 932-3111; fax: (604) 932-1204,* has the best selection of bikes for hire as well as guided mountain rides.

VANCOUVER–OSOYOOS

It's possible to drive the 370 km between Vancouver and Osoyoos in one long day, but only if you're willing to miss some of the most pleasant sights in southern BC. Manicured formal gardens, rustic hot springs, majestic mountains and splendid walking trails are only a few of the reasons to linger along the route. If time allows, take two days, with an overnight in Hope. Better still, take three to four days, stopping in Hope, Manning Provincial Park and Princeton, plus two or three days in the Okanogan Valley.

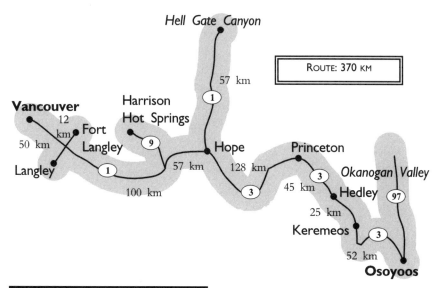

291

From Central Vancouver, take *W. 12th Ave* eastbound and merge into *Grandview Ave* near *Slocun St* on the east side of the city. Follow traffic signs for Canada 1 eastbound and enter the expressway just east of *Boundary Rd* in the Municipality of Burnaby. Follow Canada 1 over the Fraser River on the Port Mann Bridge and continue eastward past a succession of Fraser Valley towns to **Hope**, at the head of the valley. Continue east 7 km to Exit 177, BC 3, the Crowsnest Highway, heading south-east into the Cascade Mountains to Manning Provincial Park, north to **Princeton** and south-east again into the desert of the **Okanogan Valley** and Osoyoos. The Okanogan vineyards, BC's wine country, stretch north along both sides of the Okanogan River toward Kelowna, 123 km north.

The Fraser Valley is one of BC's richest agricultural areas. Immense of fields of grain, raspberries, strawberries and other crops compete with dairy herds for space along the flat plain that stretches from both sides of the Fraser River to lap at the base of the Cascades. Views across the valley to the jagged Cascade peaks are likely to remain relatively unspoiled: Most of the valley east of the town of **Langley** has been put into an agricultural preserve that offers landowners tax incentives to keep their property in agriculture rather than selling out to developers and contributing to the sprawl of **Greater Vancouver**. For a guide to the agricultural area, pick up *Farm Fresh Guide*, covering Langley, and *The Harvest Guide*, for the rest of the central Valley from Abbotsford to Sardi.

LANGLEY AND FORT LANGLEY

Tourist Information: Fort Langley and District Chamber of Commerce, *9167 Glover Rd, Fort Langley, BC V1M 2R5; tel: (604) 888-1477; fax: (604) 888-2657.*

The best choice lodging in town is the budget–moderate **West Country Hotel**, *20222 56th Ave, Langley, BC V3A 3Y5; tel: (604) 530-5121; fax: (604) 530-9763.*

SIGHTSEEING

Langley, south of the expressway, is a thriving farming community on the edge of Greater Vancouver. **Fort Langley**, north of the expressway, is a smaller town of antique stores, small restaurants and a largely reconstructed **Fort Langley National Historic Park**, *23433 Mavis St, Fort Langley, BC V1M 2R5; tel: (604) 888-4424,* open daily, $4 adults, $2 children, the birthplace of modern British Columbia. The Hudson's Bay Company built a fort at Langley in 1824 to serve as a secondary depot for inland operations. The riverside site was already a traditional meeting and trading place for First Nations from the Pacific Coast to the Rockies. The Fraser Valley was poor in furs, but the broad Langley Prairie soon became a highly profitable farming operation.

Company farming came to an abrupt end with the Fraser River gold rush in 1858. Gold fever drove farmers up the Fraser River. When news of the gold strike reached San Francisco, tens of thousands of American miners headed north, most passing through Fort Langley on their way upstream. The Fort became a profitable commercial centre, but the influx from south of the border worried the HBC. Company officials lobbied for the creation of a crown colony to prevent annexation by an expansionist America that had taken California

from Mexico a decade before. British Columbia was proclaimed on 19 Nov 1858 in the fort's **Big House** (the Manager's residence), a ceremony that is reenacted every year by BC's current Prime Minister and cabinet.

Royal Engineers pointed out that the Fort, on the south bank of the river and almost within view of the US border, was vulnerable to American attack. The capital was moved to New Westminster in 1859 and Fort Langley returned to farming. HBC finally closed the post in 1886.

The Fort, with its original storehouse and reconstructed Big House, servants' quarters, workshops, log palisade and bastions, is a living history museum. It doesn't smell as the original HBC trading post must have, but costumed interpreters convey a sense of what life was like when BC was the edge of the world, right down to the daily challenges of forging tools in the heat of summer or baking bread in the damp and dank of winter.

The Langley Centennial Museum and National Exhibition Centre, *9131 King St; tel: (604) 888-3922,* and the adjoining **BC Farm Machinery and Agricultural Museum**; *tel: (604) 888-2272,* explore other eras. The Centennial Museum houses an extensive collection of First Nation artefacts as well as recreations of farm and small town life in the late 19th–early 20th century. The Farm Museum has one of BC's largest collections of vintage agricultural equipment, from steam stump pullers to a Tiger Moth aeroplane.

Langley is also home to one of BC's most decorated wineries, **Domaine de Chaberton Estates**, *1064 216 St; tel: (604) 530-1736,* 12 km east of town. Chamberton, the only Estate Winery in the Fraser Valley, specialises in French and German white varieties. The winery is open for tasting daily and for tours at weekends.

The expressway bypasses most towns east of Langley. Abbotsford, the largest town in the central Fraser Valley, hosts a major airshow in August. The other 11 months, it's the self-proclaimed Raspberry Capital of the World.

Recreational farmers are more interested in **Chilliwack**, 83 km east of Langley, and **Minter Gardens**, north on BC 9 from Exit

135, *10015 Young Rd, Chilliwack, BC V2P 4V4; tel: (604) 792-6612* or *(800) 661-3919*, a full-colour seed catalogue come to life. Minter isn't ready to challenge Victoria's Butchart Gardens, but it follows the same tradition of generous planting and meticulous maintenance. And Butchart can't begin to match Minter's backdrop of Cascade mountain peaks dominated by 2334-m Mount Cheam. The Gardens are open April–Oct.

For a closer look at commercial agriculture, turn north (left) onto BC 9, 1 km after leaving Minter to return to Canada 1. **Agassiz** calls itself The Corn Capital of BC' for the fields of maize surrounding the community. Turn left at the town hall, drive one long block and turn right at the traffic signal. Cross the railroad tracks and immediately turn left onto BC 7 to the **Agassiz Harrison Museum**, *6947 #7 Hwy, Agassiz, BC V0M 1A0; tel: (604) 796-3545*, open May–Sept 1000–1600. The museum, in the restored 1893 train depot, focuses on agricultural development. After leaving the museum, continue 1 km east on BC 7 and turn right onto BC 9, passing farms and hazelnut orchards on the way to **Harrison Hot Springs**.

HARRISON HOT SPRINGS

Tourist Information: Harrison Hot Springs Chamber of Commerce, *499 Hot Springs Rd, Harrison Hot Springs, BC V0M 1K0; tel: (604) 796-3425; fax: (604) 796-3188*. Harrison Hot Springs is a spa, the largest lake in south-western BC and a popular recreation area. It's also one of BC's most active areas for current reports of Sasquatch, a shy, hairy over-sized humanoid that figures in First Nations lore from California to Alaska.

Hot springs facilities include a Public Pool, where mineral water from the springs has been cooled to 39°C from its initial 71°C and full spa facilities at the moderate–expensive **Harrison Hot Springs Hotel**, *Harrison Hot Springs, BC V0M 1K0; tel: (604) 796-2244* or *(800) 663-2266; fax: (604) 796-3682*, but most visitors spend more time camping, boating, fishing and walking the forest than soaking. There are also about two dozen smaller motels, bed & breakfasts, campgrounds and RV parks nearby.

Return to Canada 1 eastbound or follow BC7 east 37 km to Hope.

HOPE

Tourist Information: Hope & District Chamber of Commerce, *919 Water Ave, Hope, BC V0X 1L0; tel: (604) 869-2021; fax: (604) 869-2160*.

ACCOMMODATION AND FOOD

Hope has the largest selection of food and lodging in the area, but no chains. The budget **Skagit Motel**, *655 3rd Ave; tel: (604) 869-5220* or *(800) 667-5567*, is the best value for money in town.

SIGHTSEEING

Established as an HBC trading post at the head of the Fraser Valley, Hope became a commercial centre during the 1858 Gold Rush and the subsequent opening of eastern BC. **The Hope Museum**, *919 Water Ave; tel: (604) 869-7322*, traces local history from First Nations days through gold mining, railroads and World War II, when more than 2300 Japanese-Canadians were imprisoned at Tashame, 14 km east. Part of the $12 million Federal restitution fund established in 1988 built a Japanese garden in **Memorial Park**, across the street from the Skagit Motel. The park also has a collection of oversized chain saw carvings of salmon, eagles and other local creatures. Hope has appeared in a number of films, including Sylvester Stallone's *Rambo: First Blood*. The **Othello Tunnels**, part of the **Coquihalla Canyon Recreation Area**, *Tunnels Rd, 8 km east of town*, are popular with walkers and mountain bikers. The tunnels were cut in the 1910s for the Kettle Valley Railway, built to block northward expansion by US railroads. The KVR was abandoned after washouts in 1959. Allow an hour to walk through the five tunnels along the rushing Coquihalla River.

 **SIDE TRACK FROM HOPE**

One of the most scenic mountain drives in south-western BC is Canada 1 up the Fraser Canyon to Hells Gate, 57 km north of

293

Hope. The head of navigation on the Fraser was Yale, 23 km upstream from Hope. A rowdy steamboat port during the Fraser Gold Rush, Yale is more museum than town today. **Historic Yale Museum** and **St. John the Divine Church**, *downtown Yale; tel: (604) 863-2324*, recreate what was once the largest city north of San Francisco. As the Fraser Gold Rush declined, Yale became construction headquarters for the Cariboo Wagon Road, which opened the Cariboo gold fields in the 1860s, then a roaring recreation town for Canadian Pacific Railway construction crews.

Yale is also the southern entrance to the **Fraser Canyon**, a mass of boiling rapids that still blocks river traffic. First Nations travelled the canyon on a rugged trail that was nothing more than slippery logs lashed to cliffsides in places. Miners blasted a precarious foot trail into the cliffs, later replaced by a wagon road and finally a highway. One of the most graceful river crossings is the **Alexandra Bridge**, 21 km north of Yale. Built for the first rough automobile road up the canyon, the decaying concrete bridge is a ten minute walk down from the parking area. The open grate roadway gives a clear, if discomforting view straight down on the raging torrent.

Another 12 km of hairpin turns and tunnels leads to Hell's Gate. The canyon narrows to a rocky bottleneck just 40 m wide, creating a thunder maelstrom that is impassible even at low water. **The Hell's Gate Airtram**, *PO Box 129, Hope, BC V0X 1L0; tel: (604) 867-9277; fax: (604) 867-9279*, $9 adults, $6 children, $20 families, provides a stunning overhead view of the foaming gate. The lower tram station offers the best view from solid ground. A nearby fish ladder helps more than 2 million salmon through the rapids each year. 🔼

HOPE TO PRINCETON

Take Canada 1 east from Hope and exit onto BC 3, the **Crowsnest Highway**, which becomes a dual track road. Ten km beyond is a raw scar where 46 million cubic metres of rock and mud fell down the north side of the valley

in 1965. The Hope Slide raised the valley floor by 70 m and killed four people.

The most scenic and slowest section of the Crowsnest is **Manning Provincial Park**, *Box 3, Manning Park, BC V0X 1R0; tel: (520) 840-8836; fax: (520) 840-8700*, 71,000 hectares of rugged mountains, deep valleys, subalpine meadows and white water rapids. Two major rivers flow out of the park, the **Skagit**, which turns south into Washington and the Pacific Ocean, and the **Similkameen**, which runs east to the Okanogan and then into the Columbia River.

Visitor facilities are concentrated around the **Park Visitor Centre**, just east of the moderate–expensive **Manning Park Resort**, *Manning Park, BC V0X 1RO; tel: (520) 840-8822; fax: (520) 840-8848*. The Visitor Centre introduces park plants, wildlife trails, campgrounds and recreational activities; the Resort has the only restaurant and non-camping lodging within the park.

PRINCETON

Tourist Information: Princeton and District Chamber of Commerce, *Box 540, Princeton, BC V0X 1W0; tel: (520) 295-3103; fax: (520) 295-3255*. Princeton is the first town beyond Manning Park, a gold rush settlement that has combined farming and outdoor activities to become a regional commercial centre. The **Princeton and District Pioneer Museum**, *167 Vermillion; tel: (520) 395-7588*, the largest local museum in the Valley, concentrates on mining and ranching.

HEDLEY

Hedley sprang to life as a gold mining town in the late 19th century, but would-be miners started every day by climbing Nickle Plate, the mountain east of town, to the diggings. By 1909, the town had six hotels, a bank, a school and its own newspaper. An aerial tramway hauled miners up to the shafts each day and ore back down to stamp mills near town until the mine closed in 1956. Much of the town burned in 1956 and 1957, but the mountainside buildings are still visible hundreds of metres above. The cliffs are honeycombed with abandoned mine shafts.

Okanogan Wine

Okanogan farmers have grown wine grapes for decades, but there were few high-quality vinerifa varieties in the valley until a government-sponsored pull-out programme in 1988 encouraged growers to replace old vineyards. The replanting programme, instituted in anticipation of the North American Free Trade Agreement that would eventually open BC to cheaper, higher quality wine from the US, worked.

The two dozen wineries that line the Okanogan Valley produce nearly all of BC's wine. Although the surrounding Cascade and Selkirk mountains support three major ski resorts, the relatively warm waters of Okanogan Lake moderate winter temperatures on the hillside orchards and vineyards. The dry desert air brings long, cloudless days during the growing season. Warm days and cool nights contribute to the balance of sugar and acid needed to produce fine wine. Okanogan whites are more common than reds (and generally better) because white grapes ripen more predictably in BC's cooler, northern summers. Red grapes need more hot days to fully develop their natural sugars. BC growers note that the Okanogan shares the same latitude as leading wine areas in Germany and Switzerland. They share German and Swiss tastes in grapes as well.

Auxerrois, a French grape, produces a white wine similar to Pinot Blanc, full bodied and crisp, but with fuller bouquet. Chardonnay is known for its rich, buttery flavour when produced and aged with care. It can also produce fresh wines that taste of apples and vanilla. Chasselas is the leading grape in Switzerland, known for its crisp, delicate taste.

Gewürztraminer is a major variety in Alsace. The wines are spicy with a distinct varietal aroma and flavour that bottle ages extremely well. Ehrenfelser, another German import, produces fruity wines with fine acidity that develop well with bottle aging.

Merlot was originally imported from Washington. BC merlots are complex, soft and elegant with great aging potential. Pinot Noir is another French grape, though BC vineyards trace their heritage to Washington State and imports from Germany. The BC version produces wines that are complex and fruity but quite light.

Riesling is one of the most popular varieties in Germany. It has become the most widely planted variety in BC as well because of its affinity to cooler climates. Wines are light and flowery with clean, crisp flavours. Late harvest Rieslings develop an intense honey flavour.

295

KEREMEOS

Tourist Information: Keremeos & District Chamber of Commerce, *415 7th Ave, Keremeos, BC V0X 1N0; tel: (520) 499-5225; fax: (520) 499-2252.*

Opened during the BC gold rushes of the 1850s and 1860s, Keremeos quickly turned to the relative security of agriculture. **The Grist Mill**, *Upper Bench Rd, Keremeos, BC V0X 1N0; tel: (520) 499-2888*, is BC's only water powered mill with its machinery intact. The restored mill, operated by the British Columbia Heritage Trust, is open May–Oct. Heritage orchards, gardens and fields grow antique flowers, fruits, vegetables, and grains that have long since disappeared from commercial cultivation.

Flour ground at the mill is sold on site and used in the **Tea Room** bakery. The red bridge just west of town was originally a railway bridge, then converted for road traffic. It is the last surviving covered bridge in Western Canada.

Keremeos also has two wineries, **St. Laszlo Estate Winery**, *Site 95, Comp 8, Keremeos, BC V0X 1N0; tel: (520) 499-2856*, 1 km east of town, and **Crows Nest Vineyards**, *Box 501, Keremeos, BC V0X 1N0; tel: (520) 499-5129*, just east of Cawston.

OSOYOOS

Tourist Information: Osoyoos Chamber of Commerce, *Box 227, Osoyoos, BC V0H 1V0; tel: (520) 495-7142; fax: (520) 495-6161.*

ACCOMMODATION

Osoyoos is the commercial hub of the agricultural Okanogan Valley. There are a dozen or so motels in town, including the moderate **Desert Motor Inn**, *7702 62nd Ave, Osoyoos, BC V0H 1V0; tel: (520) 495-6525.*

Motel Row is the stretch of **Main St** (BC 3) just east of the bridge across Osoyoos Lake. **The Southwind Inn**, *Box 1500, Oliver, BC V0H 1T0 tel: (520) 498-3442*, 50 km north in Oliver, is far more convenient for winery touring.

For Bed and Breakfast accommodations, contact the **Okanogan Bed & Breakfast Association**, *Box 5135, Kelowna, BC V1Y 8T9; tel: (520) 764-2124; fax: (520) 764-2892*; or the **Okanogan Similkameen Tourism Association**, *1332 Water Street, Kelowna, BC V1Y 9P4; tel: (520) 860-5999.*

SIGHTSEEING

The Okanogan Valley, spreading east and west of the Okanogan River, is the final extension of the Mojave Desert that stretches northward from Mexico along the basin between the Rocky Mountains and the Sierra Nevada/Cascade Mountains. Originally covered with cactus and prickly brush, the Okanogan began to bloom with massive irrigation projects that put former soldiers to work after World War I. **The Osoyoos Museum**, *Osoyoos Lake in Gyro Park; tel: (520) 495-5215*, open June–Sept, depicts the early history of Canada's only desert.

Osoyoos Lake is Canada's answer to Southern California, a balmy recreation area famed for swimming and water skiing. For the best view of the lake and valley, take BC 3 west to lay-bys at the top of the ridge.

SIDE TRACK FROM OSOYOOS

OKANOGAN VALLEY

To cruise the Okanogan present, future and past, follow BC 97 north through Valley orchards and vineyards to the **Dominion Radio Astrophysical Observatory**, *PO Box 248, Penticton, BC V2A 6K3; tel: (520)* 493-7505; fax: (520) 493-7767. The highway north from Osoyoos passes a steady succession of apple, pear, cherry, peach and other orchards interspersed with expanding vineyards. Fruit stands open with the first harvests in early summer; most of the wineries are open for tasting and tours all year. The spreading green of agricultural irrigation has turned once-ubiquitous cacti into endangered species.

Turn west (left) onto Hwy 386, 6 km north of **Oliver** and begin climbing through stands of Ponderosa pines. Take *Fairview-Whitelake Rd* north (right) 4 km later through a broad agricultural valley. **Spotted Lake**, laden with minerals that deposit a mottled white layer on the surface, is on the right. The first sign of the observatory is a thick cross of telephone poles, the remains of an early radio telescope. White dish-shaped antennas come into view just beyond. The entrance is 13 km from the Hwy 386 turnoff. Look for the array of seven white dishes and a single enormous dish pointing skyward from a futuristic pylon.

The observatory was built in the **Whitelake Basin** because surrounding mountains shelter the isolated valley from the radio frequency pollution created by modern life. The observatory is open daylight hours all year, with guided tours Sundays, 1400–1700, July–Aug. Visitor parking is about half a kilometre from the main antenna to minimise electrical interference–staff vehicles are fitted with special electronic dampers.

Return 20 km along the *Fairview-Whitelake Rd* to a T junction at the *Oliver-Cawston Road*. Turn left (downhill) 2 km to a marker on the right for **Fairview**, the centre of population in the Okanogan a century ago.

The rowdy mining town declined as the mines played out, but permanent settlers began moving into the area to take advantage of cattle ranching and farming opportunities nearer the Okanogan River. Today, nothing remains of Fairview but a few foundations overgrown with sagebrush. ◄

VANCOUVER–VICTORIA

The ferry ride between Vancouver and Victoria takes around 90 mins, less as BC Ferries introduces successive generations of faster and larger ships. But whatever the length, the ride is one of the most spectacular in the world, threading between the rugged, tree-lined shores of Gulf Islands that sometimes seem almost close enough to touch. Only five of the 200 or so islands lying between Vancouver and Victoria are inhabited, but stopping at all can easily stretch the journey to anything from five days to a lifetime.

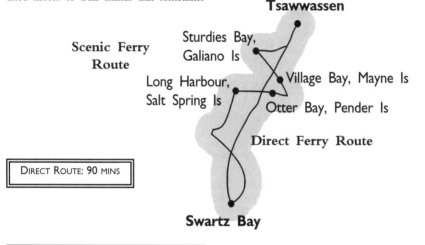

Tsawwassen

Scenic Ferry Route

Sturdies Bay, Galiano Is

Long Harbour, Salt Spring Is

Village Bay, Mayne Is

Otter Bay, Pender Is

Direct Ferry Route

297

DIRECT ROUTE: 90 MINS

Swartz Bay

ROUTES

DIRECT ROUTE

The direct ferry route runs from **Tsawwassen**, south of Vancouver, to **Swartz Bay**, north of Victoria.

SCENIC ROUTE

The island-hopping route stops at **Sturdies Bay** on **Galiano Island**, **Village Bay** on **Mayne Island**, **Otter Bay** on **Pender Island**, **Long Harbour** on **Salt Spring Island** and on to Swartz Bay. It is also possible to drive from Long Harbour north to **Vesuvius** and take a ferry to **Crofton**, on Vancouver Island, or to drive south from Long Harbour to **Fulford Harbour** and take a ferry

to **Swartz Bay**. There may also be seasonal service from **Horseshoe Bay**, north of Vancouver.

BC Ferries, *1112 Fort St, Victoria, BC V8V 4V2; tel: (604) 669-1211 (Vancouver) or (604) 386-3431 (Victoria); fax: (604) 381-5452; web: http://www.bcferries.bc.ca/ferries*. Ferries from Vancouver leave the terminal at **Tsawwassen**, 45 mins south of Vancouver off BC 99. Southbound from Vancouver, take Exit 28 to BC 17, which leads directly to the ferry dock. Northbound, take Exit 20 to BC 10 westbound, then turn south (left) onto BC 17 to the ferry dock. BC 17 lanes lead directly to ticket booths, which open onto numbered boarding lanes. Ticket takers and traffic wardens direct vehicles to the proper lane.

Advance bookings are required for vehicles (but not passengers) travelling from Tsawwassen to the Gulf Islands, and from the Gulf Islands to Tsawwassen. Reservations are neither required nor available between the Gulf Islands and Vancouver Island or between the Gulf Islands themselves. Bookings are never required for walk-on or bicycle passengers.

All advance bookings must be pre-paid. Bookings may be made in writing or by telephone with Visa or MasterCard. Advance bookings can be changed or cancelled up to five days before sailing without penalty. Changes less than five days before sailing are subject to a $10 service fee. Vehicle check-in is 40 mins before the scheduled sailing time at Tsawwassen and 30 mins before sailing at Gulf Island ports. Vehicles that arrive between check-in and sailing time revert to stand-by status and may not be allowed to board. Since there are only two daily departures on some routes, missing a sailing could mean spending an extra night in the islands.

Schedules and fares change seasonally. There are at least two return sailings daily from Vancouver to the Gulf Islands with additional departures at weekends, holidays and during the summer. There are at least six daily return trips between the Gulf Islands and Vancouver Island. Peak fares are weekends and mid June–mid Sept. Weekday and off-peak fares are reduced.

BC Ferries Gulf Island ships all have self-service cafeterias, comfortable indoor seating and a better selection of tourist literature than you're likely to find outside the main tourist information centres in Vancouver and Victoria. Passengers are allowed to ride on the car decks, but it's far more comfortable to ride on the passenger decks and enjoy the scenery. Public announcements provide ample time to return to vehicles for off-loading.

Ferries from the Gulf Islands and from Tsawwassen dock at Swartz Bay, at the northern tip of the Saanich Peninsula, 30 mins north of Victoria by car. From the ferry dock, follow signs for BC 17 southbound into Victoria or pick up the return portion of the Victoria Circular Tour (see p.313).

THE GULF ISLANDS

Protected from the worst of winter storms by

298

Vancouver Island mountains, the Gulf Islands have the mildest, most moderate climate in BC and less than half the rainfall of Vancouver. Rocky and low, none of the islands have adequate supplies of water. Open fires are often banned spring–autumn because of the wildfire danger. Accommodation is scarce on all of the islands, but less so on Salt Spring, the largest of the Gulf Islands. Advance bookings are needed all year to ensure a place to sleep. The principal activities are walking, cycling, birding, fishing, swimming, scuba diving, sea kayaking and boating. Salt Spring and Mayne Islands also have thriving artistic communities.

GALIANO ISLAND

Tourist Information: Galiano Island Chamber of Commerce and Travel Infocentre, *Sturdies Bay, Box 73, Galiano Island, BC V0N 1P0; tel: (250) 539-2233.*

ACCOMMODATION

Galiano Getaways!; *tel: (250) 539-5551*, provide bookings for most of the inns, cottages and bed and breakfasts on the Island. Most are moderate–expensive. Camping is available at **Montague Harbour Provincial Marine Park**, 40 pitches, and **Dionisio Point Provincial Park**, 15 pitches; information for both available at *2930 Trans Canada Highway, RR 6, Victoria, BC V9B 5T9; tel: (250) 391-2300.*

SIGHTSEEING

The voyage from Tsawwassen takes about 50 mins. For local **BC Ferries** information; *tel: (250) 539-2622.*

Galiano is the most northerly of the Gulf Islands, named after Spanish explorer Dionisio Alcala Galiano, who charted the area in 1792. The main commercial centre is **Sturdies Bay**, at the south end of the long, narrow and flat island. There are also settlements at **Montague Harbour** and **Spotlight Cove**, at the north end. More than 130 species of birds, as well as a number of endangered plant and animal species, make the island popular with birders walkers and cyclists. Protected waters also make swimming, scuba diving, sea kayaking and boating popular year-round. The 57-sq. km island has a permanent population of about 900

MAYNE ISLAND

Tourist Information: Mayne Island Community Chamber of Commerce, *Box 160, Mayne Island, BC V0N 2J0; tel: (250) 539-5311.*

ACCOMMODATION

Oceanwood Country Inn, *C-2 Leighton Lane, RR #1, Mayne Island, BC V0N 2J0; tel: (250) 539-5074; fax: (250) 539-3002*, expensive, is the finest inn and restaurant on the island with expansive vistas across Navy Channel to North Pender Island.

SIGHTSEEING

BC Ferries dock at **Village Bay**, which has a bay but no village. For local ferry information; *tel: (250) 539-2321*. The crossing from Galiano Island takes 25 mins.

Mayne was once a major staging area for gold miners on the way from the mining permit office in Victoria to the Cariboo Gold Rush on the mainland. **Miners Bay** remains the main town on the island. Farmers followed the miners, turning Mayne into a major vegetable and fruit supplier for Vancouver until Japanese-Canadian farmers were interned inland during World War II. Today, Mayne is one of the most popular second-home and retirement islands, with many private residences. The original 1896 gaol, Plumper Pass Lockup, is now **The Mayne Museum**; *tel: (250) 539-5286*. **Active Pass Lighthouse**, still in use, is open daily 1300–1500. The hilly island is popular with cyclists, if challenging. Permanent population is about 800 scattered across 21 sq. kms.

PENDER ISLANDS

Tourist Information: Pender Island Chamber of Commerce, *Pender Island, BC V0N 2M0; tel: (250) 383-7191*, **Pender Island Visitor Information Booth**, *2332 Otter Bay Rd*, open daily June–Sept.

Bed & Breakfasts of North & South Pender Islands, *RR #1, Pender Island, BC V0N 2M0*, makes bookings for the dozen or so bed and breakfasts on the two islands.

BC Ferries dock at Otter Bay. For local ferry information; *tel: (250) 629-3344*. The crossing from Mayne Island takes 20 mins.

North and South Pender Island are joined by a narrow wooden bridge over an artificial canal. Much of the population lives on North Pender, the larger of the two. **Driftwood Centre**, mid-island, is the major commercial hub. **Port Washington**, north of the ferry terminal at **Otter Bay**, also has several artist-owned galleries and studios. Public recreation areas include an historical archaeological dig at a traditional Salish site on the north side of the canal open for tours in summer. An annual summer tournament at the Frisbee® disk park at Magic Lake draws contestants from around the world. The 24-sq. km island has a permanent population of about 2000.

SATURNA ISLAND

BC Ferries dock is at **Lyall Harbour**; *tel: (250) 539-5423*. Crossing time to Mayne and Pender Island is 35–40 mins.

Most services and nearly all of the half-dozen bed and breakfasts are within a few kilometres of the ferry landing. With fewer than 300 permanent residents scattered across 31 sq kms, the most startling sight is likely to be the splash of an eagle fishing or a deer walking through an open meadow. The island is quite hilly, unlike Pender, creating challenges for cyclists and innumerable blind corners for motorists. Best views are from the peak of **Mount Warburton Pike**, 490 m, and **East Point Lighthouse**, atop a barren plateau surrounded by wave-sculpted sandstone formations. The US Coast Guard station on Patos Island and Mt Constitution on Orcas Island, both in the San Juan Islands, are clearly visible.

SALT SPRING ISLAND

Tourist Information: Salt Spring Island Chamber of Commerce, *121 Lower Ganges Rd, Box 111, Ganges, BC V0S 1E0; tel: (250) 537-5252; fax: (250) 537-4276.*

ACCOMMODATION

Canadian Gulf Islands B&B Reservation Service, *637 Southwind Rd, Galiano Island, BC V0N 1P0; tel: (250) 539-2930; fax: (250) 539-5390*, books more than 100 inns, cottages, houses and bed and breakfasts in the Gulf Islands, most of them on Salt Spring. A Salt Spring Chamber of Commerce booklet lists dozens of accommodations on the island, including **Salt Spring Island Hostel**, *640 Cusheon Lake Rd, Salt Spring Island, BC V8K 2C2; tel: (250) 537-4149*, budget, the only Gulf Islands hostel.

SIGHTSEEING

BC Ferries has three docks: **Vesuvius Bay**; *tel: (250) 537-2151*, with service to Crofton; **Fulford Harbour**; *tel: (250) 653-4214*, with service to Swartz Bay; and **Long Harbour**; *tel: (250) 537-5313*, with service to Tsawwassen and Swartz Bay plus Galiano, Mayne and Pender Islands. Crossings range from 10–90 mins.

Named after the salt water springs on the north end of the island, SSI (as it is usually abbreviated) is the largest (180 sq. kms) and most populous of the Gulf Islands (about 9500 permanent residents). It also claims more artists

per capita than anywhere else in Canada. More than 75 studios scattered around the island produce everything from practical pottery to whimsical macramé with no greater purpose than enlivening a dull doorway. The greatest concentrations of studios are near Ganges, Fulford and Vesuvius Bay, the major population centres.

SSI is also the most-visited of the Gulf Islands, which gives it the worst traffic problems. Hire cars are available in Ganges, but bicycles and mopeds are more popular than autos. **Island Spoke Folk**, *115 Lower Ganges; tel: (250) 537-4664*, and **Saltspring Marina at Harbour's End**, *120 Upper Ganges; tel: (250) 537-5810*, have the best selection of bicycles and scooters. Favourite destinations include **Ruckle Provincial Park**, *south-west end of SSI*, the largest park in the Islands and one of SSI's most scenic spots, **Mount Maxwell Provincial Park**, *central island*, and the **Saturday Market**, *Centennial Park, Ganges*, Apr–Oct, the most popular open market in the islands.

VICTORIA

Victoria is BC's capital and oldest city. Once a leading industrial centre, Victoria has traded the clamour and the pollution of old-fashioned metal bashing for environmental activism, tourism and, of course, government. A mild climate, attractive urban setting and easy access to some of the most spectacular outdoor scenery in the Pacific Northwest has created a bubbling mixture of artists, big-city refugees, green activists and mostly-young entrepreneurs straining to turn environmental concern into long-term business opportunity.

Victoria is unfairly known as the stuffiest, most backward looking city in Canada. 'More English than the English,' is how favourite daughter Emily Carr characterised her own father, a 19th-century immigrant, and the city itself.

It may have been true once, but modern Victoria is eagerly combining one of Canada's greatest concentrations of heritage buildings with an aggressive turn toward the future. Restored brick storefronts and century-old mansions shelter the kind of social concerns that would have moved the original occupants to call for police protection.

Urbanites from Vancouver and points east sniff at Victorians as dreamy Lotus Eaters, but these Lotus Eaters well remember the places from whence they came. They've worked hard to turn Victoria into one of the most pleasant cities in the Pacific Northwest.

TOURIST INFORMATION

Tourism Victoria, *710-1175 Douglas St, Victoria, BC V8W 2E1; tel: (250) 382-2160; fax: (250) 361-9733.* **Travel Infocentre**, *812 Wharf St, Victoria, BC V8W 1T3; tel: (250) 953-2033; fax: (250) 382-6539,* open daily. *Monday Magazine, 1069 Blanshard St, Victoria, BC V8W 2J5; tel: (250) 382-6188,* available free each Friday in shops and newspaper boxes, has the most complete listing of current events and reviews in Victoria.

WEATHER

Sheltered from storms by mountains on all sides and warmed by the Pacific Ocean, Victoria has the warmest, sunniest and mildest urban climate in the Pacific Northwest. Summer temperatures average 17°C and seldom hit 30°C. Rain is infrequent May–Sept, but not unknown. Winter averages 7°C; snow is rare. Annual rainfall is 690 mm (27 ins), less than half of what Vancouver or Seattle endure each year.

ARRIVING AND DEPARTING

By Air
Victoria International Airport, *tel: (250) 363-6600,* is west of Sidney, 20 kms and 30 mins north of the city centre. Taxi to the city centre, $20. **Airporter**, *767 Audley St, Victoria, BC V8X 2V4; tel: (250) 475-2010; fax: (250) 475-3010,* has coach service between the airport and 60 hotels every 30 mins, $13 single, children under 5 free, advance booking required. **BC Transit**, *Box 610, Victoria, BC V8W 2P3; tel: (250) 382-6161; fax: (250) 995-5639,* $2.25, exact fare only.

The **Inner Harbour** has scheduled and charter seaplane service to Seattle, Vancouver, the San Juan Islands, the Gulf Islands, Nanaimo and other destinations.

301

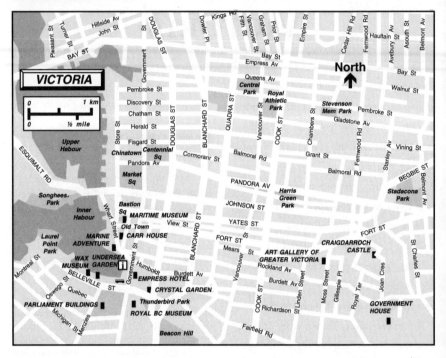

By Sea

Most of Victoria's 3 million annual visitors arrive by water. **BC Ferries**, *1112 Fort St, Victoria, BC V8W 4V2; tel: (250) 381-1401; fax: (250) 388-7754*, serves Swartz Bay, at the north end of the Saanich Peninsula, 45 mins by car from the city centre, with vehicle and passenger service from Vancouver (Tsawwassen) and the Gulf Islands. Ferry services connect with BC Transit in both Victoria and Vancouver. BC 17 begins and ends at the BC Ferries dock at Swartz Bay.

Black Ball Transport (*MV Coho*), *430 Belleville St, Victoria, BC V8V 1W9; tel: (520) 386-2202; fax: (250) 386-2207*, has car and passenger service between Victoria's Inner Harbour and Port Angeles, WA. **Victoria Rapid Transit**; *tel: (250) 361-9144*, offers passenger and bicycle service on the same route May–Oct. Advance booking required for both ferries, several days in advance in summer or at holidays and weekends.

Washington State Ferries, *2499 Ocean Ave, Sidney, BC V8L 1Tl; tel: (250) 656-1831;* *fax: (250) 656-3760*, has vehicle and passenger service to Anacortes, WA. Advance bookings required in summer and highly recommended the rest of the year. Credit cards are not accepted, but fares may be paid in either US or Canadian currency.

Victoria San Juan Cruises, *tel: (800) 443-4552*, has passenger service between Bellingham, WA and the Inner Harbour via Roche Harbor (San Juan Island, WA), May–Oct. Advance booking required.

Victoria Line, *185 Dallas Rd, Victoria, BC V8V 1A1; tel: (250) 480-5555 or (800) 668-1167; fax: (250) 480-5222*, offer vehicle and passenger service between Victoria and Seattle, WA May–Oct. Advance bookings required in summer, highly recommended the rest of the season.

Victoria Clipper, *254 Belleville, Victoria, BC V8V 1W9; tel: (250) 382-8100 or (800) 888-2535; fax: (206) 443-2583*, has daily passenger catamaran service between the Inner Harbour and Seattle with the fastest ships on the route. Advance bookings required.

By Land

All land transport between Victoria and the mainland requires a ferry connection through the Saanich Peninsula (Swartz Bay or Sidney) or the Inner Harbour. From Saanich, follow BC 17 south directly to the inner city. **Pacific Coach Lines**, *210-1150 Station St, Vancouver, BC B6A 4C7; tel: (250) 385-4411*, runs between central Victoria and central Vancouver by way of BC Ferries.

The **Victoria Coach Station**, *700 Douglas St*, is behind the Empress Hotel. Once on Vancouver Island, the main highways into Victoria are Canada 1 (the TransCanada Highway) from the north, BC 14 from Port Renfrew and the west and BC 17 from the Saanich Peninsula. **Esquimalt & Nanaimo (E&N) Railway**, *450 Pandora Ave, Victoria, BC V8W 1N6; tel: (800) 561-8630 or (250) 383-4324*, has daily return service between Victoria and Courtenay via Nanaimo.

GETTING AROUND

Greater Victoria spreads across much of the south-east corner of Vancouver Island, but most of touristic Victoria is within a compact 10-block area along the south and east sides of the Inner Harbour. Walking is the best way to explore.

Streets are busy until the last restaurants and pubs close in the early morning hours. Sex has been big business in Victoria since the boom days of the last century, though today's trade is conducted largely through escort ads in the telephone book Yellow Pages. The women and men who work *Government St* after the tourist shops close around 2200 are as discreet as their customers. As in most cities, it's best not to walk empty streets alone at night, but there are no dangerous neighbourhoods to avoid. Since Victoria is on an island with limited and easily controlled access, criminals seem to prefer to ply their trade on the mainland where escape is easier.

Public Transport

It is entirely practicable to explore all but the most distant parts of Victoria by public transport. **BC Transit**, *Box 610, Victoria, BC V8W 2P3; tel: (250) 382-6161; fax: (250) 995-5639*,

has a dense network of bus routes throughout Greater Victoria. The fare within the city centre and the southern Saanich Peninsula is $1.50 for adults, $1.00 for seniors, secondary school students and children; $2.50 and $1.50 for longer two-zone journeys. Sheets of 10 discount tickets are $13.50. **Super PASS** is $5.00 daily or $47.00 monthly; $4.00 and $30.00 concession. The Tourism Victoria Infocentre, 812 Wharf Street, sells day passes. The *Victoria Regional Transit System Rider's Guide*, available from BC Transit, lists other sales locations and all routes. Service on main lines runs approximately 0600–2400, but some routes have as few as two buses daily.

Driving in Victoria

Narrow streets, busy traffic and limited street parking make it difficult to explore the city centre by car. Best bet is to park and explore on foot, then drive to more distant attractions. There is ample parking off the west side of *Wharf St* along the Inner Harbour as well as parking garages east of *Government St*. Street parking is regulated by metres, with time limits strictly enforced.

Traffic is heavy most of the day in the city centre, but flows smoothly in other areas. Exceptions are major commute arteries, particularly BC 17 and BC 1A during commute hours, 0730–0900 and 1600–1800 Mon–Fri. Left turns are extremely difficult in the city centre due to heavy traffic and the near-total absence of left turn signals or left turn lanes. Most residential streets are wide enough to allow for parking as well as moving vehicles, but country roads on the Saanich Peninsula can be narrow, winding and slow.

STAYING IN VICTORIA

Accommodation

There are more than 6500 rooms in Greater Victoria, ranging from elegant hotels to modest bed and breakfasts. There are also 3 million visitors each year, which makes advance bookings a necessity in summer and extremely wise the rest of the year.

Most rooms at all price levels can be booked by credit card through **Tourism Victoria**;

tel: (800) 663-3883. Chains include *BW, CP, CS, DI, HI, QI, Rm* and *TL*. Inexpensive motels are clustered along BC 1A eastbound *(Goldstream Ave, Craigflower Rd* and *Gorge Rd)* and BC 17 southbound.

Best Canadian Bed & Breakfast Network, *1090 W. King Edward Ave, Vancouver, BC V6H 1Z4; tel: (604) 738-7207; fax: (604) 732-4998*, and **Canada-West Victoria Reservation Service**, *6203 Central Saanich Rd, Victoria, BC V8Z 5T7; tel: (250) 652-8685; fax: (250) 652-8679;* list and book area bed and breakfasts.

The most prestigious and most central address in town is Canadian Pacific's château-like **Empress Hotel**, *721 Government St, Victoria, BC V8W 1W5; tel: (250) 384-8111* or *(800) 441-1414; fax: (250) 381-5959,* the most imposing building on the Inner Harbour. Opened in 1908 by the same architect who built Parliament Houses, the ivy-covered Empress sits surrounded by gardens on what was once a malodorous tidal flat. Although swamped by tourists in summer, the elegant Edwardian decor makes the original lobby worth a visit, if only for a drink. Corridors in The Empress' first underground level are lined with photographs showing the upper crust from around the world at play during the first half of the century. The hotel is best known for its overpriced afternoon **High Tea**, but **The Empress Dining Room** is one of the better Northwest restaurants in town.

The modern **Laurel Point Inn**, *680 Montreal St, Victoria, BC V8V 1Z8; tel: (250) 386-8721* or *(800) 663-7667; fax: (250) 386-9547,* overlooking the Inner Harbour entrance, and **Ocean Pointe Resort on the Harbour**, *45 Songhess Rd, Victoria, BC V9A 6T3; tel: (800) 667-4677* or *(250) 360-2999; fax: (250) 360-1041,* on the west side of the Inner Harbour, offer similar luxury but without the Empress' Edwardian gloss. All are pricey.

Days Inn on the Harbour, *427 Belleville St, Victoria, BC V8V 1X3; tel: (800) 329-7466* or *(250) 386-3451; fax: (250) 386-6999,* and **Quality Inn Harbourview**, *455 Belleville St; tel: (800) 424-6423* or *(250) 386-2421; fax: (250) 386-8779,* both moderate–expensive, are directly across the street from the US ferry

docks and a pleasant 10-min walk along the Inner Harbour from The Empress.

There are dozens of bed and breakfasts in and near the tourist core. Among the best is the expensive **Inn on St Andrews**, *231 St Andrews St, Victoria, BC V8V 2N1; tel: (250) 384-8613,* a wonderfully restored mansion in a quiet residential neighbourhood equi-distant from The Empress and Beacon Hill Park.

Best budget bets are the **Backpacker's Hostel**, *1418 Fernwood Rd, Victoria, BC V8V 4P7; tel. (250) 386-4471,* **Hostelling International**, *516 Yates St, Victoria, BC V8W 1K8; tel: (250) 385-4511; fax: (250) 385-3232,* **Pacific Rim Hostelling Network**, *934 Selkirk Ave, Victoria, BC V9A 2V1; tel: (250) 389-1213* or *(800) 974-6638; fax: (250) 389-1313,* and **University Housing**, *Box 1700, Victoria, BC V8W 2Y2; tel: (250) 721-8395; fax: (250) 721-8930.*

Eating and Drinking

Victoria's most famous repast is **High Tea**, epitomised by the 100,000–plus overpriced mid-afternoon meals served in the main lobby of **The Empress Hotel** each year. Look for finger sandwiches, crumpets, scones, pots of whipped cream and jam, berries and, of course, tea. Advance booking required.

Credit an early 19th-century Duchess of Bedford with the idea. Praying that a light snack would counteract 'that sinking feeling around five o'clock', she tried snacking on tea and small sandwiches. The custom caught on, evolving into the formal Afternoon Tea and the more serious meal called High Tea.

Many Victoria restaurants offer Afternoon Tea as a light repast, with High Tea often reserved for weekends. Prices are budget–moderate, depending on location and quantity. Victorians avoid summer crowds at The Empress but return during the winter months. Local year-round favourites include **The Bedford**, *1140 Government St; tel: (250) 384-6835,* **James Bay Tea Room and Restaurant**, *332 Menzies St (behind Parliament Houses); tel: (250) 382-8282,* **Tudor Rose Restaurant and Tea Room**, *253 Cook St (near Beacon Hill Park); tel: (250) 382-4616,* **Blethering Place Tea Room and Restaurant**, *206-2250 Oak*

Bay Ave (Oak Bay Village); tel: (250) 598-1413, **Oak Bay Beach Hotel**, 1175 Beach Dr.; tel: (250) 598-4556, and **The Olde England Inn**, 429 Lampson St, Esquimalt; tel: (250) 388-4353.

Most restaurants near the Inner Harbour cater to tourist tastes for pizza, pasta and ice-cream with more emphasis on convenience and atmosphere than on taste. Advance booking is always wise and essential in summer. Best choice for a quick meal is the top-level food fair at **Victoria Eaton Centre**, Government St, Fort–View Sts; tel: (250) 389-2228.

Wharfside, 1208 Wharf St; tel: (250) 360-1808, is a moderate tourist restaurant with excellent harbour views serving respectable fish and pizza despite the crowds. **Chandlers Seafood Restaurant**, 1250 Wharf St; tel: (250) 385-3474, and **Herald Street Café**, 546 Herald St; tel: (250) 381-1441, moderate–pricey, are the best seafood restaurants. **Deep Cove Chalet**, 11190 Chalet Rd; tel: (250) 656-3541, pricey, gets the nod as the best (and most expensive) French-inspired restaurant in Victoria.

The Olde England Inn, 429 Lampson St, Esquimalt; tel: (250) 388-4353, has the best traditional roast beef and Yorkshire pudding on Vancouver Island. The **James Bay Inn**, 270 Government St; tel: (250) 384-7151, budget–moderate, is a quiet neighbourhood restaurant and pub south of Parliament Houses. **Siam**, 512 Fort St; tel: (250) 383-9911, budget–moderate, has outstanding Thai dishes. Visiting vegetarians flock to **Green Cuisine**, 560 Johnson St, Market Square, Courtyard Level; tel: (250) 385-1809, for shockingly good budget veg choices. **Bohematea**, 515 Yates St; tel: (250) 383-2829, is a popular tea house with splendid budget meals as well as tea, coffee and a good selection of local beers.

Top breakfast or lunch choice is **Sally Café**, 714 Cormorant St; tel: (250) 381-1431, with fine budget omelettes, sandwiches, soups and pastries. **Topo's Ristorante**, 2950 Douglas; tel: (250) 383-1212, is one of the best Northern Italian choices. **San Remo**, 2709 Quadra St; tel: (250) 384-5255, is a good Greek choice. **India Curry House**, 506 Fort St; tel: (250) 384-5622, and **Taj Mahal**, 679 Herald St;

tel: (250) 383-4662, are two of the better Indian possibilities. All are budget–moderate.

Pubs are the most popular spots for eating, drinking and evening entertainment. The **Elephant & Castle**, 100 Victoria Eaton Centre, Government and View Sts; tel: (250) 383-5858, cheap–budget, is the most 'English' of the city's many pubs and extremely popular with tourists. **Swans Hotel**, 506 Pandora Ave; tel: (250) 361-3310, has one of BC's best breweries, **Buckerfield's Brewery**, on the premises, as well as a fine budget–moderate Northwest restaurant and hotel in a restored heritage building. The **Charles Dickens Pub**, 633 Humboldt St (ground floor, Empress Hotel); tel: (250) 361-2600, budget, is a more traditional alternative. Technophiles and the email-starved prefer the budget **Underground Onramp**, 1414b Douglas St; tel: (250) 995-1812; fax: (250) 995-3216, Victoria's leading cybercafé.

Communications

There are dozens of post offices in Victoria. Mail can be addressed to hotels.

Money

Thomas Cook Foreign Exchange is located at Sussex Place, G3-1001 Douglas St, Victoria, BC V8W 2C5; tel: (250) 385-0088; fax: (604) 383-6169.

ENTERTAINMENT

Victoria has emerged as a fertile incubator for local bands which graduate to wider fame on the mainland. Local venues and performers change frequently, but Monday Magazine stays abreast of who's hot and who's deserted to Vancouver.

McPherson Playhouse, 3 Centennial Square; tel: (250) 386-6121, is the centre of professional and repertory theatre on Vancouver Island. The restored playhouse has a regular summer schedule of noon concerts and evening musical comedy. The McPherson is also the venue for **Victoria International Festival**, Jul–Aug, featuring international orchestral concerts, recitals and operas, and **The Pacific Opera**, 1316 B Government St, Victoria, BC V8W 1Y8; tel: (250) 385-0222; fax: (250) 382-4944, which performs Sept–May.

The **Victoria Symphony**; *846 Broughton St, Victoria, BC V8W 1E4; tel: (250) 386-6121*, performs a pop and masterworks series Sept–Apr at the **Royal Theatre**. The **Victoria Conservatory of Music**, *tel: (250) 386-5311*, also performs at the Royal. **Beacon Hill Park** and **Centennial Square** host outdoor concerts and other events May–Sept. Rock concerts and other major events play **Memorial Arena**, *1925 Blanshard; tel: (250) 361-0506*.

The **Netherlands Centennial Carillon**, *Government and Belleville Sts; tel: (250) 387-1616*, the largest carillon in Canada, plays in recital every Sun at 1500 Apr–Dec and Fri at 1900 July–Aug. Best seats are in the Sunken Gardens behind the carillon tower, the Royal British Colombian Museum plaza and the Empress Hotel Rose Garden. The bells sound on the quarter hour 0700–2200 daily.

Shopping

Victoria is not a shop-till-you-drop city, though there are ample opportunities to spend. **Victoria Eaton Centre**, *Government St, Fort–View Sts; tel: (250) 389-2228*, the largest shopping mall in the city centre, has more than 100 shops, including **Eaton's** department store.

Government St itself is one long mall from *Humboldt St* north to *Johnson St*. **Munro's Books**, *1108 Government St; tel: (250) 382-2832*, originally the Royal Bank, has one of Victoria's best selections of Canadiana and travel books. **Murchie's Tea & Coffee**, *1110 Government St; tel: (250) 383-3112; fax: (250) 383-3255*, has been a BC fixture since 1894. Best seller is Empress Afternoon Blend, the same mix of Ceylon, Keemun, Darjeeling and Assam teas served at The Empress every afternoon. The pastry, tea and coffee bar is one of the busiest budget eateries on *Government St*.

Beautiful British Columbia, *910 Government St (Harbour Centre); tel: (250) 384-7773*, specialises in made-in-BC gifts, crafts, souvenirs, clothing and food items. **Cowichan Trading Co.**, *1328 Government St; tel: (250) 383-0321*, has the largest selection of First Nations sweaters, art and crafts. **James Bay Trading Co.**, *1102 Government St; tel: (150) 388-5477*, specialises in First Nations art as well as other Canadian-made items.

Market Square, *560 Johnson St; tel: (250) 386-2441*, is a collection of nine heritage buildings, most of them originally shops and storehouses, that have been redeveloped into an arcade for shopping, public art, eating, busking and passing the time.

Just north is **Chinatown**, Canada's first Chinese community, dating from the 1840s and 1850s when Victoria was BC's only serious city. Modern Chinatown is more tourist trap than community. **Fan Tan Alley**, *between Fisgard St and Pandora Ave*, is lined with small shops selling everything from antique parasols to New Age music in what were once gambling dens, opium parlours and brothels. **Antique Row**, *Fort St, Blanshard–Cook Sts*, has more than two dozen antique shops.

Sightseeing

Nearly all of touristic Victoria lies within walking distance of the **Inner Harbour**, the carefully engineered remains of the natural harbour that lured Hudson's Bay Company trader James Douglas to the site in 1842. Douglas built Fort Victoria the next year on what is now *Bastion Square*. Envisaged as a refuge against expansionist Americans who were following the Oregon Trail into the Columbia River basin, Victoria became one of the richest and rowdiest cities in North America.

Three years later, the US-Canada border was set at the 49th Parallel. The Columbia River, HBC's highway into interior Canada, was out of bounds. So was company headquarters at Fort Vancouver, north across the Columbia River from present-day Portland, OR (see p. 134). HBC moved its Pacific operations to Victoria, setting up farms, timber operations and coal mines. Fuelled by growing commerce and gold rushes on the Fraser River and the Kootenays, the city soon outgrew its origins.

What remained of the wooden fort was pulled down in 1862 to make way for yet another round of commercial expansion. All that survives is a handful of rusted iron mooring rings set in the rocks along the Inner Harbour. The rings are buried beneath overgrown blackberry bushes, but a replica (not open to the public) of HBC's eight-sided bastion rises above

Fort Victoria RV Park, *340 Island Hwy; tel: (250) 479-8112,* west of the city.

The original blockhouse stood at what became the corner of *View* and *Government Sts.* Canada's only genuine HBC bastion is in Nanaimo (see p. 323).

Coloured bricks set into the pavement along *View St* west to *Bastion Square* and south along *Government St* to *Fort St,* then west toward the harbour, outline the original stockade. The imposing colonial buildings of **Old Town**, *Humboldt St–Pandora St, Inner Harbour–Government St,* date from the 1880s–1910s.

Architecture

Victoria's most imposing structures have nothing whatsoever to do with James Douglas. **Parliament Buildings**, *S. end of Inner Harbour; tel: (250) 387-3046,* and **The Empress Hotel**, *721 Government St; tel: (250) 384-8111,* were both built near the turn of the century by British architect Francis Mawson Rattenbury. Rattenbury arrived in Victoria in 1892 and promptly won an Empire-wide competition to design and build the province's new Parliament House – at the age of 25. The towering totem pole on the Parliament Buildings' lawn is a modern addition.

When the Parliament Buildings opened in 1898, the only dignitary not in attendance was the builder himself. Ratz, as he preferred to be called, was in London trying to raise financing for a scheme to transport miners and materials to yet another gold rush, this one in the Yukon. The Yukon scheme came to naught, but Ratz built the Empress, perhaps the continent's most opulent Edwardian edifice, the Crystal Garden (see below), and dozens of other major buildings in Victoria.

He also built a new life on a lurid divorce and remarriage to a woman 30 years his junior. Stuffy Victorian society snubbed both the new wife, who was so unspeakably modern as to smoke cigarettes in public, and the man who so openly pursued her. The couple moved to England in 1930, where Ratz was murdered by his wife's young lover four years later.

Rattenbury's other great public project is the **Crystal Garden**, *713 Douglas St; tel: (250) 381-1277; fax: (250) 383-1218,* open

0800–2000 daily July–Aug, 0900–1800 Apr–June and Sept–Oct, 1000–1630 Nov–Mar, $6.50 adults, $4 seniors and children 6–16, an immense glass hall modelled on England's Crystal Palace. Now a tropical conservatory, the Garden held the largest indoor swimming pool in the British Empire when it opened in 1925. With ballrooms, tea rooms and an elegant promenade, it became one of the most famous landmarks in Canada. The building now houses tropical butterflies, a waterfall, monkeys and a somewhat parched rain forest.

First Nations Exhibits

Between the Crystal Garden and Parliament House is the **Royal British Columbia Museum**, *675 Belleville St; tel: (800) 661-5411* or *(250) 387-3701,* open 0930–1900 July–Sept, 1000–1730 Oct–June, $5 adults, $2 seniors and children aged 6–11 yrs, $15 family. The immense museum has three floors of displays on the natural and human history of British Columbia.

The First Nations exhibit includes a full-sized Kwaktuil chief's house, complete with totems, carvings and chiefly regalia. Even more striking is the careful rendition of the full flowering of First Nations arts in the profitable decades after first contact and the even swifter collapse as smallpox and other diseases decimated the Native population between 1843 and 1885. A single outbreak of smallpox which began in Victoria in 1862 killed 20,000, 30% of the Native population.

Victoria was also largely responsible for the modern revival of First Nations arts. In the 1940s, the museum donated a section of its grounds to **Thunderbird Park**, *Belleville and Douglas Sts,* to display totem poles. Chief Mungo Martin of the Kwagiulth band from Fort Rupert led a group of Thunderbird Park carvers in the 1950s in a successful attempt to rediscover what was already a largely lost art. Replicas of Martin's original poles tower above the park; many of the originals are on display inside the museum.

Historic Buildings

Immediately behind Thunderbird Park is **Helmcken House**; *tel: (250) 387-4697,* open

1000–1700 May–Sept, 1200–1600 Oct–Nov and Feb–Apr, variable in Dec, $4 adults, $3 seniors and students, $10 family. Dr. John Helmcken built the house in 1852 for his wife Cecilia, James Douglas' eldest daughter. Helmcken, Speaker of three colonial legislatures, is better remembered for reserving Beacon Hill as a public park. Period photographs of Helmcken in front of his house show the Garry oak trees nearly as large as they are today. The squared logs of his original cabin are clearly visible through a window set into one wall. An excellent taped tour describes life in early Victoria and explains the furnishings.

Next door is **St Ann's Schoolhouse**, built about 1845, the oldest surviving building in the city. The site of James Douglas' own house, which stood until 1906, is marked by a small plaque in **Cherry Tree Square**, *on the west side of the Museum*.

Inner Harbour

The **Royal London Wax Museum**, *470 Belleville St; tel: (250) 388-4461*, open 0900–2100 July–Aug, 0930–1630 the rest of the year, $7 adults, $6.25 seniors, $6 students, $3 6–12 yrs, $22 families, offers the usual collection of wax figures of the rich and infamous. The 1924 Beaux Arts-style Roman Temple was originally the Canadian Pacific Steamship Company terminal.

Undersea Gardens, *490 Belleville St; tel: (250) 382-5717*, open 0900–2100 May–Sept, 0900–1700 the rest of the year, $6.50 adults, $6 seniors, $3–$4.75 children, $17.50 families, is an underwater observation room looking into an immense aquarium stocked with native marine life.

Broad walkways surround the southern and eastern sides of the Inner Harbour providing ample room for buskers. A kilted bagpiper is a semi-permanent afternoon fixture at the harbourside corner of *Government* and *Belleville Sts*.

The **Tourism Victoria Travel Infocentre**, *812 Wharf St*, sits atop a collection of tourist shops, restaurants, public toilets, showers and a laundromat, all designed for travelling yachters moored nearby.

Just north along the waterfront is **Victoria Marine Adventure Centre**, *950 Wharf St;*

tel: (800) 575-6700 or *(250) 995-2211*, booking and departure point for several whale watching, marine wildlife tours, kayaking, scuba diving, sea plane tours and other outdoor activity companies.

Museums and Galleries

Just inland (east) is **Bastion Square** and the **Maritime Museum of British Columbia**, *28 Bastion Square; tel: (250) 385-4222*, open daily 0930–1630, $4 adults, $2 children, $13 families. The museum includes ship models, figureheads, tools, naval uniforms and the 1860 *Tilikum*, an 11-metre dugout canoe converted to a three-masted schooner, which sailed from Victoria to England and back 1901–1904. The museum is in the elegant Victoria Law Courts building, used as a court 1889–1962. Its polished brass elevator is the oldest working lift in Canada.

Market Square, *560 Johnson St; tel: (250) 386-2441*, dates from the same era. The collection of nine red brick heritage buildings, now an open shopping arcade, were originally shops and storehouses for the docks and industrial areas built to supply successive waves of gold miners, fishing fleets, sealskin hunters, coal ships and general cargo vessels. Nearby streets, saloons, gambling dens and brothels were as wild as any on the Pacific coast, but strict law enforcement maintained a clear separation between the working classes who laboured and lived near the Inner Harbour and the moneyed classes who moved farther inland and south.

The ultimate docklands escapee was Robert Dunsmuir, a Scottish indentured labourer who built BC's largest fortune on coal, railways and the well-trampled backs of company employees.

His **Craigdarroch Castle**, *1050 Joan Cres; tel: (250) 592-5323*, open 0900–1930 Jun–Sept, 1000–1700 the rest of the year, $6 adults, $2 children, was the tallest home atop the tallest hill in Victoria. Dunsmuir died before the house was completed in 1889, but his widow and daughters lived in the 39-room rough stone castle until 1909. His grandchildren squandered the family fortune.

Dunsmuir lived an ostentatious style popularised by his California colleagues Collis

Victoria Gardens

Victorians take their gardening seriously. It's not just the trademark flower baskets hanging from lamp posts along the Inner Harbour or the famed Butchart Gardens (see p.310). The entire city is fixated on flowers.

While the rest of Canada shivers beneath the arctic snows of February, hundreds of perfectly normal-seeming Victorians can be found stooped over their crocus beds, calculators in hand, or perched on precarious ladders to count individual blossoms on flowering fruit trees. The city-wide flower total, calculated from flower totals telephoned in by gardeners from around the city, is celebrated as the end of winter.

Victoria's passion for gardens began with the first White settlers. When Hudson's Bay Company factor James Douglas surveyed what would become the Inner Harbour in 1842, he wrote to a friend 'The place appears a perfect Eden in the midst of the dreary wilderness of Northwest Coast, and so different is its general aspect...that one might be pardoned for supposing it had dropped from the clouds'.

Douglas himself was no gardener, but his son-in-law, Dr John Helmcken, Victoria's first physician, was an ardent collector of native plants.

The farmers and merchants who settled at the fort Douglas laid out in 1843, set about re-creating the look of an England they had left behind. Hawthorn hedges, cowslips, primroses and roses soon replaced the trees and brush that once covered the rolling hills of Victoria.

As commerce grew and great houses began to appear, gardens became a point of pride as crucial as any architectural detail.

By the time an abandoned limestone quarry was transformed into the Butcharts' famed Sunken Garden in 1917, Victoria had already established itself as the most beflowered city in the Pacific Northwest.

309

Huntington, Leland Stanford and Charles Crocker. The intricately ornamented castle is resplendent in carved wood, polished marble and fine paintings. His fellow magnates lost their equally ornate mansions to the 1906 San Francisco earthquake, but Craigdarroch Castle has become a public museum.

Victoria has several other open houses. The most scenic is **Fisgard Lighthouse & Fort Rodd Hill National Historic Sites**, *603 Fort Rodd Hill Rd, west of Esquimalt off Hwy 1A; tel: (250) 478-6481; fax: (250) 478-8415*. Built in 1860, the lighthouse is the oldest on Canada's West Coast. An automated light still guides ships into Esquimalt, but the keeper's house has become a fine lighthouse and shipping museum. Fort Rodd Hill was part of Canada's marine defence system 1878–1956, protecting the naval base and coaling station at Esquimalt. Both sites temper history with excellent coastal views.

Point Ellice House, *2616 Pleasant St; tel: (250) 380-6506*, open 1000–1700 May–Oct, a rambling Italianate villa, has Canada's most complete collection of Victoriana and a fine afternoon tea (advance booking required). **Craigflower**, *Admirals Rd and Hwy 1A; tel: (250) 387-4697*, open Sun 1000–1700 May–Oct, is a restored 1850s farmhouse originally built for the HBC. The property includes heirloom plantings and farm animals with extremely knowledgeable and enthusiastic interpreters in period costume.

Carr House, *207 Government St; tel: (250) 383-5843*, open 1000–1700 May–Oct, is the birthplace of Canadian painter and writer Emily Carr.

The **Art Gallery of Greater Victoria**, *1040 Moss St; tel: (250) 384-4101; fax: (250) 361-3995*, open Mon–Sat 1000–1700, Thur 1000–2100, Sun 1300–1700, $5 adults, $3 seniors and students, free on Mondays, is partially housed in an 1889 mansion. The Gallery specialises in contemporary artists from Canada and Asia and historical art from Asia, Europe and North America.

Parks and Gardens

Nearby **Government House Gardens**, *1401 Rockland Ave, open daily dawn–dusk,* has 14 hectares of formal flower beds, blossoming shrubs, lawns, ivy, heather, azaleas and rhododendrons surrounding the Lt Governor's official residence (closed to the public).

Beacon Hill Park, *from Douglas and Dallas Sts,* is 74 hectares of formal gardens, playing fields and small lakes sloping down to the sea. A seaside walkway is especially popular with runners, dog walkers and sightseers for its splendid views across the Strait of Juan de Fuca to the Olympic Peninsula. **Butchart Gardens**, *Bentwood Bay; tel: (250) 652-4422,* open daily 0900, closing varies with the season, $13 adult, $6.50 children, reduced admission Nov–Mar, is one of the most visited gardens in North America. Its 20 hectares, once a private estate, are divided into Rose, Japanese, Italian and Sunken Gardens plus several other landscape features. The Gardens are spectacular all year and breathtaking in summer – as are the crowds.

310

Tours

Many tours leave from *Belleville* and *Menzes Sts,* along the Inner Harbour, whether by motorcoach, horse-drawn coach, pedicab, or on foot. **Gray Line**, *700 Douglas St, Victoria, BC V8W 2B3; tel: (800) 318-0818 (BC), (800) 663-8390 (US) or (250) 388-5248,; fax: (250) 388-7059,* operate the most extensive schedule of coach tours in Victoria, including the bright red double-decker buses parked in front of The Empress Hotel. **Royal Blue Line**; *tel: (800) 663-1128* or *(250) 360-2249,* offer similar tours around the city and as far afield as The Butchart Gardens (see above).

Victoria Harbour Ferry; *tel: (250) 480-0971,* and **Harbour Gondola**; *tel: (250) 361-3511,* offer harbour tours by small ferry. The *SS Beaver, 1002 C Wharf St; tel: (250) 384-8116; fax: (250) 384-8933,* has harbour tours and dinner cruises aboard a replica of the Hudson Bay Company's 1835 paddle wheel steam ship of the same name.

Victoria Carriage Tours, *Belleville and Menzies Sts; tel: (250) 383-2207,* offer horse-drawn carriage tours lasting from 15–60 mins.

Greenday Bicycle Tours; *tel: (800) 469-2453* or *(250) 380-6033,* have full-day bicycle tours of Victoria as well as 3-day cycle tours of the **Galloping Goose Trail** to the town of Sooke (see p. 316).

Bird's Eye View offer historical walking tours of the inner harbour area leaving from the Tourism Victoria Infocentre each evening at 1900 in summer.

Victoria Bobby; *tel: (250) 953-2033,* guide walking tours of the old town three times daily, also from the Infocentre; advance bookings strongly recommended. **Another Way Adventures**; *tel: (250) 385-2035,* stalk back alleys in search of murder, ghosts and mayhem at 1900 in summer, advance booking strongly advised.

Les Chan, *270 Simcoe St, Apt 407, Victoria, BC V8V 1K7; tel: (250) 383-7317,* leads walking tours of Chinatown with visits to a temple, traditional pharmacy, tea shop, gallery and lunch. **Lantern Tours**; *tel: (250) 598-8870,* offer lantern tours of the Old Burying Ground at 2130 Jul–Aug.

The Old Cemetery Society; *tel: (250) 598-8870,* sponsor guided cemetery tours most Sundays throughout the year. The **Canadian Forces Base Esquimalt Nanden**; *tel: (250) 363-4395,* is open for self-guided walking tours 0800–1600 Mon–Fri at the HMCS Nanden-North Gate, off *Admirals Rd* in Esquimalt.

Victoria Garden Tours; *tel: (250) 721-2797,* offer a full schedule of guided garden tours at Government House, the Horticulture Center of the Pacific/Ravenhill Herb Farm, Saxe Point Park/Point Ellice House and Hatley Park (Royal Roads University). Advance booking required.

Western Forest Products Ltd; *tel: (250) 642-6351,* have free forestry tours leaving from Victoria, Colwood and Sooke Jun–Sept.

For a lightening look at the highlights of Southern Vancouver Island, **Grand Circle Tour**; *Box 57, Cowichan Bay, BC V0R 1N0; tel: (250) 480-7245* or *(800) 665-7374; fax: (250) 748-6525,* has a summer-only circle tour combining **E&N Railway** to Duncan, the **Native Heritage Centre**, a 3-hr sail, walking tour of **Butchart Gardens** and coach tour back to Victoria.

VICTORIA CIRCULAR DRIVE

Allow the better part of a day for this 125-km drive around Victoria. If time is short, eliminate the loops west to Fort Rodd Hill/Fisgard Lighthouse and north to Butchart Gardens. Visiting all of the museums and attractions could stretch to the better part of a week.

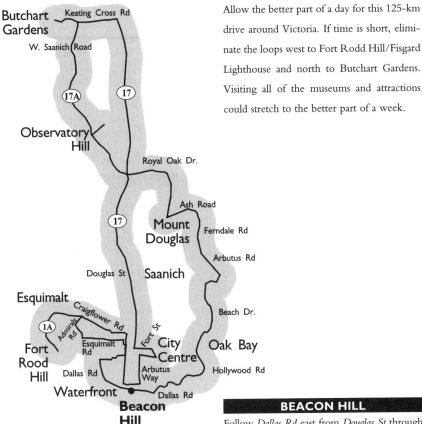

311

ROUTE

The route begins and ends at the south-west corner of Beacon Hill Park, *Douglas St* and *Dallas Rd*, but you can pick it up at any point. The circuit can be taken in either direction (except for one-way streets in the city centre), but the directions given reduce left turns and take advantage of one-way streets. Avoid the downtown and major arteries during commute hours, 0730–0900 and 1600–1800.

BEACON HILL

Follow *Dallas Rd* east from *Douglas St* through Beacon Hill Park along the Juan de Fuca Strait. The wooden sign marking Mile 0 of the TransCanada Highway is scenic, but the highway now extends west to Tofino. **Beacon Hill** is named for the signal fire that burned on the hilltop from the 1850s through the turn of the century to guide ships around treacherous reefs guarding the harbour entrance.

A shoreline walking and cycling path is as popular with runners as it is with photographers entranced by the Olympic Mountains rising across the strait. The totem pole on the left was once the tallest in the world, a record currently held by the totem in front of Parliament Buildings. **Clover Point** has good views.

Dallas Rd continues between Ross Bay and **Ross Bay Cemetery**, where most early Victorians can be found. There is ample parking and public access to a rocky beach below. *Dallas Rd* becomes *Hollywood Crescent* just beyond the cemetery, then *Hollywood Rd* as it curves around **Gonzales Bay**, better known as **Foul Bay** for the leavings of its seabirds. The fine sandy beach is busy on sunny summer days.

OAK BAY

Take *King George Terrace* to the right, following green Scenic Drive signs. The **King George Lookout**, part of **Trafalgar Park**, has Victoria's best sea level view across the strait. Port Angeles, WA is dead ahead, 37 km south. The view is even better from the **Dominion Meteorological Observatory** (see p.313), in a small park atop Gonzales Hill, accessible via *Denison Rd*, just beyond Trafalgar Park.

King George Terrace ends at *Beach Dr.* Go right (east) on *Beach Dr.* along the shores of McNeil Bay to the **Municipality of Oak Bay**. Tudor and other traditional English motifs are so popular that the municipal limit is half seriously called the Tweed Curtain. *Beach Dr.* swings north through the **Victoria Golf Club**, a popular place for a stroll. Visitors occasionally meet Doris Gravlin, the resident ghost, usually wearing a long white dress. Gravlin's body was found in a sand trap in the 1930s. Her husband was suspected of murder, but he drowned before the investigation was completed.

Just north of the golf course is the **Oak Bay Beach Hotel**, *1175 Beach Rd; tel: (250) 598-4556; fax: (250) 598-6180*, and, directly opposite, the **Oak Bay Native Plant Park**. A few hundred metres north are **Haynes Park** and the **Oak Bay Marina**; *tel: (250) 568-3369*. The **Oak Bay Rose Garden** and more than 500 plants from the private estate that once occupied the area fill the south-east corner of **Windsor Park**, west on *Currie Rd* opposite the breakwater.

Continue north past **Willows Park** and through the massive stone gates of **Uplands**. The posh 1912 housing estate was designed by the Olmsted brothers, who created New York's

Central Park. **Uplands Park** was part of the original plan. The 75-acre park is the largest tract of undeveloped Garry Oak habitat in Victoria. Known as Oregon white oak in the US, immense groves of Garry oaks once flourished in the drier meadows of Victoria. Many of the graceful trees became furniture, others were cut down to make way for homes.

The entire park is a natural area except for two boat ramps and minimal development on shore. **Cattle Point** earned its name in the last century when cattle were driven from a nearby abattoir. Continue 5 km north to **Loon Bay**, the **Royal Victoria Yacht Club** and another massive stone gate marking the northern boundary of Uplands. *Beach Dr.* becomes *Cadboro Bay Rd* at the Municipality of Saanich.

SAANICH

Continue past *Sinclair Rd* and a small shopping mall to curve right onto *Maynard Rd*, then left onto *Telegraph Rd* and a four-way stop at *Arbutus Rd*. Turn left (north) onto *Arbutus*, following the Scenic Route signs through increasingly rural countryside. Continue 2 km north to *Finnerty Rd* and bear right, remaining on Arbutus to the T-junction with *Gordon Head Rd*, 1 km north, and turn right. Continue 1 km around the left onto *Ferndale Rd* and a four-way stop. The entrance to **Mt Douglas Park** picnic grounds and beachfront play area are to the right. *Ash Rd* continues straight and *Cedar Hill Rd* climbs the slopes of **Mt Douglas** to the left.

Take *Cedar Hill Rd* 1 km to the end of the forested section on the right. Turn right onto *Churchill Dr.*, a steep 1-km road through dense forest up Mt Douglas, 229 m. Short trails lead up to the summit from the car park just below. Views across the Saanich Peninsula can be stunning on clear days.

Return to *Cedar Hill Rd* and the four-way stop. Turn left (north) onto *Ash Rd* and left (west) again onto *Royal Oak Dr.*, which runs through new housing estates past the **Broadmead Village** shopping mall. Turn right (north) onto BC 17, following signs for Sidney and Swartz Bay ferries.

Follow BC 17 for 7 km, passing Beaver Lake, Elk Lake and *Sayward Rd* to *Keating Cross Rd*. The countryside becomes increasingly agricultural, thanks to greenbelt policies. Go left onto *Keating Cross Rd*, often abbreviated on street maps as '*X Rd*', and climb 4 km through the low hills forming the spine of the peninsula. *Keating Cross* becomes *Benvenuto Ave* at West Saanich Rd, BC 17A.

On the left (south) is **Victoria Butterfly Gardens**, *Box 190, Brentwood Bay, BC V8M 1RC; tel: (250) 652-3822; fax: (250) 652-4683*, open daily 0900–dusk, a tropical garden filled with butterflies. *Benvenuto* continues 2 km to **Butchart Gardens**. The steady stream of coaches departing for Victoria can overwhelm the narrow road. Return to *W. Saanich Rd* and turn right (south). The country road winds through 6 km of scenic hills, farms and townships to **Observatory Hill** and the free **Dominion Astrophysical Observatory**, *5071 W. Saanich Rd; tel: (250) 363-0012*, open all year Mon–Fri 0915–1630, May–Aug 0900–2300 Sat, 0900–2000 Sun and holidays.

The access road climbs around the hill to a car park at the base of the observatory dome. The 1.82 m reflecting telescope inside was the world's largest when it opened in 1918, only to be eclipsed by the Mt Palomar (California) Observatory a few weeks later. The original telescope, is still in active use.

Return to BC 17A and turn left (south) for 3 km to *Royal Oak Dr*. Turn left (east), following signs for BC 17 and Victoria. Just after the first traffic signal *(Elk Lake Rd)*, turn right (south) onto BC 17. At the end of the dual carriageway, 4 km south, make a sharp left turn onto *Douglas St* at the **Town and Country Centre**.

Turn right 1 km later onto *Cloverdale Rd*, following signs and lane markings for 'Victoria by way of Douglas St'. At the second traffic signal, turn left onto *Douglas* to pass **The Mayfair**, one of the largest shopping malls on Vancouver Island, and a strip of budget–moderate motels. The left lane is often blocked by vehicles waiting to turn left.

The Bay, *1701 Douglas; tel: (250) 385-1311*, the modern department store successor to the Hudson's Bay Company, occupies the south-east corner *Douglas and Herald Sts*. The pink and grey brick **Victoria City Hall** is on the west side of Douglas at *Pandora St*.

ROCKLAND

Continue 5 blocks to *Broughton St* and turn right (west) at the red brick **St Peter's Presbyterian Church**, right again at *Broad St* and again onto *Fort St*, one-way eastbound. Follow *Fort St* 2 km past *Antique Row* to *Moss St*. Turn right (south), following green signs for the **Art Gallery of Greater Victoria**. Upon leaving the Gallery, turn right onto *Will Spencer Pl*, left onto *Moss* and right onto *Fort St*. Remain in the right lane and take the next right turn into *Joan Crescent*. Continue to **Craigdarroch Castle**. The surrounding homes stand on what was once Craigdarroch grounds; residents remain protective of their parking privileges. Use the castle car park.

Exit onto *Joan Crescent* and turn right. Continue to *Rockland Ave*, turn right and then immediately left into **Government House Gardens**. Leave Government House to the left (west) on *Rockland*. Homes are palatial to merely mansion-sized, mostly hidden behind hedges and trees. Continue across *Moss St, Cook* and *Vancouver Sts*, where *Rockland* becomes *Courtney St*, to *Quadra St* and **Christ Church Anglican Cathedral**, *912 Vancouver St; tel: (250) 383-2714*, open daily, built in 13th-century Gothic style. Turn left (south) onto *Quadra*, which becomes *Arbutus Way* in Beacon Hill Park. Veer left onto *Bridge Way*, then right onto *Circular Dr.*, to follow *Park Way* to the top of Beacon Hill for pleasant views across the city and Juan de Fuca Strait. Return to *Circular Dr.* and follow the circle left to *Douglas St*, then go left (south) onto *Douglas*. Go right (west) onto *Niagara St* 2 blocks to *Government St* and turn right (north). **Emily Carr House** is ahead on the right (east).

CITY CENTRE

Continue north past the **James Bay Inn** toward *Belleville St*, with the **Parliament Buildings** on the left and the **Royal BC Museum** on the right. Across Belleville, the **Inner Harbour** is on the left and **The Empress Hotel** on the right. Move to the right lane following *Government St* north, passing the **Infocentre** on the left.

Traffic is likely to be slow on *Government St*,

313

one way northbound, with tourists wandering across the street. Continue past *Fort St* with **Eaton Centre** on the right and **Munro's Books** on the left. At *View St*, **Bastion Square** and the **Maritime Museum** are to the left. Turn left (west) onto *Yates St*, where *Government St* becomes two-way again. Turn right (north) onto *Wharf St* one block later, and move into the left or middle lane. Turn left (west) and cross the sky-blue Johnson St Bridge over Victoria Harbour. **Market Square** is to the north-east at the corner of *Johnson and Wharf Sts*.

ESQUIMALT

Johnson St becomes *Esquimalt Rd* on the west side of the bridge. **Songhees Park**, to the south, and the **Ocean Pointe Resort**, were a dreary industrial area until the 1980s. The park was named after the Songhees First Nations band which was evicted from Fort Victoria and moved across the harbour.

Esquimalt Rd continues 4 km to *Admirals Rd*. Turn right (north) onto *Admirals*, following signs for BC 1A toward Sooke and Nanaimo. *Esquimalt* continues to **HMC Naval Dock**, which does not welcome unannounced visitors. Follow *Admirals Rd* north through the base. At the railway tracks, turn left (west) into **HMCS Nanden**, *tel: (250) 363-4395*, open 0800–1600 Mon–Fri for 30-min self-guided walking tours. The tour visits the **Esquimalt Graving Dock**, the largest civilian dry-dock on the west coast of North America.

Turn left (north) back onto *Admirals Rd*, originally a horse trail leading from the Admiral's residence at Esquimalt to **Craigflower House**, 3 km north at the intersection with BC 1A, the *Island Highway*. To visit **Craigflower**, continue through the intersection and take the first left turn. To continue on the circuit, turn left (west) onto BC 1A.

Fort Victoria RV Park is on the right, 1 km west, notable for the replica HBC bastion. Continue west into the **City of Colewood**, a strip of auto dealers, fast food outlets and small businesses. Turn left onto *Ocean Blvd* at the first traffic signal beyond the **Juan de Fuca Recreation Centre** (on the south side), following signs for *Fort Rodd Hill* and **Fisgard**

Lighthouse. Continue straight for 2 km to visit the twin historic sites, or take the first right for the route to **Port Renfrew**.

Return to BC 1A and turn right (east) towards Victoria. At the intersection with *Admirals Rd*, continue straight onto *Craigflower Rd* past the **Gorge Vale Golf Course**, on the right (south). Craigflower becomes *Skinner St* at **Banfield Park**, on the left. Turn right 2 blocks later onto *Catherine St*, then left onto *Langford St*, following signs for the Point Ellice Bridge. **Point Ellice House** is to the left immediately after the bridge.

THE WATERFRONT

Cross the bridge onto *Bay St* and turn right (south) onto *Government St* at the second set of traffic signals. The first drive on the right is **Vancouver Island Brewery**, *2330 Government St; tel: (250) 953-9000, ext 4722*, open for tours Mon–Fri and Sat in summer. VIB's Piper's Pale Ale is an island favourite.

Continue south on *Government St*. The ornamental gate over *Fisgard St* marks the entrance to **Chinatown**, with bilingual street signs in English and Chinese. Remain in the right-hand lane and turn right (west) onto *Yates St*, where *Government St* becomes one way northbound. Move into the left-hand lane and turn left onto *Wharf St*, passing **Bastion Square** and **Wharfside** along the **Inner Harbour**. Turn right down to car parks along the Inner Harbour. *Wharf St* curves east to meet *Government St* and the **Tourist Infocentre** on the right. Turn right onto *Government St*, often crowded with pedicabs, taxis and tour coaches picking up passengers at the harbour. Go right onto *Belleville* at the first traffic signal. **Parliament Buildings** are on the left, **Undersea Gardens** and **Royal London War Museum** on the right, with the ferry docks just beyond.

Follow the main road left onto *Pendra St*, then right onto *Cross St*, left onto *Montreal St*, right onto *Kingston St*, left onto *Lawrence St* and then immediately right into **Fisherman's Wharf Park** for a pleasant view across the harbour. Leave the park on *Dallas Rd*, which turns south toward the **Ogden Point Docks** and ferries to Seattle. Continue past the docks to end of the circuit at *Douglas St*.

VICTORIA–PORT RENFREW

BC 14, *Sooke Rd*, is more commonly called the *West Coast Rd*. By any name, it runs 95 kms along the southern coast of Vancouver Island to the town of Sooke, then past a succession of ever-wilder beaches to Port Renfrew and the start of the West Coast Trail to Bamfield. Views south across the Strait of Juan de Fuca are mouthdropping in clear weather and thunderous during winter storms. Views across recent clear-cuts closer to the road are equally stunning, if for different reasons. Traffic can be slow at weekends or holidays. Allow at least a full day for the return trip. Better still, overnight in Sooke and Port Renfrew.

> ROUTE: 95 KM

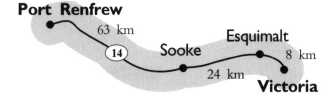

315

ROUTE

From the Empress Hotel, drive north on *Government St* to *Humboldt St*. Turn left, then right on *Wharf St* and left again over the *Johnston St Bridge* onto *Esquimalt Rd*. Continue 4 kms to *Admirals Rd*. Turn right onto *Admirals Rd* at the Tudor House Pub, pass the CFB Nanden Museum and go another 2 kms to the Island Highway at Craigflower House. Turn left onto the Island Highway, passing the Six Mile Pub and the town of **Colwood**. Just beyond the Juan de Fuca Recreation Centre (on the left), go left at the traffic signal onto *Ocean Blvd*, following signs for *Fort Rodd Hill*.

Continue straight 2 kms to Esquimalt Lagoon. At the west end of the lagoon, turn right onto *Lagoon Rd*. At the top of the hill, turn left onto *Metchosin Rd*. Pass Albert Head Lagoon Park and Witty's Lagoon Regional Park, 3 kms to **My-Chosen Café** and veer right onto *William Head Rd*. Turn right up the narrow avenue of *Lombard Poplars*, 2 kms ahead, just past Devonian Park. Turn left onto *Rocky Point Rd*, then right after 3 kms onto *Matheson Lake Park Rd* (Rocky Point continues straight to a military ammunition depot, visitors emphatically unwelcome).

Continue past East Sooke Regional Park 6 kms to *Gillespie Rd*. Turn right to save time, or continue another 9 kms to the end of the road and return to *Gillespie*. Follow *Gillespie Rd* north to BC 14 and turn west (left).

Pass *Sooke River Rd* and the Sooke Potholes, the Sooke River Hotel, the Sooke Regional Museum and **Infocentre** and continue into **Sooke**.

Take BC 14 west from Sooke past the Shearingham Light and Shirley, Point No Point and a string of undeveloped beaches and beach parks, the lumber town of Jordan, and another 42 kms into **Port Renfrew**.

Backtrack to Victoria from Port Renfrew, or in good weather, follow unpaved logging roads to Lake Cowichan and Douglas, then south along the Island Highway to Victoria.

VICTORIA TO SOOKE

Esquimalt Lagoon offers a good view east toward the Fisgard Lighthouse. The lagoon attracts large flocks of waterfowl. To seaward is *Royal Roads,* a protected anchorage first used by the Spanish in 1790.

Albert Head Lagoon Park, just past the gravel pit, is a wildlife sanctuary and cobble beach with good views back to Victoria and across the Juan de Fuca Strait to the Olympic Peninsula. The lagoon has a large wildlife population, including swans.

Witty's Lagoon Regional Park, *Capital Regional District Parks, 490 Atkins Ave, Victoria, BC V9B 2Z8; tel: (250) 478-3344; fax: (250) 478-5416*, 3 kms beyond Albert Head, is a birders paradise with luxuriant stands of Douglas-fir, sword fern, creeks running to Sitting Lady Falls, sandy beach and rocky beach. Look for seals and great blue herons.

Metchosin Schoolhouse, *Happy Valley Rd*, was BC's first school after Confederation. A local market is held across the street behind the Volunteer Fire Department on Sundays, with takeaway breads, sausages and sweets from local producers. **My-Chosen Café**, *4492 Happy Valley Rd; tel: (520) 474-2333*, cheap–budget, is a local favourite.

Devonian Regional Park, *1 km east*, is a nature sanctuary with a 1-km trail past Sherwood Pond (excellent birding) to Perry Bay and good marine mammal viewing. Low tide exposes a 5-km trail east to Witty's Lagoon. The Lombard Poplar avenue just beyond was planted by Hans Helgesen, a Nordic traveller who settled the area in 1865.

East Sooke Regional Park, *490 Atkins Ave, Victoria, BC V9B 2Z8; tel: (250) 478-3344*, covers more than 1400 hectares along the Strait of Juan de Fuca. Untouched foreshore fringed with twisted arbutus and stunted shore pine gives way to stately Sitka spruce, red cedar, hemlock and Douglas-fir. Bald eagles wait at the edge of the forest as river otters and mink scurry through tangled driftwood and cormorants dive offshore. Sea lions are common Sept–May. A complex trail system runs from easy forest jaunts to an all-day 10-km trek along the entire shoreline, but can be confusing without a map. Dozens of small beaches have offshore islands and spits, creating endless picnic spots.

Inland, **Galloping Goose Trail** follows an abandoned railroad line from Colwood to Sooke and the abandoned mining settlement of Leechtown. The park is 47 kms long and just 30 m wide.

Sooke Potholes Provincial Park, *5 kms north on Sooke River Rd*, a series of deep swimming holes in the Sooke River, is familiar to generations of local residents. The potholes are extremely popular in summer.

SOOKE

Tourist Information: Sooke Region Museum, *2070 Phillips Rd, Sooke, BC V0S 1N0; tel: (250) 642-6351*, open 0900–1800 daily in summer, Tues–Sun autumn–spring.

Get directions for the many undeveloped (and often unmarked) beaches to the west, including Gordons, Sandcut, Mystic and Sombrio. Beachcombing is best directly after storms.

ACCOMMODATION AND FOOD

Choose from three dozen bed and breakfasts and the **Sooke Harbour House**, *1528 Whiffen Spit Rd, Sooke, BC V0S 1N0; tel: (250) 642-342; fax: (250) 642-6988*. The fine expensive hotel is better known for its very pricey restaurant that lures gourmands from around the world: BC cuisine only, caught fresh from the waters just offshore, grown by local farmers or plucked from the restaurant's own gardens.

Mom's Cafe, *2036 Shields Rd; tel: (250) 642-3314*, budget, is a busy local eatery.

316

SIGHTSEEING

Sooke began as a fishing and forestry town, the site of Vancouver Island's first successful steam-powered saw mill and one of the last of BC's commercial fish traps. Both stories are recounted in detail at the **Sooke Region Museum and Art Gallery**, *2070 Phillips Rd, Sooke, BC V0S 1N0; tel: (250) 642-6351*, open 0900–1800 daily in summer, Tues–Sun autumn–spring.

Moss Cottage, built in 1870, is Sooke's oldest structure, built of lumber from the Muir Mill, opened in 1855 with a boiler salvaged from a shipwreck. In summer, local actors invite visitors into the cottage, furnished as an 1870s working class home. The cottage is closed the rest of the year. The museum collection covers local First Nations as well as early settlement and the 1864 gold rush that turned 40 kms of riverbank into gold mines and earned just $100,000.

Speculation continued with the Sooke Harbour Hotel, built in 1912 in anticipation of a land boom that never materialised. The hotel burned in 1934 but the riding stables were converted to an ever-popular roadside pub. City fish traps, immense nets and pilings sunk nearly 50 m deep, were built every summer to catch salmon returning to spawn and dismantled before winter storms swept up the Strait of Juan de Fuca. The traps were dismantled for the last time in 1954. Sooke remains a centre for sport salmon fishing.

Sooke Harbour is protected from the Strait by Whiffen Spit, a narrow gravel strip at the foot of *Whiffen Spit Rd,* a few metres from the Sooke Harbour House. Whiffen Spit was the site of the Muir Mill. Sooke's first mill was opened in 1849 by Capt Walter Colquhoun Grant, a former military officer. Grant left the island after a few years but is still reviled for planting the first seeds of the brilliant yellow Scotch Broom that has become a prolific environmental scourge as far south as California.

Sooke Harbour stretches 5 kms east from the Spit, then opens onto the Sooke Basin, an estuary twice the size of the harbour and a favourite with paddlers. Commercial fishermen frequently sell fresh fish from their boats at Government Wharf. **Shearingham Point Light**, *17 kms west of Sooke, 1 km south on Shearingham Point Rd,* a scenic red and white lighthouse, has been guiding ships along the coast since 1912. RVs should not take the dirt road due to limited turnaround space at the lighthouse.

French Beach Provincial Park, *2 kms west of Shearingham Point Rd; tel: (250) 387-4363*, is a good spot to watch the grey whale migration early–mid April (northbound) and mid–late Dec (southbound). Up to 20,000 whales pass the park yearly on a 16,000-km migration to Baja California. A few greys remain in the area all year. No one is sure why, but whales of all species spyhop, or thrust themselves vertically from the water and look around, more than usual off French Beach. Other visitors include orcas, minke whales, Stellar sea lions, California sea lions, dolphins and seals. An easy paved path leads to the beach.

Point No Point Resort, *3 kms west, 1505 West Coast Rd, RR 2, Sooke, BC V0S 1N0; tel: (250) 646-2020*, is a traditional stopping point on the way to Port Renfrew and a popular moderate seaside inn. The budget afternoon tea is a local classic worth twice the price. The point is named for confused cartographers in the last century who saw the prominent headland from one direction but lost it from the other side.

Jordan River, *7 kms west of Point No Point*, is a tiny logging town with some of the best surfing on the southern coast but no lodging. Western Forest Products Ltd, which has a large information sign on the beach, holds the local logging license. Many of the most devastating clear-cuts were made over vocal local protests.

China Beach Provincial Park, *4 kms west*, has a waterfall and sandy beach. The **Juan de Fuca Marine Trail** leads 47 kms west to Botanical Beach at Port Renfrew. The shoreline wilderness trail takes 3–4 days, with sections cut off at high tide. Access points are China Beach, Sombrio Beach, Parkinson Beach and Botanical Beach.

Mystic Beach, *2 kms west*, is a 20-min walk down a steep trail from the parking area. Best views are coming back up the trail, when drifting mists help obscure the clear-cut scars.

317

Sombrio Beach, *17 kms west*, once had the last old-growth forest within a reasonable drive of Victoria. The hillsides were logged into a wasteland despite loud protests. Resulting erosion has made the rough access road dangerous for passenger vehicles in wet weather and impassable for RVs anytime. The 10-min walk down to the beach may be muddy, but the vista is worth the effort, from a picturesque creek across a shore battered by surf to sea caves at the other end. Continue 18 kms to Port Renfrew.

PORT RENFREW

Tourist Information: Sooke Travel Infocentre (see p. 316) or the **West Coast Trail Information Centre**, *16 kms west of Sombrio Beach*, open 0900–1700 daily.

ACCOMMODATION

Most Port Renfrew lodging caters to backpackers starting or ending the tough trek along the West Coast Trail. The moderate **Arbutus Beach Lodge**, *5 Queesto Dr., Port Renfrew, BC, V0S 1K0; tel (520) 647-5458*, is notably better than its competitors and has a stunning view over Port San Juan and the San Juan River.

EATING AND DRINKING

The **Arbutus Beach Lodge**, open for lunch and dinner in summer, weekends the rest of the year, budget–moderate, is the best restaurant in town. **The Lighthouse Pub**; *tel: (520) 647-5543*, budget–moderate, is a good alternative.

SIGHTSEEING

Port Renfrew is textbook West Coast: wet weather, lush forests, rich wildlife and outdoor recreation on all sides. The entire area is used heavily by hikers, paddlers, anglers, beachcombers and hunters, depending on the season. May–Sept is the busiest season with thousands of West Coast Trail walkers pouring through town, but expect at least a few chance companions in any season.

Botanical Beach Provincial Park, *4 kms south on a dirt road from the end of BC 4*, at the entrance to Juan de Fuca Strait, is one of the island's most intriguing beaches. Deep, clear tidepools are teeming with sea life, from the waving tentacles of green anemones to the sharp spines of red and green sea urchins, purple sea stars and innumerable fish. Pounding surf has carved sheer cliffs into coves, creating natural amphitheatres surrounded by dense forest. The same forces have eroded the headlands between the cliffs into twisting, swirling sculptures of sandstone capped with Sitka spruce and shore pine.

It's best not to visit Botanical Beach without a Tofino tide chart in hand. At high tide, both beach and tidepools disappear beneath the rough waters. The rising tide sweeps in much more quickly than most visitors expect, with occasional rogue waves washing far up what had been dry rock. The best–and safest–time to visit is near the end of a falling tide or at slack water. The Juan de Fuca Trail runs 47 kms east to China Beach, a 3–4-day walk.

Red Creek Fir, *12 kms from Port Renfrew*, was for years the largest Douglas-fir in Canada, 73 m tall and 4 m in diameter. Foresters estimate the tree to have been closer to 90 m tall before the top broke off in a windstorm sometime during the past 900 years. The tall tree was left when loggers clear cut the area in 1987. Ask locally for directions and, more importantly, road conditions. The unpaved road is usually passable by passenger vehicles in good weather but can be extremely rough. It is not suitable for RVs.

A taller Douglas-fir was found in the upper Coquitlam watershed in the mid-1990s but not measured for the record book until 1996. The new tallest tree is 94 m tall, 2.5 m in diameter.

Unpaved **logging roads** lead from Port Renfrew inland to BC 117 at Mesachie Lake and Lake Cowichan, near the head of the Cowichan Valley, then 32 kms east to Duncan and the Island Highway (see p. 319). The logging roads are not recommended for RVs, but the mainlines, the major arteries, are usually passable by passenger vehicles with caution. Check locally before setting out. Unannounced road closures are common due to active logging and driving conditions can change dramatically overnight. Some car and RV hire prohibit driving off paved highways.

VICTORIA–NANAIMO

Nanaimo

20 km — Ladysmith — **Scenic Route**

20 km — Chemainus

35 km — 20 km — Crofton

10 km

Genoa Bay

Duncan — Maple Bay

15 km

35 km — Cowichan Bay

Direct Route — 24 km

Malahat Hills

25 km

Victoria

The 115-km drive to Nanaimo takes less than 90 mins outside commuting hours, or several days with stops in the small towns that dot the Cowichan Valley north of the Malahat Hills. The Island Highway, Canada 1 or the TransCanada Highway, is never far away if time presses, but the more scenic route is a taste of the rural, more relaxed side of Vancouver Island that Victoria has ignored almost from its beginnings as a frontier outpost.

DIRECT ROUTE: 115 KM

319

ROUTES

DIRECT ROUTE

The direct route leaves the Empress Hotel going north along *Government St* 4 blocks to *Fort St*. Turn east (right) onto *Fort* and continue two blocks to *Douglas St*, also Canada 1, the **TransCanada Hwy**. Turn north (left) onto *Douglas* and follow Canada 1 signs through Greater Victoria, then west along the base of the Saanitch Peninsula past Portage Inlet and through Thetis Lake Park. The highway swings north at Goldstream Provincial Park, 19 kms from the Empress, and becomes *Malahat Dr.* through the **Malahat Hills**. Lay-bys near the 352-m summit offer stunning views across the Saanitch Inlet and Peninsula to the mainland and the Cascade Range, but are accessible only from northbound lanes. *Malahat Dr.* becomes the **Island Highway**, running north

through the agricultural lands of the Cowichan Valley to **Duncan**, **Ladysmith** and into **Nanaimo**.

SCENIC ROUTE

The scenic route follows the direct route 50 kms to *Cowichan Bay Rd* at a rest area 18 kms north of the Malahat summit. Take *Cowichan Bay Rd* east (right) through 6 kms of rolling farmland dotted with small lakes to the tiny coastside town of **Cowichan Bay**. Continue north on *Cowichan Bay Rd* along the edge of Cowichan Bay. *Cowichan Bay Rd* becomes *Tzouhalem Rd* at a T-junction 1 km north of a historical marker on the west (left) side of the road, commemorating the landing of the first English settlers in 1862. Another marker lauds poet Robert W Service, who worked and published locally in the early 1900s. *Tzouhalem Rd* continues 5 kms north, then west to **Maple Bay**. Follow *Maple Bay Rd* north-east (right) 6 km through exclusive housing to *Genoa Bay Rd* and turn east (right). *Genoa Bay Rd* follows the shore of Maple Bay south, climbs through an impressive range of granite hills to emerge at tiny **Genoa Bay**.

Return 8 km to *Maple Bay Rd*. Turn north (right) 1 km to Maple Bay, with Saltspring Island just offshore. Take *Herd Rd* north and west 3 km to *Osborne Bay Rd* and turn north (right). Drive 5 km to *Chaplain St* and turn east (right) into **Crofton** and Osborne Bay. Return up *Chaplain St* to *Crofton Rd* and turn north (right) to *Chemainus Rd*, 2 km beyond the Fletcher Challenge pulp and paper mill. Follow *Chemainus Rd* across a wooden bridge and continue north 1 km to **Chemainus**. *Chemainus Rd* continues another 10 km to rejoin the Island Hwy. Turn north (right) and continue 13 kms to *Cedar Point Rd*. Turn east (right) through 3 kms of pastoral farm country to *Yellowpoint Rd*. Turn east (right) at the petrol station for 6 kms of rolling hills and forest past the Yellowpoint Lodge turnoff. Continue north 11 kms past Roberts Memorial Provincial Park and an ocean swimming beach, back onto *Cedar Point Rd*. At *MacMillan Rd,* turn right to visit the Harmac pulp mill or continue straight another 3 kms to the Island Hwy. Nanaimo begins just across the Nanaimo River.

MALAHAT HILLS

Malahat Mountain and its foothills were a formidable barrier to land travel north from Victoria until well into this century. Cliffs plunge directly into Finlayson Arm, forcing travellers to cross the inlet by ferry to Mill Bay or Cowichan Bay, then overland into the rich agricultural heart of the Cowichan Valley. The colonial government built a crude road over the Malahat in 1861, but the trail was more suited to cattle than wagons. Public pressure pushed another try in 1877, but when the road was finally finished in 1884, it was still too steep for heavy traffic. Farmers flocked to the E&N Railway to move their produce to market in Victoria. It took a new century, new public pressure and a new survey to open the present 16-km route in 1911.

A lay-by at the summit (352 m) has a totem pole and an unobstructed view across the lower inlet to the Saanitch Peninsula. A second

lay-by, 2 km north, has a spectacular view across the upper inlet, the peninsula, the Gulf Islands and the snow-capped peak of Mt. Baker shimmering on the horizon in Washington.

DUNCAN

Tourist Information: Duncan–Cowichan Chamber of Commerce, *381 TransCanada Hwy (at Coronation Way), Duncan, BC V9L 3R5; tel: (520) 746-4636; fax: (520) 746-8222,* open Mon–Fri 0900–1700, Sat 1000–1600, Sun 1100–1500, is the only tourist office in the Cowichan open year round.

BW is the only chain, but there are a number of independent motels and Bed and Breakfasts. **Cowichan Connection**, *1505 Khenipsen Rd, Duncan, BC V9L 4T6; tel: (250) 748-5192,* handles Cowichan area bookings.

SIGHTSEEING

Duncan is the commercial and tourist centre of the Cowichan Valley, but there's more than the strip mall that girdles the highway. About three dozen totem poles, all carved locally, dot city streets with one of Canada's greatest public concentrations of First Nations art. The **Native Heritage Centre**, *200 Cowichan Way, Duncan, BC V9L 4T8; tel: (520) 746-8119; fax: (520) 746-4143,* west (left) of Canada 1 just north of the Cowichan River at the south end of town, has a large collection of First Nation arts, crafts and books, a budget restaurant serving First Nation specialities, an excellent multimedia presentation on local groups and a popular lunchtime feast in summer. European immigrant history is covered at the **Cowichan Valley Museum**, *120 Canada Ave, Duncan, BC V9L 3Y2; tel: (520) 746-6612,* Duncan's old train station. Duncan began when 2000 local farmers and merchants blocked a train carrying E&N Railway builder Robert Dunsmuir because he hadn't built a station in the area. When the Duncan station opened in 1887, Cowichan Bay, which had been the commercial and shipping centre of the Cowichan Valley, went into decline. The museum has domestic and commercial tools and equipment in period room settings as well as extensive photographic holdings.

Somenos Marsh, *Box 711, Duncan, BC*

320

V9L 3Y1; tel: (520) 746-8383, 2 kms north of town on the east (right) side of the highway, is 48 hectares of waterfowl nesting and wintering habitat. Wildlife viewing is good from the parking area, even better from a short trail that begins 50m north. The **British Columbia Forest Museum**, RR #4, Duncan, BC V9L 3W8; tel: (520) 746-1251; fax (520) 746-1487, 1 km north of the marsh on the east side of the hwy, open Apr–Oct; is the forestry industry's tribute to itself. Capt. George Vancouver gets credit as BC's first logger for cutting Douglas-fir to repair spars and masts in 1778. A working sawmill and other equipment provide lumber for the museum. A narrow-gauge steam train winds through a logging camp, homestead farm and forest May–Sept; environmental issues are ignored all year. The **Freshwater Eco-Centre**, 1080 Whamcliffe Rd, Duncan, BC V9L 2K7; tel: (520) 746-6722, explores and explains the freshwater ecosystem of the Cowichan River, including a trout hatchery and walking trails along the Cowichan River dike.

COWICHAN BAY

The Cowichan River valley was heavily settled when the Europeans arrived. In the 1850s, James Douglas sent several military expeditions to Cowichan Bay from Victoria to subdue the 'fierce, treacherous and turbulent Cowichans' who took exception to HBC plans for the warm, lush valley. What the military began, smallpox and other imported plagues soon finished. The shallow bay became the centre for fishing, timber and farming, with regular steamship connections to Victoria. When the E&N Railway lured commerce to Duncan, Cowichan Bay turned to sport fishing and other gentlemanly leisure pursuits. The local lawn tennis tournament is the second oldest in the world after Wimbledon, England. All that remains of the town today is a scenic strip of buildings built on stilts over the bay shallows, a busy timber operation just north and the lawn tennis club.

The **Wooden Boat Society and Cowichan Maritime Centre**, Box 787, Duncan, BC V9L 3Y1; tel: (520) 746-4955, on the former Chevron fuel pier in the centre of town, has a fine local history museum with vintage photographs. **The Marine Ecology Station**,

RR1, Cowichan Bay, BC V0R 1N0; tel: (520) 748-4522; fax: (520) 748-4410, 100 m north on Pier 66, offers marine displays, touch tanks and microscopes to explain the cold water marine environment. Locals like the budget–moderate **Bluenose Steak & Seafood House**, 1765 Cowichan Bay Rd, Cowichan Bay, BC V0R 1N0; tel: (520) 748-2841.

To visit Duncan, follow Tzouhalem Rd west beyond the junction with Maple Bay Rd. Tzouhalem becomes Trunk Rd and intersects the Island Highway. The Chamber of Commerce is one block north at Coronation, on the west (left) side of the highway. To visit Maple Bay, follow Maple Bay Rd east to the ocean.

MAPLE BAY

Maple Bay Rd runs through a succession of expensive housing estates that block most access to Quamishan Lake and habitat for local and migratory birds. Best view of the lake is from **Quamishan Inn**, 1478 Maple Bay Rd, Duncan, BC V9L 4T6; tel: (520) 746-7028, a bed and breakfast mansion cum dinner restaurant.

BC Ferries run between Maple Bay and Salt Spring Island. For a view of the island, continue north along the bay beyond the dock. The road becomes Arbutus Way and snakes up the hillside for 2 kms through thick stands of arbutus trees and expensive homes. Saltspring Island seems to hover barely out of reach at the end of the road.

GENOA BAY

Drive the 8 kms from Maple Bay to Genoa Bay sooner rather than later. Much of the area is marked for subdivision and development, which will displace the easy calm along what is barely more than a single track road through groves of spreading shade trees clustered in a succession of tiny valleys rimmed with sheer granite cliffs. Genoa Bay itself is a small marina in an exquisite cove almost completely cut off from the outside world by forbidding cliffs. The **Good Pine Café**, tel: (520) 746-0797, open daily summer and Thur–Mon autumn–spring, lures yachties from up and down the coast.

CROFTON

Tourist Information: Crofton Museum, next to BC Ferries; tel: (520) 246-2456, summer

321

only. Crofton was an instant town, built in 1902 as a smelter site. The smelter closed, but forest industries and BC Ferries to Salt Spring Island kept the town alive. The Museum covers the copper mine, smelter and local history. Just outside the museum is a wooden statue of Adam and Eve by African carver Johann Mhlanga. The **Fletcher Challenge Crofton Pulp & Paper Mill**; *tel: (520) 246-6100* dominates Crofton. Tours are available in summer.

CHEMAINUS

Tourist Information: Chemainus and District Chamber of Commerce, *Box 575, Chemainus, BC V0R 1K0; tel: (520) 246-3944, in the red caboose at Heritage Sq.* in summer, **Arts and Business Council of Chemainus**, *across from the waterwheel; tel: (520) 246-4701*, all year.

The budget **Chemainus Hostel**, *9694 Chemainus Rd; tel: (250) 246-2809*, or ask for *Chemainus Accommodations* from the Chamber of Commerce, listing more than a dozen inns and Bed and Breakfasts.

Chemainus calls itself 'the little town that did' for a successful switch from timber to tourism after the town's major mill and employer closed in 1983. Local activists prevailed on artists to paint downtown murals showcasing regional history, sparking an artistic boom that has become a major business. Three dozen murals now lure tourists by the coachload to Canada's largest permanent outdoor art collection. Mural walking tour maps are sold at the Infocenter, a summer-only mural kiosk at *Willow and Legion Sts* and at the **Chemainus Valley Museum**, *in Waterwheel Park; tel: (502) 246-2445*. The **Chemainus Theatre**; *tel: (520) 246-9820*, has a year-round schedule of live theatre. Advance bookings suggested, but tickets for midday performances may be available shortly before curtain time. A small car and passenger ferry runs to Thetis and Kuper islands.

LADYSMITH

Tourist Information: Ladysmith Chamber of Commerce, *Box 598, Ladysmith, BC V0R 2E0; tel: (520) 245-2212*, infocentre open summer only. Ladysmith should have been a border town. The 49th parallel, the negotiated border

between the US and Canada, passes nearby, but the two countries agreed to leave all of Vancouver Island in what was then British hands – then nearly went to war over a rampaging pig (see p 269). The town was founded by coal baron James Dunsmuir. He named the streets for English generals in the Boer War in a propaganda ploy to curry favour with military clients and intimidate his often rebellious miners. *First Ave* is lined with restored heritage buildings that have been turned into art galleries and boutiques.

NANAIMO

Tourist Information: Nanaimo Tourist and Convention Bureau,(NTCB) *266 Bryden St, Nanaimo, BC V9S 1A8; tel: (520) 754-8474* or *(800) 663-7337*.

BC Ferries, *Departure Bay Ferry Terminal; tel: (520) 753-1261; fax: (604) 381-5452*, have regular sailings between Nanaimo and Vancouver's northern terminal at Horseshoe Bay. Duke Point Terminal, at the south end of Nanaimo Harbour, opens in spring 1997, for high-speed ferries from Tswassen, see p.297

The **Island Highway** is the main road link north and south. A by-pass, the Nanaimo Parkway, has been under construction for several years. When completed later this decade, it will allow through traffic to avoid the 19 traffic signals that now slow travel through the city.

ACCOMMODATION

Chains include *BW, CR, DI* and *TL*. Best value for money is **Harbourview Days Inn**, *809 Island Highway South, Nanaimo, BC V9R 5K1; tel: (520) 754-8171* or *(800) 329-7466*, moderate. Best in the area is the expensive **Yellow Point Lodge**, *RR 3, Ladysmith, BC V0R 2E0; tel: (520) 245-7422*, an immense log lodge and rustic cabins on the ocean off *Yellowpoint Rd*. Bed and Breakfast guides are available from the NTCB.

EATING AND DRINKING

Nanaimo has the best eating and drinking selection on Vancouver Island outside Greater Victoria. Fast-food outlets are concentrated in the malls lining the Island Highway north of Nanaimo. The Old City Quarter, an arc of streets east of the Island Hwy, that was once the upper class commercial district, has a number of trendy shops and eateries. One of the better choices is **Phüong**, *428 Fitzwilliam St; tel: (520) 754-2523*, for moderate Vietnamese dishes. **Javaw City**, *#8-90 Front St; tel: (520) 753-1688*, has budget breakfast and lunch, plus sweets and coffee to die for. **Pagliacci's**, *7 Old Victoria Rd (in the Old Firehall); tel: (520) 754-3443*, has some of the best budget–moderate Italian choices and friendliest service in town.

SIGHTSEEING

Nanaimo's sheltered channel and small bay were a traditional meeting ground for five Coast Salish bands. HBC explorers discovered exposed coal seams along the harbour and paid local Salish workers the equivalent of one shirt per day to work the mines. When disputes erupted over land ownership, the HBC traded 688 blankets for 20 km of coast, imported miners from Prince Rupert and erected a bastion to enforce their version of the bargain. Ten years later, HBC sold out to a London-based competitor for £40,000. The bastion still stands, the only HBC fortification to survive the ravages of time and commerce. The coal mines that made Nanaimo rich covered most of the waterfront, delving deep beneath the harbour and into the foundations of Newcastle Island. Mine owners, including a former indentured labourer named Robert Dunsmuir, got rich, got political power and got the better of their workers. Mine accidents were almost as frequent as the bitter labour actions. Owners regularly brought in strike-breakers from as far away as Mexico and turned strikers out of company-owned homes in the dead of winter. When hard-headed miners persisted in demanding safer working conditions and something more than $1 per tonne of coal, Chinese labourers were hired for a flat $1 per day. Mine owners created decades of racial tensions but kept profits high until oil began to replace coal in most industrial uses. Nanaimo's last major mine closed in 1950; the last one-man colliery shut in 1968.

A quarter century later, the only coal pit in town is a model mine at the **Nanaimo Centennial Museum & Archives**, *100 Cameron Rd, Nanaimo, BC V9R 2X1; tel: (250) 753-*

1821. The museum also has an excellent display of local First Nations artefacts as well as *Main St, circa 1900* and Chinatown, which burned in 1960. A miner's cabin in the park outside is the only public evidence of Nanaimo's mining past. Newcastle Island has become **Newcastle Island Provincial Park**; *tel: (520) 755-2483*, a popular spot for picnicking, camping and exploring caves, quarries, beaches and forests. Access is by private boat or ferry from the Nanaimo Public Market and Maffeo Sutton Park, near the city centre; *tel: (520) 753-8244.*

On the mainland, dingy coal docks have been replaced with a sparkling 4-km Harbourside Walkway from the boat basin north to the Departure Bay Ferry Terminal. **Swyalana Lagoon Park**, once an abandoned industrial area, is now Canada's first artificial tidal lagoon and a popular swimming spot. **The Bastion**, *Bastion and Front Sts; tel: (520) 754-8474*, open daily July–Sept, has become a museum focusing on 1850–1880 with period photographs. A detachment of 1850s naval guardsmen fire a noon cannon each day during the summer.

Three **Heritage Walks** leave from The Bastion exploring the harbour area, coal mining and development spurred by the arrival of the **E&N Railway**, *Selby and Fitzwilliam Sts; tel: (604) 383-4324* or *(800) 561-8630*. The line remains in daily service between Esquimalt and Courtenay with stops in Nanaimo. An even earlier bit of local history is preserved at **Petroglyph Park**, *east side of Island Hwy 3 km south of Nanaimo*. One of about 20 local petroglyph, or rock carving sites in the area, the park features sandstone carvings of humans, birds, wolves, sea monsters and supernatural creatures. Centennial Museum has directions for other petroglyphs on public lands.

The best spots to watch the giant ferries come and go from the Departure Bay ferry terminal are the beach at Departure Bay, just north of the terminal, the northern and western sides of Newcastle Island and the grounds of the Pacific Biological Station on *Hammond Bay Rd*, 2 km around the bay from the ferry terminal. The southern end of the bay is largely occupied by timber mills and booming ponds. **Harmac Pacific**; *tel: (520) 722-4315* offers free tours of its pulp and paper plant May–Aug.

323

NANAIMO–CAMPBELL RIVER

The 160 km between Nanaimo and Campbell River are a gradual transition from gentle farmland to the rougher, resource-based North Island. The coastal plain that makes South Island life and travel easy narrows to the north, squeezing the strip of civilisation along the Island Highway into increasingly smaller pockets. Allow at least one long day for this route; three days are better, with overnights near Parksville/Qualicum Beach and Courtenay.

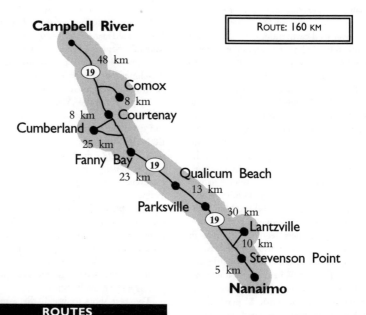

324

ROUTE: 160 KM

Campbell River
48 km
19
Comox
8 km
8 km ● Courtenay
Cumberland ●
25 km
Fanny Bay **19**
23 km
Qualicum Beach
13 km
Parksville ●
19 30 km
Lantzville
10 km
Stevenson Point
5 km
Nanaimo

ROUTES

DIRECT ROUTE

Canada 1 becomes BC 19 at Nanaimo but retains the Island Highway name. This route follows the Island Hwy north along the coast to **Parksville**, **Qualicum Beach**, **Fanny Bay** and **Courtenay**, then turns inland before returning to the coast near Oyster River and continuing to Campbell River.

SCENIC ROUTE

The scenic route follows *Departure Bay Rd* north around the end of Departure Bay, past the Pacific Biological Station to *Stevenson Point Rd* and right onto *Hammond Bay Rd*, past Piper's Lagoon Park and right onto *Dickenson Rd* to **Lantzville**. Continue through Lantzville to BC 19 and turn north (right) 16 kms to the **Parksville** and **District Chamber of Commerce** and the adjoining **Craig Heritage Museum**. Drive another 3 kms into Parksville, past the turnoff for Port Alberni and Tofino (see pp. 339 and 342), and on to **Qualicum Beach**. Pass pleasant beaches to a brant goose viewing area and a succession of small settlements where playing children and grazing deer can slow traffic. The road passes turnoffs for **Horne Lake Caves** and the **Big Qualicum Fish Hatchery**, then goes north to **Bowser**, **Fanny Bay**, the **Denman Island** ferry, **Union Bay**, **Royston** and the **Cumberland** turnoff. **Courtenay** is 4 km north.

Turn east (right) from BC 19 onto *17th Ave* toward **Comox** at the Riverside Mall, just past the Courtenay Travel Infocentre. Go right again onto *Comox Rd*, passing a wildlife viewing area on the Comox River estuary and into Comox. Fishing boats docked at the foot of *Port Agusta St* often sell fresh seafood. Turn right onto *Balmoral Ave* at the four-way stop, then right again onto *Croteau Rd* to the Comox Spit and fine views back across the harbour or out to the Georgia Strait.

Return to *Comox Rd*, turn right to *Lazo Rd* and go left onto **Lazo**, following the blue and white 'scenic drive' signs. Watch out for deer grazing along the verges. The road curves around **Pt Holmes** to the chainlink and barbed wire fence surrounding the Canadian Forces Base, Comox. The base golf course, Glacier Greens, is open to the public. Continue past the Comox Valley Regional Air Terminal to the Main Gate and Museum.

Turn left on *Ryan Rd* directly back to BC 19 or continue straight to the Griffen Pub sign and right onto *Kilmorley Rd*, then 1 km to *Astra Rd*. Turn left onto Astra, passing **Kin Beach** to a T-junction with *Prairie River Rd*. Turn right onto Prairie River and immediately left into **Wilkinson** for 1 km to *Eleanor Rd*.

Turn left for BC 19 (right for BC Ferries to Powell River), then veer right into *Anderton Rd*. Take a sharp left turn after 2 km into *Wavelander Rd* and left again after 1 km onto *Bates Rd*, following signs for BC 19 and Campbell River. Pass the **Seal Bay Nature Park** and continue 3 km to the stop sign at

Coleman Rd. Turn left for the final 4 km back to BC 19. Turn north (right) to Campbell River.

STEVENSON POINT

The blunt point forms the north side of Departure Bay and the ship channel out to the Georgia Strait. Several public beaches offer good view points to watch BC Ferries and other marine traffic.

Piper's Lagoon Park, *on the north side of the point*, looks across the Strait. The quiet lagoon is a local favourite for late afternoon walks.

LANTZVILLE

One of many picturesque seaside communities, Lantzville's biggest attraction is a herd of 400 sea lions that winter near the waterfront. The broad, sandy shores of Nanoose Harbour are good for clam digging.

PARKSVILLE

Tourist Information: Parksville and District Chamber of Commerce, *Box 99, Parksville, BC V9P 2G3; tel: (520) 248-3613; fax: (520) 248-5210, Infocentre on Hwy 19 at the south end of town*, open daily.

ACCOMMODATION

BW and *HI* are the only chains in the adjoining resort towns of Parksville/Qualicum Beach, but there are dozens of motels along BC 19. **Sandcastle Inn**, *374 Island Hwy W., Parksville, BC V9P 1K8; tel: (520) 248-2334 or (800) 335-7263*, is the newest, budget–moderate choice.

The Qualicum Beach Chamber of Commerce, *2711 W. Island Hwy, Qualicum Beach, BC V9K 2C4; tel: (520) 752-9532; fax: (520) 752-2923*, publishes a free list of bed and breakfasts.

EATING AND DRINKING

Most of Hwy 19 is lined with strip malls and fast food outlets. Two of the better alternatives are **India Curry House**, *261 E. Island Hwy, tel: (520) 954-3630*, budget, and the pricey summer dinner theatre at **Best Western Bayside**, *240 Dogwood St; tel: (520) 248-3424*.

Sightseeing

Parksville and Qualicum Beach are a well-established holiday area. Every low tide exposes hundreds of hectares of flat beach filled with large shallow pools in the sand, perfect for young children. Hot sand warms the incoming tide for comfortable swimming. **Rathtrevor Beach Provincial Park**; *tel: (520) 248-3931*, claims BC's warmest ocean water, 21°C in summer, and one of the island's busiest public campsites.

Craig Heritage Park Museum, *Box 1452, Parksville, BC V9P 2H4; tel: (520) 248-6966, at the Tourist Infocentre on BC 19*, displays local artefacts in historic buildings moved to the museum grounds. An annual mid April **Brant Festival**; *tel: (520) 248-4117; fax: (520) 248-3720*, supports the year-round brant goose wildlife viewing area between the Parksville Bypass and the Tourist Infocentre. A free *Guide to Studios and Galleries* introduces the nearly two dozen art galleries and studios in the area.

QUALICUM BEACH

Tourist Information: Qualicum Beach Chamber of Commerce, *2711 W. Island Hwy, Qualicum Beach, BC V9K 2C4; tel: (520) 752-9532; fax: (520) 752-2923.*

Sightseeing

This retirement and tourist community is known for golfing, salmon fishing and beachcombing. Development restrictions have kept the beachfront clear and open to the public. The Chamber of Commerce publishes a free area walking guide, including the village centre, 1 km inland. **The Power House Museum**, *587 Beach Rd, Qualicum Beach, BC V9K 1K7; tel: (520) 752-5533*, open June–Sept, displays local artefacts in the town's original brick power house, across the street from the disused train depot.

The Old School House Gallery & Art Centre, *122 Fern Rd W., Qualicum Beach, BC V9K 1T2; tel: (520) 752-6133; fax: (520) 752-2600*, open Mon–Sat, is a visual arts teaching centre and gallery complex.

Horne Lake Caves Provincial Park, *16 km north on BC 19, then 15 km west on Horne Lake Rd; tel: (520) 248-3931*, has two caves open for self-guided tours year-round and three caves with guided tours in summer. All caves require sturdy shoes and warm clothing for moderate climbing and at least two light sources per person. Torches and hard hats (HIGHLY recommended) are $4 per person.

Big Qualicum River Fish Hatchery, *west at the sign between Home Lake Rd and the Big Qualicum River; tel: (520) 757-8412*, rears and releases millions of salmon and trout each year. The hatchery is open for self-guided tours all year.

DENMAN ISLAND AND HORNBY ISLAND

Tourist Information: Hornby–Denman Tourist Association, *c/o Sea Breeze Lodge, Hornby Island, BC V0R 1Z0; tel: (520) 335-2321.*

These small islands, just off the coast from Buckley Bay, are accessible only by boat but have become hugely popular for camping, hiking, fishing, beachcombing and relaxing. Hornby is more mountainous; constant pounding from the Georgia Strait has carved dramatic sea caves at Tribune Bay and several other sites. Union Bay was once the major port for coal mines at nearby Cumberland.

CUMBERLAND

Take *Royston–Cumberland Rd* 6 km west from Royston, 8 km north of Union Bay. **Tourist Information: Cumberland Chamber of Commerce**, *2755 Dunsmuir Way, Cumberland, BC V0R 1S0; tel: (520) 336-8313.*

Sightseeing

Founded by coal baron Robert Dunsmuir, Cumberland had nearly 10,000 people at its height in the 1910s. British, Italian, Chinese and Japanese miners lived in segregated neighbourhoods, each with its own complement of bars, brothels, gambling houses theatres and shops. Low wages and atrocious safety standards sparked a bitter two-year Island-wide coal strike in 1912. BC Premier WJ Bowser sent 1000 troops to 'keep the peace' by forcing Cumberland miners back to work. In 1918, police killed local pacifist and union organiser Ginger

Goodwin under questionable circumstances, sparking more unrest. In a tacit admission of guilt, the BC government named a nearby section of the Island Highway *'Ginger Goodwin Way'* in 1995.

Cumberland's last mine closed in 1966, but slag heaps and derelict buildings remain. So does the fine **Cumberland Cultural Centre and Museum**, *First St and Dunsmuir Ave; tel: (520) 336-2445*, a splendid museum with restored storefronts and period facades. Its unvarnished look at life in the mines is stunning, as is the collection of photos of the local Japanese community destroyed by World War II internment.

COURTENAY

Tourist Information: Comox Valley Chamber of Commerce, *2040 Cliffe Ave, Courtenay, BC V9N 2L3; tel: (520) 334-3234; fax: (520) 334-4908*, Infocentre *on BC 19 3 km south.*

ACCOMMODATION

There are a number of bed and breakfasts north of Royston as well as motels along BC 19 in Courtenay, including *TL.*

SIGHTSEEING

The Comox Valley is one of the few spots in Canada where it actually *is* possible to ski in the morning and play golf in the afternoon, at least in winter. Courtenay's two ski areas, **Forbidden Plateau**; *Strathcona Provincial Park; tel: (520) 334-4428*, and **Mt Washington Ski Area**, *Box 3069, Courtenay, BC V9N 5N3; tel: (520) 338-1386*, are also popular summer retreats for camping, mountain biking the ski trails, fishing and hiking.

The Courtenay & District Museum, *360 Cliffe Ave, Courtenay, BC V9N 2H9; tel: (520) 334-3611; fax: (520) 334-4277*, open Tues–Sat 1000–1630, is housed in the historic Native Sons' Hall, the largest free-span log building in Canada. Inside is the fossilised skeleton of a 14-m Elasmosaur, the largest marine reptile ever found in Canada west of the Rocky Mountains. Other chronological exhibits cover 5000 years of First Nation history and art, White settlement, logging and printing.

The Bar None Café, *244-4th St, Courtenay, BC V9N 5N3; tel: (520) 334-3112*, one of the valley's best (and only vegetarian) restaurants, is just down Cliffe.

COMOX

Tourist Information: Comox Valley Chamber of Commerce, *2040 Cliffe Ave, Courtenay; BC V9N 2L3; tel: (520) 334-3234; fax: (520) 334-4908*, Infocentre *on BC 19 just south of the Comox turnoff.*

SIGHTSEEING

'Comox' is a First Nations word meaning 'place of abundance' for the rich harvest of berries and game the valley once provided. There are still extensive farmlands, nature preserves and public beaches, including **Seal Bay Regional Nature Park**, *Box 3370, Courtenay, BC V9N 5N5; tel: (520) 334-6000*, 700 hectares of peaceful forest and undeveloped beach.

Filberg Lodge, *61 Filberg at Comox Ave; tel: (520)339-2715*, the former residence of local timber magnate Robert Filberg, and 29 hectares of landscaped grounds are open for tours.

The Comox Air Force Museum, *CFB Comox, Lazo, BC V0R 2K0; tel: (520) 339-8162*, traces the history of Canada's Air Forces. The Chamber of Commerce publishes a free *Comox Valley of the Arts* guide to local artists, studios and galleries.

CAMPBELL RIVER

Tourist Information: Campbell River & District Chamber of Commerce, *Box 400, Campbell River, BC V9W 5B6; tel: (520) 287-4636; fax: (520) 286-6990*, Infocentre, *1235 Shoppers Row at Tyee Plaza*, open daily summer, Mon–Fri 0900–1700, Sat 0900–1600 in winter.

ACCOMMODATION

Motel chains haven't come to Campbell River, but there are a dozen or so motels near BC 19 as well as a wide variety of fishing inns and bed and breakfasts south of town. **The Town Centre Inn**, *1500 Elm St, Campbell River, BC V9W 3A6; tel: (520) 287-8866 or (800) 287-7107; fax: (520) 287-3944*, moderate, is good

---

Quadra Island

The large (276 sq km) island off Campbell River which forms one side of Discovery Passage is scalloped with sheltered harbours and inlets. The ferry trip from Campbell River takes about 15 mins.

Quadra is known for fishing, scuba diving and hiking, but mostly for the **Kwagiulth Museum and Cultural Centre**, *Cape Mudge Village, Box 8, Quathiaski Cove, BC V0P 1N0; tel: (250) 285-3733*. The museum was built to house part of a potlatch collection seized by federal government officials in a 1922 crackdown on First Nation ceremonies. **Potlatch**, a ceremony in which tribal leaders distributed immense quantities of food, trade goods, clothing and household furnishings to their people, was banned in 1884.

The ceremony, usually held in winter, was a central part of First Nation life along the Northwest coast. It was a time to reinforce tradition and authority through performances of sacred rites and to establish political authority. The greater the wealth a leader was able to distribute to members of his own tribe as well as to neighbouring bands, the greater his power.

Christian missionaries and government agents condemned potlatch as part of a 'decrepit' culture. Complained one government agent in 1918, 'During these gatherings, they lose months of time, waste their substance, contract all kinds of diseases and generally unfit themselves for being British subjects in the proper sense of the word'.

The potlatch ban was quietly dropped in the 1950s. Most of the items seized, including masks, headdresses, blankets and other ceremonial regalia, were returned to this museum and a similar institution in Alert Bay (on Malcom Island, off Port McNeil) in 1988. The gift shop has an excellent selection of contemporary Kwagiulth masks, prints, wooden plaques, oil paintings and jewellery.

There are also accessible petroglyphs in a small park across from the museum as well as Wa Wa Kie Beach and Francisco Point.

---

value. Book in advance to avoid being swamped by fishermen swarming north at the first mention of a good catch.

EATING AND DRINKING

Look for fast food along BC 19 and in Tyee Plaza. Elsewhere, seafood is always a good choice. **Panache**, *1090 Shoppers Row; tel: (520) 830-0025*, may be the best, and most expensive, restaurant along the Island Hwy. **Pier Street Café**, *207-871 Island Hwy; tel: (520) 287-2772*, has moderate prices and more basic preparation. **Panagopoulos**, *223 Dogwood; tel: (520) 286-0241*, budget–moderate, has the best Italian food in town.

SIGHTSEEING

Some 60% of visitors come to fish the enormous shoals of salmon and other species moving through the narrow waters of Discovery Passage connecting the Georgia and Johnston Straits. Even non-boaters do well fishing off Discovery Pier, just south of the marina. The pier is also a good vantage point to watch cruise ships and ferries passing between Vancouver/Seattle and Alaska.

Discovery Passage scuba diving is spectacular for the rich underwater life, especially in the clear winter water, but ripping tidal currents make local guides a must. **Island Dive Connection**, *1621 N. Island Hwy, Campbell River, BC V9W 2E6; tel: (520) 830-0818; fax: (520) 830-0832*, are experienced, knowledgeable and friendly.

The Museum at Campbell River, *470 Island Hwy, Campbell River, BC V9W 4Z9; tel: (520) 287-3103*, covers local First Nation history, contemporary and pioneer history. Best outdoor totems are in **Foreshore Park**, *just south of the BC Ferries terminal*, with freshly painted poles as well as a well-weathered eagle overlooking Quadra Island.

CAMPBELL RIVER– PORT HARDY

Drivers in a hurry can make the 245 kilometres north to Port Hardy in three hours if traffic and weather co-operate, but allow at least one full day to absorb the vistas. There's still a frontier feeling beyond Campbell River, albeit a frontier where more mountainsides have been scalped than allowed to retain their original forest cover. Logging trucks and heavy equipment share the roads and the infrequent hamlets with hunters, fishermen and sightseers.

Lodging, petrol and other services are rare along twisting canyons so narrow that even radio reception is problematic. Outside the frequent campsites, the only places to overnight en route are occasional bed and breakfasts on the side tracks to Sayward/Kelsey Bay and Zeballos, and basic motels at Telegraph Cove, Alert Bay and Port McNeil. Advance booking is essential, especially in summer.

329

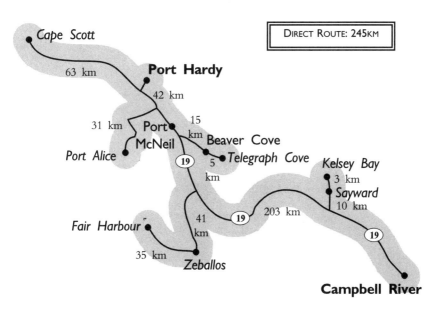

DIRECT ROUTE: 245KM

Cape Scott

63 km

Port Hardy

42 km

31 km   Port   15
McNeil   km   Beaver Cove

Port Alice   19   5   Telegraph Cove   Kelsey Bay
km   3 km
Sayward
10 km
41   203 km
Fair Harbour   km   19

19

35 km
Zeballos

Campbell River

ROUTE

Take BC 19 north past the turnoff for Strathcona Provincial Park and a major pulp and paper mill to Seymour Narrows. The road continues beyond a series of lakes to the **Sayward-Kelsey Bay** turnoff and into the twisting Nimpkish River canyon. Follow the shores of Nimpkish Lake to the **Telegraph Cove** turnoff, then north past turnoffs to **Port McNeil** (and the Alert Bay ferry), **Port Alice** and **Cape Scott** to the end of the road at Port Hardy. The entire route is paved, but traffic sometimes backs up through the scenic geologic jumble that makes up much of North Island. RV traffic is particularly heavy in summer with holiday makers on their way to and from Prince Rupert (on the mainland) via the BC Ferries terminal at Port Hardy.

Strathcona Provincial Park, *District Manager, Box 1479, Parksville, BC V9P 2H4; tel: (250) 755-2483*, is 48 kms west of Campbell River on BC 28. The 211,973-hectare park is a rough wilderness triangle straddling Vancouver Island. Highlights include 440-m **Della Falls**, the highest waterfall in Canada, 2200-m **Golden Hinde**, the tallest point on Vancouver Island and a rugged collection of lesser peaks, meadows, forests and lakes. Mt Washington and Forbidden Plateau ski areas (see p.327) border the park. There are campsites scattered throughout the park and the moderate motel-like **Strathcona Park Lodge**, *Box 2160N, Campbell River, BC V9W 5C9; tel: (250) 286-8206; fax: (250) 286-8208*, just outside, as well as lodging in Campbell River or Courtenay.

Fletcher Challenge Elk Falls Pulp and Paper Mill, *4405 N. Island Hwy, Campbell River; tel: (250) 287-5594*, rises just beside BC 19 7 kms north of Campbell River. A large lay-by overlooking the mill, barge terminal, and Quadra Island has signs explaining plant buildings and operations. Tours available Mon–Fri in summer, advance booking required.

Seymour Narrows, *7 kms north of the mill*, is a perilous pass between Vancouver Island and Maude Island. The twin peaks of Ripple Rock once lay just beneath the surface of the Narrows, creating one of the most hazardous ship passages in the world. A government

project removed Ripple Rock in 1958 with one of the largest non-nuclear explosions in history, but fierce currents and treacherous eddies still churn the Narrows into a boiling mass of white water at flood tide. Marine traffic passes a convenient viewpoint on the north (right) side of the highway. A moderate 8-km path climbs **Wilfred Pt**, overlooking the narrows, from a trailhead 6 kms north. The last ship to run aground on the remains of Ripple Rock, the *SS Sundancer*, hit bottom in 1984. The one-time Alaska cruise ship now sails the Atlantic coast of South America.

Link and Pin Logging Museum, *23 kms north of Ripple Rock Overlook; tel: (250) 287-3931*, open daily June–late Sept, claims the island's best collection of logging paraphernalia, from handsaws to stamp hammers and caulk boots, as well as antique oil lamps and early North Island photographs.

Roberts Lake and rest area, *east (right) side of the hwy, 600 m north*, is one of dozens of scenic fishing lakes along logging roads off BC 19. Most hillsides within view of BC 19 have been logged, some of them repeatedly. The surrounding mountains are at their mysterious best when fog and mist hide the scars. Widespread replanting only began in the 1950s under public and government pressure. Look for signs along the highway giving the cutting date(s), replanting year and next planned cut under the banner of 'Forests Forever'.

Most of Vancouver Island is either owned directly by timber firms or controlled by the industry under license from the provincial government. Timber companies have, however, opened thousands of square kilometres to recreational use between harvests and built dozens of highway rest areas—easily identified by sign-boards like the one at McNair Lake, 4 km north of the Link and Pin Museum, extolling the virtues of clearcutting over the 'dying and diseased' state of old growth forests.

SIDE TRACK
TO SAYWARD AND
KELSEY BAY

Sayward is one of a handful of company towns that still exist in BC, entirely owned by the MacMillan Bloedel Ltd Board Company. MacMillan's Kelsey Bay Lumber Operation, divisional headquarters and town are 10 km north (right) of BC 19. Kelsey Bay is 3 km beyond.

Turn north (right) 29 km north of McNair Lake, following signs for Sayward, and cross the single track bridge over the Salmon River. In addition to namesake salmon, the 74 km river is reputed to hold the largest steelhead on the island. The river drains into Johnstone Strait at Kelsey Bay. Just beyond the bridge on the left-hand side of the road is a steam donkey, or steam engine, once used the haul logs through the forest, being overgrown by moss and brush. The dense poplar trees just beyond are a tree farm.

Sayward is 8 km ahead, overshadowed by 1671-m **Hkusam Mountain**. A marsh and a small lake create the fog that frequently rings the peak. There are no public services.

The upper reaches of Kelsey Bay are a MacMillan Blodell log pond, protected in part by the rusting hulks of barges sunk as breakwaters. The Kelsey Bay wharf was once the southern terminus for BC Ferries' route to Prince Rupert that now ends at Port Hardy. Today, the small harbour is the exclusive domain of sailors, fishermen and charter boat captains. Return to BC 19 and turn north (right).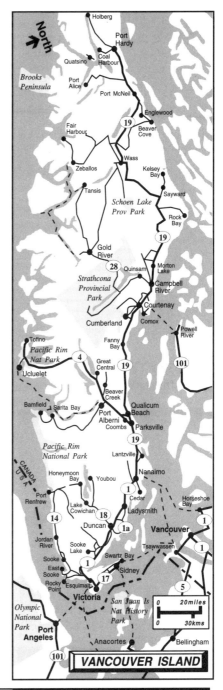

SCHOEN LAKE TO WOSS

Schoen Lake Provincial Park, *to the south (left) 54 km north of the Sayward/Kelsey Bay road; tel: (250) 248-3931,* is a stunning wilderness park. The 1802-m peak of Mt Schoen reflects in the narrow, still waters of Schoen Lake, a 5-km stretch of canoeing waters. Hikers and campers can expect to see deer, bears, beavers, wolves, cougars and Roosevelt elk, or at least sign of their recent passing. The road is passable by passenger vehicles in good weather, but chains are required in winter to get as far as the **Mt Cain Ski Area**, *19 km off BC 19, Box 1225, Port McNeil, BC V0N 2R0; tel: (250) 956-2246.* In winter, 16 ski runs and 20 kms of unmarked cross-country trails, open weekends and school holidays. Mt Cain probably gets more visitors in summer for its wildflowers, wild blueberries, alpine meadows and marshes.

Hoomac Lake, *4 km north of the Schoen Lake turnoff*, is a rest and recreation area maintained by Canadian Forest Products Ltd, better known as Canfor. A signboard clearly explains Canfor's forest cutting and replanting scheme to boost wood production by 80%, but the best reason to stop is a pleasant walking path down the lake. A few hectares of old growth forest has been left around the lake to provide habitat for elk and other creatures which don't prosper in farmed forests.

Woss, *7 km north and 2 km west of BC 19*, is another logging company town. Canfor keeps an antique steam locomotive engine on display that was once used to haul logs through local forests. In summer, the railway is still used to haul tourists about 25 kms through the Nimpkish Valley to the dryland sort and booming grounds at Beaver Cove. The tour takes about 5 hours; *tel: (250) 281-2300*. The town has one of the few petrol stations and restaurants between Campbell River and Port McNeil.

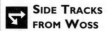

SIDE TRACKS FROM WOSS

ZEBALLOS

Zeballos, *21 km north of Woss, then 41 km south*, is a scenic village at the end of a rough gravel road that offers stunning mountain views. The road is open all year, but is too rugged for most RVs and some low-clearance passenger vehicles. The tiny settlement is a base for boat and kayak trips on the long inlets and waterways around Nootka Island.

ACCOMMODATION

Choices include the **Zeballos Hotel**; *tel: (250) 761-4275*, **Zeballos Inlet Lodge**; *tel: (250) 761-4294; fax: (250) 761-2060*, and **Zeballos Mini-Motel**; *tel: (250) 761-4340*, all budget–moderate; and several campsites.

FAIR HARBOUR

An even rougher unpaved road, not recommended in winter, continues 35 kms north-west to Fair Harbour, a favourite launching point for kayakers putting into the Kyuquot Sound and the Provincial Wilderness Recreation Area on the Brooks Peninsula. Vancouver Island's last known indigenous sea otter was killed near Fair Harbour in 1929; otters transplanted from Alaska in the 1970s seem to be re-establishing themselves along the relatively deserted coast. Return to Zeballos and BC 19 and turn north (left) toward Port McNeil.

NIMPKISH LAKE

This narrow lake skirts the highway for 22 km, finally flowing into the Queen Charlotte Strait just beyond the turnoff for Beaver Cove and Telegraph Cove.

SIDE TRACK TO BEAVER COVE AND TELEGRAPH COVE

Take a well-marked turn south (right) off BC 19 just beyond the north end of Nimpkish Lake at the **North Island Forestry Centre**; *tel: (250) 956-3844 or (800) 661-7177*. The centre is run by five forestry companies that offer a variety of tours depending on location, length and season. Some tours operate all year, but most are summer only, with departures from Port Alberni, Port Hardy, Port McNeil or Woss. Advance booking required.

The paved road ends at a T-junction 11 km from the highway. Turn left, following signs for the Telegraph Cove Resort. A fish hatchery just beyond the turn is sometimes open for self-guided tours. Fletcher Challenge's **Beaver Cove** facility is 1 km beyond. Continue another kilometre past the dryland sort to a lay-by on the left near the top of the hill.

Fletcher Challenge's facility below is the largest dryland sort in Canada, processing 1.4 million cubic metres of logs from the Nimpkish Valley each year. Logs are sorted into 35 different categories by species, size, and grade for lumber, shakes, shingles, ply-

Boats and Islands

Unless Pacific Northwest drivers take to amphibious automobiles, much of the British Columbia coastline will remain inaccessible by land. But just because you can't drive doesn't mean you can't get there. Getting about by boat is a way of life.

BC Ferries, *1112 Fort St, Victoria, BC V8V 4V2; tel: (604) 669-1211; fax: (604) 381-5452*, is one of the largest and busiest ferry systems in the world. Its 40 vessels serve 42 ports of call scattered along more than 1000 km of BC coastline. Like the Washington State Ferries that serve Seattle and Puget Sound, BC Ferries are as much sightseeing ships as they are basic transport, weaving between islands and threading narrow passages that are off limits to the immense cruise ships sailing the main channel of the **Inside Passage** (between Vancouver Island and the mainland) between Vancouver and Alaska.

The most popular ferry routes are Vancouver (Tsawwassen and Horseshoe Bay) to Vancouver Island (Swartz Bay and Nanaimo) and Vancouver to the Gulf Islands. One of the busiest summer circle routes is Vancouver to Nanaimo by ferry, by road to Port Hardy, ferry through the Inside Passage to Prince Rupert and road through the BC interior back to Vancouver. Port Hardy–Prince Rupert summer sailings are booked months in advance. Advance vehicle bookings are required all year, although drive-on space is occasionally available in winter.

Advance bookings are required for both passengers and vehicles **Prince Rupert–Queen Charlotte Islands** and the summer-only **Discovery Coast Passage** route, **Port Hardy–Bella Coola**, on BC's far north-west coast. The two-day, one-night voyage, which began in 1996, twists through some of the most scenic islands in the Northwest. The flexible schedule has as many as seven stops, depending on the sailing date. Most of the towns along the route had never before had regular transport to the outside world.

333

Namu has BC's oldest archaeological site as well as an immense abandoned fish plant, both open for tours, and a new Native art centre. **McLoughlin Bay** offers marine tours and some of the finest fishing along the coast. **Ocean Falls** and **Klemtu** provide historical walking tours. Isolation has helped **Bella Coola** preserve its combination First Nation/Norwegian history and charm. BC Ferries can arrange lodging at intermediate stops, or passengers can sleep on board in reclining seats. BC 20 runs from Bella Coola through the interior of BC and south to Vancouver.

Alaska Marine Highway car and passenger ferries, *Box 25535, Juneau, AK 99802; tel: (800) 642-0066; fax: (907) 277-4829*, sails the Inside Passage between Bellingham, WA, Prince Rupert, BC and Alaska. Book staterooms and vehicle space as early as possible for summer sailings. Winter departures can be booked a few weeks before sailing.

Every coastal town on Vancouver island has its own fleet of boats for local ferry service, fishing, scuba diving, whale watching and other waterborne activities. The *MV Lady Rose* carries passengers as well as cargo to the Broken Group of Islands, Ucluelet and Bamfield from Port Alberni (see pp. 339–342). Advance bookings are required all year.

The **MV Uchuck III**, *Box 57, Gold River, BC V0P 1G0; tel: (250) 283-2325; fax: (250) 283-7582; email: mvuchuck@goldrvr.island.net*, offers similar passenger, kayak and cargo services to Nootka Sound and Kyuquot Sound on the north-west coast of the island. The ship sails from Gold River, west of Campbell River, to Tahsis, Port Eliza, Fair Harbour, Chamiss Bay and Kyuquot on a rotating schedule all year. Expect to see migrating grey whales in spring and autumn as well as orcas, bears, seals, sea otters, and immense flocks of sea birds. A summer-only day trip to Nootka Sound includes a stop at Resolution Cove, where Capt James Cook first landed on Vancouver Island in 1792. Trips last one to two days, with overnights in bed and breakfasts along the way. Advance bookings are crucial, especially in summer.

wood, pulp, poles and log homes. Once the logs are sorted, they are weighed, strapped together and dumped into the booming grounds, or ponds, to be 'stowed up', or chained together, into rafts 21 m wide by 121 m long. Tugs tow 12 rafts at once to mills in Vancouver. Woods tours of logging operations are usually available with advance booking; *tel: (250) 928-3023.*

Continue another kilometre to a stop sign and a second T-junction. Turn left and drive 2 km to Telegraph Cove.

Telegraph Cove Resorts, *Telegraph Cove, BC V0N 3J0; tel: (250) 928-3131 or (250) 284-3426 in winter; fax (250) 928-3105,* open May–Oct, is one of BC's best-preserved boardwalk communities. The tiny town was built early in the century at the terminus of the first telegraph line to North Island, then grew into a thriving sawmill and fish salting community. The handful of surviving buildings, nearly all of them built on stilts over the cove, have been absorbed into the budget–expensive resort. Other facilities include a small marina, general store, RV park and campsite.

The cove has become as popular with environmental groups as it is with fishermen. Sixteen pods (family groups) of Orcas, or killer whales, more than 200 individuals, congregate in the nearby Johnstone Strait in summer and autumn. An ecological preserve has been established at Robson Bight, about 20 km south, a shallow area off the mouth of the Tsitka River where orcas rub on gravel beaches. **Stubbs Island Whale Watching**, *Box 7, Telegraph Cove, BC V0N 3J0; tel: (250) 928-3185 or (800) 665-3066; fax: (250) 928-3102,* runs up to 5 whale watching trips daily June–Oct. More than 90% of trips see whales (minke, humpback and grey as well as orcas) plus porpoises, seals, sea lions, bald eagles and other wildlife. Advance booking highly recommended. Return to BC 19 and turn north (right).

Nimpkish Fish Hatchery, *2 km north of the Telegraph Cove turnoff; tel: (250) 974-9556,* open daily 0900–1500 Oct–May, is run jointly by the Nimpkish Indian Bands, the Boy Scouts and Canfor. In the early years of the century, more than 10,000 sockeye salmon were caught in the Nimpkish River each year; by 1978, ocean fishing off the West Coast of Vancouver Island and habitat destruction from logging in the Nimpkish Valley had cut the annual run to fewer than 500 sockeye. The hatchery is incubating, rearing and releasing several million fish each year in an attempt to restore the fishery. The Nimpkish facility does a better job than most explaining why salmon are important culturally as well as economically, why the runs have declined and how hatcheries and habitat restoration may help. And unlike most hatcheries, this one has viewing windows as clean as any commercial aquarium, with entrancing views into swirling shoals of fish.

BC 4 crosses the Nimpkish River just north of the hatchery. On the east side of the road just over the river is an imposing totem pole carved in 1966 to commemorate the 100th anniversary of the joining of Vancouver Island with the mainland. The turnoff for Port McNeil is 6 km north to the east (right). ⚓

Tourist Information: Port McNeil Chamber of Commerce, *Box 129, Port McNeil, BC V0N 2R0; tel: (250) 956-3131 or (250) 956-4437; fax: (250) 956-4977,* **Infocentre** *next to BC Ferries dock* open daily June–Sept.

ACCOMMODATION

Most area lodging is in Port Hardy. Port McNeil choices include the **HaidaWay Motor Inn**, *Box 399, Port McNeil, BC V0N 2R0; tel: (250) 956-3373; fax: (250) 956-4710* and **Datewood Inn**, *Box 280, Port McNeil, BC V0N 2R0; tel: (250) 956-3304; fax: (250) 956-4351,* both moderate and both with restaurants.

SIGHTSEEING

Port Hardy is primarily a lumber and fishing town. **North Island Forestry Center**, *Box 130, Port McNeil, BC V0N 2R0; tel: (250) 956-3844; fax: (250) 956-3848,* offers a selection of daily tours June–Aug. Tours last about 6 hours, advance booking required. The **world's**

The Queen Charlotte Islands

The **Queen Charlotte Islands**, *Queen Charlotte Islands Travel Infocentre, 3922 Hwy 33, Box 337, Queen Charlotte City, BC V0T 1S0; tel: (250) 559-4742*, are as close to the British Columbia seen by Capt Cook and other early explorers as still exists. The 150 or so islands form an elongated triangle 250 kms long, some 90 kms west of Prince Rupert.

Early traders called them the Misty Islands for the 200 days of fog, drizzle and rain that blanket the dense rainforest each year. The original Haida inhabitants called them 'Haida Gwaii', The Land of the People.

Legendary for their art, frequent raids and fierce domination up and down the coast, precious few of those People remain today. Smallpox and other epidemics introduced by White traders and missionaries killed more than 90% of the population. The rainforest has fared somewhat better, thanks largely to the 1988 creation of **Gwaii Haanas National Park,** *Box 37, Queen Charlotte City, BC V0T 1S0; tel: (250) 559-8818*.

The park, which was supported by the Haida over the fierce objections of timber and mining interests, covers 15% of the archipelago, including much of Moresby Island, the second largest in the archipelago, from development.

The visual highlight is vast stretches of virgin rain forest with 1000-yr old trees whose 70-m tops disappear into the swirling mist most days. The park also protects several Haida villages that were abandoned during the epidemics of the last century.

The most famous – and the most scenic – is **Ninstints**, on Anthony Island. The village, which was abandoned in 1900 after 90% of the population died, was declared a UNESCO world cultural heritage site in 1981. The 200-yr old wooden buildings and towering totem poles are slowly disappearing beneath accumulating moss and crumbling back into the forest. Prior permission must be obtained from Parks Canada before visiting Ninstints and other First Nations sites.

One of the best places to explore Haida art and history is the **Queen Charlotte Islands Museum,** *RR1 Second Beach Rd, Skidegate, BC V0T 1S1; tel: (250) 559-4643*. The museum houses a number of historic totem poles as well as contemporary carvings in wood and stone, metal, glass and other media.

According to Haida legend, humanity first appeared on **Rose Spit**, which extends from the north-east corner of Graham Island, the largest of the group, 10,000 years ago. That was where Raven, the great trickster god, prised open a clamshell that contained the Haida people and released them to the earth.

A wooden carving by Haida artist Bill Reid at the University of British Columbia's Museum of Anthropology in Vancouver recounts the legend.

Archaeological evidence suggests that the islands have been inhabited at least that long. When Capt Juan Josef Perez traded with the Haida in 1774, there were about 7000 Haida in the islands. By 1915, epidemics had reduced the Native population to about 600. The Haida community has grown to around 1000, many of them living in Old Masset and Skidegate, both on Graham Island. The balance of the Islands' population of 6000 live in nearby Masset, Port Clements, Tlell and Queen Charlotte City.

The Queen Charlottes remain a naturalist's dream despite extensive logging. Tiny Sitka deer, immense brown bears and haughty bald eagles frequent the shores; seals, porpoises and whales haunt the many inlets.

Access to the islands is easy, if limited. There are regular flights from Prince Rupert and Vancouver and passenger/vehicle ferry service from Prince Rupert.

There is a small road system on Graham Island, but sea kayaks remain the most popular way to explore the archipelago.

largest burl is 1.5 km north of town on BC 19, 13½ m around and weighing more than 20 tonnes. It was found at the head of the Benson River, about 40 km south. The harbour is an active commercial and sport fishing port as well as the terminus for BC Ferries' route to Alert Bay and Sointula. **Henschel Fine Arts**, *801 Nimpkish Heights Rd, Port McNeil, BC V0N 2R0; tel: (250) 956-3539 or (800) 663-9686; fax: (250) 956-4760*, displays and sells nature paintings by local artist Gordon Henschel.

◤ SIDE TRACK TO ALERT BAY AND SOINTULA

Tourist Information: Alert Bay Tourist Information Centre, *118 Fir St, Alert Bay, BC V0N 1A0; tel: (250) 974-5213; fax: (250) 974-5470*, open daily June–Sept, Mon–Fri Sept–June.

GETTING THERE

BC Ferries *from Port Hardy; tel: (250) 956-4533 or (800) 663-7600*, daily.

SIGHTSEEING

Nowhere is Canada's mystical First Nations heritage more evident than at Alert Bay. The Nimpkish burial ground is guarded by a phalanx of totem poles towering above the beach, a sight more often seen in faded black and white museum photographs than in living colour partially obscured by swirling ocean mists.

In the 1870s, missionaries convinced the Nimpkish band to move from the Nimpkish Valley to Alert Bay on Cormorant Island, just off Port McNeil, to staff a salmon saltery. Today, the village is an ethnic mix, but the ethos is decidedly First Nations. The biggest draw is the **U'Mista Cultural Centre**, *Box 253, Alert Bay, BC V0N 1A0; tel: (250) 974-5403; fax: (250) 974-5499*, open daily, home to half of the potlatch collection taken in a 1922 raid. The remainder of the collection is on display at the **Kwakitul Museum** in *Cape Mudge, Quadra Island* (see p. 328). The cultural centre also has temporary exhibitions of contemporary

First Nations art and cultural events. A 58-m totem pole at the north end of the island is currently the tallest in the world.

Sointula, on Malcom Island, is linked to Port McNeil and Alert Bay by BC Ferries. The tiny fishing village began in 1901 as a utopian retreat organised by Finnish philosopher and playwright Matti Kurrika. The colony collapsed in 1905, but about 100 Finns remained. Finnish is still heard on the streets. The **Sointula Finnish Museum**; *left on First St after leaving the ferry; tel: (250) 973-6353*, reflects Finnish fishing and farming roots. **Misty Lake Rest Area**, *17 km north of Port McNeil Rd*, is a scenic rest area on the east side of the road. The 2-metre stumps are all that remains of the original forest cover. The road to Port Alice is 3 km north. ◣

◤ SIDE TRACK TO PORT ALICE

Tourist Information: Quatsino Chalet, *1061 Marine Dr, Port Alice, BC V0N 2N0; tel: (250) 284-3318*, open daily Mon–Fri.

SIGHTSEEING

This 1910s mill town at the head of Neroutsos Inlet in Quatsino Sound was moved in the 1960s, accounting for its relatively new look. The 33-km drive east from BC 19 passes Beaver Lake, beloved by locals for a thriving population of cutthroat and Dolly Varden trout, and two of North Island's few golf courses. The **Seven Hills Golf and Country Club**; *tel: (250) 949-9818*, has 9 holes and the island's most unusual hazard, a 40-tonne steam tractor from 1910 that bogged down while hauling logs. Since the tractor was too heavy to move, the course was built around it. The **Port Alice Golf and Country Club**, another 9-hole course, is so steep it has a periscope at the second tee. Lumber reigns in Port Alice, but sport fishing, hiking, camping and outdoor recreation are gaining ground. Return to BC 19 and turn north (left) toward Port Hardy.

Beaver Harbour, *Fort Rupert Rd east*

(right) toward the airport, 3 km north of BC Hydo's Keogh Generating Station, was the original Hudson's Bay Company settlement in the region. Today, the area is a Kwakwaka'wakw reserve. The only sign of the fort is a crumbling chimney. Several of BC's finest Native artists, including carvers from the renowned Hunt family, work, display and sell at **The Copper Maker**; *Box 755, Port Hardy, BC V0N 2P0; tel: (250) 949-8491; fax: (250) 949-7345*, open Mon–Sat. **Bear Cove**, *1 km north of Fort Rupert Rd, then 6 km east*, is the **BC Ferries** terminal for Prince Rupert; *tel: (250) 949-6722* or *(800) 663-7600*. Ferries operate weekly in both directions Oct–Apr, twice weekly May–Sept. Advance bookings required all year. Artefacts from an 8000-year old Bear Cove settlement are at the Port Hardy Museum. Port Hardy is 4 km north from the junction with BC 19.

PORT HARDY

Tourist Information: Port Hardy & District Chamber of Commerce, *7250 Market St, Port Hardy, BC V0N 2P0; tel: (250) 949-7622; fax: (250) 949-6653*, open daily June–late Sept, Mon–Fri Oct–June.

ACCOMMODATION

Year-round ferry traffic means year-round business for local motels, inns and bed and breakfasts–advance bookings are always wise and a must in summer. **North Islands Reservations**; *tel: (250) 949-7622*, books local lodging. **Pioneer Inn**, *Bying Rd, near the Bear Cove turnoff, Box 699, Port Hardy, BC V0N 2P0; tel: (250) 949-7271; fax: (250) 949-7334*, is the best budget–moderate value. The **Thunderbird Inn**, *7050 Rupert St, Port Hardy, BC V0N 2P0; tel: (250) 949-7767; fax: (250) 949-7740*, moderate, is in central Port Hardy.

SIGHTSEEING

Port Hardy is the commercial centre of North Island. BC 19 comes to an end at a broad bayfront park with a bright orange wooden carrot and handcarved 'Welcome to Port Hardy' sign. The 'carrot at the end of the road' is a pointed reminder that a generation of provincial governments reneged on campaign pledges to extend BC 19 to Port Hardy until 1979. A walkway extends the length of the scenic harbour, a favourite gathering place for bald eagles, Canada geese and other birds.

Buildings just up from the town dock are part of the original Port Hardy, founded in 1925. The original Hardy Bay Hotel had North Island's first liquor license. The town's first community hall is now the **Port Hardy Museum and Archives**, *7110 Market St, Port Hardy, BC V0N 2P0; tel: (250) 949-8143*, open afternoons Tue–Sat Oct–May, daily in summer. Exhibits cover First Nations history (including excavations at Bear Cove) and European exploration and settlement.

The port is home to a commercial and sport fishing fleet, both benefiting from the **Quatse River Salmon Hatchery**, *5050 Hardy Bay Rd (across from the Pioneer Inn), Port Hardy, BC V0N 2P0; tel: (250) 949-9022*, open 0800–1630 Mon–Fri. The hatchery raises coho, chinook and chum salmon, with pleasant walking paths along the river.

SIDE TRACK TO CAPE SCOTT

The only access into **Cape Scott Provincial Park** is by foot, but logging roads lead 63 km from Port Hardy to the trailhead. Cape Scott itself is a rugged 2-day return hike with staggering views of both sides of Vancouver island from the lighthouse perched far above crashing waves rolling off the open Pacific Ocean. Less adventurous walkers generally opt for the 45-minute walk along chip paths and boardwalks to the sandy shores of San Josef Bay.

Although the park is a wilderness area, loggers have long been working the mountains between Port Hardy and the Pacific. Gravel roads to Holberg, Winter Harbour, and Raft Cove are well maintained and passable–with care–by passenger vehicles during the summer. Not recommended for large RVs because of occasional rough patches on the road and difficulty pulling over for logging trucks.

PARKSVILLE–TOFINO

This 180-km route cuts through the heart of Vancouver Island, from the sheltered waters of the Inside Passage on the east coast, through low, wet mountain ranges to the pounding surf of the unprotected Pacific coast. Along the way, small towns nestle between some of the oldest and tallest stands of Douglas-fir on the island and the more familiar patchwork of clearcutting. The West Coast and Pacific Rim National Park are wetter, wilder and even less developed than North Island. Until the road to Tofino was paved in 1972, the West Coast was almost a private preserve. Today, the return trip can be made in a day, but deserves at least one night each in Port Alberni, Ucluelet and Tofino.

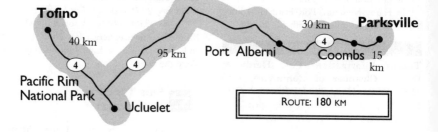

338

ROUTE: 180 KM

ROUTE

Take BC 4 west from Parksville past Englishman River Falls and the town of **Coombs** (look for goats grazing the rooftops) to **Cameron Lake**, **Cathedral Grove** and **Port Alberni**. The highway follows Sproat Lake, then swings south-west to a T-junction. **Ucluelet** is 5 km south (left), the Long Beach Unit of **Pacific Rim National Park** and **Tofino** to the north (right).

PARKSVILLE TO PORT ALBERNI

Emerald Forest Bird Garden, *1420 Alberni Hwy, Parksville, BC V9P 2G5; tel: (250) 248-7282; fax: (250) 248-7298,* open daily, is a welcome splash of brilliant colour. About 260 parrots, macaws, canaries and other tropical birds flutter and squawk in a recreated habitat. Many have been trained to perch on the nearest available arm, shoulder or head.

Englishman River Falls Provincial Park, *½ km W. of Emerald Forest to Arrington Rd, 7 km S.; tel: (250) 248-5212,* is a pleasant picnic spot with two small but photogenic waterfalls. Both falls are about ½ km through dark, mossy forest, a welcome relief from the island's usual stumps and tree farms.

On the way back to BC 4, turn right onto *Grafton Ave* (just before the highway), then left onto *Leffler Rd* at the end of the pavement, to the **North Island Wildlife Recovery Association Museum of Nature**, *1240 Leffler Rd, Errington, BC V0R 1V0; tel: (520) 248-8534; fax (250) 248-1274.* The museum re-creates several forest environments; the

MV Lady Rose

The sea remains the only way to see much of the West Coast, and **Alberni Marine Transportation**, *Box 188, Port Alberni, BC V9Y 7M7; tel: (250) 723-8313; fax: (250) 723-8314*, is the only reliable commercial service on the coast. The *MV Lady Rose*, a 1937 packet freighter from Glasgow, Scotland, runs from Port Alberni to Bamfield and Ucluelet all year. The somewhat newer *MV Frances Barkley* provides additional service in summer.

Both ships are freighters, not car ferries. Cargo runs the gamut from parcel post and soda pop to engine fittings and new clothes as well as passengers, bicycles, canoes and kayaks. The ships are also the primary access to the **Broken Group Islands** unit of Pacific Rim National Park. Spring–autumn trips almost always include kayakers starting or ending their own voyages at Gibraltar Island or the Sechart Whaling Station, the main port for the Broken Group.

Bamfield trips depart the *Argyle St* Dock in Port Alberni at 0800 and return late afternoon. The only other way to reach Bamfield is by way of the West Coast Trail or rough gravel road from Port Alberni or Lake Cowichan. Chief points of interest are a shoreline boardwalk and a marine biological station. Brady's Beach, a popular picnic and swimming spot, is a short walk away. The Broken Group–Ucluelet run leaves at the same time but returns later. Passengers can expect to see the same kind of wildlife as kayakers – seals, sea lions, bald eagles, whales, basking sharks, orcas and more – as the ship threads its way through the winding deep water channels toward Ucluelet. Kayaks, of course, can approach much more closely than the noisier motor vessel. Alberni Marine also hires canoes and kayaks for Broken Group explorers.

recovery centre treats about 700 injured animals yearly. Animals too badly injured to be released back into the wild are sent to zoos or used for education programmes.

Coombs, 3 kms west on BC 4, was founded just after the turn of the century. Part of a Salvation Army scheme that brought more than 250,000 poor English and Welsh to Canada, the tiny town is now a combination tourist trap and 1960s throwback. Goats graze the turf roof of the **Old Country Market** while tourists graze the fresh produce, ice-cream and wickerware inside. **Butterfly World**, *1 km west; tel: (250) 248-7026*, is a repeat of Butterfly World near Victoria, wooden walkways and hundreds of colourful butterflies fluttering through a semi-tropical environment.

Little Qualicum Hatchery; *8 km west of the junction with BC 4A*, is one of the island's less impressive hatcheries. **Little Qualicum Falls Provincial Park**, *2 km west on BC 4; tel: (250) 752-6305*, is a pleasant spot for a picnic. The park includes the entire shoreline of **Cameron Lake**, on the north (right), 4 km west of the park entrance. There are a number of very pleasant picnic spots on the lakefront.

Cathedral Grove, part of **MacMillan Provincial Park**, lies just west of the lake. The park was named after Harvey Reginald MacMillan, BC's first provincial chief forester (1909–13) and later head of the timber company that became MacMillan Bloedel. Easy walking trails explore the grove, one of South Island's rare bits of virgin forest. The trees, some of them layered with 800 years worth of accumulated moss, are among the largest Douglas-fir and red cedar left in BC. Smoking is not permitted on trails or anywhere else in the 135-hectare park. **Port Alberni Summit**, 375 m, is 7 km west.

Mt Arrowsmith Regional Park, *2 km west of the summit*, has winter skiing and ice climbing. The park is more popular in summer for hiking, wildflowers, fishing and expansive vistas from **Mt Arrowsmith** (1817 m) and **Mt Cokely** (1616 m). Carry chains in winter. Port Alberni junction is 5 km west. At the junction, go left into central Port Alberni or continue straight to Ucluelet and Tofino.

PORT ALBERNI

Tourist Information: Alberni Valley Chamber of Commerce, *RR 2, Site 215*

Pacific Rim National Park

Pacific Rim National Park Reserve, *Box 280, Ucluelet, BC V0R 3A0; tel: (250) 726-7721 or (800) 689-9025,* is three parks in one. The **West Coast Trail**, north from Port Renfrew, the **Broken Group Islands**, in Barkley Sound and the **Long Beach Unit**, between Ucluelet and Tofino, encompass 510 sq km of south-western Vancouver Island and some of the wildest scenery on Canada's Pacific Rim. The **Park Information Centre**, *BC 4, 3 km north of the Ucluelet-Tofino-Port Alberni Jct; tel: (250) 726-4212,* is open mid Mar–mid Oct.

The **West Coast Trail** was originally a life-saving trail along the rugged coast between Port Renfrew and Bamfield. Spectacular virgin scenery is the norm, but generally wet weather and rugged topography make this 75-km, 6–7-day walk a challenge. The Trail is open 15 Apr–30 Sept; permits are required. Advance bookings begin 1 Mar; *tel: (604) 387-1642 or (800) 663-6000,* daily 0600–1800. The $25 booking fee can be paid by Visa or MasterCard. Space-available permits are available in Port Renfrew, Nitinat Lake (mid-way point) and Bamfield. The permit wait averages 3 days, but stretches longer each season.

The **Broken Group** is more than 100 islands, most little more than rocks supporting a few windblown trees. Hundreds of ships have been wrecked on outer edge of the Broken Group in the past two centuries, competing with the mouth of the Columbia River as the 'Graveyard of the Pacific'. Behind lies a maze of semi-protected islets and passages that harbours one of the richest concentrations of marine life off North America. Canoeists and kayakers come to view the wildlife as well as stunning scenes of untouched islands rising from pristine waters on every side. The only access is by water, usually aboard the *MV Lady Rose* from Port Alberni; *tel: (800) 663-7192.* Advance bookings required.

C10, Port Alberni, BC V9Y 7L6; tel: (250) 724-6535. **Infocentre**, *Port Alberni Jct,* open Mon–Fri 0900–1700.

ACCOMMODATION AND FOOD

CS is the only chain in the area, but there are another 15 or so hotels/motels plus many bed and breakfasts and campsites. **Coast Hospitality Inn**, *3835 Redford St, Port Alberni, BC V9Y 3S2; tel: (250) 723-8111 or (800) 663-6677; fax: (250) 723-0088,* is easily the best in town, followed by **The Barclay**, *4277 Stamp Ave; tel: (250) 724-7171 or (800) 563-6590.* Both are moderate.

Seafood is always a safe bet in this long-time fishing port. **Paradise Café**, *4505 Gertrude St; tel: (250) 724-5050,* is a good choice. **Blue Door Cafe**; *tel: (250) 723-8811,* and **Steamers**; *tel: (250) 723-2211,* both at Alberni Harbour Quay, are local favourites for breakfast and lunch.

SIGHTSEEING

Fishing and forestry have been economic mainstays since Port Alberni was established as a lumber town in 1860. Tourism is gaining quickly, especially near **Harbour Quay** at the foot of *Argyle St.* The **observation tower** has good views over Stamp Harbour and Alberni Inlet, stretching 40 km to the Pacific. The **Forestry Information Centre**, *Harbour Quay; tel: (250) 724-7888,* arranges tours of local saw and pulp mills as well as lumbering operations. The Quay is also home to the *Lady Rose,* with passenger and freight service to Barkley Sound. Many commercial fishing boats now sell direct to the public at Government Pier. Others are moving to sport fishing, though Port Alberni still disputes Campbell River for the 'Salmon Capital of the World' title.

Much of the **Alberni Valley Museum**, *4255 Wallace St, Port Alberni, BC V9Y 3Y6; tel: (250) 723-2181; fax: (250) 723-1035,* explores industrial history. Best examples are the **Alberni Pacific Railway**, a restored 1929 steam locomotive engine and carriages running summer weekends, and the **R.B. McLean Lumber Company**, a family-owned sawmill under restoration. Contact the museum for

Road-building has transformed the **Long Beach Unit** from a seldom-seen island hideaway at the end of a tortuous logging road to one of the most popular parts of Vancouver Island. More than 800,000 people a year visit the 30-km of sandy beach, rocky headland, forest and bog between Ucluelet and Tofino. What were once empty beaches have sprouted busy parking lots with bright yellow payboxes – and wardens to enforce the $5 daily parking fee. Most visitors come for the day May–Oct. By late afternoon, the beaches are all but deserted except for sea gulls, sea lions and crabs hiding in the heaps of driftwood that wash up on every strip of sand. **Florencia Bay**, *S. off Long Beach Rd*, also known as Wreck Beach, is a 5-km crescent pointing toward the **Wickaninnish Centre**, *end of Long Beach Rd; tel: (250) 726-7333*, open mid Mar–mid Oct, the main interpretative centre for the park. The restaurant, museum, and elevated walkways with broad vistas across Wickaninnish Bay are particularly busy July–Aug.

Centre and Bay are named after the local Nootka chief who inadvertently sparked the fur trade. In June, 1788, Wickaninnish traded Capt. John Meares 50 sea otter pelts for two copper kettles. Meares eventually sold the fur-bare pelts, used as bedding by his crew, for $2500 in China. The surf-swept sand of Long Beach stretches 10 km north. **Combers Beach**, *5 km north on BC 4*, is the north end of Long Beach. A well-marked trail explores the distinct ecological zones between salty, inhospitable sand and the dense, moss-draped forest a few hundred metres inland. **Radar Hill**, *16 km north*, is the site of a 1954 radar base on the 'Pine Tree Line' built to defend the United States against nuclear attack from the Soviet Union. The Pine Tree Line followed the 49th Parallel, with the Mid-Canada Line running through Central Canada, and the DEW (or Distant Early Warning) Line along the northern rim of the continent. Tofino is 12 km north on BC 4.

current hours and tours. The museum also publishes a self-guided historic city walking tour brochure.

PORT ALBERNI TO UCLUELET

There are no services, including petrol, between Port Alberni and Ucluelet, more than 100 km west.

Roberson Creek Hatchery, *3 km beyond the Husky petrol station to Central Lake Rd, then 8 km north*, open 0800–1600 daily, has an excellent series of displays. Bear, deer and other wildlife share the gravel road with vehicles.

Sproat Lake Provincial Park, *Box 1479, Parksville, BC V9P 2H4; tel: (250) 954-4600*, is busy in summer, almost deserted the rest of the year. Loud aeroplane sounds mean the Mars water bombers are dumping 27 tonnes of water on forest fires. These two converted military planes, the largest water bombers in the world, are based on the lake at **Flying Tankers**, *Bomber Base Rd; tel: (250) 723-6225*. No tours, but the base is open for visitors who keep out of the way.

The road west climbs past Sproat Lake, following the Taylor River into the **MacKenzie Range**. An extensive area around the road burned in 1967 when highway construction equipment sparked a major forest fire. Replanting of the burned area began the same year. The high point is **Sutton Pass**, 175 m, which leads to **Hydro Hill**, an 18% grade that runs straight into a recent 'clear-cut'. Graffiti on the guard rail, 'telephone poles – last of the old growth' reflects growing local sentiment.

Continue 22 km to a T-junction and a summer-only **Travel Infocentre**. Go right 34 km to Tofino, left 7 km to Ucluelet.

UCLUELET

Tourist Information: Ucluelet Chamber of Commerce, *227 Main St, Ucluelet, BC V0R 3A0; tel: (250) 726-4641; fax: (250) 726-4611*, open Mon–Fri 1000–1500, daily June–Sept.

ACCOMMODATION

Moderate–expensive **Canadian Princess Resort**, *1948 Peninsula Rd, Ucluelet, BC V0R*

3A0; tel: (250) 726-7771; fax: (250) 726-7271, a former hydrographic survey ship refitted as a resort, is the best in town. The Chamber of Commerce can supply a current list of budget–moderate bed and breakfasts.

SIGHTSEEING

This scenic tourist, fishing and logging village is about a third of the way up Ucluelet Inlet from Barkley Sound and the open Pacific. The name comes from the local First Nations' word for 'people of the sheltered bay'. The calm inlet is a sharp contrast to the pounding Pacific west of **Amphitrite Point**, 5 km south of the town centre. The **lighthouse**, still operating, was built in 1906 after the *Line of Melfort* struck the point and sank with all hands.

Ha-tin-kis Park, just before the lighthouse, has an extensive boardwalk system through coastal forest and bogs. Park and lighthouse have stunning sunset views. The road ends in a housing estate just beyond the lighthouse. Return north through **Pacific Rim National Park** (see p. 340) to Tofino.

TOFINO

Tourist Information: Tofino Chamber of Commerce, Box 249, Tofino, BC V0R 2Z0; tel: (250) 725-3414; fax: (250)725-3296, open Mon–Fri 0900–1700.

ACCOMMODATION

BW is the only chain, but there are more than two dozen inns and bed and breakfasts as well as motels. Best choice is the moderate **Weigh West Marine Resort**, *634 Campbell St; Tofino, BC V0R 2Z0; tel: (250) 725-3277 or (800) 665-8922; fax: (250) 725-3922.*

EATING AND DRINKING

The Blue Heron, *Weigh West Resort; tel: (250) 725-4266,* and **The Schooner**, *331 Campbell St; tel: (250) 725-3444,* are the pricey best. **Alleyway Café**, *305 Campbell St; tel: (250) 725-3105,* has the best vegetarian meals on the West Coast.

Common Loaf Bakeshop, *180 First St; tel: (250) 725-3915,* has shockingly good breads, pastries and light meals. All are open daily.

SIGHTSEEING

Government Dock at the foot of *First St* is the end (or the beginning) of the TransCanada Highway and the entrance to **Clayoquot Sound**. Named after a 17th-century Spanish hydrographer, Tofino is better known as the land of the Nuu-chah-nulth First Nations, called Nootka by early European visitors. Commercial fishing is still important, but Tofino is growing as the supply town for Pacific Rim National Park and a growing outdoor recreation industry. Hiking, fishing, whale-watching, sea kayaking and environmental activism are favourite pastimes. A 1993 provincial government decision to allow the logging of two-thirds of Clayoquot Sound, then among the largest surviving virgin temperate rainforests on the planet, sparked Canada's largest civil disobedience action ever. The industry-controlled **Rainforest Interpretative Centre**, *316 Main St; tel: (250) 725-2560; fax: (250) 725-1252,* is one of the few local institutions to support logging.

First Nations art is a powerful local force. **Eagle Aerie**, *350 Campbell St; tel: (250) 725-3235; fax: (250) 725-4466,* and **House of Himwitsa**, *300 Main St; tel: (250) 725-2017; fax: (250) 725-2361,* are Tofino's leading First Nations art galleries. Displays are the equal of anything shown in Vancouver and Victoria, as are the prices. Himwitsa also operates the popular **Sea Shanty Restaurant** and the **Himwitsa Lodge**, both with broad views across Tofino Inlet.

Tofino grinds to a halt around **sunset**, at least in good weather. Favourite spots to watch the sun drop are **Government Dock**, **Tonquin Park**, and **Chesterman Beach**. Daylight activities include excursions to nearby islands. **Meares**, an easy kayak paddle away, is known for its virgin forests that have, so far, escaped the chain-saw. **Hot Springs Cove**, an all-day boat excursion to the island's only known hot springs, offers virgin forests and hot springs. The 50°F water cools as it plunges over a waterfall and flows through several pools toward the sea. Swimming costumes are optional, to the occasional delight of local mosquitoes.

DRIVING DISTANCES AND TIMES

Approximate distances from major cities to surrounding places and main centres are given following the most direct routes. Driving times are meant as an average indication only, allowing for the nature of the roads but not for traffic conditions, which can be very variable (see the route descriptions throughout the book). They do not include allowance for stops or breaks en route. The journey times of the main ferry crossings are also shown.

Eugene to . . .	Miles	Hours
Astoria	215	4½
Baker City	460	10
Bend	180	3½
Crater Lake	145	3
Florence	90	2
Medford	170	4
Portland	115	2
Seattle	300	5⅔

Portland to . . .	Miles	Hours
Baker City	310	6
The Dalles	85	1½
Olympia	120	2
Pendleton	210	4
Seattle	180	3⅓
Yakima	195	3⅔

Seattle to . . .	Miles	Hours
Grand Coulee Dam	295	7
Mt Rainier	110	2⅓
Olympia	60	1
Port Angeles	ferry	3
Portland	180	3⅓
Spokane	280	5⅓
Vancouver	140	3
Winthrop	195	3½
Yakima	120	3

Spokane to . . .	Miles	Hours
Clarkston	110	1⅓
Ellensburg	170	3⅓
Grand Coulee Dam	85	1⅔
Osoyoos	185	3⅔
Seattle	280	5 ½
Winthrop	185	4

Vancouver to . . .	Kilometres	Hours
Campbell River	ferry	3½
Hope	150	2
Nanaimo	ferry	1
Osoyoos	400	5
Port Hardy (incl. ferry)	385	7
Port Renfrew (incl. ferry)	210	5
Seattle	230	3
Victoria	ferry	1
Whistler	150	2½

Victoria to . . .	Kilometres	Hours
Campbell River	280	4
Nanaimo	120	1¾
Port Angeles	ferry	2½
Port Hardy	500	7⅔
Port Renfrew	90	2
Seattle	ferry	5
Tofino	315	5⅓
Vancouver	ferry	1

343

HOTEL CODES
AND CENTRAL BOOKING NUMBERS

The following abbreviations have been used throughout the book to show which chains are represented in a particular town. Cities and large towns have most except *HI*. Central booking numbers are shown in bold – use these numbers whilst in the North America to make reservations at any hotel in the chain. Where available, numbers that can be called in your own country are also noted. (Aus=Australia, Can=Canada, Ire=Ireland, NZ=New Zealand, SA =South Africa, UK=United Kingdom, WW=Worldwide number).

344

BW **Best Western**
(800) 528 1234
Aus *(1 800) 222 422*
Ire *(800) 709 101*
NZ *(09) 520 5418*
SA *(011) 339 4865*
UK *(0800) 393130*

CI **Comfort Inn**
(800) 228 5150
Aus *(008)090 600*
Can *(800) 888 4747*
Ire *(800) 500 600*
NZ *(800) 808 228*
UK *(0800) 444444*

CM **Courtyard by Marriott**
(800) 321 2211

CP **Canadian Pacific**
(800) 441 1414

CS **Coast Hotels**
(800) 663 1144

DI **Days Inn**
(800) 325 2525
UK *(01483) 440470*

EL **Econolodge**
(800) 424 6423
WW *(800) 221 2222*

ES **Embassy Suites**
(800) 362 2779
Aus *02 959 3922*
Can *416 626 3974*
NZ *09 623 4294*
SA *11 789 6706*
UK *(01992) 441517*

FS **Four Seasons**
(800) 332 3442

Hd **Holiday Inn**
(800) 465 4329
Aus *(800) 221 066*
Ire *(800) 553 155*

NZ *(0800) 442 222*
SA *(011) 482 3500*
UK *(0800) 897121*

HI **Hostelling International**
202 783 6161
(information only)
Can/US *(800) 444 6111*
UK *(0171) 248 6547*

HJ **Howard Johnson**
(HoJo)
(800) 654 2000
Aus *02 262 4918*
UK *(0181) 688 1418*

Hn **Hilton**
(800) 445 8667
Aus *(800) 222 255*
NZ *(800) 448 002*
SA *(011) 880 3108*
UK *(0345) 581595*

Hy **Hyatt**
(800) 233 1234
Aus *(800) 131 234*
Ire *(800) 535 500*
NZ *(800) 441 234*
SA *(011) 773 9888*
UK *(0345) 581666*

Ma **Marriott**
(800) 228 9290
Aus *(800) 251 259*
NZ *(800) 441 035*
UK *(800) 221222*

M6 **Motel 6**
(800) 437 7486

PP **Pan Pacific**
(800) 663 1515

QI **Quality Inn**
(800) 228 5151

Rd **Radisson**
(800) 333 3333

Ire *(800) 557 474*
NZ *(800) 443 333*
UK *(800) 191991*

Rm **Ramada**
(800) 228 2828
Aus *(800) 222 431*
Can *(800) 854 7854*
Ire *(800) 252 627*
NZ *(800) 441 111*
UK *(800) 181737*

RI **Residence Inn**
(800) 331 3131
Aus *(800) 251 259*
Ire *(800) 409929*
NZ *(800) 441035*

RL **Red Lion**
(800) 848 9600

Sh **Sheraton**
(800) 325 3535 or
(800) 325 1717
(hearing impaired)
Aus *(008) 073 535*
Ire *(800) 535 353*
NZ *(0800) 443 535*
UK *(0800) 353535*

S8 **Super 8**
WW *(800) 800 8000*

TL **Travelodge**
(800) 578 7878
Aus *(800) 622 240*
Ire *(800) 409 040*
NZ *(800) 801 111*
SA *(011) 442 9201*
UK *(0345) 404040*

VI **Vagabond Inn**
(800) 522 1555

WT **Westin**
(800) 228 3000

WEBSITES AND EMAIL ADDRESSES

Prices, opening hours and other details change as quickly in the Pacific Northwest as they do anywhere else in the world. Details in this volume were checked less than a month before publication, but you can still expect to find changes that came too late for inclusion. For the absolutely latest updates, nothing beats the World Wide Web and Email. If the idea or attraction you're looking for isn't listed, a few moments with your favourite search engine may turn up a new website.

For details of **Thomas Cook** and its services around the world, visit their website on *http://www.thomascook.com*. Thomas Cook Holidays site is *http://www.tch.thomascook.com*. (VB=Visitor Bureau; VCB=Vistor and Convention Bureau; CC=Chamber of Commerce; CVB=Convention and Visitor Bureau; CVC=Commerce and Visitors Centre.)

Alaska Marine Highway: *http://www.dot. state.ak.us/external/amhs/home.html*

Amtrak: *http://www.amtrak.com/amtrak/travel*

Bay Area CC (Coos Bay, North Bend, Chaleston, OR): *http://www.ucinet.com/~bacc*

BC Ferries: *http://bcferries.bc.ca/ferries*

Tourism BC: *http://www.travel.bc.ca*

BC Transit: *http://transitbc.com*

Bellingham-Whatcome County, WA, CVB: *http://www.bellingham.org*

British Columbia Bed and Breakfast Directory: *http://www.monday.com/tourism*

Canadian Native Art: *http://www.netbistro.com/pg/Art/native*

Canadian Pacific Hotels: *http://www.cphotels.ca*

Cascade Range Volcanoes (US): *http://vulcan.wr.usgs.gov/*

Central Oregon Visitors Assn: *cova@empnet.com*

Clarkston, WA: *http://www.clarkston.com/welcome.html*

Columbia River Gorge: *http://www.gorge.net*

Cowlitz County, WA, Department of Tourism: *cc2rism@teleport.com*

The Dalles Area CC: *tolacc@gorbe.net*

Empress Hotel, Victoria, BC: *http://vvv.com/empress/*

Eugene, OR: *http://www.efn.org/~sgazette/eugenehome.html*

Galiano Island, BC, CC: *http://www.islandnet.com/galiano*

Gold Beach, OR, CC: *http://www.harborside.com/gb/*

Tu Tu'Tun Lodge, Gold Beach, OR: *http://www.el.com/to/tututunlodge*

Harrison Hot Springs, BC, CC: email: *harrison@uniserve.com*

Hostelling International: *http://www.tapon line.com/travel/hostels/pages/hosthp.html*

Hostelling International American Youth Hostels: *http://www.hiayh.org*

Hostelling International BC: *http://www.virtualynx.com/bchostels*

Jacksonville, OR, Britt Festivals: *http://www.mind.net/britt/*

John Day Fossil Beds National Monument, OR: *http://www.nps.gov/joda*

Kitsap Peninsula, WA, VCB: *http://www.kitsapedc.org*

La Grande-Union County, OR, CC: *http://www.ucinet.com/~lagrande/*

CVA of Lane County, Oregon (CVALCO): *http://www.cvalco.org*

Lynden CC: *http://www.pacificrim.net/~lynden*

Medford, Jackson County, OR, VCB: *MEDJACCC@Magick.Net*

345

Mt Hood Meadows Ski Resort, OR:
http://www.skihood.com/mhmeadows

MV Uchuck III: email:
mvuchuck@goldrvr.island.net

Tourism Nanaimo BC:
http://www.tourism.nanaimo.bc.ca/

Greater Newport, OR, CC:
http://www.newportnet.com

North Cascades National Park, WA:
http://www.nps.gov/noca/

Northwest Trek, WA: *http://www.nwtrek.org*

Olympic Coast National Marine Sanctuary, WA: *ocnms@ocean.nos.noaa.gov*

Olympic National Park, WA:
http://www.nps.gov/olym/

Olympic Peninsula Travel Association, WA: *http://www.waypt.com/opta/opta.html*

North Olympic Peninsula, WA, VCB:
http://www.northolympic.com

Ontario, OR, VCB: *email: ontvcb@micron.net*

Oregon, Washington & California Bed & Breakfast Directory:
http://www.moriah.com/inns

Oregon Caves National Monument:
http://www.nps.gov/orca/

Eastern Oregon communities:
http://www.eosc.osshe.edu/rec_poi.html

Southern Oregon coastal communities:
http://www.harborside.com/hs/online_comm/

Southern Oregon Visitors Association:
http://www.sova.org

Oregon Brewers Guild:
http://www.oregonbeer.org

Oregon Online Highways:
http://www.ohwy.com:80/or/homepage.htm

Oregon Tourism Commission:
http://www.traveloregon.com

Osoyoos, BC: *http://alpha.ftcnet.com/~edoca/*

Out West newspaper:
http://www.outwestnewspaper.com

Portland Oregon Visitors Assn:
http://www.pova.com

Salem, OR, CVA:
http://www.oregonlink.com/~salem/scva/

San Juan Island, WA, CC:*http://www.pacificrim.net/~bydesign/chamber.html*

San Juan Island National Historic Park, WA: *http://www.nps.gov/sajh/*

San Juan Island Tourist Information Services, WA:
http://www.pacificrim.net/~bydesign/tis.html

Seaside, OR, CC: *seaside@aone.com*

Spokane, WA, Regional CV:
http://www.spokane-areacvb.org

Stubbs Island Whale Watching, Telegraph Cove, BC: *stubbs@north.island.net*

Tofino, BC, CC: *bnixon@lbmf.bc.ca*

Underground Onramp:
email: *comments@underramp.com*

Tourism Vancouver and the Greater Vancouver CVB :
http://www.travel.bc.ca/vancouver

Vancouver Island communities:
http://www.island.net/

Tourism Victoria:
http://www.travel.victoria.bc.ca/
email: *info@travel.victoria.bc.ca*

Canada-West Victoria Reservation Service: email: *canwest@netnation.com*

Wallowa County, OR, CC:
http://www.eosc.osshe.edu.~jkraft.wallowa.com

Washington State Ferries:
http://www.wsdot.wa.gov/ferries/

Washington State Lodging & Travel Guide: *http://www.travel-in-wa.com*

Washington State Tourism Division:
http://www.tourism.wa.gov

Washington Winter Guide:
http://www.skinorthwest.com/

CONVERSION TABLES

DISTANCE

km	miles	km	miles
1	0.62	30	21.75
2	1.24	40	24.85
3	1.86	45	27.96
4	2.49	50	31.07
5	3.11	55	34.18
6	3.73	60	37.28
7	4.35	65	40.39
8	4.97	70	43.50
9	5.59	75	46.60
10	6.21	80	49.71
15	9.32	90	55.92
20	12.43	100	62.14
25	15.53	125	77.67

1km = 0.6214 miles
1mile = 1.609 km

METRES AND FEET

Unit	Metres	Feet
1	0.30	3.281
2	0.61	6.563
3	0.91	9.843
4	1.22	13.124
5	1.52	16.403
6	1.83	19.686
7	2.13	22.967
8	2.4	26.248
9	2.74	29.529
10	3.05	32.810
14	4.27	45.934
18	5.49	59.058
20	6.10	65.520
50	15.24	164.046
75	22.8	246.069
100	30.48	328.092

WEIGHT

Unit	kg	Pounds
1	0.45	2.205
2	0.90	4.405
3	1.35	6.614
4	1.80	8.818
5	2.25	11.023
10	4.50	22.045
15	6.75	33.068
20	9.00	44.889
25	11.25	55.113
50	22.50	110.225
75	33.75	165.338
100	45.00	220.450

1kg	=	1000g
100g	=	3.5oz
1oz	=	28.35g
1lb	=	453.60g

FLUID MEASURES

Litres	Imp.gal.	US gal.
5	1.1	1.3
10	2.2	2.6
15	3.3	3.9
20	4.4	5.2
25	5.5	6.5
30	6.6	7.8
35	7.7	9.1
40	8.8	10.4
45	9.9	11.7
50	11.0	13.0

1 litre(l)=0.88 imp.quarts
1 litre(l)=1.06 US quarts
1 imp. quart = 1.141
1 imp. gallon= 4.55 l
1 US quart = 0.95 l
1 US gallon = 3.81 l

347

MENS' SHIRTS

UK	Europe	US
14	36	14
15	38	15
15.5	39	15.5
16	41	16
16.5	42	16.5
17	43	17

MENS' SHOES

UK	Europe	US
6	40	7
7	41	8
8	42	9
9	43	10
10	44	11
11	45	12

Unit	mm	cm	metres
1 inch	25.4	2.54	0.025
1 foot	304.8	30.48	0.304
1 yard	914.4	91.44	0.914

To convert cms to inches, multiply by 0.3937
To convert inches to cms, multiply by 2.54

MENS' CLOTHES

UK	Europe	US
36	46	36
38	48	38
40	50	40
42	52	42
44	54	44
46	56	46

LADIES' SHOES

UK	Europe	US
3	36	4.5
4	37	5.5
5	38	6.5
6	39	7.5
7	40	8.5
8	41	9.5

LADIES' CLOTHES

UK	France	Italy	Rest of Europe	US
10	36	38	34	8
12	38	40	36	10
14	40	42	38	12
16	42	44	40	14
18	44	46	42	16
20	46	48	44	18

TEMPERATURE

Conversion Formula: °C × 9 ÷ 5 + 32 = °F

°C	°F	°C	°F	°C	°F	°C	°F
-20	-4	-5	23	10	50	25	77
-15	5	0	32	15	59	30	86
-10	14	5	41	20	68	35	95

INDEX

References are to page numbers. **Bold** numbers refer to the grid squares on the planning maps at the end of the book.

348

349

READER SURVEY

If you enjoyed using this book, or even if you didn't, please help us improve future editions by taking part in our reader survey. Every returned form will be acknowledged, and to show our appreciation we will give you £1 off your next purchase of a Thomas Cook guidebook. Just take a few minutes to complete and return this form to us.

When did you buy this book? _____

Where did you buy it? (Please give town/city and if possible name of retailer)

When did you/do you intend to travel in the Pacific Northwest?

    For how long (approx.)? _____
    How many people in your party? _____

Which cities, national parks and other locations did you/do you intend mainly to visit?

Did you/will you:
- ☐ Make all your travel arrangements independently?
- ☐ Travel on a fly-drive package?

Please give brief details: _____

Did you/do you intend to use this book:
- ☐ For planning your trip?
- ☐ During the trip itself?
- ☐ Both?

Did you/do you intend also to purchase any of the following travel publications for your trip?
    Thomas Cook Travellers: Vancouver & British Columbia
    A road map/atlas (please specify) _____
    Other guidebooks (please specify) _____

Have you used any other Thomas Cook guidebooks in the past? If so, which?

Please rate the following features of On the Road around the Pacific Northwest for their value to you (Circle VU for 'very useful', U for 'useful', NU for 'little or no use'):

The 'Travel Essentials' section on pages 15–38	VU	U	NU
The 'Driving in Pacific Northwest' section on pages 39–46	VU	U	NU
The 'Touring Itineraries' on pages 52–57	VU	U	NU
The recommended driving routes throughout the book	VU	U	NU
Information on towns and cities, National Parks, etc	VU	U	NU
The maps of towns and cities, parks, etc	VU	U	NU
The colour planning map	VU	U	NU

Please use this space to tell us about any features that in your opinion could be changed, improved, or added in future editions of the book, or any other comments you would like to make concerning the book:

_____

_____

_____

_____

_____

_____

_____

_____

352

_____

_____

Your age category: ☐ 21-30 ☐ 31-40 ☐ 41–50 ☐ over 50

Your name: Mr/Mrs/Miss/Ms
(First name or initials) _____
(Last name) _____

Your full address: (Please include postal or zip code)

_____

_____

_____

_____

Your daytime telephone number: _____

Please detach this page and send it to: The Project Editor, On the Road around the Pacific Northwest, Thomas Cook Publishing, PO Box 227, Peterborough PE3 6PU, United Kingdom.

We will be pleased to send you details of how to claim your discount upon receipt of this questionnaire.

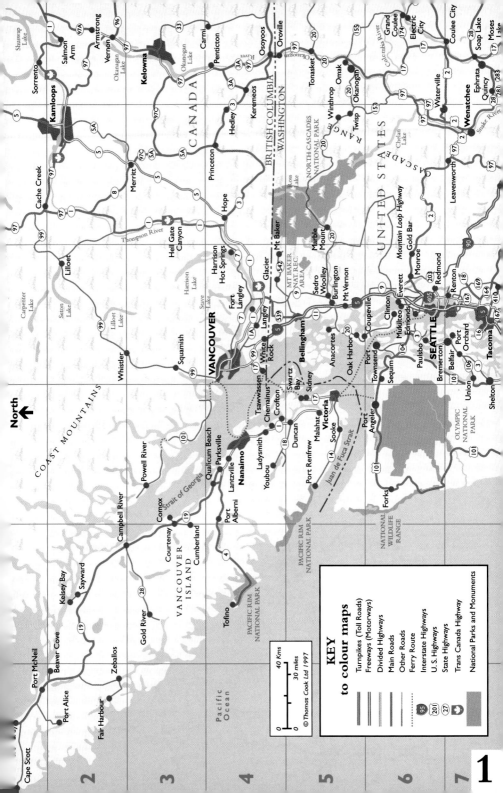